Canada:
An Economic History

William L. Marr and Donald G. Paterson

PUBLISHING LIMITED
TORONTO ONTARIO CANADA

Canadian Cataloguing in Publication Data

Marr, William L., date
   Canada, an economic history

Bibliography: p.
Includes index.
ISBN 0-7715-5684-5

1. Canada — Economic conditions.   I. Paterson,
Donald G., date.   II. Title.

HC113.M37   330.971   C79-094918-0

Originally published by Macmillan of Canada
under ISBN 0-7705-1845-1

2 3 4 5 6 THB 85 84 83 82 81

Printed and bound in Canada

CONTENTS

LIST OF TABLES

LIST OF FIGURES

LIST OF MAPS

To our children

Jennifer   *John Benjamin*
Peter   *Jennifer Ann*
               Catriona Elizabeth
W.L.M.
               D.G.P.

PREFACE

The arrangement of this book is thematic. Such an ordering of historical material, we believe, permits a clearer identification of the forces of economic change and their consequences than otherwise would be possible. Yet, there are certain themes of Canadian economic history which are so pervasive that they do not readily submit to the confines of this approach. Themes, such as the economic importance of foreign trade or the growth of government involvement in the economy, are, therefore, embodied in most chapters and no attempt has been made to give them separate treatment. Specific events also have this quality of pervasiveness in history. None has it more so than the national policy which dominated the economic history of at least the sixty years from 1879. The importance of such themes and events is, we trust, emphasized by their appearance throughout this history.

We have assumed that the readers of this book are familiar with the broad outlines of Canadian history and the basic principles of economics. To do otherwise would have required a work of encyclopaedic proportions. References of a general nature are, however, given in both the notes and bibliography. The bibliography is restricted, for the most part, to works which are directly relevant to Canadian economic history. Furthermore, it is a select bibliography with no pretention to completeness.

Throughout the book the geography of Canada is described by the historically appropriate terms. However, where the sense of argument dictates otherwise, modern terms have been employed. For instance, in order to distinguish the various regions of the prairies, much of which was the North West Territories until 1905, the names of the current provinces are used. We hope that those unfamiliar with Canadian history will not be confused by such a procedure. Thus, despite the recent tendency to neologisms, Canada West remains Canada West, the name of the (approximately) present Ontario between 1840 and 1867.

ACKNOWLEDGMENTS

No study which ranges over so many themes in the history of a nation can do so without relying heavily on the works of others. We have unashamedly borrowed from a rich body of literature. It is necessary then, at the outset, to recognize our debt to both current and past researchers. Although at all times we have sought to reinterpret and synthesize, it is our hope that no individual scholarly contribution has been misrepresented. Furthermore, we have gained much insight from our co-workers and have found through the years the Social Science and Humanities Research Council conferences on Canadian economic history a valuable forum for the exchange of ideas. Permission was given to cite material from A. E. Lunn's McGill MA thesis, J. Shepherd's unpublished paper, and P. McClelland's Harvard Ph D thesis. Full reference is in the bibliography. We wish to thank the copyright holders. In general, we must also thank our students. Their patience, gentle criticism, but most of all their enthusiasm for the subject of study, both motivated and directed us.

Both of our universities were instrumental in encouraging and indirectly sponsoring our work. In particular, office facilities were made available by the University of British Columbia so that we could work together in 1976-77. Wilfrid Laurier University generously provided typing and duplication facilities and for these we are grateful.

At an early stage in the writing of this book, we were encouraged by many individuals but particularly so by Ronald Shearer and John Weir. Others generously read chapter drafts and offered comments and insights which influenced the direction of this study. Among these colleagues whose contributions went far beyond the call of duty we would like to thank: G. Christopher Archibald, Philip Neher, Michael Percy, Ronald Shearer, and Richard Unger of the University of British Columbia; Marilyn Gerriets of Wilfrid Laurier University; Louis P. Cain of Loyola University of Chicago; Paul David of Stanford University; Kevin Burley and C. Knick Harley of the University of Western Ontario; R. Marvin McInnis of Queen's University; Phyllis Deane of University of Cambridge; Carolyn Clark of Washington State University; and James Shepherd of Whitman College, Washington. Last, we would like to thank Peter George of McMaster University and Alan Green of Queen's University who read the manuscript in its entirety. Their general and detailed suggestions were instrumental in shaping the published version of this book. Furthermore, the insights and criticisms were delivered in such a gracious and thoughtful manner that we drew a full measure of encouragement. The discipline of economic history in Canada is well served by two such scholars.

To Georgina Weisz and Elsie Grogan who cheerfully and efficiently typed the several drafts of this manuscript and to E. J. P. who proofread them we extend our warmest thanks. Virgil Duff and Beverley Beetham of Macmillan of Canada were responsible for this book through various stages. They guided both the manuscript and authors with apparent ease, good humour, and professional thoroughness. Our debt to them is substantial.

William L. Marr
Wilfrid Laurier University

Donald G. Paterson
University of British Columbia

Summer, 1979.

CHAPTER ONE

Introduction

Any contemporary economy can only be fully appreciated when its past is understood. Such an extravagant assertion can readily be justified by appeal to economic history which is the record of how economies have evolved. In all cases we observe as much diverse as common experience in the patterns of economic development and this diversity of experience, in turn, gave rise to the many unique features which distinguish one economy from another.[1] This book is about the development of the Canadian economy and the forces which shaped it, the features which it shared with other countries, and those which were unique.

The process of economic change which was to shape the modern country of Canada was, in the first instance, largely a product of the European expansion into North America. Prior to the coming of the Europeans, North America was populated by the Indians and Inuit who had centuries before migrated from Asia and who lived essentially in harmony with their environment, relying on hunting and gathering, and in some cases primitive agriculture, for their economic well-being. Numerically they were few and even this small population was fragmented into many tribal and language groups. Some of the tribes developed, over their long histories, very elaborate and sophisticated social and political institutions. For instance, the ceremony of the potlatch conducted by the West Coast Indians probably served as an effective means of redistributing income in a society which lived close to the margin of subsistence. However, for the most part, the economies of the native peoples were primitive. Very simple technology was applied to the local, available natural resources to produce most of the goods necessary for survival. There was little specialization of work and systematic trade between the tribes was rare and when conducted it was by barter. In contrast, the advanced market economies of Europe were ones in which change was ubiquitous. The expansion of European civilization into North America at the end of the sixteenth century, therefore, defines one of the limits of this study.

Where do we place the bound of our study in the recent past? In principle everything that happened before this instant is history. On the other hand, more than one economic historian has muttered in his beard that study should cease at the point at which he can remember the events in question. But since the purpose of economic history is to comprehend the *background* to the present economy, particular attention should be given to the long-run forces which shaped that economy. Consequently, while of undeniable interest, the *immediate* conditions of today's economy normally lie outside the jurisdiction of the economic historian. For instance, regional differences in per-capita income have persisted in Canada throughout that period of history for which there are accurate records. The very recent past in this case is part of an historical theme. Conversely, the Minister of Finance's budget of last year is not yet economic history because it is still impossible to tell whether the announced measures are of transitory or permanent importance. Accordingly, the bound of economic history in recent time is that period or era within which one can no longer say with certainty that the forces being examined have been of lasting consequence in shaping the structure of the economy.

All economies, no matter how advanced or primitive, fulfil several important, highly interrelated functions. Resources must be allocated to competing uses, income must be distributed in some fashion, and there must be some framework for individual and collective decision-making. In countries such as Canada, where development took place in an environment of market capitalism, the history is one of the evolution of market and economic institutions and, in turn, the composition, level, and growth of income. First insights into the economic development of Canada can be gained by a focus on resource allocation, income growth and distribution, and decision-making processes. After all, history is neither a litany nor a catalogue of facts to be recited promiscuously. By an examination of these interrelated functions, it is then possible to identify the key features of economic change and to indicate their contributions.[2]

In contrast with the economic histories of most countries which have achieved a relatively advanced state of economic development, Canada's history is marked by the persistent and powerful influence of the more mature economies with which there was contact. One aspect of this influence is the length and importance of the colonial period; another is that of the massive economy to the south, the United States.

Areas of the new world of the seventeenth century were usually given political and economic definition by European colonization. In this regard, Canada is not unique. However, the country's colonial experience is unusual in two respects. First, two powerful European nations, France and Great Britain, were instrumental in shaping the political, economic, and social structure of the country. The impact of these two colonial régimes was different in both kind and degree. The dual colonial heritage also gave rise to special problems as the economy evolved. Many institutions, such as the pattern of land ownership in agriculture, outlived the French régime to last long into the period of British colonial control. Economic development took on rather special characteristics as a consequence. Many aspects of this dual colonial legacy, of course, survive to influence today's economy. The second attribute of the colonial period is that it was long by comparison with that of other nations. As is well known, the British came to control most of what was previously French territory during the Seven Years War. For more than a century thereafter, Canada was a direct colony of Great Britain and by the time political sovereignty was achieved in 1867, the process by which the economy was being transformed into an industrial one was well under way.

The close proximity of a large economy has always been a major influence on the pattern of economic development in Canada. This influence often assumed a belligerent quality as the different colonial powers warred over territory, as Great Britain confronted the revolution which created the United States, and as the small British North American colonies struggled with the forces of manifest destiny from the United States. But apart from territorial disputes the major economic influences of the United States arose out of that economy's size and more advanced state of economic development in general.[3] Although we shall see in greater detail throughout this study the character and impact of these influences, it is pertinent to observe here that they were only occasionally forces of economic conflict. Indeed, it may be argued that the single most powerful impact that the United States had on Canada's economic development was simply in providing a model of what could be achieved in a land which shared so many characteristics.[4]

While geography of empire-building and the proximity of the United States were important determinants of economic change, the influence of the United States was in large measure due to a special feature of the Canadian economy. Throughout its history Canada's economy has been not only relatively small but also open. An open economy is first defined in terms of the importance of its international trade sector. Relative to national income the contribution of exports and imports is large. For instance, the United States has a closed economy because of the relatively small contribution of trade to national income despite a large absolute volume of trade. Canada, on the other hand, has an open economy with a lower absolute volume of trade. In terms of traded goods, the Canadian economy has always been open whereas that of the United States was open until approximately the mid-nineteenth century and gradually became closed as subsequent development took place. There are other qualities apart from the importance of trade, however, which define an economy as open: The relative contributions of capital imports, net immigration, and the flow of technology are the most important. But, inflows of foreign savings are no longer as vital to the level of capital formation as they once were and net immigration no longer causes as rapid a change in the size and structure of the population as it once did. In this respect, the Canadian economy has given up some attributes of openness.

As well as being open, the Canadian economy was small relative to those economies with which it had most contact. For instance, during the nineteenth and twentieth centuries the Canadian economy was only about one-tenth the size of that of the United States — see Table 1:1 for a contemporary comparison. This meant that the prices of many traded goods were established internationally rather than domestically and, to some extent, that factor prices were also set outside the domestic economy. In the nineteenth century, a capital market in England established the interest rate chargeable on Canadian debt, real wage movements in the United States were reflected by those in Canada, and the price of wheat in Canada was determined by the Liverpool price minus transport costs and other relevant charges. The forces of the international economy in such a manner directly influenced the pattern of economic change.

Despite the changes in the size and structure of the economy, Canadian prices have tended to remain prices taken in the world factor and product market. The successive development of exports based on the country's natural-resource endowment has contributed more than anything else to the continued openness of the economy. Staples, that is, exports with a high natural-resource content, were often the major cause of rapid economic development. When exports grew rapidly and in turn stimulated the rest of the economy, growth is said to have been "export-led". In this context, "growth" refers not to the simple short-run increase of income but to that process of change which is marked by either greater intensity of economic activity which often occurs through its geographic spread, or structural change in the organization of the

Table 1:1 Relative Size of Sixteen Economies, 1976

(Gross Domestic Product, GDP, at 1970 U.S. Prices)

Country	GDP	GDP Per Capita
(1)	(2) ($ billions)	(3) ($)
Canada	113.0 *7*	4,882 *2*
U.S.A.	1,158.2 *1*	5,385 *1*
U.K.	200.9 *5*	3,583 *15*
France	249.4 *4*	4,697 *4*
Germany	268.2 *3*	4,359 *7*
Italy	160.1 *6*	2,869 *16*
Japan	465.0 *2*	4,155 *11*
Belgium	44.4 *10*	4,515 *6*
Netherlands	59.2 *8*	4,304 *8*
Australia	58.3 *9*	4,280 *9*
Switzerland	26.9 *13*	4,199 *10*
Austria	27.9 *12*	3,713 *14*
Sweden	39.0 *11*	4,748 *3*
Denmark	20.8 *14*	4,082 *12*
Norway	18.3 *15*	4,549 *5*
Finland	18.0 *16*	3,814 *13*

Source: OECD, Main Economic Indicators, May 1977.

economy, or both. Structural change, as will be seen, took many forms, but the variation in the relative importance of industrial sectors was the most fundamental form.

Before about 1850, the principal attribute of economic development was the general geographic spread of the economy. More and more areas were brought within the range of the market forces which emanated from the international economy. There was, as well, a growth in the range of economic activity, but at this time expansion was based, for the most part, directly on the exploitation of natural resources. To be sure, there were changes in the structure of the economy and an important element was the rise of a large commercial sector to finance trade. However, such structural change, as far as we can judge from the imperfect evidence of that period, was slow and especially so when it is contrasted with that which took place later.

After about 1850, the nature of economic development was different and more and more the economy's structure changed in an apparently irreversible manner. All primary activity, such as natural-resource exploitation and agriculture, declined in relative importance to national income whereas manufacturing, construction, and tertiary economic activity increased in relative importance. Furthermore, real output and real output

Table 1:2 Long-Run Trends in GNP, Real GNP, and Real GNP Per Capita, 1850-1970

(1935-39 prices = 100)

Year	GNP	Real GNP	Real GNP Per Capita
(1)	(2)	(3)	(4)
	($ millions)	($ millions)	($)
1850	169	406	167
1860	319	582	180
1870	459	764	211
1880	581	981	231
1890	803	1,366	286
1900	1,057	1,877	354
1910	2,138	3,085	441
1920	5,543	3,844	449
1930	5,728	5,119	501
1940	6,743	6,743	592
1950	18,006	10,475	764
1960	36,287	19,199	1,074
1970	85,685	33,732	1,578

Sources: M. C. Urquhart and K. A. H. Buckley, eds., *Historical Statistics of Canada* (Toronto, 1965), pp. 14, 131; O. J. Firestone, "Development of Canada's Economy, 1850-1900", *Trends in the American Economy in the Nineteenth Century* (Princeton, 1960), pp. 222-29; and Statistics Canada, *Canadian Statistical Review*, Cat. no. 11-003.

per capita expanded at a faster rate than they had earlier. However, a fast rate of increase in income was not automatic and, as Table 1:2 illustrates, there was often a considerable difference between the general trend and decade-by-decade change. As will be seen in greater detail later, there are three distinct eras during which economic development, measured in terms of both income and changing structure, was rapid:

1) *the mid-nineteenth century (approximately 1850 to 1870)*: associated with a reciprocal free-trade treaty with the United States, the building of the first railways in central Canada, and the buoyant exports of wheat, flour, and timber to both United States and Great Britain;
2) *the so-called wheat boom (approximately 1895 to 1929)*: associated with rapid growth of wheat and flour exports as well as those of pulp and paper and minerals, the development of hydroelectric energy, and the growth of secondary manufacturing; and
3) *the decades of sustained economic growth (post-1945 to about 1970)*: associated with the postwar expansion, demand for consumer durables, large-scale immigration, the renewed vitality of the export performance of raw materials, the effects of expenditure on education

following the baby boom of the 1940s and 1950s, social services, and special projects such as the St. Lawrence Seaway.

But increases in aggregate real income did not always indicate an improvement in the welfare of individuals. Income is a very crude measure of economic well-being which fails to take into account either population growth or the social costs of increased output. In addition, only goods and services which enter a market are generally recorded and a decrease in the home production of goods, such as that in the nineteenth century, will be recorded as an increase in income when production is shifted to a factory unless due allowance is made. Generally, it is argued, real income per capita more sensitively measures the extent of economic development than increases in aggregate real income because it contains an implicit welfare criterion. That is, when aggregate real income is deflated by the population base and the resulting measure is observed to rise it is usually the case that the real income gains accrue to a very large portion of the population. Such a welfare measure must be used with extreme caution. For instance, real per-capita income gains in Lower Canadian agriculture in the late eighteenth and early nineteenth centuries were undoubtedly achieved at the expense of a growing incidence of rural poverty. Gains to the economy as a whole and gains to the individual, as an examination of Table 1:2 indicates, may be substantially different. For instance, the first decade of the twentieth century registered a very high rate of increase in real income but a much lower rate of increase in real income per capita. This paradox is explained by the very rapid increase in population during this decade which was due largely to immigration. The changing population base of the real-income-per-capita measure was dependent on the real income gains being made. Consequently, growing income attracted population and this in turn depressed the increase in individual well-being. When changes in economic society are measured over long periods of time individual welfare must be considered. So too, it must be remembered that gains in real income do not necessarily constitute immediate improvements in the well-being of the population as a whole. By the same token, the decades of the 1880s and 1890s saw relatively small gains in real income. Commentators, especially at the time, complained about Canada's slow economic growth, but it was slow only in comparison with the growth rate of real output in the United States. However, the relatively low rate of population growth in Canada during these years permitted real output per capita to expand at a relatively high rate.

Real income gains may disguise the social cost of achieving them. The most obvious example of real income and real-income-per-capita gains being achieved at a high social cost are those registered during the time of war. Wartime demands on economies are usually powerful stimuli to economic growth but war also involves the separation of families, thwarted ambitions, the wasting of towns — as happened during the War of 1812 — and death.

Social benefits are as difficult to measure as social costs. Over the very long run, the Canadian workforce has chosen to reduce the hours per week spent in gainful employment and as a consequence has foregone real dollar benefits. This has, however, been more than compensated for by the increased time spent in leisure activities. Real income and the so-called psychic benefits of leisure time are competing goals. If the workforce had not chosen the alternative compensation of leisure, the growth rate of measured real income per capita undoubtedly would have been greater. A focus on the real income measures alone understates the pace of economic development if the net social benefits are not recognized even when they cannot easily be measured.[5]

In the histories of most currently highly developed countries, the nineteenth and twentieth centuries were periods of rapid structural change symbolized by the long-run decline in the importance of primary economic activity. In terms of aggregate economic performance, Canada's growth of real output per decade measured, on average, 40.7 per cent for the years 1870-74 to 1960-62. As Table 1:3 shows, this growth exceeded that of most industrial economies. However, population also grew rapidly.

Population growth rates are generally divided into one of three groups:

1) *less than 10 per cent:* England and Wales, France, Germany, Switzerland, Norway, Sweden, Italy, and European Russia;
2) *between 10 and 15 per cent:* Netherlands, Denmark, and Japan; and
3) *greater than 15 per cent:* United States, Canada, and Australia.

Thus, Canada's economic development and achievement of high real-per-capita-income growth was substantially different, even in its general features, from that of many other industrial countries (France, for example). The Canadian experience of long-run economic change most resembles that of the other regions of contemporary settlement. It is these similarities and diversities which are the subjects of economic history.

This study of Canadian economic history, as indicated earlier, is arranged by themes. Each theme focuses attention on a particular aspect of economic change, such as the growth of the population, the mobilization of savings, or the provision of transport facilities. Two basic questions form the core of each theme: What conditions brought about the

Table 1:3 Comparison of Long-Run Trends in Economic Development: Growth of Real National Product, Population, and Real Per-Capita Product Per Decade, Selected Countries
(per cent)

Country/Period	Real National Product	Population	Real Product Per Capita
(1)	(2)	(3)	(4)
Canada			
1870-74 to 1960-62	40.7	19.1	18.1
England and Wales—United Kingdom			
1700 to 1780	5.3	3.2	2.0
1780 to 1881	28.2	13.1	13.4
1855-59 to 1957-59	21.1	6.1	14.1
France			
1841-50 to 1960-62	20.8	2.5	17.9
Germany—West Germany			
1851-55 to 1871-75	17.6	7.7	9.2
1871-75 to 1960-62	31.1	11.2	17.9
Netherlands			
1900-04 to 1960-62	29.7	14.3	13.5
Switzerland			
1809-99 to 1957-59	25.7	8.3	16.1
Denmark			
1870-74 to 1960-62	31.8	10.4	19.4
Norway			
1865-74 to 1960-62	29.0	8.4	19.0
Sweden			
1861-65 to 1960-62	36.9	6.7	28.3
Italy			
1861-65 to 1898-1902	9.7	6.8	2.7
1898-1902 to 1960-62	26.8	6.8	18.7
United States			
1839 to 1960-62	42.5	21.6	17.2
Australia			
1861-65 to 1959-62	34.1	24.2	8.0
Japan			
1879-81 to 1959-61	42.0	12.3	26.4
European Russia—U.S.S.R.			
1860 to 1913	30.2	13.8	14.4
1913 to 1958	35.7	6.4	27.4
1928 to 1958	53.8	6.9	43.9

Source: S. Kuznets, *Modern Economic Growth* (New Haven, 1966), pp. 64-65.

forces for economic change? and What effect did these forces have on the growth and structure of the economy? Not surprisingly, attempts to be authoritative meet with varying success. History presents fascinating problems but rarely obliges with easy answers.

CHAPTER TWO

Patterns of Aggregate Economic Change

Introduction

For at least two centuries after the first European settlement of the St. Lawrence valley in the early 1600s the dominant feature of economic development in Canada was the geographic spread of the economy. By the time of Confederation in 1867, however, the nature of economic change was qualitatively different: The process of modern economic development was underway. Although its beginnings can only be dated approximately to the third quarter of the nineteenth century modern economic development was evident in *both* the continued geographic spread of the economy and the rapid changes in the structure of output. The consequence was a long-run rate of growth of national and individual income which was higher than had been previously experienced. In this chapter the relationships between income growth and changes in economic structures are explored.

First, the general basis for the spread of the economy is examined in the framework of export-led growth. Second, the performance of national and individual income is linked to the changes in the structure of income or output. Third, the sources of economic growth are identified. Last, the influence of technical change is analysed in the context of its causes.

General Characteristics of Staple Production

The spread of the economy over the landscape, and the pattern of economic development, were critically dependent on foreign demands for natural resources and the ability of the new country to supply them. At the beginning of the 1600s economic activity centred on the exploitation of the Atlantic fishery. Later, as settlements were established, furs, particularly beaver pelts, became a major export to Europe. By the nineteenth century the timber industry had replaced the fur trade as the principal source of exports. It is, however, important to note at the outset that the periods in history which are characterized by the dominance of a particular natural-resource export are ill-defined. For instance, although furs were a major export commodity from New France in the late seventeenth century they were accompanied by significant shipments of codfish. A century and a half later fish, fur, and timber resources were all being exploited concomitantly. In addition, agriculture and simple manufacturing evolved to meet internal colonial demand. Thus, while early Canadian economic development was initiated and extended on the basis of a few simple exportable natural resources, the character of that development was, as will be seen, increasingly complex.

Despite the disparate nature of the natural resources which helped to stimulate economic change, the harvesting and economic consequences of them shared common features. These were first analysed systematically by W. A. Mackintosh and H. A. Innis[1] and from their writings evolved what has come to be known as "the staple thesis". Staples are defined as products destined primarily for export which have a high natural-resource content. Typically such staples received very little processing before being exported. Some staples, such as fish and certain types of minerals, were exported in their raw form although it should be noted that even the act of gathering natural resources created value added in production. Staples also include agricultural products because of the intensive use of land in their cultivation.[2] By focusing attention on staples, the thesis attempts to provide a broad framework for explaining economic development in terms of exports and natural-resource use. Yet, the staple thesis is not a theory. The scope of the staple thesis prevents the precise relationships which form the economic structure from being specified independently of the staple in question. Furthermore, the staple thesis does not have the principal attribute of a theory—it cannot be refuted. Yet, the value of this broad approach to Canadian economic history is seldom disputed because it provides an essential taxonomy—a system of classification for like economic phenomena.

Because the staple thesis attempts to demonstrate how exports promoted rapid economic development it is often referred to as "the export-led model of economic growth". Within its scope lie several central, somewhat overlapping, themes.[3] They each suggest that aggregate output in the Canadian past has been determined by:

1) autonomous demands for Canadian exports;

2) linkages or spreading effects from the export sector to the rest of the economy;

3) technical change, particularly in transport systems, which facilitated exploitation of natural resources; and

4) the natural-resource endowment.

First, the appearance of an export staple depended on the existence or emergence of a foreign demand. Changes in foreign demand were, however, unrelated to changes of income in the staple-producing region and are thus said to be autonomous. There was, of course, a great variety of forces which influenced the demands for staples and in the instance of the three earliest staples—fish, fur, and timber—no common patterns of demand can be found. Demand for the product of the fisheries was comparatively stable since it was largely determined by relatively unchanging tastes, especially in the Roman Catholic countries of Europe. The demand for fur resources, on the other hand, was volatile since it was subject to changes in fashion in the industries where fur was used, the hatting and garment industries of France and England. The highly price-inelastic demand, a characteristic usually associated with luxury goods like furs, made planning the appropriate output level difficult for the Canadian traders. It could not be assumed that all their shipments would be taken at a given price. Over-production in Canada in any year profoundly influenced total revenues and hence profits. Timber exports depended on British protection to find a market. Without this preference the British consumers would have imported timber at lower cost from the Baltic region. Furthermore, shifts in the demand for lumber in Great Britain occurred as the construction sector, which used a large quantity of the timber, expanded or declined. Movements in British aggregate income were thus transmitted to British North America. In summary, although the demand for staples was determined abroad, over time each staple faced different price elasticities and shifts in demand. These shifts were critical in determining the pace of economic development and its geographical spread. Not surprisingly, political expansion tended to follow economic expansion into those regions where the resources were found.[4].

Second, the growth of staple exports influenced income not only through the open-economy multiplier[5] but also through the other changes in the economy which they induced. Development economists have classified such induced changes into three types.[6] First, there is the backward linkage. This describes the induced creation of domestic production whose outputs became inputs into the staple sector. For instance, early agriculture developed, in part, as a response to the derived demands for food supplies in the staple trades. In general, the backward linkages can be described as strong or weak. As we shall see, the effects of the fisheries in the seventeenth and eighteenth centuries on geographic spread and growth of income was relatively weak. In turn, the fur trade stimulated more settlements than the fisheries but fewer than the timber trade. A greater stimulus to agricultural expansion was generated by the timber trade than by the fur trade because of the greater labour-input demands for the former. While these linkages will be discussed in much greater detail in subsequent chapters, it is important to note here that one of the greatest backward-linkage effects has been the demand for transport facilities to permit the efficient harvesting of the natural resources.

It also should be kept in mind that as the economy became more complex subsidiary backward-linkage effects asserted themselves. In the nineteenth century, for instance, consumer-goods industries grew in importance. Since consumer goods are the final products themselves and can only be classified as inputs into staple production in a very indirect manner, these linkages are often referred to as "final-demand" ones.

The second general category of induced change is forward linkage. In this case the original staple output became the input into some production process, the output of which was then exported. Typically these forward linkages were of great importance to the development of a manufacturing capacity. For instance, when timber was first exported in the early nineteenth century it was relatively untransformed. Timber was simply cut and roughly squared for ease of transport. However, as a workforce grew which was more skilled in the cutting and sawing of timber and as the economy was capable of financing sawmills, the more highly processed timber exports — lumber planks or sawn timber deals, as they were known — replaced square-timber exports to some extent. There were many other examples; as will be seen, the manufacturing sector in Canada was, and still is, based in large measure on the processing of natural resources. If the changing economic circumstances were such that stronger forward linkages were forged, more value added was generated within the staple region.

Lateral linkage occurs mostly in the form of external economies generated by the export and related industries which stimulated the growth of some third industry. For example, transport developments in the timber trade decreased transport costs for other industries, such as those in the commercial sector. The attraction of skilled labour capable of alternative employment with no adverse effect on wages in the staple industry is another example. During the period of the exploitation of Canada's first three staples the lateral-linkage effects seem to have been relatively weak.

A necessary condition for the emergence of export-led economic development was the existence or appearance of a technology which permitted economic exploitation of the natural-resource base. Technology, then, is the third element of the staple thesis. In the case of the early staples little value added was derived in the act of wresting the resources from nature. Exports were mainly of relatively untransformed natural resources, such as salted or dried fish, animal pelts, or squared timber, none of which required much more than the technology of a requisite transport system. Even later when the new staples of the nineteenth and twentieth centuries required more domestic processing, as in the case of mineral products, or more cultivation, in the instance of agricultural products, the transport technology was a major determinant of whether economic development proceeded or not.

The importance of transport technologies, of course, lay in their ability to reduce the cost of shipping the staple to the final market. If the costs of freight declined while the price of the staple remained constant, the area in which the resource was gathered could expand. Although the impact of transport systems on export-led growth is examined in more detail in Chapter 10, it is pertinent to note here that by anticipating staple requirements government could intervene to help provide the appropriate transport technology. For instance, government assistance aided the rapid expansion of a railway system into the prairies in order that that region might more quickly be brought within the scope of the world wheat market. Railway shipping technology highlights the fact that the transport effects were often experienced more broadly in the economy than solely within the staple sector (see Chapter 10).

In the early days of the fur trade one of the major technical improvements was the introduction of the large, freight-carrying canoes. Their use outside of the staple trade was, however, negligible. By contrast, the large cargo-carrying capacity of the early nineteenth-century timber ships reduced the costs of the trans-Atlantic passage from Europe. The problem of imbalance in cargo, from a cost viewpoint, was thus solved by employing the otherwise unused capacity for the immigrant trade.[7] So too, the development of canals in the Great Lakes–St. Lawrence water system in the second quarter of the nineteenth century, and the later development of railways, reduced the general cost of shipping goods even though the canals were rationalized as being important for the expansion of staple production. Consequently, a social product was generated which was often more than merely the direct product of the staple industry. Naturally, the more broadly the impacts of falling transport costs were felt the more rapid the geographic and economic frontiers expanded. This brings us to the last element of the staple thesis—the natural-resource endowment.

By introducing the natural-resource endowment into the general explanation of how an economy develops, the staple thesis provides a descriptive framework for the *spread* of the economy. In order to experience a growth in output, with a given technology, either the quantity or the quality of inputs must be increased. Certain effects, such as economies of scale in production, may result as a consequence of the growth in output but these are secondary. Early Canadian history affirms that the growth in output was achieved by bringing increasing quantities of natural resources into production. These resources were in demand in the markets of Europe and later also in those of the United States and they were, as noted earlier, generally exported with only a small degree of processing. The quantity of available natural resources and the effort expended in their harvest determined output and subsequent export of the staples. This can be described by a production function[8]

$$Q = f(L, K, R)$$

where Q = the output of the final good or staple; L = the inputs of labour; K = the inputs of capital; and R = the natural resources used as inputs. Increases in output can be achieved by expending more effort in the form of labour and capital services to harvest from a given resource stock. But output can also be increased by augmenting the flow of resources from an enlarged stock of available natural resources which, in early Canadian history, usually meant territorial expansion.

Geographic expansion depended on a transport system. This, however, was usually a large-scale endeavour which, once completed, sharply reduced gathering costs. This meant that the economic frontier was often pushed back in a discontinuous manner. However, as the following chapter will show, the economic mechanism which caused sudden shifts of the resource frontier was frequently complex, depending, as it did, not only on where the natural resources were located, but also on the institutional arrangements of resource exploitation—that is, whether the resource was used by many or few. Each time a harvest area was exhausted beyond economic use the staple industry expanded into a virgin resource region. But the new resource region was not necessarily a new region of settlement. Often the various resource areas were coincident with those containing other resources. For instance, in the case of the timber industry of the nineteenth century the harvest area was almost identical to that of the earlier fur trade. Such economic expansion over the same territory was, of course, a reaffirmation of political as well as economic jurisdiction.[9]

The natural resources which provided the foundation of export-led economic development were, of course, vastly different from one another. For example, those resources which were the basis of early expansion were renewable ones—fish, fur, and timber. If left to nature the stock of these resources would grow after some harvesting had taken place. On the other hand, minerals and oils were exhaustible resources; once depleted they could not be replaced. Many of Canada's later staples were based on these non-renewable resource stocks.[10] This vital distinction between renewable and non-renewable resources was bound to affect the manner in which the resources were exploited as will be shown in chapters 3 and 11. However, another distinction should be made. Some staples were agricultural products; they were technically the products of the renewable-resource base of land but were qualitatively different. As may be anticipated, the export of wheat and wheat products which was vital to the expansion of the economy at several times—in central Canada in the nineteenth century and in the prairie region in the early twentieth century—was so different in the nature of the economic spread it generated that separate treatment is warranted (see chapters 4 and 11).

Although the staple thesis is a broadly conceived description of the patterns of the economy's spread, it is evident that that description must necessarily be less complete as the economy grew to be more complex. There are those who, in fact, argue that even by the early 1800s the degree of complexity was such that the staple thesis loses its power.[11] Yet as Table 2:1 shows, natural-resource-based products remained the principal exports of the economy. The continued dominance of agricultural and timber products, along with mineral products after 1890, is evidence of this so-called staple dependence. To be sure, the individual commodities being exported changed generally to include more value added of domestic origin. For instance, pulp and paper which became a dominant proportion of wood-product exports in the twentieth century, embodied much more processing than the earlier forest-based products sold abroad. Similarly, minerals are exported after more domestic processing than was generally the case in the early 1900s. With regard to imports, manufactured goods of agriculture, textile, and metal origin were, and continue to be, the majority of purchases from other countries. Thus, the economy retained many of its staple features even when the structural composition of output began to change rapidly as modern economic development took place. Indeed, the process of staple expansion was an

Table 2:1 Composition of Exports and Imports by Value, 1851-1960
(percentage of total)

	1851	1860	1870	1880	1890	1900	1910	1920	1930	1940	1950	1960
	(1)	(2)	(3)	(4)	(5)	(6)	(7)	(8)	(9)	(10)	(11)	(12)
Exports:												
Agricultural Products	23.5	38.1	14.9	38.1	15.7	14.7	30.7	33.6	36.6	31.4	34.4	26.7
Animals and Their Products	11.8	19.0	23.9	28.8	40.4	38.4	25.5	25.3	10.5			
Fibres and Textiles	—	—	1.5	1.4	1.1	1.1	0.7	2.7	0.8	2.0	1.0	1.0
Wood, Wood Products & Paper	52.9	33.3	34.3	20.9	28.1	18.6	20.4	17.3	28.9	29.5	38.6	37.2
Iron and Its Products	—	—	1.5	1.6	1.1	2.3	3.6	6.6	5.6	10.9	9.5	14.2
Non-ferrous Metals	—	2.4	1.5	1.6	2.2	18.6	12.4	4.4	10.9	16.5	15.9	28.4
Non-metallic Minerals	—	2.4	3.0	1.7	4.5	4.0	3.6	2.4	2.7	2.9	3.6	7.9
Chemicals	—	—	—	—	1.1	0.6	1.1	1.8	1.9	2.6	3.5	5.6
Others	11.8	4.8	19.4	5.8	5.6	1.7	1.8	5.8	2.2	4.3	1.7	2.0
TOTAL	100.0	100.0	100.0	100.0	100.0	100.0	100.0	100.0	100.0	100.0	100.0	100.0
Imports:												
Agricultural Products	22.2	31.1	26.2	21.2	21.4	21.3	17.4	22.7	19.0	15.2	16.5	13.4
Animals and Their Products	18.5	8.9	7.1	9.2	7.1	7.9	6.8	8.9	5.9			
Fibres and Textiles	25.9	31.1	20.2	32.1	25.9	21.3	19.4	21.8	14.8	14.3	11.5	7.8
Wood, Wood Products & Paper	3.7	2.2	—	4.1	4.5	4.5	6.0	4.0	5.0	3.6	3.0	4.6
Iron and Its Products	14.8	11.1	11.9	13.9	13.4	16.9	20.3	17.6	22.3	29.2	30.8	37.3
Non-ferrous Metals	—	—	1.2	1.4	3.6	3.9	6.2	4.9	6.6	7.0	6.9	8.7
Non-metallic Minerals	3.7	4.4	4.8	6.8	12.5	11.8	11.7	11.5	16.4	15.7	19.2	12.1
Chemicals	—	2.2	2.4	3.3	3.6	3.4	2.7	2.8	3.7	5.1	5.1	6.3
Others	11.1	8.9	26.2	8.7	8.0	9.0	9.3	5.8	6.3	10.0	7.0	10.0
TOTAL	100.0	100.0	100.0	100.0	100.0	100.0	100.0	100.0	100.0	100.0	100.0	100.0

Note: The above are calculated from data which are in current-value terms. For the years prior to 1930 they cover all exports and imports whereas the most recent calculations are based on the adjusted declared value of domestic exports and imports.

Sources: O. J. Firestone, "Canada's External Trade and Net Foreign Balance, 1851-1900", *Trends in the American Economy in the Nineteenth Century* (Princeton, 1960), p. 761; and M. C. Urquhart and K. A. H. Buckley, eds., *Historical Statistics of Canada* (Toronto, 1965), pp. 154-57 and 174-86.

important element in the creation of the modern economy and many but not all characteristics of the changes are adequately described by the simple export-led model.[12]

In summary, the staple thesis provided the framework for explaining the spread of economic activity associated with export demand for natural-resource-based products. Emphasis is directed to the demand forces, the linkages with the rest of the economy, changes in technology, and the natural-resource endowment. As indicated, few inferences can be made about the growth of individual income because the description is that of aggregate economic development. This feature notwithstanding, the export-led approach to economic development concentrates attention on phases of rapid expansion. But more than just the spread of the economy was linked to natural-resource exploitation. As will be seen in the following sections of this chapter, staples were vital to the process of modern economic development.

The Growth of National Income

A decade-by-decade comparison of national income reveals that the rate of growth of GNP was greater during the 1850s than at any other time in the nineteenth century. There is, of course, only indirect evidence about the behaviour of national income prior to 1851 but the trends of prices of exports and imports suggest that earlier growth was less than that recorded for the mid-century period. So too, the latter part of the nineteenth century registered growth rates of national income below those of the 1850s (see Table 2:2).[13] Rates of growth of national income in the twentieth century, on the other hand, contrast markedly with those of the preceding century.

Apart from the decades between the two world wars, the growth rates of national income were consistently high. Even the average growth rate of 0.34 per cent per year gives a misleading impression of low economic performance during the 1920s because of the particularly severe slump in 1930. For instance, between 1926 and 1929, GNP rose by an annual average of 5.89 per cent. For the purpose of general description it seems prudent to regard the growth of national income in the 1930s as the lowest recorded in this century so far and that of the 1920s as much higher than Table 2:2 suggests. The rates of growth of national income at the beginning of the century during a period often called "the wheat boom era" were larger than any which had previously occurred in Canadian history. In the more recent past, since the outbreak of the Second World War, high rates of growth of GNP have also been experienced on average, for more than three decades.

Because GNP is a money or current measure of the flow of national in-

Table 2:2 Growth of Income, 1851-1970: Compound Average Annual Rates of Growth Per Decade

(1935-39 prices = 100)

Period	GNP	Price Level	Real GNP	Real GNP Per Capita
(1)	(2)	(3)	(4)	(5)
1851-60	7.31	3.10	4.08	0.87
1861-70	3.71	0.92	2.76	1.58
1871-80	2.38	-0.15	2.53	0.90
1881-90	3.29	-0.07	3.37	2.17
1891-1900	2.79	-0.43	3.23	2.15
1901-10	7.78	2.10	5.56	2.68
1911-20	9.48	7.60	1.74	-0.36
1921-30	0.34	-2.50	2.92	1.12
1931-40	1.61	-1.12	2.76	1.65
1941-50	10.66	5.57	4.83	2.89
1951-60	7.57	0.95	6.55	3.77
1961-70	8.34	2.96	5.19	3.36

Note: It should be noted that the above growth rates are computed from income figures from several sources. In addition, the price deflator is that used by Firestone which is extended by a simple linking procedure to post-1950 price indexes.

Source: See Table 1:2.

come, caution must be exercised when interpreting its rate of growth. Price inflation may contribute to the growth rate without any corresponding increase in the real flow of goods and service. It is, therefore, the rate of growth of national income in *real* terms which gives the most appropriate measure of the changing national well-being. From Table 2:2 it can be seen that real GNP increased less rapidly during decades of rising prices and more rapidly during decades of falling prices than current measures indicate. For instance, during the last three decades of the nineteenth century, the fall of prices in general led to real growth in national income. Not surprisingly, there was a connection between the rate of growth of prices and real income although that relationship itself altered as the economy changed structure.

The *real* and *nominal* growth of national income were occasionally both high during periods of low average price inflation, such as the 1950s, yet these instances were comparatively rare. More frequent was the discrepancy between the real and nominal growth of income when price inflation was high. This strongly supports the view that rapid price inflation was detrimental to the real growth of the economy. It may be conjectured that while a mild inflation often produced desirable effects on the growth rate of the economy, too rapid a price inflation introduced a great deal of uncertainty about the variability of prices. In turn, this reduced the incentive to undertake current investment while increasing the tendency to reduce savings; householders reallocated income to current consumption of durable goods. Certainly we can observe that the real and nominal growth of national income diverged substantially during periods of high price inflation. The wartime inflation of 1914-18 was such that by 1920 real income had grown on average by only 1.74 per cent whereas nominal income had grown by almost 10 per cent.

While the growth of real GNP often significantly differed from the growth of current GNP, it also was different from the rate of growth of real income per capita. In most developing countries real national income and real income per capita tended to move in concert. Yet, in Canada's past there was no such tendency and explanation lies in the manner in which populations grew. It is in the nature of the open economy that immigration and emigration profoundly affect the population size and structure; in a closed economy, immigration and emigration necessarily play a minor role. Not surprisingly, as will be seen in Chapter 6, decades of high real growth in aggregate terms were also the ones of large net immigration which, in turn, reduced the per-capita gains from the general expansion of the economy. Nowhere is the evidence more dramatically portrayed than in the 1850s. The most prosperous decade of the entire nineteenth century records one of the lowest growths of average real income. So too, during the economic expansion of the early twentieth century, the growth of real income per capita, while large, was far below the aggregate real expansion of the economy. This is the difference between intensive and extensive economic development.[14]

Although a rapid expansion of the population as a result of immigration may have caused the measured rate of growth of real income per capita to depart from the rate of growth of real GNP, it does not follow that it reduced the potential advantages to society. First, real aggregate economic growth was vitally dependent on immigration and the salutory effects it had both in terms of aggregate demand and in terms of its impact on the labour market. Extensive economic growth would have taken place more slowly without the migrants. Second, the larger population resulting from immigration provided the economic incentive, in terms of size of markets and skills within the economy, which became the basis of future economic growth. Apart from the vagaries of actual measurement, there is still one last caution about the interpretation of the rate of growth of measured real income per capita which should be noted. It is an average over the entire population which, as noted earlier, gives no information about the distribution of income.

The sustained decline in prices generally was a symptom of both a world and a domestic economy which were expanding slowly. Yet, in the longest experience of falling prices in modern history during the last quarter of the nineteenth century, Canada's long-run economic performance was surprisingly good. A depression in 1873 had had an immediate impact but by the early 1880s recovery had been such that the real growth of GNP was close to the long-run average. During this period the economy was expanding more slowly than it had earlier or would do later but the low net emigration which took place permitted an annual rise in the real income per capita well above the average of 1.53 per cent for the last half of the century. Another persistent decline in general prices also occurred during the late 1920s and early 1930s although its duration was much shorter. In this depression the growth of GNP in both nominal and real terms actually became negative as did that of real income per capita. Although a fuller discussion of these turbulent years is postponed until later, it is pertinent to note here that only towards the end of the decade was the real growth sufficient to offset the earlier declines.

In summary, economic growth, measured in aggregate, by nominal and real national income, and in per-capita terms, displayed remarkably different and often conflicting patterns over time. While the real growth of the economy is best measured in the aggregate it is a fundamental error not to consider it in conjunction with the improvement in the well-being of the population at large. The task now is to demonstrate how the pace of expansion was linked to the basic structure of the economy.

Sectoral Shifts of Output

In the early 1970s primary economic activity in Canada accounted for less than one-tenth of all output. Yet, it was agriculture, fishing, hunting and trapping, and mining, which at the time of Confederation produced about half of the income in the economy for distribution to more than half of the labour force. The long-run decline in the importance of primary economic activity is the principal attribute of the massive structural change in the economy which occurred during the process of modern economic development. But there were other characteristics. No less spectacular was the growth of the tertiary sector of the economy to a point where, in contemporary Canada, slightly more than 70 per cent of all labour income is earned there. While manufacturing, as a sector of the economy, also expanded, its relative growth was neither as pronounced as the decline in primary production nor as the growth in tertiary production. All sectors, of course, grew in absolute terms.

The best single measure of economic structure is the proportionate contribution of the three main sectors to GNP, presented in Table 2:3. From this can be seen the nature of the long-run changes which seldom

Table 2:3 Sectoral Distribution of GNP, 1851-1970

(per cent)

Year	Primary Sector			Secondary Sector			Tertiary[b] Sector	Other[c]
	Agriculture	Other[a]	Total	Manufacturing	Construction	Total		
(1)	(2)	(3)	(4)	(5)	(6)	(7)	(8)	(9)
1851	32.0	14.8	46.8	18.3	4.2	22.5	18.9	11.8
1860	38.2	12.0	50.2	15.0	4.1	19.1	19.7	11.0
1870	33.3	11.6	44.9	19.0	3.0	22.0	20.9	12.2
1880	32.0	11.5	43.5	18.9	3.8	22.7	22.4	11.4
1890	27.0	9.6	36.6	23.5	4.5	28.1	26.7	8.6
1900	26.7	9.8	36.5	20.8	4.2	25.0	29.4	9.1
1910	22.8	7.4	30.2	22.7	5.1	27.8	33.6	8.4
1920	19.4	7.2	26.6	24.1	5.5	29.7	35.3	8.4
1930	11.0	4.8	15.9	21.7	4.4	26.1	52.3	5.7
1940	10.3	7.3	17.6	24.1	2.8	26.9	45.7	9.8
1950	9.5	6.1	15.6	26.2	4.9	31.1	44.6	8.7
1960	4.8	5.3	9.6	23.2	4.8	28.0	51.0	11.4
1970	3.4	5.0	8.4	23.3	6.3	29.6	62.0	

[a] Includes forestry, fishing and trapping, mining, quarrying, and oil wells.

[b] Includes transport and communications, storage, utilities, wholesale and retail trade, finance, insurance and real estate, public administration, and personal services.

[c] From 1851 to 1920 inclusive this category includes rents, net indirect taxes, and net investment income. For later years it includes net income paid to non-residents.

Sources: O. J. Firestone, *Canada's Economic Development* (London, 1958), p. 189; Firestone (1960), p. 225; Urquhart and Buckley (1965), p. 133; and Statistics Canada, *Income and Expenditure Accounts 1961-1975*, pp. 36-37.

reversed themselves. While there were often periods of accelerated change and also of slow change, so persistent was the change itself that it is often claimed to be irreversible. Of course, in recent years there has been a distinct tendency towards stability of the economic structure. It is unlikely that the agricultural sector, for instance, could be reduced further in relative terms. Such changes in the economic structure of other countries were common. In fact, there was probably a fairly uniform set of historical forces which operated in the developing countries to ensure that this was so. Yet, there were variations and, as so often is the case, these were usually associated with whether the economy was essentially a closed or open one.[15]

In a closed economy the primary productive sector will decline in relative importance whenever there is a growth in real per-capita income. This inevitable process rests on a change in the pattern of consumer purchases as income rises and is known universally as "Engel's law". At low levels of per-capita income the greater part of income must be spent providing for the basic needs of food and shelter. However, as income rises it is no longer imperative to devote such a high proportion directly or indirectly to the output of the primary sector. More manufactured goods are consumed and better quality dwellings, more highly processed food, and more services of the tertiary sector are demanded; that is to say the products of the primary sector face a low income elasticity of demand.[16] Because of this low income elasticity the value of primary production cannot grow as rapidly as the value of the flow of goods and services produced by the rest of the economy.

In an open economy such as Canada's, more complex economic forces than those which might prevail in a closed economy governed the change of industrial structure. First, the tendency for Canada's comparative advantage to lie in the production of primary products promoted specialization in agricultural and natural-resource-based primary activity. This, of course, raises an intriguing question: If Canada's long-run comparative advantage lay in specialization of primary production, why did the primary sector decline relative to the other sectors? In part, the decline was due to the possibility of increased specialization of economic activity, and was made necessary by the exploitation of agricultural and natural resources for export purposes. Comparative advantage induced development from the simple looting of natural resources to a more complicated, roundabout method of economic expansion. This involved, as will be seen later, the creation of a transport system, increased construction, and other related developments. In addition, the manufacturing sector, particularly that portion concerned with the simple processing of primary products, tended to grow because of the proportionately greater value added incurred at that level as a response to the general specialization in primary production. While the long-run impact of comparative advantage has been to cause absolute growth in primary-product-based industries, the distinct characteristic of such specialization was the growth of a relatively large tertiary sector. The tertiary sector grew in all developed economies but its growth has been greater in economies with specializations in primary production. This is true of nations but also, as will be seen later, the regions of Canada which have specialized intensely in natural-resource-based production tend to have larger tertiary sectors than those which have not.

Domestic income-elasticity-of-demand conditions, even in an open economy, played a role in determining the industrial structure. For instance, in Canada the growth of real per-capita income brought about by staple exploitation created a proportionately greater demand for goods and services. These often could only be supplied internally and the allocation of economic resources to their production reduced the relative importance of the primary sector. Even when the goods, for which there was a high income elasticity of demand, could be imported, the existence of an expanding market as well as growing prosperity created the incentive for import-substitution industries. If the initial forces causing a rise in incomes during the wheat-boom era, for example, were based on the demand for primary products, the subsequent rapid decline in the share of the primary sector in output and the rapid growth of import-substitution industries—including foreign direct investment—was an inevitable result of the domestic income elasticity of demand. In general, the consumption of durable goods, such as household appliances and automobiles, increased more than that of clothing and housing which, in turn, increased more than the consumption of foodstuffs. This reflects the various propensities to consume different goods which evolved as income rose.[17]

Production in the open economy faced not only its own domestic income-elasticity conditions but also those of the world-wide markets in which staples were sold. This made Canada more vulnerable to larger swings in economic performance than economies with large proportions of manufactured goods among their exports. The vulnerability stemmed from the great variations in international demand often associated with primary products. As will be seen in Chapter 4, Canadian wheat exports in the nineteenth century were inversely related to the success of the British harvest. So too, the primary-product exports of other countries introduced an instability to world supply by ensuring that world supply often shifted more rapidly than world demand in the short run. Even in the long run, the relative ease of other countries' entry into the export markets for primary products often weakened the Canadian comparative advantage. A stark example occurred in the 1890s when the discovery of natural phosphate deposits in the United States eliminated Quebec producers from the world market. Less dramatically, but just as surely, in the early twentieth century, agricultural exports faced new, effective competition in the traditional market of Great Britain from countries such as Argentina, Australia, and New Zealand. In summary, there were international forces which tended to impede complete specialization in the production of commodities where comparative advantage lay. As well, the income elasticity of demand altered the structure of output, placing less emphasis on primary-product production.[18]

Despite the long operation of the above forces the composition of Canadian exports has not fundamentally changed in modern history. Exports have a high agricultural or natural-resource content as noted in Table 2:1. Indeed, it was the very success achieved in exporting these goods which induced the relative expansions of tertiary and manufacturing production and contractions of primary production. In Canada, the more rapid the rate of export expansion, the more rapid the rate of aggregate income growth and the more rapid the structural shift of output has been. The long specialization in the export of foods, raw materials, and processed materials has been achieved against a background of declining world trade in these commodities relative to secondary manufactured goods. That is, the income elasticity of demand operated globally and only the efficiency of Canadian industries permitted growth in the face of these elasticity conditions. However, it was impossible for the economy to escape entirely from their influence. For instance, in the years since the Second World War, global food exports from all sources declined and Canadian exporters were unable to win a greater proportion of this trade. The role of agricultural exports in the economy weakened and, as seen in Table 2:3, agriculture as a whole is now only a small element of the economic structure. In summary, both the growth in efficiency of Canadian agriculture and primary natural-resource exploitation and the income elasticity of local and world demand forced the economic structure to change. Indeed, it has always been the case that when attempts were made to increase staple outputs, as in the 1850s, the investment necessary for extending the simple exploitation has, itself, irrevocably altered the structure of the entire economy.

Sources of Economic Growth

The forces which gave rise to economic growth and development had their origins at microeconomic levels, in individual industries, and in factor and commodity markets. Although they often came together to exert an effective pressure, explanation of their effect at the level of the whole economy is seldom fully satisfactory. For instance, a production function may explain causal relationships at the level of the individual firm but not for the entire economy. Nevertheless, in aggregation a production function may be employed as a description of the set of stable supply conditions in an economy or, over long time periods, of steadily changing supply forces. In this sense, an aggregate production function is an important vehicle through which insight can be gained about long-run productivity growth.[19]

A production function relates inputs and outputs to each other and in its simplest form deals explicitly with only two inputs. Of the various forms of the function, the Cobb-Douglas function best approximates the relationship:

$$Q = TL^{\alpha} K^{1-\alpha}$$

where Q, L, and K are output, labour, and capital services respectively and T is some measure of a technological constant. The α and $1-\alpha$ are the long-run elasticities of the factors with respect to output; they are the respective shares of output allocated to L and K when all output is distributed to L and K on the basis of marginal contributions. When the functional distribution of output, income, is so arranged, all income is distributed to the factors, and no economies or diseconomies of scale are assumed to be operating. Of course, this was most definitely not the historical case. Why it should be appropriate to so describe the pattern of growth will be seen below.

Transformation of the production function into rates of growth yields:

$$\dot{Q} = a\dot{L} + b\dot{K} + \dot{T}$$

When weights can be assigned to a and b, which must sum to unity, the contributions of labour and capital growth can be assessed. What is not accounted for is the contribution of the *residual*, in this context often referred to as technology—hence, labelled T—or alternatively the rate of total factor-productivity growth. That is, all economic growth which occurred in the past and which was not directly attributable to a growth of either labour or capital is measured by this residual.[20]

First, it is necessary to discover historical values for a and b. In recent history, since the early 1920s, the share of income allocated to domestic labour and non-labour has been remarkably constant at about 77.5 and 25.4 per cent respectively—which comes to slightly more than 100.0 per cent because of foreign claims on assets in Canada. For early periods in history, the evidence for constant factor shares is less overwhelming. In the private sector of the economy, as seen later in Table 2:6, evidence

Table 2:4 Total Factor Productivity Growth in Canada and the United States Compared

(Measured as annual average contribution to the growth of national income with overall growth rate in brackets)

Canada		United States			
Period	Per cent	Period	Per cent	Period	Per cent
(1)	(2)	(3)	(4)	(5)	(6)
—	—	1800-55	0.3 (4.2)	—	—
—	—	1855-1910	0.5 (3.9)	—	—
1891-1910	0.75 (3.38)	—	—	1889-1901	1.07 (4.23)
1910-26	1.16 (2.46)	—	—	1909-29	1.48 (3.17)
1926-56	2.70 (3.89)	—	—	1929-57	2.31 (2.95)

Note: Because of the slightly varying weights for the factor shares the results presented above do not exactly correspond. Notice also that different degrees of accuracy are reported. Figures in columns (3) and (4) are those of Abramovitz and David while those of columns (5) and (6) are those of Denison as reported by Lithwick.

Sources: M. Abramovitz and P. David, "Economic Growth in America: History, Parables and Realities", De Economiste, Vol. 121, no. 3 (1973), p. 254 and H. Lithwick, Economic Growth in Canada (Toronto, 1967), pp. 53-54.

from the manufacturing sector of the economy illustrated a relative constancy of labour's share since Confederation. On the other hand, the economic history of the United States demonstrates that labour's share of output fell slightly in the early nineteenth century before assuming a constancy about mid-century. This was probably also true for British North America but there is no direct evidence.

Historical information since the late nineteenth century has enabled direct estimates to be made of the various contributions to the growth rate of the economy. Once adjustment has been made to reflect the declining work week, changes in education, and other qualitative changes in the direct inputs to production, it is discovered that the direct contribution of more labour and more capital has been of decreasing importance over time. In both the United States and Canada the proportion of the growth of income due to the addition of non-conventional inputs—the residual contribution—grew. During the period 1891-1910 in Canada, for instance, the long-run yearly rate of growth of 3.38 per cent was composed of a contribution of 2.63 per cent from conventional inputs of labour and capital and a 0.75 per cent residual contribution. Over the periods of study, see Table 2:4, the residual contribution has grown absolutely so that in the recent past it has been the major constituent of modern aggregate economic growth. The forces which led to this increasing factor-productivity were fourfold.

The residual contribution to the rate of growth—the rate of total factor productivity—is generally thought to be comprised of several inter-related elements: technological change, productivity gains arising from learning by doing, non-quantifiable productivity gains arising from improved education of the labour force, and the shift in the structure of industry.

1) *Technical change* and innovation in most industries was a continuous process of adaptation. Although it is impossible to discover a suitable description of this particular phenomenon at the aggregate level, it is evident from the microeconomics of most industries that invention and innovation were most rapid during periods of high investment. This was particularly so in Canada where most of the new techniques of production were not local but rather imported, often embodied in new imported capital goods.

2) *Productivity gains from learning by doing* also varied with investment. These gains in output were usually accomplished by workers increasing their familiarity with the capital equipment they operated. To be sure, such productivity gains may also have arisen in industries with low levels of capital intensity but they were usually associated with the early stages of production. Whatever signalled the beginning of learning-by-doing productivity gains, they were usually rapid at first and then slowed down as workers become more used to the capital equipment or organization of the workplace.

3) As noted earlier, *the higher education of the workforce* produced a quantifiable difference in aggregate productivity. However, in the years since the Second World War the increase in the formal-schooling experience of the labour force, measured in years, directly explains only a relatively small proportion of the rate of growth. On the other hand, since education was a factor determining occupational and geographic mobility, it significantly improved the general appreciation of alternatives in the labour market and thereby induced an allocation of labour which promoted a more rapid rate of growth. Quite understandably, quantification of the ability of the labour force to respond more rapidly must be imprecise although most observers feel that it is an important part of the residual contribution to economic growth.[21]

4) Of all the single sources of factor-productivity growth, none has proven to be as important as *the simple shifting of factors from declining to growing industries.* Factors leaving low-productivity economic activities for high ones immediately created a productivity gain which accrued to the economy at large and an increased return to the factor itself. In the years since the beginning of the Second World War, these factor shifts associated with the long-run change in the composition of

the industrial structure accounted for approximately 25 per cent of the average, annual total contribution of factor productivity to economic growth. Alone this has been the most important residual component of the growth rate.

Let us summarize the evidence about the sources of growth, so far as they are understood. The rate of growth of real output has risen secularly over the past century at least. Although an increase in the employment of labour and capital accounted for the initial rise in the growth rate, in the twentieth century the increased rate of growth was increasingly associated with total factor productivity, that is, the residual contribution to the growth rate. This contribution of non-conventional inputs, which in recent years has dominated the growth rates, cannot be adequately accounted for but is thought itself to be affected by innovation, learning by doing, and the increased education of the workforce, but dominated by the productivity gains arising from the inter-industry shifting of factors.[22] Herein lies a problem.

If the major structural shift in the composition of the economy's output is for the most part complete will the residual contribution of economic growth not become smaller in the future and the overall rate of economic growth decline? Certainly, the massive, irreversible shift of resources from primary production to manufacturing and tertiary production is, in a relative sense, almost complete. To be sure, the shift may continue but only at a slow rate. Furthermore, studies of this problem in the United States actually demonstrate the beginnings of a new downward trend in the rate of economic growth brought about, it is asserted, by a decline in the residual contribution to economic growth. Sectoral shares of output, of course, became stable in the United States before they did in Canada. Whether or not Canada is bound to suffer a decline in its real growth rate is as yet uncertain. First, the evidence that growth rates in the United States or Canada are declining secularly is unproven. Second, the total factor-productivity gains may continue to be as great as new industries emerge and as new firms are created, even though the broadly defined structural change in the economy has been for the most part completed. Last, there is no reason to suppose that, in the long run, the productivity gains from the other non-conventional inputs may grow to offset the decline in the impact of inter-industry shifts of labour and capital.

Technical Change

All studies of economic growth and development assign a central causal role to the effects of technical change. This, of course, is not surprising in light of the previous discussion, since the total effects of technical change were the major causes of economic development, along with the addition of new factors. New transport technologies permitted the opening of the prairies; the creation of new production processes in, for example, the pulp and paper industry, enabled the exploitation of new natural resources, and the introduction of inventions, such as the mechanical reaper, resulted in productivity gains in each sector of the economy. New products were also created. In short, any description of the Canadian economy and its evolution must also describe the new technology and inventions which made that evolution possible.

Technical change can be defined as the application of man's inventive capacity to an economic end use. It has appeared as either the creation of new, or the alteration of existing, production processes. New goods were designed and goods using existing designs were produced more efficiently. From time to time technical change also appeared as the reorganization of marketing activity or the restructuring of plant involving little or no new mechanical equipment. Generally, technical change conformed to one of two main types.[23] The first type was that of a wholly new invention which changed existing technique profoundly when adopted by innovators. Second, there were a great number of changes which were not the result of wholly new inventions but were more in the nature of a routine innovation by one practised in some particular art. That is, no radical change in technique was required for the exploitation of this type of change. When new inventions or innovations took place they tended to spread throughout the economy. Naturally, the individual economic circumstances associated with a new technique determined when it was first introduced and then how rapidly it was adopted by others. Often this process of diffusion required modification of the new technique to local conditions, as will be seen later. Another characteristic of new technology in the small, open economy of Canada was that much was imported from other countries. This, however, is not to imply that Canadians were less inventive or innovative than individuals elsewhere. There are many examples of new technology of domestic origin. Some of these technologies, in turn, were quickly adopted outside Canada. The long-distance transmission of electric power and the early ripening of cereals were only two of many new techniques developed in large measure in Canada. Such new techniques were commonly linked to the process of developing natural-resource use.

Technical change was a vital component of changes in transport systems which, in turn, were necessary for successful staple exploitation. However, in many cases the transport technology was autonomous. That is, it was not created, in the first instance, in response to the needs of the staple trades. Usually these changes in transport were imported from abroad: railways, steam tugs, and canal-building techniques, for example. Although their creation was not *induced* by economic necessity in Canada, their local adaptation was. So important was the local adaptation that it is difficult to distinguish between a change in technology, say the railways, and the innovations required for local use, such as the design of gravel beds for track over marsh in Northern Ontario, for example. There are many other examples of substantial modifications before employment of an existing technique in Canada.

There can be no dispute that much of the technical change in transport and other sectors of the Canadian economy was imported. Consequently, it is necessary to ask not only what determined the rate of inventive activity, the diffusion of new techniques, but also what determined the rate of import of new technology into the open economy? In general, the pace of scientific advance determined the pace of inventive activity. New scientific and engineering principles were, however, not always directly linked to the introduction of new techniques although some observers have claimed that the link between science and technology has strengthened in recent years. Invention and its subsequent application has been the work of practical men, many of whom had no particular training in science or formal education in engineering. New technologies tended to be introduced into fields of economic activity where the greatest economic rents could be earned. For instance, in a particular sector or industry the amount of inventive activity of the novel variety was directly linked to the amount of investment undertaken in the immediate past. This strongly suggests that in expanding new industries, where both the risk and the potential economic rent were higher, only the inventive and innovative spirits survived in business. The rate of routine innovation in industry, on the other hand, did not respond to the rate of change of investment activity. Rather, routine invention and application was invariant to changes in what might be regarded as potential stimulants—the movement of profits over the business cycle, the performance of exports, and others. Underlying such observations is the suggestion that the amount of routine innovation did not necessarily vary with the rate of new invention. It was, as far as is known, stochastic in the short run although affected profoundly in the long run by such influences as government policy.[24]

Government policy, in fact, played an important part in determining the pace of the development of inventions and their application because it set the general economic framework. Government action to ensure that new techniques were introduced and spread, far from being a modern activity and quite apart from the special concerns of the transport sector, was common in the nineteenth century. This was so because only through government action could certain externality problems associated with innovative behaviour be solved. As will be seen with regard to the costs and benefits of introducing new drainage techniques in the agricultural sector, the state's authority was necessary to ensure that when a new technique was introduced there was an equitable sharing of costs and benefits. Also, by the late nineteenth century the government was beginning to take a direct role in research and development as it had earlier in the century assumed responsibility for technical education. For instance, the research stations of the Department of Agriculture were instrumental in discovering new techniques in agriculture as well as being responsible for their dissemination. These agricultural innovations extended the wheat frontier in western Canada and raised agricultural productivity.[25]

Technical change was, as has been said, a product of both inventive activity at home and the importing of new techniques. New techniques brought to Canada from abroad were often used immediately. In this manner advanced techniques were introduced and, without delay, diffused throughout the economy. Imported technical change itself reached Canada in a variety of ways. There was, of course, the simple international flight of ideas carried by observant travellers, by newspapers and technical publications, and by letter, to name but a few routes of transmission. Technical change reached Canada more systematically in the form of new techniques carried as skills by the immigrants to the country and *embodied* in the capital goods imported. The skills of immigrants, for instance, included many of the best practices of eastern European and U.S. farming which made these groups so successful in the prairie wheat economy. More consciously acted upon were the techniques known to specific individuals. For example, when John Rogers, engineer, immigrated from New York to Vancouver to set up western Canada's first major sugar refinery in the 1890s he brought with him knowledge of the new techniques of that industry. A few individual Swiss-born migrants from upper New York State in the 1860s carried the initial innovation of factory cheese-making techniques to Canada. Elsewhere, the phrase "human capital" has been used to describe such knowledge, much of which contributed to the rate of innovative activity in Canada.

So too, the new foreign direct investments carried with them the new technologies, particularly those of secondary manufacturing. Often, it was this technological expertise which gave the foreign producers their market advantage in Canada. The assembly-line techniques of modern manufacturing usually made their first large-scale appearance in Canada under the aegis of firms controlled in the United States. In recent years, changes in technique have also been imported into Canada by the vehicle of licensing agreements. Foreign producers permit use of a new technique to a specific domestic firm — usually, of course, for a fee.

Yet, of all the methods by which new techniques reached Canada, none were so ubiquitous as through the importation of capital goods. Capital goods generally embodied new advances in technology made elsewhere and Canada's relatively high dependence on imported capital goods relative to other countries made this type of embodied transfer important. Not surprisingly, the rate of technical change through this medium varied directly with the performance of the Canadian economy through the investment process. Consequently, such technical change was highly responsive to the performance of the small open economy but required little domestic investment in research and design. Once introduced, a technical change tended to spread throughout the economy. However, a complex set of economic circumstances controlled both the extent to which the new technique was finally adopted and the rate of its spread. First, however, it is important to note that new and old techniques of production often existed side by side and it was in no sense inevitable that new technologies replaced old ones. A new technique often had implications for the size of economic units and furthermore might require factors to be combined in different proportions than formerly. If the minimum required scale was too large, given the state of demand, or if the supply of cooperating factors was such that input prices were radically altered, the new costs might offset the productivity gain from the new technique. Consequently the new technique might not be applied everywhere. Similarly, old techniques often continued to be the most efficient method of production in parts of industry. For instance, long into the age of steam and iron ships, shipyards in the Atlantic region of Canada continued to produce wooden sailing ships which were supplied to ready purchasers. In part, this can be explained by the fact that, lacking any comparable opportunity cost, those who supplied inputs of labour and capital permitted a bidding down of their service price in order to ensure that prices of wooden sailing ships remained competitive, in efficiency terms, with the products of the new technology. Construction of wooden sailing ships made up a sizeable proportion of Canadian shipbuilding until well into the twentieth century. Since local circumstances were so important, it is not surprising that the survival of old techniques often had a regional effect. In the case of wooden shipbuilding, the industry of Quebec more quickly succumbed to the pressure of the new technology than that of the Maritime provinces.[26]

If there were few barriers to the spread of the new technique, diffusion was often rapid and complete. The new canning techniques, for example, introduced a radical change in the Pacific salmon industry after 1880. Their spread was rapid and within a few years adoption was total because failure to innovate denied a firm entry into the quality-conscious export market. Throughout industry the proven value of a new technique forced others to adopt it in their firms; generally, this spread of a new technique conformed to a pattern. At first, the innovator alone perceived the economic rents to be gathered but after some time the slightly less intrepid imitated him. Then, with repeated demonstration of success, the rate of diffusion became more rapid. But the rate of diffusion naturally slowed down again as laggard firms either adopted the new technique or were driven out of business. This decline in the rate of diffusion arose from many circumstances. If the increase in supply drove down prices, economic rents, of course, fell because of the impact on revenues and the marginal firms succumbed. The use of the new technique often raised capital barriers in the industry as, for instance, mines were extended into poorer-grade ore deposits and the less successful firms could not marshall financial resources to undertake the adoption of the new technique.

The time it took for a new technique to win wide acceptance necessarily varied from industry to industry. Diesel locomotion, for instance, replaced steam power on the railways within ten years, which was, by historical standards, a short period of time for the adoption of such a novel technology especially given the amount of new investment required to bring about its application. Whether the new technique was fundamental or whether it was simply a routine invention and whether it required a large amount of investment or not were considerations which helped to determine the rate of diffusion. But that was not all. The spread of technique was also dependent on the market structure of the industry within which the technical change took place. For instance, oligopolistic firms often delayed the introduction of new techniques but once the initial innovation took place the subsequent diffusion was rapid. In more competitive industries, particularly agriculture, the adoption of new techniques was generally immediate once the technique became known. It is impossible to generalize, however, about their subsequent spread. Although the diffusion of certain new techniques, such as the development of cereal hybrids and new cattle breeds, took relatively short periods of time the widespread adoption of the gasoline tractor took a long time. As late as 1941, only one farm in every three on the prairies had a motor tractor. In those industries where the new technique was embodied in imported capital goods the diffusion of technology was generally more rapid than when that industry had to rely on the small capital-goods sec-

Figure 2:1 The Diffusion of New Techniques: Adoption of Diesel Locomotion

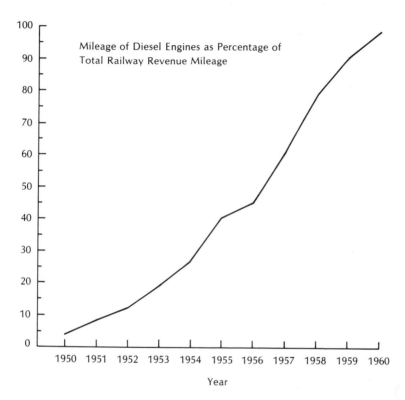

Source: Data are from M. C. Urquhart and K. A. H. Buckley, eds., *Historical Statistics of Canada* (Toronto, 1965), p. 354.

tor in Canada. As was mentioned earlier, there was a potential for storing up and then importing technological change. In general, this may have led to the more rapid diffusion of new techniques, once introduced, than in, say, the United States. Diesel locomotion on the railways was a case in point.

The invention and application of new techniques of production was a source of important productivity gains. Yet despite the income gains which have accrued from technical change some observers of the process of industrial growth have argued that the net gains have been ambiguous; technical change biased industrial development in a manner which may have been detrimental to the society's long-run welfare. For instance, Karl Marx, in *Das Kapital*, argued that the biases introduced through innovation and invention in a developing capitalist economy would ultimately drive down the wage rate of the labour force to subsistence level and create an army of unemployed. While it is manifest that this has not come to pass it is still pertinent to inquire if technology has tended to bias the economy into reducing the potential income gains to labour.

Invention, innovation, and the reorganization of production processes were the result of economic pressure to reduce costs. In the private sector of the economy, businessmen introduced cost-reducing technology in order to increase profits or to avoid unprofitability and the demise of the business venture. In the public sector, the government was also active in promoting technical change. Its motives were not those of profit but an awareness of the general benefits to society which might result from cost reductions in certain sectors of the economy. Particularly in the nineteenth and twentieth centuries Canadian governments have been well aware that certain costs retarded the spread and development of the economy. To reduce costs, a variety of measures were employed, among them subsidies to certain industries and the sponsoring of new technologies either through research and design or by making arrangements which permitted the importation of capital goods with embodied technique.

When technical change was induced by the need to reduce costs per unit it was often found later to have had an ambiguous effect on the factor proportions used in production. For example, the new technology often saved on the employment of labour and expanded the use of capital. Such adjustments are referred to as "biases" and are defined in terms of changes in the share of output—value added—with respect to the factor input. Labour-saving biases were those which economized on the use of labour thereby reducing labour's share. Biased technical change may also be capital-saving in which case it would also be described as "labour-using". Of course, new technologies may be neutral with respect to their impact on factor shares. As a response to factor prices which they could observe changing in a fairly systematic manner, entrepreneurs attempted to bias the new technology.

The long-run trend in both primary and secondary Canadian manufacturing exhibited technical change which was relatively labour-saving—capital-using. The historical evidence is threefold.[27] First, real wages in Canada grew more rapidly than the cost of capital services from at least the mid-nineteenth century. The real interest rate, in fact, remained relatively constant. Technical change which was successfully introduced, economic theory suggests, conserved on the use of the more expensive factor input. There may well have been temporary cost barriers or engineering research problems which delayed the desired labour-saving effect, but in a developing capitalist economy, these did not usually persist since factor returns were equilibrated with their marginal products or at least directed towards them. Second, since Canada was an open economy, much of the technical change in manufacturing was imported. New technology came principally from the United States, embodied in the form of capital goods, new direct investments with their innovative procedures, and also in the human capital of immigrants. Since manufacturing in the United States displayed a labour-saving bias from the earliest times, also in response to the increasing relative costs of labour to capital, the bias was imported into Canada. Third, Canadian manufacturing has displayed, throughout recent history, and it is believed earlier, an elasticity of substitution between capital and labour which was less than unity in absolute terms. This needs amplification. The elasticity of substitution between two factor inputs is defined as:

$$\varepsilon^{KL} = -(\% \text{ change in K/L} / \% \text{ change in the MRTS})$$

where K/L is the capital-labour ratio, the MRTS $= MP_K/MP_L = P^K/P^L$, where MRTS is the marginal rate of technical substitution defined as the ratio of the marginal products and where P^K/P^L is the relative price of capital to labour. It is a measure of the substitution possibilities in response to relative price changes. For instance, if the engineering characteristics of production required K and L to be combined in fixed proportions there is no possibility of substitution in response to a change in relative prices. At infinity the ε^{KL} is an indication of complete substitution possibilities.

Yet a low elasticity of substitution indicates labour-saving technical change only under certain conditions. These conditions arise from the historical tendency of the quality of inputs to change. For instance, if units of capital increase in efficiency, due to, say, the better organization of a factory, at a rate greater than the growth of labour efficiency then a capital-augmenting technical change occurs when entrepreneurs respond to this efficiency. The relative efficiency gain, in this example of capital, will dampen the tendency of the K/L to decrease when there is an increase in P^K/P^L and an ε^{KL} less than unity would be measured. On the other hand, when labour grows in efficiency more rapidly than capital, labour-augmenting technical change takes place and this alone would produce an ε^{KL} greater than unity. Consequently, it is only when there is both labour-augmenting technical change and an ε^{KL} less than unity that there is unambiguous evidence for a relatively labour-saving bias in the direction of technical change.

Strong, although indirect, evidence supports the view that technical change has been labour-augmenting. As already noted, the quality of labour inputs in Canada has increased more than that of capital and has contributed more to the growth rate of output. Furthermore, there is much individual evidence that both workers and bureaucracies "learn by doing". Given the open nature of the economy it is again possible to look to the experience of the United States: Since 1900 technical change in that country has been both labour-augmenting and labour-saving. Labour-augmentation and a long-run ε^{KL} of approximately 0.6 in Canadian manufacturing during the post-1926 years indicates that technical change was of the labour-saving variety. This was probably also true prior to 1926.

Yet within the manufacturing sector there was considerable variation in the extent of the labour-saving bias. Some industries exhibited low elasticities of substitution between capital and labour. These included the petroleum, chemicals, textile, non-ferrous metals, tobacco, rubber-goods, and leather-goods industries. When technical change took place in industries with high elasticities of substitution between capital and labour—but still less than unity in absolute terms—the labour share of output fell as a result of technical change but not by as much as in former cases. These industries were food and beverages, clothing, wood products, and non-metallic minerals. All others were close to the overall manufacturing average.

This bias of technical change in Canadian primary and secondary industry has not been confined solely to a labour-saving tendency. Expanded notions of production based on the gross value of output must include not only labour and capital but natural resources (R) and energy (E). Such production functions are written

$$Q = f(K, L, R, E)$$

This helps to pose a problem of modern economic growth. To some extent all inputs are substitutable but not all inputs come from a renewable stock. Many natural resources are non-renewable and of course much of the energy consumed by industry comes directly from fossil-fuel sources or other sources which cannot be readily expanded. Yet, natural-resource and energy prices have increased less rapidly than labour in the nineteenth and twentieth centuries. Not surprisingly there has been a tendency for innovations to be resource-using and energy-using. Where these input prices were established in international markets and Canada was simply a price-taker, they may, in the long run, have created the conditions which lead to the depletion of natural resources at too rapid a rate. There indeed may be limits to growth and the prospect of a relatively stable growth-path may be jeopardized. In many cases, both federal and provincial governments may have failed to tax resource-use at the appropriate rate thereby conferring economic rents on the exploiter, who in this case was also the innovator. As will be noted in Chapter 8, many of the industries with relatively large resource and energy inputs have a substantial foreign-business presence. The threat to long-run economic performance is that the resource- and energy-using tendencies further truncate export industry with only modest domestic-income gains which in the long run must be weighed against the potential income losses realized when natural-resource stocks and fuel stocks are further reduced.

To return to the main theme: Despite the historical tendency to introduce labour-saving innovations there is no evidence that the share of output paid to labour declined. For the entire economy, as noted earlier in this chapter, the income shares were relatively constant. Table 2:5 presents the evidence from the private-business sector. As a whole, the share of income which went to labour was fairly constant although there may have been a slight upward trend in recent years; later we shall see that this slight upward trend is mirrored by a slight downward trend of the K/Q ratio.[28] In most sub-sectors of private business the shares were unambiguously constant with the important exception of the service industry and undoubtedly the growth in the personal services of physicians or artists, for example, accounted for the growth in labour's share. It is critical to note that the tertiary sector, discussed earlier, includes not only the service industry but construction, transport, communications, and utilities as well as retail trade and financial, insurance, and real-estate services. When considered in its totality there is little evidence to suggest that aggregate factor shares in the tertiary sector have been other than constant.

Canada demonstrated an income distribution, measured by factor shares, which was essentially similar to all countries which developed in a competitive capitalist environment. Clearly, the decline in labour's share of income which may have come about due to biased technical change was offset so as to leave factor shares little affected.

In summary, economic growth, in modern times, in developed countries such as Canada, has taken place with:

1) a rising price for labour relative to the services of capital with real prices of capital goods relatively constant through time;
2) a rising ratio of capital to labour, the aggregate K/L, in the economy as a whole;
3) a relatively stable ratio of capital to output, the aggregate K/Q, in the economy as a whole with a slight downward trend over the last fifty years;
4) relatively constant distributive shares of output;

Table 2:5 Labour's Share in the Private Business Sector, 1870-1960

Wages, Salaries, and Supplementary Labour Income as a
Proportion of Income

Year	Labour's Share of Value Added in Manufacturing	Manufacturing	Transportation, Communications, and Utilities	Construction	Service	Business
(1)	(2)	(3)	(4)	(5)	(6)	(7)
1870	0.42	—	—	—	—	—
1880	0.45	—	—	—	—	—
1890	0.46	—	—	—	—	—
1900	0.54	—	—	—	—	—
1910	0.43	—	—	—	—	—
1920	0.46	(1926) 0.69	0.68	0.77	0.38	0.49
1930	0.47	0.67	0.71	0.77	0.40	0.54
1940	0.47	0.69	0.61	0.74	0.42	0.53
1950	0.47	0.68	0.71	0.68	0.51	0.56
1960	0.49	(1958) 0.75	0.70	0.72	0.54	0.62

Note: Column (2) is calculated from the value-added base which includes depreciation allowances, cost of repairs, office equipment, and supplies, as well as advertising expenses. It is a larger base than income, employed in columns (3) to (7), which excludes the above. Consequently, column (2) is not directly comparable to the rest of the table although it does provide good historical evidence that factor shares changed very little.

Sources: S. A. Goldberg, "Long-Run Changes in the Distribution of Income by Factor Shares in Canada", in The Behavior of Income Shares (Princeton, 1964), pp. 227, 266-67 and Urquhart and Buckley (1965), p. 463.

5) increasing labour productivity; and
6) a more or less continuous pattern of technical change.[29]

Without technical change, growth in an economy could only occur by the exploitation of a fixed set of investment opportunities and because of the phenomenon of diminishing returns, there would necessarily be a rise in the K/Q ratio. This is equivalent to a decline in capital productivity. As a real wage rate grew relative to the real price of capital, the K/L ratio would increase. This process, known as "capital deepening", would not produce gains in labour productivity because of the static set of investment opportunities being exploited. Output per labourer would tend to fall. Any attempt to describe the history of the economy without accounting for technical change does not come to grips with the historical facts displayed over the long run.

Technical change as a demand force altered the efficiency of capital. It delayed diminishing returns by creating a new set of investment opportunities. As the K/L ratio rose in response to the relative prices of the two

Table 2:6 Capital-Output Ratios by Industry, 1950

Industry	K/Q
(1)	(2)
Agriculture	1.62
Resource Industries	3.94
Primary Manufacturing	2.53
Secondary Manufacturing	1.69
Transport, Storage, and Communication	8.15
Trade, Services and Construction	1.04

Source: W. C. Hood and A. D. Scott, *Output, Labour, and Capital in the Canadian Economy* (Ottawa, 1957), p. 266.

factors there was a resulting growth in labour productivity. That is, Q/L grew because of labour's greater efficiency when combined with capital embodying the new technique of production. In turn, the rise in labour productivity just offset the capital deepening to produce relatively constant factor shares so long as the K/Q ratio remained constant.

If the foregoing describes the stylized facts of modern economic growth, it does not, without elaboration, accurately sketch a particular phenomenon associated with pre-modern economic development. Some time in the past the K/Q ratio rose to values of approximately 2.5 to 3.5. In the United States the K/Q ratio was about 1.8 at the beginning of the nineteenth century and rose to approximately 3.6 by mid-century. Although there is no direct evidence for Canada it is likely that the K/Q ratio similarly increased some time after that of the United States. This rise in K/Q was brought about by the rapid shifts in the industrial composition of output which were the first signs of the increasingly complex staple production and early growth of manufacturing. In particular, the growth of transport facilities was instrumental in causing the increase in K/Q and the apparent rise in the savings rate in the late nineteenth century was a source of financing it. After all, the rise of the tertiary economy to occupy a significant proportion of all output was a process which involved a shift to many capital-intensive types of economic activity, such as transport. Exploitation of staples in the twentieth century and earlier was a capital-intensive as well as natural-resource-intensive economic activity as evident in Table 2:6.

In this chapter we have presented an overview of the process of spread and change in structure of the economy. It is now necessary to examine these themes both in greater detail and in their historical perspective. We turn now to the period of early settlement and the extension of economic activity based on the early staple trades.

CHAPTER THREE

The Early Staples: Renewable-Natural-Resource Exploitation

Introduction

During the age of the great explorers many came to the land which is now Canada in search of gold and a trade route to the Indies and China. Their legacy, however, was the publicity they gave in Europe to the abundant natural resources of the areas they explored: the teeming cod fishery of the St. Lawrence, the wealth of animal furs, and the vast forests. Attracted by the possibilities of trade in these natural resources, the first Europeans to establish permanent settlements in Canada arrived in the early 1600s. For more than two centuries the trade in these particular natural resources was the main element of export-led economic development. The most distinctive feature of that development was, in turn, the vast geographic expansion of the economy.

By contrasting the three major staple trades in fish, fur, and timber it is possible to show how each influenced the spread of the economy. As noted in the previous chapter, the staple thesis provides the general framework for examination of the impact of natural-resource exploitation on economic development. As such, it leads to consideration of the linkages which were created by the staple trades, the technology of staple exploitation, and the demand for the staple products. However, the staple thesis does not suggest a mechanism which explains how the process of resource exploitation regulated the pace of economic development. It is necessary, therefore, to specify a model of resource development which takes account of the institutional features of each trade. In that context, the generalizations of the staple thesis will be examined.

The Exploitation of Natural Resources

The economic problem of natural-resource use in history is a familiar one: Should consumption of the resource today be undertaken at the expense of consumption tomorrow? That is, what is the marginal rate of time preference placed by society on the resource? Regardless of whether the natural resource in question is renewable, such as fish stocks, or non-renewable, such as coal deposits, the basic question concerning its efficient use is the same. The use of non-renewable natural resources must involve their depletion; in the absence of new discoveries, the stocks of existing natural resources must fall. On the other hand, the exploitation of renewable resources does not necessarily imply their depletion. Since Canada's earliest major staple trades were all renewable-natural-resource-based products — fish, fur, and timber — it is necessary to examine the growth of the staple trades in the context of depletion.[1]

Renewable natural resources are, of course, those which are capable of self-regeneration. This quality gives them very particular economic attributes; the biology of natural growth interacts with the economic allocation of scarce resources. First, it should be noted that any natural-resource stock will grow at a different rate depending on the size of the existing stock. In the original state of nature a resource stock of say, fish, is at its long-run equilibrium. That is, apart from short-run fluctuations, the resource stock is stable; the net recruitment is said to be zero. No net growth takes place because the resource has reached the carrying capacity of the environment so that for each death or disappearance one new recruit to the stock occurs. In the example of fish, the availability of food resources and the existence of natural predators, among other causes, determine the equilibrium size. In terms of timber, it is the density of the existing forest which determines in large measure the size of the net recruitment.

In the stationary state of nature — called "bionormal equilibrium" — the resource stock is the same throughout time (R^e in Figure 3:1). The axes of this diagram indicate the *net growth* of the stock at different *sizes* of the resource stock. If, on the other hand, the resource stock is smaller than R^e, for any reason, there is space or food in the environment to permit positive growth of the stock. That is, at stock levels such as R^m net recruitment takes place — represented here by F(R). If the stock is very small, F(R) will be small because of the limited breeding or growth capacity and as the stock grows new additions can be made without causing any diminution in the survival possibility of extant stock and net recruitment grows. However, beyond some unspecified maximum stock

Figure 3:1 Exploitation of a Renewable Resource Stock

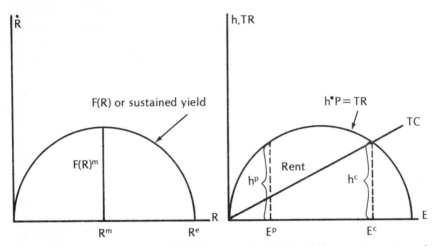

Note: The maximum sustained yield is given by $F(R)^m$ and the maximum size of stock occurs at R^e. In practice biological and botanical species may become extinct before a zero stock level. In the second diagram, care should be taken not to impute directly the stock size; it will, in fact, vary inversely with E.

R — resource stock
$\dot{R}$ — rate of growth of resource stock
R^e — biological maximum of stock
R^m — sustained yield maximum
h — harvest
E — effort
P — price
TR — total revenue
TC — total costs
Superscripts p and c refer to the private and common property rights solutions.

size the new additions are of a sufficient number that the natural mortality or disappearance rates increase and as a consequence the net recruitment falls until it becomes zero at the natural equilibrium. In the absence of man, the resource stock at any given time t, grows in the next period (t + 1) to be:

$$R_{t+1} = R_t + F(R_t)$$

If the stock is not at its natural equilibrium, and providing it is not extinct, $F(R) > 0$.

The sustained-yield curve in Figure 3:1 indicates the net recruitment to any resource stock. It is called a "sustained-yield curve" because man can harvest an amount equal to the net recruitment in a particular time period and the resource stock will remain unaltered in size. Cropping fish, fur, timber, or any other renewable resource in this manner can carry on indefinitely; the harvest is sustainable. If on the other hand, the harvest is less than the net recruitment the stock grows and if it is greater the stock declines. This can be written as:

$$R_{t+1} = R_t + F(R_t) - h_t$$

If harvesting is exactly equal to the net recruitment, then the total revenue possibilities from harvesting are given as the sustained yield times the prevailing price. When this total revenue is examined with respect to the possible levels of effort expended in gathering the resource (E) it can be seen in Figure 3:1 that both revenues and costs determine the economic decision of how much cropping should take place. Where the effort is simply comprised of the labour and capital inputs into production the total cost of harvesting is assumed to be linear. However, even with knowledge of costs and revenues from a sustainable harvesting it is impossible to predict what the eventual harvests will be because of the variability of the property rights over the resource.

In an economic context, property rights describe control of the resource; there are two basic types. First, when a resource stock is available to anyone who wishes to harvest from it, the property rights are described as common. Conversely, when there is sole ownership of the resource, property rights are described as private. The distinguishing feature between the two is the freedom of entry into the industry employing the resource. Whether a resource is a common or private one is basically determined by whether exclusive use of the resource can be defended either in recognized law, or through the use of economic or political sanctions. For example, in the sixteenth century it was extremely difficult for any individual enterprise or indeed any nation to claim control over the Gulf of St. Lawrence fishery and then to successfully defend that claim against the encroachments of others. Because the type of property rights influences the marginal rate of time preference of the resource users there is an effect on the long-run equilibrium.[2]

Consider in Figure 3:1 sole ownership of the resource in question where low effort implies a large stock and *vice versa*. A monopolist will use the resource, expand effort, to the point E^P. This is the harvest level at which net economic rent is maximized.[3] The marginal benefit of the additional resources collected by expending a unit of effort just equals the marginal cost of doing so. Of course there would be no reason for a resource user to practise sustained-yield harvesting initially. As Canadian history amply demonstrates there was often a rapacious use of new-found resources. Depletion would occur until the E^P equilibrium was reached. However, if there is freedom of entry into the industry using the resource the stock declines further and the flow of the resource harvested on a sustained basis will generally be lower than under conditions of limited entry attached to private property management. This occurs because the new entrants hope to capture the economic rent of the sole owner. However, the marginal costs incurred by society gathering the resource exceed the marginal benefit to society. Entry into the industry takes place until all the economic rents are dissipated at the equilibrium described by E^C. There is no pure profit left to attract additional exploitation. Any individual conservation attempts simply confer greater harvests on competitors. The equilibrium, in fact, occurs at the point of effort and stock size where the *average* benefit equals the *average* cost. The flow of the resource into the society is smaller than that which would occur under sole ownership.

Now we can apply the concepts of resource use to early Canadian history in order to describe the spread of the economy. Consider a renewable resource, such as fur-bearing animals, which exists in two geographically separate areas. The stocks of the resource in each area are similar in every respect. However, since one area (Area B) is far removed from settlement, there are fixed costs associated with harvesting which do not exist when nearby Area A is exploited. For instance, these fixed costs might include the cost of establishing forts, trade centres, transport routes, as well as the time cost of shipping goods. If the fixed costs were high enough, as in Figure 3:2, the resource users will harvest exclusively in Area A and Area B will remain in an unexploited natural state. Depending upon the prevailing pattern of property rights the exploitation will be either h_A^P or h_A^C.

A variety of economic forces may propel geographic expansion of this simple economy. The entire structure of variable costs in both areas may fall. Or, the fixed-cost component of exploiting the resource in Area B may fall. A rise in the price of the resource would also have the same general effect of encouraging expansion. With reference to Figure 3:2, if there is a rise in the price, the total revenue possibilities in both areas increase but the sustained yield remains unchanged by economic phenomena. Harvesting in the remote Area B is now feasible and will occur whatever system of property rights pertains. At the same time, there is more depletion of the proximate resource stock; the discovery and exploitation of the western fur reserves did not bring an end to local trapping and hunting in Quebec. The economy grew and spread.

Much of earlier Canadian history was determined in the context of

Figure 3:2 The Spread of a Natural-Resource-Based Economy

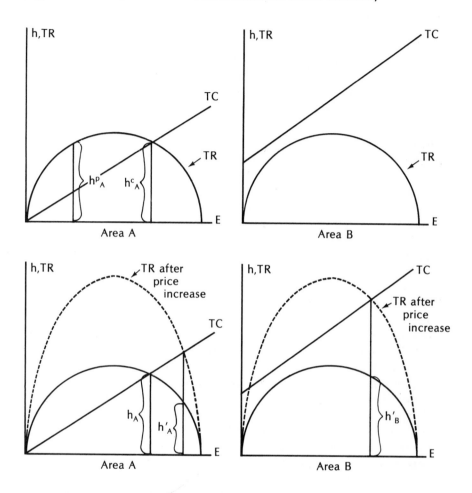

Note: The two diagrams in Row 1 illustrate the private and common property rights solutions of exploitation. The symbols are the same as those used in Figure 3:1, with A and B being the near and far resource regions, respectively.

In Row 2 only the common property rights solution is shown for the sake of simplicity. Notice that the result of the price increase is to shift upward the total revenue functions but not the sustained harvest profile. Harvesting in A increases while that in B begins, in this case, at a high level.

renewable-natural-resource exploitation. Here, a theory has been presented to aid explanation of the spread of the economy. However, it is necessary to take into account several additional features:

1) the physical characteristics of the renewable resource stock;
2) whether over-harvesting took place or not; and
3) under what economic arrangements the exploitation took place.
    Within the enlarged model the early staples are now examined.

The Fisheries

No one cay say with certainty when the Europeans first discovered the Gulf of St. Lawrence fishery. All that is sure is that by the late sixteenth century many European fishermen systematically voyaged to the area to harvest part of the resource wealth. Since no one nation or group could at this time exclude the others from the fishing grounds, entry by vessels into the Grand Banks fishery was open. Here we have an example of the classic case of a common property resource where no individual or interest group asserted jurisdiction over the resource although increases in the number of users might reduce enjoyment of the fishing grounds. By the end of the sixteenth century Portuguese, Spanish, English, and French fishing fleets were all active in the Gulf of St. Lawrence fishery. Despite the open access there has never been any evidence to suggest that aggregate catches were falling or that the resource stock was being depleted. In this case, the low extra returns anticipated from attempting to appropriate and defend exclusive jurisdictional rights maintained the common-property nature of the resource and as more vessels fished the area they tended to distribute themselves over more of the fishery. There were some exceptions, such as the intense rivalry between French and English fishing interests. But confrontation was not general and was only acute during the seventeenth century in some regions of Newfoundland's inshore waters.[4]
    Open access to the fishery depended on the roughly equal power of the maritime nations which, in turn, led to policies of non-harassment. However, with the eclipse of first Portuguese and then Spanish power in the late sixteenth century the pattern of entry into the fishery altered. It is from this time that the ascendency of the English fishing fleet began. Although the French established some control on the south coast of Newfoundland (by 1680 French vessels outnumbered the English by three to one), the French fishing effort was not as well coordinated as the English.
    There were several fundamental differences between the methods employed by the English and French in their activities in the fishery. Of these the nature of the preparation of the fish, or cure, is a vital distinction. The English landed on the foreshores and sun-dried the cod before

shipment to market. On the other hand, the French employed a wet cure which entailed that the individual vessels carry salt to the fishery to be used as a preservative. It has long been argued that the different cures were adopted because the relative price of salt in France was much lower than in England.[5] France had, by virtue of its location, a superior ability to collect and dry sea salt. Unfortunately, the evidence is not wholly convincing that the price of salt was always lower in France than in England since sea salt generally must be dried by more conventional coal or charcoal heat means even after rudimentary sun-drying in the coastal salt pans. England had very cheap sources of heat energy whereas France did not. More than likely it was the different nature of the final markets in which the fish were sold which determined the appropriate cure. Nevertheless, because the English fishermen, from the earliest times in the fishery, used the dry method of curing the cod, England was more assertive in establishing territorial claims in Newfoundland and other shores abutting the fishery than France.

The principal advantage of the dry- as opposed to the wet-cure method of preserving fish for market is that when dried the foodstuff does not spoil as rapidly. With a longer inventory life the fish could be stored more effectively and this, in turn, permitted more flexibility in the selling and subsequent use of the fish. For instance, when the French attempted to use the fishery as a source of cheap foodstuff for the large slave population of the West Indies as a general policy of encouraging sugar plantations, they, like the English earlier, adopted the dry cure. That is, the West Indies market was sufficiently different from that of France that greater inventories were required. By adopting the dry cure, and at the same time maintaining the wet cure, the French were ensuring that sufficient protein was available for both the slaves of the sugar plantations and the domestic market of France. To make this possible, the French established settlements on Newfoundland's south coast, between Cape Ray and Cape Race.[6] Although the French were not fully successful in their attempt to provision the West Indies from this source, the attempt marked a period of growth of the French effort in the North American fishery.

Because the English were forced to land to cure the fish an opportunity was presented to exploit economies of scale. Unlike the French fishing effort, which can best be thought of as a single expedition to the fisheries by individual boats—even in the case of the West Indies trade—the English increased the use of larger vessels—sack ships—on the trans-Atlantic voyage and smaller bye-boats for actual fishing effort. Thus, throughout the seventeenth century, efforts in the English fishery became more specialized.

Since the French were less dependent on the ability to land on the foreshore than the English, their fleet was more widely dispersed throughout the fishery. It was thus that individual French fishermen more easily fell prey to English harassment. Nor was the French fishing fleet homogeneous, sailing from a few specific ports in France. Rather, individual vessels sailed from ports as far apart as St. Malo and La Rochelle, and as a result presented no unified voice to the French authorities for special protection. The English fleet, on the other hand, sailed almost exclusively from ports in the West Country around Bristol and presented its views as a single pressure group. In addition, the government recognized the Newfoundland fishery as an important training ground for the navy and relied on dried cod as an element in the diet of the armed forces. Also because of the higher degree of concentration which resulted from the attempts to capture economies of scale and the consequent relative high barriers to entry into the industry, the English were able to pressure government for special considerations. Among these, which the French never achieved, were increased protection by the navy and special subsidies to support the land-based operations.

A vital distinction between the French and English fishing efforts lay in the different markets for the staple output. The French fleet sold its produce almost exclusively in the domestic market apart from that which was sold in the West Indies. In the seventeenth century the local French market was sufficient to absorb the supply at prevailing prices and the rigid mercantilistic policy, later known as "Colbertism", prohibited any other trade in cod. On the other hand, the English market for Newfoundland fish was too small to absorb the catch of the English fleet. Indeed, the expansion of the English effort was undertaken because fishing was a commercial venture involving sales to Spain and the other Roman Catholic countries of the Mediterranean. Silver brought back from the new world by Spain reached England after being traded for the humble codfish. In the years between 1768 and 1772, for which records survive, no less than 88.5 per cent of all Newfoundland dried-fish exports went to southern Europe. This became the basis of trade for many goods apart from silver; the ships which carried the catches of cod also carried sherry to the English market — hence the name "sack ships".

The English fishery also owed its ascendency to the policy of empire which then prevailed. It became government policy to integrate the Newfoundland fishery into commercial trade and into the formal structure of empire and this gave it more reason to attempt as much control over the common property resource as possible. The French mercantilistic policy which concentrated much more on the domestic market prevented the integration of the fishery into the structure of its empire. Even in the late seventeenth century there was very little direct contact between the

Figure 3:3 A Common Trading Pattern Associated with the English Fishery in the Gulf of St. Lawrence

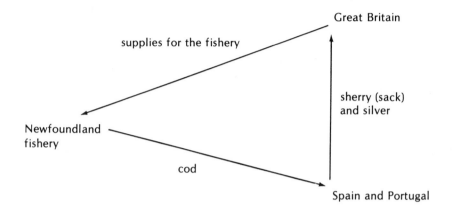

Note: This trading pattern illustrates a route often taken by the sack ships. Similar to all trading patterns in the North Atlantic, it was neither exclusively nor necessarily the route which carried the greatest bulk of the traffic in any given year. It was, however, the most consistent pattern.

French fishery, New France, and the other French colonies in the western hemisphere, despite the French government's attempt to establish a three-cornered trade with the Newfoundland fisheries and the French West Indies. Climate and distance caused high costs which prevented New France from displacing New England as a supply base of fish, agricultural products, and timber for the French West Indies. This is not to suggest that the English maintained complete control over the fishery; they did not. Nor did the early growth of the English fishery take place smoothly or without conflict between English interests themselves. Control of the foreshore and the opportunities for trading attracted London-based trading ventures and these trading companies not only competed fiercely but often came into conflict with the West Country fishermen over the control of the foreshore.[7]

At the early stages of exploitation the income generated flowed to the countries which maintained fishing fleets. No substitution possiblities existed between native and European labour. Slowly, as settlement grew, a portion of that income accrued to fishermen resident in the area; such income was, by absolute and relative standards, small. On the other hand, the effort put into the fishery helped to establish some settlement and, more important, the assertion of political control.

The Fur Trade of New France

First to explore the lower reaches of the St. Lawrence River the French were also the first to exploit the vast fur resources of the Canadian hinterland. In the early years trade with the Indians and the subsequent sale of furs provided additional income to those engaged in the fishery. Soon sufficient pelts reached metropolitan France that they became the basis of the hatting industry. From those early times beaver skins were the staple of the fur trade and the critical determinant of the survival of the major French colony in North America.

But the development of New France was not without its setbacks. These often originated from the very development of the fur trade itself which tended to be discontinuous in nature. Of course, some of these disturbances to the orderly growth of the fur trade originated in perturbations of demand in the final product market of France. Often, however, they resulted from the manner in which the search for new sources of fur pelts was conducted. Because the interior of North America was not a limitless hunting area but rather many separate harvesting areas, such as those represented by Figure 3:2, the fur-trade expansion was spasmodic. Some of these harvesting areas were determined by the nature of the geography; others were politically circumscribed.

By the early 1600s the English had established the Massachusetts Bay Colony and the Dutch, New Amsterdam.[8] Increasingly thereafter the Dutch and English provided a southern check to any French expansion. To the west the Indian nations prevented French enroachment beyond the Ottawa River. During the early years of the fur trade these checks were potential rather than real since the Indian tribes of the northeast could provide ample pelts to satisfy the traders. Thus, under the direction of *la Compagnie de la Nouvelle France* the fur trade was localized. The Indians of the region brought their pelts to the fur traders who in the early years of the seventeenth century had expanded just beyond Tadoussac, the export point to France. At first the pelts supplied were the highly prized *castor gras d'hiver* which, because they had been used as garments by the natives, were more directly useful to the felting process of the hat-making trade.[9] Later, as the highly prized pelts became less common, they were replaced, in part, by the *castor sec* pelts. These were the skins of newly killed animals which retained their coarse guard hairs and required more processing than the *castor gras*. Whenever a new territory was opened up to the fur traders the ratio of *castor gras* to *castor sec* pelts supplied increased only to fall as exploitation continued. The ability of the Indians to supply pelts to the fur traders was one of the major elements in the trade's profitability. Although the animals were a renewable economic resource, conditions existed, unlike those of the fisheries, which rendered the supply of furs unstable.

Figure 3:4 Supply and Demand Conditions of Fur Resources in a Fixed Harvest Area Over Time

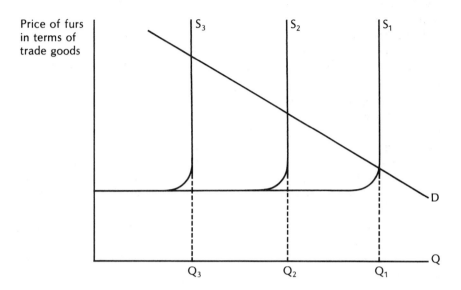

Note: Changes in the supply of furs offered by the Indians over three periods, for example, resulted from the fact that the flow was never consistent with a steady state stock. Hunting effort caused the supply shifts because it resulted in depletion.

D—the fur traders' derived demand for pelts
S—the Indian trappers' supply of furs
Q—the quantity of furs   The subscripts 1, 2, and 3 denote time.

The early fur trade can be thought of as two interrelated economic activities. First, the Indian trappers responded to the derived demand of the traders by supplying pelts and second, the traders collected and shipped furs to the final markets in Europe. These two activities can be stylized. Consider the case of hunting as output. The short-run supply of beaver pelts was probably very elastic over a given range and then perfectly inelastic (see Figure 3:4). That is, if the Indians could be induced to harvest at a rate which was substantially greater than the sustained yield they would be limited by the resource stock as it fell. Evidence supports the view that the confrontation of European and native Indian societies caused a profound change in the latter. The Indians prized highly European trade goods, such as copper pots and kettles, guns, tobacco, and alcohol, particularly rum. Consequently, they would supply pelts at a relatively low price in terms of trade goods. Prior to the coming of the white man Indian hunting territories were defined in terms of relatively simple consumption needs. However, the commercialization of hunting and the desire to possess trade goods led many Indians to abandon traditional hunting practices. Prior to the commercialization of hunting, most Indian bands harvested from relatively well-defined areas but these harvesting territories were not sacrosanct. Neighbouring tribes permitted encroachment for the purposes of food gathering when local scarcity occurred. There was, given Indian requirements, no global scarcity. Such sharing arrangements, however, broke down when the cash economy of the white traders intruded. Indian tribes established their hunting territories as private property for the gathering of furs. However, the costs of enforcing the private property rights were high.[10]

Conflict between the Indian bands often resulted as traditional values were superseded through interaction with white traders. This placed a premium both on the bands' ability to defend themselves and on their geographic mobility, each enhanced by the new trade goods. Such a preference for European trade goods, if held strongly, determined not only the elastic range of the supply curve but also the quantity at which it became price inelastic. If the hunters wished to preserve some animal stock which yielded a steady flow of pelts over time their aggregate supply curve from a given geographic area would have become inelastic at the appropriate sustained-resource flow. However, if their preference were held so strongly that they were willing to sacrifice future consumption for present consumption this high marginal rate of time preference induced a supply curve which shifted back through time as the renewable-resource base was depleted and the flow of resources to the fur trade was reduced (see Figure 3:4). From the Indians' viewpoint, the opportunity cost of ignoring the fur trade rose over time, measured in terms of trade goods foregone. By comparison, the opportunity cost of trapping and trading was quite low. So the TC curve of Figure 3:2 can be thought of as rotating clockwise, thus reducing h^c, the maximum harvest necessary to keep the stock fixed. At the same time, the TR curve shifted upwards as the price of fur rose in Europe; this encouraged more effort on the part of Indians and traders with a resulting decline again in h^c. As a consequence the natural resource stock was depleted.

Since the availability of pelts was the key element in determining their price, given a derived demand for them exhibited by the traders, then the price of furs was similarly important in influencing the level of trading profits. This can be most readily seen by outlining the salient features of the production process of the fur trade. First, trade goods were purchased and brought to the point of trade. Second, inventories of both trade and final goods had to be financed over the time spent in transit across the Atlantic and into the interior of New France. Third, trading posts were built and manned as centres to which the Indian suppliers could come. Two distinct transport systems evolved to ship the trade and final goods. Moving goods from the trade centre to the export point involved a substantially different transport mode, canoes for the most part, than that required for ocean shipment. Formally, a production function which describes the fur trade from the Indians' presentation of pelts for trade represents all the inputs, along with the output of the fur trade

$$Q = f_1 (P, K, L, T_I, T_A)$$

where Q is the output of furs in Europe; P is the input of pelts; K is capital, such as trading posts; L is labour; T_I is transport within Canada to export point at Tadoussac; and T_A is transport from Canada to Europe.

The problem of the fur traders was to minimize costs for any given output. Under constant returns to scale — where a doubling of inputs led to a doubling of output — the per-unit cost function is written, with each term the cost of the inputs noted above,

$$c = f_2 (g, r, w, t_I, t_A)$$

where c is the per-unit cost; g is the cost to the traders of a pelt in terms of trade goods; r is the rental rate of capital, including inventories; w is the wage rate; t_I is the cost of transport services within Canada; and t_A is the trans-Atlantic shipping costs. Although all input prices varied over time, to a greater or lesser extent, the effects of resource depletion can be more easily seen if for the moment all but g are considered fixed. As the Indian supply curve shifted through time because of the resource depletion of a fixed area the per-unit cost of pelts to traders rose (see Figure 3:4). Consequently, average costs rose and the fur trade profits fell. Profit-maximizing or loss-minimizing output, of course, was lowered as the marginal costs rose. This is consistent with the observation that the price of final output rose when the trade was confined to the territory of New France east of the Ottawa River. There is no consistent evidence on whether the fur traders were able to reduce the other per-unit factor prices or not although trans-Atlantic freight rates probably fell throughout the first half of the seventeenth century. This was, of course, not directly influenced by the fur trade. On balance it seems most likely that the increasing price of raw pelts offset any other cost declines since profits were declining by the end of the first quarter of the seventeenth century. In the face of falling profits there was a considerable long-run impetus to expand into new hunting territory.[11]

The westward expansion of the fur trade was delayed because the Indians who blocked the potential fur-trading routes were not only a physical threat but separate economic agents in trade. For decades in the early seventeenth century the powerful Indian nations of the Iroquois, Huron, and Algonquin battled each other for the strategic control of the Ottawa River system. Control over this river system gave the dominant power the opportunity to mediate between the French fur traders and the Indian trappers beyond the Ottawa River. As the stock of fur-bearing animals was reduced in the northeast the supply of pelts was augmented by those supplied by the Hurons and Algonquins. The augmented supply dampened the overall increase of the traders' average costs but did not prevent it entirely. Thus the role of the Indians as middlemen was temporary since they could supply raw pelts less efficiently than the French traders themselves could have had they gained access to the new western harvesting area. The power struggle between Indian nations resulted in the Iroquois wresting control of the Ottawa route from the Hurons in 1649-50. This immediately reduced the supply to the French since the Iroquois were linked with the Dutch trade to the south. Conflict between the Iroquois, whose allegiance later lay with the English, and the French was the almost inevitable consequence and it ended with the defeat of the Indians and the gaining of access to the Ottawa and St. Lawrence routes to the interior by the French in 1663.

The western expansion of the fur trade took place in a series of encroachments rather than as a single thrust. At first the simple expedient of permitting the western tribes to bring their pelts to Montreal, the town which emerged as the trade centre in the 1640s, encouraged expansion. The next phase, as the price of furs rose, was the establishment of forts as trading centres in the west itself, first at Kingston and later at Niagara—as predicted in Figure 3:2. Thus began the expansion of the French fur-trading empire based on over-harvesting practices induced by the overall common-property nature of the trade.[12]

With each new westward thrust a realignment of factor use took place. Movements up the Great Lakes system into (relatively) discrete new harvesting areas, such as Michigan and Northern Ontario, required greater inputs of transport, capital, and labour because of the increased distance from Quebec. As the trade moved into distant areas interior transport costs became a much more significant factor than they had been earlier.

The basic problem of the fur trade was to ensure profits in the face of two spatial characteristics of production, changing factor-price ratios and changing technologies of production. The enlarged scope of the total transport costs produced an incentive for technical innovation. The development of shipping on the Great Lakes, the use of large freight-carrying *bateaux* on the upper reaches of the St. Lawrence, and the development of the larger canoes were all a response to the pressure of transport costs. The large canoes were employed on the Ottawa–Nippissing route to the upper Great Lakes. Such innovations helped to offset the increased length of the transport networks.

Of all the input prices only that of interior transport was amenable to manipulation whereas the costs of capital, labour, and trans-Atlantic shipping were either all determined exogenously or could not be further reduced. When the trade required substantial new inputs of capital, barriers to entry were also created. The many independent traders, who existed in the early years despite the loosely enforced state monopoly, disappeared. However, even the resulting monopoly was unstable. Discrete expansions into new territories often drove up total costs at a faster rate than the increased total revenues from shifts in the demand for furs in Europe. As a result, from time to time the fur trade had to be rescued from bankruptcy. The two most notable reorganizations of the fur trade during the French régime took place in 1663 and 1701 at the time of the first western expansion and the expansion into the Hudson Bay drainage area.[13]

When the trade expanded into the Hudson Bay drainage basin the French came into conflict with the English. The English had asserted control of this huge area and sole rights to the fur trade had been granted to the Hudson's Bay Company. The French, however, ignored the exclusive rights of the company and encroached on the trading territory. Although the area was sufficiently large that it could tolerate two exploiters, for some time the two interest groups came into conflict. At first the French were quite successful in wresting vital trading posts from the English but the Treaty of Utrecht in 1713 which settled a European war, also re-established the English control over the area. The Hudson's Bay Company, for the remainder of French colonial rule, remained a barrier to the exploitation of fur resources close to Quebec and forced the French traders to seek furs elsewhere.[14]

The periodic bankruptcy of the fur-trade monopoly was symptomatic of weaknesses in the industry during the French régime. The demand for furs was primarily based on a demand for luxury goods in the hat trade of Europe. Consequently the demand was highly price-inelastic and any changes in supply often drove down the market price in any given year with resulting losses to the monopoly. This condition, however, is not usually associated with the monopolization of a market; a monopoly can usually identify the quantity of output which will maximize profits because of its market power. Here we must look to a further weakness, the internal organization of the fur trade. For most of the period the monopoly was operated as a multi-plant firm with a weak central organization. Leases on trading areas were given to *fermiers* or local traders but no regulation of individual output was attempted at this level. As a result the flow of furs reaching the export point was usually shipped on to Europe with only a cursory attempt at regulating the quantity. Over-production, with respect to optimal monopoly output, led to reduced profits and in some years substantial losses. In a dynamic framework, spasmodic shifts in the demand for furs in the hatting trade, which were strongly influenced by volatile changes in tastes and fashion, exacerbated this problem. Declining profits and losses were often recorded for periods as long as a decade, such as the first decade of the eighteenth century, as the monopoly strove very imperfectly to identify its equilibrium-output levels.

The expansion of the French fur trade was, as a result of its production and market characteristics, halting. Despite the vast territorial expansion the enlargement of output was modest as indicated in Table 3:1. By the end of the French régime long transport networks carried furs from as far away as the foothills of the Rockies and the headwaters of the Mississippi to Quebec. Confrontations with the Iroquois and English over control of territory were violent and inevitable. In general, this competition arose from the inability of the fur trade, at several levels, to assert private-property control over the resource and inevitably depletion of the resource followed.

Competition in the Fur Trade
The fall of New France in 1759 brought an immediate end to the French fur trade. Without access to the traditional Paris market and cut off from sources of funds to finance the substantial inventories of the trade, the French Canadians were forced to retreat from active management. Into the vacancies came the Anglo-American traders of the southern English colonies anxious to capture the extensive fur empire of the St. Lawrence route. Despite attempts of Anglo-American traders, no strong power emerged during the two decades after the fall of Quebec. Few licences were available in the early years as the new British colonial administrators groped for a policy to restore the trade to profitability and in the later years war interrupted the trade. But in the 1780s one firm emerged to dominate the St. Lawrence fur trade—the famous North West Company.[15]

The North West Company was first organized in 1775 as a loose partnership of fur traders. Initial profitability provided the incentive for a more permanent structure and although this was constructed, the com-

Table 3:1 Estimates of Annual Average Quantities of Beaver Skins Exported from New France/Quebec in the Eighteenth Century

Period	Skins[a]	Period	Skins[b]
(1)	(2) (lbs.)	(3)	(4) (lbs.)
1706-14	70,000	1701	75,993
1715, 1717	120,945	1712, 1717	109,886
1721-22, 1725-30	116,480	1722-23, 1725-26, 1728-30	123,230
1732-40	162,905	1732-40	149,228
1742-48	154,571	1742-48	165,394
		1754-55	140,725
		1769-72	134,000[c]
		1793-1808	170,000[d]

Note: The various estimates are those of Lunn (a), Lawson (b), Shepherd (c), and Innis (d), as presented in Shepherd.

Source: J. Shepherd, *Staples and Eighteenth-Century Canadian Development: A Comparative Study*, unpublished paper, Whitman College (1973), p. 15.

pany did retain a large degree of flexibility. Basically, as it took shape in the 1780s, the company consisted of partners in Montreal and wintering partners in the west, all of whom had a direct share in the profits. Clerks in both the east and west worked in hope of a partnership and, in fact, promotion was fairly rapid. The French-Canadian role was largely that of canoe man. Thus, for the partners and the clerks, the internal organiza-tion provided a great deal of incentive. Unlike the French fur trade with its *fermiers*, the partners of the North West Company were not con-strained to pay a licence fee and then to recover its costs thus output levels were more closely coordinated. Also, unlike the French fur trade, the North West Company lacked a state-granted monopoly and from time to time rival firms were formed, often among break-away partners.

During the 1790s an intense competition began between the North West Company and the other companies based in Montreal. The North West Company deliberately encouraged the decimation of the fur-bearing animal populations in some of the proximate fur-trapping regions and in particular in the present American states of Ohio and Michigan. This forced the industry deeper into the old northwest region of Illinois, Indiana, and Wisconsin. The intent of this policy was to drive rival firms into bankruptcy by forcing them to absorb high overhead costs. In any event the old northwest was ceded to the United States and the traders lost their rights under Jay's Treaty of 1796 before this policy could be firmly established. As a result of the increased distance to the nearest trading territory the fur empire of the St. Lawrence took on some characteristics of a natural monopoly. One firm could survive but the market was incapable of supporting more than one given the fixed costs which had to be borne by each company. In 1800 two rivals of the North West Company merged to form the XY Company. Named after the stamp on its bales, the XY Company fiercely competed for new sources of cheap furs. Although the North West Company had expected its rival to collapse into bankruptcy, the XY Company proved to have sufficient financial capital to weather the years of unprofitability. However, despite the financial assets there was a critical weakness in the XY Company — its personnel. After several years of intense rivalry betwen the firms, the lack of good management of the XY Company proved the deciding impediment to profitability and a merger was sought with the North West Company.[16]

The success of the North West Company in dominating the St. Lawrence fur route was based on a vigorous policy of expansion. By the early 1800s the company had established trading posts in the Athabasca region and had reached the Pacific Ocean. This expansion brought the North West Company into conflict with the only other fur-trading company with a market in Great Britain, the Hudson's Bay Company.

The Hudson's Bay Company had been founded in 1670 and had been granted sole rights to the fur trade in the drainage basin of Hudson Bay, the area known as Rupert's Land. With varying success the company had exploited the region but of course during the French régime the Quebec-based traders did not acknowledge the English firm's rights and encroachment occurred. With the British takeover of New France the Hudson's Bay Company's sovereignty of the drainage basin was secured. In this security the company drifted into a period of lethargic management.[17] However, when the European market for furs was denied to the company as a result of the Napoleonic Wars, it was forced to rationalize its corporate structure as well as to cope with the market competition of the North West Company in London. The actions taken at this time were critical.

The Hudson's Bay Company undertook three specific policy changes in its reorganization. First, the port at York Factory was reorganized and new accounting methods were introduced on the basis of which an element of profit sharing was introduced to provide incentives. Second, the transport system of the company was revolutionized with the introduction of the York boats which were capable of carrying large cargoes at a much reduced per-unit transport cost. Third, the Selkirk settlement was established primarily to supply foodstuffs for York Factory. By 1811-12 this reorganization had transformed the Hudson's Bay Company and within a decade it was in a strong enough market position to absorb the North West Company.

Not only did the reorganization improve the efficiency of the Hudson's Bay Company but it placed the North West Company at a further disadvantage. Thus, while the short haul to York Factory, using York boats, lowered average costs the transport network of the North West Company was lengthened because of the interposition of the Selkirk settlement. Further, the Selkirk settlement effectively cut off the supply of foodstuffs, pemican, to the North West Company. After bloody conflicts between the two companies over territorial disputes, šuch as that at Seven Oaks, the Colonial Office in London put pressure on the companies to merge. With failing profits the North West Company succumbed to the financially stronger Hudson's Bay Company. The year of the merger, 1821, thus marks the abrupt shift of the fur trade from the St. Lawrence. For almost two hundred years, fur exports, along with fish, were the principal medium of export-led growth. In comparison with later staples the fur trade involved little more than the looting of natural resources; nevertheless, it had profound impact on the nature of economic development. Because of the persistent need to expand into new hunting areas, the fur trade was responsible for the vast geographic expansion of both economic activity and political jurisdiction. The beginning of a transcontinental economy, albeit tenuous, was established.

The Timber Trade
The disappearance of the fur trade from the St. Lawrence represented the end of an epoch. It was not, however, in any sense the end of the fur trade which continued to grow and contribute to the economy's exports from its new base on Hudson Bay. Even the St. Lawrence economy was little influenced by the loss of the trade because a new staple industry had already emerged and was quantitatively more important—the timber trade. Although Canadian exports of timber had accounted for less than 1 per cent of the British import market in 1800, by the time of the merger of the North West and Hudson's Bay companies twenty years later Canadian timber dominated the British market. In 1820, for instance, over 81 per cent of all timber sales to Great Britain were shipments from British North America although the average was somewhat lower. The rapid growth and development of this new trade based on Canada's forest wealth more than compensated for the loss of the fur trade to the regional economy of the St. Lawrence. Between 1829 and 1845, average exports of timber and its more highly processed form, lumber, made up over 40 per cent of all exports from British North

America *via* the St. Lawrence; in some periods it constituted as much as 70 per cent. For a staple economy with a small domestic market, the appearance of such a trade had a profound impact on the pace of economic growth. As outlined below, the expansion of British North America's timber trade was a clear illustration of the influence of foreign market developments.

Prior to the American Revolution, British North America exported timber and timber-based manufactured goods, such as barrel staves, to the West Indies. In addition, timber was cut and processed for masts and spars for the Royal Navy. After the war which changed the geography of the empire, this export trade centred on New Brunswick and to some extent on Nova Scotia and by 1795 the British Admiralty regularly tendered contracts for masts and spars from the St. John's River area. Otherwise the nascent British North American timber industry was excluded from the British market by both its high costs relative to other timber-producing areas and its high shipping charges. Traditionally the British drew their timber imports from the nearby Baltic countries of Prussia, Sweden, Norway, and Poland. These Baltic states provided the required types of timber, pine and oak, and had a competitive advantage because of lower transport costs, lower wages, and, since the labour of the Baltic states was highly skilled, better quality finished timber. Baltic timber was much preferred to the rough-hewn Canadian lumber in both the general construction sector and the shipbuilding industry in Great Britain. Thus, despite the vast timber resources of British North America, access to the British market was denied.[18]

The Napoleonic Wars interrupted the free movement of market forces and in response the prevailing pattern of trade changed. The cost to Great Britain of Baltic timber rose because of the increasing hazard of depending on supplies from that area. The first reaction came in the early 1800s when the British government, at the insistence of the Admiralty, began to subsidize the timber trade of British North America through contracts in order to ensure a safe source of supply. By 1804 the British government was finally convinced of the country's vulnerability in relying exclusively on the Baltic supplies and a tariff was implemented against Baltic timber the following year.[19] Both the intent of this tariff policy and its subsequent effect were to make British North American timber more competitive. The tariff was raised in 1810 after the continental blockade and again in 1815. Although it was reduced slightly in 1821, the tariff remained high enough to guarantee to British North American timber producers the largest share of the British market. In a static framework the impact of this tariff can be seen in Figure 3:5. Prior to 1805 the joint Canadian and Baltic supply of timber in Great Britain, with a given demand, determined the market price—P_1. Because the Baltic

Figure 3:5 The Impact of the British Tariff on Baltic Timber on British North American Shipments

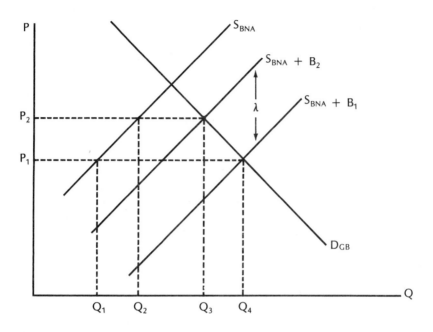

λ—the Baltic timber tariff
S_{BNA}—the British North American supply of timber in the British market
S_{BNA} + B—the joint British North American and Baltic supplies of timber in
   the British market before the tariff (B_1) and after the tariff (B_2)
D_{GB}—the British demand for timber
Q_4-Q_3—the decline in the Baltic producers' British market
Q_2-Q_1—the increase in the British North American producers' British market

Note: It is assumed for the sake of simplicity that there was no domestic British supply.

states were more efficient areas of production their share of the market was large (Q_4 - Q_1) and the British North American share was small (Q_1). The imposition of the tariff, λ, caused an upward shift in the supply curve of the Baltic producers but left the British North American supply curve unaffected. The new aggregate supply-curve shift caused the price to rise—P_2. Baltic producers experienced a decline in their market to Q_3 - Q_2, whereas, the British North American sales rose to Q_2. From 1820 until the tariff was substantially reduced in 1842 the British North American share of the British timber market averaged over 75 per cent. Stimulated by this tariff protection the rate of exploitation of timber resources became extremely rapid and as a result the economy spread.

When tariff protection was conferred on British North America the centre of the timber trade moved from the ports of New Brunswick to the greater hinterland of Quebec. The maritime ports continued to be important export points and in some years accounted for the greatest proportion of the value of exports, particularly during the 1820s, but ultimately the industry of New Brunswick was limited in a way that of central Canada was not. However, in the immediate post-1804 period the Quebec hinterland could no more readily respond to the increased quantity demanded and over the long run came to dominate the trade. Rising demand in Great Britain increased the industry's total revenue but at a cost of reducing the sustainable yield in any harvesting area. Timber cutting spread into new resource areas, first up the banks of the St. Lawrence River to the head of Lake Ontario, and in the 1820s along the river systems of the lake. During the next decade the timber cutters were active along the Ottawa River and the Lake Erie shore. Subsequently, the harvest areas of Lake Huron and the headwaters of the Ottawa were caught up in the search for new timber stands (see Map 3:1).[20]

One of the features of the spread of the timber trade in the early nineteenth century was the rapid depletion of the central Canadian forests. This much-commented-on phenomenon has often been described as symptom of the lack of any conservation ethic on the part of the frontier population of New Brunswick and the Canadas. The implication is one of prodigality. After all, a relatively small population was responsible for pushing back the forest edge in a relatively short period of time; within three decades of 1810 the harvest of the St. Lawrence and Great Lakes lowlands no longer had sufficient timber to attract the major timber-cutting firms. Yet, the forces which caused the rapid depletion of much of the forests are easily understandable and, furthermore, rapid depletion may have been not only the most reasonable alternative in a frontier society but also the most efficient method of promoting economic development.

The reason that rapid depletion of the forest took place in southern Upper and Lower Canada as well as part of New Brunswick, in particular, was that once cleared the land was well-suited for agriculture. Of course, most pioneer settlements were established to exploit the agricultural potential of the land. This meant that the land had to be cleared of trees. Since the amount of land which could be cleared in any one year by the settler was necessarily limited, it usually took several years to clear enough for subsistence farming, and, therefore, other sources of income during the start-up period were needed. Even when a level of self-sufficiency was reached, there was still a need for cash income. Well into the nineteenth century, even when markets for wheat and other agricultural outputs were well-developed, farmers discovered that the remaining timber stands adjacent to their farms could provide extra income without any direction of effort away from agriculture.[21]

The presence of pioneer homesteads on the forest frontier meant that many farmers were prepared to engage in timber cutting. There were no particularly significant barriers to entry into this stage of the timber trade. Capital requirements were modest and since cutting timber was generally carried out at that time of the year when no major farming effort was necessary, there was no hidden cost or consequence to dissuade the farmers. Since, in addition, there was no method whereby one timber cutter could effectively bar the entry of another, the industry can be characterized as a common-property one. Ease of entry, with reference to Figure 3:1, drove down the stock of trees as harvests beyond the level of sustained yield were gathered. That is, effort tended towards E^C. While cutting down the forests the pioneer farmer was also engaging in another activity—clearing land for agricultural use.

The joint activity of engaging in the timber trade and clearing land for cultivation had the effect of inducing even more harvesting than that which would have occurred otherwise. This may be seen in Figure 3:6. Land freed from the forest had value in agriculture; the measure of this value would be the discounted stream of net earnings from cultivation, or more simply stated, the present value. Since an individual pioneer would be willing to incur the cost of clearing the land so long as such an activity was profitable he would in effect be willing to absorb personally some of the costs of cutting trees for the lumber trade. Since the present value of land in agriculture would increase with the amount of land so used, measured here as effort, the direct cost of harvesting timber was reduced to, say $TC - PV_0$.[22] Such incentives led to a cropping of the forests beyond that of a sustained yield and thus to their rapid depletion because of the higher level of effort (E_0^j) applied. Of course, there is reason to believe that some land yielded a present value in agricultural use which was more than the cost of harvesting timber and in such instances, noted in the case of PV_1, the pioneer farmer would clear as many trees as possible as quickly as possible and reduce the timber stands completely.

The cash income which the pioneer farmer earned from the timber trade permitted the purchase of goods which were not produced locally. However, the cash income was also used for investment on the farm in items such as draft animals, farm implements, and seed. Since farm productivity depended on such investments, cash was more useful at the early stages of pioneering each farm than the later stages. This early cash requirement would induce a more rapid cropping of the forests and timber stands.

In the potential agricultural regions, not all of the forest stands, of

Map 3:1 Trade Routes in Major Staples

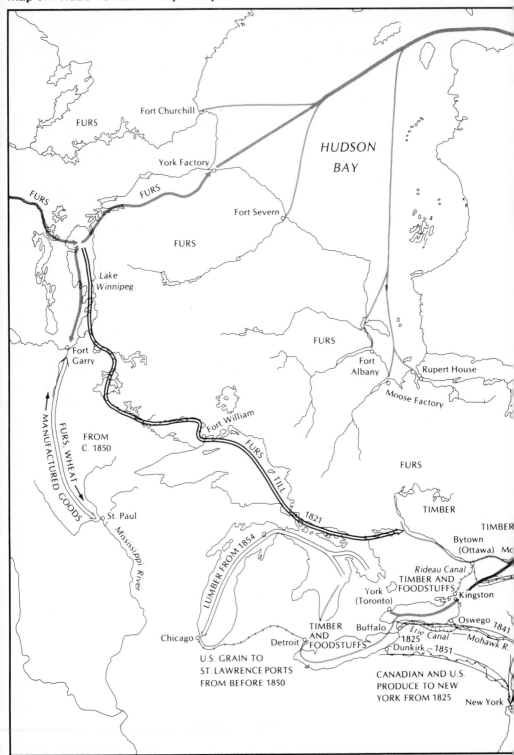

FURS

Fort Churchill

York Factory

HUDSON BAY

FURS

FURS

Fort Severn

FURS

FURS

Lake Winnipeg

Fort Garry

FURS

Fort Albany

Rupert House

Moose Factory

FROM C. 1850

Fort William

FURS TILL 1821

FURS

TIMBER

FURS, WHEAT

MANUFACTURED GOODS

St. Paul

Mississippi River

TIMBER

Bytown (Ottawa)

Rideau Canal
TIMBER AND FOODSTUFFS

York (Toronto)

Kingston

LUMBER FROM 1854

Chicago

Detroit

TIMBER AND FOODSTUFFS

Buffalo

Oswego 1841

Erie Canal
1825

Mohawk R.

Dunkirk 1851

U.S. GRAIN TO ST. LAWRENCE PORTS FROM BEFORE 1850

CANADIAN AND U.S. PRODUCE TO NEW YORK FROM 1825

New York

Source: D. G. Kerr, *Historical Atlas of Canada*, 3rd rev. ed. (Toronto, 1975), pp. 46-47.

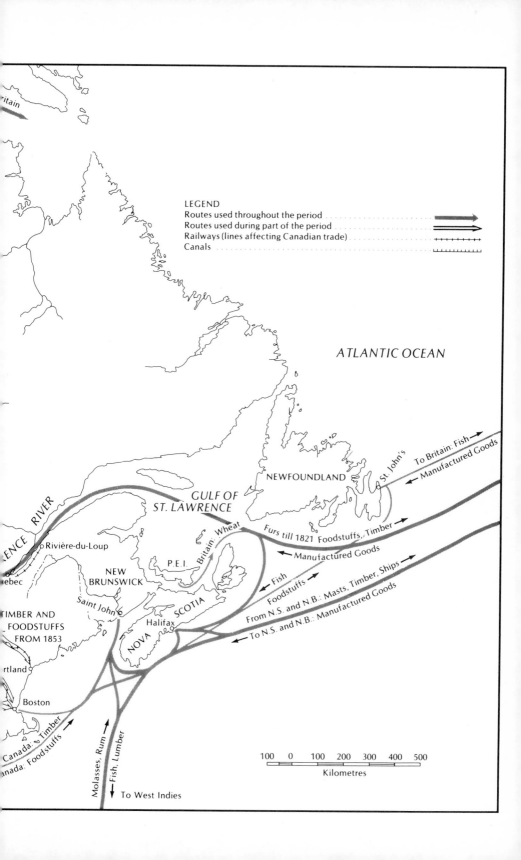

LEGEND
Routes used throughout the period . . . .
Routes used during part of the period . . . .
Railways (lines affecting Canadian trade) . . . .
Canals . . . .

ATLANTIC OCEAN

NEWFOUNDLAND

St. John's

To Britain: Fish
Manufactured Goods

GULF OF
ST. LAWRENCE

Furs till 1821 Foodstuffs, Timber
Manufactured Goods

ENCE RIVER

Rivière-du-Loup

Britain: Wheat

P.E.I.

Fish
Foodstuffs

From N.S. and N.B.: Masts, Timber, Ships

NEW
BRUNSWICK

Saint John

NOVA SCOTIA

Halifax

To N.S. and N.B.: Manufactured Goods

ebec

TIMBER AND
FOODSTUFFS
FROM 1853

rtland

Boston

Canada: Timber
anada: Foodstuffs

Molasses, Rum

Fish, Lumber

To West Indies

100   0   100   200   300   400   500
Kilometres

ritain

Figure 3:6 The Joint Impact of the Timber Trade and Agriculture on the Forest

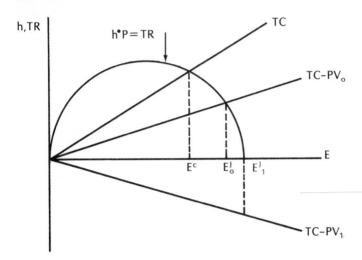

Note: The symbols are the same as those used in Figure 3:1.

PV—net discounted present value of land in agriculture

The superscript J refers to the joint activities of timber trade and agriculture and the subscripts o and 1 indicate the two possible cases where $PV < TC$ and $PV > TC$, respectively.

course, were located within access of means of easy transport of the timber, adjacent to streams, for example. Difficulty of transport gave rise to a forest-based industry which circumvented the problem of shipping bulky timber, the manufacture of potash.

Potash, like the wood from which it was derived, found a ready market in Great Britain where it was used in the manufacture of soap and as a bleaching agent in the textile industry. Indeed, the demand for potash was such that its importance as an export pre-dated the rise of the timber trade itself. The manufacture of potash was simple: Hardwoods were burned to produce ash, which was then saturated with water; the resulting fluid was evaporated in open pots to produce a crystalline potassium hydroxide or lye. Because of the crude nature of the required technology and the extremely modest capital requirements, small potasheries sprang up throughout New Brunswick and the Canadas. Often they were corporate ventures although many farmers, individually or as part of a cooperative, continued to manufacture potash for the commercial market. Such was the growth of this industry that at its peak in the 1830s, in terms of exports, over fifty thousand barrels were being regularly shipped from the Canadas to Great Britain.[23]

Because of the common-property aspects and the strong incentives to cut timber the rate of expansion of the industry was extremely rapid once discriminatory tariffs gave British North America access to the British market. This was especially so during war years, as the price of timber was driven upwards. On the other hand, there were periods of slower growth, and occasionally retrenchment, usually associated with depression in Great Britain, such as that following the end of the Napoleonic Wars, or peace-time recession, such as that in the late 1820s. Nevertheless, as indicated in Figure 3:7, the underlying trends in both timber and lumber exports from British North America was upward. The distinction between timber and lumber was as critical in both the market and the supplying region for although growth was common to both each of these two major components of the timber trade evolved quite differently.

Timber in the form in which it was exported was one of the most rudimentary of forest products. It was simply the fallen tree roughly squared along its length—hence the name "square timber". Since the forests were virgin, there was an abundance of trees which were suited to this trade and since the logs could easily be transported to the shipping ports of Quebec and New Brunswick, high prices induced a very rapid expansion in the industry and within a few years of the Baltic timber tariff, British North America dominated in the British market. In contrast, it took much longer for a similar dominance to be established in the market for sawn timber, or "deals" as this product was called. Indeed, it was not until the early 1840s that the British market was wrested from the Baltic shippers.

The trade in deals simply could not respond in volume to the demand of the British market. More substantial capital requirements, in the areas of both sawmills and transport facilities, prevented quick response in British North America which not only was relatively short of necessary capital but had no effective means of mobilizing it quickly. In addition, skilled labour was required to dress the wood and, relative to the Baltic countries, British North America possessed very little. Only as these skills were acquired, either by the local labour force or through the immigration of skilled workers, was the economy able to exploit the tariff protection it had been given. Evidence that these skills were not acquired quickly or easily was the frequent complaint of British timber merchants that the sawn planks were not up to the quality of finish of those from the Baltic region. As a consequence, British North American deals often commanded a lower price. Yet, in the long run the timber trade did adjust,

Figure 3:7 British North American Timber and Lumber and the British Market, 1800-1860

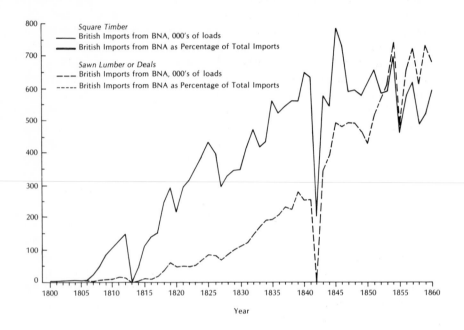

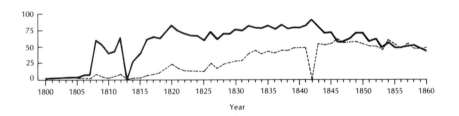

Note: A load of timber is 50 cubic feet. Prior to 1843, sawn lumber was measured in "Great Hundreds", a measure which varied from country to country but which in British North America was approximately 5.4 loads in 1800-20 and 5.6 loads in 1821-41.
[a] Complete figures do not exist for these years.
[b] Virtually all of the remainder is accounted for by the Baltic countries of Prussia, Norway, Sweden, and Russia.

Source: Data are from P. D. McClelland, *The New Brunswick Economy in the Nineteenth Century*, Ph.D. thesis, Harvard University (1966), pp. 68-88.

and after the 1830s, the shipment of deals increased relative to square timber. This was a trend which continued long after the years of high protection which ended in 1842.

In addition to the British preferences, one of the major determinants of the increased market share held by British North America in the British market was the impact of technological innovation on the supply. During the period of preference the most critical of these innovations were in the transport sector. These, in turn, were of two distinct types—changes in the method of moving timber and lumber within Canada and changes in methods of ocean shipping. In terms of both total revenue and total cost, both innovations increased output by encouraging more effort, the variable input, to be applied to the timber resource. Changes in the method of moving timber within British North America resulted in more output per unit of effort, and changes in ocean shipping reduced transport costs directly. That is, not only did the Baltic supply decline, as noted in Figure 3:5, but the British North American supply increased.

Changes in the production techniques of moving timber within Canada were rapid. In the early days of the trade, timber was cut on the banks of the major rivers, such as the Miramichi, the Saguenay, and the Ottawa, and rafted to the ports. One of the first major innovations was the simple charting of the major rivers which permitted exploitation further up the major water routes. Techniques were then developed for the speedy breaking-up and reassembly of timber rafts so that rapids were no longer an obstacle to the spread of the industry. To exploit forests along the minor streams, methods such as timber slides were developed for bringing timber efficiently to the major water routes. Then too, the process of rafting timber changed as better methods for constructing and moving rafts on the rivers evolved. Such changes in technique brought more and more of the forests within the potential harvesting area. Many of the important technical changes which permitted expansion were not, however, a direct response to the needs of the trade, but adopted from outside. For instance, the invention and subsequent use of steam tugs in the late 1830s greatly changed the pattern of moving timber on the Great Lakes. The construction of canals on the St. Lawrence and Great Lakes was not only a stimulus for the expansion of lumbering but a factor facilitating the switch from the production of square to sawn timber since finished lumber could not be moved by raft. Even during the period of the British preferences the new transport mode of the railway, for shipping to ports or to points in the United States was a vital supply-side consideration.[24]

Not only were changes in transport techniques within Canada important for the development of the timber trade but so too were changes in the techniques of ocean transport. Timber was very unlike its previous export counterpart, fur, in its transport requirements. Furs in shipment had a much higher value-to-bulk ratio than timber. Quite small ships could carry a valuable cargo of furs but only a very low value of timber. In order to reduce the per-unit shipping charges of timber, larger vessels were necessary. The response to the profits to be made in shipping was immediate. Freight rates fell and this decline was inversely related to the average tonnage of ships plying timber across the Atlantic. In the last half of the eighteenth century cargo ships clearing the port of Quebec averaged about 130 tons. By 1800, ship sizes began to increase and within fifty years, the average cargo ship registered about 400 tons. In turn, the profitability of transporting timber stimulated the shipbuilding industry throughout Nova Scotia, New Brunswick, and Quebec. Most timber carried from British North America to Great Britain was carried in domestically built ships. The consequence of the reduction in freight charges was to increase further the supply of timber in the British market.[25]

The revolution in trans-Atlantic shipping brought about by the specialization in type of goods carried reversed the traditional problem of unbalanced cargoes. High value-to-bulk cargoes on the eastward Atlantic crossing during the era of the fur trade created an imbalance in the shipping loads since goods of a comparable value imported from Europe were much bulkier. Timber, on the other hand, with its low value-to-bulk ratio created unused capacity on the westward voyage since European imports were less bulky. Many ships were forced, in fact, to sail back to British North America in ballast. Yet, the imbalance in cargoes had a subsidiary effect on the growth of the population through immigration. While this will be discussed in more detail in Chapter 6, it should be noted here that the timber trade which stimulated the growth of a labour force due to its labour-intensive production also produced the means which enabled more immigrants to flow into the country. The excess capacity on the western voyage made space available for passengers at relatively modest costs on a scale previously impossible.[26]

In 1842 the reduction in the Baltic timber tariffs signalled the end of British preference. Although the tariff was not fully removed until 1860 the British North American timber industry was increasingly forced to compete with the Baltic timber industry. In absolute terms, the quantity of British North American square-timber exports to Great Britain fell after 1842 and within a decade Baltic timber had re-established its dominance. However, the absolute trade in deals with Great Britain increased. To be sure the Baltic export of deals grew at a more rapid rate and by 1865 Baltic producers had also reasserted their majority market share but not at the expense of an absolute decline in British North

American exports. The last phase of British preference from 1842 to 1860 was one readjustment of the timber industry of British North America. While the continuing expansion of the exports of sawn timber to Great Britain tended to dampen the extent of the readjustment, it was still quite profound. However, as will be seen in subsequent chapters, new markets were found in the United States. From a trickle in the 1830s, the flow of square timber to the United States increased year by year.

Thus, the export of timber in the first half of the nineteenth century played a key role in determining the pace of development of the economy. It is, however, unlikely that in the absence of British preference the timber trade would have emerged so rapidly. The spread of the economy would undoubtedly have been slower. Within a few years the timber trade had grown from an insignificant export of spars and masts to the most significant export of the country, one which accounted for well over 50 per cent of the value of all British North American exports by the late 1820s. Other than Great Britain, no foreign market at this time appears to have had the capability to absorb such supplies of timber and lumber.

> Were ye ever in Quebec
> Hielan' laddie, bonnie laddie,
> Strappin' timber tae the deck,
> My bonnie hielan' laddie?
> *Traditional song.*

CHAPTER FOUR

Agricultural Development in Central Canada to 1914

Introduction

When economic development was based on the exploitation of natural resources agricultural activity was generally part of that development. Only in recent times have market mechanisms evolved to a degree of efficiency which obviates the need for a local food supply. Consequently, throughout Canadian history there was a large agricultural sector even when the dynamic basis of growth was derived from other parts of the economy. Of course, the agricultural sector often itself became the focus of export-led growth.[1]

As will be seen throughout this chapter many factors governed agricultural development. Where there were no particularly strong demands derived from other sectors of the economy, or where it was inefficient, agriculture often developed on a self-sufficient or subsistence basis. This was the case in early Upper Canada. In this instance, as in many others, however, it was generally expected that crops would eventually find both domestic and foreign markets. When a market for agricultural output developed, farms were no longer constrained to be self-sufficient units. However, even the existence of a market was no particular evidence of a surplus agricultural production and a region of settlement was often unable to feed itself. In New France, imports of food were required from time to time. Yet, it is important to note that, in general, the ability of a region or country to feed itself is not necessarily a characteristic of an advanced economy. Often it is a symptom of the inefficient use of a resource endowment. For instance, British Columbia, with a tiny proportion of its land area capable of supporting agriculture, has always been a net importer of foodstuffs. Given the efficiency of adjacent regions any diversion of resources—labour and capital—into agriculture to reduce food imports would lead to a net welfare loss.

Besides individual farm or regional self-sufficiency in agriculture there are may historical examples in Canada of regions capable of generating surplus agricultural output. The importance of these agricultural surpluses has been twofold. First, the surplus was often exported, as in the wheat economy of mid-nineteenth-century Canada West. Second, the surplus released factors of production, such as labour or capital, from agriculture to other sectors of the economy where they were used more efficiently. As will be noted in Chapter 6 the rural-urban shift of population was one of the major migratory movements in Canadian history.

In seeking to explain the significance of agriculture in economic development in this chapter emphasis is placed on central Canada. A discussion of prairie agriculture which was tied to the rapid industrialization of the economy in more modern times is postponed until Chapter 11. Here specific attention is directed to the economic forces which at first retarded the generation of an exportable agricultural surplus, later permitted it, and subsequently transformed the agricultural sector.

The Agriculture of New France
The initial settlement of New France was primarily based on the exploitation of natural resources and the subsequent export of their products. In order to meet the basic necessities of those involved in the staple trades and because of the impracticality of importing food, it was immediately necessary to establish agricultural activity.[2] From the initial stimulus the agricultural sector was to grow to be the largest constituent of the economy even though the staple trades continued to dominate economic development. Yet despite the relative size of the agricultural sector, New France only achieved a precarious ability to feed itself. This was so because, although the agricultural sector grew, there was little structural change within agriculture which facilitated a more rapid growth of output. From the beginning of the colony in 1606 and during the French régime, three relatively unchanging economic characteristics directed the pattern of agricultural development.

First, there was an abundance of land suitable for agricultural use. Second, the population of New France was small in absolute terms. The flow of immigrants from the mother country was insignificant after the first phase of settlement and in this vital characteristic New France was different from the British colonies to the south. Furthermore, the small population base meant that skilled labour was relatively scarce. Third, there was a scarcity of capital in agriculture, including farm buildings and livestock. In part, this capital scarcity was a consequence of the small size of the colony and in part a result of inadequate flows of capital from France to New France. Thus, there were low labour-to-land and low capital-to-land ratios.

One of the basic features of agriculture in New France which distinguished it from agricultural activity elsewhere was the institutional organization.[3] Tenure of agricultural land was held through the institution called "the seigneurial system". Although this system will be described in detail later, it is important to note here that the seigneurial system differed from a feudal system in that the individual habitant was not tied to the land. Certainly, the seigneurial system was based on European precedents and principal among these was the basis of land tenure in open-field agriculture.

In Europe, open-field agriculture developed, it is generally argued, as a response to the need for farmer-peasants to diversify land holdings. Such diversification was found desirable because it represented a mechanism by which the individual agriculturalist could insure himself against the risk of local disaster—the flooding of a stream, cattle invading the cereal field, and the like. Furthermore, because each farmer had a well-diversified portfolio of land of different soil characteristics, incomes tended to be more stable than otherwise might be the case. Diversification, especially when agricultural technique was primitive, also facilitated the cooperative use of labour and capital equipment.[4]

Under the seigneurial system of land tenure the seigneur held his land at the pleasure of the Crown. While this land was often simply granted to the seigneur, there was the possibility of acquiring seigneuries by purchase. In the years before the Crown took direct control of the colony in 1663 *la Compagnie de la Nouvelle France* distributed large tracts of land bordering on the St. Lawrence River between Quebec and Montreal. Later, under the Crown, more seigneuries were distributed and, although these tended to be smaller than the earlier distributions, there was, as before, a great variety of sizes. By 1672, most of the land between the two major cities of the colony had been distributed to seigneurs. However, there was still enough vacant land in the colony for subsequent grants to be made. These newer seigneuries were primarily those along the tributary streams of the St. Lawrence. In total, slightly more than 250 seigneuries were granted in the history of New France. Some, it may be anticipated, were of small agricultural value.[5]

Land was sub-infeued to the individual settlers. As the seigneur held his land from the Crown, the individual *censitaire* or habitant held his title in feu contract from the seigneur. For his *rotures*, that is, his fields, the individual was required to pay *cens et rentes*. These were, respectively, a fixed feudal due and a land rent, which was generally proportional to the harvest. In return, the seigneur usually provided certain facilities such as grist mills. Indeed, part of the cens et rentes may be viewed as a tax paid for the provision of public goods which included administration of the colony and measures for defence against Indian attack.[6] Although the seigneurial system was patterned on the French model, it differed in many respects, largely because of the abundance of land in the colony. For instance, seigneurs often competitively bid down the rents required of censitaires in order to attract or keep them since they were not tied to the land. Seigneurs were obliged, by their contracts with the Crown, to encourage settlement. Whether or not the rents paid by the censitaires were higher than those which might have prevailed under a more flexible form of land tenure is of course difficult to determine.

It is often claimed that the seigneurial form of land tenure retarded the generation of an agricultural surplus.[7] While there is little doubt that New France's agricultural sector was slow to develop the attribution is unconvincing because, as noted earlier, agriculture developed under conditions of land abundance and labour and capital scarcity.

The conditions of pioneer agriculture were, of course, not unique to New France. In the Thirteen Colonies in the early 1600s, or in Upper Canada two hundred years later, land was plentiful relative to other factors of production. However, land was not free apart from seigneurial claims; it had to be cleared from the forest. As a result effort was directed to land clearance and little attention paid to attempting to increase yields on the land already under cultivation. Not surprisingly many of the farm units were barely self-sufficient. However, unlike other areas in North America, the population base of New France was small and increased relatively slowly because there were so few immigrants to supplement the growth of the population. Thus, in New France the small domestic market provided insufficient incentive for the production of foodstuffs as commercial commodities. Another contributing factor was the relatively high opportunity cost associated with farming because of the alternative of employment in the fur trade or fishery. Many habitants chose to combine farming with part-time hunting and trapping in the early pioneer phase of agricultural expansion. The initial westward movement of the farming frontier towards Montreal was, in fact, as much a product of the fur trade as it was of conditions within agriculture itself.

By the 1660s, as the demand for manpower in the fur trade ceased to expand rapidly, more settlers turned to full-time agriculture. At the same time, France, through its colonial intendents, set out to establish agricultural settlement on the St. Lawrence more firmly. Under the guidance of administrators, such as the gifted Jean Talon, New France's economy was directed towards enlarging the agricultural base and wheat soon developed as the major cash crop once gristmills had been established. Other goods, such as peas, hogs, sheep and some fruit, were produced but were less important cash commodities.[8]

The long narrow lots of the seigneurial field pattern were, as noted earlier, a typical feudal response to the economic problems of risk-sharing and cooperation in relatively primitive agriculture. Such a pattern also solved the need for transport as settlement expanded from the immediate vicinity of Quebec City—the typical field pattern is illustrated in Map 4:1. In the dense forests of New France, transport facilities were scarce and costly since there was little proper capital to clear roads. Only the rivers, and especially the St. Lawrence River, provided cheap means of transport. At first almost all settlers lived within a mile of the navigable rivers and within about twenty miles of Quebec City or Montreal. To keep the cost of transport inputs at a minimum, it was imperative for all farmers in this early period to have river frontage; narrow lots gave such frontage to a maximum number of settlers. Of course, once the cost of land clearing had been borne, land transport became a more competitive means of carriage for some goods and people, but high-bulk, low-value items were usually more efficiently carried by water.

With land abundant and labour and capital scarce, profit-maximizing agriculture called for extensive cultivation. Elaborate crop rotations and selective cattle breeding, both labour- and capital-intensive activities, were inefficient. Cereals best suited the economic conditions and land was often planted with wheat for several years in succession before being left fallow. Where practised, alternating wheat and pasture on the same piece of land served as a simple rotation policy. Because the urban market for livestock in New France was small and export opportunities for these commodities were limited, the value of output to be gained from livestock and its development was slight. In addition, fencing, which was necessary for livestock-production, used scarce capital. Farmers, or habitants, kept only enough livestock for their own needs which meant that since there was little demand for feed crops, there was little opportunity to rotate them with cereals.

Agricultural development in New France was slow primarily because the growth of the domestic market was sluggish. Even as late as 1759 much potential agricultural land in the seigneuries still required clearing or draining. There is little evidence to suggest that the slow growth of agricultural output and the apparently backward technique, which was much commented on at the time, were directly a product of the seigneurial system. For instance, cens et rentes fell in real terms

Map 4:1 Strip Farming in New France

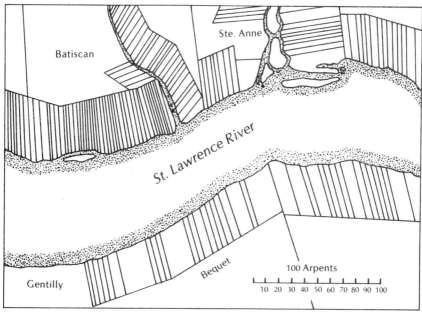

Batiscan

Ste. Anne

St. Lawrence River

Bequet

Gentilly

100 Arpents

10 20 30 40 50 60 70 80 90 100

Source: D. G. Kerr, *Historical Atlas of Canada,* 3rd rev. ed. (Toronto, 1975), p. 25.

throughout the period on most seigneuries. Rights, such as that held by the seigneur to exact labour services—*corvées*—from his *censitaires*, were either trifling or fell into disuse.[9] Land abundance and the flow of young men into the service of the fur trade introduced a flexibility into the system of land tenure which was not found in the mother country or in other feudal systems.

In relative terms, agricultural development was greatest on the seigneuries closest to the two major urban centres. Since short transport distances conferred the advantage of proximity to the commercial markets, the *censitaires* of these areas were more responsive to market forces than those elsewhere. However, it is unlikely that demand alone explains the greater efficiency of land use near Montreal and Quebec. Much of the land capable of servicing the urban demand was held by the Church. Church-held seigneuries had been granted early in the history of New France and accounted for about one-quarter of agricultural land, that is about 2.1 million *arpents* of a total of about 8 million *arpents* in 1759.[10] These seigneuries were, it is generally argued, more efficiently managed than the seigneuries held by laymen. The reason, of course, was that because Church seigneuries were not liable to sub-division, investment in farm equipment and buildings could take place with greater certainty than otherwise would have been possible. Both the proximity to markets and the more efficient estate management of the ecclesiastical bodies served the cause of higher productivity.

Although agricultural output grew slowly the colony of New France did achieve a limited ability to export cereals from time to time. The few decades after a particularly bad harvest in France in 1709 saw continued attempts by the colonial administrators to channel wheat exports to both the mother country and to the French West Indies. However, by 1740, and until the end of the French régime, an exportable surplus was not forthcoming and in many years the colony had to import foodstuffs. Apparently the changes in both domestic and export demand induced an insufficient supply response.

The reasons for the inadequate response to demand forces which was particularly evident in the last twenty-five or so years of the French régime were institutional. Only in part, however, were the institutional barriers to agricultural development created by the seigneurial system. In large measure the barriers were caused by the administration of the colony. However, it must be appreciated that, lacking any good evidence concerning the quantity of output or, indeed, the quantity of land in production, such reasoning must be in the nature of conjecture.

First, the monetary base of New France was unstable. As Chapter 8 discusses in greater detail, such instability introduced risks associated with commercial agriculture which acted as an impediment to specialized production. That is, the market did not necessarily compensate individuals for risk. Second, and in a similar manner, administrative actions made the market for agricultural products uncertain. For instance, agricultural prices in New France were seldom the result of market forces. The governor of the colony had the power to set prices by fiat and often exercised that power. Table 4:1 shows the wheat prices which prevailed during the last three decades of French rule. These nominal prices display less variation than might be expected because of the frequent assessment of an administered price. During the period from March 1742 until October 1744, for instance, a decree held the price constant. Cause for intervention was a succession of poor harvests which raised the price of wheat and flour in Quebec. Only small price increases were allowed and it is therefore not surprising that response in the agricultural sector overlooked the possibility of growing more wheat on a commercial basis and substituting less land-intensive crops for consumption on the farms. In addition to administered prices, the officials of the colony occasionally took levies of grain from individual farmers during times of cereal scarcity.

Table 4:1 Price of Wheat in New France, 1729-1758

(livres per minot)

Year	Price	Year	Price
(1)	(2)	(3)	(4)
1729	3.0	1744	4.2
1730	3.0	1745	3.0
1731	2.5	1746	2.5
1732	3.0	1747	3.0
1733	2.0	1748	3.0
1734	2.0	1749	2.5
1735	2.0	1750	3.0
1736	3.5	1751	5.0
1737	4.0	1752	4.0
1738	3.0	1753	3.5
1739	2.0	1754	3.5
1740	2.0	1755	3.5
1741	2.5	1756	5.0
1742	3.5	1757	10.0
1743	4.25	1758	18.0

Note: A *livre* was approximately the equivalent of one shilling sterling; a *minot* of wheat equalled 1.07 bushels. The above prices were calculated by Lunn from both current and official prices. It is a crude index because of the paucity of data. Nevertheless, it fairly represents the trend and is accurate for those periods when all wheat traded at the official price, for example, from March 1742 until October 1744.

Source: A. J. E. Lunn, *Economic Development in French Canada, 1740-1760*, MA thesis, McGill University (1934), pp. 118-20.

The effect of interference in incentives for agricultural development showed itself most profoundly in the lack of investment in the farm sector. Since individual *censitaires* could not be displaced from their holdings it might be expected that they would invest in their farms. Such investments might have taken a variety of forms: clearing land of forest, increasing fencing to permit diversification of agricultural output, and increasing attention to good animal-husbandry practices, among others. However, with the constant prospect of administered prices and levies of agricultural goods by the government the rewards of investment might be unrealized. In the final years of the French régime, this was compounded by the inability to consolidate *rotures* permanently because inheritance law required that all assigned land should revert to the *censitaire*'s estate upon his death and be divided among his heirs. Thus, although a rental market in *rotures* did exist, there was a limitation on the expected return to any investment on rented land.[11] The seigneurs were also unlikely to invest when they too found that the real value of their rents was falling thereby preventing them from capturing the benefits of agricultural improvements.

Any assessment of the economy of New France must note that it produced for its inhabitants a standard of economic well-being which was, in most respects, comparable with that achieved in the pioneering stages of development in the English colonies to the south. The slow growth of New France's population meant that the economy took longer to diversify, even within agriculture, and the abundance of land was the major characteristic of expansion. It is to the low ratios of labour and capital to land that we must turn in order to explain the techniques of production. What may have appeared prodigal to those from other economies was no more than the most efficient type of agriculture under the circumstances. The peculiar system of land tenure itself was not a major retarding influence. On the other hand, the oppressive and powerful administrative structure at times intruded as a progressive force, under Jean Talon in the seventeenth century, and as a retarding influence later.

In summary, the agricultural development of New France was slow only in comparison with the progress of agriculture in the English colonies in North America. There, conditions were different. It is only in the years long after the close of the French régime that agricultural development can be described as stunted.

Stunted Agricultural Development

British rule was established in Quebec in 1763. Initially the new order changed the character of French-Canadian agriculture very little since one of the major conventions was the preservation of the seigneurial system. Indeed, this archaic system was not abolished until 1854. The advent of British rule, of course, indirectly influenced the pattern of agricultural development in a variety of ways. Principal among these influences were the exposure of French-Canadian agriculture to new market forces, the introduction of non-French-speaking agriculturalists into Quebec, and the growth of an agricultural sector in the adjacent colony of Upper Canada. However, other forces emerged between 1763 and 1854 which were largely a product of internal circumstances. Most keenly felt in the agricultural sector was the growth of the French-Canadian population. By the beginning of the nineteenth century all the forces combined in a manner which produced a period of prolonged agricultural crisis. Although the exact nature of this crisis and its proximate causes are a matter of some historical controversy, as will be seen later, there is no doubt of its occurrence.[12]

Although the seigneurial system was not dismantled until 1854, few new seigneuries were granted under British colonial rule. None were created after 1790. All agricultural settlement outside the bounds of existing seigneuries took place under the English laws of land tenure—freehold property rights. Since much fertile agricultural land had not been alienated under the French régime, its disbursement in the late eighteenth and early nineteenth centuries created a sizeable part of the agricultural sector under a different form of tenure. This land attracted farmers from the southern colonies, afterwards the United States, and later from Great Britain. Because few French-Canadian farmers could establish themselves on this land, which was located for the most part in the area known as "the Eastern Townships" to the southeast of Montreal, the different legal rights to the land also distinguished two types of agriculturalists. Apart from the new settlements, non-French-speaking farmers were also able to purchase seigneuries and consequently established themselves close to Montreal.[13]

However, there were not two but three distinct sub-sectors of agriculture which evolved in Lower Canada. Apart from the growing number of English-speaking settlers, the French Canadians themselves were of two types by the early nineteenth century. There were those who farmed the older established seigneuries and those who were displaced from the St. Lawrence Valley plain onto the marginal lands close to the Precambrian Shield.[14] The displacement of the latter was caused by the growing population on the established seigneuries, the constant supply of agricultural land on those seigneuries which prevailed after about 1800, and the apparent unwillingness of French Canadians to leave their native land. Not until the decade of the 1850s did a substantial number of French Canadians emigrate and thus relieve pressure for land which had reduced many to penury.

There is little doubt that the speed of agricultural development increased in the late eighteenth century. Although there is no direct evidence about agricultural output, the rapid growth of villages in Lower Canada marked the prosperity associated with increased output and greater specialization. With the return of peace after the war with the United States came the growth of an exportable surplus of agricultural output, particularly wheat. This surplus, for the most part, was shipped to the British market. By the early 1790s the wheat exports of the colony had grown to the levels shown in Table 4:2. Most of these wheat shipments originated on the seigneurial lands farmed by the French Canadians. Naturally, as a response to the rising price of wheat in the late eighteenth century, land clearing proceeded at a fast pace. During this period farm incomes in Lower Canada grew quite rapidly although, as noted, the exact extent of the income gain is not well documented.[15]

The process of agricultural expansion in the late eighteenth century, however, changed the relative scarcity of factors. Land became progressively more scarce and thus more expensive. The growing rural

Table 4:2 Wheat Exports from Lower Canada, 1793-1808
(thousands of *minots*)[a]

Year	Exports	Year	Exports
(1)	(2)	(3)	(4)
1793	541.7	1801	663.5
1794	483.5	1802	1,151.5
1795	448.7	1803	438.1
1796	24.9	1804	273.1
1797	101.1	1805	115.0
1798	139.4	1806	151.9
1799	201.2	1807	333.8
1800	318.5	1808	399.0

[a] One *minot* equals 1.07 bushels.

Source: F. Ouellet, "L'Agriculture Bas-Canadienne Vue à Travers Les Dimes et la Rente en Nature", *Histoire Sociale/Social History*, Vol. 8, no. 3 (1971), p. 10.

population, on the other hand, made labour more abundant and less expensive in relative terms than it had been formerly. In this manner, the factor-input combinations which had earlier led to the extensive cultivation of cereals in French Canada was altered and no longer dictated a specialization in wheat. Yet, throughout the first half of the nineteenth century wheat remained the principal agricultural output of Lower Canada.

As is evident in Table 4:2 the exports of wheat from Lower Canada reached their zenith in 1802. Afterwards they declined to a level which was no greater than that achieved much earlier although there was, of course, much year-to-year variation. This failure of exports to grow took place against a background of rising wheat prices in Lower Canada, and elsewhere, until the end of the Napoleonic Wars.[16] After 1802 it is likely that Lower Canada became less effective a competitor with other wheat-growing areas of the United States and Upper Canada.[17] Was this apparent inability to sustain wheat exports due to the failure of the agricultural sector to adapt new techniques of cereal production or is it simply evidence of a diversification into non-cereal production (for which there was a growing domestic demand), or both?

A growing population and a fixed land supply in the context of the seigneurial system had at least one major deleterious effect. It altered the size of the farm unit. Upon the death of a *censitaire*, the land was generally divided among the surviving children. Formerly, when land was available at a low price or could be carved from the forest, lots which had been sub-divided were often regrouped. Even if they were not regrouped, individual farmers could acquire other acreage and farm size did not necessarily fall. In this respect the early seigneurial system was flexible. But when fertile farm land became scarce in the nineteenth century, permanent sub-division occurred. In the absence of other adjustments there would be a fall in the incomes expected from agriculture on the established seigneuries. Indeed, the income loss resulting from the decline in size of the average land holdings may have been proportionately greater than the decline in size of farms as the gains in efficiency derived from scale were lost. Furthermore, cens et rentes in real terms per arpent rose. That is, many seigneurial dues had been recontracted. In the early years of British rule it was fairly common for the seigneur to abandon the nominal dues in favour of real ones, a policy that the British permitted. A failure to innovate accompanied the small size of French-Canadian farms; this failure had two dimensions. First, there was no successful attempt to raise wheat yields. Second, there was no rapid adjustment of the output mix which might have increased overall agricultural efficiency. One major theme of Canadian history stresses that the failure to innovate was a product of the basic conservatism of the French-Canadian farmer. So powerful was the reliance on traditional methods that, despite the increased land scarcity and the steadily increasing demand for cereal exports, agricultural development stagnated. The inability to sustain wheat exports at their former levels identifies an agricultural crisis of major proportions in the immediate post-1802 years (see Table 4:2).[18]

Another interpretation of the same events suggests that while wheat prices were secularly increasing until the end of the Napoleonic Wars there was a great deal of short-run price instability. This instability was caused by shifts in the export demand which depended on the state of the British harvest, on Great Britain's access to European sources of supply which fluctuated with the wars, as well as on the ability of other North American wheat-growing areas to produce a surplus. Such price instability induced a diversification of agricultural output which was further reinforced by the fall in wheat prices in Great Britain after the end of the Napoleonic Wars and the increasing domestic demand for non-cereal output. While wheat remained the principal export commodity and the main product of domestic agriculture, in all likelihood its relative importance fell.[19] If this interpretation more satisfactorily explains the performance of French-Canadian agricultural development the crisis was one of structure and not of stagnation. Simply, the structural change in output took place too slowly in the face of changing costs and demand and resulted in retarded or stunted agricultural development.

The stunted development of agriculture on the established seigneuries was due to the inability of habitant farmers to respond adequately to market pressures. This, in turn, produced conditions of relative backwardness which were less due to habitant mendacity than to the constraints imposed by economic circumstances in the first half of the nineteenth century. Existing farms were too small to permit a restructuring of output with less cereals and more livestock. The open-field system further compounded this problem. Furthermore, as land became relatively scarce the costs of any consolidation of *rotures* rose and capital markets were too imperfect to facilitate any individual investment in farm buildings, fences, livestock, and other farm capital. Many *censitaires* were, in fact, already in debt to the seigneurs just to maintain existing farms.

Few other forces existed to ameliorate the backward condition of French-Canadian agriculture. The new agricultural societies formed for the dissemination of better techniques were geared to the pattern of farming on enclosed fields and were, as a consequence, generally restricted to English-speaking farmers. In addition, the infrastructure for change was lacking: the livestock was of relatively poor quality, there were few dealers in new and improved seeds, and there were few marketing agents. Not surprisingly, yields of wheat per acre fell. Thus, the traditional land-intensive methods prevailed with insufficient emphasis on stock raising, crop rotation to maintain fertility of the land, renewal of seed, and the reseeding of idle land with grass or clover in order to provide better pastures. Agricultural development on the established seigneurial lands progressed slowly in the first fifty years of the nineteenth century; the crisis was of long duration.

The Eastern Townships stand in marked contrast to the seigneurial lands. First settled by the so-called Loyalists from the United States and, after 1815, by English and Scots, the Eastern Townships employed real capital more widely than the seigneuries. The Crown had ceded vast areas to the British-American Land Company in order to induce settlement. The company built roads and provided much of the necessary infrastructure for commercial farming. Using the rolling terrain for pasture, the English-speaking farmers specialized in livestock and some dairy produce for the urban markets; grains were of secondary importance. The high quality of livestock, the reseeding of pastures, and the employment of the best-known crop-rotation practices—all characteristics associated with greater capital intensity—led to yields per acre which were much higher than those which prevailed on the seigneurial lands. Service and artisan activities were more common in the Townships than anywhere else in Quebec. The more commercialized nature of agriculture brought greater revenues and encouraged specialization with an attendant higher demand for local village activities. After 1830 some French Canadians took up land in the northern portion of the Townships but, owing to the capital scarcity which they faced, farming practices tended to resemble those on the seigneurial lands.[20]

The two major systems of agriculture in Lower Canada developed differently: the French-Canadian farming sector was relatively backward in contrast to that managed by the Anglo-American and other English-speaking farmers. That this separateness was due solely to the conservative practices of the French-Canadian farmer is only so because institutional and market economic forces did not permit otherwise. The seigneurial system lacked the flexibility it had had in earlier times. Such was the relative backwardness that many individuals were displaced from the older seigneuries into the newer areas of seigneurial settlement. The plight of these individuals is considered later in this chapter.

Achieving an Agricultural Surplus: Upper Canadian Wheat, 1794-1846

The development of agriculture in Upper Canada, like that in the Eastern Townships, progressed in marked contrast to that on the St. Lawrence Valley plain. While Lower Canada became a less effective competitor in the world wheat market, Upper Canada became a more effective one. Two dates, 1794 and 1846, conveniently circumscribe the first phase of rapid agricultural development in Upper Canada. The year 1794 witnessed the first exports of agricultural produce from Upper Canada; in 1846 the British North American farmers and grain merchants were set adrift from the imperial system of trade which, by means of the British Corn Laws, had protected and stimulated colonial agriculture from the beginning. Between these years, the staple export of wheat emerged as the dynamic element in agriculture based almost entirely upon entry to the British market. Only occasionally was it profitable to ship wheat exports to the U.S. market. A critical determinant of potential markets, the wheat-import policies of both Great Britain and the United States greatly influenced the prosperity of Upper Canada.[21]

Land in Upper Canada was an abundant resource while both capital and labour were relatively scarce and therefore expensive. Agriculture accordingly possessed the same characteristics as in Lower Canada: extensive cultivation, simple crop rotation, and wheat as the major cash crop. Peas, barley, rye, and buckwheat found only a domestic market and mixed farming was restricted to parts of Upper Canada such as those near York–Toronto and the Niagara Peninsula.[22] The widespread development of mixed farming for general market, which changed the focus of central Canadian agriculture, occurred only after 1846.

During the pioneer phase of agriculture, transport facilities were also scarce. Transport was first provided by the St. Lawrence River–Great

Lakes system as in Lower Canada and the only alternative mode was the growing network of roads which opened up more of the colony in the early 1800s. Yonge Street, which linked Toronto to Lake Simcoe, and Dundas Street, which joined the western end of Lake Ontario to the Grand River, were among the few major routes which existed in early years (see Chapter 10). Settlers built roads linked to the major arteries but these were neither intended for nor capable of bearing heavy traffic. The geographical extension of commercial agriculture depended on the extension of transport facilities through the construction of canals as well as on the flow of capital into the agricultural sector. Yet, these supply factors alone were insufficient to initiate and sustain agricultural change.

During this period, 1794-1846, the demand forces were the essential ones, and they, in turn, were related to the degree of preference which Great Britain showed Canada. Preferential access to the British market was ensured under the provisions of the Corn Laws which were designed to protect British home agriculture. Basically they prohibited imports of grain and flour when British prices were very low but permitted them when prices were high. Between extreme prices a variable tariff or sliding scale, which rose positively with the domestic prices, regulated the inflow of grain and flour. Canadian grain and flour were given preferential treatment as empire produce. Canadian exports were permitted to enter Great Britain at a lower price than those of non-empire countries. Also, Canadian grain bore a lower tariff rate on the sliding scale than that of foreign countries. Although the Corn Laws were modified many times during the period under consideration, often in an attempt to appease British North America, the basic structure, described above, and its effect on wheat exports remained unaltered until 1842.[23] From then until the repeal of the Corn Laws four years later a nominal duty of one shilling was levied regardless of the British price.

Access to the British market guaranteed a market for British North American grain and flour; however there was an associated cost. The Corn Laws caused a high variance in income. How this variation came about can be seen in the context of the model presented in Figure 4:1. Represented here are the domestic supply and demand conditions of wheat which prevailed in the respective economies of Great Britain (S_{GB} and D_{GB}) and British North America (S_{BNA} and D_{BNA}) as well as the trade between the two areas.

While the Upper Canadian farmer would have undoubtedly preferred unlimited access to the British market to the exclusion of all others, this was not to be. Without the tariff on British North American grain equilibrium would occur where total wheat supply equalled total wheat demand. Thus, the intersection of D_E with S_E would determine the quan-

Figure 4:1 The Wheat Trade Under the Corn Laws

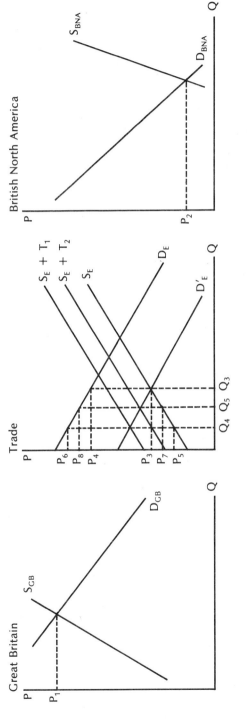

P—price
Q—quantity
S_{GB}—supply curve of wheat in Great Britain
D_{GB}—demand curve for wheat in Great Britain
S_{BNA}—supply curve of wheat in British North America
D_{BNA}—demand curve of wheat in British North America

S_E—excess supply curve of British North American wheat = $(S_{BNA}-D_{BNA})$
D_E—British excess demand for British North American wheat in
    Great Britain = $(D_{GB}-S_{GB})$
D'_E—British excess demand for British North American wheat minus
    the transport cost from British North America to Great Britain

tity exported (Q_3) and the price received in Upper Canada (P_3). The British price (P_4) was simultaneously determined by adding transport costs to P_3. By comparison, in the absence of trade between Upper Canada and Great Britain, the price in Upper Canada would be P_2 while that in Great Britain would be P_1. The policy of the imperial government prevented the establishment of an equilibrium price and export flow (represented by P_3 and Q_3) which may have promoted a more orderly development of grain production in Upper Canada in the absence of any other sources of supply. One of the principal sources was the United States. However, all foreign grain and flour, as opposed to colonial products, was denied entry into Great Britain unless the prevailing British price was high. During the period 1822 to 1842 which the model here most accurately describes, the Corn Laws did not permit the entry of foreign breadstuffs at prices below 80 shillings per quarter (8 bushels).

During the period 1794 to 1846 the Corn Laws, as they applied to British North America, changed several times:

1) Prior to 1815 the price of wheat in Great Britain was sufficiently high that the Corn Laws seldom either taxed or exluded British North American wheat from the British market.
2) The Corn Laws were modified in 1815. The revision imposed quantity restrictions based on a sliding scale attached to the British price. No wheat was permitted to enter Great Britain at prices below 67 shillings per quarter. Canadian wheat and flour were admitted at any higher price but non-colonial grain was not cleared for entry until the price was 80 shillings.
3) In 1822 the minimum entry price for colonial grain was reduced to 59 shillings per quarter but a duty was imposed until the British price was 57 shillings.
4) The next revision in 1828 guaranteed entry for British North American wheat and flour at any price. However, if the price was below 67 shillings the duty imposed was high (5 shillings) and if above 67 shillings the duty was low (sixpence).
5) No major revision was then undertaken until 1842 when the price at which the tariff rate applied to British North American grain and wheat was reduced to 55 shillings per quarter.

As may be judged from the above, Figure 4:1 captures the essential features of the Corn Laws from 1815 to 1846.[24]

How such a sliding scale affected Canadian farm income can be gauged from Figure 4:1. If the British domestic wheat price (P_1) was less than 67 shillings per quarter, colonial grain bore the higher of the two

Figure 4:2 The Average Price of Wheat Per Imperial Quarter in Great Britain, 1794-1846

Shillings & Pence

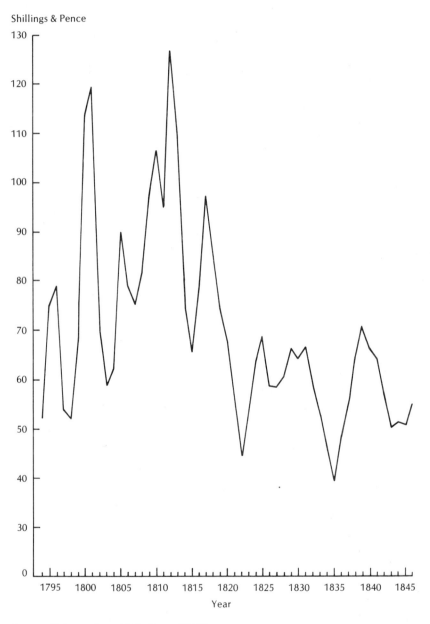

Year

Source: Data are from Michell, pp. 488-89.

tariffs. Bearing this higher tariff effective excess supply shifted to $S_E + T_1$, from the free trade alternative S_E; the difference represents the per-unit tariff of 5 shillings. The market clearing price in British North America was lower (at P_5) with this particular Corn Law provision than it otherwise would have been (P_3) and Canadian production was curtailed — a movement along the British North American supply curve — by reduced exports (Q_4). The British North American price was lower than the non-tariff alternative yet higher than that which would have prevailed in the absence of trade. In Great Britain the farm sector was protected since the prevailing price there was P_6.

On the other hand, poor harvests in Great Britain — or for that matter any factor which might influence the supply of grain in Great Britain — drove the price up. The British domestic wheat price (P_1) might be greater than 67 shillings per quarter. Under such conditions the tariff was the lower rate of sixpence per quarter ($S_E + T^2$) and although British North American grain exports were high (Q_5) they were lower than a non-tariff alternative would have dictated (Q_3). The price received by Upper Canadian grain exporters (P_7) was, similarly, lower than that which would have prevailed with free trade between British North America and Great Britain (P_3). Of course, the barrier of transport costs would have existed even with unimpeded access to the British market. Not suprisingly, Upper Canadian farmers resented the income-instability imparted by the Corn Laws even though they were the guarantee of entry to the British market.

From 1800 to 1815, a series of poor British harvests and the interruption of supply from the Baltic due to the wars with France kept the market price high in Great Britain and the full effect of the Corn Law was not felt in the Canadas. Wheat output expanded in Upper Canada. Figure 4:2 documents the relatively high British wheat prices from 1799 to 1815 when the price only twice fell below 67 shillings (in 1804 and 1815). Few complaints emanated from British North America. This continued until 1820 when good British harvests produced a situation resembling ($S_E + T_1$) and the high Corn Law duty prevailed forcing British North American exports down (Q_4); prosperity turned to depression in both Canadas. The relatively low prices of 1821 to 1824 attest to this fact. The climax, in a sense, of this staple dependence took place from about 1832 to 1840 when Great Britain experienced excellent harvests and, adding to the problems, Upper Canada suffered partial crop failures in 1835, 1836, and 1837. This caused, in a dynamic framework, supply (S_{BNA}) to decrease, which in turn decreased S_E, which further reduced exports. Note the relatively low wheat prices in Figure 4:2 from 1832 to 1838 and the corresponding small amounts of British North American exports to Great

Figure 4:3 British Imports of British North American Grain and Flour, 1800-1846

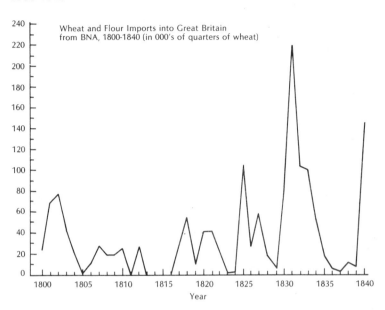

Wheat and Flour Imports into Great Britain from BNA, 1800-1840 (in 000's of quarters of wheat)

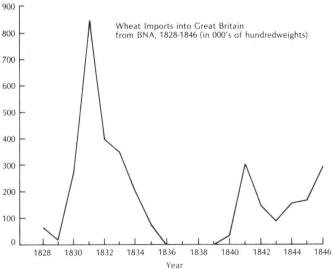

Wheat Imports into Great Britain from BNA, 1828-1846 (in 000's of hundredweights)

Note: One barrel of flour equals 5 bushels of wheat.

Sources: Data are from F. W. Burton, "The Wheat Supply of New France, *Canadian Journal of Economics and Political Science*, Vol. 3, no. 2 (1937), pp. 213 and Michell, p. 100.

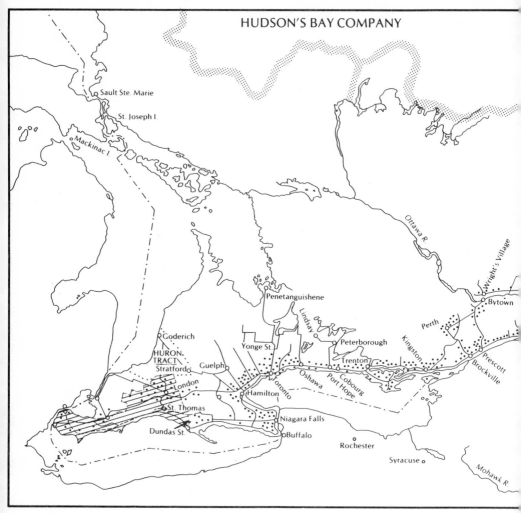

Map 4:2 Agricultural Settlement in the 1830s

Britain in Figure 4:3. Rebellion erupted in both Lower and Upper Canada in 1837; among other complaints the farmers demanded more favoured entry to the British market and high tariffs against agricultural produce from the United States entering Upper Canada.

The import of wheat to British North America from the United States was a further grievance of the Upper Canadian farmers against the commercial system which had emerged in the early nineteenth century. Moreover, the commercial interests in Montreal wanted to make the St. Lawrence-Great Lakes corridor the principal route not just from Upper

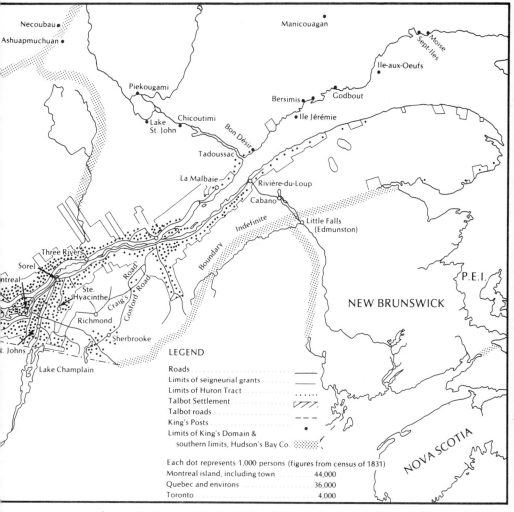

Canada but from the entire heart of North America to Great Britain. Although this problem will be discussed in detail later it is pertinent to note here that many of the actions of the merchants who supported this strategy for development were further elements inducing instability in Upper Canadian farm income. Although the terms of the Corn Laws were revised many times and the tariffs on U.S. farm export to Upper and Lower Canada varied—they were increased in 1842—the uncertainty about farm income levels remained.

Nevertheless, the British Corn Laws were the instrument, which encouraged specialized agricultural production on the frontier of Upper Canada. They protected British North America from its principal trade rival, in this case, the United States, just as the Baltic timber tariff did. Furthermore, they offset the low transport-cost advantage which other suppliers had. By the 1840s an aggregate surplus had been achieved. There were other factors which also aided the generation of the surplus. For instance, many farmers supplemented their incomes by engaging in the timber industry during the winter months of the year. Since there were few barriers to entry and it normally did not interfere with agricultural tasks the variability in farm incomes was considerably more than the variation in farmers' total incomes. That the timber trade provided another source of cash on the frontier helped to stimulate agricultural expansion. In the end, however, it was the protection of the Corn Laws which gave Upper Canada the impetus to develop its agricultural sector through the creation of an export staple.

Rebellion, Unification, and Annexation
Three events of far-reaching political consequence dominate the history of the early nineteenth-century Canadas: the rebellions in Upper and Lower Canada in 1837, the unification of the Canadas three years later, and the Annexation Movement of 1848-49. All of these events were closely related to agricultural development.

To the economist, the rebellions in Upper and Lower Canada appear in large measure to be a popular demand for land reform.[25] Seen in this light, the greater intensity of the rebellion in Lower Canada is quite explicable. Archaic even when it was introduced, the seigneurial system was, as we have seen, a complete anachronism which by the nineteenth century permitted no flexibility. Surviving into the period of British colonial rule this system of land tenure had changed only to the extent of freeing seigneurs from many of their obligations. Seigneuries were bought and sold like any real estate. Absentee landlords became more common. Since they were primarily concerned with short-run capital gains from resale and current rental streams, the investment in measures which might increase long-run productivity was neglected. If the seigneurial system had ever been a broadly based socio-economic system it had ceased to be so by the beginning of the 1800s. From then to its demise in 1854, it was nothing more than a simple method of land tenure. As new seigneuries, such as those along the Ottawa River, were opened up for settlement in the marginal farmlands, conditions of rural poverty were created the like of which have never before or since been experienced in Canadian history. On the long-established seigneuries income per farm was, if not falling, rising only slowly. The poverty was a direct consequence of the system of land tenure which prevented specialization in agriculture by keeping farm units well below their most efficient scale and an intricate debt system which often bound the habitant firmly to the land. Thus, while agricultural output rose agricultural productivity was low.

In Upper Canada the system of land tenure was broadly similar to that found elsewhere in North America. The farmer could dispose of his land, provided he had title, and was not required directly to finance amenities such as roads and land surveys. Yet the Upper Canadian farmer did have common grievance with his counterpart in Lower Canada. In both areas prime agricultural land had been alienated. In Lower Canada the British-American Land Company held much of the area of the Eastern Townships and the fact that this land was not free for settlement prevented the escape of the sons of the habitants from the seigneuries. In Upper Canada the Canada Company which held a vast amount of land in the southwestern region was thought to have effectively checked the westward push of the farm frontier. The Crown had sold this area to the company in order to promote more rapid settlement through the provision of roads and other facilities which the government was unwilling to provide directly. That the land had been alienated in the first instance caused unrest. Many frontier farmers were by their actions speculators in agricultural land as well as agriculturalists. Their scope was constrained since the Huron Tract was also closed to free or low-cost settlement. Lands set aside in both Canadas for the clergy's support also attracted popular displeasure. The Clergy Reserves, as these lands were called, were effectively removed from the public domain although they could be leased. Finally, the farmers of Upper Canada saw a common cause in their opposition to the power of the Family Compact with the opposition of the habitants to the Château Clique. Undoubtedly riddled with patronage these two groups wielded power in the executive branch of the colonial governments and since they, for the most part, represented the interests of merchants, were universally despised by the more radical farmers.[26]

The 1830s were marked not only by the instability of farm income attributed earlier to the Corn Laws, but also by a relative depression in Great Britain. The demands for grain and timber transmitted this depression to the Canadas and because the timber industry supplemented farm income the effects were particularly severe. Poor harvests aggravated agrarian discontent. When rebellions broke out in 1837 the proximate causes were the farmers' disputes with the merchants over trade policies, tightened credit brought about by declining incomes, and the control exerted by the merchants over colonial government. Although the rebellion in Lower Canada assumed overtones of the frustrated ambitions of French-speaking professionals (who were chronically under-employed) it was, as the rebellion in Upper Canada had been, a protest for agrarian reform.

Agrarian reform was less essential to Upper Canada than to Lower Canada. The increase in farm income due to rising prices, the fact that the Canada Company was, on balance, efficient in settling the Huron Tract, and positive political reform did much to remove the sources of agrarian discontent in Upper Canada. In Lower Canada structural change of some magnitude was required. There was a growing realization that the seigneurial system served neither the interests of the habitants nor the seigneurs and in the 1850s the system was dismantled.[27] However, for that change to be effective it had also to be accompanied by increased private and public investment, such as that in the agricultural colleges, in order to speed the change in agricultural production from wheat to mixed and dairy farming which the market indicated was appropriate. The rebellion of 1837 helped to force these changes on a reluctant political mechanism and only afterwards was there a rise in agricultural productivity.

The question of whether wheat from the United States should be permitted to enter Canada aroused much of the antipathy of the farm sector to the merchant interests. The Colonial Trade Act of 1831 allowed this import and although the grain could not be re-exported to Great Britain it was milled and shipped as flour which, in turn, was permitted entry under the terms of the Corn Laws. As Montreal tapped the grain flow from Upper Canada as well as from the United States the canal system, as noted earlier, was expanded. Both farmers and merchants were vitally interested in transport improvements because of the higher domestic price which would result. By the late 1830s, however, two problems were associated with this expansion of the transport network. First, the canal system was incomplete and second, the colonies had incurred a large debt to finance canal building. The size of this debt effectively prevented them from borrowing more funds. By consolidating the debt of the Canadas through the union of Upper and Lower Canada as Lord Durham recommended, the new political entity was able to exert more leverage for the mobilization of financial capital in the main capital market of London. In this sense, the Act of Union of 1840 was a victory for the merchants since it strengthened the St. Lawrence entrepôt economy at the expense of farming interests. This, of course, is not to argue that there were no gross benefits accruing from the development of the St. Lawrence canal system and the shipping of U.S. grain. Along the route there grew up a very substantial flour-milling industry which otherwise would have received less economic stimulation.[28]

Within a decade of the union of the Canadas a political movement, which enjoyed considerable support, again threatened to change radically the directions of the country. The Annexation Movement of 1848-49, principally aimed at forcing a political union with the United States, was a product of the same economic forces which governed the movement of agricultural exports on the St. Lawrence canal system. The key element of the St. Lawrence economy was its domination over the interior grain trade which the British Corn Laws conferred. However, no less than two years after the union of the Canadas the British government began to dismantle the imperial system of trade. A revision of the Corn Laws in 1842 reduced the protective effect enjoyed by the Canadian grain trade, and, as mentioned earlier, Great Britain finally abandoned the Corn Laws in 1846; the last of the protection for Canadian grain in its main market was withdrawn. Although grain production, like timber production, had become relatively efficient under protection, wheat and flour exports did decline. As they did the St. Lawrence entrepôt shipping economy suffered. This decline was aggravated by the response to the price mechanism under free trade, which no longer made the shipment of American grain to Canada, and its subsequent shipment as flour to Great Britain, a profitable alternative.

Not only was the flow of grain and flour exports down the St. Lawrence waterway system diminished because of the repeal of the Corn Laws, but much of which might have been shipped by this route was diverted to another. The economic viability of the St. Lawrence transport network was dependent on the United States' tariff on Canadian grains. Prior to 1846 Upper Canadian farmers would not ship their grain to Great Britain through the United States because grain so routed was denied access to the British market under the discriminatory Corn Law provisions. That is, the British classified grain by port of shipment and not ultimate origin. Had there been no other change than the repeal, Upper Canadian farmers would still have shipped their diminished exports via the St. Lawrence. Even though the route through the Erie Canal in the United States — via Buffalo or Oswego to New York — to Liverpool was cheaper, the tariff of the United States precluded using this route by inadvertently protecting the more costly Canadian shipping network. In 1845 and 1846, however, the United States introduced drawback legislation which in effect permitted the shipment of Canadian grain in bond through the U.S. route. Traffic immediately flowed to the more efficient, cheaper southern route. Again, the effect was not absolute but trade in grains increasingly took place across the Great Lakes rather than down them. As the volume of St. Lawrence shipping fell so the economic climate of the shipping centre, Montreal, worsened.

To these forces was added what proved to be the catalyzing force of the Annexation Movement, the removal of the Acts of Navigation. As one of the central features of the imperial system of trade, the Acts, among other provisions, restricted intra-empire shipments to those carried by vessels of British or colonial origin. Like the Baltic timber duties and the Corn Laws, a few years earlier, the last vestige of the Acts of Navigation was repealed in 1848, thus admitting U.S. shipping not only to the trade between Canada and Great Britain but to the Great Lakes coastal trade in general. It had been hoped that more efficient U.S. shippers might be induced to use the St. Lawrence route but this traffic failed to materialize. Instead the impact was felt primarily on the Great Lakes system where the growing volume of cross-lake trade increasingly fell into the hands of U.S. vessels.

Shipping and mercantile interests throughout the Canadas were dismayed. In addition to these fundamental economic forces which dictated the changing pattern of trade a series of good harvests in Great Britain reduced the price of grain and reduced the volume of British North American wheat exports. In 1848 wheat exports to Great Britain via the St. Lawrence route attained only about two-fifths of the previous year's level. Frustrated, the Annexationists argued that if the protection of an imperial system of trade was denied them their only recourse was to seek annexation with the United States. They argued that by annexation Canadian exports would be admittted to the United States without duty and thus a market would be ensured.

Despite the vociferous appeal of the Annexation Movement it faded quickly as a political force. First, the farmers failed to support it. Although agricultural recession marked these years the farmers could not agree to support the St. Lawrence route which meant lower farm-gate prices than the Erie Canal route. Second, by the late 1840s the U.S. market was able quickly to absorb much of the grain which otherwise could only have been shipped to Great Britain. Higher prices in the United States than in Canada were such that the U.S. tariff could be overcome. These high prices prevailed through the early 1850s and dropped only when the western settlements of the U.S. prairies were brought within the market economy about the time of the American Civil War. Third, there was a revival of trade in the 1850s on the St. Lawrence route; it was smaller than had been hoped for in the optimistic days of the 1840s but, in conjunction with the north-south trade to which the Canadian merchants had quickly gained access, it mollified public opinion. Finally the promise of Great Britain to negotiate a free-trade agreement between British North America and the United States drained the last political argument from the Annexation Movement.

That the three major political events of the 1830s and 1840s should spring almost solely from economic circumstances is not surprising. The economic basis for prosperity was still extremely narrow and the economy vulnerable to changes in the prices of a few simple staple commodities. Although there were many political crises and changes of great importance none were so directly a product of one sector of the economy as the rebellion of 1837, the unification of the Canadas, and the Annexation Movement. The achievement of the agricultural surplus was by no means a smooth transition.

Innovations in Agriculture

Over the course of the nineteenth century much of agriculture in central Canada developed from subsistence farming to an industry highly sensitive to market forces. This transformation, as previously noted, was first a response to an external market and only later, as urban centres grew, a response to internal demand. The extension of the market through lower transport charges dictated in part the ability of agricultural production to respond to these market forces. Growing efficiency in the farm sector also facilitated the response. Falling per-unit costs were a necessary condition of retaining a market share at a time when new agricultural frontiers were being exploited and new agricultural techniques were being developed elsewhere. New techniques in agriculture were important in terms of a retention, or expansion, of a particular commodity market, and they were the vital technological element which enabled agriculture to change structurally when economic forces dictated.

Innovations, the application of new techniques, in agriculture were many in the nineteenth century. Yet certain key economic characteristics described all of them. Innovations lowered the per-unit cost of agriculture as illustrated in Figure 4:4. By causing a shift in the production function not only was the optimum scale of output changed but a different combination of factor inputs was called for depending on the particular innovation in question. Some innovations, such as the mechanical reapers of the 1850s, induced more capital-intensive agriculture; others, such as the improved methods of drainage, induced a shift to the use of more land. In general, all innovations tended to reduce labour inputs relative to other factors because of the relative labour scarcity. Yet other innovations so altered the structure of costs of competing land uses for production that the output profile of the agricultural sector was altered as individual farmers responded to profit incentives.

Figure 4:4 Agricultural Innovation

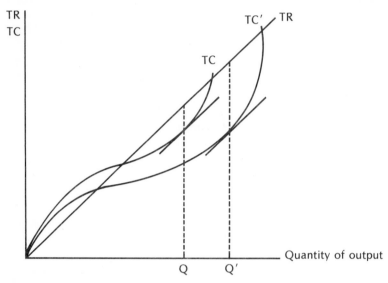

TC—total cost before the innovation
TC'—total cost after the innovation
TR—total revenue
Q and Q' denote optimum-size outputs using different technologies

However it was not only private but also public investment which initiated innovations.

Before about 1840 farming in Upper Canada employed the best techniques of pioneer agriculture. Although the application of new techniques was common it tended to consist of the simple modification of well-known practices, such as crop rotations, to the particular soil and climatic conditions. While horses and oxen drew ploughs the harvesting of crops was done by hand with a scythe and cradle—the cradle being a wooden frame which prevented the grain stalks from scattering on the ground. By the early 1840s agricultural techniques began to change at a rapid rate. Most of the technical changes were first introduced in other countries and spread into Canada and were usually brought in by new immigrants or spread by the growing agricultural press. So widespread were the new techniques and the resulting productivity increases in agriculture that the mid-nineteenth century is often referred to as "the second agricultural revolution"—the first being that which marked the initial application of scientific experimentaion in England in the late 1600s.

After approximately 1840 the rate at which new techniques were adopted increased. While it would be impossible to note all the contributions to productivity growth it is possible to delineate the broad classes to which they belong and the most significant examples. The classes were:

1) mechanical innovations using existing energy sources as well as innovations associated with lowering the cost of—and changing—energy sources;
2) non-mechanical innovations associated with improvements in the quality, or quantity, of the capital stock; and
3) new methods of increasing the quality of non-capital inputs.

There was diversity even within these three broad classes. Let us consider for the moment mechanical innovations.

Although horse or oxen power as applied to farming, and particularly ploughing, was of ancient origins its extensive use after the 1830s was in marked contrast of that of earlier times. Two mechanical innovations, the mechanical reaper and the mechanical thresher, were responsible for this gross substitution of horse-power energy for direct human effort. The magnitude of such changes can be recognized in the decline in the man-hour requirements to produce one acre of wheat from approximately 75 to 43 between about 1830 and 1850.[29] So too, mechanical reapers and threshers in the post-1850s had the effect, especially in Ontario's labour-scarce economy, of increasing the scale of the farm producing wheat or other cereals and causing a substitution of capital for labour. In 1870 about 36,000 mechanical reapers were employed on Ontario farms. The rapid adoption of this technology was primarily governed by the improving quality of the machines, their falling prices, the rise in wage costs, as well as by the increasing price of wheat until 1868.[30]

Since horses powered these innovations it was then necessary for farmers to give over more of their land to the production of oats and hay. That is, the cost of the new innovations to the farmers were the capital cost of acquiring the machinery and horses and provision for the maintenance of both. Nevertheless, the value of the productivity increases more than outweighed the costs. Much of the increase in cereal production in Upper Canada—Canada West—was a direct consequence of these mechanical inventions introduced about mid-century. The application of horse-powered energy to farming lasted until comparatively modern times. By the 1870s, however, a new energy source was introduced into the agricultural sector, steam power. Although the application of steam power was limited, where it was applied to power machinery, such as threshers and haying equipment, further productivity increases were made. For instance, the time spent threshing the cereal production of one acre of land declined from about eight man-hours to one man-hour over the three decades from 1850.

One particular mechanical innovation of the late nineteenth century was responsible for permitting a structural change in the composition of output. This was the cream separator. A disarmingly simple contraption, the cream separator was a centrifuge which, when operated by hand, produced a motion through a system of gears which separated cream from milk at a rate previously unimaginable. This innovation was alone responsible for reducing costs in dairying, increasing the size of the optimum dairy herd, and, by so doing, bringing dairying in central Canada within the framework of more than the local market. As explained elsewhere in this chapter the rise to prominence of the dairy industry in the late nineteenth century was one of the key features of agricultural development in central Canada.

Mechanical innovations, of course, were only one of the changes which deepened the capital stock in farming through the process of new investment. The introduction of new strains of wheat, primarily from northern Europe, less susceptible to blight and faster maturing than those used earlier, again dates to the early 1840s. About the same time there was growing appreciation of the value of animal husbandry. New breeds of cattle, such as those with increased milk output or more meat per animal, were introduced to increase productivity. As a result the capital stock of cattle on farms increased.[31]

The process of innovating through new investment was not always simply the result of each farmer evaluating the marginal costs and benefits and reacting. Some new techniques in agriculture carried with them external effects, most notably the new techniques of land drainage. Although Canada West was effectively settled by the time of the 1851 census many acres of potential agricultural land were vacant of settlement and many farms had unproductive acreage. This land was simply too wet. Indeed in many areas of what is now southwestern Ontario, the land was no better than swamp. The application of drainage techniques, as Table 4:3 shows, not only increased the number of farms in the area but on average increased the amount of useable land on each farm. Long past the end of the pioneer agricultural era the rural land base was significantly augmented.

Land could be drained and made useable in two ways. First, watercourses could be deepened through swampy land to drain the adjacent areas. However, it was to the disadvantage of any one farmer to undertake such an improvement since all his neighbours had to imitate him for

Table 4:3 Agricultural Acreage in Canada West (Ontario) and Canada East (Quebec) in the Late Nineteenth Century
(thousands of acres)

	Canada West/Ontario			Canada East/Quebec		
Date	Area in Farms	Improved Land	Ratio of (3) to (2)	Area in Farms	Improved Land	Ratio of (6) to (5)
(1)	(2)	(3)	(4)	(5)	(6)	(7)
1851	9,826	3,703	0.38	8,113	3,605	0.44
1861	13,355	5,042	0.45	10,375	4,804	0.46
1871	16,163	8,834	0.55	11,026	5,704	0.52
1881	19,260	11,294	0.59	12,626	6,410	0.51
1891	21,092	14,158	0.67	15,962[a]	8,671[a]	0.54
1901	21,350	13,266	0.62	14,444	7,440	0.52

[a] The measurement in 1891 is a slight overestimate of the acreage for Quebec.

Source: M. C. Urquhart and K. A. H. Buckley, eds., *Historical Statistics of Canada* (Toronto, 1965), p. 352.

drainage to be effective. Government intervention solved the problem through a series of drainage acts in the early 1870s which required all land owners along a watercourse to pay taxes to finance the improvement, where the majority favoured a drainage program. Public investment was then just the total sum of private investment that would have been necessary to achieve the agricultural benefits of improved drainage had all participated. The coercive power of the state ensured further agricultural development.

In a different manner the state also ensured increased agricultural productivity by enabling farmers to employ another drainage technique. The installation of drainage tile on individual holdings achieved land drainage where costs and benefits were internalized. As this innovative technique became popular in the late 1860s and early 1870s it was realized that few farm workers could finance such improvements since financial institutions were unwilling to extend credit. Thus, despite the potential gains in additional agricultural output the farm sector was starved of capital. Again it was the government which solved this bottleneck by implementing laws, such as the Drainage Act of 1879 in Ontario, which permitted farmers to borrow from the government on reasonable terms in order that agricultural improvement could advance.[32]

The effect of drainage improvement in particular was twofold. First, more land was made available to farmers and so the land-resource constraint was changed. As a consequence the technical possibilities of combining factors also changed. Second, because more land became

Figure 4:5 Drainage Innovations

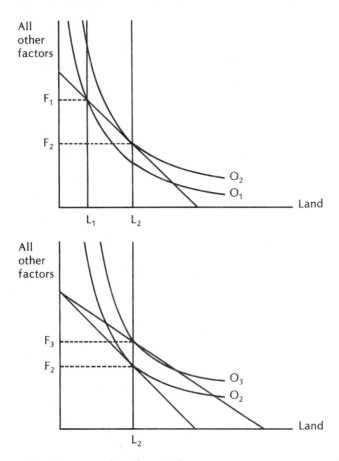

Note: In Row 1, the effect of drainage innovations on agricultural productivity and farm acreage as usable land increased from L_1 to L_2 is illustrated. F measures the use of other factors and O the output level.

In Row 2, the effect of the relative decrease in the price of land to all other factors brought about by drainage technology on agricultural productivity is illustrated.

available relative to the desired demand the price of land fell. These effects are shown in Figure 4:5 and although their resultant contribution to agricultural productivity cannot be precisely measured the causal sketch proves consistent with the pattern of agricultural development. Prior to the innovative use of drainage techniques there had been a land constraint. Agricultural production, given the factor prices, was constrained to operate at an output represented by O_1. We know that it was so constrained because individual farmers found it profitable to improve the drainage of land even with existing land prices. Here we are, of course, assuming that all factor prices were exogenously determined. The innovation resulted in a higher output (O_2). More land was used and less of other factors — L_1 to L_2 and F_1 to F_2.

While the actions of one farmer or homesteader would not influence factor prices, the actions of all might. For instance, the greatly augmented supply of agricultural land in central Canada in the years after pioneer settlement, a large measure of which was attributable to improved drainage, drove down the price of land relative to other factors. Therefore, in a dynamic sense the output was further increased — from O_2 to O_3 — as farm budget constraints adjusted to the new relative prices. As further drainage innovation took place higher levels of output were achieved, until at some point, probably about 1891 in Ontario, it became unprofitable because of the lower soil productivity of the land and the fact that very little land was left in swamp, or wet condition, to which the new drainage technique could be applied. It is worth noting at this point that while drainage could only be undertaken by the process of new investment in capital equipment it did not necessarily raise the ratio of capital to land in the agricultural sector. To the contrary, it permitted agricultural expansion at the land-using margin.

So far attention has been directed to innovations, mechanical and non-mechanical, which were introduced through the process of new investment in the capital stock. The last of the broad classes of changing techniques, mentioned earlier, encompasses that new investment in the labour stock. When a labour stock becomes more efficient — due to factors other than the influence of cooperating factors of production — the stock of human capital increases. Human capital, then, is just the embodiment of certain skills. Skills, however, can be achieved in a variety of ways. First, they can be gained by individual experimentation, otherwise called "learning by doing". Second, individuals can be taught skills in a number of ways from the simple copying of the actions of others when those actions are efficient in an economic sense, to the more elaborate methods involved in formal education. Education, of course, differs from simple demonstration effects to the extent that it involves a reasoning process in the acquisition of skills. Even the latter need not be education of the formal type as in the case of the dissemination of knowledge through the agricultural societies which began to develop in the 1840s and 1850s.

The result of increasing human capital on farms was twofold. First, given technology was more efficiently employed in response to factor and output prices than it had been earlier. Second, the interrelated phenomenon of the adoption of the best new economic techniques took place more rapidly than it would have otherwise. As farmers learned more about the use of best methods and as they had better information presented to them, new techniques were more rapidly diffused throughout the farm sector. The knowledge of new cereal types and livestock breeds was particularly notable for its rapid diffusion.

Early governments recognized that the formal teaching of agriculture as a science stimulated the two effects noted above, efficient farms and the rapid diffusion of technology. In Upper Canada agricultural colleges, such as that at Guelph, date from the 1830s. In Canada East the widespread introduction of the formal teaching of agricultural methods was introduced somewhat later. However, by the 1850s the new colleges and the agricultural research stations, such as that at Oka, proved to be elements which revolutionized the backward techniques of that region. The government was the central agent in providing formal education because of the general nature of the benefits produced.[33]

When one individual farmer introduced a new cost-saving innovation he earned an economic rent. Why, then, do we observe that groups of farmers banded together to disseminate information about new techniques? After all, the more rapid the spread and adoption of the innovation the more rapid the dissipation of these economic rents. The apparent paradox is explained by observing that in order for a hinterland to have access to a market certain scales of aggregate output must be reached. Otherwise, the necessary transport and credit facilities will not exist. This was even more critical in an agricultural economy where the output mix and the location of the final market were shifting. Part of the ability to change rested on the widespread adoption of new techniques in agriculture. Although the individual and the sectoral farm response was a necessary element of central Canada's agricultural development the state's role in ensuring a growth in aggregate agricultural productivity was also a key feature.

Transformation of Agriculture

In 1854 Great Britain signed a treaty with the United States on Canada's behalf. Known as the Reciprocity Treaty of 1854 it guaranteed the free movement of agricultural goods and some other primary products across the common border. Exactly how much of the Canadas' prosperity during the period of this treaty, 1854-66, can be attributed to free access to the United States is debatable and is discussed in detail in Chapter 5. Certainly, the United States, during this period, was a net importer of farm produce from British North America and given the excess demand forces the export base in agriculture widened. Livestock and cereals other than wheat entered the export bundle in greater proportions than they had formerly. Yet, despite the widening of the export base wheat and flour remained the pre-eminent foreign-exchange earners for the young economy after timber exports. Their position was reinforced by a recovery of the British market by Canadian wheat exporters, especially notable during the years of the Crimean War, 1854-56, when Great Britain was cut off from some of its sources of wheat imports on the European continent.

By the late 1860s the price of wheat began to decline. Although the prices of most agricultural commodities, as well as other goods, declined for much of the late nineteenth century after a general depression which began in 1873, wheat prices actually began to fall in 1868. In fact, the high price of wheat in 1868 was not reached again until the twentieth century. This specific price decline was precipitous and directly associated with the increase in the supply of wheat from the U.S. midwest, particularly Iowa and Kansas. As noted in more detail in subsequent chapters, settlement of the U.S. plains predated the similar westward push in Canada. Undoubtedly the change in price forced many of the less efficient wheat farmers in central Canada to change their output mix from cereals to other crops. In addition to the price response, a series of wheat blights and declining soil productivity hastened the initial shift in output composition.

This shift from cereal to other agricultural outputs, such as livestock and dairy products, was the major transformation in central Canadian agriculture in the late nineteenth century and gave Ontario and Quebec agriculture its present configuration. This is not to suggest either that the transformation was complete by the advent of the twentieth century or that subsequent changes of a less profound nature did not take place. However, from an examination of export performance and the agricultural response to a society which by 1900 was becoming urbanized at a very rapid rate it is evident that the period roughly from Confederation to 1914 was one of major structural change.

For instance, it can be seen from Table 4:4 that both Quebec and Ontario became more efficient producers of foodstuffs on a per-farm basis. Because of the relative backwardness of agriculture in Quebec the rate of efficiency gain there was generally greater than in Ontario. In both areas, there was a decline in the relative importance of grain and potatoes to total output of foods. As noted earlier, the stunted development of Quebec agriculture led that area to specialize in the production of grains long after comparative advantage had dictated otherwise.

Table 4:4 Long-Run Trends in Food Production in Quebec and Ontario, 1850-1970
(thousands of calories of food energy produced per farm per day)

Year	Grain and Potatoes		Meat		Poultry and Eggs		Dairy Products		Fruit, Vegetables, etc.		Total	
	Quebec	Ontario	Quebec	Ontario	Quebec	Ontario	Quebec	Ontario	Quebec	Ontario	Quebec	Ontario
(1)	(2)	(3)	(4)	(5)	(6)	(7)	(8)	(9)	(10)	(11)	(12)	(13)
1850	8.8	26.2	2.9	5.6	0.1	0.1	1.6	2.7	0.3	0.6	13.7	35.1
1870	10.9	22.5	3.4	5.4	0.2	0.3	3.1	3.4	0.5	1.0	18.1	32.6
1890	7.6	26.1	3.1	6.8	0.3	0.5	4.8	6.6	0.8	0.9	16.6	41.0
1910	12.0	25.1	6.4	12.4	0.4	0.8	10.9	9.9	0.9	1.5	30.6	49.5
1930	11.1	25.1	5.9	9.8	0.6	1.2	12.9	12.3	0.8	1.5	31.0	49.9
1950	6.0	32.2	11.7	21.8	1.3	3.0	17.3	18.6	1.5	2.9	37.8	78.4
1970	12.5	37.2	32.2	47.9	8.7	8.8	56.8	37.9	6.0	8.1	116.2	139.9

Note: This table understates agricultural output because only food items are included. This is particularly problematic when assessing agricultural output in Quebec where, in the nineteenth century, horses were a major product.

Source: J. Isbister, "Agriculture, Balanced Growth, and Social Change in Central Canada Since 1850: An Interpretation", *Economic Development and Cultural Change*, Vol. 25, no. 4 (1977), p. 682.

Naturally, part of the productivity surge in Quebec after 1850 was due to the rapid restructuring of output. Since wheat remained a viable agricultural specialization in Ontario longer than in Quebec the transition in terms of relative output was less marked in the nineteenth century. Although the long-run pattern of change continued after the First World War, it is evident that by that time tranformation in the structure of agriculture had taken place.[34]

While the falling wheat prices, blights, and declining soil productivity undoubtedly catalyzed the structural change in output, it is unlikely that this alone explains the decline in wheat growing.[35] Indeed, from roughly 1873 to 1900 the relative price of wheat to other agricultural products remained constant. But the market for agricultural produce other than wheat was expanding rapidly. Simply the demand shifts and supply shifts matched. Without a change in relative prices the transformation cannot be explained except by reference to costs. That is, wheat farmers in Ontario were unlikely to change their output mix simply because wheat farming in the mid-west was more efficient if they were still making profits. Therefore, changes in both the demand and the relative costs of agricultural production within central Canada and in the farming skills of the population explained the transformation.

Yet, there was a substantial migration of farmers to the western frontier throughout the last three decades of the nineteenth century as seen in more detail in Chapter 6. These individuals responded to the greater profits to be made there. Wheat farming could be carried out by expanding the acreage, which had a very low opportunity cost, and by reducing the proportion of labour inputs. In addition the larger farms in the west were closer to the optimum size given the technology of the day and thus capital was used more efficiently. Consequently, western farmers earned a greater net income from a given output of wheat than their central Canadian counterparts. Even if there had been no change in the relative costs in central Canada the existence of the western frontier would have induced different types of agriculture. But relative costs did change; the migratory movement which changed the component of skill of the farming population in central Canada, therefore, accelerated the transformation.

Nowhere is the transformation so complete and striking as in the emergence of a dairying industry which reduced the dependence on cereal exports. So substantial was the growth of dairy output that exports from this sub-sector of agriculture grew from insignificance in the 1860s to exceed wheat exports in both current value and real terms for some years in the 1890s (see Figure 4:6) and to become the second-ranked Canadian export item after timber. Yet as an export dairy products soon

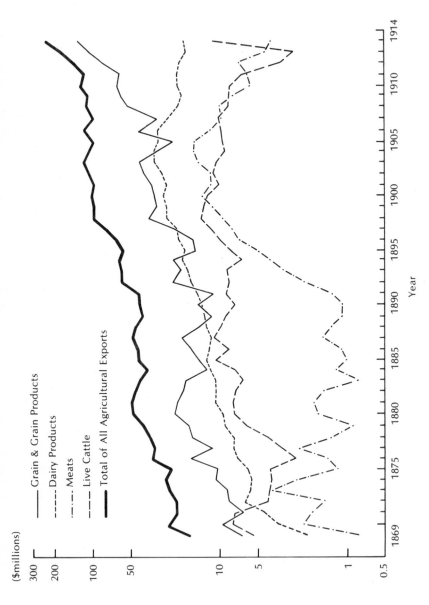

Figure 4:6 Agricultural Exports from Canada, 1869-1918, in Real 1900 Terms ($millions)

($millions)

Grain & Grain Products
Dairy Products
Meats
Live Cattle
Total of All Agricultural Exports

Year

Source: Data are from Taylor and Michell, pp. 34-35.

declined in importance. By about 1904 it was evident that other agricultural exports were growing more rapidly and dairy exports were actually declining in real terms. Why they decreased, as we shall see later, is an element of the transformation in agriculture rather than a symptom of a slow growth of output.[36]

One of the earliest of the cost changes which propelled the shift away from wheat production was that associated with declining soil productivity. The concentration of agricultural production on the raising of livestock was first noticeable in Quebec, where soil productivity had been declining for most of the period 1730-1850. The signing of the reciprocal free-trade treaty with the United States which opened up that market to Canadian producers permitted this widening of the agricultural base. Since this market became available at exactly the time that the seigneurial system was being abandoned the change in the composition of agricultural output was marked. Declining soil productivity in Canada East in most areas outside the Eastern Townships was followed in the 1860s by declining soil productivity in some regions of Canada West. An over-extension of wheat productivity in Canada West during the boom of the 1850s pushed wheat farming onto land which could not support cereal agriculture in the long run. Particularly in the regions immediately north of Lake Ontario soil productivity declined markedly. To be sure, poor agricultural practices, such as improper rotations, often contributed. Many farmers were accused of "wheat mining".[37]

In both Quebec and Ontario the closing of the U.S. market in 1866 and the possibility of a dairy trade with Great Britain speeded up the transformation. Speedier Atlantic passages and rudimentary cooling procedures — still at this time using natural ice — made the latter market accessible.[38] Although butter and cheese had been made on the farm for household consumption, new factory methods of production introduced in the late 1860s reduced the cost of dairy production. So too, the increasing quality of the herds both for dairying and the live cattle trade increased the efficiency of production. Mechanical innovations, discussed earlier in this chapter, also contributed by lowering the costs of producing hay — the major winter fodder for cattle. By the late 1890s refrigeration techniques which further reduced costs were becoming more widespread and with the reduction of transport costs removed the locational market constraint. By these and other cost-reducing changes in dairy agriculture the composition of land use became more labour- and capital-intensive.

The growth of cheese factories and butter creameries was rapid in the 1870s. Within a decade of the first introduction of cheese factories in 1863 there were at least two hundred operating in Ontario alone. Many were small because of the inability to ship fluid milk great distances from farms. Later in the century economies of scale were achieved as larger units replaced many smaller ones. For the most part the cheese production in Ontario was concentrated in the prime dairy lands of the south-central area in towns such as Ingersoll and Stratford. In Quebec, butter production in counties such as Huntingdon and Chateauquay in the Eastern Townships was of a consistently high quality. High-quality butter was exported; however, only with the introduction of the cream separator in the 1880s and the coming of refrigeration in the 1890s did the industry, organized on a factory basis, become efficient enough to supply a large export market. The cream separator aided industry efficiency by allowing the separating of cream from fluid milk on the farm. Creameries — butter-producing plants — could then simply collect the cream, a much less expensive system.[39]

All products of the dairy industry found a ready export market particularly in Great Britain. Canadian hard cheeses, such as cheddar, quickly replaced local cheeses in the British market by offering both a higher quality product and a lower price. So successful was the penetration of this market that the British dairy industry switched its efforts into products which would not compete with the Canadian ones. British soft cheeses originate from this time. Evident in Figure 4:6 is the rapid growth of dairy exports from Canada in the late nineteenth century. However, it can also be seen that other types of agricultural exports varied directly with dairy exports. This interdependence represents another element of the transformation in central Canadian agriculture. The switch in output from wheat to specific non-cereal agricultural outputs created economic conditions of interdependence in agriculture in general. For instance, dairying was complementary to hog raising. Fluid milk was used to produce cheese or butter but also, as a by-product, represented cheap inputs — whey or skim milk — which fed pigs. (It has been remarked that the distinctive flavour of many of the early Canadian cheeses was due to the fact that the hogs were raised in the cheese factory itself; whey was simply thrown out of the factory into troughs where pigs fed.) Not suprisingly the high degree of complementarity in production brought about by this lateral-linkage effect stimulated an efficient export industry in hogs and bacon (see column (4) in Figure 4:6). The domestic impact was the stimulation of a meat-packing industry.

To a lesser extent livestock production was a complement to dairy specialization. Here, however, it is important to note that dairying and livestock production was sometimes carried out in different localities. The increased proportion of the aggregate cattle herd made up of dual purpose animals — both good milk and meat producers, such as Holsteins—emphasizes this link. Excess supplies of calves and young cattle, themselves a by-product of dairying, were shipped to regions in Ontario, such as those around the town of Peterborough or Durham County, in which livestock was raised. These two sub-sectors of agriculture were often spatially separate because of the ability of livestock farming to tolerate poorer soil conditions than dairying. Livestock production often provided the early alternative to wheat and as such live cattle exports exceed those of dairying in the late 1860s and early 1870s. However, from that time onward live cattle exports moved in a consistent fashion with dairy exports. Fortunately for Canada at this time Canadian cattle received preference in the British market due to that country's quarantines and prohibitions against the importation of live cattle from the United States and South America.[40]

The surge to importance of dairy-related products as an export item forces us to consider whether or not they can be considered as an important staple in Canadian economic development. Often the late nineteenth century is characterized as a period of slow growth with no particularly dynamic staple export stimulating economic expansion. Is this appropriate? From some points of view dairy and associated exports can be considered a staple; they rose rapidly to major importance in Canada's export bundle. Linkages have been shown here to have existed though they were weak outside the agricultural sector itself. One characteristic perhaps overwhelms all others and denies an important dynamic role to dairy and associated exports; a period of absolute decline followed the period of their rapid growth.

The decline in the importance of the export of dairy products is the last phase in the transformation of central Canadian agriculture. Certainly, part of the decline in exports can be attributed to the growing domestic demand in Canada. The population was not only growing rapidly, as noted earlier, but also becoming urban at a very rapid rate in the early twentieth century. However, the growth of the domestic market is only part of the explanation. Technology again intervened. The same technology which enabled dairy exports to grow in the 1890s facilitated the decline a decade later. As refrigeration developed it became a more efficient and portable technology. In particular this permitted the bulk shipment of fluid milk which was previously impossible. This technology then permitted the agricultural sector to exploit the latent demand for fresh milk in the urban centres. The first city deliveries of milk took place just after the turn of the century. However, in response to prices, fluid milk was diverted from cheese- and butter-making for export to the domestic fresh-milk trade. Furthermore, Canadian exporters of non-cereal agricultural goods met with increasing competition within the

British market. Both British and foreign producers became increasingly able to meet the price and quality levels established by the Canadian export trade. Among the competitors the Scandinavian producers increased their share of the dairy market and the Argentinian producers increased their share of the meat market, particularly in tinned meats. These phenomena considerably reduced the export capabilities of the dairy industry, in particular, and in general affected the performance of allied agricultural exports. Thus, the transformation was complete by about 1914. Central Canadian agriculture had a domestic focus for the first time since subsistence farming in the early 1800s.[41]

CHAPTER FIVE

Commercial Policy Before Confederation

Introduction

Prime Minister Alexander Mackenzie once grumbled that tariffs were "the relics of barbarism". Within three years his successor supervised one of the major upward revisions of the Canadian tariff structure. So the attitude of Canadians about commercial policy vacillated depending on the fashion in economic thinking, the power of vested interest to convert opinion to its particular cause, and the goals which changes in commercial policy were intended to serve. Since the external trade of Canada from early colonial times was an important constituent of aggregate economic activity, political and economic concern about changes in its composition and direction of flow was considerable. This concern was directed not only at our own commercial policy but also at the trade policies of Canada's major trading partners.

The ratio of foreign trade in commodities — exports plus imports — to national output best measures the extent of the openness of the Canadian economy. This ratio was 30.9 per cent in 1870-80, 32.2 per cent in 1911-13, 41.5 in 1926-29, and 31.2 per cent in the more recent period of 1956-60 and, as seen in earlier chapters, the foreign-trade sector was just as important before Confederation. The continued importance of foreign trade to the growth, spread, and structural change of the economy contrasted markedly with economic development in the United States. There, the ratio of foreign trade to national output fell through time and by the third quarter of the nineteenth century the United States had become essentially a closed economy. Canada, on the other hand, largely remained an open economy, its trade policy influenced by the importance of natural resources to its export trade.

Trade Barriers and Their Effects

The economic gains from trade arise from international specialization.[1] While it is often argued that free trade permits full advantage to be taken of these possibilities of international specialization it does not necessarily follow that the absence of restrictions on trade best promotes economic development. For instance, a major trading partner may have achieved a higher level of industrial maturity and its exports may forestall the emergence of a domestic manufacturing sector. Not surprisingly then commercial policies were often invoked to foster rapid economic change. Policies established elsewhere also influenced Canadian economic performance.

Commercial policies have generally taken the form of either tariffs or special legislation, such as the Navigation Acts, which impart a bias to trading patterns. Tariffs, the taxes levied on commodities when they cross the boundary of a customs area, are of three types. These are transit duties placed on goods passing through a customs area en route to a third country, export duties placed on commodities leaving a country, and the more familiar import duties placed on merchandise entering a country. All three were important in Canadian economic development. In the 1840s, for example, the United States eliminated the transit duties on Canadian products passing en route to Great Britain and Europe; this encouraged merchants in Canada West to use the Erie Canal–New York route to the Atlantic making it more difficult for Montreal merchants to establish the St. Lawrence artery from the interior of North America.

The first known tariff in what is now Canada was levied in 1650; it was an export duty on beaver and moose pelts taxed at 50 per cent and 10 per cent respectively, and payable in kind.[2] During the last two decades of the nineteenth century and the first of the twentieth century, some provincial governments levied export duties or bounties on logs in their unmanufactured state; this was designed to encourage further processing in Canada.[3] More recently, export duties were levied on some petroleum products. However, import duties were the most common element of the commercial policies which affected Canadian economic development.

Before 1763, the two political entities comprising part of present-day Canada both imposed tariffs, namely New France from 1650 and Nova Scotia from 1758. Later New Brunswick, shortly after separation from Nova Scotia in 1784, also enacted tariffs. The Constitutional Act of 1791 divided Quebec into Upper and Lower Canada, and while the imperial government retained regulation of trade and tariffs, the new colonial governments were allowed under the terms of the Act to levy their own tariffs in addition to the imperial duties. It is important to note that they were not permitted to raise tariff barriers to trade between each other.

Thus, this particular Act set the basic framework for free trade within Canada. Upper and Lower Canada each imposed their own tariffs until the Act of Union in 1840 reunited them to form a customs union—an area sharing a common external tariff. Finally, Confederation in 1867 consolidated the tariff structures of Canada, Nova Scotia and New Brunswick, and later Prince Edward Island and, still later, British Columbia.[4]

Tariffs are either specific, *ad valorem*, or a combination of the two, compound duties. Specific duties are levied as a payment per physical quantity of the commodity, whereas *ad valorem* duties are calculated as a percentage of the value of the good traded. However, the point at which the value is taken can vary. For example, the *ad valorem* duty on a product imported from Great Britian might have been calculated using the average British price of the product prior to export or the price of the good landed at Montreal, the latter including the cost of transporting the product. The real burden of *ad valorem* tariffs remains constant as the price of a good varies, while the real burden of specific duties varies inversely with changes in price.

The imposition of import duties has complex results and, as will be seen, some of the consequences may conflict with each other. If, as in Figure 5:1(a), there is a Canadian demand for a particular good the domestic price in the absence of trade would be P_1 given the domestic supply. However, domestic suppliers are less efficient producers than foreign suppliers and when trade takes place the price falls to P_2 as Canadians can purchase the good in any amount without affecting the world price. Domestic producers experience a decline in output from Q_1 to Q_2 whereas imports of Q_2 to Q_3 occur. As a result of the lower prevailing price more Canadian consumers purchase the good in question.

When a tariff of T is placed on the imports, the domestic price increases to $P_2 + T$ as in Figure 5:1(b). The tariff simultaneously produces the following effects:

1) the volume of consumption of the good falls from Q_3 to Q_5 as the price rises—the *consumption* effect;
2) the Canadian producers' sales rise from Q_2 to Q_4 because more domestic firms will supply at the higher price—the *protective* effect; and
3) the authority which implements the tariff raises revenue of the tariff times the imports, now at $Q_5 - Q_4$—the *revenue* effect.

In addition, the economic rent accruing to the domestic industry is measured to be the excess of income over costs and from the point of

Figure 5:1 Effects of a Tariff in Partial Equilibrium

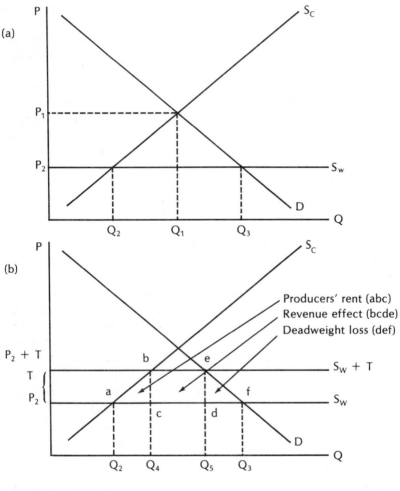

D—domestic demand   T—tariff (measured in money terms)
S_C—Canadian supply   P—prices
S_W—world supply   Q—quantities

view of the consumers as a whole there is a deadweight loss. This loss is equivalent to the reduction in welfare associated with the decrease in the quantity demanded. Notice that if the goal of commercial policy is to maximize the incidence of protection for domestic producers both the rent which they acquire and the deadweight loss increase but the revenue effect diminishes to zero. On the other hand, policy designed to raise revenue must necessarily reduce the protective effect below its potential. In this sense, there is a conflict among the effects. Yet, it is also important to recognize that all tariffs designed to increase revenue will confer protection.

Revenues raised from the imposition of tariffs were the major source of government funds in early British North America. Even as late as 1908-12 they accounted for 59 per cent of all federal government receipts.[5] However, with the implementation of direct taxes on income, and other taxes, tariff revenue has fallen to less than 10 per cent of government receipts in recent decades. Prior to the 1850s, British North American legislators claimed that import duties were for revenue purposes only; whether this was their only purpose or not, a loss of consumer welfare inevitably occurred and domestic producers were protected. It is impossible to distinguish between tariffs implemented for revenue and those implemented for protection.

Tariffs were often placed not only on finished goods but also on raw materials and intermediate goods destined to be used in production in Canada. The cost of the input to domestic producers was thus raised which generally had the effect of reducing the supply of the particular finished goods for which that commodity was an input. This introduces the important distinction between the nominal rate and the effective rate of tariff protection. This distinction is necessary in order to examine the impact of a tariff levied on a finished good which contains imported material inputs on which import duties are also applied at a different rate from that on the finished good. If, say, clothing bears a 40 per cent import duty, while its material inputs are duty free, and if these inputs contributed half of the value of the finished article, then the effective rate of protection for Canadian manufactured clothing is much higher. An industry's net protection can be increased simply by reducing tariffs on the inputs it uses. Net protection also increases if the proportion of the imported inputs to the value of the finished commodity rises. These two outcomes have important consequences for Canadian commercial policy, as we shall see later when actual import duty rates are investigated.[6]

Apart from the argument that tariffs were needed for revenue purposes, several other arguments supporting import duties appeared throughout the last 150 years of Canadian economic history.[7] All of these arguments were first made before Confederation, in some cases as early as the 1820s. First was the argument for infant-industry protection which was based on the notion that Canada had a *latent* comparative advantage in an industry or group of industries; in the short run import duties were required to cultivate this advantage in the face of foreign competition. Comparative advantage after protection would flow from currently unrealized internal and external economies of scale. New production could expand behind a tariff wall and experience internal economies; as the optimum-sized plant was attained the import duty could be removed. Otherwise production would be forced to a small and uneconomic scale with little prospect of competing with established foreign producers. External economies could also be experienced as expansion of the protected industry, or group of industries, lowered costs for all firms by training a labour force or by acquiring and spreading knowledge of production techniques. As early as the 1820s, British North American writers advocated import duties on manufactured commodities in order to stimulate economic growth. They often noted that the United States and Britain reached their states of advanced development through highly effective import duties. It was easy to point to the relatively small Canadian population and the lack of skilled workers and entrepreneurs in order to rationalize the infant-industry protective argument. Whatever the long-run benefits this form of tariff protection justified, the economic development engendered by it must in potential income gains, discounted to the present, exceed the cost of protection to consumers.

Employment arguments for protection often accompanied the infant-industry rationale. Business interests in British North America pleaded for import duties in order to stimulate employment. Such claims often arose when emigration to the United States grew in size. We saw in Figure 5:1 that import duties increase the quantity of output of the protected industry; this would attract labour, capital, and other inputs away from alternative uses. If these inputs have no higher opportunity cost in the protected industry, then this is a gross gain for Canada. Otherwise, the gain is only a net of losses in other industries. In the Canadian case, the additional inputs of labour and capital often had to be attracted to the protected industries from abroad through net immigration and foreign investment. Therefore, import duties failed to reallocate a fixed amount of resources from non-protected to protected industries, but instead increased Canada's productive resources. This increased Canadian gross national product but not necessarily its GNP per capita since these inputs were used inefficiently. Consumer welfare was undoubtedly reduced whether or not employment rose. Often, such Canadian tariffs led to the retaliation of other countries, although Canadians argued in turn that their own tariffs were simply retaliation measures to particular tariffs introduced by the United States and other countries.

In the 1820s and 1830s, farmers in Upper Canada complained about U.S. farmers' wheat "dumping" practices and demanded import duties. Three decades later, manufacturers in Canada West suggested that tariffs be used to prevent dumping of foreign goods in the Canadian market. In fact, foreigners were probably not dumping; they were selling at prices lower than Canadian prices in that market. Dumping occurs if sales in the Canadian market take place at prices below those in the foreign market; this may happen if foreigners can practise discrimination between their domestic and Canadian markets. Dumping may be predatory if price cutting is undertaken to destroy Canadian competition faced by foreign producers. There is little evidence to suggest that much dumping actually took place although in recent years the federal government has felt the necessity to introduce anti-dumping legislation.[8]

Open economies, historically, were more prey to international economic disturbances than closed ones. As early as the 1830s, farmers and manufacturers argued that Canada should reduce its vulnerability to such disturbances by instituting import duties. Vulnerability to external forces can be reduced, but only at the cost of reducing the gains from trade. This argument for tariffs had some effect on the imposition of agricultural tariffs during the 1830s and 1840s, but declined in popularity as Canadians came to realize that their comparative advantage lay with trade in agricultural and natural products. Writers both before and after Confederation coupled these arguments with the desire to diversify the Canadian economy. Once again economic-development experiences in Britain and the United States were held up for emulation. It was believed that a reduction in vulnerability would follow as Canada reduced dependence on primary exports. Price fluctuations would be reduced and the stability brought about would provide the economic conditions in which average incomes would rise.

In summary, tariffs as the main element of commercial policy were perceived as an important tool of economic development especially during Canada's formative years. Great Britain and the United States were, it was thought, the examples to follow. Yet the impact of any commercial policy was seldom fully understood and, as seen here, there were many ramifications. Arguments for import duties remained almost unaltered for about a century from the 1850s as Canada developed behind a wall of tariffs. To be sure, the height of this wall changed over time and the requirement to raise revenue by tariffs lessened in the twentieth century, but these represented only changes of degree.

Empire Trade and the Revenue Tariff to 1822

> O praise the Lord with one consent
> And in this great design
> Let Britain and the Colonies
> Unanimously jine.
> *W. Billings, 1770.*

Whether or not there was ever any divine blessing of "this great design", as the system of empire trade was once described, it must have seemed so to the early colonists. Empire trade was characterized by total regulation imposed from afar. So it had been during the French régime and so it continued to be after the establishment of British control.

The imperial system of trade to which the colonies of British North America had to conform was comprehensive but never inflexible.[9] The system was modified many times, not least of all when changes were brought about by Great Britain's loss of her most important overseas possession, the Thirteen Colonies. Less turbulent events of empire also caused modifications to be introduced, such as the reforms needed to ensure adequate revenues from tariffs to finance the administration of Quebec. Yet, while it was flexible, the system was designed for the benefit of the imperial power rather than the economic welfare of British North America although, as we have already seen, the specific regulation of trade sometimes coincided with the colonial interest. At the heart of the imperial system of trade were two types of regulation, the Navigation Acts and a set of imperial duties.

The Navigation Acts were a set of statutes governing shipping within the empire and prohibiting trade with non-empire countries. Although these statutes were altered many times during the period of their enforcement from 1660 to 1849, they retained their essential features. Designed to guarantee trade for "British bottoms", as the phrase goes, only British ships were permitted to carry cargoes within the empire. The statutes also held colonial ships to be British. Only one exception to the exclusively British and colonial carrying trade was generally permitted. This was the establishment of "free ports". Quebec City, designated as the only free port in Quebec — and later the Canadas — was permitted to receive foreign goods in foreign ships but it was not until the 1820s that ships from the United States were permitted general entry.

All British North American imports shipped by water routes as a consequence of the Navigation Acts were required to come from Great Britain or the West Indies in ships carrying the British flag. The former restriction probably imposed no burden whatsoever since most manufactured goods would have come from Great Britain in any event. However, the requirements governing goods from the West Indies, such as rum and molasses, generally meant that British North America was restricted to using the products of the British West Indies at higher prices than those often prevailing elsewhere in the Caribbean and to using British and colonial ships on this particular route where they were less efficient than the U.S. carriers. The early distillers of Nova Scotia found in this restriction particular complaint. Yet, there is no evidence to suggest that the Navigation Acts alone were responsible for the substantial cost borne generally by the colonies.

Exports from British North America of almost all goods destined for Europe were shipped to Great Britain first because of the prohibition on entering foreign ports.[10] The only exceptions were the lumber shipments from Quebec, which occasionally were permitted to go directly to southern Europe and fish exports, which were not subject to regulation. The export of furs *via* Great Britain caused the only major distortion in trade because some of the final demand was from the European continent. By themselves, the Navigation Acts probably did very little to structure the trans-Atlantic trade to a pattern it otherwise would not have assumed since the source of demand for most of the exports of British North America at the time was in Great Britain. Although forcing trade through a London entrepôt transshipment centre probably caused only a small loss of income, there was an unintended consequence: It gave British businessmen a competitive advantage over the French Canadians who had earlier controlled the fur trade through Montreal.[11]

By the 1820s, the increasingly liberal Navigation Acts left trade by ships using the free ports relatively unfettered. Trade on the Great Lakes was, however, an exception. The Navigation Acts had been formed and subsequently modified on the premise that a sea barrier separated all British colonies from foreign trading partners. This was not the case in the interior of North America. At the time there were long debates about whether the Navigation Acts should legally be applied on the Great Lakes. When it was decided that the Acts were enforceable, American shipping was prohibited from the coastal trade on the lakes and prevented from using the St. Lawrence canal system. Paradoxically, this was most important during the decade of the 1840s when for all other purposes the Navigation Acts were of no consequence. Indeed, they were not repealed until 1849 almost, it would seem, because they had been forgotten, that is, forgotten everywhere except on the Great Lakes.

More important than the Navigation Acts in the regulation of trade was the second element of empire policy, the systems of imperial and colonial duties on imports. As already seen, the imperial duties on wheat and timber, the Corn Laws and the Baltic Timber tariffs respectively, were of vital importance to early British North America. Yet this was a result of the duties diverting British purchasing power from cheap non-empire supplies to relatively expensive empire ones. The British consumer bore the burden of the discriminatory policy. While exports of wheat and timber were stimulated, British North America itself had to bear a cost.

The imperial duties, which were the product of many separate pieces of legislation, were tariffs which each colony was required to levy on imports. While many tariffs applied only to the imports from non-empire countries others were applied on the products from other colonies within the empire. For instance, in 1733 a duty was placed on molasses and sugar entering British North America, including the Thirteen Colonies, from the West Indies. This was reinforced by a subsequent ban, in 1764, on all such imports from non-British colonies. In almost all cases the tariff specified a duty, a good, and a port of origin. Thus British West Indian goods entering British North America in the 1780s bore a high duty if imported directly but a low duty if imported from Great Britain. The intent of imperial trade policy was to route shipments through Great Britain whenever possible. Although by the nineteenth century colonies were permitted to levy their own tariffs, ostensibly for revenue, they were not permitted to distort trade from the pattern specified by the imperial duties. Great Britain was always to be at the apex of the triangular trade patterns of the North Atlantic economy. From the point of view of the colonials the tariffs were pure taxes on consumption. Imported goods, such as wine, clothing, tobacco, and other luxuries, bore the main tariffs as they had done earlier during the French régime. As illustrated in Figure 5:2 the small size of the colonial market ensured that the entire burden of the tariff was shifted to consumers, a fact not lost on those in the Thirteen Colonies. There the new tariffs of the 1760s and 1770s were fuel to the fires of revolution. Ironically, many of the new tariffs at this time were intended as reforms. The Quebec Revenue Act, for instance, which permitted the retention in Quebec of the revenues raised from the duties, was intended to be a solution to the chronic need for funds for local government. Those to the south viewed it as discriminatory and it has since been enshrined as one of the Intolerable Acts promulgated by the British government.

Within the British Empire, as it was constituted prior to the American Revolution, the principal trading body, apart from Great Britain, was the Thirteen Colonies.[12] Not surprisingly then, the events of 1776 had immediate consequence for the system of empire trade. First, the trade between Quebec, Nova Scotia, and New Brunswick on the one hand, and the United States on the other, was made illegal. Second, the West Indies, which had formerly depended on the Thirteen Colonies for imports of foodstuffs and lumber, had to seek a new source of supply.

Trade with the United States could not be prevented for long. In particular, the remaining British North American colonies were too vulnerable to economic crises brought about by bad harvests to survive without trade. Only rarely could they generate an agricultural surplus and often they could not provide the foodstuffs for their small local populations. In the early 1780s, for instance, an acute food shortage in

Figure 5:2 Effects of an Imperial or Colonial Duty on Imported Goods

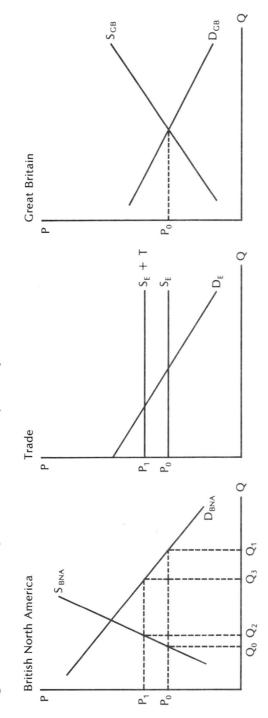

Note: The supply curves S_{BNA} and S_{CB} reflect the relative supplies in British North America and Great Britain, respectively. Because of scale differences, the excess supply of British goods to satisfy the excess demand, S_E and D_E respectively, in the trade sector is infinitely elastic. Without regard to transport costs, the price of P_0 would prevail in all sectors. However, implementation of the tariff, T, raises the price in British North America by exactly the amount of the tariff. Notice that the left-hand diagram, British North America, is the same as Figure 5:1.

Nova Scotia and New Brunswick forced the governors to ignore the legal barriers and admit livestock and provisions. In recognition of this an imperial order-in-council permitted products from the United States to enter British North America in emergencies. Soon afterwards Lord Dorchester in Quebec sanctioned trade between the state of Vermont and Quebec and a good part of that trade, in the form of naval stores, found ultimate destination in Great Britain.[13] Indeed, it shortly proved impossible to prevent trade with the United States. Temporary prohibitions due to war, the Navigation Acts, and the imperial tariffs were without substance given the inability to enforce them along the vast interior frontier. In many products, smuggling may have surpassed the legally enumerated trade. At various times the British tried to stop the import of products like tea, rum, and molasses from the United States but because of the high value of these goods relative to their volume, smuggling proved too lucrative to prevent. The Great Lakes area, especially in Quebec, and later Upper Canada, became a great "free-trading" region.

The second consequence of the realignment of empire was the entry of Nova Scotia and New Brunswick into the West Indies trade. By the mid-1790s over one hundred vessels had been built in the maritime colonies, many in response to the demand for carriers between British North America and the West Indies. With the withdrawal of the United States from the empire, it was hoped, both in London and in the colonies themselves, that Nova Scotia and the other maritime colonies could provide the basic exports of fish, agricultural, and timber products, to the West Indies as well as some manufactured goods such as barrel staves. The United States could supply these goods more cheaply than maritime British North America but was for many years prevented from doing so; this situation is represented in Figure 5:3. Before the American Revolution, and from about 1793 to 1807, the trade curve S_E depicted the situation—the largest share of British West Indian imports of fish, agricultural products, and the like came from the Thirteen Colonies or the United States by virtue of their lower costs, both in production and in transport. From about 1783 to 1793, the Navigation Acts excluded American shipping from the British West Indies and again from 1807 until the end of the War of 1812, the U.S. Embargo and Nonintercourse Acts outlawed this trade. In terms of the British North American exports depicted in Figure 5:3, only the S_M supply curve then prevailed, the only excess supply was S'_E and the price of British West Indian imports rose to P_1 from P_0. With this type of cost-of-living and/or input price increase, it is no wonder that the plantation owners in the West Indies complained. In maritime British North America product prices rose, sales abroad increased, and agricultural and timber frontiers were pushed back. Both periods were ones of prosperity for Nova Scotia, New Brunswick, and Prince Edward Island. As

Figure 5:3 Import Prices of Natural Products in the British West Indies Due to the Exclusion of the United States from the Trade

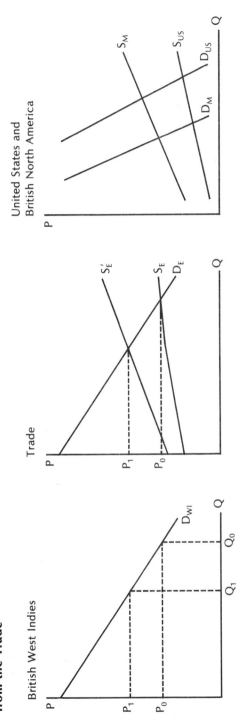

Note: The separate U.S. and maritime British North American markets (M) are superimposed here. The aggregate excess supply in the trade sector is given as S_E and represents supply when both areas of continental North America exported to the British West Indies. The S_E' is the situation which results in a price rise from P_0 to P_1 when only maritime British North America was permitted to export.

well as the trade in their own products, maritime shipping interests took advantage of the exclusion of the United States by re-exporting British goods to the Caribbean — "A Golden Age".[14]

The American Revolution also inadvertantly brought about one of the major changes in empire trade. As seen earlier, the movement of peoples into western Quebec — now Ontario — from the United States was of sufficient magnitude to generate support for a separate colonial status for that region. Quebec had been permitted to retain, for instance, many features of French law and the application of this type of law in the west was felt inappropriate to those who professed loyalist sentiments. The Constitutional Act of 1791 formally divided Quebec into Lower and Upper Canada. For trade policy this division had two important features. Of primary importance was the requirement that barriers to trade between the two colonies end. This departure from past colonial policy is ultimately the principle upon which the free trade between the provinces of today rests. However, the same Act also gave the colonies the right to levy local import duties provided they did not conflict with imperial tariffs. Thus began the long, and tediously complex, history of the dual import-duty schemes with each colony attempting to raise its own tariff revenue. It can be immediately appreciated that since Quebec City was the only major seaport for both Lower and Upper Canada, and since each colony levied different tariffs but Upper Canada was unable to collect duties, as goods passed between the colonies, the dual-import scheme in this form was administratively divisive. As will be seen later, the granting of these new colonial powers engendered intercolonial disputes which took almost fifty years to settle.[15]

In the aftermath of the American Revolution and during the subsequent wars which interrupted trade between empire countries and the United States there emerged what may be called "the entrepôt syndrome". The Montreal merchants attempted to assume the role of middlemen between Great Britain and some other country or area. Goods would be moved in both directions via Montreal along the great trading networks that joined North America, including the Caribbean, to Europe. Particularly lucrative was the trade between Great Britain and the United States. Direct trade was, in fact, the most efficient because the U.S. tariff of 20 per cent took the Montreal price as the base when levied on Canadian exports of British goods. Montreal had two advantages, albeit temporary ones, which favoured the routing of the U.S.–British trade northward. First, war often interrupted legal trade but the British did not wish their export performance to suffer; the vast interior with few customs posts gave ample scope for smuggling. Second, in periods of peace, the U.S. tariff could be evaded. It was not until the 1820s that the increased vigilance of the U.S. customs service greatly affected this smuggling trade. Despite a variety of measures, legal and illegal, Montreal merchants never did manage to capture much of the trade flowing between the West Indies and Great Britain or between the West Indies and the United States. Once the temporary advantages of Montreal's location were gone increasing attention was paid to a third entrepôt gambit—the routing of U.S. produce through Canada to Great Britain and Europe.[16]

The American Revolution destroyed the notion of a homogeneous empire with all elements participating in trade flowing along predetermined routes. The Thirteen Colonies had been the largest colonial market for Great Britain and the major source of imports for the British West Indies. As a consequence, from the 1770s to the end of the Napoleonic Wars in 1815, the imperial system of trade was continually readjusted as Great Britain defined new roles for its remaining colonies in North America. Many of these roles were key elements in stimulating economic development, as shown by the Baltic timber duties. On the other hand, some could only confer transitory economic gains. As a supplier of foodstuffs to the British West Indies the small economies of Nova Scotia and New Brunswick were inadequate and only decree achieved the golden age of Caribbean trade. Economic pressure soon grew in the West Indies to dissolve the connection. So too, the strength of Montreal's trading position as an entrepôt centre for Great Britain was fragile, based as it was on routes which were inefficient in the normal course of events.

Internal Discontent and the British Betrayal
The peace that came with the defeat of Napoleon was expected to restore order once again to the imperial system of trade. It did not. In part this was due to the influence of the United States and the altered vision of empire which it inspired.[17] Formerly the most vital component of the empire, the United States, once peaceful intercourse was restored, became in its liberty, one of Great Britain's major trading partners. Economic pressures dictated that the United States would still be a lynch-pin of Great Britain's trade policy. British consumers increasingly bore the costs of protected empire trade—the Corn Laws and timber tariffs—and they were being increasingly recognized as a heavy burden. Unlike earlier times the benefits of protected trade largely accrued to areas outside Great Britain such as British North America. In turn this gave impetus to the growing free-trade sentiment within Great Britain. From 1815 to 1846 imperial trade regulation was continually redefined as a consequence.

Although the British North Americans were shocked when Great Britain began to dismantle protected empire trade in 1842 it was the almost inevitable result of the redefinition of empire. In the colonies themselves there were forces which created a certain instability, and although much economic development and the achievement of an exportable agricultural surplus dates to this late phase of empire, trade policy was continually being reassessed.[18] The three consequential issues of trade policy during the years from the early nineteenth century to 1846 were:

1) the dispute between Upper and Lower Canada over the revenues from the colonial duties;
2) the struggle between the agriculturalists and merchants to assert their own particular views in commercial policy; and
3) the end of trade prohibitions and the final settlement of the Navigation Acts issue with respect to trade with the United States.

These will be examined in turn in the context of the decline of empire preference and final repeal of its main tenets.

The Constitutional Act of 1791 gave both Upper and Lower Canada the right to impose separate import duties against all but each other's products. Both Canadas exercised their powers but the prevalence of smuggling meant, in effect, that Upper Canada was wholly dependent upon revenues collected at the port of Quebec on goods destined for Upper Canada. The proportion in which the import revenue collected at Quebec City should be divided between the two Canadas was a continual source of disagreement. Various schemes were tried, such as dividing the revenue according to the estimated proportion of imports destined to Upper Canada, but they all proved unsatisfactory.[19] In 1822, an agreement was reached whereby Upper Canada received one-fifth of the revenue, and each three years thereafter, until 1840 the proportion was recalculated according to the percentage of imports consumed in each province. This meant that Upper Canada's government revenue to a large extent depended upon the import duties which Lower Canada enacted. The obvious arbitrage which could take place minimized the power to levy separate tariffs and the fact that the two colonies had separate tariffs simply ensured unending dispute. With the relatively greater commitment to infrastructure expenditure, the disbursements of this revenue to Upper Canada were a constant source of complaint. As the primary source of colonial government revenues both Upper and Lower Canada were extremely sensitive to variations in the tariff structures. The fiscal need had dictated the creation of the general *ad valorem* tariff of 2.5 per cent in 1813 — New Brunswick and Nova Scotia had instituted a general *ad valorem* tariff earlier. By the Imperial Act of 1825, the imperial duty was raised to 15 per cent, but during the following fifteen years so many different exemptions were permitted that the tariff structures of Upper and Lower Canada could only be described as chaotic. In part, the impetus for the Act of Union of 1840 stemmed from this conflict over the division of revenue and the desire to harmonize the tariff structures. Consequently, the Act joined Upper and Lower Canada into the united Canadas with a common tariff system. Apparently to raise revenue, the first commercial act of the new union was to raise the colonial general *ad valorem* import duty from 2.5 per cent to 5 per cent. Most of the specific duties from the pre-union period were continued.

The farmers and merchants of Upper and Lower Canada agreed on one thing: The preferred position of the Canadas in the British market must be enhanced. As noted earlier, the British preferences for colonial goods, especially wheat, flour, and lumber, formed the backbone of this position. Canadian interests desired free access to the British market but opposed British free trade; they wanted to be part of a customs union made up of the empire. This, of course, was never achieved since Great Britain always maintained a tariff on colonial wheat, flour, and lumber although higher import duties were charged on non-empire produce. However, almost until the eve of repeal in 1846, the British continually modified the Corn Laws which were construed as being in the Canadian interest. Before 1825, for instance, Canadian exporters were not assured of sales of wheat and flour since they might ship a cargo to a British port only to find that the prevailing price excluded much of their product from the market. Accommodation was made and after 1825 colonial wheat and flour were admitted at all times to the British market, although as noted in Chapter 4, the duty varied according to the prevailing price. The Canada Corn Act of 1843 reduced the duty to a nominal one shilling per quarter on Canadian wheat imports into Britain and abolished the sliding scale.

Timber exports fared similarly to wheat. The duty on foreign timber stood at 25 shillings per load in 1805 and reached its maximum of 65 shillings per load in 1814. This was subsequently reduced to 55 shillings in 1821 where it remained until 1842 when the duty was lowered to 30 shillings. Colonial timber, on the other hand, entered the British market free of duty before 1821 and afterwards was charged only a nominal duty. Be that as it may, colonial timber merchants and firms complained bitterly about their loss of advantage in the British market. The growth of an export trade in sawn lumber and of a market for Canadian timber in the United States and at home partially offset this loss. All evidence suggests that the removal of British preferences on timber came as less of a shock to the Canadas than the repeal of the Corn Laws since colonial preferences on timber either fell or were constant from 1821 onward. In contrast, farmers increased wheat acreages and extended milling facilities after the passage of the Canada Corn Act only to be confronted with the loss of all preferences within three years. This undermined all the endeavours of the Montreal merchants to make the St. Lawrence a viable trade route. They began at once to look for alternatives to the British market.

If farmers and merchants agreed on British preferences, they disagreed on the entry of the U.S. produce into Canadian trade. In their plan to make the St. Lawrence a great trading route, the merchants wanted Great Britain to regard U.S. goods, especially natural products, shipped by this route as colonial goods for import-duty purposes while excluding non-U.S. products from entering the Canadas from the United States.[20] Therefore, the merchants and milling interests desired that U.S. wheat and flour enter the Canadas at low or zero import duties and then receive the favoured treatment of the British market as Canadian produce. Naturally enough Canadian farmers opposed the merchants; the agricultural interests wanted U.S. agricultural products entirely excluded. Faced with uncertain income prospects because of the Corn Laws, the farmers were concerned that easy importation of agricultural products into the Canadas and Great Britain would further increase the supply of such products, reduce their price, and depress incomes further. Such fears were well founded. At the same time, the United States in 1824 imposed an import duty of 25 cents a bushel which, in most years, precluded Canadian farmers from selling there. Only in years of poor harvests in the United States, for example between 1835 and 1838, did the wheat price rise high enough there to allow Canadian exports to scale the U.S. tariff.

From 1822 to 1831, import duties were charged on United States agricultural products entering Canada. The merchants won a partial victory in 1828 when Great Britain agreed to accept flour ground in British North America from U.S. grain as colonial, although U.S. flour and wheat were still not admitted as colonial. Much to some farmers' dismay, these duties were too low to prevent the import of other agricultural goods, such as oxen, pigs, and sheep, from the United States. The merchants strengthened their position with the passage of the Colonial Trade Act in 1831 which repealed all duties on agricultural products entering the British North American colonies. This had at least three results. First, since U.S. grain shipped through the St. Lawrence to Great Britain faced the non-preference import duty, U.S. wheat was shipped to Upper and Lower Canada where it was sold domestically. Second, since flour manufactured in Canada from U.S. grain was admitted to Great Britain as colonial, a Canadian milling industry developed as mentioned earlier. Third, with depressed agricultural conditions continuing throughout most of the 1830s, farmers generally saw their *bêtes noires* as the merchants and those in Great Britain whose culpability permitted the Colonial Trade Act. However, balance of power changed in the 1840s to favour the agricultural interests, at least in part, because Canadians believed that Great Britain would enlarge the preferences if substantial shipments of U.S. wheat were prevented, appeasing British farmers. As a result, the Canadian legislature in 1843 levied an import duty of 3 shillings per quarter on imported U.S. wheat and imposed import duties on most agricultural products. But in the same year, the Canada Corn Act was legislated and because of the lower duties it imposed on grain entering Great Britain, U.S. grain continued to enter Canada in most years; the effect of the Act was to offset the 3-shilling colonial duty. It is interesting to note that the agricultural tariff of 1843 may have been Canada's first tariff designed for protective rather than revenue purposes although it had effect only in the domestic market since re-exports of U.S. products continued.[21]

The farmers and merchants were divided also on the admittance of non-primary production from the United States. The farmers wanted low consumption costs and inexpensive inputs so they favoured importation while the merchants and manufacturers desired protection. While the Canada Trade Act of 1822 permitted importation of the natural products of the United States, most manufactured articles and non-U.S. goods were still excluded. Manufactured products, it was supposed, were produced domestically or, more likely, imported from Great Britain. In addition, this Act required the Canadas to apply the Navigation Acts to inland navigation. Previously, ships from the United States had freely entered Upper Canada's inland ports because uncertain requirements and actual practice were quite different matters as the illegal trade continued. In 1822, Quebec City was still the only "free" port in the Canadas; foreign ships could carry certain cargoes to that city and return with Canadian produce. The same privilege was later extended to Montreal. However, by 1825 trade between the Canadas and the United States was liberalized; only fire arms, ammunition, sugar, rum, coffee, tea, salted fish, fresh and salted provisions, and a few other items were forbidden entry. With the exclusion of sugar, rum, coffee, and tea, the British authorities were still attempting to monopolize the West Indian–British North American trade for the maritime and Montreal merchants. By 1830, Great Britain recognized the absurdity of the Navigation Acts as a barrier to trade with the United States, and opened all ports in British North America to vessels from the United States. Even the British North American–West Indian trade was opened to the United States in 1842 when the imperial government permitted coffee, sugar, molasses, and rum to enter Canada from the United States; the list of non-tradable goods was reduced to only weapons, munitions, counterfeit coins, and objectionable books.*Banning of the last is not a theme pursued here. Of course, colonial import duties prevailed on most products, but at least trade could take place. Trade prohibitions, for the most part, had been lifted and the Navigation Acts were of little practical significance as a barrier to trade.

To the maritime British North American colonies the West Indian trade was still of primary concern in the 1820s. Yet, based on the arguments of the West Indian planters, there was increasing pressure on the imperial authorities to re-open the direct West Indies trade to the United States. Four interest groups required appeasement: The United States wanted to enter the trade, West Indian plantation owners demanded the cheapest food and transport, British shipping interests wanted to maintain their virtual monopoly on the trans-Atlantic route, and Nova Scotian and New Brunswick interests wanted the United States excluded. The long struggle lasted about fourteen years, from 1816 to 1830. There were two periods of restrictions on shipments from the United States, 1818 to 1822 and 1826 to 1830, and during these periods the shipping interests of Nova Scotia and New Brunswick prospered. Between 1822 and 1826, and after 1830, the opposite occurred: U.S. shipping was allowed into the West Indian trade and prospered at the expense of Nova Scotia and New Brunswick. In 1830, U.S. merchants and shipowners gained equal treatment with the British in the West Indies carrying trade. British North American interests were not, as it turns out, totally excluded because additional duties were placed on some commodities entering the West Indies when brought directly from non-empire countries. The direct trade with Europe, now permitted where markets were developing for natural products, further softened the blow.

One last feature of Nova Scotian and New Brunswick duties bears mention because legislators there showed a curiously advanced appreciation of how tariffs can be used to foster domestic production at the expense of foreign manufacturers. Here is a case of increasing the effective rate of protection by lowering tariffs on imported inputs. In 1834, Nova Scotia lowered its 15-per-cent duty on fishing equipment imported from the United States; this source had the lowest production costs and diverted imports from Great Britain to the United States. After 1835, imperial duties on flour, salt beef, and pork were remitted if the goods were used in the fishing industry. Yet, in the case of most manufactured imports, duties in maritime British North America throughout this period were at least as high as in the Canadas. As in the Canadas, a preferential rate favoured most imports of empire manufactured products. All of British North America felt a sense of betrayal when Great Britain ultimately refused to give preferences for colonial goods.

Free Trade and Protection, 1846-1866

The passing of the old preferential system of empire trade conferred on the British North American colonies a measure of autonomy in establishing commercial policy. Using their new-found freedom, the colonies, in the twenty or so years prior to Confederation, set the tenor of trade policy for at least the rest of the nineteenth century. Also, since many new economic pressures were being felt as the relatively simple staple economy diversified, the manner in which commercial policy pacified or accommodated them was to have lasting importance. In particular, the years between 1846 and 1866 witnessed three radical changes in commercial policy all of which were designed to transform trading patterns:

1) the establishment of free trade between all British North American colonies previously limited to the two Canadas;
2) the creation of a free-trade area, in certain non-manufactured products, with the United States; and
3) the increased tariff on manufactured imports which was in part a response to the claims of manufacturers for protection.

The 1840s, as will be recalled, was a turbulent decade. British preferences were lost. The U.S. drawback legislation drew Canadian traffic to the Erie Canal by permitting the shipment of grain and flour in bond through New York for re-export. In addition, the United States imposed a 20 per cent *ad valorem* tariff on unmanufactured lumber and two years later, in 1848, a specific tariff of $2.00 per quarter on wheat. Together these actions caused widespread consternation in British North America since the economy was still almost totally dependent on its ability to export these staple commodities. Initially, there were two reactions: to increase intercolonial trade and to seek entry into the U.S. market. The Annexation Movement of the late 1840s most vehemently expressed the latter reaction. Later, a third reaction took the form of claims for protection for the small manufacturing sector.[22]

The commercial union of the British North American colonies was intended to enlarge the domestic market for all participants. However it should be immediately noted that the commercial union was of a very limiting type. It was a free-trade area only in certain natural-resource and agricultural products. Since each colony retained its own tariff the extension of the reciprocal free-trade privileges was far from creating a customs union, that is with a common external tariff. Yet, as might be expected, this laid the framework for an eventual customs union in 1867. More immediately, it laid the foundation for seeking reciprocal free trade in natural-resource and agricultural products with the United

States. With a common free-trade policy in these particular products British North America could bargain with the United States as a unit. In 1854 such a bargain was struck with the United States and incorporated in the Reciprocity Treaty of 1854.[23]

We can examine how the treaty integrated markets by the use of a simple model which isolates the main features of such an extension of free trade. First, with respect to the exports of British North America of such goods as grain and timber included in the treaty, a representation is given in Figure 5:4. Domestic prices in Great Britain and the United States in the absence of foreign supply would have been those illustrated in the left-hand diagram of Figure 5:4. Panel B, on the other hand, represents the excess supply of the good in question and the excess-demand curve of the United States and Great Britain combined. It is assumed that the United States levied a tariff on the goods coming from British North America, as in fact was the case. The world price is P_0 and the total of British North American exports is Q_0 of which Q_2 are shipped to Great Britain and Q_0-Q_2 to the United States. The price that prevails in the United States is P_0 plus that country's adjustment to the tariff. This represents the situation prior to the trade treaty between the United States and British North America.

By allowing free trade in the products which British North America had traditionally exported, the treaty increased the excess demand of the United States for such goods. As a result of this shift in demand in the international market two effects were introduced. First, the price of the goods increased from P_0 to P_1, because British North America had the ability to supply the commodity and the increase in production induced by the price rise was offset by the decline in production in the United States where the price fell because of the withdrawal of the tariff. Thus, production shifted from high- to low-cost producers created trade. Second, trade was also diverted. British North America here switched its exports from destinations *outside* the treaty area to destinations *within* the treaty area; before the treaty Q_2 of exports were destined for Great Britain and afterward only Q_3. The trade creation and trade diversion effects[24] would demonstrate themselves as:

1) an increase in British North America's exports, in value as well as quantity;
2) an increase in British North America's exports to the United States, as a treaty trading partner, in value as well as quantity; and
3) a decline in the quantity of exports to Great Britain, as a non-treaty trading partner; in this instance the value of these exports may fall or rise depending on the price elasticities of demand.

Figure 5:4 British North American Exports of Goods Incorporated in the Reciprocity Treaty of 1854

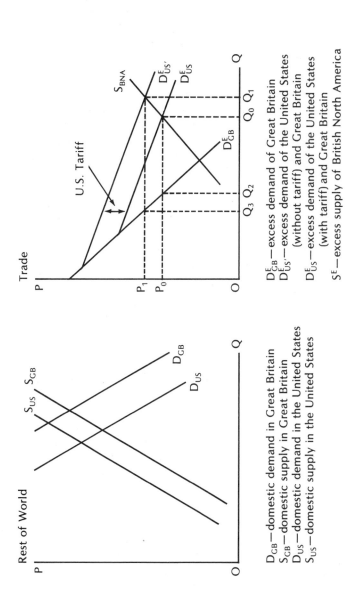

D_{GB}—domestic demand in Great Britain
S_{GB}—domestic supply in Great Britain
D_{US}—domestic demand in the United States
S_{US}—domestic supply in the United States

D_{CB}^E—excess demand of Great Britain
$D_{US'}^E$—excess demand of the United States
(without tariff) and Great Britain
D_{US}^E—excess demand of the United States
(with tariff) and Great Britain
S^E—excess supply of British North America

Note: Were the above diagrams to be relabelled Canada, Nova Scotia, and other trading partners, it could be demonstrated that the trade creation and trade diversion effects following from the free-trade union of the colonies in 1850 were the same as in the above case.

Conversely, it can be shown that if after the reduction of tariffs, the United States was a lower-cost producer than British North America in some goods, production would be diverted to the treaty trading partner and imports of the goods would increase. Of course, no trade-creation or trade-diversion effects would be expected among those commodities omitted from the treaty. For instance, the flow of manufactured goods between Great Britain, the United States, and British North America should not have been directly influenced.

Observers in the 1850s and 1860s witnessed the rapid growth of trade as well as the general prosperity and attributed these changes to the effects of the treaty. Yet there were other powerful forces, perhaps less obvious to contemporaries, which operated to produce the buoyant economic growth of the period:

1) the relatively rapid pace of economic expansion in the United States which created temporary excess demands for such goods as cereals and timber;
2) the Crimean War, 1854-56, which temporarily severed Great Britain from sources of cheap grains in the east and forced British importers to turn again to British North America;
3) the Civil War in the United States, from 1860 to 1865, which not only created many new demand forces in the international market but also produced an inflation upon which British North America could capitalize; and
4) the impact of railway construction, which was felt in most parts of British North America but particularly in Canada East and Canada West.

In the early 1850s Europe, in general, entered a period of prosperity marked by rising prices which gold discoveries in California and Australia and railway construction in both Europe and North America stimulated. British North American exports not only found new markets in the United States but began to recapture some of the lost market in Great Britain. Indeed, long before the Reciprocity Treaty was signed or the impact of local railway construction was felt; British North America began to experience improved economic conditions. Despite the U.S. tariff the end of imperial preferences had no long-run depressive effect on the British North American economy. The expansion of the U.S. economy, particularly in the mid-west, soon reduced the local supply of timber and the United States turned to foreign supplies. Even before 1854 when British North American timber exports faced a U.S. tariff they had kept pace with the growth of British North American trade in general. At the same time, British North America's increasing population and growing cities created a domestic market which for the first time was reaching significant proportions.

Higher breadstuff prices, improved shipping facilities, and fertile farm lands enabled British North America to expand its grain exports after the late 1840s. When the Crimean War excluded Russian grain from Great Britain, a large excess demand for Canadian grain developed. This occurred at a time when the United States bought more imported grain. Even the relatively inefficient agricultural region of Canada East gained markets in New York and New England for coarse grains, livestock, and dairy products, reversing the trend towards rural decline described earlier.

The first seven years or so of the 1850s witnessed general prosperity in both British North America and its main trading partners. Coupled with the domestic effects of railway-building expenditures and the consequences of a fall in transport costs, the spread of the economy was rapid. Even later, in the 1860s, in the United States, falling supplies of goods occasioned by the diversion of resources to war production, and rising demand occasioned by the increase in money wages caused the price inflation which accompanied the American Civil War. Excess demand, therefore, developed for British North American products, and the rising prices of U.S. products made them less attractive to British North American consumers. The fact that the general prosperity of the 1850s began before 1854 masked the impact of the treaty itself. Forces were already at work before the signing of the treaty which would have increased British North America's exports and imports. Because of the various stimulants to trade, it was difficult at the time, and is no less so now, to measure the effect of reciprocity alone on the exports and imports of British North America.

Table 5:1 demonstrates the dramatic shifts in the export and import of goods enumerated under the treaty which occurred almost immediately in Canada East and West. Since reduction in imports from the rest of the world offset only a small amount of the increase in imports of such goods from the United States almost all the increase in imports from the United States was created trade. Canadian exports of articles included under the reciprocity agreement increased dramatically in 1855. In addition, there appears to have been some trade diversion as exports of reciprocity articles to the rest of the world declined substantially. But note that they regain their previous level by 1856, probably as a result of the railway and building boom in Great Britain. As might be expected, total Canadian exports and imports were higher after 1854 than before but exactly how much of this can be credited to reciprocity is questionable. Exports and

Table 5:1 Trade Statistics of Canada, 1850-1868
(thousands of dollars)

	Imports into Canada of				Exports from Canada of			
	Reciprocity Articles from		Non-reciprocity Articles from		Reciprocity Articles to		Non-reciprocity Articles to	
Year	U.S.	Rest of World	U.S.	Rest of World	U.S.	Rest of World	U.S.	Rest of World
(1)	(2)	(3)	(4)	(5)	(6)	(7)	(8)	(9)
1850	1,238	187	5,358	10,197	4,756	5,684	196	1,324
1851	1,039	355	7,325	12,713	3,860	7,188	212	1,704
1852	940	453	7,536	11,355	6,048	6,672	236	1,100
1853	1,281	657	10,499	19,543	8,696	10,524	340	2,452
1854	1,976	855	13,556	24,141	8,412	10,508	236	2,092
1855	7,726	649	13,102	14,608	16,508	6,652	228	1,536
1856	8,083	1,083	14,621	19,797	17,776	10,400	204	1,428
1857	8,642	1,025	11,582	18,183	12,912	10,640	296	1,600
1858	5,565	1,036	10,070	12,407	11,656	9,190	274	909
1859	7,106	1,424	10,487	14,538	13,625	8,455	297	725
1860	7,069	1,407	10,204	15,766	18,096	12,787	332	1,146
1861	9,981	1,316	11,088	20,670	13,972	18,646	414	1,685
1862	14,431	1,700	10,742	21,727	14,566	15,289	498	1,326
1863	12,339	1,667	10,770	21,188	17,573	16,608	2,477	2,689
1864[a]	4,876	657	5,551	12,799	6,769	4,118	953	1,067
1865	9,132	1,851	10,457	23,180	20,567	13,994	2,372	2,675
1866	8,752	2,213	11,672	31,165	31,337	13,245	3,433	2,242
1867	6,114	1,925	14,159	36,852	22,051	16,108	3,533	3,278
1868	5,461	1,451	16,993	33,343	19,376	15,516	4,974	4,672

[a] Data available for half year January 1 to June 30 only; 1850-63 data for year ending December 31; 1865-68 data for year ending June 31.

Source: L. H. Officer and L. B. Smith, "The Canadian-American Reciprocity Treaty of 1855 to 1866", *Journal of Economic History*, Vol. 28, no. 4 (1968), p. 600.

RECIPROCITY INTRODUCED

* only apparent significant differences (however, not surprising)

imports of reciprocity articles with the rest of the world were also higher after 1854. However, as contemporary theory had predicted, the proportion of reciprocity articles going to the United States rose: imports from 73 per cent in 1850-53 to 87 per cent in 1855-59 and exports from 43 per cent to 61 per cent over the same interval. After 1856 little growth or shift in the structure of imports and exports was recorded; the treaty, it appears, had a dramatic once-and-for-all trade-creating effect but did not substantially affect growth. The extent of trade diversion was small.

Timber and lumber exports of individual items to the United States increased steadily between 1850 and 1870 and although there was a sudden increase in 1855-56 it was the only departure from the trend. The treaty opened convenience trade in wheat and flour whereby Canada East and Canada West, and the Maritimes, traded in these commodities across the border.[25] Since this meant that imports offset exports there were few gains in economic welfare except from the saving in transport costs. In summary, while there were once-and-for-all gains from reciprocity with the United States there was little growth in the economic performance of the trading sector throughout the period which was directly related to the treaty. The Crimean War boom and the demands which the American Civil War created proved the more important contributors to prosperity. Perhaps one of the most telling observations which can be made about the relatively minor part played by the treaty is that when the United States abrogated the agreement in 1866 no profound change in the structure of net exports took place.

The maritime colonies of New Brunswick, Nova Scotia, and Prince Edward Island, which had also signed the Reciprocity Treaty in 1854, similarly experienced rapid economic growth during its term.[26] But here too there was little in the pattern of expansion which suggests that the treaty did anything other than reinforce the existing trends. In trade—see Table 5:2—there was a pronounced increase in the proportions of all imports and exports originating in and destined for the United States which dated from the early 1850s. The treaty strongly reinforced the increase in the proportion of agricultural exports to the United States, but here, as in the Canadas, the effect was of a once-and-for-all nature. To be sure the rise was substantial—between 1853 and 1860 agricultural exports to the United States as a proportion of all agricultural exports grew from 10.3 to 26.6 per cent, from 12.8 to 37.9 per cent, and from 5.0 to 50.9 per cent for Nova Scotia, New Brunswick, and Prince Edward Island, respectively. But, given prices in the regions of the adjacent country, much of this increase could have been expected, treaty or not.

More generally the maritime regional economy of British North America both grew and developed, propelled by economic forces apart

Table 5:2 Trade Statistics of Maritime British North America, 1848-1866
(thousands of dollars)

Year	Nova Scotia				New Brunswick				P.E.I.			
	Imports		Exports		Imports		Exports		Imports		Exports	
	Total U.S.		Total U.S.		Total U.S.		Total U.S.		Total U.S.		Total U.S.	
(1)	(2)	(3)	(4)	(5)	(6)	(7)	(8)	(9)	(10)	(11)	(12)	(13)
1848	846	295	523	150	629	244	639	44	133	16	40	1
1852	1,194	347	980	266	1,110	393	796	83	171	34	106	28
1853	1,417	415	1,078	277	1,716	574	1,072	121	210	37	117	24
1854	1,791	575	1,247	318	2,068	711	1,104	97	273	39	152	16
1855	1,882	738	1,472	481	1,431	782	826	123	268	43	147	33
1856	1,869	678	1,372	413	1,521	714	1,073	173	356	52	167	28
1857	1,936	—	1,393	—	1,418	628	917	158	258	50	134	50
1858	1,615	583	1,264	408	1,162	564	810	163	186	42	153	65
1859	1,620	576	1,377	456	1,416	675	1,073	236	234	62	178	89
1860	1,797	651	1,323	446	1,446	688	916	248	230	56	205	79
1861	1,522	611	1,154	304	1,238	628	947	175	209	43	163	48
1862	1,689	605	1,129	362	1,291	616	803	185	211	47	150	44
1863	2,040	771	1,309	373	1,595	739	1,029	259	293	71	209	106
1864	2,520	860	1,434	489	1,863	691	1,052	263	337	83	202	78
1865	2,876	865	1,766	723	1,476	636	1,153	361	381	91	291	124
1866	2,876	808	1,608	645	2,083	779	1,327	386	444	74	246	24

Source: S. A. Saunders, "The Reciprocity Treaty of 1854: A Regional Study", *Canadian Journal of Economics and Political Science*, Vol. 2, no. 1 (1936), p. 165.

from those which the treaty brought about. Railways helped to extend the cropping of the forests since timber was shipped to the United States in increasing quantities. More vessels from British North America were able to force their way into the Atlantic carrying trade with the growth in trade between North America and Europe and during the distress of the American Civil War the reduced capacity of that country provided more shipments for British North American vessels—including, it may be added, blockade-running to the Confederate States. So too the diminished fishery in the United States caused an increased demand for the fishery products of other countries. British North America managed to capture temporarily a larger proportion of the West Indies trade than formerly. In most respects the pace of development of the Atlantic economy of British North America resembled that of the Canadas during the period of reciprocal free trade with the United States. The economic forces at work in the international economy induced parallel economic development in the two principal regions.[27] Yet, as later chapters will show, the maritime economy was essentially too weak to withstand the economic pressures of the late nineteenth century.

With respect to transport, the earlier loss of British preference was perceived as a tragedy in the trading centre of Montreal, in that it coincided with the completion of the St. Lawrence canal system which was designed to exploit trade with the interior. As was seen earlier, an increase in trade shipments failed to materialize and in the early 1850s when the U.S. authorities suggested that the St. Lawrence River should be completely open to their ships—foreign ships were not yet permitted to travel the full length of the entire system—commercial policy became embroiled with transport policy. So, within the Reciprocity Treaty there were clauses which permitted vessels from the United States to use the Canadian canal system at the same rates as domestic carriers and the United States allowed Canadian vessels free use of Lake Michigan. The intention was simply to generate some revenue on the canal system, since the Atlantic carrying trade of U.S. produce had been lost.[28] How low the ambitions of earlier times had sunk.

The attempt to capture traffic for the St. Lawrence system was unsuccessful. For instance, shipments on the St. Lawrence canal system increased by only 282,000 tons compared to an increase of 1.5 million tons on the Erie Canal route between 1850 and 1860.[29] The combination of free trade and cheaper transport costs drew an increasing proportion of Canadian grain exports southward. As we will see in more detail later, illustrated well by Table 5:3, it was the cheap trans-Atlantic shipping rates which gave New York its ability to capture the interior trade with the North American mid-west. Although the St. Lawrence system was a

Table 5:3 Transport Charges from Chicago to Liverpool in 1856 for a Ton of Wheat/Flour

Erie Route		St. Lawrence Route	
(1)		(2)	
Chicago to New York	$ 5.56	Chicago to Quebec	$ 4.77
New York to Liverpool	$ 5.00	Quebec to Liverpool	$ 9.00
Total	$10.56		$13.77

Note: Although rates changed from time to time the proportionate differential was maintained.

Source: S. McKee, "Canada's Bid for the Traffic of the Middle-West", *Canadian Historical Association Report* (1940), pp. 26-35.

cheaper route to salt water, it seemed it was the expensive alternative for shipments from many points on the Great Lakes. To be sure, the St. Lawrence traffic, and canal revenues, increased markedly in the early 1860s but not as a consequence of reciprocity. Closure of the Mississippi River during much of the American Civil War diverted traffic northward. Even then the St. Lawrence canal system operated much below capacity. The clauses in the treaty designed to promote the Canadian route to Europe had no effect.

Despite the Reciprocity Treaty of 1854 the general, nominal trend of import duties in British North America was upward during the entire period between the loss of British preference and Confederation. The Canadas adjusted duties upwards in 1849, 1856, 1858, and 1859 and the maritime colonies followed suit towards the end of the period. In 1851 Canada had a general tariff rate of 12.5 per cent which covered the major part of her import list; Nova Scotia's rate was 6.5 per cent, New Brunswick's 7.25 per cent, and Prince Edward Island's 5 per cent.[30] All colonies levied higher *ad valorem* duties on specific items and had a free list of foodstuffs and natural products. In the Canadas the generally higher rates stemmed from the need for greater revenue than the Atlantic colonies to build infrastructure.

Two particular events of lasting significance highlighted Canadian tariff history in this period. First, as a reaction to lost preferences in the British market, in 1847 the Canadian legislature repealed all previous tariff acts and levied a new uniform set of duties upon imports from all countries, including Great Britain. This lowered the average rate of duty on U.S. manufactured imports from 12.5 to 7.5 per cent and increased that on British manufactured imports from 5 to 7.5 per cent. A single tariff replaced the former two-tier tariff, one level for British and another for non-British goods; a reconstituted British preference replaced this one-tier tariff at the end of the century. Subsequently, in 1849, the general rate was raised to 12.5 per cent. If Canadian merchants thought that higher duties against imports from Great Britain would move that country to re-establish preferences, they were mistaken. The British government only regretted that Canada rejected their splendid example of free trade.

Second, despite the Reciprocity Treaty of 1854 two successive Finance ministers revised the tariff on dutiable imports first, in 1858, to 15.0 and then to the unprecedented 20.0 per cent in 1859. This was the highest level they were to attain prior to Sir John A. Macdonald's national policy tariff of 1879. Known as the Cayley–Galt tariffs, they were invoked because a recession in 1857 caused a fall in government revenues. As government expenditures rose because of railway guarantees and other investments in infrastructure duties were increased in order to maintain the government's solvency and Canada's respectability in the British loan market. There is no reason to doubt Galt's insistence that protection, which must follow from an increase in tariff rates, was only an incidental motive for the higher duties. Nevertheless, it appears that these new rates did raise the level of effective protection and that this was at least in part a response to growing pressure.[31] In the late 1840s and throughout the 1850s, protectionist sentiment became more common in the Canadas. The first organized group to achieve prominence was the Association for the Promotion of Canadian Industry, formed in 1858. As the first organized body of Canadian manufacturers, the association petitioned the legislative assembly for an increased tariff on articles competing with Canadian industrial products and a decline in tariffs on those that could not be produced in Canada. Protectionism became firmly ingrained in Canadian tariff history. As a consequence of this pressure and in response to the need for revenue by government the tariff rate was increased. This, in part, offset the free trade in natural-resource products and agricultural goods. This is demonstrated in Table 5:4.

After his revision of tariffs, Alexander Tilloch Galt proposed a plan in 1859 for intercolonial free trade within British North America since at that time the Reciprocity Treaty covered only specified items. However the Maritime colonies were unwilling to assume the heavy revenue duties of Canada East and West and hesitated to place their manufacturing industries in competition. Also, people in the Maritimes were used to relatively low duties and the increased price of imported goods was unattractive. It must also be noted that the largest part of the trade of both the Canadas and the Maritimes was with Great Britain and the United States, and with reciprocity, the advantages to a formal union were obscure. After all, trade within the maritime colonies was greater than

Table 5:4 Measures of Tariff Rates, 1850-1870

Year	Ratio of Tariff Revenue to Value of Imported Goods	Ratio of Tariff Revenue to Value of Dutiable Imported Goods
(1)	(2)	(3)
1850	14.5	15.6
1851	13.8	14.9
1852	14.6	15.5
1853	12.9	13.6
1854	12.1	13.0
1855	9.8	13.7
1856	10.3	14.2
1857	10.0	14.5
1858	11.6	16.3
1859	13.2	18.9
1860	13.8	19.9
1861	12.0	19.1
1862	10.1	19.4
1863	12.5	22.5
1864	13.6	21.9
1865	14.2	22.4
1866	15.3	22.0
1867	13.3	19.6
1868	13.1	20.2
1869	13.1	20.2
1870	14.1	20.9

Note: The general rate cannot be considered in isolation because of the many specific tariff duties. Note the impact of the Treaty of 1854 and the Cayley-Galt tariffs of 1858-59 on the above measures.

Source: J. H. Young, Canadian Commercial Policy (Ottawa, 1957), pp. 23-24.

that with Canada, and trade between the Maritimes and the West Indies ranked next in value after the trade with Great Britain and the United States, and was, in turn, more important than that with the Canadas. But, in 1865 the United States announced that it would abrogate the reciprocity treaty. Nova Scotia and New Brunswick had by this time committed themselves to substantial new expenditure in public works, especially railways, and had increased duties to raise revenue when the reciprocity treaty ended. This brought their duties more into line with those of Canada East and West; subsequently Galt lowered Canada's tariff rates in 1866 in anticipation of a union. The expense of establishing railway connections with Canada and the United States, as we shall examine in detail later, threatened to bankrupt the maritime governments without guaranteeing that they would remain an entrepôt centre. The tariff basis of Confederation was established.

CHAPTER SIX

Population Growth in Canada

Introduction

The European settlement of Canada began in the early seventeenth century with a few thousand souls eking out a livelihood in small enclaves on the Atlantic coast. Within three and a half centuries the population had grown and spread to people the northern portion of the North American continent. How this came about is the subject of demographic history.

Population change in the Canadian past was of two distinct types. First there was the natural growth of the resident population and, second, there was that change brought about by the settlement of peoples from other countries. These basic features can be represented by:

$$P = (B - D) + (I - E)$$

where P is the change in population over some given time, (B - D) is the excess of births over deaths, and (I - E) is the excess of immigrants over emigrants. The excess of births over deaths is referred to as "natural increase" and the excess of immigrants over emigrants as "net immigration".[1] In common with other areas of the Americas, South Africa, New Zealand, and Australia, net immigration was responsible for permitting the population to grow at a faster rate than natural increase alone would allow. However, both natural increase and net immigration contributed to population growth in a different manner and often, as will be seen, the effect of one swamped that of the other. Net immigration, for instance, was often of only minor significance in determining the growth of population. Canada, although largely a nation of immigrants, has also been a nation of emigrants.

The history of demographic change records that both natural increase and flows of people to and from Canada were highly responsive to economic conditions. As will be seen in more detail later, the mechanisms governing the economic influence on these two types of population growth were both complex and themselves subject to change. For instance, the changing economic role of children as society became more urban appears to have changed attitudes towards family size and thus to have affected the manner of population growth. With respect to net immigration, the closer economic ties between Canada and the United States which evolved in the last half of the nineteenth century changed the mechanism which governed emigration by integrating the two countries' labour markets in a way not previously experienced. The economic influence on population change was not only national in scope but also regional. Because of the highly regional nature of Canada's economy, natural increase displayed considerable local variation and, not surprisingly, new immigrants tended to settle in those areas where economic opportunity was expanding most rapidly. Differences in the intensity of economic activity also caused Canadians to migrate within the country. Demographic change in the Canadian past, therefore, had a third dimension apart from natural increase and net immigration—the geographic distribution of the population among the country's regions. In the broader context of Canadian economic development, the number of consumers, whether they were individuals or family units, whether they were located in urban or rural areas, and whatever social characteristics they displayed, in part determined the structure of the demands for consumer and capital goods. Population growth changed the nature of the domestic market for goods and services by setting the basic requirements of food, clothing, shelter, and services, and influenced the demand for "population-sensitive" capital investments such as housing, transport facilities, and schools. On the production side of the economy, rates of population growth had consequences for the size and distribution of the aggregate labour force as well as its pattern of participation in work. Since economic development required investment, the savings which augmented Canada's capital stock were again partly a function of the size of the labour force, its participation rates, and its age structure. Also, since population growth rates influenced both the demand for and supply of capital, it also helped to determine international flows of savings. One of the principal historical features of a developing economy is a population which is growing, and being geographically distributed, in such a manner that it produces neither chronic long-run excess demand nor excess supply forces in labour or other markets.

The earliest census of what is now Canada was undertaken in 1851.

Table 6:1 Trends in the Size of the Canadian Population, 1668-1971
(Rounded to nearest 1,000)

Year	Population	
(1)	(2)	
1668	4 ⎤	
1685	16 ⎟ New France	
1713	19 ⎟	
1763	65 ⎦	
1790	192	Upper and Lower Canada
1806	473 ⎤	Upper and Lower Canada, Nova Scotia, New
1831	1,124 ⎦	Brunswick, and Prince Edward Island
1851	2,436 ⎤	The Canadas, Nova Scotia, New Brunswick, and
1861	3,230 ⎦	Prince Edward Island
1871	3,689 ⎤	
1881	4,325 ⎟	
1891	4,883 ⎟	
1901	5,371 ⎟	Canada excluding Newfoundland
1911	7,207 ⎟	
1921	8,788 ⎟	
1931	10,377 ⎟	
1941	11,507 ⎦	
1951	14,009 ⎤	
1961	18,238 ⎟	Canada including Newfoundland
1971	21,568 ⎦	

Source: *Census of Canada*, various years.

Prior to that time, only an occasional enumeration was attempted.[2] Nevertheless, even these figures from the early history of Canada's population corroborate what is known about pre-1851 growth (see Table 6:1). For instance, prior to the third quarter of the eighteenth century the population levels reflect primarily the impact of natural increase, apart from the initial settlement of course. Only after the British maritime colonies were used to settle the displaced populations of late eighteenth century Great Britain—particularly that of highland Scotland—did net immigration significantly augment the population beyond the limits imposed by natural increase. Later, in addition to the trans-Atlantic migratory movement from Great Britain, the influx of American-born United Empire Loyalists into Upper Canada and Nova Scotia caused the population to expand rapidly in the first part of the nineteenth century.

Between 1851 and 1971 Canada's population grew from 2.5 million to over 20 million. As noted this growth was often extremely rapid, as was the case in the 1850s, the prosperous years from approximately 1900 to 1914, and the post-Second World War years. Census information reveals that during three of the decades contained in these episodes of rapid growth, the population grew by more than 30 per cent. Since accurate historical information is only usually available for census years, this dating is somewhat artificial. For instance, the large net immigration of the early twentieth century continued beyond 1911 to 1913-14. These three epochs of population growth, as noted later, produced economic conditions which facilitated, and in turn were sustained by, this rapid population change.

Net immigration must be distinguished from gross immigration since Canada's history also records a steady loss of population to other countries, principally the United States. This immediately raises the question of who the emigrants were. Were they the recent immigrants to Canada using the country as a way station to the United States or were they Canadian-born? Only during relatively prosperous periods was Canada able to retain sufficient numbers of its population to ensure that net immigration remained positive. Thus, while net immigration accounts for the pronounced decade-by-decade fluctuations in the Canadian population, it has, in an accounting sense, contributed very little to the long-run growth of the population. For instance, over the 120-year period from 1851 the increase in the population of over 18 million is attributed mostly to natural increase, net immigration accounting for only 14 per cent of the growth in the Canadian population (see Table 6:7). A gross immigration of over 10 million was reduced to a net immigration of approximately 2.5 million. As can be seen in Table 6.2, so powerful a force has emigration been that net immigration was negative during the four decades from 1861. Only the relatively high rates of natural increase prevented the Canadian population from declining during these years.

In contrast, Canada's population almost doubled during the first thirty years of the twentieth century. From 1901 to 1911, the growth of population was 34.2 per cent, the highest rate for any decade since 1851, and over one-third of this was attributable to net immigration. Not only was net immigration high but increasingly the economy was drawing immigrants from other than the traditional western European sources. The retentive economic power of the economy remained for part of the next decade but a decline in gross immigration as a result of the First World War and an emigration of 1.38 million dampened the overall effect. In the 1920s, population growth slowed; although gross immigration remained relatively high at 1.2 million, over 900,000 emigrated. During the 1930s depressed economic conditions reduced birth rates and net immigration was negative for the only time in the twentieth century.

Table 6:2 Population Growth by Decade, 1851-1971: The Contributions of Natural Increase and Net Immigration

Increase as % of Population at Start of Decade

Decade	Total	Natural Increase	Net Immigration
(1)	(2)	(3)	(4)
1851-1861	32.6	27.6	5.0
1861-1871	14.2	20.1	-5.9
1871-1881	17.2	19.5	-2.3
1881-1891	11.7	16.5	-4.8
1891-1901	11.1	14.8	-3.7
1901-1911	34.2	20.9	13.3
1911-1921	21.9	18.7	3.2
1921-1931	18.1	15.5	2.6
1931-1941	10.9	11.8	-0.9
1941-1951	21.7	20.2	1.5
1951-1961	30.2	22.5	7.7
1961-1971	18.3	14.3	4.0

Note: The table refers to the present area of Canada except that Newfoundland is excluded prior to 1951-61. The estimates made by Keyfitz are used from 1851-61 to 1911-21. McDougall (1961) presents different estimates made by constructing new life tables and making independent estimates of immigration.

Sources: 1851-61 to 1941-51: M. C. Urquhart and K. A. H. Buckley, eds., *Historical Statistics of Canada* (Toronto, 1965), p. 22. 1951-61 to 1961-71: D. Kubat and D. Thornton, *Statistical Profile of Canadian Society* (Toronto, 1974), p. 18.

In the post-Second World War period the earlier trend reversed as both the gross immigration and the rate of natural increase rose. From 1951 to 1961, population grew 30.2 per cent, the third highest rate since censuses have been taken. As a consequence of the immigration, the number of marriages remained high, even though the number of Canadian-born young people reaching marriageable age was relatively low—a reflection of the relatively low birth rates in the 1930s.[3] The inflow of immigrants, largely in the age groups 20 to 35 years, sustained the marriage rate and contributed to the temporary rise of the birth rate. In contrast again, the 1960s witnessed a fall in Canada's population growth rate. While net immigration declined absolutely, it maintained its proportionate contribution to the change in population during this decade. It is perhaps the continuing downward trend in the birth rate, interrupted by the postwar baby boom, which more than anything else has accounted for the decline in the population growth rate.

With these general trends in mind, it is now necessary to turn to a more detailed examination of the elements of population growth and ask both how they were affected by economic circumstances and how they contributed to the process of economic development.

Vital Statistics

The simple effect of births and deaths was the most important component of population growth in Canada over most periods of history. Yet, the patterns of births and deaths not only varied in the short run, but also in the long run and since Confederation at least both birth and death rates have declined secularly. While biological effects, in part, determined the rate of natural increase, both birth and death rates responded to economic forces which generally operated on some underlying demographic variable.[4] This, in turn, influenced the crude birth and death rates—births and deaths per thousand of population. Noted below are those underlying changes which have been the most important historically.

1) *Nuptiality* or the pattern of marriages in society affects the number of births by placing more or fewer women at risk to have children. This, of course, assumes that most children are born within wedlock. Variations in the ratio of females to males in the country or changes in the age composition of the population can cause changes in the pattern of nuptiality. Since women are, on average, fertile only between the ages of 15 and 49, any tendency to, say, postpone marriage leaves a shorter period over which the partners of the marriage can produce children. Because of the increase in the average age at marriage, the pattern of nuptiality changes.
2) *Age-specific fertility* is the child-bearing pattern of women of a certain age. This may, as we have seen above, be directly influenced by nuptiality patterns. Changes in age-specific fertility, however, may also be the result of changing attitudes to family size brought about by socioeconomic forces. For instance, the greater use of contraceptive controls can make effective decisions to limit family size. Some birth-control practices were known in the past.
3) *Mortality patterns of individuals over twenty years of age* are an important component of the overall pattern of death. Yet the mortality experience of adults, apart from the incidence of epidemics, changed very little over most of Canadian history. The number of years a twenty-year-old male should expect to live, on average, has increased only by about 3.5 years since Confederation—life expectancy of a twenty-year-old male in 1871 was 47.9 years. On the other hand, the life expectancy, at age twenty, of a female has increased by about twice that of the male population over the same period—from 47.3

years. This has largely been due to the lower incidence of female death associated with pregnancy and child-bearing.

4) *Infant and adolescent mortality rates* have historically been the largest component of the overall crude death rate. Improved techniques of medical science, better hygiene, increased nutrition, and other economic effects associated with a growing income greatly influenced these rates. Crude death rates which averaged between forty and sixty deaths per thousand persons in the pre-industrial world, have been reduced to fewer than ten in most western countries, almost exclusively as a result of the reduction in infant and adolescent mortality. In Canada, for instance, in the modern period 1931 to 1960, the incidence of infant mortality, largely due to diarrhea and enteritis, fell from 1,226 to 119 per 100,000 live births.[5]

Natural Increase in New France

In 1665, when the company territory of New France became an official French colony, its population numbered only 3,215 persons. Not only was this population small but the sex ratio was unbalanced. Within the age range 16 to 40 years there were 719 males and only 45 females. In order to bring about stability in the colony, and particularly to induce the French soldiers to settle, young women were shipped out to the colony — the famous *filles du Roi*. The immediate consequence of the adjustment in the sex ratio was an increase in the marriage rate and a crude birth rate above 60 per thousand (Table 6:3). Despite the improvement in the male-to-female ratio the population was still demographically unbalanced in its age composition. Because the age distribution centred on a low age — a full one-third of the population of 1665 was below the age of eleven — adult mortality was low in the years 1690-1700. Not until 1700 did the crude death rate reach the level of 20 to 35 per thousand which, apart from fluctuations, was consistent with the long-run trend (Table 6:3). The age composition of the population also had an impact on the birth rate. For instance, the low birth rate of the 1680s simply echoes the period when the new generation, the offspring of those married in the 1660s, was not of marriageable age. Like the crude death rate, the crude birth rate probably did not reach its long-run trend until the decade of the 1690s.[6]

The difference between the long-run trends in birth and death rates was such that the population of New France doubled about every thirty years. Although this rate of population growth was high, it was remarkably similar to the pattern of the British colonies to the south despite the different religious composition of the two areas. Furthermore, while high, population growth was still well below the upper limit

Table 6:3 Crude Birth and Death Rates in New France
(annual averages per decade)

Period	Crude Birth Rate (births per 1000 of population)	Crude Death Rate (deaths per 1000 of population)
(1)	(2)	(3)
1660-70	63.0	14.8
1670-80	60.1	10.3
1680-90	35.9	15.7
1690-1700	50.2	16.2
1700-10	56.8	23.8
1711-20	56.8	24.4
1721-30	53.5	23.4
1731-40	56.2	25.4
1741-50	51.0	29.3
1751-60	52.9	33.9
1761-70	56.8	28.2

Sources: G. Langlois, *Histoire de la Population Canadienne-Française* (Montréal, 1934), p. 252 (for pre-1711 to 1720 figures) and J. Henripin and Y. Peron, "The Demographic Transition of the Province of Quebec", in D. V. Glass and R. Revelle, eds., *Population and Social Change* (New York, 1972), p. 218.

of breeding potential. This was the result of age at marriage in the period 1700-30 being about 24 years for females and 27 years for males and an infant mortality rate which was only slightly less than that which prevailed in Europe at the same time.[7]

In summary, although the population of New France grew rapidly, this growth rate was slightly greater in the years prior to 1700. Yet throughout the French régime the crude birth rate was high by European standards; this can be attributed in part to the population's age composition and also to the economic fact that New France was a frontier area with more economic opportunities for young people to acquire farmland or find employment in the expanding fishing and fur trades. Nevertheless, the relatively late age at marriage of young people by the early eighteenth century suggests that some modest limitation of family size was brought about and that the range of economic opportunity or potential family income was limited. With respect to the death rate, New France after 1700 experienced the ravages of high infant mortality often, and wrongly, associated only with the countries of pre-industrial Europe. Although epidemics were less common in the New World than in Europe, their relative absence lowered the crude death rate only slightly. Even under normal circumstances only 50 per cent of the children born in New France survived to age twenty. The incidence of death associated with the process of birth, the effects of diseases of the digestive system, and the communicable diseases of childhood were as common in New France as elsewhere.

Long-Run Trends in Natural Increase
In 1765 the population of Quebec numbered about 70,000. The only other area under British control which was destined to become part of Canada was Nova Scotia, which included New Brunswick, and was at this time only sparsely populated. This maritime colony had only 12,000 inhabitants, many of whom were the dispersed Acadian population of Champlain's first colony. In subsequent years, English-speaking immigrants flowed into both the maritime colonies and Quebec. Quebec at this time stretched down the St. Lawrence–Great Lakes valley into what was later to become the Ohio Territory. The flow of English-speaking immigrants into Quebec was of sufficient size that political pressure was exerted to divide the jurisdiction. The Constitutional Act of 1791 created Upper Canada from the western part of Quebec in order to accommodate the growing English-speaking population and its apparent wish for separate political and legal jurisdiction. Lower Canada was the other colony roughly corresponding to the present-day province of Quebec.

The population of Upper Canada in 1790 was approximately 7.5 per cent of that of Lower Canada. Yet within sixty years, with both growing rapidly, the population of Upper Canada exceeded that of the older area (see Table 6:6). Critical to the rapid increase in the size of the English-speaking population was its high fertility. All evidence suggests that the crude birth rates to be found in the frontier areas of Upper Canada, New Brunswick, and Nova Scotia, prior to 1851 were at least equal to those of the French-speaking population.[8]

Children, of course, have the economic attributes of both consuming family income and adding to it. The importance of each effect varies under different conditions. If, as settlement pushed on to the more marginal lands in Quebec in the early 1800s, young people forming families foresaw a decline in their standard of living they might tend to limit the size of their families so that per-capita consumption would fall more slowly than aggregate family income. At this time there was a decline in the marriage rate consistent with such behaviour. In Upper Canada, on the other hand, the agricultural and timber frontiers provided scope for a growing family income which put less pressure on families to limit the number of children conceived and provided more opportunity for children to contribute to family income. Since young children are capable of performing most farm tasks at an early age their potential contributions to family welfare served further to remove the need to control family size.

Some time in the second quarter of the nineteenth century crude birth rates in both English- and French-speaking Canada began to decline (see Table 6:4). Not only was less land available at low prices but because of specialization in the economy more and more of the population was located in villages and the new urban centres. When such specialization took place the economic role of children as family-income earners became more limited and new families had more incentive to limit the number of children. Over the same period, although the evidence is incomplete, there was probably a slight decline in the infant mortality rate due to advances in innoculation techniques. Clearly evident as early as the 1851 census was the first stage of the long secular decline in both crude birth and death rates throughout Canada. From 23 per thousand in 1851 the overall death rate declined to fewer than 7 per thousand in the early 1970s. Birth rates also dropped, and to such an extent that today's population will barely replace itself numerically if the present rates persist. However, the closing of the gap between birth and death rates has been a recent phenomenon; for most of the past 120 years the gap has been such that 86 per cent of the growth of the Canadian population has been due to natural increase (Table 6:7). The downward trend of birth and death rates was similar in Quebec (Canada East) between 1840 and Confederation although at a somewhat higher level. Crude birth rates, and to a lesser extent, crude death rates, fell more slowly there than elsewhere in Canada. Whether this discrepancy can be attributed to religious or ethnic reasons is a moot point. It may have been a direct consequence of the lower than average per-capita income of that area and its high proportion of population which until recently lived in rural areas. In recent years, as they were in the pioneering society earlier, the vital statistics of the French-speaking population have again become almost identical with those of the rest of Canada.[9]

An explanation of this secular decline in the crude birth rate may be seen in the context of the decision to have children.[10] It is generally argued that this decision is determined by:

1) the benefit to a married couple of an additional child relative to the benefit of things which they might otherwise achieve (preference system);
2) the cost of an additional child relative to the cost of other things if another child was decided against (price system); and
3) the parents' income defined as both earned income and the amount of time and energy available.

It may be hypothesized that the likelihood of deciding to have another child varies directly with the relative benefit from that child and income

Table 6:4 Vital Statistics of Canada, 1801-1970
(annual averages per decade)

Period	Crude Birth Rate (births per 1000 of population)		Crude Death Rate (deaths per 1000 of population)	
	Canada	Quebec	Canada	Quebec
(1)	(2)	(3)	(4)	(5)
1801-10	n.a.	51.5	n.a.	26.5
1811-20	n.a.	50.6	n.a.	25.7
1821-30	n.a.	52.3	n.a.	25.3
1831-40	n.a.	51.4	n.a.	26.1
1841-50	n.a.	51.3	n.a.	23.0
1851-60	45.2	48.9	21.6	21.0
1861-70	39.6	47.0	20.8	21.9
1871-80	36.9	43.6	18.8	24.5
1881-90	33.6	39.5	18.0	22.0
1891-1900	30.3	36.7	16.2	20.1
1901-10	30.7	35.8	12.9	18.5
1911-20	29.2	37.8	12.4	17.8
1921-30	25.2	33.0	11.0	13.6
1931-40	21.0	25.6	9.8	10.6
1941-50	25.3	29.4	9.7	9.4
1951-60	27.8	29.0	8.2	7.7
1961-70	21.1	20.4	7.5	6.1

Note: The figures for Quebec (Lower Canada and Canada East) prior to 1870 for births are the rates appropriate only to the Roman Catholic population. After that date they are based on the entire population. The figures on death rates for Quebec prior to 1880 are those based on the Catholic population and for the entire population thereafter. The death rate for Quebec in 1881-90 actually covers only the years 1884-90.

Sources: Henripin and Peron (1972), pp. 230-31; Urquhart and Buckley (1965), p. 43, and *Vital Statistics*, Cat. no. 84-202.

available for all goals, and inversely with the relative cost from that child.

Canada has had a long history of increasing income as it is defined above. Between 1850 and 1970, real GNP per capita rose from $167 to $1,578 as shown in Chapter 1; also, there has been a decline in hours devoted to gainful employment and increased amounts of leisure time. Therefore, examining only the income effect, we expect a long-term upward trend in the crude birth rate. Since it declined in Canada, changes in the preference and price systems discouraged fertility. What have these changes been?

One change in the preference system that tended to reduce family size was the mortality decline seen in Table 6:4. This factor has several effects. First, if fertility had not declined over time while mortality declined, the ratio of population under fifteen years to that aged fifteen to fifty-nine years would have risen dramatically. Thus the benefit of an additional child would fall as the level of mortality declines. Second, if parents want to ensure that a certain number of children survive to maturity, declining mortality reduces the need for additional children as protection against the death of one or more of the existing children.

Another element of the preference system is the benefit which parents derive from their children's productive labour. This declined as the amount of land per capita fell and restrictions were placed on the use of child labour in factories and other urban employments. We would therefore expect to observe a long-run decline in fertility. Furthermore, the development of formal institutions to support the elderly further reduced the relative benefit to parents of additional children. With social security and more adequate pension arrangements, it became unnecessary for parents to bear children in large numbers to assure that one or more children would support them in old age. The preference system also changed and the social rewards from a large family probably declined. When mortality was high, governments and religious organizations encouraged high fertility as a means of national survival and economic growth. But as mortality levels fell, these institutions changed their position to one of neutrality. Preferences also changed in a manner which encouraged the limitation of family size as more alternatives such as travel became available. It may be the case that social status is more and more determined by conspicuous consumption, a tendency which would lead to decline in fertility.

Turning now to the influence of the price system, several factors have increased the cost associated with an additional child relative to the cost of alternatives. First, urbanization in Canada resulted in a rise in the relative price of living space, thereby tending to lower fertility. Second, the labour cost of child care (hours necessary to care for a child) rose because of both the increased possibility of a female finding employment and the increased remuneration from a job. Third, as the quality of education that parents demanded for their children or was demanded of them increased, the relative cost of an additional child rose making child-raising less attractive. Fourth, if birth control methods are crude and parents lack information about them, the decision not to have an additional child involves inconvenience or even danger if resort is to the primitive means of abortion. But new and improved methods of birth control not only made contraception more efficient and less costly in terms of health, but also helped to restructure attitudes about desired family size.

Thus, with economic development there were changes in the

preference about family size and changes in the patterns of benefits and costs which actually depressed fertility to such an extent that the income effect was more than overcome.

While the trend of birth and death rates was downward, fertility, nevertheless, varied substantially from that trend from time to time. One such episode occurred at the beginning of the twentieth century when the effect of the large net immigration into Canada was felt. The previous decline in the birth rate was forestalled by the immigration of young, working-age people whose own family formation held the fertility rate constant until about 1921. Subsequently, during the interwar period, the fall in the crude birth rate was precipitous, reaching a relatively low rate of 20.1 per thousand in 1937 as the result of both a fall in the marriage rate and the number of children born within wedlock. Both were the consequences of the depressed economic conditions. Furthermore, the new contraceptive techniques enabled the population to respond more effectively to the induced changes in the desired number of children. In contrast to the 1930s, the postwar economic boom after 1945 and the postponement of child-bearing until after the war caused a further reversal in the crude birth rate. Overall, it can be seen that, while the pattern of fertility has declined since 1851 at least, there have been temporary reversals due to the effects of immigration and the combined psychological and economic impacts felt in the years after the two world wars.[11]

The behaviour of the crude death rate responded to economic forces in a very different manner from that of the birth rate. This was so because changes in scientific, medical, and hygienic practices which often had little to do with contemporary economic stimuli profoundly influenced the pattern of mortality. For instance, the introduction of the small-pox vaccine, the adoption of sterile techniques in the nineteenth century, and many other medical practices were essentially simple, though their use, of course, depended on the ability to devote resources to making their use widespread. The result of scientific advances produced better public hygiene, better and more widespread medical practices, and a higher standard of nutrition, all of which contributed to a steady decline in the crude death rate.

The reduction of the crude death rate over the past few centuries has been largely due to one of its components — the infant mortality rate. Indeed, the greatest single reduction in the crude death rate in absolute terms occurs in the first year of life. Even over the course of recent history this rate has been reduced from 81 per thousand live births in the early 1930s to the present ratio of 20.8.[12] So too, most of the mortal diseases of childhood have been checked and it is to their relative rareness and the control of their virulence that the low crude death rate can be ascribed.

The long-run downward trend in the age-specific fertility rate also affected the size of population and played an important part in its age distribution. The years from Confederation to approximately 1901 witnessed a gradual aging of the population with the proportion under twenty years of age falling and the proportion over forty years of age rising (see Table 6:5). However, the trends in crude birth rates, net family formation, and the aging of the population were temporarily reversed in the early twentieth century. Since the majority of immigrants were in the age range 20 to 39 years this particular age category expanded and prevented the proportion of young people from declining as rapidly as it might have done since the new immigrants themselves both contributed to net family formation and, as noted earlier, delayed the long-run trend in fertility. A large new immigration also accompanied the so-called baby boom of the post-1945 years and, as expected, had the same effect on the age distribution. Yet it is evident from Table 6:5 that even this effect was reversed by the time of the 1971 census and the proportion of those over forty years of age is once again growing.

In Canadian demographic history natural increase is the principal component of long-run population growth. In the process of this growth, the age distribution of the population has changed with implications for the markets for both labour service and finished goods. At present, the gap between births and deaths is such that natural increase will not continue to play its historical role; undoubtedly Canada is currently experiencing very fundamental demographic change since neither crude birth nor death rates can decline much further.[13] Emphasis on the role of natural increase in the growth of population seems to stand in contrast to the notion that Canada was, and is, a nation populated by those from other countries.

Population Movements: A Framework
The geographic movement of people — and for that matter other resources — both internationally and internally usually reflected choices made by individuals and families about their economic and political environments. For that reason, economic historians are interested not only in describing the magnitude of population movements and their direction of flow but also in discovering their causes. This section sets out a framework in which this may be accomplished; attention then shifts to the history of population, and hence labour, movements into and throughout Canada.

Table 6:5 Age Distribution of Canada's Population, 1881-1971
(per cent)

Age Group	1881	1891	1901	1911	1921	1931	1941	1951	1961	1971
(1)	(2)	(3)	(4)	(5)	(6)	(7)	(8)	(9)	(10)	(11)
0 – 19	49.8	47.1	44.6	42.3	43.5	41.6	37.5	38.0	41.8	40.3
20 – 39	29.4	30.5	30.3	33.1	30.5	29.8	31.3	30.4	27.1	29.6
40 – 59	14.4	15.3	16.6	17.0	18.3	20.0	21.0	20.3	20.3	21.7
60+	6.4	7.1	7.6	7.1	7.5	8.4	10.2	11.4	10.8	12.3

Sources: R. Caves and R. Holton, The Canadian Economy: Prospect and Retrospect (Cambridge, Mass., 1959), p. 58; G. W. Wilson, S. Gordon, and S. Judek, Canada: An Appraisal of its Needs and Resources (Toronto, 1965). p. 70; and Statistics Canada, Canadian Statistical Review, Cat. no. 91-202.

International and internal migration are similar phenomena; in theory they can be treated analogously. Nevertheless, it is true that there are practical problems which, as will be seen later, lead us to distinguish between these two types of migratory movements. For the purpose of setting a framework, the similarities are stressed. When migration takes place in response to economic stimuli it is generally based on expectations.[14] First, it is necessary to note the obvious fact that there is a country *in which* the potential migrants' expectations are formed. Second, there is a country *about which* expectations are formed. Economic conditions in both areas jointly determine whether the potential migrant actually moves. Generally, a person contemplating migration has many countries from which to choose and expectations are formed about these alternatives. By comparing all the additional costs and benefits, over his lifetime, an individual chooses among the alternatives, one of which, of course, is for the person to remain in the home country. But how are these additional costs and benefits calculated and how does the process of forming expectations influence the calculations? The determinants of migration, or the costs and benefits which influence the decision to migrate, are of two types, pecuniary and non-pecuniary.

The potential migrants can evaluate pecuniary costs in a specific manner. First, people form expectations about the future lifetime income streams that might be received in the countries which they are considering, which, among other things, are influenced by the current price for labour in specific occupations and the likely pattern of wage rates. Wage rates, as noted elsewhere, vary because of changes in labour productivity and the growth or decline of employment opportunities in the industry in which the potential migrants might work. Since future lifetime income streams in the various countries probably exhibit different time patterns, comparisons can only be made by reducing all alternatives to present-value terms. Of course, the present age of the potential migrant also influences possible future income streams.

Since future income may be uncertain, the potential migrants act as if there is objective probability on receiving the present value of the future income stream in the countries to which they might migrate. Therefore, for a potential migrant of some occupation and age, the expected income from employment in a specific country is the product of the present value of the future income stream and the objective probability of receiving that income stream. Although benefits are important, individuals are unlikely to make decisions about migrating without considering costs.

The pecuniary costs absorbed by the migrants can be separated into three categories:

1) *Opportunity costs* are the foregone income streams, and other benefits to the individual migrants in their home country or the other countries of potential residence.

2) *Transport costs* include not only the cost of each individual's migration but also that of his family, as well as the cost of shipping moveable property. As will be seen later, these exogenously determined costs were often of a critical nature in determining the flow of migrants into Canada.

3) *Capital losses* associated with the sale of property, usually fixed property such as farms or houses, constitute the third category of costs. Not only will expected capital losses, or for that matter capital gains, influence the decision to migrate but they will affect its timing since capital-asset prices in most countries behave in a cyclical fashion over time. Property owners therefore have a more complex decision to make if they wish to minimize capital losses when migrating.

By comparing benefits and costs a specific worker of a given age can evaluate the net expected returns. Since there are probably several areas to which a potential migrant may go he can review the alternatives and, if unconcerned with non-pecuniary benefits and costs, select the country which will yield him the highest net expected return. If all net expected returns are negative the potential migrant will presumably remain at home and count himself fortunate.

Certain implications may now be drawn about the size of labour flow from one country to another. It will increase if, in the potential receiving country, the present value of the future income stream or the probability of receiving that income rises, if the opposite effects are observed in the home country, if the two countries are near each other, if transport rates fall, or if the number of dependents per family in the home country falls.[15] The labour flow will decline if the opposite happens to any of the above determinants. If it is assumed that the present value of future income streams is inversely related to the age of potential migrants and that the costs associated with migration are directly related to age, then the migrants will tend to be young. Implications may also be drawn about the geographical distribution of immigrants in their new country. They will migrate to regions with the highest present value of future income streams. Since transport costs may also be vital, the regions will often be close in a geographical sense to the home country. In reality many of the determinants of migration change at the same time and often do so in contradictory ways; it is a matter of relative strengths. For example, someone in Germany in 1976 can migrate to, say, France or to Canada; France is nearer but Canada offers a higher present value of the stream of future income. The subjective calculation of the net expected return to the individual from migrating to France or Canada determines ultimately where, if at all, the person will migrate.

To the forementioned pecuniary benefits and costs must now be added the non-pecuniary determinants of migration. Climate, urban-rural living, differences in community culture, and political factors, all were among the issues confronting the potential migrant. The non-pecuniary costs of migrating also include divorce from established social and family ties, and the educational uprooting of children. Because of these benefits and costs it cannot be assumed that all those who do migrate will go to the region of highest expected net pecuniary return. Nor will it be the case that all of those with positive expected net returns will migrate. After all, most people did not become international migrants. Turning for the moment to migration within Canada, a potential migrant in the Maritimes may achieve the highest net return when migrating to Ontario, and yet migration rates are higher for the *intra*-Maritime movement of people than migration to or from the Maritimes; this may partly be explained by the fact that non-pecuniary factors like social ties outweigh the pecuniary determinants. The two kinds of determinants are interdependent in that some non-pecuniary factors affect pecuniary benefits and costs; for example, non-pecuniary factors become more important with older age groups, a larger number of dependents, and greater property holdings which in turn lower gross pecuniary returns and/or increase pecuniary costs. In any event, both types of determinants appear throughout the history of labour migration into and throughout Canada.

Many of the international migrants who came to Canada did so as a means of escaping their homelands. In the late nineteenth century an increasing number of Russian and Polish Jews fled the pogroms for the more congenial conditions of other countries among which Canada was one. Religious refugees often came in groups as in the case of the Mennonites. Some of these groups, particularly such Christian sects as the Hutterites and the Doukhobors, sought the relative solitude of the Canadian west. Other individuals sought political freedom and among the first immigrants from continental Europe in the nineteenth century the Germans were often so motivated. In recent years, emigrés from Hungary, Czechoslovakia, and Chile have sought escape in Canada from turbulent political upheavals in their own countries. In the rubric of the above discussion, to such individuals the non-pecuniary benefits dominated the decision to migrate. This being so, it is often, however, difficult to ascribe any simple motive. Perhaps this is most obvious in the instance of the first major flight of political refugees into Canada, the United Empire Loyalists of the years during and after the American Revolution. As will be claimed later, the greater availability of land in British North America relative to those areas in the United States from which they came as well as the timing of the migration suggest a more complex motivation than the simple loyalty to the Crown.

Immigration and Settlement Before Confederation

The trans-Atlantic migration of the French was small.[16] As noted earlier, the expansion of French settlement in New France was primarily based on the natural increase of the initial immigrants of the seventeenth century. Neither the fur nor fishing trades of France acted as a continuing stimulus to immigration and permanent settlement. Such labour as was required in these resource industries was induced away from the only permanent settlements which were, of course, agriculturally based. Agriculture, unlike that in the English colonies to the south, never played a dynamic role in encouraging immigration and settlement, as noted earlier. The net expected return to migration to New France was apparently so low that the French felt little emigration fever. Even the great Voltaire dismissed New France as *quelques arpents de neige*.

To the British, on the other hand, North America, as early as the mid-seventeenth century, represented the new frontier where the net expected returns to migration were high and the non-pecuniary benefits often outweighed all costs of migrating. Initial waves of migrants from Great Britain went primarily to the British colonies which are now part of the United States. By the mid-eighteenth century, some of the settlement was, however, reaching north. For the next one hundred years the immigrants to present-day Canada were almost exclusively either British or English-speaking Americans.

Military concerns dictated the first British settlement patterns. In 1749 Halifax was established as a military counterbalance to the fortress of Louisbourg. Immigration from Britain was encouraged but by 1775, of about 18,000 people in the maritime region, fully two-thirds were New Englanders. If the expected gross returns from migrating to areas such as the Annapolis Valley from England or New England were about equal, the actual migration of New Englanders no doubt reflected lower migration costs. Both the pecuniary costs associated with transport and the psychic ones associated with already having lived in the colonies were lower for those nearby. New Englanders probably had more information about the Annapolis Valley than people in England, thus leading them to make more practical decisions about expected income streams. In addition New Englanders may have been better able to cope with the agricultural technology of the new colony, thus raising their net returns from migrating relative to those of the British.

The history of immigration, emigration, and settlement from the downfall of New France to 1867 is one of separate settlement of geographical areas, namely the Great Lakes–St. Lawrence Valley, the maritime colonies, and the west including British Columbia. Economic links between these regions were weak for most of this period and were not strengthened until the few decades before Confederation.

During the pre-Confederation period the balance of population shifted between Upper and Lower Canada. In 1784, Lower Canada's population was approximately 113,000 while that of Upper Canada was a mere 10,000. Although the absolute gap grew—in 1831 the provinces' respective populations were 553,000 and 236,000—the rate of growth of population in Upper Canada was more rapid (Table 6:6). The tide eventually turned, and by 1851, the population of Canada West—Upper Canada—was 952,000, about 7 per cent greater than that of its eastern neighbour.[17]

After 1763 there was a surge of English-speaking immigrants into Lower Canada. These included people from New England and New York, led of course by the United Empire Loyalists, farmers from England and Scotland, and merchants bound for Montreal and Quebec City. But as a destination for farmers Lower Canada was distinctly less attractive than Upper Canada, as noted in Chapter 4. Farm settlement by the non-French-speaking was limited to the Eastern Townships. By the beginning of the nineteenth century, the majority of immigrants to the St. Lawrence Valley went to Upper Canada. Montreal, the centre of British North American commerce, and Quebec City continued to attract English-speaking immigrants but their prosperity was linked as much to Upper as Lower Canadian development.

In Upper Canada, immigration also began with the United Empire Loyalists during and after the American Revolution. Loyalists and later immigrants from the United States constituted about 80 per cent of the population of Upper Canada in 1812. Some of the Loyalists fled to the protection of the Crown as they were burned out of their homesteads in the most approved modern style by the U.S. freedom-fighters. Others, undoubtedly, were genuinely motivated by a wish to remain loyal subjects even although they themselves were not in jeopardy. Yet, much of the so-called Loyalist migration was not so simply motivated. During the revolutionary turmoil, many merchants from New England, for instance, moved to Nova Scotia in order to continue their business of trading with the British West Indies which had been interrupted by the British blockade of

Table 6:6 Population of British North America by Area for Selected Years Prior to Confederation

(thousands)

Year	Lower[a] Canada	Upper[a] Canada	Nova Scotia	New Brunswick	P.E.I.	Nfld.	Assiniboia
(1)	(2)	(3)	(4)	(5)	(6)	(7)	(8)
1790	160	12	30[b]	—	—	17[c]	—
1806	250	71	63	35	10	27	—
1812	—	—	70	60	—	—	—
1814	335	95	—	—	—	—	0.3
1822	427	—	—	—	23	52[d]	—
1824	—	150	—	74	—	—	—
1831	553	237	168	94	33	76	2
1840	—	432	—	156	—	—	5
1841	—	455	—	—	47	—	—
1842	—	487	—	—	—	—	—
1844	697	—	—	—	—	—	—
1851	890	952	277	194	72	102	5[e]
1861	1,112	1,396	331	252	81	125	—

[a] Also designates Canada East and Canada West; [b] Excludes Cape Breton; [c] British population only; [d] 1823; [e] 1849.

Source: For official and unofficial estimates see *Census of Canada,* 1871 and 1931.

the ports. In Upper Canada the migratory stream from the United States continued for many years—well into the nineteenth century. While we may question the motives of those who took decades to make up their minds about where true allegiance lay, the migrants themselves were under no illusions. Upper Canada was located on the route from the Atlantic to the Ohio and Mississippi valleys and was in many respects the next natural frontier after settlement of upper New York State. The migrants came as frontier settlers in search of cheap land. Government grants of land of 200 acres per family between 1783 and 1815 were as much the attraction as any supposed intangible benefits derived from loyalty to the Crown.[18]

During the Napoleonic Wars the level of immigration from Great Britain was generally lower than in the periods before and after. Once peace-time prosperity had been established in the 1820s, British North America began again to present an attractive alternative to many. At first the new wave of British immigrants included some on assisted passage. British government schemes to encourage migration to Canada were seen as a policy to ameliorate unemployment, poverty, and social unrest in Great Britain in the immediate aftermath of the wars with France. However, most migrants generally came unaided; they reacted to improved economic conditions which can be traced to development stimulated by the timber trade during and after the Napoleonic Wars as well as to high unemployment among some trade and farm groups in Great Britain. As Upper Canadian agriculture itself became more efficient, many immigrants were drawn directly into this sector by rising farm incomes.

The return-cargo problem associated with the timber staple aided immigration directly by lowering the costs of the trans-Atlantic voyage. Lumber's bulk relative to the return cargoes from Great Britain resulted in a cargo imbalance and, as noted earlier, many ships sailed back to British North America in ballast. This, in turn, meant that there was an incentive for the shippers to carry some cargo on the westward voyage in order to increase gross revenues without, it was hoped, adding very much to total costs.[19] So low fares to British North America were offered which very much enlarged the pool of potential migrants and caused many to consider emigration from Great Britain for the first time. Despite growing income in British North America and the falling cost of migration, the inflow of settlers was not always large. Epidemics of cholera in 1832 and 1834, the rebellions in Canada of 1837, and a recession in the same year combined to keep immigration relatively low in the 1830s.[20] By this time land settlement was also hampered by private individuals and government officials alienating land which they withheld from the market for speculative purposes. Policies reserving land for specific purposes, as in the case of the Clergy Reserves, had the same effect. During this troubled decade Canadians first began to fear the spectre of destitute immigrants; in French Canada once again there was a growing concern about cultural domination by the growing English-speaking population as there had been in the first years of British control.

In contrast, the rise in net immigration in the 1840s can be attributed more to the poor economic climate in Great Britain than to an improved one in Canada. The progressive movement towards free trade and, in particular, the free trade in grains after 1846 caused widespread economic hardship among the British tenant farmers and small business proprietors. At the same time, the early stages of a recession, with their attendant urban unemployment, caused many to consider the alternative of trans-Atlantic migration. To this flow must be added the Irish immigration of 1846-51. Fleeing from one of the worst famines to ravage a European country, the Irish flocked to the ports for passage to North America. Many were landed in Canada.

The catastrophic nature of the Irish migrations in the face of famine in the years from 1846 to about 1850 marks one of the most tragic phases of the trans-Atlantic movement of people.[21] On the voyage, the incidence of disease and death was extremely high, even by the standards of the day. When landed at the ports of entry, most of the Irish immigrants were emaciated and at the principal receiving station of the Grosse Isle quarantine facility, the death rate was extremely high. Since Grosse Isle could barely cope with the number of Irish immigrants — 54,000 were landed in the 1847 shipping season which marked the peak year — most immigrants were admitted to Canada in a wretched condition, whence they were shipped up the St. Lawrence. Each town en route charged with the responsibility of caring for the destitute and diseased immigrants shipped them on as quickly as possible. Major outbreaks of cholera were experienced and the Irish themselves were the principal victims. Many quiet acts of heroism were performed in an attempt to minister to the sick and dying; none were more valiant than the efforts of the nursing sisters of the Church.[22]

Many, probably the majority, of the Irish immigrants who survived did not settle in the Canadas. Since very few had any skills, even of rudimentary farm practice, they soon found that employment opportunities were limited. Furthermore, the demand for unskilled labour in the United States afforded more jobs to which the Irish quickly migrated. Of course, a large number did remain to settle and influence the character of the population.

Based on railway construction, the growth of agricultural products as a staple, and the continuance of lumber as a product of some importance, economic development was rapid in the 1850s. Staple prices were rising and foreign savings, principally British, were available for railway and other capital projects. The immigration which these economic conditions induced contribution to a population growth of an exceptional 16 per cent. Although net immigration was lower later in the decade, this was probably due to a better economic climate in Great Britain rather than a slackened pace of Canadian economic expansion. By this time information about the Canadas was more readily available. The best source proved to be the former immigrants who sent back favourable reports of conditions as well as money to finance another migrant's passage. This may be interpreted as creating higher probabilities of receiving income and lowering transport costs.

Immigration into the maritime provinces was much smaller than that into the St. Lawrence Valley. Because of the inability of agriculture to produce for a large export market and the relatively poor soil conditions in some areas, a population scattered in sea-cost settlements, a scarcity of good roads, and a scarcity of savings, limited agricultural productivity and hence the net returns to migration. While the population of Nova Scotia grew from 11,000 in 1767 to 330,000 by 1861 and New Brunswick's population rose from 1,100 to 252,000 over the same period, population growth was below that in the St. Lawrence Valley. Immigration probably peaked in the 1840s, and later waves of immigration by-passed the area.

Before 1867 population growth in the Canadian west was sparse and settlement was beyond the scope of the market economy. Although the first agricultural settlement was established in the Red River Valley in 1812, by 1871 Manitoba still had a population of only 25,000. Settlement in the present provinces of Alberta and Saskatchewan was equally sparse. The western population in 1871 consisted almost exclusively of the original settlers of 1812, their descendants, retired employees of the Hudson's Bay Company, and the free-spirited Métis. Similarly, British Columbia's population before Confederation consisted mainly of Hudson's Bay Company employees and those drawn in by the gold discoveries on the Fraser River. The lure of gold often gave rise to spectacular inflows of immigrants from other areas. However, gold provided a loose base for settlement since, as the gold rush ended, the net return from migrating became negative for many people and emigration resulted. This area's long-run economic development was tied to economic diversification around a longer lasting natural-resource base than placer gold mining. Because of the need to develop closer economic links with other areas, and to find markets for the region's coal and timber, British Columbia in the 1860s was ripe for union.

The Nation of Immigrants
The years from 1867 to 1900 are often referred to as the "years of frustration".[23] But this was so only in the sense that they fell short of the expectations of men like Sir John A. Macdonald. They were years of economic growth slow only in comparison with either that of the United States of the same period or Canada itself at the beginning of the twentieth century. However it has yet to be shown that Canadian growth or development between 1867 and 1900 was substantially below its potential for these years. If the compound average annual rates of growth per decade in real GNP per capita (see Chapter 2, Table 2:1) are used as a guide, growth in the 1880s and 1890s of 2.17 per cent exceeded the rates during the 1850s, for example. Furthermore, as Table 6:7 shows, immigration continued at high levels in the period 1870-1900. Yet, despite the ability of the economy to draw in immigrants from Europe, or perhaps because of it, emigration from Canada was also high. By increasing employment in Canada through policy of growth and development, it was hoped that emigration to the United States would be dampened. In this respect the Conservative's national policy failed. However, the situation reversed itself in the first two decades of the twentieth century. Rapid industrial

Table 6:7 Immigration and Emigration, 1851-1971
(thousands)

Period	Immigration	Emigration	Net Immigration	As a % of the Population at Start of Decade			Net Immigration as % of Change in Population
				Immigration	Emigration	Net Imigration	
(1)	(2)	(3)	(4)	(5)	(6)	(7)	(8)
1851-61	209	86	+ 123	8.6	3.5	+ 5.0	+15.5
1861-71	186	376	- 191	5.8	11.7	- 5.9	-41.5
1871-81	353	438	- 85	9.6	11.9	- 2.3	-13.7
1881-91	903	1,108	- 205	20.9	25.6	- 4.8	-40.4
1891-1901	326	507	- 181	6.7	10.5	- 3.7	-33.6
1901-11	1,782	1,066	+ 716	33.2	19.8	+13.3	+39.0
1911-21	1,592	1,360	+ 232	22.1	18.9	+ 3.2	+14.7
1921-31	1,203	974	+ 229	13.7	11.1	+ 2.6	+14.4
1931-41	150	242	- 92	1.4	2.3	- 0.9	- 8.1
1941-51	548	379	+ 169	4.8	3.3	+ 1.5	+ 6.8
1951-61	1,543	462	+1,081	11.0	3.3	+ 7.7	+25.6
1961-71	1,377	639	+ 738	7.2	3.6	+ 4.0	+22.4
TOTAL	10,172	7,637	+2,534				+13.9

Source: See Table 6:2.

development and expansion of prairie agriculture combined to turn the tide of net immigration.[24]

The problem in essence becomes: Why did the post-1900 boom with its relatively large, positive net immigration not occur earlier? The answer explains why the apparent net returns from migrating to Canada changed so markedly after 1900 and introduces a new element, the influence of the prairie west.

Some appreciation of the west in the history of Canadian population growth may be gained from Table 6:8. From 1881 to 1921, by census years, the "older" provinces accounted for a diminishing percentage of Canada's total population whereas the West, including British Columbia, accounted for a larger proportion. The growth of population in this area exceeded the national average population-growth rates in every decade from 1881-91 to 1911-21. While population-growth rates differed among provinces after 1921, they were more closely aligned together than in the boom years of 1901 to 1921.

Although there was settlement of the prairies prior to 1900, there was also a variety of reasons why a large wave of permanent immigration came to rest there only after that date.[25] First, until 1885 the prairie region lacked the full range of transport facilities which were a necessary condition of integration with the world commodity markets. Before the coming of the Canadian Pacific Railway some regions such as southern-Manitoba could ship grain southward *via* the Red River to railways in the United States. The area which could be so serviced was, however, very limited. Consequently it was only after the railroad connection was established that settlement patterns were based on economic conditions other than the desire to undertake subsistence farming. Second, the prices, and terms, the CPR set for land close to the rail lines were higher than comparable land in the United States. Although homestead land in Canada was free, like that to south, since the railroad held alternate blocks of land, the density of settlement was affected. Third, much of the southern prairies in what is now Alberta and Saskatchewan were adaptable only to dry farming. The techniques of dry farming, which involved letting land lie fallow, were not well-known prior to the 1890s in Canada, and dry farming itself was more risky than farming the sub-humid lands elsewhere. Immigration to the prairie West was, as a consequence, delayed until the major portion of homestead land in the United States was settled. As land in the western United States became more scarce, the flow of continental immigration to agricultural regions more and more came to Canada. About 1900 settlement of the southern prairies began to proceed rapidly, based upon the new technology of dry farming, made practical in turn by rising wheat prices. Until this time prairie

Table 6:8 Percentage Distribution of the Canadian Population by Province by Census Year, 1881-1971

Province	1881	1891	1901	1911	1921	1931	1941	1951	1961	1971
(1)	(2)	(3)	(4)	(5)	(6)	(7)	(8)	(9)	(10)	(11)
P.E.I.	2.5	2.2	2.0	1.3	1.0	0.8	0.8	0.7	0.6	0.5
N.S.	10.2	9.3	8.6	6.8	6.0	4.8	4.9	4.6	4.0	3.6
N.B.	7.4	6.7	6.2	4.9	4.4	3.8	3.9	3.7	3.3	2.9
Que.	31.4	30.8	30.7	27.8	26.9	27.2	28.2	29.0	28.8	28.1
Ont.	44.6	43.8	40.6	35.1	33.4	32.2	32.1	32.8	34.2	35.7
Man.	1.4	3.2	4.8	6.4	6.9	6.5	6.2	5.5	5.1	4.6
Sask.	—	—	1.7	6.8	8.6	8.5	7.6	5.9	5.1	4.4
Alb.	—	—	1.4	5.2	6.7	6.9	6.7	6.7	7.3	7.5
B.C.	1.2	2.0	3.3	5.4	6.0	6.6	6.9	8.3	8.9	10.0
Nfld.						2.6	2.6	2.6	2.5	2.4

Note: Figures do not add to 100.0 because of the exclusion of the population of the territories. The figures for Newfoundland are included from 1931 even though that province did not join Confederation until 1949.

Sources: Kubat and Thornton (1974), pp. 12-16; and Statistics Canada, *Vital Statistics*, Cat. no. 84-202.

settlement had been limited to the sub-humid prairies of the area around the North Saskatchewan River and Manitoba. Transport costs, which were lowered internally by the railroads and externally by improved ocean-shipping techniques, firmly brought the prairies within the bounds of the world wheat market—a discussion of the mechanics of prairie settlement is postponed to Chapter 11.

The emigration of eastern Canadian farmers to the plains of the United States was also reversed in the years around the turn of the twentieth century. Emigration in the period 1871-1900, however, took place from all parts of Canada. Thousands of French Canadians left Quebec for New England and New York.[26] With the lack of opportunities for them at home, the growing demand for labour in that part of the United States attracted the emigrants to that country. Table 6:7 shows clearly that emigration continued even during the boom period. While the net returns attracted many foreigners to Canada, the structure of rewards was such that many Canadians felt they could do better elsewhere.

For the first twelve years of the period between the two world wars, the pattern of large-scale immigration and only slightly smaller emigration continued. With the outset of the depression, this pattern was markedly altered.

Between 1931 and 1941 not only was net immigration negative but both immigration and emigration were absolutely lower than in any single decade since Confederation. This of course resulted from the generally depressed economic conditions of the 1930s which directly influenced the net returns to migration. It should be noted here that Canadian authorities, fearing an inflow of unemployed people, tightened regulations and reduced their efforts to attract people to Canada.

But immigration and emigration also rose and fell with the level of economic activity in Canada during the 1920s. Part of the inflow of people was offset by an outflow especially to the United States where a boom associated with the First World War and its aftermath and the beginnings of a phase of rapid industrial growth meant that there was a high positive net return which some could capture by leaving Canada. In these years the United States imposed quotas on immigrants by birthplace in an attempt to draw immigrants specifically from northwestern Europe and Canada. After the First World War, as earlier, the majority of immigrants found employment outside the farm sector. Organized labour, imitating its U.S. counterparts, generally opposed large-scale immigration. This cautious attitude of organized labour appears consistently throughout Canada's immigration history.[27] As early as 1880 to 1902, the Trades and Labor Congress argued against assistance to immigrants since they feared that large-scale net immigration, so induced, would lower real wage rates; they also opposed "contract" labour and immigration from the Orient because of the imagined danger to living standards.

Not until the 1950s did Canada again experience large-scale net and gross immigration. This began after the Second World War when many thousands of Europeans, some displaced by the ravages of war, moved to Canada. Net immigration increased with a buoyant Canadian economy typified by rising rates of wage increase and relatively low unemployment rates. In 1957, a large immigration occurred when the Hungarian Revolt and the Suez Crisis aroused temporary fears of another war in Europe. Subsequently, however, in the years from 1958 to 1961, net immigration fell as Europe's economic condition improved, while in Canada unemployment rates rose to over 7 per cent. But starting in 1962, job opportunities in Canada improved relative to those in western Europe resulting in rising levels of net immigration until 1968. Since then immigration from Europe to Canada has declined.

In the decade of the 1950s net immigration accounted for 25 per cent of the change in Canada's population. About 50 per cent of postwar immigrants, which of course included women and children, became active in the labour force as compared with about 33 per cent for Canada as a whole. In 1953, about 200,000 native-born persons reached the age of seventeen; because of departures, retirements, and deaths the labour force increased by 111,000 of which immigrants contributed 91,000. These postwar immigrants were drawn from very different sources than the earlier waves of settlers.

The settlers of the pre-1850 decades, apart from the earlier French, were almost exclusively English-speaking from either the British Isles or the United States. An exception was the German immigrants to Nova Scotia. During the 1850s, however, a substantially increased proportion of immigrants came from continental Europe. This represented about 30 per cent of total immigration. Until 1900 the source of these non-English-speaking immigrants was, for the most part, northwestern Europe. An exception was the Chinese labourers who were brought to western Canada to help build the railroad.[28] The new century brought a change in the proportion of immigrants from Great Britain. It fell and has continued to do so. This was not the result of a decline in the numbers coming from that area but a result of the gradual opening up of new sending areas over time: eastern and southern Europe during the first half of the twentieth century and Asia, South America, and Central America, including the Caribbean, since 1950. For instance, between 1946 and 1966, 83 per cent of Canada's immigrants came from Europe, with 3 per cent from Asia, 9 per cent from North and Central America, and 1 per cent from South America. The corresponding data for 1971 are: 43 per cent from Europe, 18 per cent from Asia, 30 per cent from North and Central America, and 4.5 per cent from South America.[29] The widening of the recruitment areas dated from 1962 and the immigration policy change of that year. The decline of travel costs as well as the broader dissemination of knowledge about Canada through the establishment of immigration offices in more countries were also contributing factors.

Vital evidence about the relative drawing strengths of the Canadian regions is provided by the locations chosen by immigrants for homes. It is clear from Table 6:9 that Ontario was the principle choice of immigrants in 1901, but that that area's dominance was eroded during the period 1901-31 when Canada experienced the large inflow of people to the prairies. As will be indicated fully in Chapter 13 (Table 13:2), the prairie provinces may have generated personal incomes per capita above the national average in 1910-11, 1920-21, and also above that found in Ontario. Sometime after 1941 but before 1951 Ontario re-emerged as the major magnet for the immigrant population, experiencing relatively high personal incomes per capita and low unemployment rates; the foreign-born reacted as expected. It is particularly noticeable that the foreign-born population tended to avoid settlement in the Maritimes. For the most part, the distribution of the foreign-born among the ten provinces over time corresponds to the distribution of per-capita income.

Table 6:9 Percentage Distribution of the Foreign-Born Population of Canada by Region of Residence by Census Year, 1901-1971

Region	1901	1911	1921	1931	1941	1951	1961	1971
(1)	(2)	(3)	(4)	(5)	(6)	(7)	(8)	(9)
Maritime Provinces	6.7	3.6	3.4	3.1	3.1	2.7	2.3	2.2
Quebec	12.7	9.3	9.6	10.9	11.1	11.1	13.7	14.2
Ontario	46.3	32.0	32.9	34.9	36.4	41.3	47.6	51.8
Prairie Provinces	20.3	40.7	40.7	37.2	34.2	28.3	21.3	16.6
British Columbia	11.3	14.1	13.3	13.8	15.1	18.5	14.9	15.1
Yukon and N.W.T.	2.7	0.3	0.1	0.1	0.1	0.1	0.2	0.1

Note: Figures after 1941 include Newfoundland.

Source: Calculated from Kubat and Thornton (1974), p. 74.

The Displacement Thesis

That emigration from Canada has, in a cumulative sense, so nearly equalled immigration since at least 1851 raises questions about the economy's ability to absorb immigrants. While some of the emigrants were disappointed immigrants who returned to their native lands the principal emigration was to the United States and was of people who were themselves born in Canada. The dimensions of this emigration noted earlier in Table 6:7 may also be seen in Table 6:10 which records the Canadian-born population of the United States. Between 1870 and 1900, for instance, over 20 per cent of the Canadian population emigrated. The proportion of Canadian-born individuals in the United States similarly reflected this vast movement southward.

To explain this outflow historians offered a mechanism called "the displacement thesis".[30] This mechanism assumes that immigration tended to displace native-born Canadians or naturalized foreign-born citizens. An inflow of immigrants increased the labour supply; since the demand for Canadian output was set externally and increased only slowly, supply shifts in the labour market more than offset demand shifts. Therefore, real wages in Canada fell, and as a result, emigration to the United States took place. Canadian-born or naturalized foreign-born were the most likely emigrants because recent Canadian immigrants were often prepared to work for lower real wages than the domestic labour force. The Canadian-born are presumed to have borne the burden of unemployment or resulting lowered wages. Therefore, native-born Canadians emigrated to the United States. The displacement thesis is one of supply shifts.

In order for the displacement mechanism to have operated there must

Table 6:10 Migration of Canadians to the United States, 1850-1960

Year[a]	Canadian-Born Living in the U.S.[b]	As Percentage of U.S. Population	As Percentage of U.S. Foreign-Born Population	As Percentage of Canadian Population[b]
(1)	(2)	(3)	(4)	(5)
1850	147,711	0.6	6.6	6.2
1860	249,970	0.8	6.0	7.9
1870	493,464	1.3	8.9	13.4
1880	717,157	1.4	10.7	16.6
1890	980,938	1.6	10.6	20.3
1900	1,179,922	1.6	11.4	22.0
1910	1,204,637	1.3	8.9	16.7
1920	1,124,925	1.1	8.1	12.8
1930	1,286,389 PEAK	1.1	9.1	12.4
1940	1,065,480	0.8	9.3	9.0
1950	1,003,038	0.7	9.6	7.1
1960	949,322	0.5	10.1	5.2 OK

[a] Canadian population figures used are from the Canadian census for the year following the date indicated.

[b] Newfoundland is treated as a part of Canada in some census, and is excluded in others. In no year, however, did migration of persons born in Newfoundland account for more than two per cent of total Canadian-born living in the United States.

Source: R. K. Vedder and L. E. Gallaway, "Settlement Patterns of Canadian Emigrants to the United States, 1850-1960", *Canadian Journal of Economics*, Vol. 3, no. 3 (1970), p. 477.

have been some shift in the supply of immigrants to Canada independent of the real wage level. While at first encounter such a phenomenon seems to contradict the framework of migration as a response to change in the pattern of possible net returns, it need not. For instance, during the wheat boom decade of 1901-11 many immigrants arrived intending to engage in farming. When they discovered that there were capital barriers to entry into farming, many, who also happened to be skilled in other pursuits, offered their services in the labour market. This, then, caused the real wages to fall relative to those in the United States and tended to displace Canadian residents of long standing from employment. Those displaced simply migrated to the United States. Because the immigrants did not intend to enter the labour market in which they eventually found themselves, existing real wages were not relevant to the decision to migrate in the first place. Otherwise, they would not have come to Canada at all but would presumably have gone to the United States where real wages were higher anyway. Despite the assumption of the displacement thesis then, it is likely that displacement operated to some extent, at least in the first decade of the twentieth century when both immigration and emigration were high.[31]

In opposition to the displacement thesis is an explanation of Canadian emigration based on shifts in the demand for labour in the United States.[32] If the excess demand for skilled labour expanded in the United States more rapidly than the demand for unskilled labour then there would be the growth of the real-wages differential between the United States and Canada for skilled labour. Historically, real wages in Canada were generally lower than those in the United States for any specific type of labour service. That is, there probably existed a labour-market condition which we might call "an equilibrium wage-gap". Because of the costs of relocating, including the physic ones, the higher real wage in the United States was not sufficiently greater to induce Canadian workers to move. However, if the wage-gap departed from its equilibrium for any reason and real wages in the United States rose relative to those in Canada a flow of emigrants to the United States would occur. Thus, when the demand for skilled labour in the United States increased more rapidly than that for unskilled workers, the flow of emigrants from Canada might be expected to contain a high proportion of skilled workers. If Canadians of long residence, and in particular the native-born, had better access to information on U.S. labour-market conditions or were simply in a better position to finance any move, they would disproportionately enter the emigrant stream.

The historical record of labour flows shows that immigration and emigration were highly correlated and that peaks in emigration tended to follow peaks in immigration into Canada. Also, real wages in the United States were generally higher than those in Canada. Furthermore, the flow of emigration from Canada tended to be one of skilled, as opposed to unskilled, labour and tended also to be made up largely of Canadian-born individuals. Thus, the evidence might support either the displacement or demand-pull mechanism.

Yet, as noted earlier, displacement depends on an inflow of skilled migrants who are not sensitive to the level of real wages. It is only during the wheat-boom immigration of 1900 to 1914 that this was likely so. In addition, although immigrants to Canada were increasingly skilled ones, thereafter, many were prevented from going to the United States because of that country's restrictive immigration policy introduced in 1921. Since, under the policy, Canadians were given favoured treatment, it is not surprising that they responded to an increase in the real wage between the United States and Canada with more alacrity.

Internal Migration — Interprovincial

One by one they all clear out,
Hoping to better themselves, no doubt.
They don't care how far they go,
From the poor little girls of Ontario.
Traditional song.

Not only did the Canadian population grow rapidly in the long run but its distribution within the economy also changed markedly. In general those regions which presented the greatest economic opportunity tended to find their populations growing more rapidly than regions where the pace of economic development was slow. International migrants, as just noted, concentrated in the expanding regions. Those who left Canada for other countries tended to come from the less prosperous regions. But there was another migratory movement which more than any other explains the regional distribution of population — migration within the country. Canadians have been one of the world's most mobile populations. However, internal migration was more than simply the movement of people from one region to another; it was the movement within regions, from one urban centre to another, and from farms to city. It should come as no surprise that the framework laid out earlier in this chapter to explain international migration is of equal value in explaining internal migration from one province or area to another. In this framework, it is to be expected that trends in provincial income and regional unemployment rates should then govern interprovincial migratory flows.

Throughout the years for which information has been compiled, unemployment rates have consistently been relatively high in the Maritimes, Quebec, and British Columbia, and relatively low in the prairie provinces and Ontario.[33] Income per capita, on the other hand, has been relatively low in the Maritimes and Quebec, relatively high in Ontario and British Columbia, and unstable in the prairie provinces. While the prairie provinces recorded a relatively high income per capita from 1900 to 1920 it subsequently hovered around the national average. The history of internal migration between the Canadian regions might be expected to be dominated by people leaving the Maritimes and Quebec for Ontario, and the prairie provinces, at least between 1900 and 1920. Movements to British Columbia may have been caused by the area's relatively high income per capita, but was partly offset by the lower probability of receiving that income — relatively high unemployment rates. Does history show these expected flows?

Before Confederation, the Canadian population showed little tendency to leave the traditional areas of settlement in the Maritimes and lower St. Lawrence Valley. Although the Pacific coast was part of British North America, its two colonies of Vancouver Island and British Columbia were not initially settled by a westward movement of people from the east. In this respect, the settlement of the west coast of the United States was quite different. Because of a lack of transport and communication facilities, the cost of moving and the uncertainty associated with it, even between places such as Halifax and Montreal, was relatively high. With obstacles of costs and uncertainty gradually being overcome during the last four decades of the nineteenth century, people started to move westward: from the Maritimes to Ontario and the west, from Ontario to the west.[34] As the historical information about the migration of the native-born reveals in Table 6:11 the prairie areas and British Columbia gained migrants. Clearly evident is the force of prairie development from 1901 to 1931 attracting large and positive flows of migrants. By the 1930s, the main migration to Manitoba and Saskatchewan was over, and these areas became net losers of migrants; Alberta continued to experience a net gain of internal migrants based on relatively high per-capita incomes generated by the non-agricultural resources industries. It appears that income prospects outweighed any fears of unemployment in the minds of migrants to British Columbia. The west-coast province has consistently had a large net inflow of people. For some, especially the retired middle class, this province continued to be an attractive place for retirement, irrespective of prevailing economic conditions. Tea time at the Empress Hotel in Victoria is remarkable testimony to this claim. As might be expected the maritime provinces lost population to other areas every decade of this century. Ontario, on the other hand, lost migrants prior to 1921 as many persons left Ontario for the west, but this was only a loss on balance. Ontario had gained, in a gross sense, many migrants during the years 1901 to 1931. It may be speculated from the province's structure that inward and outward migrants were dissimilar in their employment characteristics. In-migrants, skilled and semi-skilled, were drawn by industry in the urban centres. Out-migrants tended to be agricultural workers and farmers. The migratory movements were occupation-specific. By the 1930s the Ontario economy, depressed as it was, displayed more ability to retain its population than earlier, although to be sure, there were few attractive alternatives. From that time on Ontario gained more population through interprovincial migration than it lost to other parts of Canada. By the 1950s and 1960s, the three provinces which recorded the highest number of Canadians living outside their province of birth were Ontario, British Columbia, and Alberta. All are provinces with per-capita incomes above the Canadian mean.[35]

Table 6:11 Internal Migration, 1871-1961

A—Estimates of Net Internal Migration of Native-Born Canadians, 1871-1931 (thousands)

Period	P.E.I.	N.S.	N.B.	Quebec	Ont.	Man.	Sask.	Alta.	B.C.	Yukon and N.W.T.[c]
(1)	(2)	(3)	(4)	(5)	(6)	(7)	(8)	(9)	(10)	(11)
1871-81[a]	—	- 2.0	+ 1.0	- 11.1	- 14.2	—		- 4.1	—	—
1881-91[a]	-1.8	- 2.3	- 3.2	- 10.2	- 45.6	+ 22.2	-123.8		+ 17.0	—
1891-1900	-3.1	+ 2.1	- 2.5	- 4.5	- 51.7	+ 18.5	+ 22.3		+ 18.9	+ 2.0
1901-11	-5.7	-12.9	- 8.4	- 24.0	-147.3	-16.0	+184.9		+ 41.1	-11.6
1911-21	-3.0	- 6.3	- 0.5	- 14.6	- 2.7	-18.5	+ 8.0	+ 20.4	+ 16.3	+ 1.0
1921-31	+0.8	- 9.6	- 6.4	+ 24.1	+ 51.4	-36.1	- 41.8	- 13.5	+ 30.2	+ 0.8

B—Estimates of Net Internal Migration of Native-Born and Foreign-Born, 1931-1961 (thousands)

Period	P.E.I.	N.S.	N.B.	Quebec	Ont.	Man.	Sask.	Alta.	B.C.	Yukon and N.W.T.
1931-41	-2.6	+ 5.7	- 7.9	+ 24.3	+ 96.9	-37.8	-140.5	- 36.3	+ 89.1	+ 1.5
1941-51	-8.3	-43.7	-31.1	+ 6.0	+320.7	-41.0	-156.6	+ 22.4	+234.0	+ 3.7
1951-61[b]	-9.8	-31.7	-27.2	+168.3	+665.3	- 0.4	- 70.0	+124.3	+223.3	+ 3.0

Note: Because the procedure for estimating the internal migration of Canadians is based on census records only the internal migration of the native born can be measured with any accuracy prior to 1931. The estimates for 1931-41, 1941-51, and 1951-61 are from George who used the census survival ratio method in his calculations. These estimates differ from those of Anderson in part because she used the vital statistics method.

[a] The records for these years are inaccurate and the rows do not sum to zero.

[b] Newfoundland in 1951-61 is –11.9.

[c] Included in columns (8) and (9) prior to 1891.

Sources: M. V. George, *Internal Migration in Canada: Demographic Analysis* (Ottawa, 1970), pp. 58-59; Urquhart and Buckley (1965), p. 21; and I. Anderson, *Internal Migration in Canada* (Ottawa, 1966), pp. 63-69.

Since 1881, persons born in Manitoba, Prince Edward Island, and Saskatchewan showed the greatest propensity to migrate to other provinces—measured by the proportion of a province's native-born residing outside the province. Conversely, the tendency for native-born residents to be living outside their province of birth has been least evident in British Columbia, Quebec, and Nova Scotia. For recent decades at least, French Canadians have been the least mobile of Canadians. Undoubtedly this reflects the non-pecuniary costs associated with migration and helps give Quebec's economy its unique characteristics.

The trend of interprovincial migration over Canadian history has been one of movements from low- to high-income areas. Migration is an income-induced labour flow. When that flow was smaller than might be suggested by relative income per capita, such as the outflow from Quebec, evidence can be found for the heavy weighting of non-pecuniary factors. Nevertheless, the actual flow has been large. Yet, despite the shifts of labour supply which we might expect to have influenced the pattern of per-capita income there has been little tendency in history for provincial per-capita income differences to diminish. Why these migratory movements have not resulted in narrowing regional income differences, as they have done in economies such as that of the United States, suggests further consideration of the effects of internal migration (see Chapter 13). So far concern has been focused only on the causes of migration.

Internal Migration—Urbanization
Of all the internal migratory movements the largest has been the shift of population from rural to urban locations.[36] As the relative importance of agriculture declined so labour flowed to the growing manufacturing and tertiary sectors. These, by their economic nature, were located in population centres or urban centres grew up around their location. Structural change in the economy, analysed in Chapter 7, induced this rural-urban shift by ensuring that there were positive net returns to migration. Wages in expanding sectors generally grew more rapidly than those in sectors suffering a relative decline in importance. But factors other than the relative growth of sectors of the economy dictated the extent of the rural-urban migration. Absolute growth in agriculture also caused a movement from rural areas since it induced specialization in the service sectors linked to agriculture. For instance, the decade of the 1900s witnessed the greatest growth in the size of the prairie rural population and the urbanized population of the prairies grew even faster, both primarily due to immigration into the region.

So strong was the tendency towards urbanization that only in rare circumstances did the net flow reverse itself. Also, the rural-urban shift was not wholly an internal phenomenon. Many Canadian farmers and agricultural labourers left the land for employment in the urban United States. For instance, during the decade of the 1870s, the emigration from Canada was both rural and relatively unskilled in character and went primarily to cities and towns in the U.S. north-east and mid-west. Later, as Canadian urban centres grew, the proportion of this type of labour in the emigration flow decreased, so that emigrants were more and more of the skilled variety as noted earlier. The changing focus of the rural-urban shift to Canadian cities and towns was neither a reversal of its pattern nor even a slowing down of its pace.[37] Reversal of some of the rural-urban migration was only once of consequence in Canadian history and that was during the depression of the 1930s. High unemployment rates in central Canadian industry drove some people back to their rural birth places in the prairie and the maritime provinces. On the whole, however, the rural-urban shift has been the least reversible of the internal migration flows.

The growth of urban centres based on increasing specialization and increasing manufacturing output not only attracted people from rural areas but also attracted immigrants. Most immigrants who came to Canada after 1851 were drawn to urban locations. As a consequence the growth of the urban population has always exceeded that of the rural population.

Little is known about the extent of urban growth before 1851, but probably only 10 per cent of the population of Upper Canada, Lower Canada, and the Maritimes together were urban dwellers. By 1851 and the first major census of British North America, 13 per cent of the population were located in towns and villages of over 1,000 persons. While the rate of urbanization declined between 1861 and 1871 as the general pace of economic development slowed somewhat, it increased markedly over the next decade, only to fall again for the rest of the nineteenth century. While the actual rates of growth of urban populations varied, they were still sufficiently high; by 1901, 34.9 per cent of Canada's population were urban dwellers. The most rapid urbanization was in Quebec, Ontario, and British Columbia (Table 6:12).

The late 1890s and early 1900s witnessed the emergence of the wheat economy which stimulated relatively high net immigration and extensive-intensive western settlement; the rural population grew 21 per cent during the first decade of the twentieth century. This was by far the largest growth since Confederation. But the growth rate of urban areas in the same period was even greater at 62 per cent. The First World War increased the demand for manufactured goods relative to wheat, which led, in turn, to further concentration of population and economic oppor-

Table 6:12 Population of Canada, by Regions, Resident in Urban Areas in Census Years, 1851-1971

(per cent)

Year	Nfld.	Maritime Provinces	Quebec	Ontario	Prairie Provinces	British Columbia	Canada
(1)	(2)	(3)	(4)	(5)	(6)	(7)	(8)
1851	—	9.0	14.9	14.0	—	—	13.1
1861	—	9.9	16.6	18.5	—	—	15.8
1871	—	11.9	19.9	20.6	—	9.0	18.3
1881	—	15.3	23.8	27.1	14.9[a]	18.3	23.3
1891	—	18.8	28.6	35.0	23.3[a]	42.6	29.8
1901	—	24.5	36.1	40.3	19.3	46.4	34.9
1911	—	30.9	44.5	49.5	27.9	50.9	41.8
1921	—	38.8	51.8	58.8	28.7	50.9	47.4
1931	—	39.7	59.5	63.1	31.3	62.3	52.5
1941	—	44.1	61.2	67.5	32.4	64.0	55.7
1951	43.3	47.4	66.8	72.5	44.5	68.6	62.4
1961	50.7	49.5	74.3	77.3	57.6	72.6	69.7
1971	57.2	50.6	80.6	82.4	65.3	75.7	76.1

[a] These figures are for Manitoba only.

Note: The definition of urban is a densely settled built-up locality with a population greater than 1,000 persons. Figures after 1941 include Newfoundland.

Sources: L. O. Stone, *Urban Development in Canada* (Ottawa, 1968), p. 29 and Kubat and Thornton (1974), pp. 12-14.

tunities in urban areas. At the same time, mechanization in agriculture turned many farmers, or their children, into underemployed workers. The 1930s brought a dampening influence of the urbanizing factors: Immigration and population growth in general declined, demand for the products of non-primary industries fell, the rate of investment declined, and as a result the rate of urbanization fell to its lowest level since 1851.

With the Second World War there was a return of conditions which stimulated rapid urbanization. Industrial research began on a large scale and many new industries emerged, such as synthetic rubber, Diesel engine, and aircraft manufacturing; in industries like steel, capacity was permanently enlarged. These changes were interrelated with an upsurge in the level of urbanization in the postwar decades of prosperity which were accompanied by the development of oil, natural gas, pulp and paper, automobile industries, and changes in transport and communications. In contrast, the rural population, in absolute terms, declined at about an average of 2 per cent per decade from 1941 to the present.[38]

In summary, although the long-run trend was a shift from a rural- to an urban-based society, no trend emerged in the rates of urban population growth. There are upswings and downswings in the pace of urbanization.

Relatively high peaks appear for 1851-61 and 1901-11, with less prominent peaks in 1871-81 and 1951-61, and troughs in 1861-71, 1891-1901, and
1931-41. This dating is entirely in keeping with what might be expected
from the earlier discussion, that urban growth was a reflection of the net
expected returns from migrating. In view of the earlier commentary on
international migration, it is no surprise that the rates of net immigration
and urban population growth moved in a consistent fashion.

CHAPTER SEVEN

Labour

Introduction

In Canadian history, most labour supplied to employers in the economy has been voluntarily offered. While economic circumstances often narrowly circumscribed the range of choice which each worker faced, it was, nevertheless, this freedom which marked labour as the unique factor of production. Because, historically only the individual worker supplied labour service, certain rights became associated with labour and the manner in which it was supplied in the factor markets.

Labour, unlike any other factor, remained free to set its own reservation price. This simply means that each worker decided whether the wage benefits which accrue to an extra hour of work offset the personal benefits which result from that hour spent at leisure. The long-run decline in the average length of the working week in manufacturing industries is generally attributed to the individual's increasing ability to indulge preferences for leisure as real income rises. The second feature of labour in production, which distinguishes it from all other factors, is the capacity for workers to learn on the job which leads to increased productivity. "Learning by doing" is the term which describes this ability, evident throughout history, which marks people's adaptability. The learning ability, as judged by productivity gains, proceeded most rapidly when the worker was relatively new at his assigned task, and was common in every endeavour which required human labour. Third, labour in modern history has been accorded the right to offer its services collectively. Suppliers of other factors have been denied such a right; in fact, such combination is usually forbidden by law. Undoubtedly, labour's right to unionize evolved as a response to the apparent unfairness of final- and factor-market distortions in which labour alone was usually the price-taker. "United to support, not combined to injure" was the motto of the Toronto Typographical Society, adopted in 1844 by its fifteen founding members. These three characteristics give labour its unique status as a factor of production.

Since part of Canada's industrialization, which will be examined in more detail in the following chapters, was to encompass the emergence of secondary manufacturing and the growth of specialized trades and professions, a skilled labour force was essential to economic development. Temporary labour-market shortages tended to retard the speed of expansion. This chapter will examine the historical evolution of labour markets in the context of labour's twofold economic role as producer and consumer.[1]

Growth and Composition of the Workforce

Between 1851 and 1961 the Canadian work force grew from 762,000 to 6,621,000 persons. Although the average annual growth was at a rate of less than two per cent, the more than sevenfold increase in the labour force was not always smooth or continuous. Often the workforce grew very rapidly due to large net immigration. When it did the economy necessarily escaped the costs of investment in the training of workers induced to migrate to Canada. The economy was also spared the time cost of training workers. Within a short time period, new types of labour could be imported fully trained. In this manner, the open economy proved responsive to industrial demands and the pace and type of labour-force expansion seems seldom to have been a serious constraint on economic growth. However, while this rapid expansion of the labour force was a vital factor of aggregate economic growth, it sometimes produced little or no per-capita income gains in real terms.

The economic circumstances which produced the growth and change in the composition of the labour force varied. Nevertheless, certain trends can be seen. If the labour supply, for the moment, is considered to be the total number of people in the labour force, then its growth depended on:

1) the growth of the population;
2) the proportion of the population in the labour-force age group; and
3) the proportion of this group which offered itself to the aggregate labour market—the labour-force participation rate.

For instance, if L is the labour supply, P_{+14} the Canadian population which is fourteen years old or older, and P the total Canadian population then the labour supply may be represented by:

$$L \equiv (L/P_{+14}) \cdot (P_{+14}/P) \cdot P$$

Any combination of a rising labour-force participation rate (L/P_{+14}), rising proportion of the population in the working-age group (P_{+14}/P), or rising total population (P) increased Canada's labour supply. Since these three measures indicate the sources of labour-force growth, it is necessary to examine their long-run behaviour (Table 7:1).

The main outline of labour-force growth was similar to that of the total population. While the factors accounting for this population growth are mentioned elsewhere, it is worth noting again that the contribution of domestic sources to population, and therefore to labour-force, growth overshadowed that from net immigration except in the early twentieth century and during the early 1950s. About two-thirds of the labour-force growth came from net immigration during these two periods. But normally it was the almost continuous rise in the proportion of the population fourteen years and older from 1851 to at least 1941 which increased the labour force. The only exception was in the aftermath of the First World War when, due to an increase in the number of births, there was a general lowering of the age of the population. In general, had the P_{+14}/P ratio been the same in 1851 as it was in 1931, then the labour force in 1851 would have been about 951,000 instead of 762,000. So, the long-run rise in the proportion of the population fourteen years and older over these years ranks as a significant contribution to labour-force growth. Since 1941, this proportion has fallen because of the postwar baby boom although it will undoubtedly rise again in the late twentieth century.

In contrast to the changing age distribution of the population there was no significant trend in the overall labour-force participation rate. It was relatively stable throughout the years from 1851. Yet, this relative constancy hides divergent trends in the male and female labour-force participation rates which altered the labour force's composition. When L^f represents the female labour force, P^f_{+14} the total female population fourteen years and older, L^m the male labour force, P^m_{+14} the male population fourteen years and older, and since the overall labour-force participation rate is a weighted average of the male and female rates, the weights being the proportions of the population fourteen years and older which are respectively male and female, then the overall labour-force participation rate may be represented by:

$$\frac{L}{P_{+14}} \equiv \left(\frac{L^f}{P^f_{+14}} \cdot \frac{P^f_{+14}}{P_{+14}} \right) + \left(\frac{L^m}{P^m_{+14}} \cdot \frac{P^m_{+14}}{P_{+14}} \right)$$

Table 7:1 Labour-Force Growth and Its Components, 1851-1971

Year	L(th)	$\dfrac{L}{P_{+14}}$	$\dfrac{P_{+14}}{P}$	P(th)
(1)	(2)	(3)	(4)	(5)
1851	762	.560	.559	2436
1861	1053	.566	.576	3230
1871	1201	.557	.584	3689
1881	1474	.556	.613	4325
1891	1732	.563	.636	4833
1901	1885	.530	.662	5371
1911	2799	.574	.677	7207
1921	3303	.562	.669	8788
1931	4042	.559	.697	10377
1941	4652	.552	.732	11507
1951[a]	5250	.545	.688	14009
1961[a]	6621	.553	.656	18238
1971[ab]	8539	.576	.706	20993

[a] Excludes Newfoundland.
[b] For those fifteen years of age and older.

Sources: F. Denton and S. Ostry, *Historical Estimates of the Canadian Labour Force* (Ottawa, 1967), p. 20-29; D. Kubat and D. Thornton, *Statistical Profile of Canadian Society* (Toronto, 1974), pp. 12-15; and Canada, *Census 1971: Labour Force and Individual Income*, Vol. 3, pp. 1-2.

Therefore, any trend in the overall rate was a function of changes in the male and female participation rates and in the proportion of the population fourteen years and older which was female. Since the female participation rate was historically lower than the male rate any upward trend in the adult female population proportion alone tended to lower the overall rate. But as we shall see, the trend in L^f/P^f_{+14} dominates and is the more interesting.

Sex-specific participation rates and the relevant population proportion are illustrated in Table 7:2. From 1901 to 1961, by census years, distinct trends emerged. They were:

1) a rise in the female participation rate;
2) a decline in the male participation rate;
3) a rise in the proportion of the population fourteen years and older which was female. Immigration tended to prevent the adjustment of the sex ratio to natural symmetry, although this has not been the case since 1945.

In addition to the effects of the population changes, there was a drop in the male participation rate mainly in the age groups fourteen to nine-

Table 7:2 Labour-Force Participation Rates, by Sex, 1901-1961

Year	$\dfrac{L}{P_{+14}}$	$\dfrac{L^m}{P^m_{+14}}$	$\dfrac{L^f}{P^f_{+14}}$	$\dfrac{P^f_{+14}}{P^{f+m}_{+14}}$
(1)	(2)	(3)	(4)	(5)
1901	.530	.878	.161	.486
1911	.574	.906	.186	.461
1921	.562	.898	.199	.480
1931	.559	.872	.218	.478
1941	.552	.856	.229	.486
1951	.545	.844	.244	.498
1961	.553	.811	.293	.498
1971[a]	.573	.757	.392	.504

[a] For those 15 years of age and older.

Sources: S. Ostry, "The Canadian Labour Market", in R. U. Miller and F. Isbister, eds. *Canadian Labour in Transition* (Scarborough, 1971), p. 20 and *Census 71*, Vol. 3, pp. 1-2.

teen years and sixty-five years and over. These were brought about respectively by the necessity for longer periods of formal education and the possibilities of early retirement due to the increased old-age assistance, the extension of pension benefits, and the institution of compulsory retirement. Alone this age-specific change accounted for a reduction of approximately ten per cent in the male participation between the beginning of the twentieth century and 1961. Female participation, on the other hand, increased for every age grouping below the retirement age of sixty-five. Especially for women between the ages of thirty-five and sixty-four there was a doubling of proportionate representation in the workforce—from 16 per cent in 1901 to approximately 33 per cent in the late 1960s.

There were many reasons for the trends in the female participation rate.[2] Yet, behind each cause which induced a greater female participation in the workforce was either a fall in the opportunity cost of females working or a rise in the opportunity cost of females staying out of the labour force. As the state of the economy changed from agricultural and rural to manufacturing, service, and urban, employment opportunities for women in the lower- and middle-level white-collar jobs expanded, especially in education, health, welfare, recreation, government, retail sales, and secretarial and clerical activities. Similarly, on the supply side, industrial and academic education for women became more common in the late nineteenth century than it had been earlier and expansion during the twentieth century made many more women employable. The trend in recent years toward a shortening of the work week, the growth in part-time employment, and increased specialization has also made it possible for more women to enter the labour force.

So too, changes in employer and community attitudes led to greater social acceptance of women who work. During the two world wars, this increasing social acceptance was accelerated by the labour shortages which drew women into occupations previously restricted to men. The new social attitudes formed in a highly urbanized society and the secular increase in salaries and wage rates likewise attracted females to the workplace. Labour-saving household appliances and factory-prepared food for the home also introduced a new flexibility in to the pattern of family life which permitted more women than formerly to work for wages while still maintaining the household. Yet, of all causes, it was the decline in the number of children which had to be cared for which most readily permitted release from household duties. Of course, the decline in family size might also, in a less immediate sense, have been an effect. Of all the changes in the composition of the Canadian labour supply it is the change in its sexual make-up which is one of the most interesting and significant.

However, it should not be imagined that the role of women was historically unimportant. To the contrary, to the extent that women were part of a production team—on farms, for example—their services generally went unrecorded as historical evidence; the same is probably also true of children. In the early nineteenth century the unrecorded role of women must have made a substantial contribution to actual value added in the economy. So too, it might be noted that in the nineteenth and early twentiety centuries the direct employment of women in domestic service may have accounted for as much as three to five per cent of GNP.

If labour force is measured by man-hours, rather than by numbers of people, then the average hours worked per unit of time becomes an important consideration in determining the total labour force. Since Confederation, the standard hours worked per week in manufacturing—the only consistent measure recorded for this entire period—fell from over 60 to about 40 hours.[3] This was almost exactly the same as the U.S. experience. A decline of over 8 hours from 1901 to 1921 and of over 7.5 hours since the 1940s accounts for most of the change. It seems likely that the trend in manufacturing was also true for the economy at large. Certainly, corroboration exists in more recent history. One reason for this decline was the pressure from trade unions expressing the desire of their members to take more of their available hours as leisure when incomes rose. Begun in the 1870s, with workers' groups aptly styled "the Nine-Hours Leaguers", labour pressure to reduce the length of the work week continued well into recent times. As well, the minimum age of employment rose along with the maximum number of hours worked. Direct government attempts to reduce the length of the work week were probably of little consequence, however, and as the experience of the 1930s demonstrates, when a maximum number of hours was placed on the work week of most adult males the actual number of hours worked barely registered any change.

Coupled with the growth in total labour force was a regional reallocation of labour within Canada. Before about 1900 Canada's labour force was concentrated east of Manitoba; in fact, in 1891 the four western provinces or territories contained only approximately 8 per cent of the total labour force. But this increased dramatically to 26 per cent by 1911 and held steady at that percentage thereafter. This period, from 1891 to 1911, saw the largest displacement of Canada's labour force in its history and attests to the significance of prairie settlement in Canadian economic history. By 1911 the spatial distribution of Canada's labour force was virtually complete and very little displacement took place after that date; in other words, provincial labour-force growth rates converged around the overall, national growth rate after the so-called frontier stage of settlement.

The determinants of labour-supply growth were of course closely linked to its changing composition by industry and occupation. Although the extent of the shifts in labour-supply composition can only be precise for the census years after 1851, enough is known of early industrial development to give a fairly accurate description of labour-force structure prior to the census of 1851.

In early New France, for instance, the vast majority of labour was devoted to fur trading, fishing, and agricultural and related pursuits.[4] By the middle of the seventeenth century more and more of the workers were not directly involved in primary production and a new managerial, professional class of workers emerged. Under Jean Talon in the 1660s and 1670s, manufacturing industries expanded rapidly, as they were also to do in the 1740s and 1750s, but the growth of the demand for labour emanated entirely from the sectors of manufacturing closely allied to natural-resource exploitation: shipyards, iron smelters, breweries, tanneries and mills. Yet because of the small scale of the enterprises few of these new occupations were actually practised in urban centres. While a relatively large proportion of New France's population was urban by 1750 (25 per cent), it reflected more the growth of employment in commercial activity, administration, and military pursuits. The towns and villages outside Quebec City, Montreal, and Trois-Rivières served as rural service centres. In sum, the labour force of New France reflected the relatively unsophisticated economy in which people worked mainly in primary industries, farming and trapping, with some lumbering, or in industries which transported or processed the primary products.

One hundred years later, in 1851, in Upper and Lower Canada combined, 37 per cent of the occupied population belonged to the "agricultural class" alone whereas an additional 38 per cent were miners,
fishermen, and lumbermen.[5] Thus, the primary-industry workers were an
exceptionally large proportion of the working population. On the other
hand, 2.6 per cent were of the "professional class", and 16 per cent of the
"industrial class". While non-primary occupations grew and expanded
from 1763 to 1851 — foundries, boot and shoe factories, brickyards,
tobacco factories, banks, furniture plants, and shipyards, to mention only
a few — the working population was concentrated in the primary occupations during the first half of the nineteenth century, and the proportion in
these occupations may have in fact increased from, say, the 1790s.
Likewise, in both New Brunswick and Nova Scotia, the "agricultural
class" was the largest grouping of the employed population in 1851.

Twenty years later, in 1871, the expansion of primary production other
than agriculture was such that for Canada as a whole, 51.3 per cent of all
gainfully employed persons were in the primary occupations.[6] Although
the structure of employment was virtually unchanged by 1881, the proportion of the workforce in primary production did fall to 49.4 per cent
over the course of the next decade. As will be seen in more detail later,
the 1870s and 1880s marked an important turning point in the occupational structure of Canada. Prior to this time, employment in the primary
sector expanded in relative importance to the Canadian labour force, but
afterward there was a long-term decline in its importance. Even during
the first two decades of the twentieth century when commercial agricultural production on the prairies expanded rapidly the downward trend in
the proportion of employment in the primary sector continued as non-
primary employment increased.

We may hypothesize that two factors caused these changes in the
structure of the labour force: the invariant structure of human wants (the
demand side) and changes on the production side that affect the structure of final demand (the supply side). Implicitly, if demands among the
major expenditure sectors are relatively constant over time, income
elasticities of demand will be constant also. If it is further shown, or
assumed, that the income elasticity of the primary sector is low and for
the other sectors high, then the rising incomes which Canada experienced
can explain the broad sector changes noted above. Earlier we identified
the above as Engel's law. But changes on the production side have
perhaps been even more important than this supposed invariance of demand.

The technology of modern industry and urbanization meant that consumers, now living in cities, required products that were not essential in

the more usual setting of the nineteenth century. Even for food, urban demand needed greater fabrication, transport, and distribution, all outside the primary sector, than it had in an earlier period. This imposed pattern of consumption, caused by changing styles of life, brought with it a greater increase in demand for the products of the construction-manufacturing and tertiary sectors than for the products of the primary sector. As well, greater specialization and the increase in the national pattern of concentration of production caused a greater need for transport and distribution than that required by smaller plants serving local markets. In addition, technological change during the last two centuries, even with an invariant structure of human wants, pushed the balance of consumption, and employment, to construction-manufacturing and tertiary production. For example, there has been a long-run substitution of railways, automobiles, and aeroplanes for the horse in transport.

Part of the expansion in the tertiary sector was also due to the greater demand for government services. An explanation for this covering both the causal factors above, can be found in the so-called "Wagner's Law". Adolph Wagner reckoned that there would be a long-run expansion of state expenditures relative to total expenditures as per-capita income rose.[7] He offered three reasons for this. First, an expansion would come about because of the increasing administrative and protective duties of government brought about by the substitution of public for private activity. New needs for public regulation and protection would develop from the increased complexity of legal relationships and communications that accompany greater labour division with modern industry. Increases in population density and urbanization lead to increased government expenditures on law and order and on economic regulation in order to maintain the efficient performance of the economy in the face of urban complexities. Second, the income elasticity of demand for many government-supplied products, like education and welfare, is greater than unity so that proportionately more of them would be demanded as incomes rose. Third, the inevitable changes in technology and the increasing scale of investment required would create an increasing number of large private companies with a great deal of market power whose effect the government must offset in the interests of economic efficiency. In other cases, like transport, the scale of capital formation was so great that it could only be financed, directly or otherwise, by the government.

The major shifts in the composition of the Canadian labour force by *industry* of course had a direct bearing on the *occupational* distribution of labour.[8] Table 7:3, for instance, records the broad features of industrial change: the increased relative importance of tertiary activity, the

Table 7:3 Percentage Distribution of Persons Working, by Industry, 1881-1961

(omitting 1941)

Year	Primary Sector	Manufacturing and Construction Sector	Tertiary Sector
(1)	(2)	(3)	(4)
1881	51.2	29.4	19.4
1891	49.5	26.3	24.2
1901	44.3	27.9	27.8
1911	39.5	27.1	33.4
1921	36.6	26.5	36.9
1931	32.6	16.5	50.9
1951	23.3	33.2	43.5
1961	14.2	30.2	55.6

Sources: O. J. Firestone, *Canada's Economic Development* (London, 1958), p. 185 and S. G. Peitchinis, *Canadian Labour Economics* (Toronto, 1970), p. 73.

decreased relative importance of primary activity, and the relative long-run constancy of the proportion of the workforce in the manufacturing sector. The occupational structure of the workforce mirrors this change:

1) From over 50 per cent in 1881 the proportion of the workforce with occupations directly associated with primary economic activity fell below 16 per cent in 1961.
2) There was a long-run expansion of the personal-service occupations, from 8.2 to 12.4 per cent between 1901 and 1961.
3) The number of white-collar jobs — managerial, professional, clerical, commercial, and financial, among others — expanded so rapidly that they currently form the most prevalent type of occupation in Canadian society. No less than 57.3 per cent of the work force were white-collar workers in 1961 compared with only some 15 per cent at the beginning of this century.

A detailed account of the changing industrial composition of employment is only available for the twentieth century. However, from the information presented in Table 7:4, it can be seen that the growth of the tertiary sector took place mainly in the sub-sectors of trade, education, health and welfare, and public administration. Of those classes whose percentage fell between 1911 and 1961, agriculture accounts for 70 per cent of the total relative losses and, of course, was reflected in the rural-urban shift noted earlier. The expansion of other labour-market opportunities was, on the other hand, widespread. Even within manufacturing,

Table 7:4 Workforce, by Industry, 1911 and 1961

| | Industry Class | Percentage Distribution | |
		1911	1961
	(1)	(2)	(3)
I	Agriculture	34.19	9.90
II	Fishing and Trapping	1.28	0.54
III	Forestry	1.57	1.68
IV	Mining	2.14	1.85
V	Manufacturing	17.38	21.81
VI	Electricity and Gas	0.39	0.97
VII	Construction	7.31	7.22
VIII	Transportation	6.65	7.02
IX	Trade	9.54	15.34
X	Finance, Insurance, and Real Estate	1.35	3.54
XI	Services	12.11	19.49
XII	Public Administration	2.87	8.21
XIII	Others	3.22	2.45
Total Workforce		100.00	100.00
Number of Workers		(2,725,140)	(6,458,156)

Note: Manufacturing includes primary as well as secondary manufacturing such as pulp and paper, primary steel production, and others.

Source: R. M. McInnis, "Long-Run Changes in the Industrial Structure of the Canadian Work Force", *Canadian Journal of Economics*, Vol. 4, no. 3 (1971), pp. 356-57.

where employment grew least rapidly, some sub-sectors such as pulp and paper, chemicals, petroleum refining, electrical apparatus and rubber goods, which represented the new industries of the twentieth century, expanded in relative labour employment terms.

At the level of sub-national units, the structure of the labour force differed, but what concerns us here is whether the structures of these units converged with or diverged from the national structure.[9] Dividing the labour force into three sectors, namely primary (excluding mining), mining-manufacturing, and services-construction, provincial labour-force structures were more dissimilar in 1956 than in 1891 but less so than they had been in 1910 or 1929. The frontier, wheat-boom era saw structures diverge dramatically, but they showed a tendency to converge thereafter. The main shift towards structural divergence took place in the years of greatest population growth and internal migration, 1890 to 1914 (see Chapter 6); the decades of vast immigration and western settlement contributed to regional specialization.

Of the three sectors, the primary and mining-manufacturing sectors clearly demonstrate a divergence of regional structures, suggesting that the distribution of workers in these sectors among the provinces became more concentrated. Structural rigidity sets in through time in the composition of production and employment between provinces. For the primary sector as defined here, it became increasingly concentrated in the prairies as we might expect given the nature of the westward population movements. Mining and manufacturing became increasingly concentrated in Ontario and Quebec with the biggest increase occurring between 1890 and 1910; as has been argued elsewhere, central Canada established early its dominance in secondary-manufacturing activity and mining. The nature of the products from the services and construction sector suggests that this kind of activity will be widely dispersed with little regional concentration: high transport costs prohibit long-distance trade. This expectation is true; production has been widely diffused among the provinces as each requires a certain minimum level of output from this sector regardless of income level.

The Structure of Wages

The long-run expansion of the Canadian economy produced two effects on labour's aggregate and individual rewards. First, the *share* of income distributed to labour has demonstrated a relative constancy over most of recent history—a constancy which of course has a bearing on any assessment of the influence of organized labour. Second, one of the most striking features of modern economic development has been the long-run increase in real wages, both in absolute terms and relative to the returns to other factors of production.

To be sure, the evidence for the constancy of labour's share of income is less complete than one would wish despite its consistency. In general, labour of all types received approximately 75 per cent of all income; capitalists received the bulk of the remainder.

Within labour's share, however, there has been no such constancy. For instance, there has been a general rise in the share of income paid to wage and salary earners—employees—and a fall in the share of receipts to entrepreneurs and self-employed. Between 1926-29 and 1954-60, in Canada, there was an increase in the share of national income as the compensation of employees from 59 to 66 per cent, while the share going to entrepreneurs and the self-employed fell from 25 to 13 per cent.[10] The major factor in the expanded share of compensation of employees was probably the rise in the share of employees in the total labour force; this was due to shifts in industrial structure and primarily reflects the transfer of labour from self-employment in agriculture to employee status elsewhere. Agriculture and related industries have been characterized by small-scale firms and high proportions of entrepreneurs and self-employed to the labour force attached to the sector. In addition, even in the manufacturing and service sectors producing units tended to increase in scale and become incorporated, and therefore led to a reduction in the ratio of entrepreneurs and self-employed to the total labour force or an increase in the share of employees in the labour force. This shift had other ramifications. There were changes in the basis of economic life and planning which, in turn, reshaped attitudes toward family and children, in patterns of consumption, and in the propensity to invest in education and training relative to the inclination to save for investment in business and elsewhere. Trends in the relative shares of compensation of employees and of income of entrepreneurs tend to reflect shifts in the distribution of the labour force by status and these reflect changes in the economic base of life of the persons involved and hence changes in the patterns of behaviour.

The calculated share of national income which accrued to wage and salary earners of course did increase before the twentieth century. From at least the 1850s onward there was a significant rise in the number of employees, wage and salary recipients, and a long-run rise in the compensation of wage and salary earners relative to the return of labour in farming—as opposed to land rents and the return to capital. The number of self-employed as a proportion of the total labour force also declined. In the late nineteenth century, the size of production units in the tertiary and secondary sectors increased and as many businesses became incorporated the measured self-employment of the labour force was reduced. For the modern period of 1926-30 to 1954-58, approximately 70 per cent of the change in the share going to wage and salary earners was a direct consequence of the structural shift of industry. The remaining 30 per cent of the change seems, in all likelihood, attributable to improvements in the quality of labour and other efficiency gains.

The established structure of wages at any moment in history was the market clearing wages for various occupations. Occupations with high skill components tended to be better rewarded than those with relatively low skill components because of the relative abundance of unskilled labour. This is evident in Table 7:5 which presents the structure of wage rates for a year in the last quarter of the nineteenth century. The relative position in the ranking, in fact, changed little in subsequent years. Scarce types of labour, of course, earned an economic rent which, in Canada, was directly associated with the opportunity cost of labour in the United States.

Exactly what standard of living was achieved by the urban, industrial wage earner is little understood. Yet, in all likelihood, most families whose members depended on earned income, found that saving was impossible and that all of their income was spent on the most rudimentary

Table 7:5 Structure of Wages in Ontario, 1884

Occupation	Number of Hours Worked Per Week	Weekly Wages	Hourly Rate
(1)	(2)	(3) ($)	(4) (¢ per hour)
Butcher	58.42	10.00	17.1
Carpenter	59.08	9.85	16.7
Cotton Mill Workers—Corder	59.55	8.26	13.8
—Loom Fixer	59.46	10.71	18.0
—Spinner	59.45	7.69	12.9
Labourer	58.56	6.79	11.6
Machinist	59.25	9.96	16.8
Millwright	60.17	12.22	20.3
Paper Mill Machine Tender	59.00	12.06	20.4
Plumber	60.00	10.84	18.1
Printer	58.33	9.37	16.1

Note: The sample of wages used to compute the above averages was based on returns for the last weeks of both April and October. Data are for male workers over sixteen years of age.

Sources: M. C. Urquhart and K. A. H. Buckley, eds., *Historical Statistics of Canada* (Toronto, 1965), p. 93.

basic requirements. In 1900, in the city of Montreal, for example, the average weekly income for males employed in manufacturing was about $7.78; wages for women in Montreal were about $3.65 per week; young boys and girls earned even less.[11] Using a Department of Labour family budget study, we can deduce that it would have required a weekly expenditure of $9.64 for basic food and shelter and $13.77 for the total needs of a five-member family.[12] By 1911, adult male workers averaged only $10.55 per week in Montreal with women and children averaging $6 and $4 per week respectively. Inflation over the decade increased the level of expenditure to $12.82 per week for basics and $18.31 for the total budget. At this time, skilled building tradesmen earned only $13.70, building construction labourers $10.21, and trainmen $18.67. By 1921, the average situation of the Montreal wage earners had changed relatively little. The average weekly income of $23.40 for hourly wage earners in the peak earning years, even when taking into consideration the fact that 1920-21 were years of recession, is below the minimum necessary to meet basic needs as established by the Department of Labour. Yet, the average weekly incomes for adult male workers employed on an hourly basis—about two-thirds of the city's employed—were about 20 per cent below the apparent poverty line. Only if more than one person in the family worked would family incomes rise beyond the level necessary to purchase basic food, shelter, and clothing requirements. In terms of family income, the situation does appear to have been somewhat better: $28.54 per week in manufacturing; $28.50 per week in construction; and $29.52 per week in transport. Indeed, during the first thirty or forty years of the twentieth century and earlier, Montreal's wage earners were unable to make the minimum required income for basic family food, clothing, and shelter unless relatively full employment prevailed and there were two wage earners in the family. It has yet to be established if this was characteristic of other Canadian urban areas.

For the wider economy it is extremely difficult to trace the pattern of real wages in history. On the other hand, the course of money wages, at least in the twentieth century, is better known (see Figure 7:1). During the wheat-boom decade of 1901-11, for instance, money wages in general rose by 29 per cent. Although there is considerable controversy about how much of this money gain was real, the best current estimate is that real wages might have risen by as much as 11.1 per cent. Despite the rise in real wages, in the decade 1901-11 there were subsequent declines which were only offset by the next spurt in real wages during the few years after the First World War.[13]

Both money and real wages increased only modestly in the 1920s but this was immediately followed by a fall in money wages during the depression of the 1930s. This was due to the more rapid contraction of the demand for than the supply of labour. Yet, real wages may have risen at this time. From 1929 to 1933, money wages fell by about 14 per cent while the cost-of-living index declined by approximately 22 per cent. The worker with a job may have been better off, but unemployment rose dramatically. For the rest of the decade, money wages increased faster than prices. Such a trend of wages increasing more rapidly than prices gave rise to the longest sustained real gain in history, after the Second World War. Figure 7:1 records that money wages rose 131 per cent from 1946 to 1960, whereas the consumer price index rose approximately 65 per cent. At the level of the individual industry, real wages tended to reflect the direction of labour shifts required in the factor markets: real wages were nearly always higher in expanding industries than in contracting ones and patterns of rewards were such that they induced the pattern of employment described earlier. The demand for labour was, after all, a derived demand.

Organized Labour: Unionism

The growth of and changes in the composition of Canada's labour force took place within labour markets where institutional frameworks were continually changing. One of the earliest labour-market institutions to

Figure 7:1 Index of Average Wage Rates for Industry, 1901-1960 (1949 = 100.0)

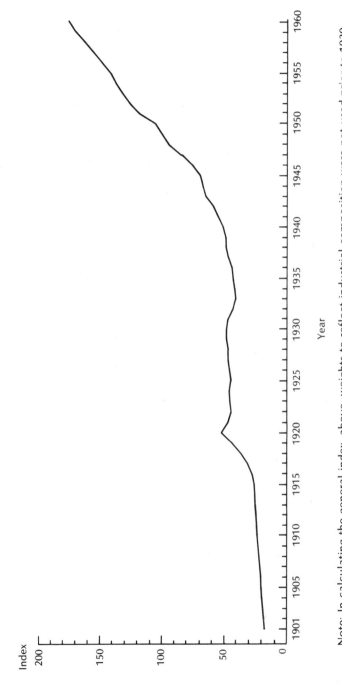

Note: In calculating the general index, above, weights to reflect industrial composition were not used prior to 1939.

Source: Data are from M. C. Urquhart and K. A. H. Buckley, eds., *Historical Statistics of Canada* (Toronto, 1965), p. 84.

emerge in Canadian history and one which played a varying but ever-present role was the union. Trade unions, labour unions, and their modern offshoot, the trade association, have all been dedicated to the collective protection and enhancement of their members' economic and social well-being. Exactly how effective these institutions have been is a matter of some controversy.

An examination of the economic impact of unionism must consider three issues:

1) What were the conditions which caused labour to organize? Distinction must be made between those long-run determinants which induced a growing proportion of the Canadian labour force to join trade and labour unions and the proximate economic conditions which often caused relatively intense support for but also benign neglect of these labour institutions.

2) The history of Canadian trade unionism differs markedly from that of other industrial countries. In particular, the economic development of the open economy created a hybrid labour institution, the international union. Its development, in turn, often inspired anti-U.S. labour sentiment, the creation of national and regional labour organizations, and increased government participation in the labour markets.

3) Trade and labour unions had an impact on labour markets by affecting labour mobility, the pace of technological change, and the relative employment of labour to other factors of production.

What is the evidence that these influences were important historically?

Returning to the first issue, what general, long-term conditions carried trade-union membership from a negligible proportion of Canada's total non-agricultural paid workers in the pre-1850 period to over 30 per cent of such workers in the 1960s?[14] Neglecting for the moment fascinating short-term trends, such as the nearly static position of the trade unions in the 1920s, there were three main determinants of organized labour's growth:

1) the evolution of attitudes and ideologies in support of unionism;

2) changes in the structure of labour markets often gave support to the cause of united labour activity; and

3) the strategic role of the employer in the industrial structure which often caused working persons to consider the collective solution.[15]

Both individual and community attitudes towards the collective action of labour became more tolerant as an increasing proportion of workers found employment in the manufacturing and tertiary sectors and as the workforce became more highly urbanized. But this had not always been the case. When the naval dockyard workers in Quebec City combined to strike in 1750, Intendant Hocquart incarcerated the leaders as, in his view, it was the only way to deal with such rabble and forestall other action. Throughout the nineteenth and early twentieth centuries, the Canadian community, as evidenced by government legislation for instance often viewed trade-union leaders as "radicals", even "outlaws", whose actions had to be curbed by controls. Only in more recent years has there been a more flexible attitude towards union activity.

The development of Canada's industrial structure strongly influenced the changing attitudes and beliefs of both employees and the wider society. Trade-union movements, for instance, were more likely to develop in urban settings where employment was concentrated in manufacturing, construction, and transport than in rural societies where primary industries, especially agriculture, predominated. As noted earlier, the Canadas of the eighteenth and nineteenth centuries, with its reliance on primary production and small related manufacturing concerns, lacked the impetus for a trade-union movement of any consequence.[16] In such a society it was often thought that only work led to personal advancement, that leisure was a vice, that economic destiny depended only on a person's ability to work and save, that poverty aptly rewarded sloth, that the poor deserved their fate, and that social-welfare schemes encouraged idleness. What might be called the "rural ethic" put a person's economic state into his own hands. Even though trade unions and their supporting social philosophy appeared in Great Britain and the United States before 1850, inadequate communications networks, the small size of firms which produced only for the domestic market in most manufacturing and service industries, and the small and scattered population hindered their spread and acceptance throughout Canada. Whether rural or urban workers, most people expected to advance by their own efforts to the employer's role: The farm hand looked forward to owning his farm; the urban labourer did not see himself as permanently trapped and cherished some notions of being upwardly mobile in both an occupational and social sense. Trade-union growth was generally slow where employees expected to rise from the status of wage earners. Whether warranted or not such attitudes were widely held in the Canadas of the eighteenth and early nineteenth centuries.

But from the last three decades of the nineteenth century attitudes began to change with the experiences of modern industrialization and its better communications, its urbanization, factory system, division of labour, the rise of manufacturing and tertiary sectors, foreign influences, and market concentrations of power. Modern industry created a society which was predominately made up of wage and salary earners who expected to spend all of their productive lives as wage earners. As the location of manufacturing stablized a large proportion of any Canadian work community expected to remain in the same circumstance indefinitely. The vision of upward occupational and social mobility if not lost was tarnished. As well as individual values, community views and standards changed. New social attitudes were imported from the labour movements of Europe and rapidly assimilated and so an atmosphere grew within which trade unions were tolerated. In Canada, the change in attitude markedly gathered pace during both world wars and in the depressed 1930s; the result was legislation supporting trade unions and their activities as well as the creation of state facilities to aid the process of labour bargaining.

The creation of a tolerant legal environment was, in the long term, an important factor permitting trade- and labour-union growth. Employees may have the will to establish trade unions, but if such organizations are illegal or if the law narrowly constrains their activities then union growth is stunted. Government policy in Canada tended to accelerate growth of trade unions. This was accomplished within the federal system, which gave provincial governments the power to set the legal terms for most labour-organization and collective bargaining. Compared with other countries, Canada responded rapidly to labour demands to create the necessary legal framework.

The third factor stimulating the growth of organized labour appears to be the change in the strategic role of employees in the industrial structure. Employers naturally enough tended to resist the growth of trade unions within their particular business because it diminished their ability to command. Especially during the nineteenth and early twentieth centuries, before employees' rights to organize were clearly delineated, the organization of workers by use of the strike was often the only course available. Successful trade-union growth so often took place when employees had a strategic position within the labour market and their disruptive tactics gained the attention of management. The changes in production techniques, which gave power to some workers while denying it to others, were often associated with the new workplaces of the factory system and mass-production assembly lines. Such workplaces appeared more commonly in Canada during the last three decades of the nineteenth century. Trade unions generally appeared first in factories, and subsequently grew most rapidly among the skilled tradesmen—whence their name. Tradesmen were usually in relatively short supply and therefore occupied a strategic position in the workforce. By the mid-twentieth century employees' rights were established and organization by use of a formal ballot replaced organization by picket. With this change the creation of unions was less dependent on groups of strategic employees and more and more on the susceptibility to appeals for votes.

No working community is completely without organization since any group of people associated together for any length of time develop recognized standards of conduct and leadership. Historically, such informal organization precipitated formal trade and labour unions. However, since Canada has always been an open economy, labour markets within Canada were, not surprisingly, connected with similar markets in Great Britain and the United States. From early in the nineteenth century organized labour in Canada displayed an international character. While Labour Circles existed in Lower Canada in the 1820s and skilled workers like printers, carpenters, coopers, stonemasons, and shoemakers had organized themselves in Ontario and Quebec during the first half of the nineteenth century, the first major surge of trade unionism occurred subsequently between 1850 and 1870. Leadership and direction often came from U.S. unionists and British skilled workers.

The joint influence of the United States and Great Britain early determined that labour organization in Canada should have an international affiliation, and that trade unions should be organized along craft-skilled lines. British union influence extended in an explicit form only until about the 1870s, and while branches of the British-based unions of the Amalgamated Society of Carpenters and Joiners and of the Amalgamated Society of Engineers appeared, no further links were established. The reasons for this are arguable, but perhaps since labour flowed only from Great Britain to Canada, British trade-union leaders saw no threat from Canadian workers and therefore saw no sense in further organization. On the other hand, the rising mobility and competition between Canadian and U.S. labourers caused local unions in both countries to join during the 1860s. The International Typographical Union and the International Iron Moulders and Foundry Workers' Union of North America were among the leaders in this movement. Long before Canada had a "national" body representing its trade unions international unionism based on the usually larger U.S. local was firmly established.[17]

In the early years of Canadian trade unionism, craft organization was more prevalent than organization along factory lines. It suited best the groups of workers who, although employed in many industries, were concerned to limit competition within their craft. Any organization of labour along industrial lines would, of course, make any one craft a small minority in each union with a consequent loss of influence. Consequently, in order to maintain their exclusive role the craft or trade unions long sought to prevent its rise. Industrial unionism had to await the day when technology undermined the old craft distinctions by turning workers into semi-skilled people with jobs peculiar to one industry. Despite the relatively long dominance of the craft unions over the labour movement the rise of industrial labour could not be forestalled. As the new factory system placed more emphasis on the employment of unskilled or semi-skilled workers the pressure for the creation of this new type of organization grew. Often it was accompanied by new institutions spilling over from the United States.

There have been at least four distinct instances of U.S. labour organizations entering Canada since 1870. Perhaps spurred on by the common construction of railway lines, the railway brotherhoods of the United States were established in Canada during the 1870s and 1880s. Second, the Noble Order of the Knights of Labor, dedicated to the unionization of the unskilled and semi-skilled, organized its first local Canadian assembly in 1881. By 1890, the popularity of the Knights had spread and several affiliated locals and district assemblies were active in Canada. Next, U.S.-based organizations opposed to the politically conservative craft-union policy of the American Federation of Labor (AFL) such as the American Labor Union and the Industrial Workers of the World, organized branches among loggers, miners, and railway workers in British Columbia and Alberta during the early 1900s. Last of the major international affiliations, was the creation of new Canadian labour unions organized along industrial lines which joined the newly formed Committee for Industrial Organization (CIO) in the United States in the 1930s and 1940s.

Canadian trade and labour unions of purely domestic antecedents in industries such as baking, tailoring, bricklaying, bookbinding, and longshoring also appeared during the 1860s. However, there was no specific coordination of their activities which came only with the market expansion and the formation of trade councils in central Canadian cities in the next decade. The establishment of central organizations followed but because of the lack of adequate communications between workers in the east and west, the formation of a national organization was premature. At best the central organizations were only provincial in scope. However, as the economy spread, trade councils became more common in the cities, and a national centre, the Canadian Labour Congress, was finally established in 1883. This body took the name Trades and Labour Congress of Canada (TLC) in 1892, a name which it kept until 1956.

The other national organization which came to represent labour rather than trade unions, the Canadian Congress of Labour (CCL) was formed only in 1940. Its origins are complicated and go back to the beginning of the century. The American Federation of Labor and its member affiliates in the TLC representing the crafts brought pressure to bear in order to force the adoption by the TLC of exclusive jurisdiction of its member unions, over workers in specific trades, and the elimination of organizations which competed with affiliates. After several years of armed neutrality, the TLC in 1902 expelled trades assemblies of the Knights of Labor and some purely Canadian trade unions on the grounds that they competed with existing craft unions for members. In opposition to this rigid policy and subservience to the AFL, the expelled unions found a nationalistic labour federation, the National Trades and Labour Congress, which later renamed itself the Canadian Federation of Labour (CFL) in 1908. This organization was dedicated to organization along national rather than international lines, and merged labour's Canadian nationalism with that of the usual union functions. During the first decade of the twentieth century, it supported measures which promoted the development of Canadian industry and jobs, protested the import of boots and shoes from the United States, and backed the notion of a Canadian shipbuilding industry. Opposed to U.S. domination of Canada and AFL-TLC craft unionism, and supportive of a united Canadian union movement, the CFL carried forward in other organizations. In 1927 the CFL, the Canadian Brotherhood of Railway Employees—expelled from the TLC in 1921—and remnants of the western Canadian-based One Big Union, of which more later, formed the All-Canadian Congress of Labour (ACCL) which advocated the independence of the Canadian labour movement from foreign control and the organization of workers along industrial lines. Finally, in 1940, Canadian branches of several CIO international unions, expelled in the 1930s from the TLC, joined with the ACCL, itself riddled with defections, to form the CCL which operated in opposition to the TLC until 1956. The CCL was based on the appeal of industrial labour unionism, a policy of political action, and a more radical philosophy of government intervention in economic affairs.

In 1955 the AFL and CIO merged in the United States. The merger caused the Canadian labour movement's members to pause and consider the potential of a new organization. It seemed expedient and efficient for the CCL and the TLC to unite. After all, it was argued, the old issue of the prevalence of craft unions in central affairs was fast waning. Unification took place in 1956 with the formation of the Canadian Labour Congress, the new national body.[18]

Regional labour organizations as well as national ones also emerged in the early twentieth century, particularly in the areas west of Ontario and Quebec. In western Canada, this regional movement first appeared when some U.S.-based labour organizations, opposed to the AFL's conservative craft policies, set up locals in Canada. These encroachments during the first and second decades of the twentieth century caused western-based affiliates of the TLC to criticize their own leadership. Criticism was five-fold: an inability to organize unskilled and semi-skilled workers, domination by the AFL, too politically neutral, failure to oppose conscription during the First World War, and the concentration of labour power in Ontario. Above all, we see a militancy and an apparent working-class consciousness with anti-U.S. affiliation. In 1919, the British Columbia Federation of Labour called for a general strike to back support for a six-hour working day; a vote was to be taken among Canadian locals to decide on the strike, and U.S. locals were to be excluded. In the same year, the Western Labour Conference called for organization along industrial lines and a referendum among its Canadian memberships designed to settle the issue of disassociation from international unions.[19] Finally, in 1919, a group of western Canadian unions formed the One Big Union (OBU) in opposition to the TLC. A year earlier, the TLC had defeated a motion by Winnipeg locals to hold a referendum on the question of reorganizing workers on an industrial instead of a craft basis; resolutions from the west charging Ottawa with antagonism toward labour were also rejected. As a result, about two hundred labourers from the west met in Calgary in early 1919 and decided to set up the rival organization to the TLC.

But before the new body could be formed, the Winnipeg General Strike began. By mid-May of 1919 about 27,000 work people, and later others, had left their jobs. Sympathy strikes took place in Calgary, Brandon, Edmonton, Saskatoon, Regina, and Prince Albert. At the same time, the OBU was formed to provide for industrial organization where desirable. While the OBU gained support at the time of the Winnipeg General Strike, this union, with a number of others, declined in the 1920s and finally amalgamated with the All-Canadian Congress of Labour in 1927.

The growth of Quebec's labour movement was one of the unique features of Canada's trade unionism. In 1921, the *Confédération des Travailleurs catholiques du Canada* (CTCC) began as a group organized and controlled by the Roman Catholic clergy. The goals of this union were, of course, to better the lot of employees, as the organizers perceived the situation, but also to maintain the rights of the French-Canadian workers to work in the French language and to support the Roman Catholic religion. In part, this was a defensive reaction to English-Canadian and U.S. influences. However, altogether Catholic trade unions represented no more than half of French-speaking, Catholic trade unionists in Quebec. While the CTCC and its antecedent clergy-organized trade unions initially stressed cooperation between employees and employers and prohibited the use of strikes, increasing urbanization of French Canadians, wage gains by unions associated with the TLC and CCL outside Quebec, and organizational campaigns of these rival organizations within Quebec forced the CTCC to become more militant. The new lay leaders soon found themselves in conflict with the régime of Maurice Duplessis; small wonder, as he said in 1948: "Workers have the right to organize and the right not to organize. Labour has the right to organize, but not to disorganize." Throughout the 1950s and 1960s, the CTCC pressed for social and political reforms within Quebec. In 1960, it renamed itself the *Confédération des Syndicats Nationaux* (CSN). In short, Quebec-based unions with their more aggressive political stance and early church association are in contrast to other elements of Canadian trade unionism.[20] Apart from the western-based unions, such as the OBU, few have played a political role. Only recently has the Canadian Labour Congress endorsed a single political party, and clearly its rank-and-file membership do not vote solidly for that party.

Government policy on the rights of trade unions and public attitudes towards collective bargaining both reflected and shaped union attitudes, beliefs, and ideologies. The Canadian tradition, it has often been claimed in this context, has been to stress private property rights over collective rights. Changes in Canada's labour legislation have lagged behind British or U.S. best practices.[21] In 1872, for instance, the Canadian federal government passed the Trade Unions Act and the Criminal Law Amendment Act, identical with British law. These declared trade unions legal entities, exempt from criminal conspiracy and strike damages. In order to settle the industrial disputes which subsequently arose some provinces passed legislation designed to speed settlement of disputes. Thus, the legal or institutional basis of trade unionism and collective bargaining was established and its general acceptance proved important to the growth of Canadian trade unions. By the first decade of the twentieth century the passage into law of the Conciliation Act (1900), the Railway Labour Disputes Act (1903), and the Industrial Disputes Investigation Act (1907), all dispute procedures, helped bring order to the process of collective bargaining. Notably the last two of the above mentioned were patterned directly on U.S. precedents. The Industrial Disputes Investigation Act established principles which proved lastingly effective and existed in law until after the Second World War: one-stage, tripartite compulsory investigation, strikes and lockouts forbidden pending complete investigation, a cooling-off period, and judgements on issues in disputes. The act was an attempt to promote necessary intervention in industrial disputes when they restricted the freedom of both sides to engage in strikes and lockouts. With the Wagner Act of 1935 in the United States as an example, an Order-in-Council (PC 1003) was issued in 1944. It guaranteed employees' rights to form trade unions, established the criteria for determining a bargaining agent, laid down procedures for compulsory collective bargaining, and set up labour relations boards to investigate and correct unfair labour practices. The Order contained many of the most useful provisions of the earlier Industrial Disputes Investigation Act: compulsory conciliations, prohibition of strikes and lockouts during investigations, and compulsory arbitration during the life of a contract. It passed into law during wartime and both federal and provincial governments passed legislation to have it apply also in peacetime. In this manner, the legislative or legal rights of employees were established and the present-day institutional framework put in place.

While the membership of trade and labour unions grew absolutely and as a proportion of the non-agricultural labour force, that growth has, of course, affected the economy. However, the effects of this growth were complex and little concrete historical evidence can be brought to bear on their exact nature. In examining the labour supply it may be assumed that trade unions desired to improve the welfare of their members by negotiating higher money wages; this could only be achieved by restrictions on the supply of labour—assuming a negatively sloped labour-demand curve—providing everything else was the same. Trade and labour unions actively restricted the supply of labour throughout the nineteenth and twentieth centuries by negotiating reductions in working hours, restrictive immigration policies, and membership control of their own unions. In the late nineteenth century, for instance, some trade unions actively organized the Nine-Hour Day Movement, an attempt to reduce the working day and therefore limit the labour supplied by any one worker. The work-leisure choice was being exercised in the only way it could in a complex industrial society, through the union. It is likely that by such activities the long union campaign to reduce working hours brought about the forty-hour work week sooner than it might otherwise have.

Also on the supply side of the labour markets, since the late nineteenth century, at least, trade and labour unions sought restrictions on the flow of immigrants into Canada, especially during periods when unemployment increased. Their voice was often loud in restricting shifts of the labour supply through reduced immigration which might have proven prejudicial to their members' wage levels. Some trade unions exercise an additional power by setting the limit on the number of persons admitted for training and by varying the length of the training period. The setting of examinations, admission requirements for the trade, conditions

Table 7:6 Union Membership in Canada, 1911-1961
(annual averages per period)

Period	Total Union Membership (thousands)	Percentage of Union Membership with International Affiliation
(1)	(2)	(3)
1911-15	155.7	84.8
1916-20	273.1	74.9
1921-25	279.9	73.9
1926-30	301.5	71.6
1931-35	288.2	60.0
1936-40	361.8	58.9
1941-45	628.0	64.7
1946-50	931.7	69.3
1951-55	1,186.1	70.3
1956-61	1,421.9	86.1

Note: Figures include Newfoundland in and after 1949. International, of course, means United States in this context.

Source: Urquhart and Buckley (1965), p. 105.

necessary for good standing, and basis of termination from the trade all had the potential for limiting the labour supply. In seeking to restrict the labour supply, however, trade unions may have increased the supply of female labour in their actions to improve working conditions and reduce the hours of work; it became more attractive for females to enter the labour force, and work was more available because of the limitations on the number of hours worked by any individual.

Trade unions often achieved higher wages for their members by shifting the demand for labour. For example, unions often asked employers to place identifying marks on goods produced by union labour and then appealed to trade unionists to buy only union-made products. Since the demand for labour is a derived demand any such successful action would lead to a contraction elsewhere; there was nothing which unions could do to increase the aggregate demand for labour. Along similar lines, trade unions requested subsidization for transport, shipbuilding, coal mining, and other industries, in the hope that this would sustain demand for labour by creating a demand for their goods and services. Similar reasoning lay behind trade-union support for tariffs and "Buy Canadian" advertising campaigns; this reduced the number of substitutes for home-made goods and services, increased the demand for labour services to the right, and made the demands for products and labour more inelastic which might be expected to cause increased money wages. In their efforts to increase the demand for labour which they represented, trade and labour unions inevitably worked against each other. The global total of jobs, at a particular wage rate, could not be manipulated. For example, in the 1930s Canadian railway trade unions formed a "ship-by-rail" association which spent money to persuade Canadians to use railway services instead of truck transport; both truck and railway unions later opposed the St. Lawrence Seaway project, arguing that it would divert traffic away from land-based transport.

As the economic structures change in response to economic forces any rigidity in factor markets which creates bottlenecks is inimical to economic growth. In post-Confederation Canada labour mobility from low- to high-productivity jobs was crucial to the pace of structural change—as Chapter 2 described. This simple shift alone raised total output in the Canadian economy without augmenting the supply of labour.[22] It is easy to demonstrate that trade and labour restricted this mobility. What is not so easily shown is the reduction in social costs which the same practices brought about and how the quality of workers lives have improved as a consequence. Any trade-union activities which controlled entry into a union also prevented labour mobility in employment: high initiation fees, quotas on new members, and high admission qualifications. On the other hand, a labour market which did no better than echo Dickensian labour conditions would be inconsistent with economic development.[23]

Trade unions have generally not opposed technological change and innovation, and there is no evidence to show that trade unions impeded the ultimate implementation of new technology. However, from time to time, unions opposed the implementation of labour-displacing technology when no prior notice was given nor adequate compensation made to affected workers. Yet, such instances are, in a historical context, rare. Of course, the type of action was part of a broad argument that labour was more than an inanimate factor of production like capital, and so deserved greater consideration than other inputs. The external costs to the firm of introducing labour-saving technological change should be internalized to that firm. Only if the benefits outweighed costs, including adequate compensation for displaced labour, could the new technology be justified; that is, if the social benefits exceeded the social costs.

In summary, the growth of organized labour in Canada owed much to its British and U.S. antecedents. Like the unionism of those two countries organized labour first coalesced around skilled differences (trade unions), and only later around industrial distinctions (labour unions). Yet, the union movement, as it developed in the labour market, came to be unique. It was unique in terms of numbers dominated by unions with so-called international affiliations — with head offices in the United States. Undoubtedly, this perpetuated the schism between trade and labour unions which may have weakened the power of organized labour to advocate change. On the other hand, there was a reaction against the power of the crafts unions which was strongest in areas of the country where the trade unions were least attractive, particularly in areas such as British Columbia where labour unions were more appropriate to the natural-resources-based industrial composition of the labour force. Political radicalism became vehement. In turn, this political radicalism helped spawn a direct participation in politics and the creation of a political party which espoused the cause of organized labour — the Cooperative Commonwealth Federation and later its decendent, the New Democratic Party. So too, the overwhelmingly Roman Catholic workforce of Quebec and the attitude of the Church to unionism created conditions in the labour markets of Quebec which sharply differentiated that part of Canada from the rest of the country.

With regard to the impact of unionism on the labour markets, there can be no doubt that labour mobility was diminished as a consequence of collective action and that labour markets equilibrated differently than they would have in the absence of union interference. Yet, it is well, perhaps, to remember that measures of national income miss some benefits of economic development. After all, a society which achieves a high rate of economic growth by tolerating, say, a high rate of industrial accidents, or by preventing labour from exercising its work-leisure choice, is not necessarily ensuring that its workers' well-being is being improved. Despite any apparent threats to efficiencies in the workplace, and that is unproven, the growth of unions ensured that, on balance, labour would not be regarded simply as another factor of production.

Labour Productivity and Education

The phrase "human capital" is meant to convey the notion that it is possible for an individual, or society, to invest in improving the quality of human skills. While the exact relationship between such investment in education, the quality of the labour force, and economic development is hard to quantify, its appreciation is old. Early in the nineteenth century individuals such as Egerton Ryerson and Bishop Strachan established the basis of widespread education in Upper Canada on the grounds that it had utilitarian ends as well as moral ones. In Lower Canada the Church took responsibility.[24]

There has been a long-standing debate throughout Canadian history concerning the appropriateness of education provided in the nineteenth century, particularly in Lower Canada. It is often argued that the skills needed by a labour force for fully exploiting the opportunities for economic development were neither appreciated nor taught. First, there is much counter evidence to suggest that the Church in Quebec was vitally interested in the promotion of education to provide farm skills. Particularly in the aftermath of the troublesome decade of the 1830s, the Church, through its teaching orders, was instrumental in creating agricultural research stations and colleges. Second, the involvement of the Church in the promotion of industry in the late nineteenth century, to the extent that entrepreneurs were occasionally given papal knighthoods for establishing factories, seems curiously at odds with the claimed conservatism in education. Third, while it is true that the educational system in Quebec was late to adopt vocational training, it has not been convicingly shown that this was inappropriate given labour-market conditions. Indeed, it is likely that the major influence on the quality of labour is simply the achievement of basic literacy—which makes the worker better able to improve through learning by doing. Furthermore, the gains from education were often indirect and, as argued in Chapter 2, were probably more important during the later years of economic development than in the earlier ones.

Investment of two types achieved literacy and its associated skills.[25] First, there were the current expenses incurred by an individual to acquire an education. These costs should, of course, include taxes for education and, from society's viewpoint, subsidies received. In addition to the expense was the opportunity cost of the time spent acquiring an education—the income which could otherwise have been earned. The costs of investing in one's own human capital was, and is, largely comprised of the latter. Any decision to undertake formal education is based on future returns being large enough that when discounted to the present they at least compensate the individual for both time and money costs of acquiring skills. Thus, historically there was a structure of wages which ensured that compensation was made available to those who acquired skills. To the extent that wages were greater or less than the required compensation the labour market signalled to its new entrants the type of skills most and least in demand.

The relationship between education, the size and composition of the labour force, and economic development was threefold. First, education of a worker tended to raise earnings since it altered his physical productivity, at the margin, and thereby effectively increased the demand for his labour. Second, from the point of view of society as a whole, there were benefits derived from the experience of increased individual productivity which can be measured as a contribution to the rate of economic growth. Third, education raised overall productivity in the economy in less direct ways than simple increased efficiency. Improved knowledge and skills which increased efficiency in the production process also made people more flexible in adapting to the opportunities for new jobs; therefore workers were more mobile, and overall productivity further increased. External effects accrued to both the person and society. These were the benefits to be found in a literate society capable of making decisions which might be better informed than otherwise would be the case. With regard to solely productive activity, education has probably stimulated inventions and innovations. As well, education influenced the attitudes of corporate managers towards carrying out their functions, inspiring in them a willingness to assume risks and adopt innovations, efficient work scheduling, efficient handling of labour relations, and support of research and development programs seeking new and better production methods.

Throughout the nineteenth century, the emphasis of formal education was placed on cultural development through traditional courses in languages, mathematics, and philosophy. The humanities and arts at universities supplemented basic education at the primary and secondary levels.[26] Only when more skilled workers were required to maintain competitiveness in international trade around the turn of the twentieth century was interest aroused in technical education. The educational institutions were increasingly expected to produce skilled craftsmen for the economy. By the 1950s and 1960s, much greater emphasis was attached to higher learning and to technical post-secondary education and the school system was restructured in part to train more professionals.[27] While the proportion of gross national product devoted to formal education averaged about 1 per cent from 1867 to 1896, and less than 2 per cent from 1896 to 1950, it grew to 2.6 from 1950 to 1967 and to over 5 per cent for the 1960s (Table 7:7). The latter reflected the baby-boom phenomenon of the post-1945 years and the expansion of the country's university and higher educational systems.

From an historical viewpoint, it is convenient to think of some stock of education embodied in the labour force of the day. Changes in this stock were affected by: inflows of people in the younger age groups into the labour force, flows of people in the older age groups out of the labour force, and additions to and deletions from the labour force due to immigration and emigration. The first two raise the education stock as measured in terms of median or mean years of schooling, while the effect of the third is difficult to determine without further information. Table 7:8 demonstrates the improvement in education stock of the Canadian male labour force between 1911 and 1961.[28] Its features are:

1) a fall in the proportion of persons with only elementary schooling from about 75 to 46 per cent;
2) an increase in percentage of persons with some further schooling from about 21 to 37 per cent; and
3) an increase in the proportion of persons with some university education from approximately 4 to 16 per cent.

It might be noted that no recognition is given in Table 7:8 for 1961 to the burgeoning of technical and vocational post-secondary institutions. Since both the median and mean years of schooling for the average Canadian rose continuously, inflows of younger people and outflows of older persons from the labour force raised the stock of education.

When immigration and emigration were examined in Chapter 6, it was seen that Canada experienced negative net immigration during the last three decades of the nineteenth century and between 1921 and 1931 for males 25 to 64 years of age. The net effect of this net emigration during these periods was to lower the education attainment of the labour force. In the decades since 1914, the effect on the stock of education from immigration and emigration was likely small as net additions to the labour force relative to the size of that labour force were small.

In total, the effect of changes in the educational attainment—the stock of education—cannot be accurately assessed. However, from 1926 to 1956 the quality of the labour force increased by 6.85 years and this directly led to the rate of growth of GNP being 0.17 higher than it otherwise would have been.[29] While this figure may at first appear small it should be noted that it was equal to the entire contribution of machinery and equipment to real output. And such a measure understates the effect to the extent of the indirect contributions of education to economic growth which are believed to be substantial.

In Conflict
Labour markets in Canada evolved to meet the new demands for labour services. Seen in perspective, they have performed with an efficiency which at least produced no critical labour shortages to act as an impediment to economic development. In addition, the workforce has proven sufficiently mobile, both geographically and occupationally, that no chronic excess supply existed in any sector of economic activity. However, when considered in detail the evolution of labour markets can

Table 7:7 Expenditures on Formal Education in Canada, 1867-1967

Year or Period	Per-Capita Expenditures on Formal Education	Percentage of GNP
(1)	(2) ($)	(3)
1867-96	(1 ±)[a]	(1 ±)[a]
1896-1915	(2 ±)[a]	(1.25 ±)[a]
1926	15	2.7
1929	16	2.6
1939	14	2.7
1945	16	1.6
1950-67	34[a]	2.6[a]
1961	103	5.0
1967	222	7.3

[a] Refers to the beginning of the period.

Source: O. J. Firestone, *Industry and Education* (Ottawa, 1969), p. 185.

be seen to have been less than smooth. The tensions which occurred, and which were part of the labour-market mechanism, took a variety of forms. Conflict was often associated with bargaining for wage rates, working conditions, and the establishment of unions. It arose also between the workers themselves as they strove to protect their jobs and real wages and as they competed for new employment. Occasionally, the conflict took on a belligerent quality.[30]

Perhaps, the single most important incident in Canadian labour history was that of the Winnipeg General Strike of 1919. Although it started as a simple walkout by certain building trades in support of higher wages the strike spread and gathered momentum. It did so for a variety of reasons but most importantly because so many other workers found common grievance and willingly gave support. While the government claimed that revolutionary elements were at work—this was demonstrated later to be absurd—there was a political theme to the strike: Western unionism, especially in the case of the One Big Union, had greater political ambitions than unions or federations elsewhere at the time. In this case it was the recently demobilized veterans of the First World War who, as an association, decided to side with the strikers and march with them in protest. The men who had returned from the Flanders mud, who had survived the agony of Passchendaele, had been left to rot in the postwar unemployment. It is well known that during a demonstration march the striking workers and unemployed soldiers were confronted by the authorities. A riot followed. Whether it is sensible or not to attempt to apportion blame, one fact remains: The Winnipeg General

Table 7:8 Educational Attainment of the Male Labour Force, by Age Groups, 1911 and 1961
(percentage distribution)

Age group	Total	0-4 Years Elementary School		5-7 Years Elementary School		8 Years Elementary School		1-3 Years High School		4 Years High School		Some University Education		Complete University Education	
		1911	1961	1911	1961	1911	1961	1911	1961	1911	1961	1911	1961a	1911	1961
(1)	(2)	(3)	(4)	(5)	(6)	(7)	(8)	(9)	(10)	(11)	(12)	(13)	(14)	(15)	(16)
Total	100.0	24.2	7.5	34.5	20.8	16.1	17.6	18.1	29.7	3.2	8.7	1.5	10.1	2.4	5.6
24-34	100.0	18.4	3.9	33.2	14.6	18.3	19.5	21.3	33.8	4.3	8.7	1.8	13.5	2.7	6.0
35-44	100.0	23.4	6.1	34.9	21.4	16.1	15.0	18.2	31.6	3.2	9.5	1.6	10.1	2.5	6.3
45-54	100.0	28.7	9.5	35.8	23.4	14.2	17.8	15.7	27.3	2.3	8.5	1.3	8.4	2.0	5.0
55-64	100.0	34.6	15.3	35.7	29.1	12.4	18.3	12.7	20.3	1.7	7.4	1.1	5.3	1.7	4.2

a Includes Grade 13 for provinces in which Grade 13 is given.

Source: G. W. Bertram, *The Contribution of Education to Economic Growth* (Ottawa, 1966), p. 18.

Strike became the rallying symbol of organized labour. It is still the metaphor used to invoke the claimed intransigence of employers and government in the problems of union conflict.[31]

It is a well-tended myth of Canadian history that industrial relations have been essentially harmonious.[32] Yet certainly in the twentieth century, and probably earlier, strikes and lockouts have occurred with high frequency and have been long-lasting. The Canadian record in this regard is much worse than that of the United States. Furthermore, the seasonal patterns of many natural-resource-based industries often result in long periods during which the workers were laid-off, or received no wages, or both. Exactly what caused the frequency and length of strikes is not well understood. The answer probably lies both in the high degree of local labour-market power exercised by a single employer — monopsony power — and the ability of the firm, or in recent times the government, to withstand strikes. This ability is itself a product of the high degree of market concentration in final-goods markets and the ability of many natural-resource-based industries to maintain sales simply by the expedient of depleting their usually large inventories.

Although often obvious, conflict in the labour market was also quiet, almost unnoticed. Competition for employment has produced opposing views among workers. While this conflict has taken many forms, the most blatant has been the arbitrary discrimination against certain types of workers. Discrimination based upon sex, race, nationality, and language have all been common and indeed are still so. As noted earlier in this chapter, the radical changes in the sex-specific participation rates were brought about, in part, by evolving social attitudes of tolerance and by the observation that the various types of workers were not necessarily in competition for the same jobs. Yet, this type of arbitrary discrimination still exists in many sectors of the economy although today it seldom openly takes on unsavoury characteristics.

In summary, while the long-run adjustment of labour markets has been relatively tied to changes in the structure and location of labour demand, the process was not without its human conflict.

CHAPTER EIGHT

Capital Formation and Mobilization

Introduction

Capital, as we have now seen in several instances, was fundamental to the development of the early staple economy. It came in many forms: the establishment of transport services, the financing of the inventories of the fur trade, and the introduction of new strains of cattle, among many others. All of these forms represented part of the flow of investment which enlarged the stock of capital, the capacity of the economy to produce goods and services. Here, the importance of capital to the process of modern industrial growth will be examined. However, it is first necessary to distinguish between the related concepts of capital formation and capital mobilization by examining the changing composition of the real capital stock. The responsiveness of the process of financial mobilization to demand as well as the ability of the economy to generate savings were basic to meeting capital requirements of the growing economy. The evolution of markets in which savings were allocated was fundamental to long-run economic performance and ultimately it was these capital markets which determined the rate at which investment augmented the real capital stock, thereby adding to productive capacity.[1]

In the process of producing goods or services, inputs or resources were used, primarily labour, land, natural resources, intermediate inputs, and real capital. Within the constraints imposed by non-capital inputs, some levels of investment allowed the Canadian economy to produce more output. This enlarged the economy's potential, which included improvements in the quality of life such as the ability of its residents to consume more leisure time. This may be called "the capacity-creating effect of investment". On the other hand, an increase in investment expenditure, from one time period to the next, operated through the multiplier to raise the level of effective demand and shifted actual output close to potential output.

In Chapter 2 the aggregate impact of capital as a source of economic growth was examined. Here attention is directed to the evolution and consequences of the dual role of investment creating both capacity and demand. In the following chapter account is taken of the role played by foreign investment in capital formation and mobilization.

Long-Run Trends in Capital Formation
Like most countries experiencing rapid economic development, Canada faced special problems both in creating real capital and in mobilizing sufficient savings to finance this new investment. The flow of investment grew and changed in composition creating two economic strains which were acute in the nineteenth and early twentieth centuries—strains which to some extent are still present. First, Canadian investment opportunities provided the incentive for the mobilization of increasing amounts of domestic and foreign savings and when this mobilization was unsuccessful the rate of economic progress was impeded. Second, as the composition of investment changed to include more geographic areas, more sectors of economic activity, more varieties of real capital, and more capital users, mechanisms had to be created to facilitate the transfer of savings to meet the new demands. The creation of financial institutions which more efficiently marshalled savings and directed them as financial capital in what is known as "the capital market", and the process called "the mobilization of capital" eased both strains. This, then, was the function of capital markets: to direct the savings to the most appropriate method of forming real capital. Although capital markets assumed formal structures in later history, it is important to recognize that in the early years they were often very informal mechanisms for the transfer of savings to the demanders of real capital. Although the processes are interrelated, the process of capital mobilization was distinct from the process of capital formation in that it was being undertaken by a different group in society with different motives. The responsiveness and ability of the economy to bring these groups together in changing circumstances proved to be a major factor in altering the pace of economic expansion.

As previously mentioned, the capital stock is one of the basic determinants of a society's ability to produce goods and services. It is defined as that part of the economy's past production which is reserved to produce goods and services in the next period. However, in time capital stocks wear out or depreciate. In an agricultural society, herds of cattle may age and fence posts may rot. In a more modern industrial economy, machinery declines in capacity or breaks down if forced to operate beyond its useful life; technological change makes some equipment redundant. Unless provision is made for this obsolescence of the capital stock, it will decline in size and the productive capacity of the economy will fall. It is, therefore, necessary for the capitalists to undertake some investment to replace the real capital by reserving part of current production simply to ensure that future production does not fall. This is the familiar concept called "depreciation". To provide for increases in future production the capital stock must be enlarged and this will only happen when the gross flow of investment is greater than depreciation costs. Since the ability to increase the capital stock is an elemental part of economic development it is important that such concepts be given some precision.

The flow of gross investment, most broadly defined as gross national capital formation (GNCF), includes depreciation. It comprises all additions to capital *stocks* undertaken by Canadians. When depreciation charges are subtracted the measure becomes one of net national capital formation (NNCF). The counterparts from the national-income accounts which measure the gross and net flows of income accruing to Canadians are gross national product (GNP) and net national product (NNP), respectively. During most of Canada's history, domestic savings were used almost exclusively to finance home investment and few net exports of capital occurred. Yet, domestic savings were often insufficient and imports of foreign savings were required as an important supplement. However, GNCF omits real investment by foreigners.

In order to account for foreign investment in the Canadian capital stock another measure must be employed, that of gross domestic capital formation (GDCF). The GDCF, or its equivalent net of depreciation (NDCF), indicates the amount of real savings committed to investment in Canada irrespective of source. As gross domestic product (GDP) and net domestic product (NDP) give measures of the flow of income derived *in Canada*, so GDCF and NDCF respectively give measures of gross and net investment in Canada by Canadians and foreigners alike.[2] Since Canada has been for most of its history a net capital importer, the demand for capital has been greater than the domestic supply of savings — GDCF has been greater than GNCF. At the height of capital imports in the years 1911-15, during the wheat boom period, GDCF was approximately 185 per cent greater than GNCF (see Table 8:1). What impact this foreign capital inflow had on the pace of Canadian economic growth has been a matter of some controversy, as will be seen later. But for the moment it may simply be noted that the addition to domestic savings from foreign sources to finance

Table 8:1 Capital Formation, 1870-1970

Year	GDCF/GNP	GNCF/GNP	Period	GDCF/GNP		GNCF/GNP	
(1)	(2)	(3)	(4)	(5)		(6)	
1870	14.9	7.2					
1890	15.5	8.6					
1900	13.4	9.4	1901-05	22.7		17.4	
			1906-10	27.0		17.7	
1910	26.5	13.5	1911-15	26.9		14.5	
			1916-20	19.3		18.0	
1920	23.2	18.4	1921-25	16.1		16.4	
			1926-30	(20.3)	21.6	(18.3)	19.7
1929	23.0	17.9	1931-35		9.7		9.3
1930	21.2	15.1	1936-40		14.8		17.8
1939	16.3	19.4	1941-45		9.1		12.4
			1946-50		20.6		21.4
1950	23.9	21.2	1951-55		23.3		21.9
			1956-60		25.1		21.4
1960	23.2	20.2	1961-65		23.3		21.7
			1966-70		23.5		22.6
1970	21.4	22.4					

Note: The figures for the years prior to 1926 are from Firestone (1958), p. 72 and Buckley (1955), p. 15 and are presented in columns (2) and (3), and (5) and (6) respectively. The official figures differ slightly and the calculation are the sum of gross fixed-capital formation and the value of the physical change in inventories for GDCF less non-resident savings for GNCF. No adjustment has been made for the residual error of estimate.

Sources: K. A. H. Buckley, *Capital Formation in Canada, 1896-1930* (Toronto, 1955), p. 15; O. J. Firestone, *Canada's Economic Development, 1867-1953* (London, 1958), p. 75; and Statistics Canada, *Canadian Statistical Review*, Cat. no. 11-505.

domestic investment was large for most periods of post-Confederation history.

From Table 8:1 it can be seen that extremely high investment rates were recorded in the years immediately before the First World War. After depreciation, Canada achieved a net investment rate (the ratio of NDCF to NDP) of approximately 17.2 per cent. This is striking when compared with the historical experience of other countries. At the height of the Industrial Revolution, Great Britain exhibited an investment ratio of only 8.2 per cent. Japan, during its rise to industrial prominence (1917-26), registered an NDCF-to-NDP ratio of 13.4 per cent. Only the United States, during its post-Civil War recovery, and the Scandinavian economies of recent years have experienced investment booms of such magnitude. Unfortunately, for Canada there is no accurate evidence for investment ratios prior to Confederation. Nevertheless, most economic historians agree that the investment boom which centred on railroad development in central Canada in the 1850s occurred during a time of high ratios of investment to income. For more modern periods the economic growth experienced during the 1950s often associated with the exploitation of the "new" natural resources of oil and gas was both caused by and responsible for high investment ratios. Not surprisingly high investment ratios are usually registered during times of large-scale immigration because of the sensitivity of certain types of capital formation, such as housing, to population.

Aggregate investment ratios are an extremely reliable gauge of an economy's performance. Nevertheless, they give no specific information about the growth of sectors within the economy nor do they indicate regional differences in the patterns of economic growth. For instance, the decade of the 1880s is generally thought to be one of relatively sluggish economic performance—some observers favour the designation "slow but sustained" economic growth. The rate of growth of output in most sectors of the economy was usually less than three per cent per annum in real terms. As Chapter 6 pointed out, Canada, on balance, lost immigrants to the United States; yet, in contradiction, gross immigration into Canada was large. Some clue to this apparently perverse economic behaviour may be found in the sectoral pattern of investment, particularly in transport where substantial investment took place. During the 1880s the building of the Canadian Pacific Railway was begun and completed and net capital formation in the railroad and telegraph sector averaged about $25.3 million annually. This was much higher than during the following decade which is generally thought of as being a more prosperous one. Since the average ratios may mask strong sectoral patterns of increases in investment it may be argued that the 1880s, as an example, displayed some structural strength and failure to take account of this creates a misleading impression.[3] Suffice it to note that although it is possible to isolate periods of vigorous aggregate investment, economic growth and development may on occasion take place with a sectoral or geographical bias which the national figures ignore. Chapter 13 will investigate some specific cases.

A change in the capital stock's composition which reflected the growth of the complex industrial economy accompanied its secular growth. This is best observed by considering the four major types of capital and their subdivisions. These are:

1) Construction
   a. plant
   b. residential dwellings
   c. publicly owned institutions

2) Producers' equipment (machinery)
3) Inventories
   a. finished goods
   b. intermediate goods
4) Consumers' durables.

All components of the capital stock have grown over the long run but some categories have become more and some less important. In the agricultural economy of Upper and Lower Canada farm buildings and fences constituted the fixed capital or plant. Horses, for the purpose of farm work, are best categorized as producers' equipment, and stocks of grain and other produce as finished goods. All constituted part of the capital stock. The early exploitation of renewable resources, such as fur and timber, demanded a capital stock largely composed of inventories. Seasonal harvesting of the resources which had to be shipped great distances with slow transport facilities required large inventories of final products and, in the case of the fur trade, inventories of intermediate trade goods.

On the other hand, early industrial growth was, for the most part, based on relatively simple production processes. Requirements of machinery and plant were quite modest. Inventories and physical plant were the most significant forms of capital in such early industries as grain milling. In time, the need for larger plants was felt as industries, such as brewing and furniture manufacturing, began to exploit economies of scale. Production within the plant was still based on fairly simple techniques and while the importance of plant grew, that of producers' equipment did so only after the mid-nineteenth century. About this time new industries began to emerge. These embodied many of the technical innovations and techniques of the new industrial age which, in turn, demanded a greater machine input. At least from the beginning of the twentieth century, probably slightly earlier, machinery and equipment became more important constituents of capital formation than the building of plant (non-residential construction; see Table 8:2). Persistent labour-saving technical change in manufacturing accentuated this trend, as was noted in Chapter 2.

Canada was similar to other developing countries in experiencing a growth in the importance of machinery and equipment in manufacturing production. However, the country was also dissimilar in that construction investment—non-residential—grew at a more rapid rate than elsewhere and, in fact, increased its share of gross investment proportionately. This was almost solely due to the importance of staple-producing

Table 8:2 Components of Gross Domestic Capital Formation, 1870-1970
(Percentage of GDCF)

| | Construction | | | | Machinery and Equipment | Value of the Physical Change in Inventories | Capital Consumption Allowances (Depreciation) |
| Year | Non-Residential | Residential | Government | Total | | | |
(1)	(2)	(3)	(4)	(5)	(6)	(7)	(8)
1870	—	—	—	48.5	30.9	20.6	52.9
1880	—	—	—	—	—	—	—
1890	—	—	—	58.7	31.0	10.3	55.6
1901-05	28.5	11.3	7.3	53.1	29.6	17.3	a
1906-10	31.6	20.5	10.8	62.9	25.6	11.5	—
1911-15	30.5	17.3	13.4	61.2	27.8	11.0	a
1916-20	29.4	15.9	7.3	52.6	32.8	14.6	—
1921-25	29.9	20.4	12.1	62.4	33.3	4.4	a
1926-30	29.7	18.0	13.1	60.6	28.5	10.9	53.5
1931-35	31.4	19.9	24.8	80.0	30.0	- 9.9	131.5
1936-40	21.8	13.5	17.1	52.4	34.3	13.3	81.1
1941-45	30.0	21.3	10.8	62.1	45.8	- 7.9	107.9
1946-50	24.8	20.9	18.9	64.6	27.3	8.1	46.4
1951-55	27.7	21.2	13.6	62.5	30.5	7.0	45.3
1956-60	31.1	21.6	15.8	68.5	27.7	3.8	48.3
1961-65	27.7	19.5	18.3	65.5	28.5	6.0	52.3
1966-70	28.1	19.0	16.9	64.0	31.5	4.5	49.3

Note: Columns (5), (6), and (7) sum to 100 per cent subject to rounding errors. The figures presented here are from several sources and are not exactly compatible. However, the variations are such that they present a reasonably accurate summary of the disposition of GDCF. The pre-1900 figures are calculated from Firestone. All estimates for 1901 to 1925 are from Buckley. Post-1925 figures are calculated from official data.

"a" Firestone estimates (8) to be 69.1, 39.3 and 31.8 for 1900, 1910, and 1920 respectively.

Sources: Buckley (1955), pp. 2-17 and Appendix; Firestone (1958), pp. 100, 112, and 114; and Statistics Canada, *Canadian Statistical Review*.

industries and the transport sector, used to facilitate resource exploitation. Expenditures on steam railways dominated construction in the late
nineteenth and early twentieth centuries, and even as late as 1926-30
constituted 26 per cent of gross investment. In 1945 railways constituted
no less than 38 per cent of Canada's private sector stock of construction
capital. With less emphasis placed on the expansion of railways in
modern times, their importance to construction investment and to the
capital stock fell. This helped to account for the relative growth of
machinery and equipment. On the other hand, investment in inventories
declined in relative importance throughout the evolution of the industrial economy and the extension of the transport system which permitted such savings.

Over the course of history, the private business units controlled the
bulk of the industrial capital stock. In recent years, the development of a
more mixed economy has witnessed increased government participation
in the direct production of goods and services through such Crown cor-
porations as Air Canada. However, three items in the capital stock are
not considered part of the industrial sector. These are residential dwellings, government institutions, and consumers' durables. Residential
dwellings remained an important item in the capital stock, growing absolutely over the long run and slightly increasing in proportion to the
population. Most periods of rapid economic expansion which attracted
large net immigration have also been periods of building booms in
response to the increased demand for housing. This is not to say that the
dwellings in the capital stock have always been sufficient in number.
From time to time, in the 1920s, for example, Canada has been under-
capitalized in residential dwellings. Acute excess demand for residential
living space has often occurred in specific urban centres. In passing, the
recent emergence of publicly owned buildings or government institutions as important items in the country's capital stock should be noted.[4]

The third item in the capital stock which the household sector holds
directly is consumers' durables. Many economists choose to exclude this
category of capital from their definition of the capital stock because of
the obvious difficulty of placing a value on it. However, to exclude this
item in an historical context may be inappropriate since consumers'
durables are inputs into the production process, albeit indirect ones. Sudden dramatic changes, by historical standards, took place in the absolute
investment in durable consumer goods which have undoubtedly had a
significant if unquantified impact on labour productivity by permitting
more mobility and a more efficient allocation of time. Rare in the nineteenth century, the consumer holding of a stock of durable goods increased so rapidly in the first quarter of the twentieth century that some

observers refer to this period as the beginning of "the consumers' durables revolution". Since the 1920s, expenditure on consumer durable goods—jewellery and watches, home furnishings, furniture, household appliances, radio and television sets, and automobiles—rose from about 8 per cent of total personal expenditure to about 12 per cent by the mid-1950s and remained at this high level.

New goods characterized the early phases in this revolution: radios in the 1920s and 1930s, mechanical refrigeration in the 1930s and 1940s, electrical cooling equipment and radio equipment after 1946, television sets in the 1950s, and automatic washing machines, clothes dryers, air conditioners, and home freezers in the 1960s. Yet, it is perhaps the private automobile which more than any other good typifies the growing importance of the consumers' durables revolution. Only the United States surpassed Canada in the number of cars per thousand of population. Explanations for this revolution on the demand side are found in the rising real personal disposable incomes with relatively high income elasticities of demand for durable products, and cheap home electricity and household appliances as compared with the more costly alternative of domestic service, and, on the supply side, in the development of credit to finance purchases.[5]

In aggregate, the changing composition of the capital stock had a direct influence on the flow of gross investment. This is partly because different items in the capital stock depreciated at different rates. For instance, in the primary and secondary manufacturing sectors the relative growth, within the capital stock, was greater in the categories subject to fast depreciation. More and more gross investment has been required simply to preserve production capacity. On the other hand, the persistent significance of dwellings as an item in the capital stock and the now important category of consumers' durables allows for variable depreciation. Both of the above items have long useful lives. This permits flexibility in the investment process as the economy can permit these items of the capital stock to age with only modest losses in economic efficiency. At other times, the average age of dwellings and durable goods may be adjusted down. This then prompts consideration of the quality of, say, the housing stock, in order to make some judgment about individual economic welfare.

Here only the broad features of changing investment and the composition of the capital stock have been noted. In later chapters it will be necessary to examine them in more detail. Railways, as noted, have been so important in the process of Canadian economic development that they warrant separate consideration. Similarly, a discussion of the rise of modern industry in Chapter 12 is the most appropriate context in which to examine the impact of specific demands for capital.

Capital Markets, Risk, and Uncertainty

It was only from the years immediately after the First World War that the capital market was at all national in scope, although far from perfect. Yet there were, by the 1920s, enough types of financial intermediaries offering sufficient varieties of debt instruments that the spatial differences which characterized earlier capital markets were substantially reduced. Such geographic differences are best measured by the differential interest rate between areas for similar investments with a known distribution of risk. When the demand for real capital services is based on the marginal productivity of capital, a difference in interest rates indicates that in one capital market the savers are foregoing a higher return (see Figure 8:1) which in turn indicates that savings are being allocated inefficiently. A barrier to the movement of capital exists.[6]

Historically, the absence of debt instruments, such as loans for the provision of certain types of capital formation, was an indication that efficient capital mobilization was hindered. Interest-rate differentials occurred because of the inability of capital-scarce regions or industries to draw in savings from other regions or industries in sufficient quantity. When there was a barrier between regions or industries it was caused by the savers' attitude towards risk and uncertainty. The absence of the possibility of arbitrage in the form of debt instruments, either wholly or in sufficient volume to ameliorate the capital scarcity, was only the indication that there was a barrier to efficient capital mobilization.[7] It was *uncertainty* about the *distribution of risk* associated with capital-formation projects which prevented capital from being efficiently mobilized.

The potential failure of an investment project to produce a positive rate of return is the risk inherent in a business venture. This risk is distributed, in some fashion, over a range of probabilities. Canadian history provides ample evidence that different distributions of risk are associated with different types of business ventures. For instance, mining ventures were extremely risky in comparison with, say, manufacturing ones. Not only were new mining enterprises faced with the problem of discovering and exploiting mineral deposits at an economic cost, but, even when producing, were subject to the vagaries of world prices because of the highly competitive nature of world commodity markets. In contrast, a manufacturing firm's manager possessed more accurate knowledge about the cost and availability of factor inputs, and the output of the firm faced a relatively less price-elastic and more stable demand. However, factors other than the nature of the firms' activities determined part of the distributions of risk. Risk also depended on the size of the business, the presence of tariff protection, and the degree of industrial concentration.

Figure 8:1 Capital Market Inefficiencies

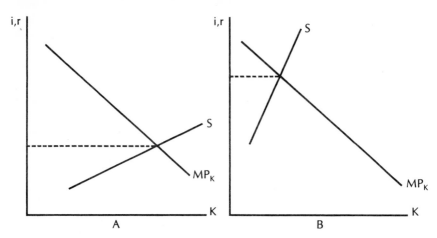

MP$_K$—marginal productivity of capital
S—supply of savings for capital formation
r—rate of return
i—interest rate
K—capital

Note: For a set of given investment projects with a known distribution of risk, the low interest rate in A permits low-yielding enterprises to be created and the high interest rate in B permits only high-yielding projects to be initiated. Perfect capital markets would permit the costless flow of funds between the markets and the equilibration of a market interest rate common to both A and B. The capital markets A and B may be those associated with a region of the country, of an industry, or, as will be seen in the next chapter, the rest of the world and Canada.

That some investment projects were more risky than others did not in itself dampen capital formation in those sectors where the chances of failure were high. As long as some savers were risk-takers, financial capital flowed into these ventures. Even when savers were neutral in their attitude towards risk, as long as a compensation in the form of a high expected rate of return enticed investors, savings were forthcoming. Indeed, there is even the possibility that savers who preferred to play safe—that is, were risk-averse—contributed to capital formation in risky industries. This often happens when, in order to save, use is made of financial institutions which have broadly diversified portfolios of investments. Although the investment behaviour is, on average, cautious and therefore appealing to the prudent saver the portfolio may contain what are often called "speculative" elements whose presence little influence the overall investment behaviour. Few of us, after all, replan our lives when we purchase a lottery ticket. There are no reasons to suppose that funds have been totally denied to industries or regions of the country simply because there was a particular distribution of risk associated with the investment which made it less favourable than others.

It was uncertainty — ignorance of the distribution of risk associated with investment — which held back the inter-industry and inter-regional flows of capital. This uncertainty had two aspects. First, the entrepreneurs themselves may have had only an imperfect knowledge about the riskiness of the business venture they were undertaking, especially when success depended on exploration for natural resources, such as minerals. Even in a given mining area, such as the Timmins gold field just prior to 1914, the probabilities of discovering an exploitable stock on particular mining claims ranged, perhaps almost randomly, between zero and unity. Mining promoters were often carried along in a wave of unwarranted optimism based on an unrealistic appreciation of a particular mining claim and its economic potential. So too, in industries which were not prey to such technical misinformation, or where no information existed, the risk was often unknown. Especially in new industries, there was often only a very imperfect knowledge of market-demand conditions. As a consequence, entrepreneurs often misunderstood the risk distribution of an investment project.

The second feature was that the riskiness of a particular investment was unknown to savers who were unable to gauge whether the entrepreneur or investor accurately stated the risk. The absence of efficient methods of communicating information and the lack of a standard of comparison determined this uncertainty. While uncertainty often increased with the geographic distance between the saver and the investor, it was also associated with the technical distance and difference in market conditions between established and new industries.

Risk and uncertainty were seldom so severe as to deny completely a flow of savings to new industries and regions. Risk-taking savers who were relatively unconcerned about the degree of risk subscribed their savings to many high-risk ventures especially during periods of economic boom. Risk-neutral individuals required extra compensation in the form of a promised rate of return in order to cover both risk and uncertainty. If the uncertainty premium savers demand was high, it alone might deny an adequate flow of savings to the potential capital-users.

In the United States, in the nineteenth century, the imperfect capital markets displayed their inefficiency by demonstrating interest-rate differential between regions, for a common use of capital, and between industries, for a different use of capital. In Canada, the barriers to efficient capital mobilization were so high that in many instances it is impossible to measure the interest—or rate-of-return—differential because not enough savings flowed to establish an observable market-interest rate. The housing market of mid-nineteenth century Canada demonstrates the phenomenon. Mortgage interest rates were high relative to other debt instruments of comparable risk and there was a substantial interest-rate differential between various regions, which for the purpose of this discussion were usually towns or townships, depending on local supply and demand conditions. In time, as capital markets became more integrated and as uncertainty was dissipated, mortgage interest rates declined absolutely and the disparity between local mortgage rates shrank.[8]

The uncertainty which characterized early capital markets tended to diminish in the late nineteenth and early twentieth centuries as entrepreneurs acknowledged the possibility of making a profit by arbitraging funds between these imperfectly linked capital markets. When someone or some agency acted as an arbitraging agent, large profits usually accrued in the form of short-run quasi-rents. This itself, of course, is evidence for the existence of interest-rate differentials. Successful experience meant that savers no longer required such large premiums to allay fears of uncertainty and more capital flowed inter-regionally and between industries. Later this chapter explores in more detail the entrepreneur's role as an economic agent reducing the barriers to capital mobility.

It is often claimed that Canadians throughout history have been relatively reluctant to take risks.[9] If this is true, we should seek a sociological explanation of what influences made investors more hesitant to lend their savings. A more satisfactory explanation from the point of view of economic history is that Canadian capital markets lost their inefficiency slowly—more slowly than in the United States, for instance. In large measure, this can be traced to the absence of well-defined debt and credit instruments which permitted rational risk-taking, that is, accepting risk without *uncertainty* of that *risk*. Risk and uncertainty, as noted above, are quite different concepts; the former is an objective probability distribution whereas the latter is the degree of knowledge about such a distribution. The absence of mechanisms through which investment could take place was a twofold problem. First, there was a great variety of risky ventures where technical and economic information was muddled, such as in natural-resource exploitation. Second, the scale of the economy in the nineteenth century, because of its small size, offered few concrete examples on the basis of which uncertainty could be dispelled.

Although the barriers to efficient capital mobilization have been reduced there are still difficulties. The recent founding of the Canada Development Corporation by the government was an attempt to provide so-called "venture capital" to those business enterprises which still were denied the use of savings because of imperfect capital mobility. Yet, the barriers fell historically as more accurate assessments could be made about the distribution of risk and as that information was disseminated more efficiently. This happened to such an extent that the post-1918 capital market was national in scope whereas earlier capital markets had been regional.

Primitive Capital Markets and Early Industry
Exploitation of the early staples of fish, fur, and timber relied on a relatively large capital stock of inventories. In the case of the fur trade the inventories consisted of intermediate trade goods, such as tools, axes, pots and pans, firearms, and other items of the European industrial age, as well as inventories of the final product. Fish and timber-trade inventories were largely of the final product. Each of these export industries were organized in a different manner. The fur trade, under the dominant influences of the Hudson's Bay Company and the North West Company, was financed almost entirely by these firms, from the initial purchase of trade goods to the final sale of furs in London. The timber trade, on the other hand, comprised two distinct operations: timber cutting and shipping by firms located in Quebec or in the other ports of maritime British North America. Shippers financed the inventories until the timber was sold, either in the British market or, increasingly after 1842, in the U.S. market. Due to the delayed method of compensating the timber-cutting firms the shippers managed to conserve their financial capital. This often meant that the bush camps were starved of financial reserves for operating capital and they often employed methods to ration their financial resources. The none-too-popular delaying of payment of wages was common practice. Despite these differences in organization, many businesses in the natural-resource industries relied almost exclusively on generating financial capital within the firm or within the industry to meet their gross investment needs.[10]

With the influx of settlers into Upper Canada in the late eighteenth century and early nineteenth century, small commercial centres developed in response to the needs of the agricultural sector. Military spending during the War of 1812 was a further stimulus. Lines of credit were established reaching from the small traders of Upper Canada to the merchants at Montreal who imported consumer and industrial goods from Great Britain. Using their market power with respect to the interior of Upper Canada, the Montreal-based merchants were able to generate sufficient business savings to finance the inventories of the Upper Canadian traders. With their control over the process of marshalling savings and of the flow of goods along the St. Lawrence and Great Lakes trade route, they thwarted the efforts of the interior traders to accumulate their own savings. Throughout the early nineteenth century the Upper Canadians had felt, with varying degrees of intensity over the years, that they were under the domination of the Montreal merchants and the control over the commercial sector in Upper Canada fed this sentiment. Only with the rapid commercial expansion in the late 1840s and early 1850s did the Upper Canadians escape from the financial control of Montreal.[11]

The early agricultural sector of both Upper and Lower Canada was capital-scarce. Of course, the government financed homesteading in some measure and the monolithic giants of the Canada Company in southwestern Upper Canada and the British-American Land Company in the Eastern Townships of Lower Canada did the same. However, the effect was transitory and achieved at a very high private cost. With respect to crops, cattle, and seed, farmers in the early-nineteenth-century Canadas were forced to carry their own inventories. In most cases the farmer himself similarly financed fixed-capital formation. Indeed, it was only about one hundred years later that farm credit became readily available. In an attempt to smooth out the very imperfect and traditional capital market the community often cooperatively built buildings, usually barns, for an individual farmer — often in a weekend. In turn, the individual in question was obliged to contribute his labour to the barn-building projects of others. The unavailability or relatively high cost of capital services relative to land created an agricultural sector which expanded production at the land-intensive margin.

Directly linked to the staple trades the first industrial enterprises in Canada were small and locally based. Sawmills and forges, grist mills and mills for carding wool, all emerged as the frontier passed through the districts of the British North American colonies. These primitive industries were usually located on streams because of their dependence on water power. Often they served as a nucleus for the small villages which grew up in response to the growing demands for the increasingly specialized agricultural sector. Distilleries, tanneries, wagon makers, cooperages, the occasional small cloth mill, as well as a commercial sector developed at sites strategically placed on the water-transport networks of the rivers and the Great Lakes–St. Lawrence system. Villages such as Kingston in Upper Canada also attracted other industries related to the transport sector. By 1820 Kingston had a thriving shipbuilding industry. In the older settled regions of Lower Canada the agglomeration of local industry had predated the coming of the Bitish. Towns such as St. Maurice had early become a centre of the metal-working trades.[12]

Most of the early industrial enterprises were self-financed. Under the seigneurial régime in New France, for example, an individual seigneur was responsible for providing and financing investment in the grist mills and under British colonial control the mobilization of capital for industry changed little. Seigneurs, as well as the Anglo-American settlers, continued to function as rudimentary capitalists. Often the industrial undertaking was a family concern. In Nova Scotia the relatively wealthy United Empire Loyalist families became actively engaged in the creation of new industries such as distilling. Similarly in Upper Canada, in the early nineteenth century, it was the more affluent of the United Empire Loyalists who established, on a private basis, the first elements of the industrial capital stock. Occasionally, as in the case of William Hamilton Merritt who became famous as the promoter of the first Welland canal linking Lake Ontario and Lake Erie, the regional capitalist controlled more than one type of enterprise — to the ownership of a grist mill was added a distillery, and so on.[13] Persons with no particular history of wealth founded some business enterprises, especially grist mills. A successful farmer often turned his local agricultural surplus into an investment in primitive industry. In virtually all cases of early industrial investment the savers and the investors were the same individuals.

With certain exceptions, notably the transport industries, many industrial enterprises of the nineteenth century mobilized financial capital from within the firm or from within the household. Real capital requirements usually remained within the capacity of individuals to finance. Not until very late in the nineteenth century did the industrial sector turn to the public on a systematic basis for the mobilization of financial funds. More formal processes for the mobilization of savings were then necessary.[14]

The absence of even modestly efficient capital markets prior to the mid-nineteenth century acted as the main impediment to capital formation. Even in the twenty years or so before Confederation, to which can be dated the emergence of some specialized manufacturing not *directly* linked to the staples, capital mobilization usually still took place in a traditional manner. Reliance on family wealth or on a business's retained earnings made capitalists reluctant to invest in new industries where there was a great deal of *uncertainty* about the *riskiness* of the ventures. Consequently, the real cost of financial capital to a new entrepreneur in a new industry, particularly in secondary manufacturing, was usually substantially higher than the degree of risk warranted. It was, of course, much higher than the real cost of capital to the already established industries. Often the cost of mobilizing savings was sufficiently high that it was an effective, if temporary, check. But the growth of existing industry proceeded and the emergence of new industries was not wholly impeded. For the most part, expansion of new industry was most efficiently financed in the traditional capital-market setting when an entrepreneur from an established sector diverted savings in response to a profitable undertaking which he perceived in a new sector. Horizontal movements from one type of business to another were quite common. The early railroad promoter Sir Casimir Gzowski, although more flamboyant than most, was typical as he founded new firms in first the railway sector and then in iron and metal-working trades.

The migration of the capitalist to new industrial ventures was commonly to one with similar techniques of production. Because of the familiarity with techniques which gave him more certain information on the nature of risk, he was the first to perceive potentially profitable new enterprises. If this occurred and the capitalist was able to undertake his own intermediation when marshalling savings, the barrier to efficient capital mobilization was minimal. On the other hand, when entrepreneurs who had no foothold in the established industrial sector attempted to raise financial capital, the barrier to efficient capital mobilization was often substantial enough to thwart their efforts and retard the pace of industrial development.

Although early industry relied on a traditional method of capital mobilization, it does not follow that the economy was short of financial capital. Although agriculture was slow to generate a surplus it was nevertheless the case that by the 1850s capital services in some sectors were relatively plentiful. One factor in the generation of the surplus, large by historical standards, was the buoyant market for agricultural goods during the period of the reciprocal free-trade treaty with the United States. But this market was also linked intimately with the extension of the railroads throughout eastern Canada which, in conjunction with other forces, permitted more effective specialization. Coming when they did, the railroads helped to shape a structural shift in the industrial sector as the proportion of the capital stock in investment in plant and machinery grew. The Grand Trunk Railway Shops in Montreal and the Great Western Shops in Hamilton were important new enterprises in the early 1860s with capital demands remarkably greater than any industry which had preceded the railway era.[15]

Until the twentieth century the control of industrial enterprises usually remained the prerogative of a single individual or family. The family firm or the public firm in which a family held a majority of voting equities remained the most common form of corporate control. However, reliance on personal sources of wealth ultimately became an impediment to industrial expansion. First, by the late nineteenth century, the scale of industrial enterprises was growing so rapidly that the financial resources mobilized in a traditional manner were inadequate to meet industrial-investment needs. Second, as the industrial firms became more complex, often through vertical integration, they were less amenable to personal control. Third, investment opportunities in new industries were expanding at a pace which induced the creation of institutions and which in turn lowered the cost of mobilizing savings. Local stock exchanges emerged in many communities. The Montreal and Toronto stock exchanges steadily expanded and by the First World War most major cities and towns in Canada boasted a formal exchange.[16] Many of these exchanges specialized in the sales and trading of particular industrial issues, such as those given over to mining shares. However, all attracted savings from a wider economic base than traditional methods of capital mobilization permitted.

The Entrepreneur

The years from the mid-nineteenth century to 1914 are often characterized as "the age of finance capitalism". This phrase describes the period of rapid transition from a simple, staple-based society to an industrial society at a time when capital markets were circumscribed. As a consequence, the individual entrepreneur or capitalist assumed a personal role in the mobilizing of financial resources for industrial and financial enterprise which accounted for a large proportion of capital formation. Of course, entrepreneurs were time-honoured, if not wholly beloved, economic agents even in the early periods of the staple trade. But then the investment which they helped to finance was either simple agriculturally based capital formation or trade inventories, and the process of economic change in which they operated placed less emphasis on new types of capital formation than in the emerging industrial economy of later times.

As less imperfect capital markets developed and as new corporate forms of organization emerged, reflecting the scale and diversity of business enterprise, the original functions of the entrepreneur were distributed over more individuals. Modern industrial society, some observers claim, witnessed bureaucracies within the large multinational and national firms usurping many of the major entrepreneurial functions —the word "technocracy" is often used to describe a society in which entrepreneurial functions are performed by cadres of highly technical managers.[17] Be that as it may, today there are individuals whose power to direct financial resources is very great.

Entrepreneurs are, by definition, those who mobilize resources and produce a real output or provide a service in the pursuit of profit. They control, therefore, the pace and type of capital formation which creates the capacity for growing output. Since capital is generally the scarce factor of production, their individual successes are usually dependent on the ability to identify a source of saving and convert it to a real capital — hence the usual synonym "capitalists". However in the process of pursuing their individual business enterprises they fulfil another economic role, that of reducing the barriers to efficient capital mobilization for society at large. Through individual entrepreneurs capital tends to flow from the economy's capital-abundant to the capital-scarce sectors and regions. Although this is more obviously the case when the particular business enterprise is a financial intermediary, entrepreneurs in a whole variety of business pursuits shift capital from one region to another. By so reallocating factors a reduction of excess demand, at a given interest rate, reduces the cost of capital to others; an external effect is created which is an important element in the evolution of relatively smoothly functioning capital markets.

During the era of finance capitalism there were insufficient information and inadequate credit and debt instruments necessary to direct savings to the most pressing demand. The importance of the entrepreneur, as discussed above, was drawn from his control over information processes. While in industry the capitalist self-financed many business ventures he rarely undertook an enterprise technologically very different from that in which he was first established. Personal information directed his transfer. For instance, the entrepreneurs of Canada's transcontinental railways were experienced in the art of transport finance. Those associated with the Grand Trunk Pacific started with the Grand Trunk; the members of the syndicate which constructed the Canadian Pacific Railway were owners of the successful St. Paul and Pacific Railway in Minnesota; the Canada Northern Railway's entrepreneurs contracted for parts of the Canadian Pacific Railway and operated lines in the West before 1900.[18]

When it was necessary to mobilize savings from others, the entrepreneur's success depended on his ability to allay fears of uncertainty. This was usually accomplished by personal contact which was most efficiently achieved when there was some degree of trust between the investors and those who controlled pools of savings. Not surprisingly a capitalist elite existed which performed both of the above functions. They tended to have similar social backgrounds; many were personally known to each other. The most important members of this group went to the same schools — Upper Canada College and the Montreal High School were two; they worshipped in the same churches — Presbyterian and Anglican most commonly; they often married each other's daughters to their sons, belonged to the same clubs, and in most respects were a closed society. Their common denominator was a shared cultural background. Even in the late nineteenth century the most important men in this group were usually of Scottish, American, English, or Irish ethnic origin and were only in a minority of cases Canadian-born.[19] Most obvious was the group of Scottish-born entrepreneurs in Montreal. Headed by lords Mountstephen and Strathcona, who were involved in railways, banking, and the Hudson's Bay Company, the group included prominent industrialists and financiers such as Sir Edward Clouston, banking and steel; Duncan MacIntyre, textiles; James Wilson, steel; and the Irish-born Robert Meighen, milling. Many of them had actually started work in the employ of the Montreal peers. Only a generation later the majority of the elite were Canadian-born, the sons of the earlier generation of capitalists.[20]

A common background, of course, reinforced the social ties. The Canadian capitalist elite was in this respect distinct from its counterpart in the United States. In that country nearly all important industrialists and financial managers were born in the United States.[21] This reflects not only the later settlement of Canada but also the smaller size of the economy and the somewhat lagging pace of expansion in the manufacturing industries. Less well-defined capital markets along with the potentially greater risks of staple-based business ventures ensured the continuance of the economic function of the class into the twentieth century, long after it had outlived its usefulness in the United States. The Molsons of banking and brewing fame and the Masseys of the agricultural machinery business bear more resemblance to the business elite of Boston in the early nineteenth century than to their contemporaries, H. W. Mellon and J. D. Rockefeller, in the United States.

There were many Canadian capitalists who did not belong to that group of the industrial and financial elite of the country but who exercised the same control of regional information flows. On a smaller scale than those in Toronto and Montreal these individuals marshalled local pools of savings which existing financial intermediaries left untapped. For instance, many small industrial enterprises, whether sawmills in British Columbia or shipping firms in Nova Scotia, relied on the raising of local financial capital from relatively few wealthy individuals.[22]

When it is argued that capitalists controlled information flows there is no implication that the particular undertaking for which savings were mobilized represented the best use of savings. For instance, capitalists often convinced governments, usually drawn from the same socioeconomic class, to undertake projects which generated a return to society which was less than might have been achieved. Were, for example, the promoters and builders of the Canadian Pacific Railway given too large a subsidy by the Macdonald government whom they convinced to initiate the project? Questions such as this will be considered in Chapter 10; it is sufficient at the moment to note that there were many inefficiencies which could not be or were not rectified by the capitalist's functioning in the capital market. His reduction of uncertainty barriers did not dissolve them; evidence is found in the fact that capital markets continued to evolve new debt and credit instruments and less personal methods of communicating.

The entrepreneur played a socially useful role in establishing more orderly capital markets so long as the exercise of his other powers did not offset that efficiency gain. In a position to monopolize factor markets, they could, and often did, make factors less sensitive to the allocation by market mechanisms. When this occurred a welfare loss resulted unless it was offset by some externality, such as a gain to society at large, which the entrepreneurs could not capture. So too, if capitalists sought to increase the amount of industrial concentration the resulting loss of income might not warrant the contribution to more smoothly functioning capital markets than would have otherwise existed.

Not all capitalists were honest promoters. Guile and manipulation produced individual fortunes which resulted in little or no social product.[23] It is unwise, however, to regard all the fortunes made as the ill-gotten gains of a social elite; many fortunes were true quasi-rents to those who disspelled uncertainty.[24] Many of the most successful entrepreneurs were those who recognized potential profits in newer industries and effectively transferred savings to them from older industries. For instance, in his early business career, George Stephen, later Lord Mountstephen, became involved in the take-overs of the Montreal Rolling Mills in 1869 and the Canada Rolling Stock Company in 1870 after initial success in the textile industry.[25] While the role of the capitalist or entrepreneur as an innovator is left unexplored here, it is nevertheless true for his role as a producer of goods and services and for his role as an agent who disspelled uncertainty (and obviously these two roles were inter-related), that once a rent was demonstrated others sought to achieve it. In so doing, they competed the level of rents down.

As economic agents smoothing the process of transferring savings inter-regionally and between industries, the capitalists were of importance as long as they provided the best alternative. However, they were not by any absolute standards efficient and the new financial intermediaries which emerged in the early twentieth century increasingly assumed their functions. The control over information flows which individuals exercised was too idiosyncratic and while their actions reduced the cost of capital, and thus facilitated indirectly the creation of investment, the possibilities of arbitrage remained. This, then, attracted the new generation of financial companies.

The Banking System

Capital mobilization is the process of identifying and marshalling savings so that they can be employed by the ultimate investors who create real capital. Throughout Canadian history the main source of savings has always been the household and private-business sectors. Fragmentary evidence, such as that presented in Table 7:1, suggests that gross investment-to-income ratios prior to the twentieth century generally averaged between 10 and 15 per cent. About the beginning of this century the ratio drifted upward to approximately 20 to 25 per cent and since then, except during the 1930s, has remained at this level. This once-and-for-all change in investment, and hence savings rates, appears to be linked to the pace and extent of industrial activity. As the industrial capital stock grew and incorporated new technologies so more and more savings had to be reserved for depreciation and further enlargement of the capital stock. Major increases were achieved only with the use of foreign savings although since then there has been more and more reliance on domestic savings. Income grew and savings rates, it is supposed, were sensitive; saving is often characterized as the ultimate luxury good. The growth of the savings rate in Canada followed a similar phenomenon in the United States by about three to four decades, reflecting the later industrial development of the Canadian economy.

Fundamental to the efficient mobilization of savings in Canada was the emergence, in the early nineteenth century, of a banking system.[26] Banks were the first financial intermediaries. In the same way as they later established financial intermediaries, such as insurance and trust and loan companies, entrepreneurs formed banks in response to a demand for real capital services and for savings instruments. That is, for providing the service of linking the surplus savers with the investors, a charge was made which constituted the banks' revenue. Interest rates indicated the relative shortages of financial funds for real investment and the existence of funds requiring savings instruments. Where there was need in an industry for capital services the interest rate was bid up as the market rationed the limited funds. However, as soon as institutions, such as banks, intermediated there was a tendency for the interest rate to fall because more funds were made available. The first institution likely made large quasi-rents from intermediation because its activities reduced the interest rate in the capital-scarce sector by an insignificant amount. But as more intermediation was undertaken by new entrants into the financial sector the rents were bid away, or at least down, as the interest rate fell.

The provision of all new financial services, except for some provided by government in recent years, such as the Canada Pension Plan, has been an entrepreneurial response to profit-making potential.[27] New institutions emerged when the existing ones were either incapable under law or unwilling to provide new intermediation services for a particular type of capital formation. Such was the case in the later 1840s. Since the banks were unable to meet a rapidly growing demand for home mortgages, a new institution, the building society, emerged as a financial intermediary directing savings into home construction. When existing financial intermediaries responded rapidly with a new financial service or when new institutions quickly supplied the new service, the economy experienced excess-demand pressure in a sector for only a short time. If, on the other hand, there was a long lag in the adjustment to new conditions, a restraint was placed on new types of real capital formation and economic development fell short of its potential.

Banks were established as a response to the growing capital requirements of the early-nineteenth-century staple economy. Paradoxically, however, in the long run banks played only a modest role in the *direct* mobilization of capital for investment purposes. This is explained by the fact that, over time, the banking system came to perform functions only indirectly associated with capital mobilization. One of these functions was the provision of a store of value and a medium of exchange—a money supply. Recall that the major element of the money supply in a developed economy is the bank money held in the form of deposit accounts and the long run conundrum comes into focus. A banking system which proved too responsive to all new demands for financial funds might endanger the stability of the monetary base if the risks associated with the new demand were misunderstood. Inflation would result that would prejudice economic growth. In Canada, because the prices of internationally traded goods were established externally and the trade sector in the overall economy was large the bankers and the legislators consistently adopted a conservative attitude. They sought monetary stability rather than a banking system which was directly and readily responsive to new investment needs.

The conservative posture of Canadian banking practices was set early in history.[28] First, there was the continual need to deal in foreign exchange and from early colonial times Canadian banks maintained branches in New York in order to conduct this aspect of their business.

Second, the major bank to dominate early banking history, the Bank of Montreal acted as the government's fiscal agent and tended to set the standard for the later banks. Through these and other activities the banking system served the interests of real capital formation only indirectly and, as will be noted later, only slowly because of its inability to respond quickly to new capital demands.

Although it is impossible in a few short pages to examine all the major developments in Canadian banking, attention here is directed to three issues which were central to long-run economic growth and change. They were:

1) the contribution of the banking system to capital formation by the provision of intermediary services;
2) the influence of the banking system on the money supply and in turn its influence on economic development; and
3) the banks' role in the creation of an increasingly efficient capital market.

An examination of the present-day chartered banks' balance sheets reveals that long-term corporate securities still constitute an extremely small proportion of the banks' total assets. As mobilizers of savings for the private sector the banks have been much more effective intermediaries for the provision of short-term and call loans. The banking system has concentrated its efforts directly on financing that part of real-capital formation known as inventories. (It is interesting here to note that when banking first evolved in Great Britain in the late eighteenth century a principal item in the capital stock was inventories. They could be financed directly with short-term loans.)[29] Banking in Canada has retained a basically conservative posture, when contrasted with the other financial intermediaries, with respect to its lending to the corporate sector for fixed-capital formation. Only since 1954 have banks financed home mortgages. Yet, this should not overshadow the importance of banks as mobilizers of short-term financial capital.

The provision of funds for the financing of inventories remained a vitally important form of capital formation. For instance, the banks lend so much to the grain dealers that this item alone is seen as worthy of a separate entry in the balance sheets. Over the decade of the 1950s, loans to grain dealers rose to some $500 million. It may be noted, for the sake of comparison, that the chartered banks' holdings of long-term corporate securities approximately equalled the loans to the grain dealers in 1960. Yet, the latter was only about 9 per cent of all short-term loans to the private sector. Similarly, in other sectors the provision of funds for inventory financing was critical; the inventories financed were frequently in the export sector.

To see how the financing of inventories became critical to early economic development it is necessary to consider the pre-banking economies of the seventeenth and eighteenth centuries. It is apparent from these times that capital formation was dependent on there being an accepted form of money. The virtual absence of an agreed-upon medium of exchange was one of the principal barriers to capital mobilization in early colonial Canada.[30] For example, New France was drained of specie, gold livres, under Colbertist policies by the simple expedient of persistently failing to ship enough coin to match the export earnings of the area and to pay the civil and military lists. Credits accumulated in France and while individuals' claims on these credits provided a tentative medium of exchange they were not universally acceptable because of their specificity. In 1685 the intendant of New France undertook bold action to surmount this problem. He declared a money which only indirectly had gold backing. This money, in the form of simple playing cards appropriately denominated, was essentially a substitute for specie which the French government owed as military pay and civil servants' salaries.

The playing card experiment of New France was remarkably successful between 1685 and 1717. It fulfilled the vital function of money as a medium of exchange because it could be redeemed in Quebec, once specie arrived from France and it became generally accepted. In fact, when France financed the war of the early 1700s by over-issue of playing-card money in New France and debasement of the coinage at home, the playing-card money depreciated less in value than its nominal backing. This is strong testimony for the argument that money is what people accept as money. It was, in fact, the subsequent growth of claims on the French Treasury which caused France to abandon this separate colonial money. Without doubt the experiment, which was repeated in the 1730-63 period, permitted the more orderly transaction of business, labour contracts, and consumption than the otherwise fluctuating amount of specie would have permitted.[31]

The British North American colonies of the eighteenth and early nineteenth centuries faced a similar problem to New France. Since the colonies were net importers, specie tended to be drained abroad. In the years immediately after the American Revolution, the vast amount of smuggling between the new United States and British North America stimulated a continual flow of sterling coin to the south. However, the problem was continental; all of North America faced the problems of insufficient specie and of a great variety of coinage circulating as money. In fact, British gold sovereigns were less common in British North America in the early nineteenth century than Spanish and Mexican coins. The values of the coins were legislated with the standard being set at its declared value in Halifax—whence the phrase "Halifax currency". In Upper Canada the accepted standard was that of New York State—"York currency". To be sure, other items such as bills of exchange—claims on specie held in a British bank or, after 1820, a domestic one—and even simple commodities—muskrat pelts among others—all functioned to some extent as money. On the other hand, bills of exchange were generally discounted, usually in direct proportion to the distance from where the claim could be made and while a backwoods storekeeper of Upper Canada might accept a muskrat pelt in payment for goods the urbane Montreal merchant would not. These substitutes were imperfect as money and their circulation only partly solved the basic liquidity problem.

It can be seen how small and unstable money supplies might limit the growth of real output from the following tautology:

$$M \cdot V = \sum_{i=1}^{n} (P_i \cdot Q_i)$$

where M is the money supply, V is the velocity of circulation of the money supply, P is prices, and Q is the quantity of the "n" goods and services produced in the economy. The velocity of circulation (V) is the number of times the money supply must be turned over each period to ensure that the transactions made with the money exactly equal output. But V tended to be stable in the long run since it was determined by habit, customs, and the technology of transactions. While V was probably capable of some short-run adjustments, it is apparent from the tautology that in the long run a growth in physical outputs, Q's, with stable prices could not take place unless matched by a growth in the money supply. On the other side of the coin, capricious movements of the money supply with relatively modest changes in physical output might cause a period of volatile price change.

Banks were founded of course as private profit-making ventures. In the process they provided the economic conditions for more rapid growth in real output. How this came about can be seen in the charter of the first bank founded in Canada, the Bank of Montreal. In 1817 the Bank of Montreal was permitted to issue bank notes to the extent of three times its registered business capital of £250,000.00 provided gold, silver, or government bonds backed the issue. Banks notes could be redeemed in specie but as long as there was confidence in the bank then there was confidence in its note issue and notes were seldom presented for redemption. The bank was also authorized to receive customers' deposits. Together the note issue and the deposits in the bank provided the mechanism for a non-inflationary growth of the monetary base in the long run although deposits did not become a perfect substitute for notes until the development of chequing privileges in the 1850s. Because of the near monopoly power of the Bank of Montreal in the early nineteenth century there was a relatively stable monetary base.[32]

In addition to issuing notes and receiving deposits, the Bank of Montreal was empowered to deal in foreign exchange, in bills of exchange, and in gold and silver bullion. Because the Bank of Montreal was the first bank and because it grew rapidly relative to the later entrants into the banking business, it came to play the role of the government's fiscal agent. While modern banking practice developed during the Industrial Revolution in England, the model for the Bank of Montreal was the United States first national bank, chartered under Alexander Hamilton. The intent was to concentrate banking power by the establishment of a branch-banking system so that credit expansion could be controlled. A branch-banking system was, it was felt, less likely to feel the pressure by frontier areas to inflate. During the presidency of Andrew Jackson, the United States succumbed to the pressure of frontier farmers and businessmen to dissolve the concentrated banking power.[33] Canada withstood such pressure and the branch-banking system became a permanent feature of the economy.

Branch banking, with power concentrated in the established trading centres, particularly suited the interests of the early Canadian capitalists who, for the most part, were either directly or indirectly associated with the staple trades. Montreal was the entrepôt centre whose merchants financed the inventories of staples and imported goods to the interior. The early banks actively supplied much of the necessary credit to merchants. As the market spread geographically into Upper Canada there was complaint that the banking system responded too slowly. Yet, as is apparent in Table 8:3, there was, in the long run, both a growth in the number of banks, most of which were based on the Bank of Montreal, and a growth in the number of branches. Bankers could not overlook the profits to be made on the extension of credit. As long as the public subscribed to the shares of the banks, the expansion of the banking system and, as a consequence, the monetary base of notes and bank deposits grew. This willingness on the part of the public was generally greater during times of rising exports and incomes than during the doldrums into which the staple industries sometimes fell.

Table 8:3 Number of Chartered Banks in British North America, 1820-1870

Year	Number of Banks Operating in B.N.A. (and Canada)
(1)	(2)
1820	1
1825	5
1830	6
1835	14
1840	16
1845	16
1850	15
1855	23
1860	30
1865	34
1870	34

Source: M. C. Urquhart and K. A. H. Buckley, eds., *Historical Statistics of Canada* (Toronto, 1965), p. 246.

Originally the note-issuing privilege of the chartered banks was the major contribution to the money supply. However, cash deposits in the banks grew more rapidly. By the early 1850s the note issue and aggregate deposits were approximately equal. The generally prosperous period which followed and lasted until Confederation witnessed a more rapid growth of credit than notes and by the eve of the first Bank Act of the new Canada in 1870, deposits in the chartered banks were more than twice as great as the circulating-note issue. In part, the rise in the importance of bank deposits relative to bank notes was due to the increased acceptance of deposits as a medium of exchange and to the government's desire to limit the banks' note-issuing privileges. It feared that competitive note issues would lead to inflation as the number of chartered banks increased and wished to take over the issue of notes. The issue of notes was after all, a cost-free debt to the issuer. Finally, in 1866, the government convinced the legislature to end the chartered banks' monopoly over the note issue by passing the Bank Note Act. This Act, although it had little immediate effect, became the basis of the Dominion Note Act of 1870 which marked a major step towards the concept of a monopoly note issue by government; however, it was well into the twentieth century before the effective bank control over the note issue was broken.[34]

Early banking in Canada was, with its concentration of power, well suited to the staple economy. Through the intermediation process between savers and investors it provided funds for the short-run financing of capital formation. The banks ventured only rarely into the financing of fixed-capital formation. The Bank of Montreal did marshall some funds for the construction of the first Lachine canal which by-passed the famous rapids on the St. Lawrence above Montreal, but such instances were rare. The troubles of the Bank of Upper Canada in the later 1850s gave the fullest support to the apparent wisdom of the conservative banking practice. This bank, along with many others, was caught up in the mania of the first railway boom. By 1857-58 the bank had over-committed itself to loans to the Grand Trunk Railway. When the railway failed to produce revenue as quickly as had been projected, its bonds and shares, as will be seen in more detail in the next chapter, were substantially discounted. Not only did the Bank of Upper Canada not expect payment of loans under the circumstances but the security which was held as collateral also depreciated. As it turned out, the loans to the railway were made to a large extent from the funds deposited by the government. During the period 1850-64, the Bank of Upper Canada acted as the fiscal agent for the government and therefore had sizeable government deposits at its disposal for loans. The bank was thus indebted to the government and although it functioned for several more years it finally succumbed to the heavy burden of debt just before Confederation. Learning from this experience, few banks directly sponsored fixed-capital formation until very recently and even now, as indicated earlier, banks are careful that it forms an extremely small proportion of a well-diversified portfolio.

Indirectly, the banks did permit fixed-capital formation but usually in the public rather than the private sector of the economy. Consequently, the mobilization of funds for the purchase of government securities was critical. The domestic banks in the pre-Confederation years were the major purchasers of government debt. Banks seldom held less than 10 per cent of their paid-up capital in this form. They were induced to do so because the only method of expanding a note issue—interest-free debt—was to back the expansion by government bonds and shares. In turn, the government debt was usually associated with capital expenditures on public works, such as the provision of roads and bridges, the building of a canal system linking the Great Lakes, and the building of harbours. These elements of fixed capital were the infrastructure without which the economy could not grow and evolve as will be seen in greater detail in Chapter 10.

In the pre-Confederation period, the most important contributions of the banking system were:

1) to provide a medium of exchange and to establish a money supply which was fairly stable;
2) to mobilize capital directly for the staple trades and internal trading sector; and
3) to channel savings indirectly into the fixed-capital formation of government.

However, to accomplish these ends, as we have seen, the government advocated, and the banks followed, a conservative banking policy. Inevitably this meant that the banking system was unresponsive to the new and growing demand for financial capital. As a consequence, new financial intermediaries evolved and displaced the banks as the major mobilizers of financial capital.

At the time of Confederation banks were still the major financial intermediaries. Alone they accounted for just under 75 per cent of all the assets held by all financial intermediaries. During the subsequent hundred years this proportion fell to less than 30 per cent as new institutions eroded the banks' pre-eminent position by the creation of new debt and credit instruments. Yet the banking system did not atrophy. On the contrary, it grew vigorously in the two decades after 1867 and over the very long run, 1870 to 1970, registered a rate of growth of real assets of 4.2 per cent per annum which was, in fact, slightly greater than the growth of real income.[35]

During the immediate post-Confederation period the banking system's absolute growth was based on the opening of new banks and branches and the increasing willingness of the public to hold deposit accounts as a medium of exchange. Although there had been a few flirtations with populist banking policies, the Bank Act of 1871 re-established the conservative principles of Canadian banking by setting high barriers to entry into this industry in terms of paid-up capital. Nevertheless, many new banks were created (see Table 8:4) and surprisingly there were no bank failures in which depositors lost their funds.

The demand for credit instruments which the banks served was primarily a demand for liquid assets. In order to control both the long-run and short-run behaviour of these particular instruments, deposit accounts, the government sought increasing control over the operation of the banking system. While the simple regulation by charter of bank activities served tolerably well in the pre-industrial years, it was too insensitive a regulatory mechanism for the requirements of the increasingly complex open economy and the growing needs of government.

As a consequence, and in contrast to the United States, the banking

Table 8:4 Number of Chartered Banks in Canada, 1870-1970

Year	Number of Chartered Banks	Number of Chartered Bank Branches		Number of Bank Insolvencies in Decade Beginning in the Year
(1)	(2)	(3)		(4)
1870	34	(1868)	123	6
1880	44	(1879)	295	7
1890	41		426	5[a]
1900	35		708	5
1910	28		2,367	3
1920	18		4,676	1
1930	11		4,083	0
1940	10		3,311	0
1950	10		3,679	0
1960	9		5,051	0
1968	9		5,922	0

[a] Includes two insolvencies in Newfoundland.

Source: Urquhart and Buckley (1965), p. 246.

system in Canada remained highly centralized. Branch banking did not yield to the populist pressure of the frontier interest and the creation of segmented unit banking. Yet there is no strong evidence to suggest that either of the banking systems served the needs of the respective developing economies better.

In the Canadian case, the continuing open nature of the economy demanded a banking system with well-developed foreign-exchange-transaction mechanisms. The individual bank's foreign-exchange expertise in the New York and London money and capital markets facilitated both trade and capital flows. In the next chapter, the banks will be seen as a critical feature of the international transfer of savings from Great Britain to Canada. It was the openness of the economy and the possible consequences of gold flows affecting changes in the money supply which made the government and the bankers favour a credit-creation system which could impart a more stable monetary base than a unit-banking system. While the unit-banking system in the United States was effective in mobilizing the savings of the frontier areas it must be recalled that in Canada frontier-based development lasted for a longer time, well into the twentieth century. This in itself was not necessarily an obstacle to the success of a unit-banking system except that the Canadian frontiers were generally more sparsely populated than those in the United States. The scale of the economy was smaller and the natural-resource exploitation, other than of agricultural land, less of an immediately attractive feature to the quick emergence of a local pool of savings which could be mobilized for investment purposes.

Yet there was a cost to the branch-banking system. In order to achieve stability of the money-supply process, industrial concentration of banking was not only permitted but at times encouraged. Successive Bank Acts raised the barriers to entry into the industry by requiring increasingly larger financial capital of new entrants. New foreign-owned banks were prohibited by 1871. The number of banks steadily declined (see Table 8:4) in the twentieth century as entry was forestalled, mergers took place, and insolvency caused failures. Despite this concentration the branch-banking system was sensitive to frontier banking needs. The establishment of new branches generally followed the pace and geographic pattern of expansion; a bank's profits were those for its entire operation and not that of a single branch; uneconomic branches were often subsidized in the short run in the anticipation of future profits. Although the banks were conservative lenders in frontier areas they did help integrate these areas into the market economy by the provision of credit instruments.[36] It is unlikely that a highly competitive banking system constrained to undertake all credit and debit transactions in one locality would have provided the same basis for economic development in the Canadian case.

In the post-Confederation period the government strove to achieve full control over the process of money creation. There were three separate phases in this evolution of control each of which centred on a specific set of events. They were:

1) the Dominion Notes Act of 1870 and the Bank Act of the following year;
2) the Finance Act of 1914; and
3) the establishment of the Bank of Canada in 1935.

The first, the Dominion Notes Act of 1870, was based on the precedent established four years earlier which permitted the government to issue notes. Only partly backed by gold the Dominion notes were in small denominations whereas the bank notes usually did not have a face value lower than $5. However, banks were required to hold one-half of their cash reserves in Dominion notes. By means of this gold-backed issue, Canada was effectively integrated into the prevailing gold standard of international exchange which then existed. Prior to this Act, the banks' holding of specie or government securities regulated money-supply creation though the note issue was limited to a proportion of paid-up capital. When the upper limit was removed the gold-backed Dominion notes became the most prevalent form of security. Gold in-flows and out-flows regulated the money supply. Dominion notes were "high-powered" money since they were used as security for bank notes which in turn permitted a multiple expansion of deposits.[37] In fact, Dominion notes circulated narrowly but were held by the banks for exactly this purpose and relative to government notes, they grew to be more than one-half of the total note issue by 1909 (see Table 8:5). Even though only a small proportion of this note issue circulated in the hands of the public its creation was an important step in the assertion of control over the process of money supply.

The Bank Act of 1871 was also critical in establishing control over the banking system, both in itself and because it became the model for subsequent Bank Acts. As mentioned earlier, the capital requirements of banks were raised but control was extended by incorporating in law the prohibitions previously outlined in each individual charter and by instituting double liability provisions for shareholders. Subsequent Bank Acts raised capital barriers further and extended the amount of reporting which governments required of the individual banks.

Regulation of the money supply under the gold standard of international exchange was relatively autonomous. But Canada abandoned the gold standard, following the example of all the belligerent countries, at the beginning of the First World War. The war crisis justified to parliament the passing of the Finance Act of 1914 which contained many provisions previously disallowed by the Bank Act. Chartered banks were no longer required to make payment in specie on demand. The most important of the new provisions was the authority given to the Minister of Finance to issue Dominion notes to the banks on promise of acceptable security. The banks could use such advances from the Department of Finance to expand their note issues and so to be multiplied by deposit creation to a larger change in the money supply. An important by-product of this system of advances was the establishment of a discount rate, the rate at which bank securities were discounted into Dominion notes. This discount rate later became what is now known as "the bank rate", the movements of which act as a signal for economic expansion and contraction: by setting the standard the bank rate governs the rate charged on loans and consequently the amount of new investment.

However, the Finance Act of 1914 and its revision of 1923 was a method of avoiding runs on banks for specie rather than a mechanism by which the Department of Finance could control short-run movements of the money supply. Yet, the advance of Dominion notes was the immediate precursor to a mechanism which could also be so used. During the entire history of advances, 1914 to 1934, there is little doubt that any bank was ever denied Dominion notes on the posting of securities.[38] Although short-run movements in the money supply are not of immediate concern it is pertinent to note that the easy access to Dominion notes gave the monetary base unstable characteristics: the effects of high-powered money were felt.[39]

The experience of the 1920s of the temporary return to gold and resumption of specie payment (1926 to 1929), and the precipitious contraction of the money supply in the early 1930s, increased the pressure for the establishment of an institution more capable of fine adjustments in the money supply than the crude policy alternative of the Finance Act. Although the immediate claim for the creation of a central bank was based upon the necessity of having independent managers of the public debt there can be little doubt that the inability of a direct arm of government to exercise short-run control over the money supply was a major force behind the founding of the Bank of Canada in 1935. Separate from the government, yet responsible to it, the central bank was given sweeping powers.

The note-issuing rights of the chartered banks were repealed and the Bank of Canada assumed sole rights to issue paper money. Begun in 1866 by the passing of the Bank Note Act, the government monopoly over paper money was now complete. Regulation of bank money, that is, deposits, was also achieved by the establishment of formal reserve ratios: reserve ratios which governed the size of the money multiplier were previously not required. As the lender of last resort the Bank of Canada had the power to set the rediscount rate which was reinforced by the establishment of a money market functioning under the authority of the central bank. The money market was simply the trading of short-term securities on specified days and the interest rate established there, the short rate, was the vital first signal to the behaviour of the long-term interest rate. Consequently, the money-market dealing in short-term bills was an element in reducing uncertainty about overall interest-rate behaviour; a more efficient capital market followed.

The evolution of the Canadian banking system continued after the creation of the Bank of Canada. As noted earlier, new credit and debit instruments were permitted and their appearance marked a more visible and direct contribution of the banks to capital formation. Regulation of the money supply was found to be more effectively accomplished through the use of open-market operations and the unexercised authority of the Bank of Canada to change reserve requirements in the form of the cash ratio was abandoned. Of course it was not coincidence that when government control over the money-supply creation process had been firmly established in 1935 there was a relaxation of the old conservative

Table 8:5 Growth and Changes in the Composition of the Money Supply, 1867-1975

(millions of dollars)

Year	Chartered Bank Note Issue	Dominion or Bank of Canada Note Issue	Canadian Deposits in Chartered Banks	Dominion Note Issue Held by the Chartered Banks	Total Note Issue in Circulation Relative to Deposits[c] (per cent)
(1)	(2)	(3)	(4)	(5)	(6)
1867	9.8	4.3[b]	32.6	—	43.3
1870	18.5	7.4	52.1	62.7	49.7
1875	23.3	11.3	60.1	75.2	43.4
1880	27.3	14.2	79.2	73.9	39.1
1885	32.4	17.8	101.9	69.7	37.1
1890	35.0	15.6	133.9	62.2	30.6
1895	32.6	22.4	197.3	71.4	19.8
1900	50.8	28.4	308.2	69.7	19.3
1905	70.0	49.0	529.5	77.8	15.3
1910	87.7	90.7	860.6	83.8	11.9

1915	122.2	178.8	1,207.7	87.6	12.0
1920	228.8	311.7	1,993.4	89.6	13.1
1925	173.9	227.2	1,972.8	93.8	9.8
1930	148.0	175.4	2,127.8	83.1	8.4
1935	118.9[a]	99.7	2,208.4	—	8.1
1940	84.0	360.0	2,805.0	—	12.2
1945	26.0	1,129.0	5,942.0	—	16.7
1950	14.0	1,367.0	7,979.0	—	14.3
1955	—	1,739.0	10,848.0	—	13.4
1960	—	2,062.0	12,921.0	—	13.4
1965	—	2,380.6	18,594.0	—	11.4
1970	—	3,632.3	29,888.0	—	10.4
1975	—	7,283.1	66,873.0	—	9.1

[a] No chartered bank notes were issued after 1935 and those outstanding retired when they were presented for payment.

[b] Refers to the Provincial Notes which were the precursors of the Dominion Notes.

[c] Note issue in circulation is defined as Dominion or Bank of Canada notes in the hands of the public excluding the chartered banks and all chartered bank notes outstanding.

Sources: *Bank of Canada Review*, various issues; and Urquhart and Buckley (1965), p. 231.

attitude towards the borrowing and lending activities of the banks. It could not have been otherwise: there was a fundamental trade-off between the long-run stability of the money-supply process and the responsiveness with which the banks could react to new investment demands.

In summary, the banking system evolved to meet two coincident needs: the demand for liquid assets and the demand for short-term credit. Because deposit liabilities and bank notes were the essential components of the money supply the banks fulfilled the need for and profited from the establishment of a medium of exchange. The consequent critical nature of the services provided increasingly focused the attention of both government and the banks themselves on the maintenance of a money supply which neither expanded too rapidly nor too slowly. Direct capital formation, undertaken through the use of loans from the banks, continued to grow absolutely but declined as a proportion because the financing of fixed-capital formation was usually indirectly financed. Indirectly, the banks aided fixed-capital formation by the purchase and holding of government securities. Particularly in the year of the railway booms, high proportions of bond holdings were government-backed railway securities. However during the years since Confederation these have almost been completely replaced by government securities.

In very recent history, banks have once more become vigorous intermediaries for direct financing of the capital stock. Under special arrangements farmers can now borrow for the purpose of improving buildings and equipment and carrying their inventories of seed and grain. In the housing market, banks now lend funds; the sign in a bank window "mortgages available", common now, would not only have been unusual but illegal two decades ago. New long-term savings accounts and debentures were created to service demands for long-term loans. So too, consumer credit for the acquisition of durable goods is readily available — at a price.

Vital contributions of the banking system to the relatively smooth process of economic development in Canada were the provision of a medium of exchange and of foreign-exchange transactions. As will be examined in the following chapter, from its earliest years in this country, the banking system operated in the foreign-exchange market and idle bank balances invariably found their way to the New York exchange market; this proved historically to be one of the most profitable accounts.

Non-Bank Financial Intermediaries
Central Canada of the 1850s was much more urban than it had been a decade earlier. The transition from a rural to an urban society gathered

momentum, stimulating a demand for home mortgages which could not be met at reasonable interest rates. In response many small cooperative ventures evolved to aid individual financing of home purchases. Later these institutions, the building societies, were empowered to accept deposits and so provide an effective mechanism for mobilizing savings. It appears that as more funds became available, as might be predicted, mortgage rates of interest fell. Many of these building societies remained local and naturally the price of mortgages varied between towns and counties.[40]

The existence of mortgage-rate differentials was simply a signal that there was the possibility of financial intermediation between the locations of the two different rates. Responding to such profitable opportunities many building societies became mortgage and loan companies. With wide powers to manage portfolios of assets and with greater flexibility than the smaller building societies to undertake financial arbitrage, mortgage and loan companies had grown by the 1870s to be the principal institution through which funds were mobilized for privately owned residential dwellings, farms, and industrial buildings. The first building society was formed in Canada West in 1846 but within two decades these societies, as mortgage and loan companies, had grown to the second largest type of financial intermediary in the country. The new residential building, represented in Figure 8:2, reflects the extent of all urban building in Canada in the immediate post-Confederation years. Its population sensitivity is readily appreciated from the evidence in Chapter 6.[41] Continued rapid growth of the mortgage and loan companies occurred until by 1885-90 they held about one-quarter of all financial assets in the hands of financial intermediaries in the private sector of the economy. There was an excess demand and no other institution could provide a similar financial service.

The rapid growth of the building societies and mortgage and loan companies immediately reduced the proportion of financial intermediation undertaken by the chartered banks and the Quebec Savings Bank. As noted earlier, from 1870 onwards the banks' share of the market declined although as is evident from Table 8:6, the banks remained the largest single intermediary despite their declining relative importance. The decline was a result of the growth of demand for mortgages which the banks could not satisfy and, later, the growth of financial institutions meeting highly specialized demands which occupied significant positions in both absolute and relative terms in the process of capital mobilization.

Not until the end of the nineteenth century did any non-bank financial intermediary hold more Canadian assets than the building societies and

Figure 8:2 Residential Dwellings Built and Completed Per Year, 1872-1921

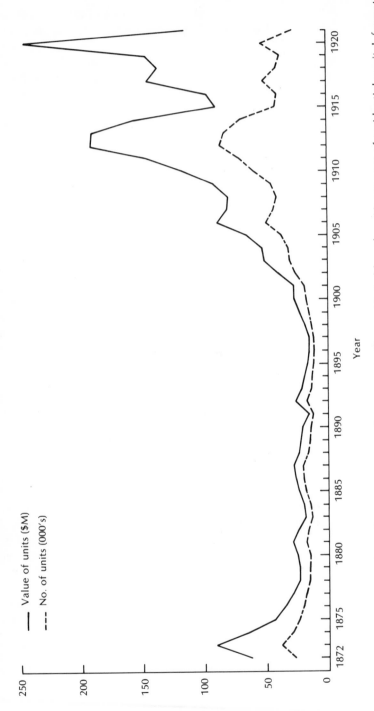

Note: Major alterations and improvements to houses generally constituted less than 10 per cent of residential capital formation. However, as a contributor to all residential capital formation, it varied less than the value of units completed.

Source: Data are from Pickett, pp. 47 and 51.

Table 8:6 Distribution of Canadian Assets Among Financial Intermediaries in the Private Sector, 1870-1968
(per cent)

Year	Chartered Banks	Quebec Savings Bank	Life Insurance Companies	Fraternal Societies	Fire and Casualty Insurance Companies	Mortgage Loans Companies	Trust Companies	Consumer Loan Companies	Investment Companies	Caisses Populaires and Credit Unions	Trusteed Pension Funds	Other Companies
(1)	(2)	(3)	(4)	(5)	(6)	(7)	(8)	(9)	(10)	(11)	(12)	(13)
1870	79.3	4.1	2.6	—	3.5	10.5	—	—	—	—	—	—
1875	75.1	3.6	3.0	—	3.7	14.7	—	—	—	—	—	—
1880	61.8	3.5	3.8	—	3.5	27.4	—	—	—	—	—	—
1885	60.0	3.1	5.9	0.4	2.9	27.9	—	—	—	—	—	—
1890	55.6	2.9	9.7	0.8	3.9	27.5	—	—	—	—	—	—
1895	60.9	3.4	15.1	0.8	4.3	28.3	—	—	—	—	—	—
1900	58.6	2.8	14.6	1.1	3.7	18.1	1.4	—	—	—	—	—
1905	63.3	2.6	13.8	1.7	3.4	13.4	1.9	—	—	—	—	—
1910	65.1	2.3	13.0	2.0	3.6	11.9	2.1	—	—	—	—	—
1915	61.9	1.9	15.9	3.0	3.2	11.4	2.8	—	—	0.1	—	—
1920	68.2	1.7	14.6	2.2	3.8	7.4	1.8	—	—	0.1	—	—
1925	58.9	1.9	22.9	2.4	4.0	7.2	2.7	—	—	0.2	—	—
1930	49.9	1.5	28.3	2.0	4.1	5.4	4.8	0.8	3.2	0.2	—	—
1935	48.0	1.4	33.0	2.3	3.9	5.0	4.1	0.7	1.5	0.3	—	—
1940	47.9	1.3	32.2	2.0	3.5	3.6	3.3	1.3	1.3	0.4	3.4	—
1945	57.5	1.2	25.5	1.5	2.9	2.3	2.5	0.6	1.2	1.2	3.5	—
1950	52.9	1.3	24.5	1.1	3.4	2.4	2.7	2.9	1.3	2.1	5.3	—
1955	47.3	1.1	22.8	1.0	3.7	2.4	2.9	5.1	3.4	2.9	7.5	—
1960	40.4	0.9	22.7	0.9	4.0	2.7	3.7	6.6	3.9	4.2	10.2	—
1965	36.6	0.8	19.7	0.8	3.3	4.2	5.9	7.3	4.7	5.1	11.3	0.5
1968	37.7	0.8	17.8	0.7	3.3	3.9	6.5	6.4	5.6	5.5	11.6	0.1

Source: E. P. Neufeld, The Financial System of Canada (Toronto, 1972), pp. 611-32.

mortgage and loan companies. When this came about, it was the life-insurance industry which assumed the new leadership. The rapid growth of the life-insurance companies dominates the history of financial intermediation in the last quarter of the nineteenth century. Foreigners first started the life-insurance industry and although its origins predate Confederation there was only one domestic life-insurance company active in 1869. On the other hand, there were thirteen British and nine other foreign companies, mostly controlled in the United States.[42] Canadian participation grew as restrictions were imposed on foreign companies partly in response to local requests — foreign companies were required to match their Canadian liabilities with Canadian assets — and as domestic entrepreneurs, who had learned from the experience of others, entered the industry. By 1890 domestic companies held approximately 60 per cent of the industry's assets. This industry stands as one of the few examples of Canadians having wrested control from foreigners (Table 8:7).

Prior to 1899 all insurance companies were required to confine their portfolio of assets to the provisions of their individual charters. The Insurance Act of 1899, which permitted a wider asset choice, brought a conformity to the industry. The driving force to extend the range of assets permitted to be held, without the time-consuming changes to individual charters, was the excess liquidity which characterized the industry of the 1890s.[43] The efficiency with which the insurance industry mobilized savings undoubtedly had a profound, if unquantifiable, effect permitting the upward shift of the GNCF-to-GNP ratio. From 1891 to 1901 the corporate bonds, mainly railroad securities, in the aggregate portfolio of the life-insurance companies rose from 3 to 13 per cent but since that time the proportion has remained relatively constant. There has been a long-run tendency, however, to hold a smaller proportion of government bonds and this decline is most noticeable in terms of municipal bonds. Mortgage loans, which were a critically large proportion of the insurance industry's portfolio in the nineteenth century, declined in importance about the turn of the century only to grow again in the years after the Second World War.

The breaking of barriers which had previously imposed rigidities on the flow of savings enabled the insurance industry to respond to market forces in the acquisition of assets. Capital mobilization was becoming more efficient with respect to sectors and regions of the economy and in the years immediately preceding the First World War the life-insurance sector, more than any other non-bank financial intermediary, helped lay the foundation for the formal Canadian capital market.

Unlike the mortgage and loan companies, the life-insurance companies had, from their inception, held broad portfolios of assets. Mort-

Table 8:7 Assets of Federally Registered Life Insurance Companies in Canada, 1888-1960

(millions of dollars)

Year	Assets of Canadian Life-Insurance Companies	Canadian Assets of Foreign Life-Insurance Companies	
(1)	(2)	(3)	
1888	16.0	18.2	(1889)
1890	20.7	22.4	
1895	35.3	37.9	
1900	59.5	51.8	
1905	102.4	66.1	
1910	170.8	78.9	
1915	274.2	115.3	
1920	423.3	166.6	
1925	812.2	268.5	
1930	1,509.9	464.0	
1935	1,880.7	561.7	
1940	2,455.8	606.4	
1945	3,449.8	838.1	
1950	4,611.7	1,133.6	
1955	6,278.4	1,524.7	
1960	8,095.3	1,900.5	

Note: Column (2) gives market values and (3) book values. Also, Canadian life-insurance companies often held non-domestic assets.

Source: Urquhart and Buckley (1965), pp. 255-57.

gage loans, although the main asset prior to 1900, were held in conjunction with bonds, mostly government, collateral loans, and real estate. This meant that life-insurance companies were more flexible than intermediaries which concentrated their attention on only one asset and when legislative action permitted them to hold more corporate bonds they rapidly absorbed them into their portfolios. Thus, the life-insurance industry was the first of the major financial intermediaries to serve directly the needs of fixed-capital formation of industry in general and when they so responded corporate and government securities became, by value, their principal asset. Yet the life-insurance industry was incapable of unchecked expansion because the types of credit instruments which could be offered to savers was limited. By the Second World War this industry too began to experience a relative decline in importance.

Even in the last quarter of the nineteenth century more and more financial institutions emerged in response to a need to provide other vehicles for saving. Trust companies, for instance, developed in the 1880s to fulfil the need for estate management. In the process funds became available to the industrial sector as the demand for corporate securities increased. Loan companies, *caisses populaires* and credit unions, mutual funds, and a variety of smaller financial intermediaries in more recent times have all become active mobilizers of the country's saving (Table 8:6). Very recently the private pension funds and the Canada Pension Plan in the public sector became major pools of savings.[44] As the demands for investment in the capital stock grew, so too have the amount of savings supplied grown through the market mechanism. The knowledge of alternatives expanded with the capital market. Consequently, the *uncertainty* about the *distribution of risk* associated with investment projects declined and the inter-sectoral and inter-regional barriers to the efficient mobilization of capital fell.

CHAPTER NINE

Foreign Investment

Introduction: Trends in Foreign Investment

Few countries have experienced for so long in their histories so much foreign investment as Canada has. At one level of analysis this foreign investment was no more than an international inflow of foreign savings which, like domestic savings, facilitated the process of real-capital formation. At another level it was the mechanism whereby foreign business interests established a major presence in the Canadian economy. It is a characteristic of rapidly developing, open economies that capital inflows and outflows occur, persist, and relate directly to a country's performance on the balance-of-payments current account. As an open economy, Canada experienced long-term capital imports which often permitted higher levels of capital formation than otherwise would have been possible. For example, in the prosperous years, 1901-15, capital imports were more than half as large as domestic savings and thus financed a major part of new investment. They were no less than 12.4 per cent of GNP.[1] The objectives of this chapter are to examine the determinants of capital imports, to account for their magnitude and timing, and to judge how they affected the pattern of Canadian economic development.

The capital flows into Canada were, of course, changing economic forces. Their composition, origin, and impact differed both with the changing nature of the economy and with the ability of foreign countries to supply excess savings. The flow of capital into Canada was not always positive or substantial. Long-term capital imports were, for instance, modest during the early phases of economic development, associated with the exploitation of the first staples. On the other hand, the Canadian economy at this time, displayed no aggregate shortage of savings, despite capital-scarce sectors, as wealth was channelled into speculative ventures such as the purchase of seigneuries.[2] The first major need for foreign savings was not felt until the nineteenth century when it was needed to help finance the canal system of the St. Lawrence. Although committed to the St. Lawrence route, the Montreal merchants were incapable, during the 1820s and 1830s, of marshalling sufficient domestic savings to complete the project, as will be seen in more detail in the next chapter. Even the addition of British savings, through debenture bonds, was insufficient for the rapid completion of the project prior to the Act of Union. Only after 1840 was sufficient capital imported to speed construction of the canal system.[3]

Canada was also unable to attract foreign savings during some periods of modern history (see Table 9:1). For instance, during the two decades from 1930, the economy was, on balance, a capital exporter. To be sure, these were extraordinary times for the international economy, first, as most economies were depressed and, second, as war and postwar demands attracted Canadian savings to Europe. Few of the countries from which Canada usually borrowed were capable of generating a surplus of savings for export. The aftermath of war had had a similar affect on the economy of the early 1920s. Then, the economy of Great Britain, on which Canada traditionally relied for capital imports prior to 1914, was depressed and incapable of supplying funds to overseas investors at the rate it had been before the war.[4] During such periods a net capital export was the result of retirement of outstanding foreign indebtedness. Too often it was impossible to refinance such debt. However, it is important to note that *gross* capital imports did continue even though the *net* balance shows an export of capital. For instance, the flow of direct investment from the United States, in particular, continued for the decade of the Second World War. In summary, while the Canadian economy usually required capital imports to expand and develop, these inflows were not always forthcoming in the magnitudes needed.

In terms of the quantitative significance of capital imports, the early-nineteenth-century economy placed increasing reliance on these inflows. This reliance increased although it varied somewhat. As can be seen from Table 9:2 even during the years of relative slow growth, 1873-96, capital imports were large as a proportion of GNP. Paradoxically, the proportion of capital imports to GNP decreased in 1896-1900 due to the growth in income which was not matched by a growth in the inflow of foreign savings. While the inflow of capital as a percentage of GNP for the first quinquennium of the twentieth century was only slightly above than the long-run average, in the following ten years it reached remarkably high proportions. Thereafter, capital imports were less important and modern ex-

Table 9:1 Net Capital Inflows into Canada, 1871-1975
(millions of dollars)

Period	Hartland	Buckley	Official	Capital Inflows as a Percentage of GNP
(1)	(2)	(3)	(4)	(5)
1871-75	166			7.0
1876-80	93			3.3
1881-85	167			5.2
1886-90	242			6.4
1891-95	202			4.6
1896-1900	124			2.5
1901-05	(317)	301		5.3
1906-10	(829)	784		9.2
1911-15		1,515		12.4
1916-20		262		1.3
1921-25		−72		−0.3
1926-30		(563)	527	1.8
1931-35			−159	0.0
1936-40			−690	−2.5
1941-45			−853	−1.6
1946-50			−812	−1.1
1951-55			2,783	2.2
1956-60			6,071	3.5
1961-65			3,939	1.7
1966-70			7,249	2.0
1971-75			7,837	1.4

Note: Columns (2) and (4) measure long-term inflows whereas column (3) measures both long- and short-term flows. The compatibility of the estimates may be judged from the overlaps in parentheses. See Bloomfield for the Hartland series. The GNP base for the years 1871 to 1900 are based on a linear interpolation of Firestone's data reported in Urquhart and Buckley. They include the reinvestment of earnings.

Sources: A. I. Bloomfield, *Patterns of Infrastructure in International Investment Before 1914* (Princeton, 1968), pp. 42-44; K. Buckley, *Capital Formation in Canada, 1896-1930* (Toronto, 1955), p. 99; Statistics Canada, *Canadian Statistical Review: Historical Summary, 1970*, Cat. no. 11-505; Statistics Canada, *Canadian Statistical Review*, Cat. no. 11-003; and M. C. Urquhart and K. A. H. Buckley, eds., *Historical Statistics of Canada* (Toronto, 1965), pp. 142-72.

perience is one of reduced reliance on them. What distinguished the pre-First World War economy from that following was that more commitments to large capital projects were undertaken relative to the size of GNP. The building of the transcontinental railways even in comparison with projects such as the St. Lawrence Seaway placed proportionately more strain on the balance of payments. In more recent history, as the role of domestic savings became more important, relatively less reliance has been placed on foreign savings. However, one might well ask whether the flow of capital imports, required to finance mammoth projects such

Table 9:2 Percentage Distribution of Foreign Capital Invested in Canada, by Source and Type, 1900-1967

Year	Great Britain	United States	Portfolio	Direct Investment
(1)	(2)	(3)	(4)	(5)
1900	85	14	75[a]	25[a]
1905	79	19	—	—
1910	77	19	—	—
1916	66	30	—	—
1920	53	44	—	—
1926	44	53	70	30
1930	36	61	68	32
1933	36	61	68	32
1939	36	60	67	33
1945	25	70	62	38
1950	20	76	54	46
1955	18	76	43	57
1960	15	75	42	58
1967	10	81	40	60

[a] above is a crude estimate based on Lewis, Paterson (1976), and Viner.

Sources: Canada, Foreign Direct Investment in Canada (Ottawa, 1972), p. 15; Statistics Canada, Canada's Balance of International Indebtedness, 1960-70, Cat. no. 67-202; D. B. S., The Canadian Balance of International Payments: A Compendium of Statistics from 1946 to 1965, Cat. no. 67-505; and Urquhart and Buckley (1965), p. 169.

as the Mackenzie Valley Pipeline would restore the ratio of foreign-capital imports to GNP to levels found in much earlier periods of history. While it has been argued that the relative importance of the inflow of capital has declined since the early years of this century it is still high. Canada continues to import more foreign savings relative to income than most countries.

Financing large projects by the use of foreign savings became characteristic of Canada's economic development. By the mid-1840s the new method of transport, railways, superseded the project of the St. Lawrence canal system. The size of these capital projects and the associated spreading effects to other sectors of the economy were important demand forces stimulating income growth. When such capital projects were undertaken during periods of rapid expansion of demand for Canada's exports, very high levels of income growth were experienced. This was so in the mid-nineteenth and early twentieth centuries. Even when the railway construction took place in the absence of strong demand pressure for exports, the construction expenditures were often sufficiently large to have a general expansionary fiscal effect. Undoubtedly, income growth in the 1880s would have been very much slower without construction of the Canadian Pacific Railway.

The capital imports of a long-term nature were essentially of two types: portfolio and direct foreign investment. The former is debt issued on security whereas the latter is the action of foreigners establishing business ventures in Canada. Quantitatively, the long-term gross inflow of portfolio capital has usually been greater than the inflow of long-term direct investment capital. The gross inflow of direct investment capital as a percentage of new Canadian security issues abroad averaged less than 50 per cent even in recent times, 1966 to 1975. Because portfolio debt is contracted for a stated period of time there has been a continual retirement of Canadian securities. Direct investment, on the other hand, takes place through business firms and does not normally give rise to the retirement of securities. Only when the business venture fails or is taken over by Canadians is there a reduction in the foreign claims on assets located in Canada. Thus, one of the main trends in foreign investment has been a growth of direct investment as a proportion of the *stock* of the economy's international indebtedness as may be inferred from Table 9:2 and as seen later. At the time of Confederation only an extremely small percentage of the stock of foreign investment was in the form of direct business participation in the economy. This increased to about 25 per cent in 1900. Although the absolute stock of direct investment grew, particularly in the years 1900 to 1926, it was not until the post-Second World War period that its relative importance grew to the predominant type of foreign capital invested in Canada.

Accompanying the rise to dominance of foreign direct investment as an element in Canada's international indebtedness was a change in the geographic composition of debt holding. The importation of capital into Canada prior to 1900 was primarily from Great Britain. The United States, a lender in later years, was itself still a net-capital importer.[5] However, increasingly after 1900 more and more gross-capital imports came from the United States, initially in the form of new direct investment. Great Britain was still the major supplier of portfolio debt. In a very few years, 1910 to 1926, the roles of the two major suppliers switched. By 1926, the United States held over half of Canada's foreign indebtedness. More and more new portfolio issues of Canadian securities were being subscribed in New York rather than in London. The depression of the 1930s froze the profile but as soon as the depression was over, about 1940, the proportion of the stock of foreign investment held in the United States again increased. The post-1945 period also witnessed the rise of countries other than Great Britain and the United States as claimants on Canadian assets. From 1952 to 1960, foreign capital invested in Canada from countries other than these two increased from $502 million to over $2.1 billion.[6] For instance, municipal bonds in 1905 were as often as not denominated in sterling. In the 1920s the debt was often issued in U.S. dollars whereas many debt issues in recent times have been denominated in Deutsche Marks.

Most countries which have been *net*-capital importers experienced a small but growing *gross*-capital export as they became more industrialized. Canada was no exception. Beginning about the turn of the twentieth century, small amounts of Canadian savings found their way abroad. This savings flow went initially to the United States, the West Indies, and Latin America and to industries where there was a Canadian business presence and in Latin America was concentrated in electric-light and power-generation companies. This gross outflow grew in modern times so that Canadian per-capita direct investment in the United States actually became larger than U.S. per-capita investment in Canada as seen later in this chapter. This, of course, does not suggest that the dimensions of the foreign direct-investment problem are less in Canada.

In summary foreign investment in Canada displayed many long-term characteristics which affected the pace and character of Canadian economic development:

1) Capital in-flows were often large but also often not forthcoming for sustained periods of Canadian history.
2) While the size of capital imports grew secularly their relative importance to GNP declined. This decline was most marked in the post-First World War years.
3) The *flow* of direct-investment capital relative to portfolio debt increased, especially in the twentieth century, but today still remains less than 50 per cent of gross long-term capital imports.
4) The composition of the *stock* of foreign investment changed slowly over the past one hundred years. Formerly dominated by portfolio debt, foreign direct investment is now the major element.
5) Accompanying the change in the composition of the stock of foreign investment was a change in composition of claims. Prior to 1926 Great Britain held most claims; later it was the United States. This reflected not only the different types of claims but the fact that after 1914 the United States became the major supplier of all long-term debt.
6) Although Canada has been a country which throughout its modern history required foreign savings to augment gross-domestic-capital formation, it also exported capital. For most of this century the gross export of capital has been growing absolutely and relative to gross-capital imports.

The Balance of Payments and International Indebtedness

Throughout most of modern history Canada has been a net importer of capital; Canada has also had a persistent deficit on current account. Of course, these were related facts or tautological truths. It will aid digestion of the rest of this chapter if the reasons for this are recalled.[7] Merchandise exports generate a capital export and merchandise imports a capital import; all items in the current account of the balance of payments, in fact, have the same effect. Why? Exports of goods give rise to increased Canadian claims abroad and therefore can conveniently be thought of as imports of little bits of paper, the paper on which these claims are recorded. While this capital flow need not necessarily balance the net current-account position it will when exchange- and interest-rate effects are added. For instance, a positive balance on current account—an excess of receipts over payments—will be balanced by a capital export of approximately the same amount. However, more than simple offsetting entries link the current and capital accounts and the capital account itself measures a variety of capital flows. In order to examine these links and categories more closely Table 9:3 presents a representative balance-of-payments schedule.

If the flow of capital into Canada was large in any given year, it served to increase the level of Canadian indebtedness to foreigners. That is, the stock of foreign-owned assets in Canada rose. The rise would be identical to the capital import but, in addition, would be composed of two items. First, the claims could be extended by the simple expedient of the reinvestment of earnings within Canada. Such reinvestment was no less a part of the capital inflow than the second component, the creation of wholly new claims based upon the issue of new equities. If, instead of a capital inflow, there was a capital outflow the net level of indebtedness to foreigners fell. Indeed, it was usually the case that when there was an outflow of capital it was used to reduce indebtedness in Canada rather than increase the Canadian asset-holding in other countries.

Short-term capital movements in and out of Canada were not directly of importance in determining the pattern of economic development, determined as they were by international interest-rate differentials, exchange-rate movements, or the necessity of financing international trade. However, these short-term capital flows were important in another respect. Movements of international capital on a short-term basis played an equilibrating role in the international adjustment mechanism which governed the trading ability of the economy and, as will be shown later when discussing the transfer mechanism, they facilitated the importation of long-term capital which contributed to new investment. Before studying these long-term capital movements it is important to note a unique

Table 9:3 Balance-of-Payments Schedule, 1900
(millions of dollars)

Current Account

1. Merchandise Exports less Imports (the balance of trade)	-20.5
2. Gold Trade Balance	+16.0
3. Interest and Dividends Receipts less Expenditures	-32.0
4. Tourist and Travel Receipts less Expenditures	+ 1.2
5. Freight and Shipping Receipts less Expenditures	
6. Immigrants Funds less Remittances	
7. All Other Current Receipts less Expenditures	- 1.3
8. Overall Balance on Current Account	
	-36.6

Capital Account

A. *Long-Term*

9. New Canadian Issues of Securities Abroad (less Retirements) less New Foreign Issues in Canada	+ 6.4
10. New Direct Investment in Canada less New Canadian Direct Investment Abroad	
11. Miscellaneous	+23.4

B. *Short-Term*

12. Change in Canadian Dollar Holdings of Foreigners	
13. Change in Official Holdings of Foreign Exchange (and Gold)	12.1
14. Other Net Capital Movements	
15. Overall Balance on Capital Account	
	+41.9
16. Balancing item; error or omissions	- 5.3

Source: Urquhart and Buckley, eds., *Historical Statistics of Canada* (1965), pp. 158-59.

historical entry in Canada's balance of payments, namely the immigrants' funds and remittances.

As a nation which experienced large gross flows of immigrants and emigrants Canada found the associated capital movements large enough to be recorded as separate entries in the balance of payments. They are accounted for in the current rather than capital account similar to export sales since they are not investments *per se*. The importance of the flows of immigrants' funds and settlers' effects on real-capital formation should not be over-stressed. Since in most years, capital inflows associated with immigration were only about 1 per cent of overall capital imports. However, in some years they significantly added to domestic savings. During the years of the migration of the United Empire Loyalists to British North America (see Chapter 6) many of the individuals who came brought substantial savings and effects with them. Of the two streams, those who moved to Upper Canada and those who went to Nova Scotia, the latter was, on a per-capita and probably on an aggregate basis, the richer of the two streams. Since many of these Loyalists were merchants and professionals, their substantial savings helped to invigorate the early timber and trading economy by new investment in lumbering, shipping, and shipbuilding.[8] Others, such as English tenant farmers, often brought sufficient savings to finance new farms. Undoubtedly, the effect of this flow of immigrants' funds in the first half of the nineteenth century was felt almost exclusively in the farm sector. Similar to the Loyalists fifty years earlier, the Germans who migrated to Canada after the year of revolution in Europe, 1848, brought more funds than most other groups. Although these inflows were significant it was the early years of the twentieth century which recorded the greatest capital inflow of this type. No less than $636 million in funds and settlers' effects were brought in by immigrants between 1905 and 1911.[9] Although it nearly equalled the long-term capital inflow in these years, the migrants' funds were not easily mobilized for investment purposes although again there can be little doubt that real-capital formation in western agriculture was significantly augmented. As noted in Chapter 6, a large proportion of this gross immigration was composed of immigrants who came from the United States to farm in the Canadian prairies.

Not only was this inflow of funds substantial but its composition was uneven. Nothing gives as good an insight into the first few years of immigrants' lives as the endowments they brought with them to Canada. On average, between 1905 and 1911, the wealthiest group were the migrants from the United States who brought $500 cash and $350 of settlers' effects per person. Immigrants from Great Britain were substantially poorer with about $100 cash and $50 of settlers' effects. However, the near abject poverty of immigrants from continental Europe is obvious from an average total of cash and settlers' effects of only $15.[10]

Last, it is essential to note that funds left Canada through this same category in the current account. Canadians, who on average were much wealthier than immigrants, left for new jobs in the United States thereby reducing the net balance. So too immigrants resident in Canada who remitted funds overseas reduced the net balance. As noted earlier, the remission of funds by an earlier migrant to Canada to a relative or friend often financed successive immigration. In this manner immigration waves were usually self-financed.

Important as these short-term capital movements were, it was the long-term capital imports which shaped the structure of the Canadian economy. However even these capital imports came in two different forms which were to have dramatically different consequences—portfolio and direct investment.

Portfolio investment is a pure flow of savings from a foreign country to Canada. Domestic businesses or governments decided that some project, such as the expansion of a business or the building of a railway, was necessary and in order to finance the undertaking debt instruments were sold to foreigners. Typically, these debt instruments were in the form of bonds, debentures, and non-voting share equities. Usually the debtor paid interest on a yearly basis to the purchaser of the security and presumably the security was purchased in the first instance because it yielded more than any other security of commensurate risk. Debt instruments such as these were normally of a fixed term, such as twenty years.

In contrast, direct investment is a capital flow which stems from a decision made in a foreign country. Foreign businesses decided that Canada presented superior business alternatives and therefore they located in Canada to exploit that opportunity. Since foreigners were the agents initiating the capital inflow into Canada they also controlled the real-capital formation financed by that inflow. Share ownership maintained control. This raises an important consideration: At what levels of share ownership were businesses essentially foreign? In legal terms, control is exhibited by a group holding 51 per cent of voting equities. However, there is ample evidence to suggest that effective control of firms is achieved by voting equity holdings of often much less than a simple majority. It is, therefore, necessary to know in each investment case whether the domestic or foreign shareholders directed the business concern.

The history of direct investment differed radically from portfolio investment because of its corporate nature; it was not a pure flow of savings. Typically, when new foreign direct investment took place in Canada, an inflow of technology, skilled labour, and entrepreneurship accompanied the capital inflow. Because of these associated inflows of resources some individual direct investments—the foreign firms undertaking the investment in Canada— grew from relatively small to large businesses without much reliance on savings actually mobilized in a foreign country. For instance, direct investments often expanded by mobilizing Canadian savings and as long as control was not sacrificed as a result the extent of foreign ownership of business in the Canadian economy increased. Often the superior ability to mobilize funds from Canadians, as compared with domestic capitalists, aided the extension of foreign control. In summary, direct investment increased because foreign entrepreneurs

1) mobilized foreign savings for investment in Canada;
2) mobilized domestic savings for investment in Canada while maintaining control; and
3) reinvested the profits made by their businesses in Canada.

Although only (1) above required the marshalling of foreign savings any causes of the extention of foreign direct investment gave rise to foreign claims on assets located in Canada and were, therefore, part of the capital imports.

Both portfolio- and direct-investment capital imports give rise to expenditures which also effect the overall balance of payments. The simple issue of securities requires interest payments of a fixed amount while direct-investment yields, in the form of dividends, vary with the prosperity of the business enterprise. Interest payments are invariant to the economy's performance and thus place more stress than direct investment on the current account where they are recorded. That is, resources must be diverted from the domestic economy in times of slow economic growth in order to meet the interest-payment commitments to foreign bond-holders.

While both portfolio and direct foreign investment were elements of the same capital inflow to Canada they grew and influenced the economy in completely different ways. In the following sections of this chapter which analyse the importance of foreign investment these differences must be kept in mind for although the quantitative significance of early foreign direct investment was small it was the root from which that investment grew to importance.

Portfolio Investment Before 1914
The canal system of the St. Lawrence was no sooner complete than the new transport demands for railway services were asserted in the 1840s. Compared to the canals the financing of the early railways in central Canada was far beyond the capacity of the domestic economy.[11] Even at the beginning of the railway era complete reliance was placed on mobilizing capital in Great Britain. If any boom in Canadian economy history can be said to have depended on foreign capital for its initial impetus, it is the railway boom which began in the later 1840s. Virtually none of the initial capital for these early railways was subscribed domestically and the government was unwilling publicly to support them given the size of the canal debt.

When A. T. Galt travelled to London in 1845 to promote shares in the St. Lawrence and Atlantic Railway he was simply the first of a great many railway entrepreneurs to do so. Early funding successes encouraged others to attempt to mobilize financial capital in Great Britain. However, London financiers considered Canadian railway securities to be extremely risky investments. First, there were many attractive low-risk alternatives such as the railways of France and Germany. Second, since a railway's ability to generate a freight traffic ultimately determined its success, ignorance about the Canadian economy and invidious comparison with some U.S. railways made the British savers reluctant to subscribe their savings in all but the most buoyant years on the London market. Consequently, some attempts to float railway securities in London were not the successes which had been hoped for by the Canadian promoters.

The powerful railway lobby in Canada convinced the Government of Canada that radical measures were required to reduce the uncertainty about Canadian railway security issues in London. In 1849, Francis Hincks brought down what was known as the Guarantee Act. Under its provision the government guaranteed to pay the interest on railway bonds — up to 6 per cent interest on up to one-half of the total bonded debt of a railway company. Yet because this guarantee was only given to existing railways which were more than 50 per cent complete, it did little to help the flotation of the securities of new rail ventures. Similarly, because the railway had to be at least seventy-five miles long, the smaller projects were not assisted. A few years later the government agreed to guarantee half of the principal on the bonds of the Intercolonial Railway, up to $3,000 per mile, in order to ensure financing. Although the government was slowly drawn into the capital markets as a guarantor, its actions resulted in only a limited success.[12]

Many small railway projects were financed indirectly by foreign savings through appeals to municipalities. These municipalities in turn floated bonds in London. Because of the many failures of municipal bonds as a consequence of the over-commitment to railways, British investors came to consider Canadian securities of all types, but especially those of railways, as speculative ventures. Even the creation of the Municipal Loan Fund to consolidate the municipal debt-commitment to railways and its subsequent issue of bonds in London did little to dispel the prevailing disfavour of Canadian railway securities. Issuing almost $7.5 million in securities in the 1850s, the Municipal Loan Fund could not effectively control the railway mania of the many small towns of Canada East and West; no new debt was issued after 1859 when the fund was wound up as the Government of Canada was forced to assume more and more of the obligation to the foreign bond-holders.[13]

Perhaps no single security issue in London did more to prejudice British investors and to embroil the Canadian government in the British capital market than that of the Grand Trunk Railway. Within six years of its founding the Grand Trunk was bankrupt and the bond- and share-holders in Great Britain found themselves holding securities which were very heavily discounted. When the company issued its first securities during the buoyant trading of 1853, the railway projected rapid and high profits. As will be seen in more detail in Chapter 10, the railway encountered construction difficulties and traffic was, in the initial years, much lighter than had been anticipated. By 1854 the market discounted its shares and bonds. Inevitably the company drifted towards bankruptcy and in 1859 the interest payments on the debt were not made. The Grand Trunk fiasco, as it was called in London, lasted for another three years.[14] Most of the debt on which the Canadian government guaranteed the interest was in fact held by the construction company of Brassey Brothers rather than by the ordinary bond-holders. Similar to most early railway issues there was a close link between the British financiers, in this case Glyn, Mills & Company and Baring Brothers, and the construction company, also British. Brassey agreed, during the troublesome times prior to 1859, to accept debt as payment for construction services but only that portion of the debt on which payments were guaranteed.

Suit and countersuit followed and the Canadian government took no action apart, that is, from themselves obtaining a judgement against the railway company. Not until the Macdonald–Cartier government was re-elected in 1862 did it act to protect the various groups of debt-holders. By a total financial reorganization and a compulsory conversion of some classes of bonds to stock and an arbitrary reduction of the interest rate on the remaining bonds the immediate crisis was over. Most debt-holders did lose heavily in terms of the opportunity use of their savings and heavily in terms of the high expectations which had been generated in the early 1850s. The Grand Trunk fiasco scarred all subsequent Canadian issues to London. For a suprising long time the memory of 1850 to 1862 remained. So prejudiced was the London market that for the next fifty years only a minority of railway securities issues found subscribers without some pledge of government backing.[15]

In the years after the Grand Trunk fiasco the proportion of Canadian securities which found British subscribers fell. From Table 9:4 it can be seen that the successful issues were still low in absolute terms in 1865-69. As is well-known, it was partly a response to the need to finance their individual railway debt that brought the British North American colonies into the conference which resulted in Confederation in 1867.

During the period from Confederation to the First World War about 80 per cent of all Canadian security issues in Great Britain financed investment in infrastructure or social-overhead capital.[16] Although this in-

Table 9:4 Canadian Security Issues in Great Britain, 1865-1914

| Period | New Canadian Issues (millions of dollars) | Percentage of All Foreign Issues in Great Britain | Percentage Distribution of Canadian Security Issues by Type | | |
			Private	Government	Mixed
(1)	(2)	(3)	(4)	(5)	(6)
1865-69	16.5	2.5	9.8	71.6	18.6
1870-74	94.6	5.5	18.5	53.3	28.2
1875-79	74.7	9.8	15.0	70.8	14.3
1880-84	69.8	4.7	50.7	27.1	22.2
1885-89	165.9	7.8	27.5	32.8	39.8
1890-94	128.0	9.0	38.6	42.1	19.3
1895-99	63.1	3.4	68.5	26.9	4.6
1900-04	87.8	5.0	74.0	9.4	16.6
1905-09	373.5	11.8	41.6	27.4	31.0
1910-14	929.3	19.4	53.4	32.5	14.1

Source: M. Simon, "New British Investments in Canada, 1865-1914", Canadian Journal of Economics, Vol. 3, no. 2 (1970), p. 241.

cluded Dominion government public works and many municipal projects, such as water and sewage systems, the bulk financed railways. Over the entire period 1865-1914 Canadian governments and business enterprises issued approximately $2.795 billion in securities. Except during the five years prior to 1915, private, non-railway business was relatively starved for capital. British investment in Canada through the subscription to portfolio debt was directed into securities where the risk was perceived as minimal. The government backed either fully or partly no less than two-thirds of the entire railway debt to finance, among other smaller ones, the transcontinentals. Typical of the issues are those presented in Table 9:5 for a representative month near the height of the pre-1914 capital inflow.

Canada depended on Great Britain for over 85 per cent of imported portfolio capital prior to 1914. Yet, British investors were neither willing nor able to provide Canada with an infinitely elastic supply of savings. As already noted few Canadian security issues found subscribers in London in the late 1860s. In contrast fifty years later, more British savings found their way to Canada than any other country. However, the time pattern of Canadian portfolio issues in Great Britain was not one of a smooth increase over the intervening period. To the contrary, capital inflows from Great Britain were highly variable. This variability behaved in what appears to be a regularly cyclical fashion. However, Canada was not unique. Most other countries which borrowed heavily in London expe-

Table 9:5 Major Canadian Security Issues in London During July 1909
(£1 = $4.85)

Issues	Amount	Type of Security	Price Relative to Par
(1)	(2)	(3)	(4)
City of Vancouver	£ 286,400	4% debentures	101
Dominion Iron and Steel Company	1,200,000	5% consol mortgage bonds	93
Standard Chemical Co. of Toronto	100,000	5% first mortgage debentures	98$^{1/2}$
City of Edmonton	187,300	4$^{1/2}$% sterling debentures	102$^{1/2}$
Grand Trunk Pacific	2,000,000	3% first mortgage bonds	82$^{1/2}$
Dominion of Canada	6,500,000	3$^{1/2}$% stock	98$^{1/2}$

Source: F. W. Field, *Capital Investments in Canada*, 3rd ed. (Montreal, 1914), pp. 264-65.

rienced the same cyclical variability in the importation of capital from Great Britain.[17]

From at least 1865 to 1914, but not later, the successful issue of new Canadian securities in London followed a pattern which was in fact simply another dimension of the cyclical activity which dominated the international economy. These cycles which are evident in many of the indicators of economic performance of the time roughly conform to what are known as "Kuznets cycles". Kuznets cycles are fluctuations of about fifteen to twenty-five years' duration. However, Canada was not a passive economy experiencing fluctuations in capital imports arising from the supply side alone. Reasonable explanation of these international long-swings all assign some importance to the demand forces within Canada.

A complex set of international economic forces governed the importation of long-term portfolio capital into Canada. First, much of the export of capital from Great Britain was destined for the regions of recent settlement in both North and South America and also in Australia and South Africa. Over the period 1865-1914 Canada alone accounted for about 10 per cent of all the new foreign-security sales in the London capital market. Yet even such a figure belies the importance of Canada's role in the international mechanism. For instance, at the height of pre-1914 capital imports, Canada was one of the major borrowers from Great Britain. During the years 1910 to 1914 about 20 per cent of all foreign security issues in London were Canadian. Second, Great Britain was one of the few major countries which exported capital. Although France also exported capital it was not as significant as that of Great Britain and was directed primarily to continental Europe and Russia. The United States,

Figure 9:1 Representation of Canadian Capital Imports, British Capital Exports, and British Home Investment, 1865-1914

% deviation from trend

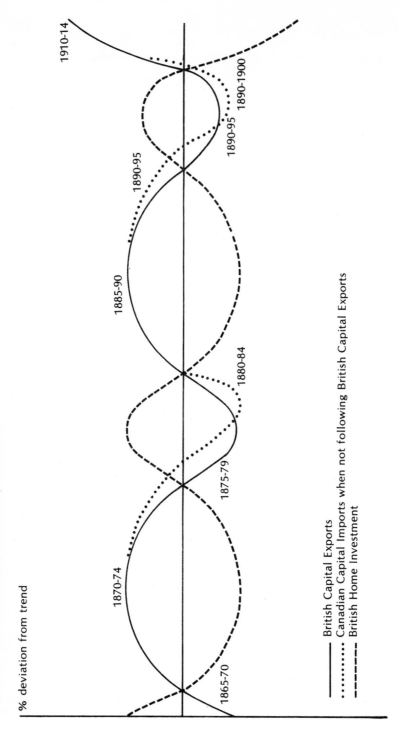

British Capital Exports
Canadian Capital Imports when not following British Capital Exports
British Home Investment

for example, did not achieve a persistent positive balance on current account until the early years of the twentieth century. Great Britain, in contrast to the experience of most countries, achieved an overall current-account surplus not by a superior ability to export goods relative to their importation but by the earnings from shipping, insurance, and the stock of investment overseas. These items, known as "invisibles", turned a negative balance of trade into a positive current-account balance making Great Britain capable of exporting savings.[18]

British capital exports in general, and those to Canada in particular, not only behaved in a cyclical fashion but were inversely related to British home investment (see Figure 9:1). As profits and interest rates in countries like Canada were rising, for a given distribution of risk, funds were channelled from domestic-capital formation to export abroad. Conversely, as these profit and interest rates outside of Great Britain fell, the financing of home investment became a more attractive and therefore more frequent use of savings. Why the profit and interest-rate differentials should vary in the first place can be seen in the nature of the economic frontier in the capital-scarce, rapidly developing countries of recent settlement. The three booms in British capital exports and troughs in home investment were associated with rapid expansion. Listed below are the particular episodes which contributed to the rise in British capital exports and the subsequent peaks.

1) 1873 — U.S. westward expansion in the aftermath of the Civil War;
2) 1889 — opening of the South African goldfields, expansion in Latin America and Australia, and building of Canadian Pacific Railway; and
3) 1913 — Canadian prairie settlement, wheat boom, and industrial expansion and South American expansion.

The frontiers expanded in a discontinuous fashion. In most cases exploitation of the new lands necessitated a transport network; once that network was completed a whole range of new demands were manifest in a relatively short period of time. As factors flowed to the new economic frontiers many economic rents of scarcity were bid down and profits and interest rates naturally fell. As they fell the rate of subscription to new security issues, based on investment in the frontier, also fell. The most reasonable explanation is, then, that the features of frontier expansion in the regions of comparatively recent settlement gave rise to the Kuznets cycles in the international economy between about 1860 and 1914.[19]

During the first of these North American frontier episodes of western expansion, Canada was little involved. Although growing rapidly in the years immediately before and after Confederation, Canada was still smarting from the effects of the Grand Trunk fiasco. She contributed very little to the increased demand for British savings. Yet, despite this, Canada experienced a small peak in the long-term portfolio imports at this time. This type of experience was actually quite common. A small region, or a region with relatively few new security issues in London, often found these security issues following the general pattern of new issues. Attitudes towards risk on the part of the savers often spilled over from the securities of one country to those of another, particularly for similar types of issues. Of course, all countries suffered when the international economy was dealt a shock such as happened in 1873 when the collapse of the New York money market spread to other financial centres.

The second upswing of 1880-89, as indicated earlier, witnessed Canada playing a larger role as an international borrower. The railway building of the 1880s, unlike the railway projects of earlier and later times, however, did not have immediately profound spreading effects as will be noted in the next chapter. Built ahead of demand, the rail network did not generate many frontier economic opportunities, such as those associated with urban construction, and therefore the expansion of the Canadian economy was arrested. In contrast, the boom associated with the intensive settlement of the prairies in the 1900-14 period was much more broadly based. Consequently it sustained itself over a longer period and although there were signs that Canadian capital imports, and British capital exports, peaked in 1913 the intervention of war in 1914 disturbed the underlying mechanism which regulated the capital flows. Critical was the suspension of the international gold standard.

In the first half of the nineteenth century Great Britain exported capital but the inverse relationship between those capital exports and domestic investment was less evident than later. Building cycles within Great Britain appear to have offset capital exports.[20] The differences between the early and later parts of the century rest on three factors. First, the London capital market became more efficient and thus more discriminating in terms of the varying degrees of risks associated with the securities offered for sale. Second, the demands for capital from countries such as Canada were quantitatively larger than any that had been experienced earlier. Third, capital flows interacted with the other major resource flows, intercontinental migration, to an extent they had previously not done.

In Canada, flows of immigrants, many from Great Britain, often predated the inflows of capital as was seen in Chapter 6. Otherwise these inflows followed similar patterns. Migrants, of course, were young and concentrated in the age group associated with setting up a first home.

The result of migration in this age group was increased demand for housing in Canada but also a decreased demand for housing in the capital-exporting region. As was noted previously, there was a rapid rate of house construction in the period 1905-13.[21] Counterposed building cycles, as a consequence, may have played an important role in establishing the long-swings in international borrowing. One of the features of the wheat-boom era, as mentioned earlier, was the accelerated pace of the rural-urban shift which compounded the building boom.[22] If capital inflows were population-sensitive then there is adequate explanation of why the expansion of 1900-13 had more impact on the international economy than the less protracted expansions of the mid-nineteenth century.

The Transfer Mechanism
It is evident that the nature of economic development in Canada changed from its previous pattern some time in the mid-1890s. The demand forces which drove up international prices as well the domestic demand acted as a stimulus to the economy which was in a position to exploit the use of the infrastructure laid down in the previous decade. Every indication is that it was these real, as opposed to monetary, forces which first promoted a quickening of the pace of economic growth. Through the initial phase of this growth, approximately 1896 to 1904, the economy displayed the ability to finance internally most of the new investment in the capital stock. Much of this economic growth was based on export performance. It was not until about 1904 that massive amounts of foreign savings began to supplement domestic savings.[23]

The inflow of capital was firmly based on the growing ability of the economy to finance import surpluses. It was a prosperity based largely on export performance which permitted the growth in aggregate income and which in turn stimulated imports. Quite possibly, but there is no concrete evidence, the Canadian economy displayed a growing average propensity to import goods.[24] The greater output and specialization in the economy created a demand for capital goods which could only be supplied externally. In addition, as domestic prices grew more rapidly than import prices, there was the inevitable substitution. Thus, not only the growth of imports associated with a growing income but a shift in the import function itself helped to create the growing import surplus through which the real transfer of savings from Great Britain to Canada took place.

Canadian borrowing abroad reached its zenith, in per-capita terms, during the ten years prior to 1914. As indicated earlier Canada as a major borrower, and Great Britain as the principal world lender, were two major influences on the international economy at this time. Not surprisingly, many economists turned to the international capital flows of this period to answer the question of how savings—purchasing power—could be transferred internationally. Would not the attempt to shift purchasing power be frustrated by movements in prices? The price-specie flow mechanism gives an important insight.

The price-specie flow mechanism applicable to Canadian borrowing in the fifteen or so years prior to the First World War was thought to have operated as a sequence of events.

1) Canadian security issues in London put pounds sterling in the hands of issuers. But of course the issuers wanted dollars and took the sterling to Canadian bank branches in London who traded sterling for dollars. These banks in turn bought the dollars on the foreign-exchange market in order to sell off their sterling and replenish their dollar holdings. This was usually accomplished through the New York market because the Canadian dollar market in London was too small.

2) Under the gold standard each country's currency was denominated in terms of a physical quantity of gold. Yet exchange rates varied to the extent that arbitrage between foreign-exchange markets involved the cost of shipping and insuring gold movements (see Figure 9:2). The excess supply of sterling in the market at the established rate of exchange drove the dollar price of sterling to the gold-import point from Canada's perspective. It was the gold-export point from the British perspective.

3) As the price of sterling reached the gold-import point a flow of gold occurred from Great Britain to Canada.

4) This would have given rise to an expansion of the money supply in Canada and a contraction of the money supply in Great Britain. Prices would respond by increasing in Canada and decreasing in Great Britain.

5) The real transfer then would have taken place as Canadian physical imports from Great Britain increased relative to exports since Canadian goods were now more expensive and British less so. Canada would exhibit a deficit on the balance of trade and Great Britain would exhibit a positive trade balance.

6) As the trade flow continued Canadian importers had to purchase sterling in order to pay the British manufacturers and so the money supplies, prices, and the initial balance-of-trade positions were reestablished. Only when the value of goods imported into Canada exactly equalled the initial gold inflow was this adjustment and the real transfer of savings complete.

Figure 9:2 The Price Specie Flow Mechanism (from the Canadian perspective)

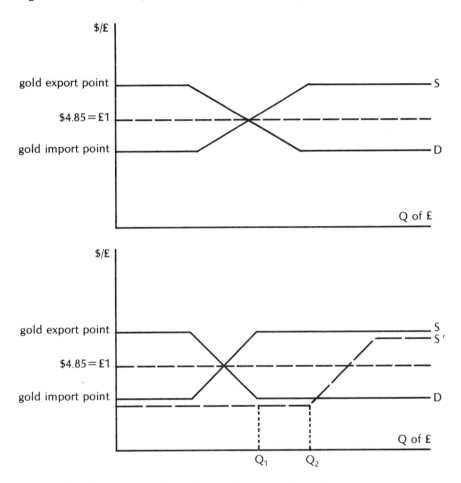

D—demand of pounds sterling   S—supply of pounds sterling

Note: The Canadian dollar was worth 23.2 grains of gold. Since sterling was also fixed in terms of gold, the rate of exchange was about $4.85 per in gold. As long as the monetary authorities were willing to buy and sell gold at the established values of the currencies, a band existed within which foreign exchange rates varied. This band was determined by the transport and insurance charges in moving the gold from, say, London to Montreal. If market exchange rates were, say, $4.86, it would not be worth shipping gold across the Atlantic at a cost of 2 cents because a loss would ensue. On the other hand, at the point where a gain could be made from shipping gold enough shipments would take place to force the exchange rate back within the band. In the above diagram, the excess supply of pounds sterling forces the exchange rate to the gold export point from Great Britain's point of view and a gold outflow of Q_2-Q_1 value in pounds sterling occurs. This is a gold inflow from Canada's perspective.

The price-specie flow mechanism is a plausible, but alas an incomplete, explanation of the transfer of savings between Great Britain and Canada—as the rather unsubtle change of tense in the previous paragraph indicated. First, very little gold flowed from Great Britain to Canada. However, this historical fact does not invalidate the price-specie flow mechanism. Recall from the previous chapter that Canadian banks were extremely active in the New York money and foreign-exchange markets. Any sterling acquired by the banks as a result of a security sale in London was transferred within the bank to New York where the majority of the foreign exchange was held. Any downward pressure on the value of sterling led Canadian banks to make loans in sterling rather than to repatriate the dollars to Canada long before the price reached the gold-export point. The effect of these foreign-exchange dealings on the part of the Canadian bank branches in New York smoothed the process of the transfer. Transfer, if it followed the price-specie flow mechanisms exactly, would be lumpy. As the Canadian banks observed a weakening of the pressure on the pound, loans were called in, sterling sold for dollars, and the transfer was accomplished smoothly. Not all loans were called in at once since the subsequent sale of sterling immediately changed the price. Sensitive to even the most minor foreign-exchange price fluctuations, the banks, as well as other dealers, seldom allowed the price to reach the gold-import or -export points.

A more important historical criticism of the price-specie flow view of the transfer, and what prevents its complete acceptance, concerns the timing of capital flows, price changes, and the performance of commodity exports and imports. Did exports and imports respond to changes in the financial flows or did the financial flows respond to changes in exports and imports? That is, was the transfer of savings between Canada and Great Britain brought about by monetary or real forces?

Capital imports, as may be judged from Table 9:6, did not reach and maintain a high volume until after 1904. In the 1890s and in the early years of the 1900s, the import of capital was, indeed, quite low by historical comparison. Yet, domestic prices relative to world prices began to increase during the period of modest capital imports thereby reversing the long secular decline in prices in the mid-1890s. Domestic prices rose more than those of traded goods and export prices rose much more rapidly than the prices of imports. However, the fact that these price changes were not synchronized with the capital imports, and in fact predated them, strongly suggests that the price-specie flow mechanism fails to explain the full history of the real transfer of savings. Similarly, the trade sector's performance appears to be linked to real forces in the Canadian economy as much as to the price effects created by the capital

Table 9:6 Capital Movements and Prices, 1900-1914

Year	($ millions) Net Balance of Commodity Trade	Net Balance of Current Account	Net Movements of Capital	Indices Wholesale Domestic Prices	Export Prices	Import Prices
(1)	(2)	(3)	(4)	(5)	(6)	(7)
1900	− 20.5	− 36.6	+ 41.9	100.0	100.0	100.0
1901	− 12.4	− 23.1	+ 10.6	99.8	102.5	101.0
1902	− 13.0	− 32.0	+ 38.3	101.3	104.3	98.0
1903	− 49.9	− 74.1	+ 72.1	102.6	107.6	100.7
1904	− 73.1	− 97.5	+ 35.5	101.1	108.7	103.1
1905	− 58.4	− 87.3	+ 99.1	106.1	105.3	102.7
1906	− 58.3	−102.0	+115.6	111.8	113.4	107.7
1907	−109.2	−166.9	+117.0	117.4	118.5	113.8
1908	− 33.3	−134.4	+119.1	116.3	124.2	117.0
1909	− 70.6	−158.3	+217.6	114.0	123.5	108.6
1910	−148.2	−251.3	+341.7	118.5	124.8	109.3
1911	−222.2	−363.7	+352.1	121.8	123.7	110.5
1912	−274.3	−421.3	+324.5	130.9	120.7	107.2
1913	−212.0	−408.2	+525.8	129.3	122.5	110.0
1914	−101.7	−288.2	+341.8	131.3	116.9	112.9

Note: Column (3) includes the gold movements on Canada's current account and column (4) includes all capital imports. In theory columns (3) and (4) should be numerically equal, however, because of errors in the balance of payments accounts they do not exactly balance. Columns (6) and (7) report data for the fiscal year up to June 31st prior to 1908 and up to March 31st thereafter.

Source: Urquhart and Buckley (1965), pp. 159, 291, 299, and 300.

imports. For instance, Canadian exports were rising long before 1905; the volume and the value of all Canadian exports almost doubled over the decade of the 1890s with most of this increase occurring after 1895. Imports, too, exhibited the same profile over time although their increase was less marked than that of exports in the 1890s. Of course, the changing terms of trade had their impact and the real transfer of savings took place by the net import of foreign goods, particularly capital ones.

The price-specie flow mechanism posits that the original disturbance to the domestic economy, as well as the international one, was the issue of securities and the associated capital flow. Trade flows, influenced by prices, were the factors which adjusted to bring the international order back to equilibrium. Since the timing of the various economic changes noted above did not coincide with the capital imports this suggests a more complex model of the transfer process in which the initial economic shock or disturbance was not the capital flows themselves.[25]

Not only was the mechanism of the real transfer of savings more complex than the simple price-specie flow model might predict but it involved more than simply Great Britain and Canada. As seen earlier in this section, the Canadian banks operating in New York were the key agents in smoothing the process of transfer.[26] Similarly, the United States played a major role as the third key country in the Atlantic economy in the 1900-14 period. Indeed, the greatest share of Canada's exports went to the United States and not to Great Britain. Great Britain, on the other hand, never achieved a balance-of-trade surplus; it was the surplus on overall current account which facilitated the export of capital. The British earnings, interest, and dividend payments from previous capital exports, much of which was in the United States, largely achieved this surplus on current account. Canada, Great Britain, and the United States were all involved in the process of transfer because the latter was the destination for most Canadian exports and the source of most imports.

In summary, the price-specie flow mechanism of adjustment helps to explain the process of the real transfer of savings from Great Britain to Canada. However, it is incomplete. Real, not monetary, forces, such as increased Canadian exports and income, were the disturbing elements which gave rise to the transfer of savings of which both commodity and capital flows were part of the adjustment process.

Benefits and Costs of Foreign Direct Investment

When the Hudson's Bay Company won the long struggle with the North West Company in 1821, as noted in Chapter 3, it was a victory for the most efficient resource exploiter. From an entirely different and somewhat unusual perspective we might also note that it was the victory of a foreign business over a domestic one. Many of the early business ventures in Canada were, of course, foreign enterprises. While the character of foreign direct investment, as well as its impact, changed remarkably over history it is well at the outset that we recognize that the phenomenon is old; it has deep historical roots.[27]

Throughout history the openness of the Canadian economy attracted foreign entrepreneurs and foreign business. This process of foreign direct investment, as was anticipated by those who framed the National Policy, conferred benefits on Canada. But the variety of costs associated with the foreign penetration of Canadian business was unanticipated. Perhaps it is not surprising since many benefits accrued quickly but the costs tended to be long-term in nature.

The immediate effects can be shown with the aid of Figure 9:3. Domestic savings provided domestic capitalists with sufficient savings to

Figure 9:3 The Effects of Foreign Direct Investment

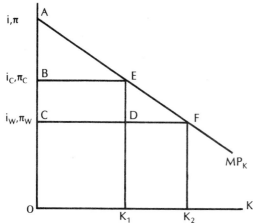

MP—marginal productivity
K—capital
i,π—interest rate and profit rate where the subscripts W and C indicate the i,π
    prevailing outside and inside Canada, respectively.

undertake real-capital formation of K_1. The establishment of an equilibrium at E guaranteed that since the marginal productivity of capital was different for all investments only those projects which had an expected profit rate of π_C or greater were undertaken. At this level of capital formation total output in the economy was AOK_1E, that is, the sum of the marginal products of K_1. Domestic capitalists received $EBOK_1$ and all other factors earned ABE. These other factors mainly included labour and tax revenues associated with, in part, the revenues from forestry and mining leases. In the short run, if there was no effective way of increasing the amount of savings offered at the prevailing interest rate no new investment took place.[28]

If profits were higher in Canada than elsewhere foreigners would be attracted and would respond by building branch plants. Foreign direct investment of K_1K_2 had three effects. They were

1) to increase Canadian income by EK_1K_2F;
2) to distribute the income gain to domestic factors other than capital (EDF) and foreign capitalists (DK_1K_2F); and
3) to redistribute the income among Canadians. Domestic factors such as labour gained the economic rents ($BCDE$), which were bid away from domestic capitalists.

Foreign direct investment would not proceed beyond K_2 because if it did the prevailing profit rate would be less than the opportunity cost of capital, the interest rate. Of course, in a dynamic framework the marginal productivity of capital shifted and population grew due to immigration. Yet, the static analysis indicates the nature of the short-run benefits from foreign direct investment. Often neglected is the important function of the reduction of economic rents of domestic capitalists. Later, as will be argued in Chapter 12, the very tariff protection desired by Canadian capitalists in 1879 was the instrument which helped stimulate the penetration of the economy by foreign business.

Earlier in this chapter it was argued that foreign direct investment was more than simply an international flow of savings — it was an international flow of technology and entrepreneurship. Any such flow of factors, of course, could shift the production function in any given sector by, say, introducing a new technology. Consequently, the marginal productivity of capital shifted outward and in turn, new investment, domestic and foreign direct, took place. To the extent that this induced shift favoured one particular factor, the distribution of gains was affected. Such effects naturally took time and had a long-term impact on the way different sectors, and the aggregate economy, grew. Whatever the long-term impact, there was an addition to Canadian income and part of that increase went to labour. Indirectly the Canadian economy may have benefitted by the technological transfer which later became available to the domestic entrepreneurs. Despite the increase in income, foreign direct investment imposed costs on the Canadian economy. However, it is impossible to say whether, at any moment in time, these costs outweighed the benefits as the lively current debate about the subject indicates.[29] Certainly, the costs have been large.

Basically the costs associated with foreign direct investment have been fourfold. They may be grouped as follows:

1) the bias introduced into industrial development;
2) the balance-of-payments problems;
3) the direct losses of tax revenue; and
4) the external influences on public policy.

None of these costs are simple ones and can only be appreciated in their historical context. The first element of that context is the examination of forces which induced foreign direct investment into Canada.

Foreign Business Penetration of the Canadian Economy
Prior to the mid-nineteenth century most of the foreign direct investment was based on special privileges won from the colonial power. Mercan-

tile trading as well as land-settlement companies, such as the Canada Company and British-American Land Company, held large domains granted under charters which conferred monopoly power.[30] Even the early commercial exploitation of Nova Scotian coal by the General Mining Association was a Crown-granted monopoly use of the coal fields much of which was held as the private property of the Royal Family.[31] While many of the foreign business enterprises, and it is often difficult to think of them as such, played vital roles in shaping history they were not the immediate antecedents of today's foreign business presence.

Foreign direct investment which was essentially modern in character first occurred in Canada in the years around Confederation.[32] It was, of course, associated not only with the growth in complexity of the Canadian industrial structure but with the growth of manufacturing in the United States and the capacity of the British economy to export capital. Both British- and U.S.-controlled companies became active in Canada in the years between Confederation and the First World War. In quantitative terms the U.S. firms probably rose to dominate the British ones at some time during the years 1895-1905. Although early foreign direct investment had for the most part been British, reflecting the colonial tie, that of U.S. firms was more rapid during the early twentieth century. This is not to say that little British direct investment in Canada took place. On the contrary, the growth of British participation in Canadian business grew rapidly with no less than $197 million of British savings being channelled into the initial equity sales of these firms during the period 1890-1914 alone. But U.S. direct investment, as a stock, grew more rapidly than its British counterpart because it was directed into business ventures which were more successful survivors in Canada. For instance, in 1897, 34.5 per cent of U.S. as compared to only 9.4 per cent of British direct investment was in manufacturing industries. Manufacturing firms tended to survive longer than firms engaged in real estate, mining, mortgage and loan, and other financial activities. Consequently, a gross inflow of long-term direct-investment capital had a greater impact on the stock of foreign direct investment when that stock included more manufacturing than when it included less. No single feature, as evident in Table 9:7, accounted so much for the early domination of U.S. direct investment in Canada over that of other countries.

U.S. direct investment in Canada was not solely restricted to manufacturing activity. In fact, it is possible to distinguish several separate types of corporate penetration. First, there was a direct investment associated with natural-resource exploitation. Second, the growing Canadian market for consumer and capital goods attracted direct investment activity. Third, cost considerations, apart from the above, often led to the establishment of branch plants in Canada.

Table 9:7 Stock of U.S. and British Direct Investment in Canada, 1910

U.S.		British	
Sector	% of Total	Sector	% of Total
(1)	(2)	(3)	(4)
Branch Companies	41.4	Manufacturing	13.5
Packing Plants	2.0	Timber	2.0
Lumber, timber and pulp		Land	14.2
and paper	22.8	Mining and Oil	36.9
Land	9.7	Finance	13.6
Mining (B.C.)	19.7	Distribution	0.2
		Utilities	19.5
TOTAL	100.0		100.0
$ millions	254.1		120.7

Note: U.S. figures for 1909. The sectors are only roughly comparable.

Source: D. G. Paterson, *British Direct Investment in Canada, 1890-1914: Estimates and Determinants* (Toronto, 1976), pp. 50, 55.

Often U.S. direct investment occurred simply because there was a relatively high rate of growth in a sector of the economy. For instance, in the 1890s the sweep of American mining companies into British Columbia was a response to the rapid rate of growth of output of these newly discovered fields. Here, at the period of intense new business registrations in October through December of 1895, no less than 35 U.S. mining companies were formed as compared to 52 domestic ones. This substantial foreign participation was, in many senses, inevitable. The south-central mining district of the Kootenays was more effectively linked by rail to the neighbouring state of Washington than to other parts of British Columbia. Also, such investment was a natural progression, given the geology of the region, of the mining frontier which had earlier focused on Colorado, Montana, and later Idaho.[33] In such ventures U.S. direct investment was simply a spillover of home investment.

Similarly, the silver and gold booms in northern Ontario, centring on Cobalt and Porcupine, attracted American attention because they were the most dynamic mining areas in North America in the 1906-14 period. Most spectacular in this regard was the impact of the Klondyke which for its few historical moments held centre stage. When American firms were created in Canada for exploitation of natural resources they were often responding to relative simple economic stimuli as in the cases of these examples from the mining sector. They acted as if no international boundary existed apart from the economic one of exchange rates and such barriers to trade and factor flows as tariffs.

In some instances the simple mining firms evolved in a manner which spanned the international border. A classic example is the firm now known as the International Nickel Company of Canada.[34] This company sprang from two U.S. firms which operated in Canada and from the earliest time, the early 1880s, their sole refining capacity was located in New Jersey. The initial decision to so locate was based on the limited and essentially non-industrial use of nickel. By the turn of the century the two companies had grown on the basis of new metallurgical demands for the metal. After the merger to form one company, the main refining capacity remained in the United States, a decision based on the fact that the initial refinery was located there. To the Ontario government of the time the problem was obvious. If domestic industry exploited the Sudbury copper-nickel deposits more jobs would be located in Canada. In an attempt to force such an outcome the government resorted to threats of export bounties on unrefined ore and although partly successful the principal refinery of the company was still the New Jersey one.[35] Ironically, the only other major company in the copper-nickel industry was British and its refining capacity was located in Great Britain. In the 1920s these two firms, the International Nickel Company and the Mond Nickel Company, merged to form the huge multinational firm of today.

Expansion into the Canadian resource sectors was often based on an attempt to control resources and thereby to ensure a flow of them to an industry in the United States at relatively low and stable prices. Not surprisingly there was a tendency for U.S. domestic firms to integrate vertically backward to this supply. Such a tendency was quite evident before the First World War, particularly in the pulp and paper industry where this integration was performed to supply newspaper firms in the United States.[36]

The second type of foreign direct investment was that associated with the growing Canadian market for consumer and capital goods. Similar to that investment in the natural-resource industries, the U.S. investment in the manufacturing sector began long before 1914.[37] In a world without tariffs there is no incentive for manufacturing to locate close to the final goods markets except where dictated by efficiency considerations such as transport costs. Foreign exporters could retain their share of, say, the Canadian market without necessarily establishing a corporate presence. However, as soon as any barrier to the free flow of trade goods emerged the foreign exporters would begin to lose their share of the Canadian market and potential exporters to Canada would be increasingly excluded. Essentially, this is what happened when the Macdonald government decided to raise the Canadian tariff.

The National Policy tariff of 1879 effectively decreased the market share, or prevented entry, of foreign firms exporting to Canada. In order to exploit the Canadian market, U.S. firms had to jump the tariff wall in order to escape the tariff and remain competitive. Parenthetically, it may be noted that the full impact of the tariff was not always avoided if the U.S. branch plants imported manufactured inputs from the United States. Many firms responded by jumping the tariff wall to locate in Canada. This eroded some of the protection guaranteed domestically controlled firms and although some domestic firms could not meet the competition on balance employment increased in the economy at large. The double-edged nature of the tariff in this respect was in fact fully appreciated by the Conservative government which had pledged itself to create jobs. The jobs created by these U.S.-controlled firms were principally in the secondary manufacturing industries, such as rubber goods, sewing machines, and later, automobiles.[38]

The tariff was not the only action of Canadian governments taken to attract U.S. firms. Canadian patent law, which required the operation of a patent within a short period after registration to ensure protection under law, encouraged some manufacturers. The system of bonuses, municipal tax concessions to attract firms to a specific locality, common in the late nineteenth century attracted footloose industries — where the firms were not required by cost considerations to locate near either their sources of raw-material inputs or their final markets. Federal-government subsidies to domestic firms, irrespective of where control lay, further induced U.S. penetration of Canadian business. This last feature was particularly evident in the iron and steel industry when the Dominion Railway Act of 1900 precluded the use of foreign rails in railway projects receiving assistance from the government.

The third of the broad categories of foreign direct investments which entered Canada, and which date to the years prior to the First World War, was firms which located on the basis of the cost of inputs. Although the lower price of Canadian labour often acted as an inducement to firms selling in Canada to locate here, the U.S. tariff on manufactured goods has prevented the location in Canada of those plants which wished to export their output back to the United States. Branches which located in Canada either had to sell in the domestic market exclusively or find an overwhelming cost saving sufficient to overcome the disadvantage of the U.S. tariff when shipping output to that country. The differential price of labour was never sufficient to be an attractive force. Only those industries which were intensive resource users found such an advantage and most of these located in Canada because of cheap energy. Low-price hydroelectric power stimulated the in-flow of firms into the aluminium industry in Quebec and the electro-chemical industry in southern Ontario.[39]

In summary, all the patterns of foreign direct investment in the Canadian economy which were of later importance were established in some form before 1914. Despite various changes in the forces of the Canadian economy attractive to direct investment, the basic forces remained. Similarly, the costs of the foreign-business presence were beginning to be felt although they had not assumed their later dimensions.

During the interwar period, 1918-39, the growth of foreign direct investment continued. Although much slower in the 1930s than in any other decade in this century the growth was such in the 1920s that between the outbreak of the First World War and 1936 the stock of U.S. direct investment alone expanded at a rate of about 6 per cent, compounded annually. Particularly in manufacturing and merchandising, as shown in Table 9:8, this expansion was rapid as the new mass-production techniques of consumer-goods industries were exploited. In the automobile industry alone all major American producers were established in Canada by this time. The Ford Motor Car Company was drawn into Canada not only by the potential of domestic sales but also of sales to the other British Empire countries under the British preferential tariff. In the automobile industry we find examples of an increasingly common method of foreign firms gaining entry to the Canadian market, the corporate takeover. For instance, General Motors gained its Canadian branch by absorbing the McLaughlin Buick Company of Oshawa. Although Colonel Sam McLaughlin continued to chair the company, the Canadian branch was fully integrated into the larger U.S. parent firm.[40]

It was during the interwar period that the Canadians first recognized, at the political levels, that substantial proportions of industry were controlled from other countries, particularly the United States. The *Royal Commission on Pulpwood* in 1924 detailed how much of the forest wealth had been alienated to foreigners.[41] In New Brunswick, U.S. firms owned about 30 per cent of the private holding of timber lands and non-Canadian firms leased a similar proportion of the public timber lands. Although most of the provinces, as well as the federal government, introduced regulations to prevent the export of unmanufactured pulpwood around the turn of the century, some provinces, such as Ontario, also introduced further restrictions on the export of valuable hardwoods in a raw state. In so doing, an attempt was made to force the foreign direct investors to export at the highest value-added level possible. Other natural-resource sectors exhibited the same truncated export performance where there was a high and growing foreign presence. The seeds of what was to become a problem in the post-1945 economy were sown.

Natural-resource industries became increasingly capital-intensive over time. As foreign control in the natural-resource industries grew, so did the import of capital goods for investment. For instance, in the 1930s, over 20

Table 9:8 Foreign Direct Investment in Canada, by Source, 1936
(millions of dollars)

Sector	Equity of Common Shareholders		Equity of All Shareholder and Par Value of Funded Debt	
	U.S.A.	U.K.	U.S.A.	U.K.
(1)	(2)	(3)	(4)	(5)
Manufacturing	654.8	121.3	836.5	173.0
Mining	192.1	37.6	220.0	57.0
Utilities	143.7	18.2	364.9	67.3
Merchandising	90.3	6.1	101.0	38.1
Financial	24.0	35.0	159.3 (38.1)	154.2 (61.5)
Miscellaneous	35.6	0.8	44.1	2.4
TOTAL	1,140.5	219.2	1,725.8 (1,604.6)	492.0 (399.3)

Note: Figures in parentheses exclude insurance companies.

Source: D.B.S., *British and Foreign Direct Investments* . . ., pp. 43-58.

per cent of new mining equipment and machinery was imported largely from the United States.[42] This tendency to import capital goods later put a strain on Canada's balance of payments since it was a leakage which increased domestic output had to finance.

First, clearly evident in the 1920s was the rise of foreign-controlled firms to commanding proportions of Canadian industry. In 1926, non-residents directed about 17 per cent of the book value of all Canadian industry and although this foreign control increased only modestly in the 1930s the expansion was rapid in the post-1945 years (see Table 9:9). In less than forty years from 1926 the extent of this foreign control doubled. Non-residents dominated such vital sectors as manufacturing, mining, petroleum, and natural gas. High though these figures are, if anything they understate the economic control exhibited. For instance, by the mid-1950s virtually all of the automobile industry was controlled from outside Canada. Many of the large industries of the economy are highly concentrated ones with six firms accounting for a high proportion of industry output; within those six, foreign firms dominated in crude-petroleum production and refining, asbestos, chemical fertilizers, primary plastics, electrical apparatus, rubber goods, and many other industries. Since the 1950s that concentration of foreign control has grown. Of all industries only the utilities sector experienced a decline in non-resident control. This was almost exclusively due to the nationalization of major public utilities in many provinces.

Foreign takeovers of Canadian firms as well as the growth of aggregate foreign direct investment in the post-Second World War years tended to

Table 9:9 Non-Resident Control of Canadian Industry, 1926-1967
(percentage of total book value of capital employed controlled by non-residents)

Industry	1926	1930	1939	1948	1954	1963	1967
(1)	(2)	(3)	(4)	(5)	(6)	(7)	(8)
Manufacturing	35	36	38	43	51	60	57
Mining and Smelting					51	59	65
	38	47	42	40			
Petroleum and Natural Gas					69	74	74
Railways	3	3	3	3	2	2	2
Other Utilities	20	29	26	24	8	4	5
TOTAL (including merchandising and construction)	17	20	21	25	28	34	35

Sources: I. Brecher and S. S. Reisman, *Canada–United States Economic Relations* (Ottawa, 1957), p. 101; Statistics Canada, *Foreign Ownership and the Structure of Canadian Industry* (Ottawa, 1968); and Canada, *Foreign Direct Investment in Canada* (1972), p. 20.

vary with the general level of prosperity in North America. Since economic prosperity in Canada and the United States has been very closely linked in recent years, the periods of shared prosperity witnessed the largest growth in U.S. foreign direct investment (see Table 9:10). Over the 1945-70 period foreign direct investment grew by a remarkable 9.5 per cent compound rate of growth. However, this growth was uneven. It was particularly rapid in the early to mid-1950s, an increase associated with Korean War demands spilling over into the Canadian economy, but more particularly with the natural-resource booms in iron ore, natural gas, and petroleum. The long prosperous period of the 1960s witnessed further growth in foreign direct investment in all sectors of the economy.[43]

It is obvious that when foreigners control such a large proportion of domestic industry their actions may affect real-capital formation profoundly. Returning to the question of the costs of foreign direct investment: When does such a control bias industrial development and impose a cost? As we have already seen truncated export industries may be created. As a consequence the value added in Canada is extremely low and the availability of cheap raw materials to foreigners frustrates the attempt to stimulate a larger secondary manufacturing capacity. Especially in the natural-resource sectors, such as mining, natural gas, petroleum and to a lesser extent timber and pulp and paper, modern economic growth dictated a change to capital-intensive industries and as a consequence not only is the value-added impact small but so also is the employment effect. It might be added that the social costs of rapid

Table 9:10 Book Value of Foreign Direct Investment in Canada, by Source, 1945-1970

Year	Total	Percentage		
		United States	United Kingdom	Others
(1)	(2) (millions of dollars)	(3)	(4)	(5)
1945	2,713	85.0	12.8	2.2
1950	3,975	86.2	11.8	1.8
1955	7,728	84.3	11.5	4.2
1960	12,872	82.0	11.9	6.1
1965	17,356	81.0	11.7	7.3
1970	26,485	81.2	9.5	9.3

Note: The figures for 1960 and earlier are not exactly comparable to the later ones.

Source: Department of Industry, Trade and Commerce, Direct Investment in Canada by Non-Residents, Cat. no. A10-11.

natural-resource exploitation in the form of pollution and environmental damage are not always adequately compensated for by the income effect. The landscape of Sudbury is offered as evidence.

Biases may also be introduced within the manufacturing sector. For instance, foreign direct investors in Canada usually have larger parent companies elsewhere and it is often the parent company which undertakes the fundamental research and development. Canada, relative to most industrial countries, has a low ratio of expenditures on research and development to gross national product—about 1.4 per cent in 1967. To be sure, it may be more efficient for the economy as a whole to import new technologies through the multinational firms. Nevertheless, neither branch plants nor domestically controlled firms have expanded their research and development capabilities as much as most other industrial countries. If new technologies are not readily available, this low commitment to research and design may well have dampened the emergence of high-technology industries and contributed to the out-migration of skilled scientists and experimental engineers.[44]

The growth of foreign direct investment also created balance-of-payments effects. However, not all of the balance-of-payments effects of this investment are costs as some trends indicate. For instance, the ratio of interest and dividend payments to GNP has consistently fallen through time. This burden of foreign investment has diminished. Also, as the stock of foreign direct investment grew relative to portfolio debt, and as dividends became much more important than interest, payments to foreigners tended more and more to be pro-cyclical. Since dividend outflows vary with business conditions in Canada and since interest payments do not, the financing of debt is somewhat eased by the fact that it is large exactly when the economy is prosperous and has much foreign exchange from trade and *vice versa*. The major problem, according to the critics of foreign direct investment, is that while the relative strain on the current account is diminishing, it is still large, about 1 per cent of income, and accounted for by a growth in non-resident control in large measure financed from retained earnings made in Canada. Furthermore, acquisitions of Canadian businesses can be undertaken with portfolio debt. Another major balance-of-payments problem relates also to biased industrial development. Export sales of raw and semi-processed natural resources, themselves a feature of truncated industrial development, force an appreciation of the Canadian dollar in foreign-exchange markets which dampens the exports of manufactured goods and further locks some sectors of industry into continued primary manufacturing production. So too, the balance of payments is sensitive to the policies of the United States. For instance, in the 1960s the forced repatriation of dividends placed a strain on the economy which was directly related to the size of Canada's foreign indebtedness.

The third cost is the loss of tax revenue which may occur as a result of the growth of certain types of direct investment. There is the lost tax revenue associated with the lost value added due to the truncated export industries but in recent years critics have identified, but not with any precision, another loss of tax revenue. Large multinational firms with operations in Canada pay tax on their profits made in Canada. However, sales are often made solely within the firm but across the national boundary. By adopting a particular pricing policy for intra-company shipments profits can effectively be transferred to other jurisdictions where the corporate-profits tax rate is lower. This is known as "corporate transfer pricing". The larger multinational direct investment in Canada becomes the more of the costs might be borne in lost taxes. Certainly, even at present, one can indicate a large number of international firms whose Canadian taxes belie their profitability.[45]

The last cost, and certainly the hardest to define, is that associated with a loss of sovereignty over public policy. To what extent have Canadians suffered a loss in potential income and to what extent adopted policies which have frustrated non-monetary ambitions such as cultural aspirations? it has been a long-held tenet of U.S. law that extra-territorial control of U.S.-owned companies in Canada, and elsewhere, exists. Consequently, these companies in Canada often constrained their activities to conform to U.S. law. For instance, the notorious Trading with the Enemy Act is believed to have forced many U.S.-controlled companies to forego potential export sales to many countries with whom Canada has full and cordial diplomatic relations. There is a similar prohibition on the export to particular countries of certain goods which contain a high technology component. Obviously the loss of potential income cannot be quantified and even if it is small, as it well may be, the political embarrassment to a government undertaking foreign policy in the country's interest may be extremely costly.

Perhaps the major concern about an undue influence on public policy arising from the high proportion of foreign direct investment in some industries is that associated with the rate of non-renewable-resource depletion. The resource flows controlled by foreign direct investment, even though they contribute to current income, may be so great that they prejudice future income gains accruing to Canadians. Either a different time structure of natural-resource export sales or the development of a broader based industrial structure less prey to movements in primary-product prices, accompanied by a relative decline in the importance in the truncated export sector, may be in the long-run interest. In the years since the late 1950s a substantial proportion of the Canadian population believes that the private rate of discount employed by the foreign-controlled firms in the resource sector is greater than the social rate of discount used by Canadians—that is, the rate of exploitation and depletion of non-renewable resources is deemed too great.[46]

The last dimension of the influence over public policy is that associated with non-economic aspirations. U.S. control over much of Canadian industry integrates Canada culturally with the United States in a manner that might not otherwise exist. While one may disagree with the argument, or the extent of so-called cultural domination, it is a view which has been strongly held by many.

This section traced the roots of foreign direct investment and in the process noted that it has grown with an inner dynamic to control much of Canadian industry. Invited by various policies of government and attracted by the profitability of natural-resource exploitation, foreign direct investment, even prior to 1900, exhibited characteristics which called for intervention in the market and while it contributed an ever-increasing amount to private-capital formation, it resulted in substantial costs accompanying the resulting income gains.

Recent Trends

Just as residents of the United States came to control the majority of foreign direct investment in Canada some time before 1914, there was a switch in the source of the long-term portfolio debt. In the late 1920s Great Britain ceased to be the principal source of these foreign savings;

from then on most foreign savings came from the United States. Canada was principally dependent on the United States within twenty years of the massive capital imports from Great Britain of the early twentieth century.

A change in the composition of foreign portfolio debt accompanied the change in the source of foreign savings. Prior to the First World War, as noted earlier, railway and government security issues dominated the debt profile. As New York rose to importance as an international financial centre and London declined, mainly as a result of the respective growth and deflation experienced by the two major economies, more and more Canadian corporate debt was issued there. The Americans did not imitate the conservative lending pattern of British investors. Railways, after the last building mania of the wheat-boom era, ceased to be the major issuers of new debt instruments. Governments in Canada, on the other hand, continued to be major issuers but even they were eclipsed by the industrial sector, probably at the time of the First World War. In recent years the industrial issue of securities, including those of the public utilities, has been about five times that of the government sector in the international capital markets. So too, the security issues of the public sector abroad changed in composition. Since the early 1950s the foreign debt of the provinces has become greater than that of the other levels of government; the foreign debt of municipalities has become greater than that of the federal government. The pattern which prevailed through most of history was reversed and the new trend demonstrates no tendency to revert.

With respect to foreign direct investment, Canadians now appear to be more fully aware of the non-resident control of industry. The high social costs of this investment were first brought to widespread public attention in 1958 by the Royal Commission on Canada's Economic Prospects chaired by Walter Gordon; subsequent studies intensified the amount of public concern about them.[47] As a result of this increase in public perception both federal and provincial governments sought more power to regulate and monitor the non-resident-controlled firms. For the most part, the measures were designed to prevent increasing foreign concentration rather than to force it to decline. Of these measures, the Foreign Investment Review Agency, created in 1973, is the most recent. It has yet to be seen whether in the long run such measures contain the extent of foreign-business penetration in both the existing and newly emerging industries of the Canadian economy. Here, alas, we must conclude that the history of this issue will not be fully written for some time yet.

CHAPTER TEN

Transport: Investment in Infrastructure

Introduction: Economic Significance of Transport Improvements

Transport improvements were fundamental to economic growth and development because they permitted an increasingly efficient movement of goods, resources, and people. The fact that much of Canadian economic development was conducted at the margins of land and natural-resource use placed particular emphasis on large-scale transport networks. For instance, before the coming of railways, overland transport of bulky goods was slow and costly. Canada's commerce was restricted to areas which could be serviced by means of water routes, originally natural routes and later canals. All important commercial centres, such as Halifax, Quebec, Montreal, and Toronto, were ports. The application of steam power to transport in the first half of the nineteenth century not only reduced the costs of water shipments through the use of steamboats but also created a whole new mode of transport, railways. Cheap rail transportation made possible the economic exploitation of vast areas of the country previously beyond the impact of market forces. By the twentieth century new forms of transport had emerged and many older ones were improved. Pipelines were developed for the transport of oil and natural gas and the motor vehicle and airplane respectively revolutionized the short-haul carriage of goods and passengers. Waterways, such as the St. Lawrence Seaway, were improved and more efficient boats were operated. In short, transport improvements reduced the costs of shipping goods and resources and improved the quality of service. These improvements in transport contribute to economic development in several ways.[1]

First, falling transport costs tended to equalize prices in geographically separate areas by creating national and international markets. At any given price, over-supplies in one area were transferred to areas of excess demand, thus tending to reduce the price disparities which arose between isolated markets. As markets grew, natural monopolies also tended to break down because of the exposure to competition which the larger market usually ensured. The falling cost of both domestic and international transport, especially in the nineteenth and twentieth centuries but also earlier, permitted Canadian exports to penetrate world markets. Since most of the goods which Canada was historically capable of exporting were income inelastic and price elastic—they faced competition from other exporting countries—the country's export performance was directly related to transport charges. So the farm-gate price of wheat at Brandon, Manitoba, in the 1890s, was generally the Liverpool price, which represented the effective international one, less transport costs. A small exporting country such as Canada invariably found transport cost critical to the pace of its economic development.

Second, more efficient transport services also integrated various regions in Canada with world import markets. Thus, the income generated from export sales was consumed in such a manner that self-sufficiency was no longer required in the production of tradeable goods. Efficiency gains were made and the consumers' range of choice was enlarged.

Third, as product markets were more fully integrated, so too were resource markets. For instance, no single force permitted the vast flow of immigrants to North America as much as the decline in passenger transport charges in the nineteenth century. Variations in transport charges usually help to explain the variation in the source of the immigration flow and its eventual destination within Canada. Earlier it was noted that the excess capacity created in the shipping of timber was instrumental in causing a reduction in trans-Atlantic passenger rates. Of course, resources other than people were carried in or out of Canada. For instance, a steel industry emerged at Hamilton, Ontario, in the nineteenth century, largely because it was the location which minimized transport charges for the producers, given the final market; at this time Canada imported most of her iron ore for processing having no exploitable deposits of her own as noted in more detail later.

Cheap transport greatly extended the area of profitable production for a given market.[2] This is illustrated in Figure 10:1 where land is of uniform fertility, producing a single product for which there is perfectly elastic demand. If P is a port and, for simplification, it is assumed that the only means of transport for a particular good is wagon haulage, the area of economic exploitation or cultivation of a staple is already defined. Based

Figure 10:1 Economic Expansion Due to Transport Improvements

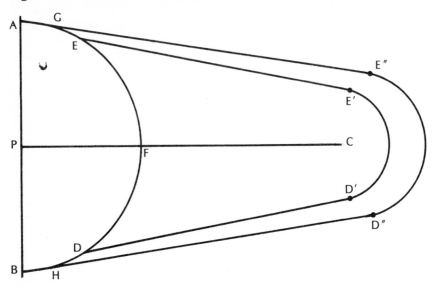

P—market (port) where prices are established
AFB—hinterland of P with existing transport
AEE′D′DB—hinterland after transport improvement to C
AGE″D″HB—hinterland after transport improvement to C and efficiency gains
   (or rise in price)

on the requirement that the costs, including transport costs, be at most
equal to the price obtainable at P for the product, the economic
hinterland becomes the semi-circle AFB. Producers within AFB earn an
economic rent whereas those on the frontier earn no profits. Imagine a
railway is constructed from P to C; the extensive area of cultivation ex-
pands because the product can now be hauled to the railway by the
relatively expensive wagon *and* carried to the port by the relatively inexpensive railway. The area of cultivation is AEE′D′DB. Producers of the
staple on the boundary make zero rent, while those operating inside of
the boundary earn positive rents. This expansion of the area of profitable
cultivation will encourage settlement in the area and increase output
and income by the extent of the new area of cultivation. Since the
population of the area rises, per-capita income increases more modestly
or not at all, depending on the savings in transport costs on shipments to
market. If the railway becomes more efficient over time, the area of

cultivation or exploitation enlarges still more, say to AGE "D"HB; the same may happen if the government forces lower transport rates on the railways, all other things being equal. This illustrates what may be called the "basic" effect of transport on an economy.

This analysis can be extended to cases where settlement had already occurred between P and C, port P specializes in new types of production, fertility variations appear, demand is less than perfectly elastic, and capital-construction costs are explicitly introduced. In order for the railway to be economically viable, the additional total benefits which it produces must exceed its additional total costs which include capital costs when the decision to build or not is being taken. If capital costs are high, the new transport may be left unbuilt even though benefits will accrue.

This direct benefit from the railway or any other transport improvement points up the identity between the reduction in financial cost and the reduction in real inputs required per unit of transport output. The real inputs saved by the transport improvement may be used to increase total output which is a net gain to the Canadian economy. This constitutes the social saving of the improvement.[3] Social savings provide a measure of the net benefit to society of the new transport system after other factors have been rewarded for their contributions. While it is readily apparent that social savings from transport improvement must be positive before that improvement is undertaken by a rational planner, it is not the case historically that all new roads or railways did constitute a net economic benefit to society.

Several important features of the social-savings measure bear closer scrutiny. First, social savings accrue to society at large and not necessarily to the individual builders of the transport system. Consequently, there is usually a divergence between the profitability of the transport project and the net benefits to society. Therefore, all levels of government, as examined below, became involved in providing transport links to overcome the great geographical distances which characterize Canada. Until very recently, Canada's transport innovations took the form of private companies working with subsidies from governments to bridge the actual or supposed gap between private profitability and net social benefit from the improvement. Only if the transport charges were applied to each individual in such a manner as to reduce his economic rents of location to zero would the two be coincident. Such discriminatory pricing seldom, if ever, took place because it was impossible to implement. Second, as illustrated in Figure 10:1, the social-savings calculation is made on the basis of constant prices and a uniform distribution of land quality or natural resources. In practice, prices vary through time and the difference in geographic distribution of land and natural-resources quality is substantial. While recognition of these facts makes computation of the social savings extremely difficult it in no way negates the use of the concept.

The social savings generated as a consequence of a transport improvement constitute the direct benefits to society. However, there are also indirect benefits in the form of linkage effects which are engendered by the general lowering of the costs of production brought about by the lower transport costs. These take many forms and include:

1) a reduction in the cost of getting goods from the point of production to the consumer;
2) a reduction in the assembly cost of materials used in the manufacturing process;
3) a greater opportunity for the geographical division of labour and the resulting advantages of specialization;
4) an inducement to undertake large-scale production with its resulting economies of scale; and
5) an increase in the number of sellers in a market, and an attendant increase in competition as a result of low freight rates.

While some of the above may have operated at different times, each has been an important outcome of transport innovations in Canada.

Because of the difference between private and social returns to transport improvement, political and social considerations also played their role in the provision of transport infrastructure. For instance, both in 1841 and in 1867 the political leaders of British North America believed that a unified political unit required adequate communications and interchange among its constituent parts. National defence considerations too influenced the choice of transport routes. Some early Canadian roads, canals, and railways were built over less economically desirable routes than possible in order that they would be relatively safe from military encroachment; lines of transport and communications, it was felt, must be united. Therefore, decisions about transport investment were not always based on the best economic alternative.

With the need for transport facilities, a small internal market, vast resources, and little domestic saving, Canadian governments were usually called upon to finance, directly and indirectly, much of the transport infrastructure. Of course, left to its own, the private sector could either underproduce or overproduce transport services. If the transport improvement caused further investment and technological change in other sectors, the private transport company would be insufficiently rewarded.

Historically, Canadian governments appear to have feared insufficient transport facilities and thus offered their continual encouragement to build more. Only recently have governments begun to realize that the social costs of some transport facilities exceed their private costs.

Finally, certain characteristics of the supply of transport services, and the size of the infrastructure, make it prone to monopolistic or oligopolistic market structures:

1) it is extremely costly;
2) it is exceptionally long-lasting
3) it has little alternative use; and
4) it is subject to economies of scale.

In order to prevent transport firms from exacting monopoly profits, the government was called upon actively to regulate rates and/or to encourage competition.

The main motives which lay behind the transport improvements to be discussed now—namely, roads, canals, railways, pipelines, airlines—were common to all and can be categorized as attempts to capture benefits from:

1) the direct reduction of transport costs;
2) the indirect linkage effects, either forward or backward, from the innovation; and
3) national unity and defence, including regional interests.

These recur throughout Canada's economic history of transport development.

The King's Highway, 1763-1850
Both direct and indirect economic benefits as well as non-economic, military considerations motivated the provision of roads in British North America. In 1763, the cheapest form of transport was by water and settlement spread, as we might expect, to those areas adjacent to navigable rivers and lakes. By 1850, British North America was laced with a well-articulated system of trunk and branch roads encompassing most of Nova Scotia and New Brunswick as well as the southern portions of Canada East and West.[4] The economic benefits which the roads created were not, however, based on the supplanting of the waterways. Carriage of goods over water was still cheaper than that by road for the bulk of commodities. Rather than a low-cost substitute for water transport the road system was intended to be complementary to it.

Map 10:1 The Canal System of the Canadas

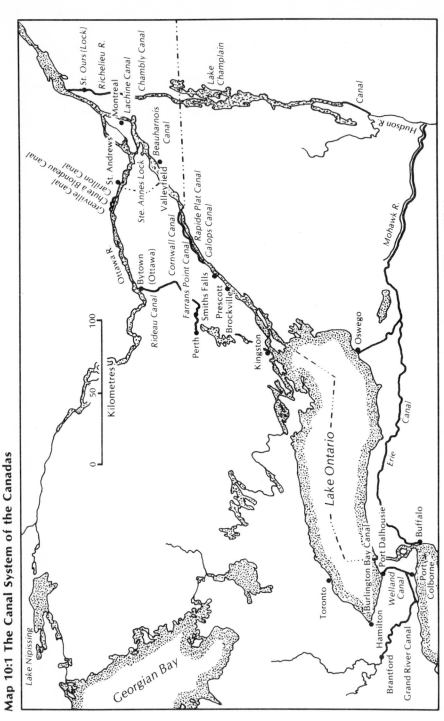

Source: W. T. Easterbrook and Hugh G. J. Aitken, *Canadian Economic History* (Toronto, 1970), pp. 260-61.

Much of the early road-building was based on the military need to defend territory. As such, road-building was undertaken by government to establish communications with the fragmented settlements. In Upper Canada, the first main road was built parallel and close to the St. Lawrence River and Lake Ontario; its apparent vulnerability to invasion from the United States prompted Governor Simcoe to build Dundas Street, connecting London, York, and eastern Upper Canada, well inland from the shore of Lake Erie (see Map 10:1). Military considerations similarily motivated his other road-building venture, Yonge Street. By connecting York with Lake Simcoe and later Georgian Bay to the north, Niagara and Detroit could be avoided. Other than at York, road systems spread out from Niagara-on-the-Lake and Hamilton only after these towns became centres of local government.[5] Because land holdings had to be registered, licences obtained, and court cases tried, communications were essential to the establishment of political hegemony. Roads were built to facilitate this communication. An overland route between the Maritime colonies and the Canadas was also regarded as essential to good government because of the need to move troops and mail when the St. Lawrence was frozen in winter.

The concern of the state with the financing of roads set an early tradition. While most colonies initially tried to build roads by statute labour this proved impractical. The lack of skilled labour and the vast distances soon led all governments to make cash grants each year for road and bridge construction. As early as 1801, the New Brunswick Assembly made regular money grants for this purpose. Upper Canada followed in 1804 with a grant of £1,000, and after 1815 the Legislature of Lower Canada regularly financed road construction and maintenance.[6] The size of these grants grew as the economy spread geographically. In the 1850s, Canada East and West passed the Municipal Loan Fund Act which made it easier for municipalities to borrow funds for road construction while the colonial government shouldered the ultimate financial responsibility. Mail-carrying contracts were let to private companies and chartered turnpike companies were often contracted to build and maintain roads.[7]

As for non-governmental considerations, roads were built to complement the waterways by reducing inland transport costs and by moving the extensive margins of cultivation outwards. First, long-distance routes for mail, passengers, and light freight were required in the winter months. Without roads, transport costs were prohibitive in the winter. In part, this was the rationale for roads such as Yonge Street, Dundas Street, Iroquois Road—Queenston to Ancaster—and the roads on both side of the St. Lawrence in Lower Canada. For example, during the twilight of the St. Lawrence fur-trading era Yonge Street became such an important route from Montreal to the West that the Northwest Fur Company funded part of its construction. This particular road construction allowed cargoes to be diverted from the Ottawa and French rivers to the St. Lawrence-Lake Ontario–Yonge Street route with an estimated saving of $10 per ton of goods. Also, roads were expected to overcome the physical barriers to trade on the St. Lawrence River and the Great Lakes. Roads were built in the Niagara Peninsula to by-pass Niagara Falls and along the St. Lawrence above Montreal to by-pass the rapids. A combination of water and land transport was used to move goods and people between Montreal and lakes Ontario and Erie in the days before canals and steamboats.

Second, local roads opened up new areas for extensive settlement by reducing transport costs as illustrated in Figure 10:1. More settlers meant more sales of Crown land although as noted earlier not necessarily sales to settlers. Also, it meant more tax revenue. However, apart from Dundas and Yonge streets, both of which were built for military reasons, there were few occasions of roads being built in anticipation of demand. In most other cases, the construction of roads and settlement progressed together. There was a lack of so-called improved roads but this does not appear to have handicapped settlement; as late as 1850 the majority of roads in British North America were little more than paths cleared of trees and stumps. Planked or macadamized roads were the exception. The settler simply did not require improved roads in order to get his produce to market. Once land was taken up, the settlers themselves cut a rough road to an improved road, or to a river, stream, or lake. Often produce was moved to market during the early winter when the ground was frozen and such roads were quite passable. Therefore an improved road was unnecessary for settlement, rough roads were carved out as land clearance took place.[8]

As mentioned, improved transport reduced natural monopolies and tended to reduce price differences between regions. There is evidence of these effects for road improvements. For instance, an editorial in the *Quebec Gazette* of 1815 noted that farm produce prices were higher in New England than at Quebec, and therefore that improved transport would lower prices in the former and raise them in the latter. The editorial concluded that road transport between the two areas should remain unimproved. Five years later, cattle were being driven over the new road to Quebec which had been constructed despite the newspaper's views.[9] While it can be argued that the 1820 trade did not follow directly from the price difference that existed in 1815, it is evident that the road integrated the markets and probably helped to drive the prices towards equality.

Third, the development of roads in the Canadas reduced the cost of land transport and therefore enabled a wider area to be settled because crops could economically be brought to a port for export. This, in turn, helped stimulate demands for the improvement of water-transport services on the Great Lakes and through the St. Lawrence. In the Maritime colonies, roads were used as a means of extending hinterlands by reducing the cost of bringing products to the major centres of Halifax and St. John, often for export to the West Indies. The major river valleys in New Brunswick all had roads by the 1830s, along which growing volumes of imports, such as foodstuffs, flowed. The complementarity between waterways and roads emphasizes the fact that most major and minor rivers in the settled areas of British North America had at least one road running beside them. The settlers' goods were moved initially by water while the people and animals walked along the shore eventually clearing a path. This path naturally developed into a road which served the transport needs of the settlers during the winter months when the waterways were frozen and thus lowered transport costs. Taverns and inns quickly sprang up to serve the travellers' other needs.[10]

The government felt little or no pressure to devolve road-building and maintenance to private companies. The precedent of public highways had been set. Private toll roads in sparsely populated areas, of course, would have generated insufficient traffic to provide revenues quickly enough to offset costs in the case of improved roads. Local unimproved roads, on the other hand, were numerous, and could be easily constructed. No private road could have maintained its monopoly. Indeed, the only instances of private roads were on the holdings of the large land companies and they were undertaken to make settlement more attractive rather than to provide a continuing source of profit; no tolls were charged.[11]

But roads could not totally serve the needs of the expanding staple economy, especially in Upper and, to a lesser extent, Lower Canada. Land transport was relatively expensive when compared with water transport. Following the U.S. example, a clamour developed for improved water transport, a demand, of course, to which the effects of improved road transport had contributed.

Way to the West: Canal Projects of the Canadas
A great era of canal-building occurred in Canada during the first half of the nineteenth century. Improved water transport, like the road transport which helped stimulate it, was based on a twofold need: to reduce transport costs on both outward and inward trade, and to provide greater defence for British interests in North America. It is convenient to sub-

divide this period into three intervals, namely pre-1826, 1826 to 1848, and 1848 to Confederation, because of the separate forces at work in the economy and the different consequences which resulted.

Farmers in Upper Canada and the north-central United States wished, of course, to send their produce by the cheapest route to the major trading centre which in the case of wheat was Liverpool. This gave them the highest farm-gate price for the item. Recall that improvements in transport shifted out the extensive margins of cultivation (see Figure 10:1) and raised the farm-gate price. In the early years of the nineteenth century the St. Lawrence route from the interior to Liverpool provided the least costly transport artery for Canadians and for many in the northern United States. The only alternative was high-priced wagon transport through New York State to the port of New York. Many counties in western New York State were important grain-producing areas by the 1820s, and before 1823 these grain exports moved to Liverpool via Lake Ontario and Montreal. Imports of manufactured goods moved along this same route in the opposite direction. At this time Montreal merchants, as well as the Imperial government, hoped to establish a major entrepôt centre on the St. Lawrence.

In the 1820s a number of events coincided to dislodge the St. Lawrence route from its pre-eminence. This caused, in turn, the merchants of Montreal to seek, over a period of at least a quarter-century, a new solution to the problem of capturing trade. The principal reason for disquiet was the opening of the Erie Canal in 1826 through upper New York State; it ran from Buffalo on Lake Erie to Albany where it connected with the Hudson River providing a continuous water route to the port of New York.[12] Shipments by this route were cheaper than via the St. Lawrence (see Map 10:1). Montreal's hinterland was substantially reduced; this may be envisaged in Figure 10:1 by the shifting inward of the extensive margin. The Canadian defence of the St. Lawrence route was further undermined in 1829, when a feeder canal was constructed from Oswego on Lake Ontario to the Erie Canal in order to tap the cereal-growing areas around the most eastern end of the Great Lakes. Thus, the Erie Canal system threatened the commercial hegemony of Montreal in both the U.S. mid-west and Upper Canada. It was evident at the time that if the city wished to expand its extensive margin, improvements on the St. Lawrence route were necessary in order to recapture the trade. The Erie Canal by itself did not destroy the social savings which accrued to Canada; to the contrary, it enlarged them. Conflict between the Canadians and Americans which later ensued was solely over the private and indirect benefits from the transport system.

The Montreal merchants were concerned not only about the loss of export traffic but also about import shipments. In the 1820s, as mentioned earlier, Upper Canada developed as a staple producer of lumber and grain. Lumber had a low value in relation to its weight which made transport costs a crucial element. While some boats and rafts could be moved downstream through the St. Lawrence River rapids, the upstream journey was more difficult, that is more expensive. Settlement brought a demand for imports and so a derived demand for improved transport. By this time steamboats had been introduced on Lake Ontario, but the rapids between the eastern end of the lake and Montreal prevented their use for transport. Improvements were necessary if full advantage of this new transport technology was to be taken.[13]

Considerations other than commercial ones were behind the improvement of Canadian waterborne communications. As it had roads, the Imperial government looked upon canals as a means of better defending the country. The War of 1812 emphasized the difficulties of supplying military forces in Upper Canada and fleets on the Great Lakes if reliance was placed soley on land transport. A by-pass to Niagara Falls and the St. Lawrence rapids had to be constructed. (Recall that the United States won the phase of the war on the lakes during this confrontation.) A canal across the Niagara Peninsula would end the necessity for separate British fleets on lakes Erie and Ontario. Therefore, the Imperial government was interested in improvements although initially unprepared to finance them.[14]

Because of the changes in economic and political circumstances the period from 1826 to 1848 in Canada was one of substantial canal construction. Three aspects of this construction campaign were of crucial significance in determining the pattern of construction and its ultimate impact. First, as Figure 10:1 emphasizes, there are in reality two parts to the St. Lawrence route: from the interior, say Chicago at C to Montreal at P; and from Montreal to Liverpool where the cost of ocean transport is reflected in the Montreal price. Naturally, canal construction could reduce transport costs only on the first part of the route. However, from the point of view of farmers in Canada or the United States, the transport cost over the entire route was the crucial consideration when deciding which alternative to use. Second, the governments' role was crucial to the successful completion of the canal network. Lacking inputs, especially savings to purchase capital, individual entrepreneurs turned to the colonial governments for financial aid. Or, the government built the canal itself. As Canada had an undiversified staple economy with dependence on external markets and a small population, foreign savers were reluctant to become directly involved in the financing of canals because of the risk. Only with government guarantees of interest payments could British savers be persuaded to subscribe heartily to the stock and bond issues which financed canal building.

A third aspect of canal construction was also of critical significance. The Imperial government's emphasis on the defensive aspects of canals eventually forced it to support canal routes which could be defended. In other words, the St. Lawrence River route *per se* was unattractive. Therefore, financial support was put behind the construction of the Rideau Canal which was completed in 1834. In combination with three canals on the Ottawa River, the Rideau provided Canada with a by-pass of the St. Lawrence rapids but the circuitous route had little effect on the reduction of transport costs of the St. Lawrence system.[15] There were no tow paths, its depth was insufficient for large steamboats, the Grenville Canal on the Ottawa River, permitting only shallow draught vessels, constrained the entire system, and there was no lock for general traffic at the rapids near St. Anne's until 1843. In short the opportunity to make the Rideau system a substantial economic alternative was unrealized. While this emphasis on an inland canal route diverted attention away from the St. Lawrence itself there was another reason for the delay on construction of a canal system on the St. Lawrence. Until the Union of 1840, political problems of the Canadas proved to be a barrier to the cooperation between the two colonies on canal financing.

After 1791 and until 1840, separate governments ruled Upper and Lower Canada. As a result neither could command credit in the capital market of Great Britain commensurate with investment needs. In the face of financial difficulties it proved impossible to coordinate even the most elementary canal-construction to ensure that canals were built to a uniform depth. The allocation of costs and benefits was also troublesome. A large number of canals were required in Upper-Canadian territory. Given the Erie Canal route, Upper Canadians felt that their expenditure on canals would mostly benefit Lower Canadians. Finally, in both Canadas, the commercial interests supporting canal construction associated with the Executive, which was usually opposed by the Legislature, leading to bitter debate and delays. Montreal was the centre of the English-British North American commercial class which controlled and therefore focused the financial and commercial interests of the colony. From about 1763, any French-Canadian interest in commercial pursuits found little scope and outlet so it is not surprising that divergent opinions on the usefulness of canals developed between the two cultural groups. Although the Legislative Assembly of Lower Canada, with a French-Canadian majority, allocated money for the improvement of the St. Lawrence it always asked the value of such infrastructure charges to the colony. As early as 1822, union of Upper and Lower

Canada was suggested, but the act never passed. The Act of Union was a prerequisite to the successful completion of the St. Lawrence canal system. Union eased political difficulties, facilitated constitutional changes, and provided a more solid foundation for borrowing in Britain. In addition, the British government offered to guarantee the interest payment on a new Canadian loan of £1.5 million; the proceeds were used to complete the St. Lawrence and Welland canal systems.

By 1848 a system of ship canals had been constructed, by-passing the major physical transport obstacles on the St. Lawrence–Great Lakes route, namely Niagara Falls and the St. Lawrence rapids. All of these canals were either constructed or deepened to uniform dimensions. In the process, the government amassed a debt of approximately £2.5 million, based on the assumption that the canals, along with British preferential tariffs, would suffice to make the St. Lawrence a cheaper route than its U.S. rival.[16]

The improved system achieved one goal admirably: the costs of transport from interior points such as Chicago to Montreal were now lower than the costs from Chicago to Albany. In 1847, it cost 77 cents to ship a barrel of flour from Buffalo to Albany, but only 35 cents from Port Maitland to Montreal, the same distance.[17] There was a similar cost differential on goods moving into Canada or the U.S. mid-west. Was this saving sufficient to divert traffic from Upper Canada and the U.S. trade to the St. Lawrence route? It appears not since, while trade along this route grew during the late 1840s and 1850s, trade on the Erie Canal increased by an even larger percentage. The St. Lawrence route was used far below its capacity in marked contrast to the route through the United States. Three factors prevented the St. Lawrence route from gaining the trade that the merchants expected.

First, before 1846 the U.S. tariff, colonial preferences, and the Canada Corn Act kept the St. Lawrence route sheltered behind a political barrier which enabled it to monopolize at least Upper Canada's external trade and to attract some agricultural trade from the United States. But the repeal of the Corn Laws in 1846 ended the possibility of offsetting the higher overall transport costs on the St. Lawrence route to Liverpool by lower entry costs to the British market.

Second, in the same year, the United States passed drawback legislation which permitted Upper-Canadian grain to be shipped to Liverpool in bond through the United States. Previously, the U.S. tariff on imported grains had prevented Upper Canadians from enjoying the full cost-saving of the Erie route. Shipment of grain *via* the U.S. route was now done without prejudice.

Third and most important, the cost of transport from Montreal to Liverpool exceeded the cost from New York to such an extent that the total transport charge from say, Chicago to Liverpool, was lowest over the Erie Canal–New York route. This cost advantage *via* New York was as true in 1826 as it was in 1848, and the improvements to the St. Lawrence-Niagara area could not eliminate it. Therefore, it is important to examine the entire route from the upper Great Lakes to Great Britain, as emphasized earlier. The important cost advantages for New York were:[18]

1) New York's lower insurance costs: Beyond New York harbour there is open sea, while downstream from Montreal there is a narrow channel often with fog and icebergs;
2) New York, being ice-free all year round, became a regular port of call: Ships were more certain of picking up a cargo, so both incoming and out-going freight shared the transport costs;
3) pilotage charges were less at New York than on the St. Lawrence;
4) the necessity of towing vessels between Montreal and Quebec increased the costs of that route;
5) wharfage and stevedorage costs were, for a 700-ton vessel, three times more at Quebec than New York;
6) because ships made better time on the open sea and faster vessels were attracted to New York, the average sailing time between New York and Liverpool was shorter; and
7) before 1848, the St. Lawrence route was preferred by merchants carrying emigrants from the United Kingdom because it gave them a cargo on the westward voyage which otherwise would have been in ballast; after 1847, most emigrants sailed to New York and this presented Montreal with a return-cargo problem.

These costs militated against the success of the St. Lawrence route as the principal link from the U.S. mid-west to Great Britain. While some Canadians in the early 1850s spoke of enlarged and new canals, the attention of the leading merchants and entrepreneurs was turning already to another transport mode, the railway.

While the social saving associated with the St. Lawrence canal system before 1867 has not been calculated it cannot be convincingly argued that it was indispensable to economic development since there was a viable alternative, namely shipping *via* the Erie–Oswego canal system. It appears that in 1848, say, all of the downward cargo carried on the St. Lawrence system could have been switched to the Erie without straining its capacity. Therefore, looking only at the resource saving, and acknowledging that there may have been overwhelming defence and political motives for these canals, the social saving of the St. Lawrence–Great Lakes canal system may have been small.[19]

Since canals failed entirely to redress the transport disadvantage of Montreal, perhaps the construction of a different kind of infrastructure would. Attention in the Canadas belatedly turned to railways.

The Coming of the Railways

While the canal system of the Canadas was being completed a new era of transport had already begun in the United States, the movement of goods and people by steam railway. By the early 1850s all of the British North American colonies had embarked on at least one railway venture. The building of this new infrastructure was to preoccupy the dreams of the political leaders for many years. When Sir Allen McNab stated in 1853 that "railways are my politics" he was being neither flippant nor unrealistic. Indeed, he was accurately predicting the unstated premise behind many political actions of at least the next seventy-five years. As in the earlier era of trunk roads and canals, fiscal policy was directly linked to the problems of transport. While it has weakened in recent years, this link had, nevertheless, been permanent.

The first railway-building era coincided with the first years of operation of the completed St. Lawrence–Great Lakes canal system. In addition the St. Lawrence canals and the railways were similar in the sense that the rationale for the construction of both was identical. Both were designed to centralize the trade of Canada on Montreal making it a metropolitan centre by reducing transport costs thereby capturing the local trade as well as that of the U.S. mid-west.[20] Like canals, the railways achieved only partial success for Montreal. Nevertheless, Montreal did assume the economic functions and attributes of a metropolitan centre, albeit slowly as:

1) commercial facilities were provided for the hinterland trade;
2) industries were established to process the products of and imports for the hinterland;
3) transport services were developed to channel trade to and from urban centres, including other cities with their own hinterlands which were still subordinate to Montreal; and
4) financial facilities for investment in the hinterland were created.

As earlier, in the case of roads and canals, two aspects of Canada's early railway experience repeated themselves. First there was the conscious attempt to extend hinterlands by reducing transport costs and, second there was the massive government involvement in the economy of the staple-producing areas. It is these themes which are explored here.

By the late 1840s, two things were painfully obvious to British North Americans with respect to transport costs. As mentioned before, while the St. Lawrence–Great Lakes canal system reduced transport costs from their former level on goods shipped *via* Montreal to Liverpool the alternative U.S. route was cheaper. Also, the railway era had already begun in the United States. Together they implied that Montreal faced the prospect of losing both the through trade of Canada and the United States, while shouldering a relatively large portion of the public debt incurred to construct the already out-dated canal system. The solution was to construct a Canadian railway network centring on Montreal. By the early 1860s, the following railways accomplished this in large measure:[21]

1) Grand Trunk Railway: Montreal, Brockville, Port Hope, Toronto, Guelph, Berlin, Sarnia; connections to Portland and Detroit,
2) Great Western Railway: Toronto, Hamilton, London, Sarnia, Windsor, Buffalo;
3) Northern Railway: Toronto, Collingwood; and
4) feeder lines: Ottawa to Prescott, Perth to Brockville, Peterborough to Cobourg, Lindsay to Port Hope, Port Dalhousie to Lake Erie, London to Lake Erie.

In 1850 British North America had 66 miles of railway track but by 1860, as evident in Figure 10:2, this had grown to over 2,000 miles. But did this infrastructure achieve the ends expected of it, mentioned above, any better than the canals? The answer is ambiguous.

Examining only Canadian trade, the railways' contribution to social savings and indirect benefits are clearly positive and large. Unlike the canals, which for the most part, with the exception of the Rideau Canal, paralleled the St. Lawrence–Great Lakes, the railways were expanded into territories which previously relied on relatively expensive wagon haulage for transport. In terms of Figure 10:1, visualize several lines like PC—the railways—being constructed, each one increasing the extensive margin of cultivation in a staple-producing country and reducing the costs of importing goods as well. Canadian commerce was freed from the dependence upon water transport and from a seasonal closing of the transport system during the winter months. The railways of Canada West shifted agriculture and lumbering westward and northward, and centres like London, Berlin—now Kitchener—Guelph, Collingwood, and Welland expanded as a result. As railways broke down barriers to trade by reducing transport costs in the Canadas they also accentuated the economic differentiation which appeared. Sawn timber rose in importance relative to square timber and agricultural specialization was also achieved as farmers responded more effectively to the different market prices. There was, for instance, a drift from cereal to mixed agriculture.

Figure 10:2 Railway Mileage in Central Canada, 1850-1868

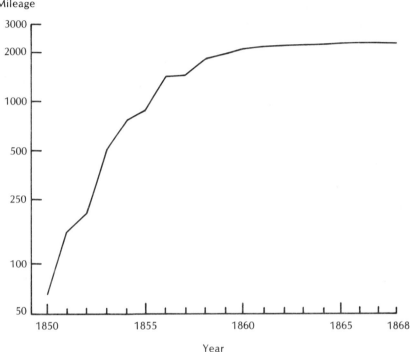

Source: Data are from M. C. Urquhart and K. A. H. Buckley, eds., *Historical Statistics of Canada* (Toronto, 1965), p. 528.

The development of the Niagara fruit belt, the tobacco-growing area along Lake Erie, and the concentration of grain cultivation in the extreme southwest part of Canada West dates to this period. Notice that there are many hinterlands for any central location such as P in Figure 10:1, one for each commodity produced or crop grown.

The railways of central Canada were, on the other hand, not an unqualified success. For instance, Montreal failed yet again to capture the trade of the U.S. mid-west. In the first instance this was due to the bulky nature of commodities such as grain. Railway transport did not confer a great cost saving as compared to water transport; the St. Lawrence–Great Lakes and Erie Canal waterways proved to be competitive with railways for many decades after their construction.[22] Second, during the 1850s, the major U.S. ports constructed their own railways across the Appalachians to tap the interior trade and this eroded Montreal's position.

The cost advantages of Atlantic shipments from New York, in contrast to Montreal, were still present and of course there was no obvious reason why Canadian railways should be more efficient than their U.S. rivals. In fact, the latter had better connections in Michigan and further west, and the adoption by Canada of a wider gauge track — 5'6 " — than that used in connecting — 4'8½ " — meant that through traffic had to be transshipped twice when using Canadian railways. While the wider gauge helped monopolize the Canadian rail traffic, it thwarted the capture of that of the United States. Therefore, Montreal failed again, and many railways constructed in expectation of a greater traffic than materialized were in financial difficulties by the 1860s.

The railways of this first period of construction, like the canals before them, often ran into financial difficulty because of their inability to secure British funds. This forced government involvement of the most direct type. Assistance was given in several ways including:

1) direct cash grants;
2) railway charters which involved the government purchasing bonds or stocks of the railway;
3) the Guarantee Act, 1849 — The Canadian government guaranteed interest, at a rate not over 6 per cent, on half of the bonds of any railway over 75 miles long if half of the railway had already been constructed;
4) the Municipal Loan Fund Act, 1852 — Municipalities in Canada issued debentures that were purchased by provincial governments who issued their own debentures which were sold in London and the proceeds were given to transport companies; and
5) grants of a non-cash variety: land, rebates, rights of way, among others.[23]

Whether in any individual case less aid could have been given without destroying the inducement to build a railway is debatable. On the other hand, there was undoubtedly an over-capitalization in rail lines, particularly in the case of the small local railways sponsored by municipalities. By the 1860s the Canadian railways were deeply in debt to the government — with little hope of repayment — and had driven many municipalities near to bankruptcy. This caused the government to close the Municipal Loan Fund and assume responsibility for its obligations. Such was the sorry plight of Canada's first railways.

By the end of the first era of railway building in British North America, and indeed even by 1867, there was no railway linking the Canadas and the Maritime colonies despite the energetic work of Joesph Howe over several decades. So too, the Pacific coast colonies of Vancouver Island

and British Columbia were as remote as ever. The failure to secure British financial aid, intercolonial disagreement over routes, and the rail line to Portland, Maine, delayed the direct Maritime link. But with Montreal's inability to capture the U.S. trade and become the entrepôt centre of more than Canada, political attention again turned to the intercolonial rail links. This was to give further scope to Sir Allan McNab and like-minded politicians.[24]

The Transcontinentals

The canals and first railways of central Canada were designed to bring already settled areas within the scope of the market economy. During the next phase railways were to press into virgin, unsettled territory. At the time of Confederation the first transcontinental railway was being built in the United States—completed in 1869. This railway and its imitators substantially lowered the costs of transport compared to the existing alternative. Yet, such was the spread of hinterlands as a result of the U.S. railways that all of British North America west of the Precambrian Shield was at risk to American settlement. The trade created by settlement would have flowed south over foreign railways. Without the physical presence of Canadian settlers the claim to full sovereignty over the prairie West was weak. To the prime minister, Sir John A. Macdonald, a railway to the West, as it was envisaged in the years after Confederation, was as much an instrument of national unification as a means of immediately lowering transport costs although, in the long run, the two results were inseparable.

Economists can point to the political considerations which governed the creation of the first Canadian transcontinental railway and claim there was a cheaper alternative. Use of U.S. railways, with additional spur lines, could have integrated the entire prairie West into the wider market economy. However, such an argument is both specious and uninteresting: The political reality was that in order for the old Hudson's Bay Territory to become part of Canada, let alone British Columbia, a Canadian railway was required. This political constraint also had a profound effect on the route which the railway would take. It was to be an all-Canadian one. In 1870, British Columbia entered into Confederation on the strength of a promise that a transcontinental railway would be built as a link with Ontario and Quebec.

Likewise, many in central Canada and the Maritimes looked to a railway as the only means of forging the eastern Confederation link.[25] Such a railway, it was argued, would spur the regions to specialization and lead to rapid improvement in income and welfare. In 1867, there was no overland transport link other than the relatively costly roads. A railway to the East would give central Canada an ice-free port at Halifax and open up the markets of both regions to the products of the other. But, as with the railway to the West, political priorities determined the route to be followed. While a railway had been proposed before 1867, construction was delayed because the Imperial government would not support it because it ran through U.S. territory which was, in fact, the shortest route. Rather, the line was destined to travel along the sparsely populated south shore of the Gulf of the St. Lawrence. Even after Confederation, this was the only politically acceptable route and the possibility of finally completing it attracted maritime British North America, especially Nova Scotia, into Confederation.

The Intercolonial Railway between Nova Scotia and Quebec through New Brunswick was not completed until 1876. Being unable to interest private companies in the project, the government built the line and supervised its subsequent deficits which stemmed from a variety of factors. First, commercial considerations, as mentioned above, were secondary in the selection of a route; with military and political considerations so prominent, deficits were perhaps to be expected. Second, the Intercolonial Railway was longer in miles than its competitors (which soon appeared) and as a result incurred higher variable costs than the others even when managed as efficiently as possible. Third, the Intercolonial was located in territory where the snowfall was heavy and floods were common both increasing maintenance costs which the small volume of local traffic in the sparsely populated areas could not offset. Fourth, freight competition by water along a large portion of the Intercolonial route proved to be effective. Last, being a political creation, freight rates were set at unremunerative levels. Since water transport and other railways provided competition for the Intercolonial, higher rates reduced the total revenue earnings due to the relatively elastic demand for its services.[26]

The transcontinental railway to the West provided a different set of problems. Throughout the late 1860s and 1870s the federal government was unable to enter into a lasting commitment to construct the railway to British Columbia. Either private interests suggested a line running partly through the United States, which was unacceptable to the government, or they were reluctant to proceed without large subsidies.[27] They foresaw relatively low private rates of return on their investment. In the operation of such a railway, large amounts of capital were necessary for construction but earnings were likely to be small for several years after its completion. But finally in 1880 an agreement was struck between the federal government and a private company, and within five years the Canadian Pacific Railway linked central Canada and British Columbia.

The basic problem, which in the first instance delayed construction and in the second bedeviled the first few years of the CPR's operation, arose from the distinction which we may categorize as that between the private and social rates of return on investment in a transcontinental railway. These need amplification.

Private businessmen contemplating the construction of the railway unaided by the government, were considering implicity the present discounted value (PV) of the future stream of net earnings from the railway for a given number of years, say, n.[28] This may be written as:

$$PV = \sum_{t=0}^{n} \frac{(GR_t - OE_t - GI_t)}{(1 + r)^t} + \frac{V_n}{(1 + r)^t} \tag{1}$$

where GR is the gross operating receipts of the railway, OE is the operating expenses of the railway, GI is gross investment in the railway, V_n is the value of the railway in year n to, say, a prospective buyer, and r is a rate of discount. The internal rate of return which a private entrepreneur may expect from the calculation of PV above is determined by setting the present value equal to zero and solving for r. If the opportunity cost of funds invested in other enterprises or bonds was greater than r, then the railway project offered insufficient inducement to be constructed by unaided, private interests. What was the situation with the CPR? While the evidence needed to answer this question is elusive, a rough comparison of the ratio of real average earnings to price of all common stock on the New York Stock Exchange from 1881 to 1900 to the private rate of return to CPR shareholders provides a first approximation. The opportunity cost was about 6.8 per cent and the r was 3 to 4 per cent; this suggests that private interests alone would not have constructed the railway.

The Canadian government correctly rationalized that there were returns from a transcontinental railway which private businessmen could not capture; there were unpaid benefits, in the form of greater national income, which the railway brought about. In other words, the social rate of return exceeded the private, internal rate of return, and the former may be represented as:

$$\sum_{t=0}^{n} \frac{(CS_t + GR_t - OE_t - GI_t + Y_t)}{(1 + s)^t} + \frac{L_n}{(1 + s)^t} = 0 \tag{2}$$

where GR, OE, and GI are as above, CS is the additional consumer surplus or social savings created because of lower transport prices, Y is the sum of all externalities or indirect benefits from the building of the railway exclusive of CS, L_n is the value to society as a whole in year n of the railway (this is the social equivalent to V_n in equation (1) above), and s is the calculated social rate of return. It was argued at the time, although not in these terms, that s exceeded r, and the government conceded cash and land subsidies, imports freed from duty, the granting of partial monopoly powers, tax concessions, and other inducements to the railway builders. We do not know what the social rate of return accruing from the CPR was; it is extremely difficult to quantify because of the unknown indirect benefits. Indeed, it is impossible to claim that this railway was the single greatest contributor to growth in modern Canadian economic history. Like the canals and railways of the 1850s, there were alternatives to the all-Canadian transcontinental. Perhaps, as suggested earlier, the most efficient alternative would have been a railway from Winnipeg to the Pacific, but using U.S. railways south of Lake Superior. Lower transport costs were necessary for the development of Canada's prairies; it does not follow that this had to be achieved with the Canadian Pacific Railway.

Be that as it may, it can be claimed with some certainty that the Canadian Pacific Railway was built ahead of the demand for its services. This being so it may have played a causal role in the relatively rapid growth of the Canadian population and income after 1900, especially in the Prairies. There were three consequences of this building ahead of demand. First, since private interests expected the railway to yield relatively low internal rates of return over its early life, government aid was required to build the line. The Dominion, provincial, and municipal governments provided several types of subsidies:

1) completed sections of railway were handed over from the government contractors to the CPR (Thunder Bay to Selkirk, Kamloops to Port Moody);
2) cash ($25 million from the Dominion);
3) land (25 million acres from the Dominion);
4) tax concessions: free import of construction materials, capital stock free of taxation, land without taxation for twenty years;
5) right-of-way and road-bed concessions;
6) freedom to take construction materials from Crown lands; and
7) twenty-year prohibition against construction of a railway south of the Canadian Pacific mainline in the Prairies within fifteen miles of the U.S. border and the Dominion restricted its rate-regulation activities.

While a subsidy was required for the reasons already mentioned, an excess amount of subsidy appears to have been paid to the company estimates of which vary in value from approximately $61 million to $40 million depending on the assumed rate of return.[29] The various government bodies apparently wanted to be certain that the Canadian Pacific would be built.

Second, building ahead of demand meant that the railway, in its early years of operation, had excess capacity so that single-year rates of return were low at first although they did rise later. Given that the government had subsidized the railway, part of this aid was used to finance a prairie route which was less likely to generate quickly a rise in traffic compared to the alternative route which might have been chosen. This was the third aspect of building ahead of demand. Rather than construct the railway through the more populous Fertile Belt of the North Saskatchewan River, the CPR followed a route closer to the U.S. border in what proved to be land less amenable to immediate settlement (see Map 10:2). The reasons for the choice of the more southern route were never clearly articulated although both the CPR and the Canadian federal government wanted to prevent the encroachment of U.S. railways into Canada.[30] Also, entrepreneurs in the Hudson's Bay Company, such as Lord Strathcona, feared that a northern route would bring competition to the Company's fur trade and so brought pressure to bear on the route selection. The builders of the CPR, for their part, had learned from bitter experience that building a railway too close to established settlements like Edmonton and Battleford, but not necessarily through them, caused problems about the right of way. Furthermore, a route chosen where fewer long-settled places existed gave greater opportunity to capture capital gains associated with town sites. It is also possible that there may have been cost savings on the southern route, irrespective of any compensating benefits, which were found attractive during the final construction phases. Building, prior to the clear identification of demand, of course, suggests that the CPR had a substantial influence on the pattern of prairie settlement and future economic development.[31] We shall return to this theme later.

The profits of the CPR attracted rival interests into transcontinental railway building and its apparent success caused many to underestimate the uncertainties of such mammoth projects. Fortified by government subsidies and interest guarantees, two additional transcontinentals were built during the twenty years from 1896 to 1915. These were the Canadian Northern Railway, and the Grand Trunk Pacific–National Transcontinental network (see Map 10:3). As a consequence, railway miles in operation, excluding second tracks, yard track, industrial track, and sidings, rose from 2,617 miles in 1870 to 13, 151 miles in 1890 and a staggering 34,882 miles by 1915 (see Figure 10:3). Wilfrid Laurier, when speak-

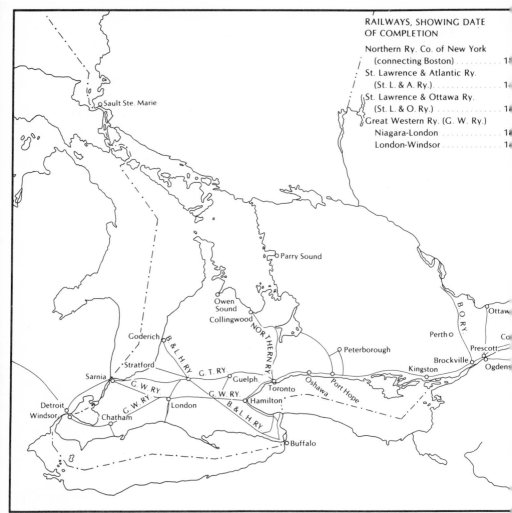

RAILWAYS, SHOWING DATE
OF COMPLETION

Northern Ry. Co. of New York
  (connecting Boston) 1₄
St. Lawrence & Atlantic Ry.
  (St. L. & A. Ry.) 1₄
St. Lawrence & Ottawa Ry.
  (St. L. & O. Ry.) 1₄
Great Western Ry. (G. W. Ry.)
  Niagara-London 1₄
  London-Windsor 1₄

Map 10:2 Early Railways of the Canadas

ing of the Grand Trunk Pacific in 1903, expressed the tenor of the times:

> We cannot wait, because time does not wait; we cannot wait because
> in these days of wonderful development, time lost is doubly lost; we
> cannot wait, because at this moment there is a transformation going
> on in the conditions of our national life which it would be folly to ig-
> nore and a crime to overlook.[32]

Heady stuff, but unfortunately considerable government assistance
enabled everyone involved to overlook the duplication of facilities that

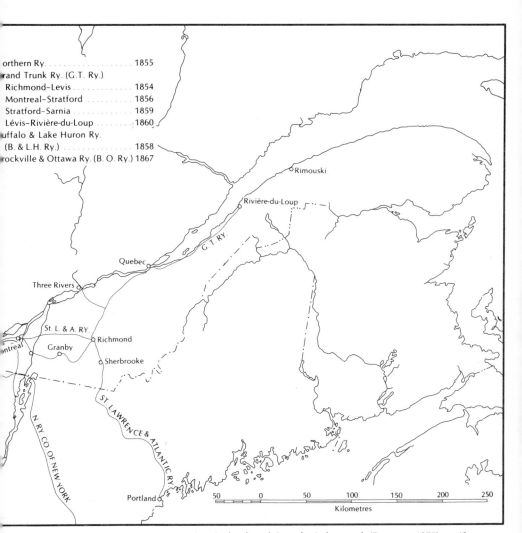

orthern Ry. 1855
rand Trunk Ry. (G.T. Ry.)
  Richmond–Levis 1854
  Montreal–Stratford 1856
  Stratford–Sarnia 1859
  Lévis–Rivière-du-Loup 1860
uffalo & Lake Huron Ry.
  (B. & L.H. Ry.) 1858
rockville & Ottawa Ry. (B. O. Ry.) 1867

Rimouski

Rivière-du-Loup

G.T. RY.

Quebec

Three Rivers

St. L. & A. RY.

Richmond

Granby

Sherbrooke

ntreal

N. RY. CO. OF NEW YORK

ST. LAWRENCE & ATLANTIC RY.

Portland

50   0   50   100   150   200   250
Kilometres

Source: D. G. Kerr, *Historical Atlas of Canada*, 3rd rev. ed. (Toronto, 1975), p. 49.

resulted in comparison to the traffic which could be generated. The West was, by the early twentieth century, over-capitalized in railway infrastructure. Not only were no, or at best small, additional social savings being created but the railways were driving each other into abject unprofitability.

The Canadian Northern's main sources of funds were cash subsidies, land grants, and guarantees on bonded debt, all involving the direct participation of Canadian governments. Under pressure from Manitoba, the Dominion government cancelled the Canadian Pacific's "monopoly

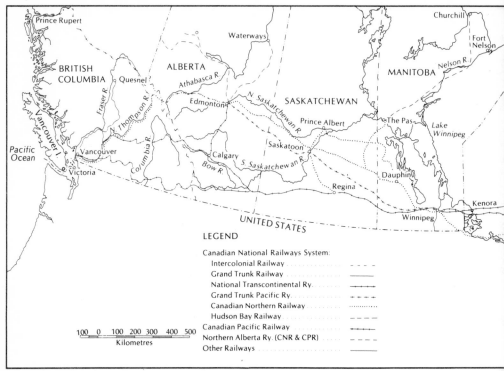

Map 10:3 Transcontinental Railways

clause" in 1888; this led to the construction of lines in southern Manitoba which eventually fell into the Canadian Northern's hands. This railway received land grants totalling about six million acres, mostly on charters under which it was built. Cash subsidies from the Dominion, Ontario, Quebec, and Manitoba governments equalled about $29 million. Finally, in order to make it easier for the Canadian Northern promoters to market their bonds, various governments guaranteed their interest to the extent of millions of dollars.[33] This practice had been abandoned previously because of the associated problems which arose in the 1850s. But this century's first decade flowed with optimism.

The Grand Trunk Pacific–National Transcontinental was similarly blessed by governments' largesse. For political reasons this transcontinental railway was destined to end in the Maritimes rather than in Maine and pass through the "clay belt" of Quebec and Ontario. For this reason, the Dominion undertook its construction from Winnipeg eastwards; it was then to be leased to the Grand Trunk. The western section from Win-

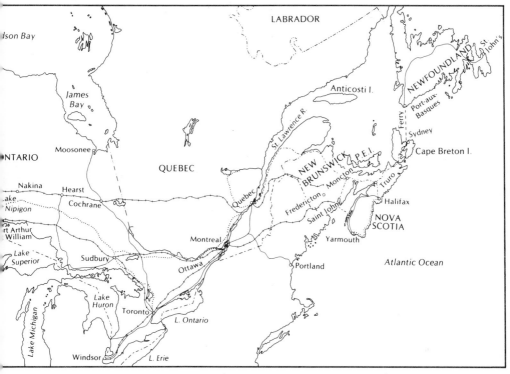

Source: D. G. Kerr, *Historical Atlas of Canada*, 3rd rev. ed. (Toronto, 1975), pp. 64-65.

nipeg was built by the Grand Trunk with substantial bond-interest guarantees from the Dominion government.

By 1914 it was evident that even with government assistance the Grand Trunk Pacific and the Canadian Northern would be unable to generate positive private rates of return. Investment had proceeded to the point where duplication of facilities occurred and the technical characteristics of the new railways left little basis for choosing among them. Therefore, the indirect benefits of additional railway mileage declined dramatically. When the railways sought more aid, the federal government established a Royal Commission which eventually recommended that a board appointed by Parliament operate these railways, along with the government-owned lines. Faced with bankruptcy the railways assented and the government, from 1917 to 1923, nationalized the Canadian Northern, the Grand Trunk, and the Grand Trunk Pacific, and, along with the government railways—Intercolonial, Prince Edward Island, and National Transcontinental—formed the Canadian National Railway. There

Figure 10:3 Railway Mileage in Canada, 1868-1920

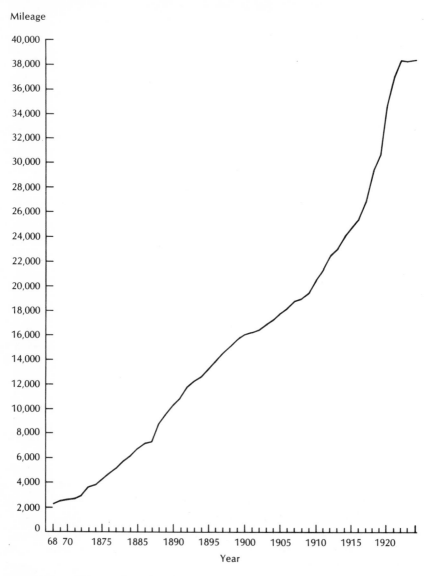

Notes: From 1907 to 1919 the figures are for the year ending June 30; subsequent years are given on a calendar basis. From 1920 to the present there has only been a modest net expansion of track (approximately 6,000 miles).

Source: Data are from Urquhart and Buckley, eds., *Historical Statistics of Canada*, pp. **528** and 532.

was no great principle at stake for the government and little popular sentiment supporting the public ownership of railways in 1917. The decision to nationalize part of the railway sector was based on sheer pragmatism. However, the framework for subsequent railway development was established. There were to be two railways, the privately owned Canadian Pacific Railway and the publicly owned Canadian National Railway.[34]

Transport Policy and Recent Trends
Long before the last section of transcontinental track had been laid government transport policy was forced, by public pressure, to consider an issue related to that of railway extension, the structure of rates charged on traffic.[35] Regulation of the rates charged by first the railways and later other transport modes, became a permanent feature of government transport policy. It is, of course, easy to understand why this was so when it is recalled that the freight charges to the market directly controlled the extent of social savings. Less obvious is the fact that various rate structures have implications for the regional distribution of social savings and the indirect benefits derived from a transport improvement.

To be sure the railways were not completely free to adopt monopoly or oligopolistic pricing practices. Several instances of competition have already been mentioned. For instance, the cost of shipping by sea governed the freight-rate charges per ton-mile from Montreal to Vancouver—costs which in fact fell in real terms when the Panama Canal was opened in the early twentieth century. However, in both the Prairie and Maritime regions there was a great deal of fervent concern about transport rates, and the government's growing responsibility for the general regulation of transport services. The ill will that soon appeared between these regions and central Canada stemmed from the alleged characteristics of railway transport.[36] Many local producers and provincial leaders regarded the railways as the creatures and instruments of national policy. Since, as we have seen, the railways were constructed with government assistance, it was argued that rail lines should be extended and provide services at, so-called, favourable rates. Competition was non-existent or controlled. While the railway managers argued that their rates were fair and justified, others claimed that a thoroughly complicated rate structure disguised rate discrimination; a lack of complete cost information being presented to all concerned fuelled these arguments. Such allegations led to the assumption by many—especially provincial political leaders—outside of Ontario and Quebec that transport costs were the most critical component of business costs and thereby in the pattern of regional growth. Railways did not represent the interest of those people of the regions and rate differences with central Canada were unjustified. Those who held attitudes similar to those above looked to the federal government to uphold their rights against the railway interests, and from this pressure came some important and long-standing concessions to regional interests. First, in the 1890s, the Canadian Pacific Railway's monopoly on the Prairies was broken, and with this came a new competition from the other transcontinental railways in that area, the Canadian Northern and the Grand Trunk Pacific.

Second, in 1897, the federal government and the Canadian Pacific Railway entered into the famous Crow's Nest Pass Agreement. In return for a subsidy of about $3.4 million for building a line from Lethbridge, Alberta, through the Crow's Nest Pass to Nelson, British Columbia, the railway agreed to reduce rates on two commodity movements of importance to the prairie region.[37] These were "settlers' effects", such as agricultural implements, farm supplies, and household furniture, moving westward from Ontario, and, second, grain and flour moving eastward to the Lakehead. The management of the Canadian Pacific agreed that these reduced rates should remain in effect *"hereafter"*. From 1899, when the reduced rates came into effect, until 1925, the agreed rates on grain and flour were effective only for seven years because the rates were first reduced to meet the lower rates that the governments of Manitoba and Saskatchewan negotiated with the Canadian Northern Railway and later raised to meet inflationary tendencies of the First World War. By 1922, these rates were back to their 1899 level. As well, specific rate changes on various commodities altered the agreed rate on westbound settlers' effects. In 1925, an amendment to the Railway Act ended the Crow's Nest Pass Agreement but made the 1899 grain and flour rates moving eastward statutory rates; the special rates for westbound settlers' effects were discontinued and grain and flour rates were applied to all traffic moving from all points on all railway lines west of the Great Lakes to the Lakehead. Subsequently, the 1899 rates for grain and flour were applied to the movement of those products by rail to ports on the Pacific Ocean and to Churchill.

Over the past seventy years, therefore, certain rates had a ceiling while production costs of the railways on this traffic rose. From the point of view of prairie grain producers, costs were lower than they could have been without the Crow's Nest Pass Agreement. This price distortion fed back into the prairie economy and was undoubtedly a contributing factor to the excessive amount of resources to be found in grain production by the 1920s. From the viewpoint of the railways' management, they were required to supply services at less than remunerative rates and, as might have been expected, this forced them to lower the quality of their service, charge higher rates elsewhere (for example on westbound traffic), and reduce investor earnings. The best measure of the distortion of resource allocation was given by the Royal Commission on Transportation in 1961 which stated that the Crow's Nest Pass rates annually fell short of covering variable costs by about $6 million.[38]

The third concession to regional interest was the establishment of the Board of Railway Commissioners by the government in 1903. In effect, the Commission heard the grievances of the regional interests and acted upon them. It was, of course, argued that for long-distance land movement the railways had only minimum competition and therefore, they charged "excessive" rates, and should be regulated. The fact that the federal government even established a board meant that railways were regarded as different from other businesses in Canada.

Fourth, since almost 1876 and the completion of the Intercolonial Railway, the political leaders of maritime Canada were unhappy with its impact on their regional economy. Some of the railway's handicaps were mentioned in the preceding section. After decades of complaint, the Maritime interests received the Duncan Royal Commission on Maritime Claims in 1925 which, in turn, led to the Maritime Freight Rates Act two years later. Similar to the Crow's Nest Pass Agreement, the Act brought about rate reductions on certain all-rail or partial-rail movements both within the Maritime region and on westbound, outward traffic. The intent was to permit producers in the Maritimes to capture more of their own market in the face of competition from central Canada and the United States, and to enable some Maritime industries to penetrate the market of central Canada with their products. Federal government subsidies to the railways allowed them to recoup their losses on the traffic. The economic effects on the Maritime economy and on railway interests were again similar to those of the Crow's Nest Pass rates.

However, there was the additional issue of the subsidy provided under the authority of the Maritime Freight Rates Act. Since the railways received a subsidy, no losses were incurred on the traffic with the result that railways received a preferred position in the transport system of the maritime region until the late 1960s. Yet, in the recent past, the subsidy scheme has been extended to other types of transport, particularly trucking. Benefits to the Maritimes from the Act came from isolating the local market area from the products of other Canadian regions. It was a simple case of trade diversion. The Act was counterproductive also in the sense that it distorted the efficiency in the transport sector as well as more generally in maritime industry. It cannot be claimed that maritime interests were well served by the Act. Truck competition soon forced railway rates below those set in the Act but yet the railways continued to receive a subsidy.

Until the end of the Second World War, as illustrated, regional interests had some success at pressing their special transport claims before the federal government. As long as the railways seemed to lack effective competition, these claims appeared to have some justification. But, the main thrust of Canadian transport policy after 1946 changed emphasis from special consideration to competition. Increasing competition destroyed the calcified railway-rate structure over which so many hours of disagreement before the Board of Railway Commissioners had been spent. With the encouragement of competition as the new basis of Canadian transport policy, how could regional interests argue that rates were unjust or showed undue preference for one region over another?

Competition for commercial traffic came from three transport modes: trucking, water transport, and pipelines. Table 10:1 demonstrates the decline in the railways' carrying thrust since 1938, but especially since 1944 when they still carried about 74 per cent of domestic freight ton-miles. From that date, while water transport increased only slightly, the relative road and pipeline shares of the traffic rose dramatically. Air freight, another new competitor, grew in importance during the early decades of the twentieth century, but despite its absolute growth, by the early 1970s still accounted for less than one per cent of aggregate ton-miles by all modes. This, however, understates the importance of this carrier since it specializes in the shipment of high-value/low-bulk cargoes.

In contrast, the trucking industry grew from what was a short-haul transport service in the 1920s and 1930s to become a transport carrier over all distances. Within two decades, certain developments on the supply side reduced costs of this transport mode. First, road surfaces were improved. In particular, after 1949 the Trans-Canada Highway Act provided assistance in building a hard-surfaced, all-weather road from coast to coast. To this trunk line were added thousands of miles of other roads and highways which made trucking more efficient. Second, improvements were made in vehicle design: Diesel motors, longer trailers, and dual-trailer units among others. The railways responded by introducing their own innovations such as Diesel power, agreed charges, trailer-on-flatcar service, but they could not fully contain the growth of long-haul trucking.

Although the growth of railway transport was the politics of the day interest in the St. Lawrence waterway did not wane after the 1860s. With the growth of grain exports after the 1880s, interest revived the potential

Table 10:1 Freight and Passenger Traffic, 1938-1968

A: Percentage Distribution of Domestic Freight (Ton-Miles)
by Mode of Transport

| Year | Rail | Road | Water | Pipelines | |
				Oil	Gas
(1)	(2)	(3)	(4)	(5)	(6)
1938	51	3	46	—	—
1944	74	3	23	—	—
1948	68	5	27	—	—
1962	41	11	26	16	6
1968	38	9	26	18	9

B: Percentage Distribution of Inter-City Passenger-Miles by
Commercial Carriers

Year	Bus	Air	Rail
(1)	(2)	(3)	(4)
1949	48	6	46
1951	48	8	44
1966	39	38	23
1968	40	38	22

Source: H. L. Purdy, *Transportation Competition and Public Policy in Canada* (Vancouver, 1972), pp. 58, 74.

of shipment by canal. The Welland Canal was deepened to fourteen feet in 1887 and a canal of eighteen feet was completed on the Canadian side of the St. Mary's River in 1895; the shallow sections of the St. Clair River, and the St. Lawrence canals were dredged or rebuilt. Even at the height of railway fever in 1907 serious consideration was given to a new canal project linking the Ottawa River and Lake Superior over the old fur-trading route.[39] However, a new Welland canal was calculated to be a cheaper alternative to handle western grain shipments and end the annual bottlenecks at the entrance to the old Welland canal. Construction of the new canal, with a depth of 30 feet, was begun in 1913.

The most spectacular improvement of the St. Lawrence system took place in the 1950s. Canada and the United States cooperated to enlarge the Great Lakes–St. Lawrence system to provide a deep waterway of minimum 27-foot depth from the head of Lake Superior to the sea. The Seaway opened in 1959. It reduced transport costs essentially by opening the St. Lawrence River to large vessels which no longer had to transship their cargoes to the shallow-draught vessels which the old 14-foot canals made necessary. Movement through the Seaway since 1959 has been distinguished by the importance of a relatively few commodities: wheat, corn, barley, soybeans, coal, coke, iron ore, fuel oil, and manufactured iron and steel. The first four commodities have tended to move eastward from Canada and the United States, while the last five commodities moved westward: within Canada — coke; from Canada to the United States — iron ore; and from other countries to the United States — manufactured iron and steel. These flows remained relatively unchanged in the recent past.[40]

While pipelines for petroleum products existed in Canada prior to 1947, the oil discoveries at Leduc, Alberta, in 1947 and subsequent natural-gas finds dramatically changed the transport of fuels in Canada. Since the main markets for oil and natural gas lay outside of the Prairie provinces, an efficient transport mode had to be found. After the Interprovincial Pipeline Company completed its pipeline from Edmonton to Lake Superior, the cost of transporting a barrel of oil fell from $1.86 by bulk rail freight to $0.55 by pipeline.[41] In comparison with other transport modes, pipelines are in continuous operation; they are not interrupted by bad weather; they have no problems of return empty capacity; they reduce the costs by avoiding urban centres; and they require less maintenance, and variable costs are a small percentage of total costs — especially wages and salaries. As well, various technological changes since the 1940s reduced both fixed and variable costs. From 1,400 miles of trunk pipelines in operation in 1950, the system expanded by, the early 1960s, to well over 9,500 miles of gathering and trunkline pipe for oil and 5,000 miles for natural gas. The system then fell into six separate divisions:

1) lines for natural gas and crude petroleum from Alberta to Vancouver;
2) similar lines to important Prairie cities;
3) a line for petroleum from the Prairies to the U.S. boundary roughly south of Winnipeg, then to Duluth, and via the Straits of Mackinac to Sarnia;
4) a pipeline for natural gas from the West, north of Lake Superior via Kapuskasing to Toronto, Ottawa, and Montreal;
5) lines in the area between Sarnia and Montreal for petroleum products; and
6) the Montreal–Portland pipeline.

For the products which they carry, pipelines provided the most efficient means of transport and they soon lured shippers from train, truck, and water modes.

The impact of transport improvements of all types was felt primarily through the augmented income which the social savings stimulated. Cheapening passenger transport has also played a role by permitting a pattern of labour mobility more responsive to economic demands. Since 1920 this has of course meant the automobile. By 1928, the private car provided about 60 per cent of total passenger miles in Canada. Throughout the 1920s and into the next decade private automobiles in use per million population grew from 47,800 to 98,700; in this respect Canada was exceeded only by the United States. Although forestalled by the depressed condition of the 1930s and subsequently by the Second World War, the growth in the use of the private car rapidly expanded again after 1946. This was stimulated by the greater number of paved roads and highways, financed by the governments, and the rise in consumers' incomes. Perhaps no other single transport mode has so changed the face of society. The growth of suburban areas from which workers could daily travel to the place of employment was subsequently rapid. However, as noted in the next chapter, suburbs of the large cities and towns were not necessarily a creation of the automobile; the automobile simply made them more practical for more people. By the 1960s, the automobile accounted for about 85 per cent of total passenger miles and a relatively small percentage by other types of transport.

While the ascendency of automobile transport has been decisive, competition among bus, rail, and airplane for the remaining portion of passenger traffic was vigorous. Table 10:1 chronicles the growth of air travel in recent years and the decline in its substitute—an imperfect substitute—of rail travel. The most important factors in the relative growth of air travel were a rise in real per-capita income, increases in average fares which were less than the increase in real per-capita income—at least in the 1950s and 1960s—a greater acceptance of air travel, better scheduling, greater punctuality of flights and reliability of schedules. In addition to Trans-Canada Air Lines, later Air Canada, founded by Parliament in 1937, and Canadian Pacific Airlines, established formally in 1942, the twenty-five years after the Second World War witnessed the addition of several regional air carriers: Pacific Western Airlines Limited, Transair, Nordair, Quebecair, and Eastern Provincial Airways. No effective competition to the airlines developed until about 1963 when the railways finally decided to innovate their services and attract intercity passenger back to rail. As a footnote it might be added that the government has taken over the passenger-carrying function of both the Canadian National and Canadian Pacific railways. Undoubtedly this is an economic sign that the rails have not yet reached the point of being an efficient passenger carrier.

In summary, the twentieth century dawned with growing resentment of the regional interest against the railways and their practices. At first, special rate regulation rectified apparent inequities but after the Second World War the government placed increasing emphasis on encouraging competition. Of course, the development of effective competition to the railways was well underway by this time, propelled by market forces. As in no earlier period, the various transport modes came into direct competition and were encouraged to do so under the terms of the National Transportation Act of 1967. No longer was the sole concern of policy to protect, stimulate, or regulate the behaviour of railways.

In this chapter attention has, rather single-mindedly, been directed to transport improvements and their significance in extending hinterlands and creating social savings. Little attention, on the other hand, has been paid to the indirect benefits which transport systems conferred on the evolving economy. Rather, it is easier to gauge their impact in context. For instance, we have already seen how the early staple economies were affected. In later chapters, more precision will be given to the effects of transport improvements in the evolving manufacturing and service economy of more recent history. In conclusion, it is worth repeating that the spectacular innovations such as steam railways derived their importance from the spread of the market economy which they could bring about. But, given the variety of transport modes, in terms of real or simply potential alternatives, it is unlikely that any one mode by itself was indispensible to economic development.

CHAPTER ELEVEN

Natural-Resource Development to 1929: The New Generation of Staples

Introduction

At the end of the nineteenth century the economy began to show signs of more vigorous expansion than had been experienced during the previous twenty-five years. It was the beginning of a phase of economic development unprecedented in its impact on both the spread and the structure of the economy as we have seen. Similar to earlier periods of rapid economic change, this one too was stimulated by exports, which for the most part were derived from natural resources. Yet, unlike earlier episodes of export-led growth the exploitation of natural resources was wholly new in character. Minerals and their products became important exports for the first time. Forest products were sold in a new form as pulp and paper with more domestic value added than formerly. New sources of energy were developed. Wheat exports, which came to typify the prosperity, came from the newly settled prairies. It is this new phase of natural-resource development which is the subject of immediate concern.

The rapid economic expansion experienced in the early years of this century are often referred to as "the wheat boom". This is a very appropriate metaphor. In a general political, social, and economic sense, the nature of the country was being redefined as western settlement filled up the still largely empty prairies. On the other hand, the phrase "wheat boom" is somewhat misleading. Wheat exports did not change significantly until the new prosperity was well established in the middle of the first decade of the twentieth century. The subsequent rapid increase in wheat exports was further stimulated by wartime demands but once these had dissipated in the early 1920s, it was evident that the wheat economy was over-extended. Yet, the overall economy continued to expand, albeit with some setbacks in the immediate postwar years, and the basis for this expansion lay in many of the other staples. Thus, the period from approximately 1896 to 1929 is best described as one of general natural-resource development and export-led growth and not as one which had its origins of growth in a particular resource.

In order to trace the emergence of the new staple industries, it is first necessary to place them in the context of Canada's international trade. Next, the major staples are examined in turn: wheat, minerals, pulp and paper, as well as the new energy resource of hydroelectricity. In each case the determinants of their development were different. So too, each had different implications for the spread and structure of the economy as did the early staples examined earlier in this study. By focusing on the emergence of the new staple industries in the late nineteenth and early twentieth centuries, their spreading effects can be examined, leading to, in the following chapter, the wider consideration of overall industrial development and the growth of manufacturing.

Exports and Prices, 1870-1915

Six years after the founding of modern Canada the economy, along with most of the then developed world, was reeling from the shock of an economic depression of unprecedented severity. This contraction of international economic activity began in 1873 and lasted for varying lengths of time in different countries. In Great Britain, the Great Depression, as it was often called, probably continued to exert its influence until almost the end of the century.[1] On the other hand, the contraction of the pace of economic activity in the United States was much more pronounced than elsewhere but also shorter lived. In Canada, as already seen, the Depression was responsible for creating high unemployment, the problem to which the framers of the national policy addressed themselves. Although there is no direct evidence about the extent of the unemployment, the concern at the time, as well as the drop in imports of more than twenty per cent in the 1870s, suggest that the problem was acute; imports changes provide a reasonable proxy for the movements of national income in a simple economy.

There has been considerable debate among Canadian historians about the severity and extent of the Depression. Some would say that the Depression lasted until well into the 1890s.[2] In part, the confusion about this period rests on the inability to distinguish fully between the influence of domestic and international prices. For the entire last quarter of the nineteenth century the trend of prices was, in general, downward. The growth of income in nominal terms was actually less than it was in real terms. Export prices rose, for the most part, more than import prices, hence the rising terms of trade of Figure 11:1.

In a world where the prices of most traded goods were declining the prices of Canada's major exports either declined very little or even experienced increases. In general, the export bundle of 1896-1900 sold for prices only 3.7 per cent lower than in 1871-75 whereas the import bundle was bought for prices which had fallen almost 35 per cent. In particular, the prices of wood and wood-product exports remained about constant and those of dairy and other animal products rose significantly. It was, as seen in Chapter 4, the latter which became the principal export of the last quarter of the nineteenth century. The expansion of the market in Great Britain for Canadian foodstuffs grew at a sufficiently fast pace that there was both an increase in the prices of these goods and an increase in the real volume of shipments (see Figure 11:2). The maintenance of the wood-products market and the expansion of the dairy- and animal-products staple, while insufficient to fuel an export-led boom, was of a magnitude which forestalled a real long-run contraction of exports and, in fact, permitted modest growth.

The overall contribution of staples to GNP (Table 11:1) was relatively fixed throughout this period of slow growth. Indeed, during the most severly depressed years of the late nineteenth century, approximately 1873 to 1883, the ratio of staple exports to income actually rose, evidence that the economy was falling back on traditional sources of specialization and income.[3] This is consistent with the observation that the rates of growth in primary manufacturing generally were greater than those in secondary manufacturing. Notwithstanding the performance during the depressed years, it can be observed that as wheat gained importance as an export in the early twentieth century, the overall contribution of staple exports to income actually fell, the usual result when dynamic and new staple industries emerge. In this context the dairy industry was not essentially new and transmitted only weak spreading effects.

Despite short-run variability in the trade-to-income ratio over the long run the economy remained open. Even the generally depressed world markets of 1873-96 and attempts to encourage import-substitution industries within the framework of the National Policy tariff had little effect on the course of exports plus imports as a proportion of income. At just below 30 per cent in the nineteenth century, this proportion rose only slightly in the twentieth century. Although there is no reason to believe that any particular outcome is inevitably part of the development process, the small size of the Canadian economy, particularly

Figure 11:1 The Terms of Trade, 1869-1915

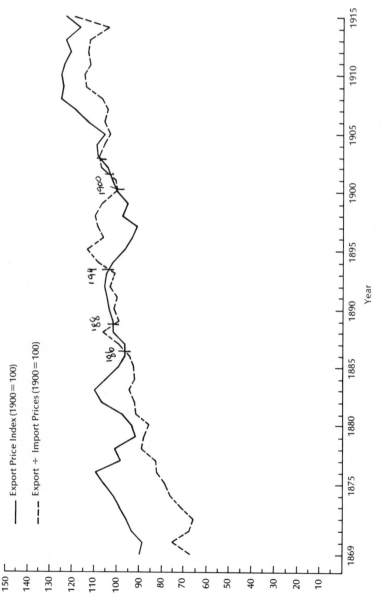

——— Export Price Index (1900 = 100)

– – – Export ÷ Import Prices (1900 = 100)

Year

Note: The terms of trade correspond to the definition of the net barter terms of trade. Figures for 1907 are for the fiscal year ending June 30, 1907, and those for 1903 are for the fiscal year ending March 30, 1908.

Sources: Data are from *Statistical Contributions to Canadian History*, p. 6 and M. C. Urquhart and K. A. H. Buckley, eds., *Historical Statistics of Canada* (Toronto, 1965), p. 184.

Figure 11:2 The Growth of Exports: Major Export Groups and Total Exports, in Constant 1900 Prices

($ millions)

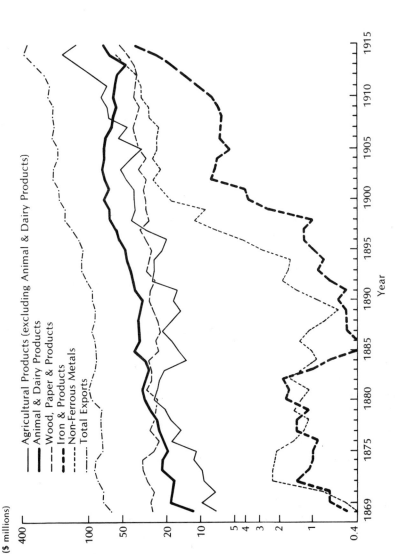

Note: Figures for 1907 are for the fiscal year ending June 30, 1907, and those for 1908 for the fiscal year ending March 30, 1908. Figures include exports of both Canadian and foreign produce.

Source: Data are from *Statistical Contributions to Canadian History*, Vol. II, pp. 12-13.

Table 11:1 Staples and Income, 1851-1912

| | Percentage of GNP | |
Period	Wheat Exports	Staple Exports
(1)	(2)	(3)
1851-1860	2.9	10.5
1860/1868-72	2.6	11.9
1868-72/1873-77	2.3	13.9
1873-77/1878-82	2.9	13.5
1878-82/1883-87	2.7	11.6
1883-87/1888-92	2.0	10.0
1888-92/1893-97	2.0	10.4
1893-97/1898-1902	2.7	12.5
1898-1902/1903-07	2.8	12.9
1903-07/1909-12	3.1	11.6

Source: W. E. Vickery, "Exports and North American Economic Growth: 'Structuralist' and 'Staple' Models in Historical Perspective", Canadian Journal of Economics, Vol. 7, no. 1 (1974), p. 51.

relative to its natural-resource endownment was among the features which sustained the open nature of economic development.[4]

It was natural resources which yet again became the basis of the prosperity of the economy and was responsible for the rapid structural change at the beginning of the twentieth century. Lasting from approximately the mid 1890s until the Depression of the 1930s, this was the period during which the settlement of the Canadian plains was at last achieved. However, wheat exports themselves were not alone the impetus for rapid aggregate income growth. To be sure, by 1912-15 cereal grain had grown to be 32 per cent of all exports, by value, but such pre-eminence was only achieved long after the period of prosperity had begun. For instance, the export of dairy and animal produce was greater than that of wheat and all other agricultural produce until 1908. Yet, the dating of the upswing in Canada's prosperity is usually to a full twelve years earlier, 1896. Undoubtedly, there was a rise in wheat production and exports in that year and the rise in world wheat prices, although not great, marks the end of the decline which had started in the late 1860s. The export-led boom of the period 1896 to 1929 was more broadly based. The new generation of staples was bound to affect the economy in a different manner than the more simple staples of earlier periods in history.

Wheat and Prairie Settlement

The rapid expansion of the wheat economy into the western prairies of Canada between approximately 1896 and 1921 was one of the most profound episodes in the country's economic development. The wheat boom was felt so strongly that the prosperity of the period was attributed to this expansion. Whether wheat exports themselves were important to the early phases of the rapid growth or not has been a matter of considerable controversy as noted earlier. Yet, by the end of the first decade of the twentieth century, their importance was not doubted. There were two types of benefits from westward expansion: the direct economic benefits of the expansion of the wheat-based western economy and the indirect benefits associated with the spreading or linkage effects induced. Because of these links the pace of development in the west had immediate consequences for the performance of eastern manufacturing. In order to isolate these consequences attention will be focused first on the nature of prairie settlement and, second, on its general impact on the process of industrialization.

Settlement on the prairies dated from the Red River colony of the early nineteenth century, but it was sparse and even the surrender of the Hudson Bay Territory to the newly confederated Canada produced no rush of settlement. Beyond the frontiers of economic settlement the flow of settlers into the west was spasmodic. Even after the completion of the Canadian Pacific Railway, settlement was slow and a premature land boom crashed in the late 1880s. At this time only Manitoba had an agricultural economy which responded to market forces. In the North-West Territories — the present Saskatchewan and Alberta — farming, when undertaken, was primarily designed for small, local markets at best and subsistence more commonly. At the very end of the nineteenth century this changed.[5] A wave of settlement reached the West and by 1901 approximately 15 million acres of prairie land were occupied, as shown in Table 11:2. Within twenty years this had expanded to 87 million acres. But economic frontiers are not simply the margin of settlement; they are the margin of economic activity. That is, settlers not only had to claim or purchase land but also to decide how much of their farms should be brought into production and how quickly. The significance of westward expansion thus lay both in the amount of settlement and the proportion of settled land which was set in crop or used for some other farming activity. The acreage on farms cultivated at least once, improved land in Table 11:2, rose from 23 to 55 per cent of the total between 1891 and 1926. This land was brought into production partly in response to an increased world demand for wheat and partly by the adoption and spread of technological change which made much of the land capable of being cultivated for the first time. The prairies soon attained a pre-eminent position in Canadian agriculture. Improved acreage on the prairie as a percentage of all such land in Canada increased from about 19 per cent in 1901 to over 63 per cent in 1921. Agricultural employment rose correspondingly.

Table 11:2 Spread of Prairie Settlement, 1881-1931

Year	Occupied Land (thousands of acres)	Improved Land (thousands of acres)	Percentage of Improved to Occupied Land
(1)	(2)	(3)	(4)
1881	2,698	279	10
1891	6,312	1,429	23
1901	15,412	5,593	36
1911	57,643	22,970	40
1916	73,300	34,330	47
1921	87,932	44,863	51
1926	88,930	49,265	55
1931	109,778	59,820	54

Sources: M. C. Urquhart and K. A. H. Buckley, eds., *Historical Statistics of Canada* (Toronto, 1965), p. 352 and W. A. MacKintosh, *Prairie Settlement: The Geographical Setting* (Toronto, 1934) p. 58.

Between 1881 and 1931, not only did wheat become the major western cash crop but the entire structure of agricultural production in western Canada was reorganized. Dairy farming, for instance, emerged in the areas surrounding Manitoba's cities and mixed farming in the Park Belt. Ranching, which had previously been the most important form of agriculture in southwestern Saskatchewan and southeastern Alberta, declined in importance in all but the southern and foothill regions of Alberta. Wherever soil and topology permitted, ranching commonly gave way to arable agriculture. By 1931, about 75 per cent of the arable land was devoted to cash crops of which the most important was wheat; the remainder was in feed for livestock. Alone, wheat constituted about 36, 65, and 67 per cent of the total cash crop for Manitoba, Saskatchewan, and Alberta respectively.[6] As wheat production in the west increased, there was, of course, a movement of the agricultural centre of Canada from Ontario and Quebec to the prairies. We have already seen that the transformation of central Canadian agriculture from cereals to other crops, such as corn, dairy products, and vegetables, for the new domestic urban markets was itself in part as a result of the expansion of prairie agriculture. Unquestionably the wheat boom was responsible for a major structural change in the agricultural production of the various regions of Canada.

In the west itself, the spread of settlement generally followed the course of the railways or their planned routes. Virtually all settlement prior to about 1901 was within ten miles of a railway. Consequently population density was greatest where the greatest number of rail lines ran; however, in areas such as southwestern Saskatchewan which were not well served by railways, settlement was still thin as late as the turn of the century. This, however, changed; over the course of the next decade settlement began to move into new areas. From 1901 to 1906, railways moved into eastern Saskatchewan and by 1911, the Canadian Northern and the Grand Trunk Pacific railways stretched across western Saskatchewan and Alberta. In addition, branch lines were added in Manitoba and Saskatchewan and in time, more sections of the Canadian Northern were brought into operation. Also, by 1911, Palliser's Triangle, avoided even as late as 1906, was settled, albeit thinly. The next ten years saw a continuation of this pattern: The spread of settlement was coincident with the spread of the railways.

No single measure better describes how the prairies were settled than the registration pattern of land grants and homestead entries.[7] Homesteads were 160-acre blocks of Crown land which a settler could claim for farming purposes. If, within three years, progress had been made in bringing some of the land into production, the settler received the title or patent to the land. These homesteads were, apart from some minor administrative charges, free to the settler, and were first granted in 1872; although homesteading policy was not fully articulated until the passage of the Dominion Land Act of 1879, the basic features of the policy did not change. The only major modification of homesteading policy was made in 1890 when pre-emption rights were disestablished. Pre-emption rights permitted the settler who received a patent to lay claim to an additional quarter-section of 160 acres. The amount of land available for homesteading was vast. In each prairie township, every even numbered section was reserved for sale by the Crown or turned over to the railways (see Chapter 10).

In Figure 11:3 is presented the number of homestead entries issued each year. The net number of new homesteads, however, was smaller depending on the number of cancellations in any year. There were three distinct periods of homesteading:

1) from the late 1870s to about 1886 with a peak in 1882;
2) from 1887 to 1897, generally a period of less settlement or homesteading; and
3) from 1898 to about 1916, with a rising number of homestead entries which reached a plateau about 1905 and a decline in the early war years. There was a subsequent spurt of claims in the late 1920s in Alberta.

During these three phases of prairie settlement different economic conditions prevailed. Nevertheless, it is possible to think of homesteading within a consistent framework.[8] At any particular time there might be

Figure 11:3 Homestead Entries by Prairie Province, 1872-1931

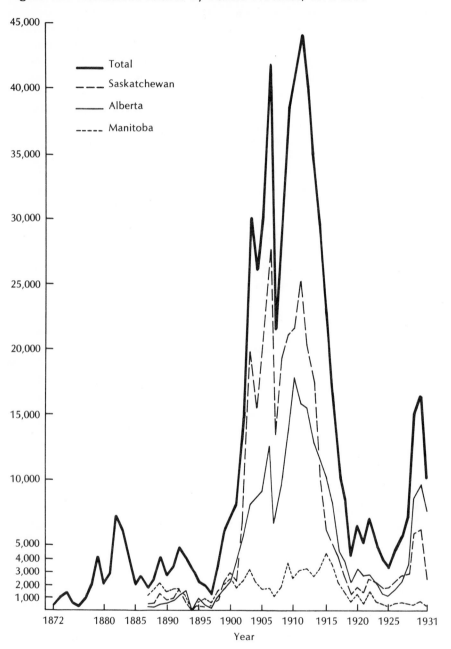

Note: Prior to 1906 Alberta and Saskatchewan were the North-West Territories. For the years 1872-80, 1883-86, and 1894 only total land grants are available.

Source: Data are from Urquhart and Buckley, eds., *Historical Statistics of Canada*, p. 320.

some optimal amount of settlement defined by the existing home-steads—aggregate entries less cancellation. This may be referred to as "the equilibrium net stock of homesteads". This optimal amount of homesteads would, of course, be determined by the prevailing prices in the same manner as the zero-rent frontier of the transport hinterland in the last chapter. However, the *actual* stock of homesteads would likely differ from the equilibrium stock in any given year and economic incentives would act to produce pressure for homesteading to adjust the actual to the equilibrium stock over time. Therefore, there are two elements which determined the actual stock of homesteads at any time: economic incentives in prairie agriculture, and the speed of adjustment of actual to equilibrium stocks of homesteads; of course, the latter changed itself over time. In this context the process of homesteading was the response to shifts in the economic incentives of agriculture. The economic returns from homesteading were twofold. First, there was the return to the homesteader's labour and capital. Second, there were the potential capital gains arising from title to land since under the Dominion Lands Act a homesteader could patent land at less than its capital value.[9] Hence those factors which influenced the pattern of the return to land and labour in agriculture were the principal inducements for homesteading to continue until the optimal level was reached.

The two most important determinants of the derived demand for labour and land in prairie agriculture, as noted above, were the relative price of wheat and the level of railway investment. A rise in the relative price of wheat increased the demand for labour in wheat farming and also shifted out the zero-rent frontier. It does not seem likely, however, that the decision to homestead would be based on the price of wheat in just one year. It is more likely that an individual's expectations of future wheat prices were based on some evaluations of the past trend—a weighted average of previous wheat prices. In addition, the level of railway investment, as measured by miles of track in operation in the prairies, also determined the equilibrium level of homestead entries, as argued earlier. The stock of land within the zero-rent frontier, for any level of the relative price of wheat, was determined by the miles of railroad track in use. The link between railroad expansion and population flows to the prairie frontier, not unnaturally, has been a continual theme in Canadian history. In particular, the speculative element in the homesteading process of capturing potential capital gains from land was ever present.

The speed of adjustment of the actual to the equilibrium stock of homesteading was influenced by many factors of which the government advertising of homestead possibilities was an important one. Throughout the period under study the Canadian government advertised extensively in the United States, the United Kingdom, and on the continent of Europe the opportunities for farmers and farm labourers on the Canadian prairies. Salaried agents, whose main function was to promote immigration to Canada, were maintained primarily in the United Kingdom and the United States. Even within Canada there was a network of immigration agents who acted to funnel immigrants upon their arrival in Canada to the prairies. These agents provided a number of services such as information on regional labour markets and farming conditions and reduced-rate rail tickets to immigrants arriving at ocean ports destined for central or western Canada. The Canadian government at times even maintained immigration agents on the Grand Trunk and Intercolonial railroads to persuade those immigrants en route to the U.S. mid-west that the Canadian prairies were a superior alternative.[10]

The government spent substantial amounts of money promoting immigration throughout the period: Annual expenditures on immigration net of expenditures in quarantine facilities averaged $228,000 from 1878 to 1886, $196,000 from 1887 to 1896, and $748,000 from 1897 to 1913.[11] The sharp rise in government expenditures on immigration in the last period and the increased activity of Canadian immigration agents in the United States were evidence of a significant difference in focus of these efforts from that of earlier years. Such government efforts to disseminate information on agricultural opportunities and to accelerate the flow of settlers in the prairies facilitated the adjustment of the actual to equilibrium stock of homesteads. Essentially, information flows reduced the uncertainty associated with the decision to homestead for any level of relative wheat prices and railroad mileage.

Within such a framework of economic incentives determining the extent of new settlement and its pace, the three distinct phases of homesteading can be discussed. In general terms, the lull in settlement between the first two periods of expansion was due to the virtual disappearance of unpatented sub-humid land on the prairies by about 1886. In addition, the absence of a dry-farming technology and early-maturing wheat varieties thwarted agricultural extension onto the semi-arid lands. From 1879 to 1886, agricultural expansion was confined largely to the sub-humid areas where farming techniques already known could be employed. This type of land was available in Manitoba and branch and trunk lines of the CPR made it accessible. Fully 96 per cent of all homestead entries occurred in Manitoba in the first period, the majority in the south-central part of that province. Immigration advertising and services, which included expenditures of over $500,000 in 1884 alone, sped the pace of settlement, and as noted, railroad mileage influenced

Map 11:1 Railway and Settlement Patterns in 1929

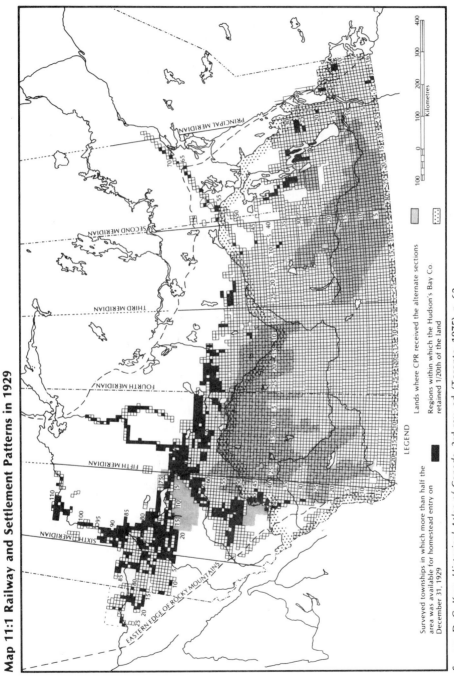

LEGEND

Surveyed townships in which more than half the area was available for homestead entry on December 31, 1929

Lands where CPR received the alternate sections

Regions within which the Hudson's Bay Co retained 1/20th of the land

Kilometres
100   0   100   200   300   400

EASTERN EDGE OF ROCKY MOUNTAINS

SIXTH MERIDIAN

FIFTH MERIDIAN

FOURTH MERIDIAN

THIRD MERIDIAN

SECOND MERIDIAN

PRINCIPAL MERIDIAN

Source: D. G. Kerr, *Historical Atlas of Canada*, 3rd rev. ed. (Toronto, 1975), p. 62.

homestead entries. The stock of homestead entries was higher during this first period of settlement, 1872-86, than during the next period, from 1887 to 1897, taken alone. Indeed, there was probably more settlement than was justified by economic opportunities. In part, this was the reaction which so often characterized pioneer agriculture, the romance of the frontier.

The traditional view of the years from 1887 to 1896 is that of a period of realignment. With the disappearance of unclaimed sub-humid land, the potential homesteader could either venture onto the semi-arid land, move northward where the growing season was shorter, or settle in the United States where sub-humid land was more abundant than in Canada. Even the amount of new railway construction was limited to:

1) lines into southwestern Manitoba;
2) a direct link between Regina and Prince Albert; and,
3) a line from Calgary to Edmonton and Fort MacLeod, Alberta.

With little railway construction, no significant long-run change in the relative price of wheat, and a low level of immigration expenditures, the number of new homesteaders on the prairies was lower than it had been before 1887 or than it would be after 1896.

In the 1890s the economic forces which governed the extent of prairie settlement began to change. First, two technical problems which had previously limited geographic expansion were solved. Dry-farming techniques had been developed and their use had become widespread in this decade. New varieties of early-maturing wheat became available which permitted the northward expansion of cereal agriculture. Second, the amount of settlement in the U.S. prairies over the past decade had, by the 1890s, exhausted the amount of sub-humid land available for homesteading in that country. The agricultural frontier shifted to the Canadian prairies. Third, as seen earlier, the years from 1898 to 1916 were marked by another phase of rapid new railway expansion which brought more land within the economically feasible range of settlement. This, in turn, prompted the government to increase the amount spent on publicizing farming opportunities. This campaign later became part of a well-articulated and well-financed policy to settle the west under the vigorous leadership of Clifford Sifton, the minister responsible for immigration in the Laurier government.[12] Last, the relative price of wheat increased.

The relative price of wheat has traditionally been linked to the process of homesteading. It enters the scheme of this analysis too but not as part of the traditional view of this process which places particular emphasis on the role played by changing wheat prices. Indeed, price changes do not correspond very closely to changes in the stock of homestead entries. To be sure, the economic incentive motivating western farmers and potential settlers would be the farm-gate price. But it is more probably the case that the decline in ocean freight rates, and the decline in domestic transport costs through railway extension, along with the roles of technical change and immigration expenditures, were more important than simple changes in the world price of wheat *per se*. Indeed, in the years just after 1895, there were only very slight upward movements of wheat prices which by themselves explain little about the pattern of prairie settlement. The mechanism directing expansion into the west was more complex. If increases in the relative price of wheat were ever by themselves significant enough to stimulate rapid settlement, it was in the late 1920s when another short-lived expansion took place.

The westward expansion of the economy, especially after 1896, had a significant impact on the pattern of economic development. In the first instance, to produce a large surplus of exportable wheat, a large market was required. That this market was found, primarily in Great Britain, is attested to by the rapid rise in wheat exports from 4 to 25 per cent of all exports, by value, between 1901 and 1921. Total exports in 1921 constituted just slightly less than a quarter of GNP. Wheat exports were clearly important. It was, of course, the changes in supply which permitted the expansion and gave Canada a comparative advantage over most cereal-exporting countries.[13]

From 1870 to 1910 raw-material exports as a proportion of total exports of domestic produce rose from about one-third to over 50 per cent. This occurred chiefly because of the increased importance of wheat and other agricultural products in Canada's export trade. However, shortly after the census of 1910 this trend reversed itself so that by 1930 raw materials made up only about 38 per cent of total commodity exports. Over this same period, fully or chiefly manufactured products rose from 33 to 45 per cent of total commodity exports. This, in part, reflected the industrialization that took place during these years. The rise in wheat and other staple production and the shift to manufacturing were part of the same economic phenomenon. One influenced the other through a pattern of linkages.

Backward linkages, it will be recalled from Chapter 2, were those which induced production of input factors to the staple production. In the case of the Canadian wheat economy, the induced investments included farm equipment and transport. For instance, in 1901, the prairie region had about 4,100 miles of rail line; by 1914, an additional 7,500 miles of track had been added and railway building on such a magnitude caused an increase in gross domestic-capital formation, as well as an increased proportion devoted to transport investment—16 per cent in 1901-05 to over 25 per cent in 1911-15.[14] It remained at almost this level well into the 1920s. Apart from transport, prairie farm investment itself became a large component of aggregate capital formation, about 16 per cent throughout the 1901-15 period on average. Of this investment land and machinery were the most important items whereas buildings and livestock lost the significance they had had prior to the rapid expansion of settlement.

The infrastructure of development was there for all to see: train stations as local distribution points; grain elevators in Fort William, Port Arthur, the interior, and on the Pacific coast; loading platforms; and stockyards, among others. In addition each commercial centre in the west supported merchant and service industries, professional occupations, and financial institutions. Because of the specialization in agriculture in the west, that area's residents depended on primary and secondary producers in other regions for non-agricultural goods. An extensive marketing structure developed to facilitate their supply. Secondary manufacturing grew in Ontario and Quebec, spurred on by the increasing demand for manufactured goods in the west. Wheat exports were one of the main sources of foreign exchange which permitted the import of capital goods and technology from the United States. This strengthening of regional specialization and the accompanying regional integration has been viewed as a logical consequence of the overall national policy of prairie settlement, railway construction, and effective tariffs. Between 1901 and 1911, although the percentage of the total labour force in manufacturing actually declined, it was more than offset by an increase in average labour productivity in manufacturing of approximately 66 per cent. The railway linked the western wheat producer to the eastern manufacturing centres as never before. For their part, the eastern manufacturing interests had access to a wholly new market, captive as it was by the tariff.

The economic impact of the wheat boom, thus, had two dimensions: the direct benefits and the linkage or indirect effects. Direct benefits included the rise in prairie land rents, the rise in tariff revenues as a result of increased manufactured imports, the returns to entrepreneurial risk-taking, and the effect of immigration on aggregate demand. While various attempts have been made to measure the quantitative significance of these direct benefits, none has proven sufficiently authoritative. In terms of income per capita, the direct contribution of the wheat boom was probably slightly over 8 per cent during the years 1901 to 1921. This, of course, is not large, but then it must be recalled, from Chapter 2, that the real growth in individual well-being was quite modest—less than one per cent annually—in the first two decades of the twentieth century. Even then, the real gains, in per-capita terms, were gathered at the end of the period, not at the beginning.[15]

Yet, the importance of the wheat boom was its impact on the economy as a whole and not so much its influence on the course of real income per capita. National income grew rapidly and it was the opportunities presented by this expansion which drew in immigrants in numbers never previously or subsequently experienced. The arrival of these immigrants had the consequence of depressing the real income gains of all who were resident in Canada, at least in the short run. In the long run, it was the ab- solute growth, largely attributable to the indirect or linkage effects, which had the major consequences for a restructuring of the economy. The inflow of foreign savings, the link of cereal agriculture to the farm- machinery sector, the induced railway building, and the general growth of the domestic market for manufactured goods were all attributes of this structural change. The rapid expansion of the western wheat economy and the rise of modern industry were far from inconsistent economic forces; they were part of the same process.

The Mining Industry

For most of the period prior to the twentieth century Canada's mineral in- dustry was traditional in character. Output was primarily for domestic consumption, the industrial organization of mining was local and most of the mines were small, the discovery of new deposits of minerals was generally haphazard, and there was often considerable variation in the quality of the minerals taken from the ground. Unlike the dominance of metallic minerals in the modern mineral industry, during this early stage of mining development the minerals exploited were primarily coal and non-metallic minerals—principal among the latter were asbestos, clay, cement, building stone, and other minerals used in the dometic construc- tion industry. There were some exports—coal from Vancouver Island to San Francisco and asbestos from Quebec to the industrial United States, for example—but they were not of national economic significance. Even the production, and export, of the precious metals of gold and silver was spasmodic, growing only during such times of discovery as the Cariboo gold rush of the 1870s. As in the case of the early staples, the type of resource exploited, naturally enough, determined the centres of activity. The overall importance of coal meant that Nova Scotia was the province or region with the greatest mining industry. It also accounted for a large proportion of the gold output of Canada in these years prior to the rapid development of the industry. More and more, however, the attention of the mining industry focused on the Laurentian Shield of Ontario and

Quebec and the mining fields of British Columbia as the railways began to open up these previously remote areas. So too, the diligent work of the Geological Survey of Canada brought more scientific expertise to bear on the discovery of new mining areas.[16] As a consequence, by the late 1880s the known reserves of many previously unexploited mining areas were ready to be brought into production by those holding the claims. The reduction of costs brought about by the railway, particularly in Northern Ontario, was extending the market for the products of the mines. However, it was the pressure of demand rather than supply shifts, in the first instance, which changed the extent and pattern of mining activity in Canada.

During the last half of the nineteenth century there was a revolution in the metal industries of the world. The basis of the change undoubtedly lay in the iron and steel industry where improvements in the quality of steel, as well as a declining real price, led to the ready adoption of steel as a structural building material and permitted the growth of a machine-tool industry, based upon, in part, the greater malleability of steel or the greater ease with which it could be machined. It was soon discovered that by the addition of certain other minerals to the steel in production, the resulting product took on particular characteristics. Nickel-toughened steel is a good example. In the 1870s Canada's nickel output, primarily from the New Orford mines in Quebec, was used for its only known purpose, the production of cheap costume jewellery. Within two decades steel toughened by Canadian nickel, by this time from Sudbury, was widely used for industrial purposes. New military technology also produced further demands for the nickel alloy for the production of both armour plate for warships and (cruel symmetry) armour-piercing shells. A completely new set of demands similarly existed for other metals at the end of the nineteenth century. The metallurgical revolution provided the stimulus to exploit previously unexploitable minerals.[17]

The search for new metallic minerals stimulated by the new metallurgy indirectly lowered the costs of exploiting some of the more familiar metals. Canada had no known source of iron ore in the nineteenth century apart from some small deposits in the Marmora district of Ontario. The modern iron-ore mining industry has a relatively short history dating from the opening of the Quebec deposits in the 1940s and 1950s. But while there was no known iron ore, there were deposits of copper and lead as well as new deposits of precious metals to be exploited. Of the traditional metals, copper and lead were usually found in complex ores. The prevalence of nickel-copper ores in Ontario and zinc-lead-silver ores in British Columbia meant that cheap processes had to be developed to separate the ores before the Canadian industry could be competitive. In the 1890s and early twentieth century, the development, and later improvements, of the chemical and mechanical processes for separating the various complex ores into their constituents were important because they permitted full use of the joint products. That is, copper could not be produced without producing nickel; lead could not be produced without producing some fixed quantity of zinc and silver.[18]

The pattern of mining in 1890, shown in Table 11:3, was typical of the last half of the nineteenth century both with respect to the types of mineral production and its location. Within twenty years these patterns were entirely different. By 1910, metallic minerals dominated the profile of output. Non-metallic minerals dropped from more than 40 per cent of production to one-quarter by the First World War, the relative value of mineral-fuel output fell slightly, and the position of gold rose slightly. Although price movements often altered the 1910 pattern of the discovery of new ore deposits and the depletion of others, the basic profile of mining has not changed in the recent past with the exception that ferrous metals are now of greater importance. On the other hand, the rise to prominence of the crude-petroleum industry, especially after 1947 with the discovery of the Leduc well in Alberta, were offset by a decline in the relative contribution of coal to total mining output. The shift in the pattern of output was accompanied by, and was in part responsible for, a change in the geographic pattern of exploitation.

The economic problems associated with the exploitation of non-renewable resources such as minerals are almost identical to those discussed in Chapter 3. How production, if profitable, is spread over time depends on many of the same features of the economy which governed the use of the early staples: the property-rights régime under which the resource was held, the knowledge of alternatives, as well as the social rate of discount. Even the mechanism of spreading from one mining area to another bears a remarkable resemblance to the spread of the fur or timber trades, despite the overwhelmingly different characteristic that one resource is renewable and the other not.

If a resource is not renewable it might be expected that the closest region to the market will be fully exploited before production is moved to more distant reserves or before prospecting is undertaken. This indeed would happen were it not for two phenomena: the additional costs of exploiting new areas are often borne in large measure by others, and the quality of mineral deposits tend to vary with the quantity of mining already undertaken. First, it is evident from the history of Canadian mining that new discoveries of reserves of minerals and new production tended to follow the new railways of the late nineteenth and early twentieth centuries. In terms of production, the mining industry did not have

Table 11:3 Distribution of Mineral Output, by Region and Type, 1890-1910

(per cent)

Region	1890	1900	1910
(1)	(2)	(3)	(4)
Nova Scotia	24.7	9.8	13.3
British Columbia	16.1	25.9	22.9
Ontario	17.6	17.5	40.8
Quebec	18.3	5.1	7.7
Prairie Provinces	2.4	1.7	10.3
Yukon	—	34.9	4.5
Other[a]	20.8	5.2	0.5
	100.0	100.0	100.0

Type			
(1)			
Metallic minerals (excluding gold)	14.0	18.6	35.0
Gold	6.9	43.3	9.6
Non-metallic minerals	40.0	14.4	25.6
Fuels	33.9	21.3	28.9
Miscellaneous (ind. petroleum)	5.4	5.2	1.6
	100.0	100.0	100.0

[a] Includes petroleum irrespective of source although this was almost exclusively Ontario.

Sources: Department of Mines, *The Annual Report on the Mineral Production of Canada during the Calendar Year, 1914* (Ottawa, 1915), p. 33; The Canada Year Book, 1915 (Ottawa, 1916), p. 239; and "Historical Summary of Canada's Mineral Production", *Annual Report 1944* (as above), pp. 29-34.

to cover all the costs of opening up a mining area: the railway through nothern Ontario was located there whether there were exploitable mineral deposits or not. Throughout the period from approximately 1890 to 1914, areas such as British Columbia and the Laurentian Shield were opened up to systematic mining activities.[19] It is not being suggested that the spread of mining was always dependent on such cost reduction between regions or mining fields; the Klondyke gold rush of 1898 is a case in point. Nevertheless, the bulk of mining output generally required such externalities.

Despite reductions in the costs of expanding into new and more remote mining areas expansion would not have taken place based on this alone. Expansion was only economic because of the differential quality of ores. In general, ores in a mining area—or in a simple mine—will be very rich as the deposit is first exploited and will diminish in grade as more ore is extracted (see Figure 11:4). High-grade ores in remote mining

Figure 11:4 The Grade of Ore by Output

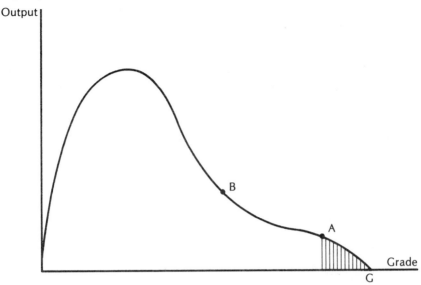

Note: If production of the mine begins at G, high-grade ores are exploited first and as exploitation of the mineral increases, the grade of ore declines. Beyond some point, the grade of ore becomes so low that economic use is prohibitive and output declines. When the price of the refined mineral increases this will induce movement along the grade-output distribution from, say, A to B. Hence, it may be found that all ore of high grade—the shaded area—is exploited and production ceases only to start again when the price change makes it economic to do so. The gradations would, of course, vary from mine to mine.

areas might be more profitable to extract and sell than lower-grade ores in less remote areas, neglecting transport costs for the moment. Indeed, the high-grade ores as well as the low cost per unit of extracting ore during the initial phases of mining an area were the principal reasons for the rush of activity into a mining area once a discovery had been made or once a price increase changed the nature of profitability.

High-grade minerals, paradoxically, because of their ease of exploitation, earned the distinction of being a "bad" staple. This was largely so because, once a virgin resource area was opened, collecting the mineral was only a little more difficult than gathering manna. There were few spreading effects, due mainly to the absence of any requirement to invest in capital equipment, or to seek a large labour force. The initial discoveries of precious-metal deposits are the most blatant historical example. Low-grade minerals, where their exploitation was justified, provided much more of the spreading effects which gave rise to permanent settlement. However, any mining activity of either high- or low-grade ores was subject to the vagaries of world-price movement. In the short run these price movements gave rise to changes in the pattern of employment. Mining areas in northern Ontario, Quebec, and British Columbia have always registered high unemployment patterns as a consequence.

Returning to the turn of the century, the rise to importance of mineral exports in Canada was due to a complex interaction of both demand and supply phenomena. For instance, the long run price of most minerals continued to decline throughout the 1890s and in the years leading up to the First World War. Yet, there is no doubt that the world's consumption of ferrous and non-ferrous metallic minerals increased; put simply, the world supply of such minerals generally increased more than demand and therby produced slightly falling prices (see Figure 11:5). But the profitability of the mining industry grew and apart from discovery, it was the reduction in variable costs which accounted for the spread of the mining frontier.

The discovery of many new mineral deposits in northern Ontario and British Columbia in the 1880s and 1890s caused a shift in the regional pattern of mineral-resource importance. However, the inaccessibility of the Laurentian Shield proved to be a slightly greater transport barrier to the wide expansion of mining than the problems of remoteness in British Columbia. There such areas as the Kootenays were opened up by both U.S. and Canadian railways. In addition, the possibility of shipping ore, or concentrate, by water on Kootenay Lake opened up a very large hinterland for the railway. It was with dramatic suddenness, in the late 1890s, that British Columbia became the self-styled "Mineral Province of Canada".[20] In 1900 that province accounted for over one-quarter of all mineral production by value in Canada. Slowly, however, as transport facilities were pushed further across the Precambrian rock and as the nickel-copper separating processes became economical, Ontario established her dominance. This occurred in 1904 and since that time the main mineral industry of Canada has been located there.

Apart from wheat, no other new commodity or group of commodities expanded proportionally as part of Canada's export bundle. Of trivial magnitudes in the early 1890s, non-ferrous-metal exports alone grew at a compound rate of over 15 per cent per year in the twenty-five years prior to 1915 (see Table 11:2). Nor did that growth end in 1915 as wartime demands stretched production of most minerals well beyond that which could be sustained in peacetime. For instance, nickel production rose to 46,300 short tons in 1918, only to fall again to 8,800 short tons in 1922. Exports in this later year were in fact greater than production due to the depleting of stock accumulated in the immediate postwar years. Such over-production was common in virtually all classes of metallic minerals

Figure 11:5 The World Mineral Market

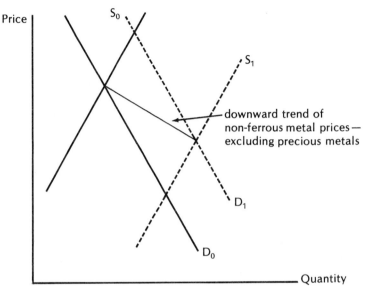

Note: D and S represent world supply and demand for minerals at times 0 and 1. The trend of price is downward. Notice that the supply shift dominates the demand.

and was by no means unique to Canada; it was a world-wide phenomenon.[21]

In the mid-1920s the mining sector slowly recovered as once more export demand reasserted itself. Metallic-mineral prices, for instance, increased in response to the rapid pace of industrial growth in the United States, the destination now of most of Canadian mineral exports. As a consequence of the rising prices many mines which had previously closed down operation because of low-quality ore grades began to reopen. And, as will be noted later in this chapter, some innovations in mining technology substantially reduced the costs of many Canadian producers.[22] The combined effect was to stimulate a growth in metallic-mineral production of well over 50 per cent between 1926 and 1929. Most of this was directly a result of export sales which averaged about 83 per cent of the country's production. However, the boom of the late 1920s was short-lived. The world-wide depression intervened to force another period of major readjustment in the minerals industry.

Forest Industries
During the late nineteenth century the forest-product industries changed in many vital respects. Principal among these was the decline of the

white pine trade. With respect to supply, the over-cropping of the central Canadian forests reduced the profitable white pine harvest. Peak production of pine timber of 2.75 billion board-feet in 1881 has never been equalled; in fact, production fell and has since remained barely more than one-tenth of that amount. The great white pine forests of central Canada were almost gone.[23]

As total production from pine fell so the absolute amount of square-timber exports declined. But, in addition, the trend which had begun much earlier, the declining proportion of squared timber in the exports of the forest-products industries, took on a more rapid pace. At Confederation about one-third of all output, by value, of the forest industries was shipped as squared timber. By 1887-90 it averaged 20.2 per cent of the output but fell to 2.4 per cent in 1912-15. In its place sawn lumber rose as a proportion of wood and wood-products output. Apart from the decline in the size of the harvestable pine forest this was accounted for by the changed structure of demand. Throughout the late nineteenth century the United States slowly replaced Great Britain as the principal market. Although Canadian exports of timber were diverted by the more rapid expansion of demand in the United States, which itself resulted from the more rapid recovery from the world-wide recession, this shift in the source of Canada's exports was of a permanent nature. Prior to 1885-89 the majority of Canadian wood and wood-product exports were destined for Great Britain. In subsequent years there was no clear pattern but by 1903 the majority of forest-product exports was destined for the U.S. market.

More than any other reason it was the depletion of the eastern and central Canadian pine forests which changed the regional pattern of forestry. In all the major forest provinces production of timber and lumber fell after the turn of the century with only one exception, the western-most province of British Columbia. There, production increased (see Table 11:4) and increased so rapidly that it offset declines in lumber and timber output elsewhere.[24]

The conditions which facilitated the rise of the west-coast forest industry to pre-eminence in the economy were several. First, although a small lumber and timber industry had existed for about fifty years the vast forest reserves were still largely unexploited. In addition, while not pine, the wood of British Columbia—Douglas fir and cedar—was a good substitute. Second, the urban building boom in the prairies, after the beginning of the twentieth century, gave impetus to the building of sawmilling capacity and the systematic use of rail as a method of shipment from the province. However, and third, even more market penetration of both eastern Canada and the United States was achieved when

Table 11:4 Estimates of British Columbia Forest Cut, 1848-1930

Period	Timber Harvest (millions of board feet)
(1)	(2)
1848-70	250
1871-80	350
1881-90	550
1891-1900	1,327
1901-10	4,754
1911-20	13,493
1921-30	24,081

Source: W. A. Carrothers, "Forest Industries of British Columbia", in A. R. M. Lower, *The North American Assault on the Canadian Forest: A History of the Lumber Trade Between Canada and the United States* (Toronto, 1938), p. 270.

the Panama Canal substantially reduced lumber-shipping costs in 1916. Fourth, because most of the prime timber was located in the coastal area of the province, ease of shipment by water to a sawmill tended to lead to economies of scale in lumber production. By the late 1920s this scale effect relative to other forest areas was readily apparent (see Table 11:5).[25]

Although lumber and timber exports were increasingly from the west coast, a new industry which used the low-quality forests of other areas emerged. Pulp and paper had been of trivial importance at the turn of the century. By 1912-15 wood pulp and paper rose to be 35 per cent of exports—14 and 21 per cent, respectively. Although still relatively small, in the pre-1914 years, newsprint production expanded tenfold within the next thirty years. While in 1910 Canadian exports of newsprint made up only one per cent of U.S. consumption, within a decade Canada supplied over one-third of the newsprint used in the United States. Initially, the U.S. paper manufacturers had looked to Canada for unprocessed pulpwood. This, however, was only the first phase of development and was followed by a transition of the industry from simply exporting raw materials to exporting a finished product—paper. The transition had its origins in both economic and political forces.

The comparative advantage Canada had in the paper industry was based, naturally enough, on the low cost of material inputs. Sulphite and ground wood together constituted about three-fifths of the charges against total costs in the industry of the early 1920s.[26] Average production costs in the United States were higher than in Canada. Pulpwood was a less expensive input in Canada for a variety of reasons. First, pulpwood stands were more accessible and they were exploited using water transport. The United States, on the other hand, had depleted much of

Table 11:5 Distribution of Canadian and British Columbian Sawmills, by Volume of Annual Production, 1921-1929

Annual Production (millions of board feet)	Canada			British Columbia		
	1921	1925	1929	1921	1925	1929
(1)	(2)	(3)	(4)	(5)	(6)	(7)
Less than 1	2,776	2,304	2,437	157	199	152
1 to 5	216	230	274	39	47	55
5 to 10	56	71	74	13	22	24
10 to 15	26	27	24	8	11	10
15 to 20	14	25	13	5	8	5
Over 20	38	43	51	23	27	37

Source: Carrothers, "Forest Industries of British Columbia", p. 253.

her pulpwood forests and those which remained by the First World War could only be harvested by making use of expensive rail transport. Second, Canadian companies—many of which were U.S. direct investments as outlined in Chapter 9—were exempt from any of the social costs associated with the industry. Both leases on Crown lands and water power were supplied at only nominal rates and fire-protection services were provided free of charge. Third, many Canadian companies by 1914 were using larger newsprint machines than any companies in the U.S. industry thus gathering any scale efficiencies. In summary, an adequate supply of inexpensive pulpwood, cheap hydroelectric power, and satisfactory facilities for the transport of pulpwood and paper put Canada in an excellent position to supply to the U.S. market. As the U.S. demand rose after 1910, Canadian companies filled the orders.

Politics too played a part, though a smaller one, in the development of newsprint production. Provincial governments, such as those of Ontario and Quebec, placed an embargo on the export of pulpwood from Crown lands or alternatively imposed a stumpage charge which declined if the wood was manufactured into pulp in Canada. On the other side of the border before 1911, relatively high import duties on newsprint paper had reduced imports but by 1913 growing pressure from newspaper interests in the United States had resulted in newsprint being placed on that country's free list.[27]

Canada had gained a new export, newsprint and other papers, and also a greater degree of processing within the country. Pulp and paper, unlike many of the earlier staples, was linked to the expansion of income in markets unimpeded by very low income-elasticity-of-demand conditions. The demand for newsprint, after all, expanded on the basis of a

Table 11:6 Paper Industry, 1917-1929

Year	Total Paper Production (thousands of tons)	Production of Newsprint as a Percentage of Total Paper Production	Percentage of Newsprint Production Exported
(1)	(2)	(3)	(4)
1917	856	80.6	81.4
1918	968	75.9	82.1
1919	1,090	72.9	89.1
1920	1,215	72.1	86.0
1921	1,019	79.0	85.9
1922	1,367	79.1	86.2
1923	1,589	78.7	83.9
1924	1,719	80.7	80.2
1925	1,885	81.5	79.7
1926	2,266	83.4	80.4
1927	2,469	84.4	78.7
1928	2,849	84.7	79.2
1929	3,197	85.2	75.2

Sources: Urquhart and Buckley (1965), p. 335 and K. H. Burley, *The Development of Canada's Staples, 1867-1939: A Documentary Collection* (Toronto, 1970), pp. 339-40.

growing literacy, and a growing appetite for the printed word in general spawned by the new printing technologies of the mass-production daily newspapers. Although the Canadian pulp and paper industry was plagued by excess capacity from time to time the long run basis for growth was sound. Even before the Depression of the 1930s newsprint and wood pulp together had become the major export of the country. A new and more complex staple had emerged.

Energy Resources: Hydroelectricity

Relatively abundant and cheap energy was critical to the process of industrialization in most national economies. This was also so in Canada. Many of the new exports of the post-1890 years could not have been produced as cheaply or have found markets without low-cost energy; other exports owed their very inception to it. Energy resources, of course, are capable of being exported and, at present, Canada finds ready customers for hydroelectricity, natural gas, and uranium, to name a few. However, historically Canada did not export much energy and indeed was often a net energy importer. This was the case when the principal energy source was coal. Yet, when hydroelectricity was made practical and economic in the late nineteenth century, it was one of the elements which helped to restructure both industry and the wider society during the natural-resource boom of the years from approximately the mid-1890s to 1929.

One of the apparent anomalies of Canadian international trade is that raw materials constituted not only important exports but also important imports. Tariff distortions, of course, explain some of these imports, as in the case of raw cotton which fed the highly protected textile industry. Less obvious were the imports of unprocessed minerals. These imports illustrate two vital features of natural-resource development. First, not all minerals were available from domestic sources. Others could not be exploited because the costs of doing so were too high relative to the price of imports or were simply not discovered.[28] With only small deposits of known reserves, the iron and steel industry purchased virtually all of its iron ore outside the domestic economy in the late nineteenth and early twentieth centuries. That the industry existed at all was mainly because its output was protected by tariffs and other restraints on trade. The second reason for the importance of mineral imports to economic development was connected to Canada's energy supply. There was a relative scarcity of certain types of energy and a relative abundance of others.

Historically, the principal energy resources available in Canada were coal and hydroelectricity power. Recently, oil and natural gas have also become major sources of energy but their importance is a post-1945 phenomenon. Energy, however, is not of a single type. Coal is used to produce heat energy, in the first instance, and electricity used primarily to produce motive power. Heat, of course, can be used to generate electricity and electricity can be used directly for some industrial heating purposes. The latter proved to be of great importance to the develoment of the pulp and paper industry as was noted earlier in this chapter. This distinction between fuel and water power is critical because the central region of Canada developed without any important domestic source of fuel and only after the late nineteenth century with plentiful and usable water power. But this was long after the establishment of that region as the manufacturing centre of the country.[29]

The coal resources of the economy are located in two distinct locations—far eastern and far western Canada. In the east the coal mines of Nova Scotia, and specifically those of Cape Breton Island, were the first to be developed in the 1820s. However, even when the railway links were established between central and maritime Canada, as noted earlier, the eastern coal could not be shipped profitably to the industrial centres. Coal from Pennsylvania was always cheaper in Ontario than Nova Scotian coal except when tariffs forced consumption of the domestic resource. Thermal energy from coal was important in many manufacturing industries but in none more so than in iron and steel production. Yet, the development of an iron- and steel-manufacturing capacity in Nova Scotia never equalled that of Ontario, mostly at Sault Ste. Marie and

Figure 11:6 Spatial Representation of the Primary Iron and Steel Industry in 1918

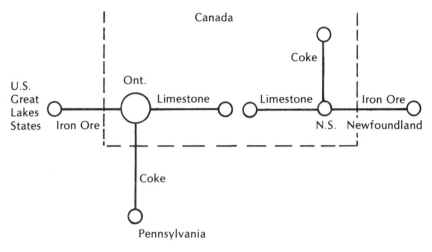

Note: In 1918 iron and steel production in Canada reached its pre-Second World War peak. Most production took place in three locations: Hamilton and Sault Ste. Marie in Ontario and Sydney in Nova Scotia. The major material inputs were all imported apart from limestone, the fluxing agent in steel-making. In thousands of short tons, the imports of iron ore were: 1,392.3 from Michigan and Minnesota to Ontario and 754.6 from Newfoundland, which was, at the time, still a British colony. In contrast only 93,100 tons of domestic iron were used and this mostly in Ontario. Ontario producers also relied on imported coking coal (861,500 tons) but in Nova Scotia, coal consumption was from the mines in Cape Breton for the most part (561,100 tons). See A. W. G. Wilson, *Development of Chemical, Metallurgical and Allied Industries in Canada* (Ottawa, 1924), pp. 188-89.

Hamilton. Ontario was the location which conferred on the producers the lowest aggregate transport costs in terms of both the inputs of energy and iron-ore and the final product itself. The advantage of local coal sup-plies in Nova Scotia could not offset the locational advantages of the Ontario-based industry for the maritime producers. Furthermore, the Dominion Steel and Coal Company of Cape Breton had to import its iron ore too, in this case, from Newfoundland (see Figure 11:6).[30]

The abundance of a natural resource, as seen in Chapter 3, was not suf-ficient to guarantee its usefulness; it also had to be strategically located. Without alternative sources of thermal power from coal and coke, im-ported from nearby locations in the United States, the rate of growth of manufacturing would have undoubtedly been lower in the post-Confederation years. In contrast to non-renewable coal-based energy,

Figure 11:7 Hydraulic Turbine Installations, 1890-1929

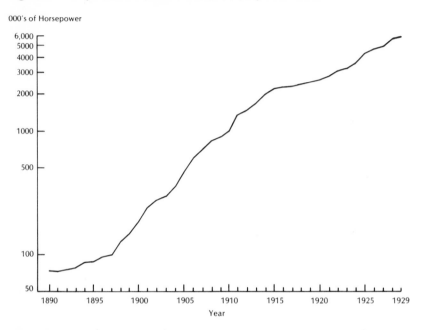

000's of Horsepower

Year

Note: The proportion of electricity generated in central electric generating stations was 83 per cent of the total in 1928 (the first year for exact compara-bility).

Source: Data are from Urquhart and Buckley, eds., *Historical Statistics of Canada*, p. 454.

however, was that derived from water power — hydroelectricity. Not only were hydroelectric power sources strategically located but the power could be produced in such a volume and at such a low cost that there were important spreading effects. Indeed, during the period from the late nineteenth century to 1929, as an input, probably no other natural-resource-based economic activity had as many direct consequences for industry as hydroelectricity. But electricity was more than an industrial input, it was also consumed in the home as light and as cheap motive power. Thus, the phenomenal growth of Canada's electric-generating capacity, noted in Figure 11:7, was based on an increasing demand which was widespread in the economy.

The export of hydroelectric power to the United States, as noted earlier, was generally of a relatively small magnitude despite the rapid growth in the demand for electricity in the economy to the south and the abundance of water-power sources from which hydroelectricity could be

Table 11:7 Hydroelectricity Exports to the United States, 1910-1929

Year	Exports (millions of kilowatt hours)	Exports as a Percentage of Domestic Production
(1)	(2)	(3)
1910	475	33
1919	1,143	21
1920	950	16
1921	1,020	18
1922	862	13
1923	1,054	13
1924	1,200	13
1925	1,239	12
1926	1,253	10
1927	1,609	11
1928	1,675	10
1929	1,604	9

Sources: A. E. D. Grauer, "The Export of Electricity from Canada", in R. Clark, ed., *Canadian Issues: Essays in Honour of Henry F. Angus* (Toronto, 1961), pp. 257 and 267 and Canada Year Book, various issues.

generated. At first, in the 1890s, the transmission of electrical energy was extremely inefficient and impractical. However, by the beginning of the twentieth century, the technical problems were solved and while this resulted in a rapid increase in hydroelectricity exports they were not maintained in the long-run (see Table 11:7). From at least 1919, the export of hydroelectricity fell as a proportion of domestic production. This was a conscious act of policy to promote the manufacturing industry.[31]

The policy to limit the export of electricity to the United States was the response to the first two decades of experience in the hydroelectric power industry. While it was never a simple codified policy it was nevertheless effective, being widely supported by municipal, provincial, and federal governments as well as private and public business enterprise. Of all the various groups which contributed to the policy, none was more consistent in its advocacy of the use of hydroelectricity power to create and stimulate domestic manufacturing than the Ontario Hydro-Electric Power Commission under the direction of its vigorous chairman, Sir Adam Beck. In the first instance, Ontario Hydro, as the Power Commission came to be known, was established in 1910 to solve one of the classic economic problems of the provision of utilities. That is, the manufacture and sale of hydroelectricity tends to be a natural monopoly either because of an exclusive property right over the fall of water or because of the high fixed costs associated with the distribution of electricity. As Ontario Hydro became more and more responsible for both electric-power generation and distribution so its imaginative chairman became convinced of the industrial advantages of cheap hydroelectric power supplied to a wide range of manufacturing: a social benefit which could only be achieved through public enterprise.[32]

Cheap hydroelectricity had given rise to many new industrial pursuits in the early 1900s. None, however, exemplified the importance of this cheap energy as much as electro-chemical and aluminum manufacturing. In both there was an extremely rapid rate of growth of output. However, growth in these industries took place at the same time as high exports of hydroelectricity and while this occasioned no major problem, shortages of electricity for domestic use did occur later during the First World War. In particular, the electro-chemical industry, which was important to the war effort, fell behind its projected production as the Imperial Munitions Board forcibly pointed out in 1917. If Adam Beck needed support for his position in restricting electricity exports, he got it when the royal commission of Sir Henry Drayton reached the conclusion that domestic shortages had resulted from the commitment to honour export contracts.[33]

The manufacture of electro-chemicals, which was the subject of so much concern during the First World War, was, in fact, one of the first industries created by the new hydroelectricity technology. Its development was important for its own sake but also important because it drew to public attention, many new problems associated with harnessing the country's hydroelectric potential. Principal among these was the benefits from public as opposed to private control over the resource. Public control by regulation and later by direct operation was one of the early features of the development of Niagara Falls. However, no such policy was practised by the Americans on the other side of the Niagara gorge. Needless to say, the economies of scale in production lowered the cost of industrial energy much more on the Canadian side of the border; at an early stage, U.S. firms were purchasing power from Canada. But power remained cheaper in Canada and by the time of the First World War, the Ontario-based industry was growing much more rapidly than its U.S. counterpart. Some of this growth was in fact due to the migration of some electro-chemical firms from one side of the Niagara River to the other.[34]

Another of the many practical results of scientific advances in metallurgy in the late nineteenth century was the creation of the new light metal called aluminum. In a very short time Canada became one of the world's major producers of aluminum despite the fact that there were no domestic sources of the basic mineral resource. What Canada had in relative abundance was cheap hydroelectricity. The process of refining aluminum is based on separating out aluminum oxide from impurities found in the major exploitable source of bauxite. Separation takes place by electrolysis — in a bath of mineral cryolite — and therefore production requires vast inputs of electricity. Since hydroelectricity was readily available in Quebec, at or near salt water, and since natural bauxite could be easily shipped from its main source in the West Indies, Quebec became the rational location for aluminum production. This locational advantage was first captured at the hydroelectric development at Shawinigan Falls and later at Arvida. Later still, British Columbia too became an important production centre. Such was the efficiency of these locations that from its inception the Canadian aluminum industry accounted for about 10 per cent of world production between 1900 and 1930. Later, as noted in Table 11:8, the Canadian production generally outpaced that elsewhere.[35]

Similar to the iron and steel industry, aluminum production in Canada required substantial imports of raw materials from elsewhere. What distinguished the two industries, however, was the use of energy. Whereas iron and steel production required energy imports, aluminum production was based soley on the advantages of location at the domestic energy source. Without protection in the domestic market, iron and steel would undoubtedly have been imported. Aluminum, on the other hand, was produced principally for the export market. It was, in the sense, the mechanism through which hydroelectric energy was exported to the rest of the world.

The exploitation of hydroelectric potential not only created new industries but transformed existing ones. New and powerful links were established between electricity and mining, for instance. These links, in turn, did much to extend the natural boom into the 1920s as in the case of base-metal mineral exports from British Columbia. Because many of the base metals were found in complex ore forms, such as silver-lead-zinc, it was natural that early exploitation concentrated on those ores which were relatively simple in nature and, of course, high grade. However, by the 1920s, it was necessary to turn to the more complex base-metal ores or cease production. Indeed, base-metal production had fallen after the First World War and at least part of this decline must be accounted for by the rising real costs of production. The froth flotation process of separating base-metal ores was well-known; however, until they were forced to adopt it, the major producers resisted the procedure in response to their growing competitive disadvantages. Critical to the use of the process was, of course, the availability of cheap electrical energy. Thus, when the demand for mineral exports expanded in the last part of

Table 11:8 Aluminum Production, 1902-1955

Year	Production in Canada (thousands short tons)	Canadian Production as a Percentage of World Consumption
(1)	(2)	(3)
1902	1	11.2
1910	5	10.0
1915	9	9.9
1920	11	7.9
1925	16	7.8
1930	38	13.0
1935	23	8.1
1940	109	12.0
1945	216	22.5
1950	397	24.1
1955	584	18.0

Source: J. Davis, Mining and Mineral Processing in Canada (Ottawa, 1957), p. 394.

the 1920s, the mining industry was capable of meeting competition with output levels which were greater than otherwise would have prevailed because of cost-reducing effects of hydroelectricity.[36]

Electricity was used for more than the industrial purposes of manufacturing. In the first quarter of the twentieth century it became the most common source of domesic lighting, at least in the urban areas. Subsequently, it provided cheap motive power for domestic appliances and certain types of light farm machinery. However, electricity was also employed as a source of motor traction and that application, in the form of urban tramways and electric railways, did much to transform the nature of urban life. The growth of the use of electricity in late-nineteenth-century Canada was intimately linked to the electrified transport service. So much was this the case that many of the major hydroelectric companies carried on the two activities of selling electric power and transport with an unclear definition of the principal part of their business. The major supplier of hydroelectric power on the west coast of Canada was, for instance, the British Columbia Electric Railway Company.

To the town dwellers of late-nineteenth-century Canada, the electric tramways and railways were the demonstrable signs of modernity.[37] As the first major application of electric power in the consumer sector, the new electric power transport was ideally suited to the movement of passengers within the urban areas, and from the surrounding hinterland to the urban centre. In both applications, the result was cheap transport which was made available at least two decades before the popular use of the motor car began to reshape urban Canada. Suburbs were linked to the towns by the electric railways — sometimes called "inter-urbans" — which by 1900 had 154 miles of operating track around and in most major urban areas. Hamilton, for instance, had four distinct radial lines, links to adjacent towns, all of which were owned by the Dominion Power and Transmission Company by 1907. The importance of the electric railways lay in the fast and cheap movement of people. However, they did have a limited freight-carrying capacity and this capacity was sufficient to permit the shipment of fluid milk to the towns. This, as noted in Chapter 4, was one of the forces which reshaped the dairy industry of the time.

The growth of the electric tramways and railways was ultimately limited by another source of motive power, the gasoline and Diesel engine. As early as 1918, more electric inter-urban rail track was taken out of commission than was laid down. In fact, only nine miles of new track were brought into commission in the post-1918 years. Automobiles and motor buses proved to be an apparently superior form of linking the suburban populations to the workplaces and amenities of the towns. So too, short-haul trucking more than adequately replaced the freight-carrying capacity of the electric railways. Although the decline in the intra-urban electric tramway was not as rapid, it was just as inevitable as the bus, a more flexible form of urban transport, replaced the clanking tramcars.[38] In general, however, any decrease in the demand for electricity for this service was more than offset by increasing domestic and industrial demands elsewhere in the economy.

In the long run, the ability of the economy to provide relatively abundant and cheap hydroelectric power to the industrial sector has created much electric-power-intensive manufacturing. For instance, the per-capita industrial use of electric power in Canadian history — 4,193 kilowatt hours in 1964 — has generally been about 50 to 60 per cent greater than in the United States. Nor should this be surprising since the per-unit cost of industrial electric energy is much lower in Canada than in the United States. Specifically, this lower cost results from the very high proportion of electricity generated from water power in contrast to the high proportion of less efficient thermal-fuelled electric generation in the United States. Of all major western economies only Norway uses as much electricity per-capita for industrial purposes, although Canada, in absolute terms, generates more electricity and has a larger industrial sector.[39]

From the last few years of the nineteenth century to 1929, Canada's economy had undergone a transformation. Whereas primary economic activity had previously dominated all others by the close of this era, the secondary sector of manufacturing and construction had become a larger contributor to national income. But as this chapter has emphasized, this resulted because of increased natural-resource use not despite it. As natural-resource development spread into new areas, as it took new forms, and as new products resulted, the links to manufacturing were strengthened. Other periods of rapid natural-resource development followed, notably in 1950s and 1960s, and are discussed in the next chapter. None, however, was as vital.

CHAPTER TWELVE

Manufacturing and Commercial Policy

Introduction

The origins of much of Canada's manufacturing industry were in the prosperity of the mid-nineteenth century. Yet, even by Confederation the manufacturing base was still narrow. Only in a few industries such as transportation equipment, agricultural machinery, and textile production had sizeable manufacturing firms emerged. Most firms in most industries were small; they produced for a local market, purchased many inputs in the surrounding region, and seldom engaged in export trading, unless of course they were directly part of the staple trades. Within sixty years, however, manufacturing was completely different in character. Most industries had some large firms, production was for a wider market than the local one, inputs were purchased and often transported over long distances, and there was a greater proportion of manufacturing output exported. Manufacturing, as a whole, had taken on the irreversible features associated with modern industry.

The manufacturing industries of Canada were, of course, subject to many of the same international pressures which had provided the impetus for change in the primary sector. As will be seen, not only was this so in manufacturing which produced goods for export but also in that part which produced goods for domestic consumption. Here domestic production and imports often contested for their share of the Canadian market in what is known as "the import-competing sector" of the economy. Thus, the international economy, to some degree, shaped all manufacturing. Not surprisingly, businessmen and politicians turned to tariff policy as an instrument to promote the development of manufacturing, particularly secondary manufacturing. This was evident as early as 1858-59 in the Cayley-Galt tariffs. Yet, Canadian manufacturers occasionally sought a commercial policy alternative—reciprocal free trade with the United States. Because this involved a reduction of the U.S. tariff, the free trade strategy was not necessarily inconsistent with the policy of unilaterally erecting barriers to trade.

In its variety of forms commercial policy became the single most important element of the strategy to both widen and deepen the manufacturing base. It was viewed as the mechanism by which the impediments to the growth of a large manufacturing sector—the small size, openness, and apparent comparative advantage of the economy in primary production—could be offset. Here we shall examine the consequences for manufacturing of the major commercial policies of Canadian history. This facet of openness, however, cannot be examined in isolation from the cyclical movements of the economy and business concentration since all were inter-related. These two themes of manufacturing development occupy the last two sections of this chapter.

Prelude to National Policy, 1867-1878

The abrogation of the Reciprocity Treaty by the United States in 1866 made British North Americans, for the second time in two decades, feel bitter about the degree and manner with which their principal trading partners abruptly changed commercial policy. They regarded reciprocity, as they had previously regarded Empire preference, as the touchstone of economic success. The U.S. government, on the other hand, felt that reciprocal free trade in staples was no longer defensible. As that country expanded westward there were pleas for the protection of agricultural markets; timber resources were no longer scarce; and, among other political pressures, the Cayley-Galt tariffs had done much to make manufacturers suspicious of Canadian motives. Canadian commercial policy was again adrift and it was to remain so for about thirteen years.[1]

The political union of the larger British North American colonies was founded on many economic assumptions.[2] One of these was that the Confederation, by expanding British North America from a quasi-free-trade union to a fully free-trading area, would create a larger market for all products of the regions and facilitate trade through the use of a common currency and a common base for taxation. However, this was not the case. The Canadas were already a free-trade area; indeed they had been so since the Constitutional Act of 1791. For the manufactured goods of Canada East and West—Quebec and Ontario—the Maritime provinces of the new union did not provide a large additional market. The agricultural, timber, and trading merchants of the Atlantic region, on the other hand, could not compete with the producers of central Canada in that market. Although the lack of direct transport links was blamed for the failure of the Maritime provinces to penetrate the main Canadian market it was in large measure the relative efficiencies of production which were the root cause (see Chapter 10).

The failure of the United States to renew the reciprocal-free-trade pact with Canada in 1866 left both the pattern of trade and its rate of growth virtually unchanged. This did not dissuade the majority of Canadians from their strongly held view. On no less than four occasions in the eight years after the end of reciprocity Canadian representatives made pilgrimages to Washington. In 1866, 1869, 1870, and 1874 the pleadings for a renewal of the reciprocal-trade agreement fell on unsympathetic ears. Even after 1873, when both the Canadian and broader international economy experienced depression, much of domestic opinion clung to the view that economic salvation lay first in reciprocity and only failing that in a high protective tariff. Before the Select Committee on the Causes of the Present Depression in 1876 many businessmen stated that they preferred free entry into the U.S. market to highly protective tariffs at home.[3] Despite popular sentiment, within three years of the committee's meetings a highly protective tariff was legislated.

The shift in commercial policy indicated by the National Policy tariff of 1879 was not as mercurial a change in political, business, or public sentiment as it first seemed. Commercial policy, as it was articulated in the late 1860s and 1870s, was the result of several forces, some contradictory, in addition to the desire for reciprocity. Each of the forces exerted represented a different priority in economic development. First, there was the need for revenue to finance government activity. Second, regional interests in the Maritime provinces had to be placated. Third, despite statements to select committees, there was a strong and growing business support for high tariffs—a feeling which strengthened remarkably as the possibility of reciprocity grew more remote.[4]

Revenue raised from tariffs was a binding constraint on the adoption of certain changes in commercial policy. For instance, the revenues from the tariffs represented the single largest source of government funds—about 60 per cent in 1868-78. In addition, Canada had assumed at Confederation a large debt from its constituent parts of over $88 million and had further committed itself to major transport improvements. Although bound more by expediency than by constitutional legality, the government failed to consider other forms of taxation in periods of falling imports and tariff rates were raised in an attempt to maintain a constant flow of funds. In 1870, for instance, Francis Hincks, noting that revenue from import duty had fallen in 1869 as compared to 1868 and that government expenditures would likely increase, revised the general tariff rate upwards by 5 per cent, increased some specific rates, and removed a number of items such as flour, wheat, coal, and coke from the free list. While the Liberals, who came to power in 1873, generally favoured freer trade than the previous Conservative government, the exigencies of raising revenue forced the new Minister of Finance, Richard Cartwright, to raise the general rate by 2.5 per cent in 1874. Despite their professed philosophy, between 1874 and 1878, the Liberals were unable to lower tariffs and by 1878, the general tariff rate was 17.5 per cent with higher specific rates on some items.

Opinion in the Maritime provinces generally favoured low import duties and some supported reciprocity with the United States in manufactured products as well as agricultural and natural commodities. Maritime representatives in the House of Commons tended to blame the failure to renew reciprocity on central Canada's unwillingness to include manufactured goods in any agreement and at least twice, tariff policy changed in deference to this low-tariff sentiment. In 1858 Finance minister John Rose removed the duty on bread, reduced the duty on molasses, overhauled the sugar tariff, and abolished tonnage duties on shipping. Some of these reductions were designed to promote the trade with the West Indies. Hincks' higher duties in 1870, and especially the new tariffs on coal and flour, were attacked bitterly in the Maritimes. So, in 1871 the Conservatives removed the 5 per cent increase, repealed the duties on coal, coke, wheat, and flour, and, a year later, those on tea and coffee. Whether or not Confederation had actually caused a diversion of trade, many in the Maritimes believed that that diversion would come about, to the detriment of their economic welfare, if tariffs became more protective; they envisaged commercial policy forcing them to purchase manufactured goods from high-cost central Canadian producers rather than from low-cost producers in the United States.[5]

In antithesis to the arguments for low tariffs were the protectionist opinions of some Canadian manufacturers. They argued that since the high tariffs of the United States restricted them in that country's market then at least the Canadian market should be theirs. Recall that concerted efforts were made to promote protective import duties in the 1850s, especially during the recession of 1857-59. The Depression after 1873 stimulated the same reaction from manufacturing interests. Between Confederation and the adoption of the national policy in 1879, commercial policy became the vehicle for placating various interests. It was adrift in a sea of pragmatism and consequently not used as an instrument to promote economic development. Conflicts between Maritime and manufacturing interests, between those who saw the tariff only as a revenue device and those who wished it used as a protective one, between advocates of reciprocity with the United States and proponents of more diversified trade were too well balanced to produce a consensus upon which government could act. Action was delayed until 1879.

Manufacturing and the National Policy Tariff

The election of 1878 was fought over economic issues as no election campaign in the past had been. Sir John A. Macdonald had given clear warning a year earlier in the House of Commons:

> We have no manufacturers here. We have no workpeople; our workpeople have gone off to the United States ... These Canadian artisans are adding to the strength, to the power, and to the wealth of a foreign nation instead of adding to ours. Our workpeople in this country ... are suffering for want of employment ... if Canada had had a judicious system of taxation [tariffs] they would be toiling and doing well in their own country.[6]

Aimed at increasing domestic employment in manufacturing, the new Conservative government introduced a tariff revision of wide-sweeping importance. The National Policy tariff of 1879, as the revision came to be called, was, however, only part of a set of policies designed to stimulate the domestic demand for domestically produced manufactured goods, to expand the Canadian market by accelerating the pace of western settlement, and to attract relatively scarce capital resources from abroad. Immigrants who would not exacerbate the unemployment condition in manufacturing—measured both by actual unemployment and by the emigration of skilled labour to the United States—were also sought. Altogether this represented a fundamental new strategy for economic development. One of its key elements was the tariff revision.

The roots of the National Policy lay in the thwarted economic expectations of the late 1870s. The abrogation of the Reciprocity Treaty by the United States in 1866 and the Confederation of the British North American colonies a year later appear to have had little net effect on economic performance. Exports and imports continued to expand and the feared recession after the end of limited free trade with the United States failed to materialize. Indeed, manufacturing output grew so rapidly in the early seventies that the average annual rate of growth for the entire decade subsequently proved greater than the long-run trend despite poor performance in the last half of the decade. This poor economic performance can be dated to 1873, a year which witnessed the beginnings of a world-wide Depression.

The falling commodity prices, reduced quantity of imports into

Canada, and rising unemployment were all results of the Depression of 1873. This was compounded in Canada when economic recovery in the United States was more rapid, resulting in an emigration of Canadian workers to that country. Following so soon after Confederation and the buoyant economic growth of the early 1870s and in comparison with the swifter recovery of the United States later, there was a general feeling among political leaders and others that the economy was falling short of its potential. It was in this mood of pessimism that, after the United States once more rejected any reciprocal free-trade arrangement, the high tariff policy was conceived. It was intended that the economy should grow and diversify behind a highly protective tariff—slightly higher on finished manufactured imports than on intermediate goods and raw materials. Although the import duties were slightly reduced in the 1890s and again subsequently, it was nevertheless true that for most branches of Canadian manufacturing the tariff's effectiveness was greater than at any time prior to 1879 or, indeed, after 1939. The National Policy and its amendments were commercial policy for sixty years, years which witnessed varying patterns of economic growth from the rapid economic expansion of the early twentieth century, to the catastrophic Depression of the 1930s.

During the sixty years of the National Policy tariff Canadian manufacturing was transformed. Many attributes of this transformation were in fact evident as early as the time of the First World War. These were the economic characteristics of modernization and included: large-scale production units, multi-product and multi-plant firms, the use of new energy sources such as hydroelectricity, and new forms of corporate control, among others. While this modernization was to continue almost unabated until the Depression of the 1930s, it was between 1867 and 1914 that manufacturing lost its traditional basis.

Exactly how the National Policy tariff altered the pattern of growth of manufacturing is a matter of considerable controversy.[7] This is so for two reasons. First, as we have seen, it is extremely difficult to separate the impact of the tariff from the real forces shaping the economy. Second, there is no general agreement about the strength of the real economic forces of the period. For instance, those who argue that the years from 1873 to the mid-1890s were years of stagnation and little economic development also argue that the transformation of manufacturing was subsequent and rapid. Such a view of Canadian manufacturing development is one of long-standing and has come to be known as the "take-off" hypothesis. Another view disputes any take-off and considers the transformation more prolonged, less revolutionary than evolutionary.[8]

The transformation of manufacturing and the influence of the tariff upon it had three dimensions:

1) the growth of manufacturing;
2) the structural change in the composition of output; and
3) the structural change in the geographic distribution of output.

Furthermore, it is necessary to inquire if the transition was compact and in particular to isolate the role played by the new staples and wheat in the immediate pre-1915 years.

In terms of the growth of output of the manufacturing sector the transition was both significant and smooth. By value, output increased at a long-run compound annual average rate of 4.2 per cent between 1870 and 1915. This also approximated the real change. Such rates were high compared with the performance of other industrializing countries and within Canada was well above the growth in aggregate income (see Table 2:1). In absolute terms this represented a growth of manufacturing output from $221 million in 1870 to $1.398 billion in 1915. Not only was this growth large but it seldomly differed from the trend over the census intervals. There were only two exceptions. In the 1890s real output of manufacturers grew annually at only 2.1 per cent whereas in the next decade it expanded at a rate of 8.0 per cent.[9] Thus, only the last decade of the nineteenth century deserves any term such as stagnation; all other decades witnessed a significant growth in manufacturing output, particularly accelerated during the period from 1900 to the First World War. Otherwise, the ratio of primary to secondary manufacturing changed little and the widening of the scope of manufacturing took place smoothly as less and less of total value added was accounted for by the five major industries.

On the whole the rank of secondary manufacturing output was relatively unchanged throughout the period (see Table 12:1). Iron and steel products, still without any basis in primary iron and steel production, dominated all others. The leather-products industry, the food and beverage sector, transport, and clothing production followed in order. In primary manufacturing the wood and agricultural industries were paramount with primary pulp and paper products and non-ferrous metals gaining in relative importance by the 1920s. Thus, the remarkable growth in output in manufacturing was achieved without any major realignment of manufacturing-industry groups. Only in the types of output produced, that is, in the increased importance of construction goods, was there any structural change and that was not of major importance. This stable pattern of sectoral development strongly suggests that the linkage mechanism between the staples and manufacturing did not qualitatively change as the economy moved into the prosperity of the 1896-1918 period. Growth took place within the confines of existing manufacturing industries.[10]

Table 12:1 Rank of Manufacturing Industry Groups, by Value Added, 1870-1957

Industry Group	1870	1890	1910	1926	1939	1957
(1)	(2)	(3)	(4)	(5)	(6)	(7)
1. Food and Beverages: Primary	4	4	3	4	3	5
2. Food and Beverages: Secondary	5	6	5	2	2	3
3. Tobacco Products: Secondary	15	14	15	11	18	22
4. Rubber Products: Secondary	19	20	22	14	14	18
5. Leather Products: Secondary	3	5	7	15	16	21
6. Textiles (excluding clothing): Secondary	9	8	8	6	4	11
7. Clothing: Secondary	7	3	4	9	9	13
8. Wood Products: Primary	2	2	2	7	11	12
9. Wood Products: Secondary	8	9	11	13	15	16
10. Paper Products: Primary	17	16	16	3	5	4
11. Paper Products: Secondary	18	18	20	21	20	17
12. Printing, Publishing, and Allied Products: Secondary	11	11	9	8	7	8
13. Iron and Steel Products: Secondary	1	1	1	1	1	1
14. Transportation Equipment: Secondary	6	7	6	5	6	2
15. Non-ferrous Metal Products: Primary	22	17	12	18	8	10
16. Non-ferrous Metal Products: Secondary	16	15	13	20	19	19
17. Electrical Apparatus & Supplies: Secondary	21	21	18	12	12	6
18. Non-Metallic Minerals: Primary	20	22	19	23	23	23
19. Non-Metallic Minerals: Secondary	10	10	10	17	17	14
20. Petroleum and Coal Products: Secondary	13	19	21	16	13	7
21. Chemical Products: Primary	21	23	23	22	21	20
22. Chemical Products: Secondary	12	12	14	10	10	9
23. Miscellaneous: Secondary	14	13	17	19	22	15

Note: The distinction between primary and secondary manufacturing is that the former involves only minor processing or natural resources mainly for export.

Source: G. W. Bertram, "Historical Statistics on Growth and Structure of Manufacturing in Canada, 1870-1957", in J. Henripin and A. Asimakopulas, eds., *Conference on Statistics 1962 and 1963* (Toronto, 1964), pp. 104-05.

The relatively stable rank structure of manufacturing industry does not imply an unchanged industry. Manufacturing was, in fact, changing rapidly as new techniques were adopted and as a scale and location effects were felt. Scale and location raise the issue of how the growth of manufacturing helped the integration of the various regional economies of Canada at Confederation. In 1870, the distribution of per-capita output of manufacturing was already skewed in favour of Ontario and, to a smaller extent, Quebec. As demand for manufactured products increased between 1870 and 1915 agglomeration economies occurred and regional specialization increased. In addition, forces developed after 1870 which pushed the economy towards greater integration. Three such forces, dealt with earlier, were prairie settlement, the construction of all-Canadian transport routes by the CPR and later transcontinental railways, and the high tariff rates on manufactured imports introduced in 1879.

The railroad policy caused expansion of transport facilities which brought more agricultural land within the feasible margin of production. Freight rates were also reduced as central Canada was linked to the West and the Maritimes. In turn, the protective tariff deflected the demand of people drawing income from the export industries to domestic rather than foreign products. These forces stimulated regional specialization by breaking down natural monopolies and allowing regions to take account of their comparative advantage albeit behind a tariff wall. Table 12:2 bears out the fact that Ontario, as Canada's manufacturing centre, became more and more specialized between 1870 and 1915 with growth being particularly rapid in the first fifteen years of the twentieth century. At least part of this change can be attributed to linkages from Prairie expansion. On the other hand, Quebec manufacturing output per capita remained close to the national average throughout the period whereas that of the Maritimes and prairie provinces declined. In British Columbia there was relative expansion between 1880 and 1900 based on the expansion in the number of small-scale manufacturing firms but by 1900 the transport systems had brought that province into greater competition with Ontario and Quebec.

The same economic forces which brought about the regional growth of manufacturing output also brought about changes in its structure. Locational advantages were exploited as transport costs declined. There was a relative expansion of secondary manufacturing in Ontario and to some extent Quebec. The rest of Canada, on the other hand, concentrated more on primary manufacturing. For example, Ontario and Quebec tended to specialize in the production of processed foods, iron and steel products, textiles, secondary foods, clothing, transport equipment, and

Table 12:2 Per-Capita Manufacturing Output of Regions as a Percentage of the Canadian Average, 1870-1915

Region	1870	1880	1900	1915
(1)	(2)	(3)	(4)	(5)
Ontario	112	115	123	153
Quebec	101	107	103	100
Maritimes	69	65	59	61
Prairies	—	40	40	38
British Columbia	—	80	132	86

Source: Bertram (1964), pp. 122-23.

secondary wood products. The prairie region specialized in agriculture with little emphasis on processing foods. Primary wood products and primary non-ferrous metals became the dominant primary manufactures of British Columbia. The only important exception was the rapid growth of the secondary manufacture of primary pulp and paper in Quebec, in the period immediately prior to 1914.

The central issue is the linkages which developed between primary and secondary activities, and among the manufacturing sectors. These linkages, as noted earlier, were for the most part established before the wheat-boom era of prosperity. Through them were passed the induced investment demands brought about by staple expansion which increased the ratio of investment to total manufactured goods produced. To be sure, Canada's import of capital goods increased but this was not the result of domestic bottlenecks. Industries rapidly responded to produce more agricultural machinery, railway cars and engines, rails, and iron and steel bridges, to name but a few. Although a property of all staple booms, it was especially so in the period 1896-1921 that the exploitation of staples set up forces which, in terms of national income, gave rise to a growth of manufacturing. This, in the long run, diminished the importance of the staples themselves.

At the same time, urbanization progressed rapidly. Between 1901 and 1921, the population resident in urban areas rose from 35 to 47 per cent on average. Ontario became overwhelmingly urban. Even in the Prairies, the proportion of the population in towns and villages grew (see Chapter 6). Indeed, it is not surprising that construction materials became a larger proportion of manufacturing-commodity output along with investment goods given net immigration and its urban character. This resulted directly from a greater aggregate demand for finished consumer and producer commodities that required the expansion of plant or construction in manufacturing, and indirectly from conglomeration in urban areas with its attendant residential construction.

Although the general tariff rate was raised from 17.5 to 20 per cent and agricultural duties were reinstated the main attempt to create employment was directed at industries such as iron and steel, agricultural implements, and textiles. Products from these sectors received nominal and effective rate increases immediately in 1879 and over the next eight years. The National Policy took some ten years to implement fully, and by 1890 the highest tariffs yet levied protected most sectors of Canadian manufacturing. Nor did the Conservatives forget that reduced tariffs on imported inputs raised effective protection: for instance, textile machinery entered Canada without duty and some iron and steel items used in shipbuilding were placed on the free list. In summary, the average rate of duty increased from about 20.5 per cent in the 1870s under the Liberals, to approximately 25 per cent in 1884, and 30 per cent in 1890.

Certain individual sectors of manufacturing were stimulated and grew in a pattern which would not have been possible in the absence of the 1879 tariff. One such industry was textiles which expanded solely on the basis of protection. New mills opened, production expanded, and raw cotton imports tripled over the period 1879-90. Other industries, such as iron and steel, which performed better than most during the late nineteenth century, appear to have grown on the basis of both protection and increased demand from the railway sector in the 1880s. The expansion from one important iron and steel works to twenty-nine establishments manufacturing iron and steel products by 1891 was assisted by government decrees for the use of domestically produced rails, bounties to steel producers, and the tariff on imported iron and steel products. Similarly, agricultural-machinery producers found that they were able to charge a price for their output which was generally about 15 per cent greater than that of the pre-tariff import price of U.S. implements. But in this sector as well, it is likely that the growing output was only in part due to the protective effect and as much a consequence of the shifts in demand due to prairie settlement. After a period of relatively slow growth in the 1890s, most manufacturing sectors expanded rapidly during the first decade of the twentieth century. This period derived its impetus from the expanding wheat economy and the resource boom in pulpwood, minerals, as well as the cheaper source of energy, hydroelectricity. Even without protection manufacturing output growth would have been accelerated.

In one unambiguous respect the National Policy tariff was successful: It attracted foreign savings. Often overlooked as a goal of tariff revision, it was well understood by individuals at the time that the expansion of the protected sectors could take place only by a transfer of resources from the relatively unprotected sector unless additional resources, particularly savings, could be secured from abroad. The tariff, of course, raised the price of imports to consumers and conferred an economic rent on domestic producers. As domestic manufacturers expanded the production of import-substitutes, so too the foreigners, in this case U.S. manufacturers, saw their Canadian market contract. As Chapter 9 showed in greater detail, the economic conditions which stimulated the establishment of U.S. branch plants in Canada were created. The increased presence of U.S. firms in Canadian manufacturing thus occurred at a time, the 1870s and 1880s, when the economy was showing few signs of dynamic economic performance. Undoubtedly this would have happened to a lesser extent if economic rents accruing to Canadian manufacturers had been smaller or non-existent.

In a wider context the tariff was held to have increased manufacturing rents at the expense of the west.[11] It has been a long-standing and generally accepted tenet of Canadian economic history that the National Policy tariff distorted the inter-regional distribution of income gains. Staple-producing regions, such as the Prairies, sold their exports in world markets which were fairly competitive but were forced to purchase their inputs of capital goods and consumer goods in protected markets. Income, it has been argued, was redistributed from the west to central Canada by the tariff. Rents which accrued to eastern manufacturers were, in part, financed by western farmers.

An alternative and increasingly accepted viewpoint suggests that the tariff caused an intra-regional rather than an inter-regional transfer of income. For instance, the high price of farm equipment relative to that in the United States caused Canadian prairie farmers to adopt a different mix of inputs than they might have in the absence of the tariff of 1879.[12] With any reasonable degree of substitution of inputs in wheat production, there was a transfer of use from the imported factor, farm equipment, to domestic labour and land. The weight of evidence strongly suggests that these transfers were the important ones and since domestic factors were supplied, for the most part, by the farmers, net transfers out of the staple region may have been extremely small or non-existent. If this was so it is unlikely that the National Policy tariff itself altered the pace of prairie settlement although it clearly defined the manner in which factors were used to extend the prairie economy.

Although the Liberals complained about certain aspects of the National Policy while in Opposition, they made only two significant rate reductions during their nearly total domination of federal politics from 1896 to 1939: the duties during the second half of the 1930s — among them Canada-United States treaties of 1936 and 1938 — and the Canada-United Kingdom agreement of 1937. While these lower rates were again associated with Liberal governments, the Conservatives did at least initiate the first agreement between Canada and the United States when the absolute economic folly of the earlier tariff increases became apparent. As in 1858-59 and 1879, recovery of the economy had little to do with import duties, and it can be traced to general recovery in the world economy with the attendant growth in demand for Canada's exports.

One might have thought that the adoption of protective tariffs would end the call among Canadians for reciprocity with the United States but this was not so.[13] It is true that as the protected industries became more important to the economy both Liberals and Conservatives became more reluctant to include reciprocity in manufactured goods in any proposals. However, some form of reciprocity remained part of both parties' platforms, and almost every tariff bill after 1879 included some provision for reciprocity if the United States was willing. In the 1880s, for instance, the Liberals called for unrestricted reciprocity, the complete removal of customs duties between Canada and the United States. After somewhat predictably losing the 1891 election on this issue, the Liberals endorsed a more limited form of reciprocity, chiefly in natural products but including some manufactured goods. Throughout the 1880s and the 1890s, the Conservatives too were amenable to a limited reciprocity in natural products. However the United States proved unreceptive to such advances until 1911. In that year, the United States suggested reciprocity and the Laurier government negotiated. The agreement which was struck provided for a free list of natural products along with the removal of duties on a few manufactured items. The reaction to this agreement well illustrates the developing conflict between those of low-tariff sentiment in the Prairies and those who generally supported protective tariffs—the National Policy—in central Canada. Reciprocity gave the Liberals an opportunity to reduce the pressure from western farmers, and Prime Minister Laurier used this in his support of the agreement. But Canada's business community was frightened by what they believed reciprocity foreshadowed, namely future tariff reductions on manufactured items. The issue split the Liberal party as it went into the election of 1911 and the Conservative victory brought an end to the Laurier negotiated pact. Reciprocity, in its nineteenth-century form, never again became a political issue.[14]

The other significant tariff development during the National Policy years was the resurrection by Canada of the British preference. From time to time after 1879, Canada attempted to negotiate preferences from Great Britian in return for Canadian tariff concessions. But Great Britain, maintaining its free-trade policy, was unwilling to restructure her commercial policy. When the new and higher Dingley Tariff in the United

States in 1897 precluded any arrangement for lower tariffs between the two countries, Laurier introduced a revamped concept of British preference. Under its terms British manufactured goods entering Canada had duty advantage over the same product from the United States. This was one-quarter of the duty payable in 1897 and subsequently was raised to one-third. It was followed by preferential agreements between Canada and most other dominions and colonies in the first decade of the twentieth century.

The Canadian example became the model for later Empire preference schemes when Great Britain again established tariffs. There were three consequences of the admission of British goods at reduced tariff rates. First, some trade diversion took place as Canada substituted higher-cost Empire goods for lower-cost U.S. goods (see Table 12:3). Second, the government lost some tariff revenues. Third, these preferences further attracted U.S. manufacturing branch plants to Canada since once within Canada their exports received preferential treatment in the other Empire countries.

The extent of trade diversion, at least with respect to Great Britain, was little. As evident in Table 12:3 the relative importance of British imports into Canada had declined steadily from 1870 to 1901 but that trend was reversed by 1901; a relatively constant 24 per cent originated from Great Britain for at least a decade. There was a corresponding change in the proportion of imports from the United States during the same period. Non-tariff changes in commercial policy, on the other hand, favoured imports from the United States during the immediate pre-1914 years. Inputs for the expanding Canadian manufacturing sector made up the bulk of her imports, especially capital goods. As this emphasis on imported inputs shifted more and more towards iron and steel products, coal, petroleum, raw cotton, and producer goods in which the United States had a comparative advantage over Great Britain the special preference came to mean less and less. As U.S. manufacturers made progress in technology and took advantage of economies of scale they recaptured their expanding share of the Canadian market which was of course reinforced by the establishment of branch plants which bound up Canadian industry and U.S. imported inputs even further. While Great Britain depended on textile exports to hold up its proportion of the Canadian market, Canada was in the process of protecting and therefore expanding its domestic textile industry at British expense. British preference temporarily froze Canada's import profile but by the 1920s, the British share of the Canadian market for imported goods fell again. Only between 1929 and 1933 was this trend again reversed and then as a result of wider preferential margins for British goods as Canada retaliated against U.S.

Table 12:3 Canada's Commodity Trade with Great Britain, the United States, and Other Foreign Countries as a Proportion of Total Commodity Trade, 1870-1939

| Year | Great Britain | | United States | | Other Foreign Countries | |
	Imports	Exportsb	Imports	Exportsb	Imports	Exportsb
(1)	(2)	(3)	(4)	(5)	(6)	(7)
1870a	57.1	37.9	32.2	50.0	10.7	12.1
1880	47.8	51.2	40.0	40.5	12.2	8.3
1886	40.7	47.2	44.6	44.1	14.7	8.7
1891	37.7	48.8	46.7	42.6	15.6	8.6
1896	31.2	57.2	50.8	34.4	18.0	8.4
1901	24.1	52.3	60.3	38.3	15.6	9.4
1906	24.4	54.2	59.6	35.5	16.0	10.3
1911	24.3	48.2	60.8	38.0	14.9	13.8
1916	15.2	60.9	73.0	27.1	11.8	12.0
1921	17.3	26.3	69.0	45.6	13.7	28.1
1926	16.3	26.4	66.3	36.3	17.4	27.3
1929	15.0	25.2	68.8	42.8	16.2	32.0
1933	24.0	39.0	54.0	32.0	22.0	29.0
1937	18.2	40.3	60.7	36.1	21.1	23.6
1939	15.2	35.5	66.1	41.1	18.7	23.4

Note: In order to assess completely the trade diversion effects of the tariff change of 1896 with respect to Great Britain a disaggregate analysis of commodity flows — those covered by the preferences and those not — would be required. However the aggregate figures appear conclusive.

a Figures for Ontario, Quebec, Nova Scotia, and New Brunswick only.

b Domestic product only.

Sources: For 1870 and 1880: O. J. Firestone, "Development of Canada's Economy", *Trends in the American Economy in the Nineteenth Century* (Princeton, 1960), p. 766. For 1886 to 1939 (excluding 1933): The Canada Year Book (1935), p. 1045. For 1933: M. C. Urquhart and K. A. H. Buckley, eds., *Historical Statistics of Canada* (Toronto, 1965), p. 183.

tariff increases and negotiated agreements with Britain and the dominions for more intra-Empire trade.[15] However, as noted before, trade agreements with the United States after 1934 returned both the tariff structure and the trends of imports, in percentage terms, to the level of the 1920s.[16]

From 1847 to the first decade of the twentieth century, a single rate applied to all countries — except for special concessions. However, in 1907 another change was made, one which still applies; this is the three-tier system:

1) the General Tariff, which had the highest rates and up to the late 1930s at least applied mainly to imports from the United States;

2) the Intermediate Tariff, with rates lower than the General Tariff which
   could be extended to any country by order-in-council; and
3) the British Preferential Tariff, which had the lowest rates.

The agreements between Canada and the United States in the late 1930s
represented one example of imposing intermediate rather than general
tariffs against some U.S. products.

Between the cessation of hostilities in 1918 and the outbreak of war
again in 1939, economic forces of unprecedented severity buffeted the
Canadian economy. Behind this volatility lay an international economic
system reeling from the profound changes which the war wrought. Indeed, it is arguable that the international economy was unstable
throughout the interwar period. Within Canada, the long-run economic
trends in the shifts in relative importance of the major sectors continued.
Although the forces giving rise to these structural changes originated in
the pre-1914 economy and they continued to operate after 1945, it was
during the interwar years that the fundamental switch took place as
manufacturing became a more important source of income than primary
production (see Chapter 2). This was shaped, however, by a variety of
new economic circumstances. From 1919 to 1925 real manufacturing output grew at a compound rate of 4.0 per cent. For the next three years it
reached an abnormally high level of 9.8 per cent. However, for the next
decade, 1929 to 1939, growth was reduced to a meagre average of 1.2 per
cent. All aggregate economic indicators trace out the same pattern.
Thus, the interwar years contained three distinct phases of Canadian
economic expansion.

The general effect of the First World War on the economy was to extend the prosperity of the prewar economy. It was not until the end of the
short, sharp postwar Depression of 1920 that the effect of this stimulus
was evident. The prairie agricultural economy was over-extended beyond
any level sustainable by peacetime prices. During the entire first period
of 1919-25 the wheat economy was depressed and some actual contraction of acreage in crops took place. Not surprisingly this had an effect on
the primary manufacturing of food and beverage products which
throughout the interwar years declined in relative importance. On the
other hand, the impetus of the demand forces which gave rise to the new
staples of the years before 1914 continued to exert their influence and
the primary manufacture of paper products, non-ferrous metals, and
chemical products expanded proportionately throughout the interwar
years. Although these industries had their adjustment problems in the
volatile economic environment of the period their long-run expansion
continued into the post-1945 prosperity. Within secondary manufactur-

ing the proportionate growth of individual industries was less pronounced than in primary manufacturing although there were exceptions: electrical apparatus, rubber products, and petroleum and coal products. However, secondary manufacturing on the whole was to shift in structure more profoundly after the Second World War.

At the regional level, Ontario and Quebec retained their positions as the centres of manufacturing in Canada; they did not, however, increase their share markedly. Yet, it was the case by 1929 that some manufacturing industries had over 90 per cent of their net production in central Canada: electrical apparatus and supplies, automobiles, rubber tires, machinery, castings and forgings, hardware and tools, agricultural implements, cigarettes, cotton yarn and cloth, boots and shoes, rubber footware, clothing, hosiery and knit goods, and furniture. This list attests to that region's dominance in manufacturing. At the same time, British Columbia began to develop a manufacturing base but the position of the Maritime provinces deteriorated further. Change in the western-most province originated mostly in the primary manufacturing of the forest and mining industries. This growth can be traced to the opening of the Panama Canal in 1916 and technological changes that allowed the non-ferrous metal ores of the Kootenay District to be more effectively exploited.

Similarly with respect to forest products the earlier rail freight rates precluded the Pacific Coast exporters from shipping to eastern Canadian and U.S. markets and from effectively competing with other timber exporting areas. By the mid-1920s, the lower ocean freight rates via Panama allowed penetration of eastern markets. In the mining industry there were a variety of scale economies which were gathered. Based on high wartime prices, larger plants, more complex technical equipment, experimentation, and, especially, inexpensive hydroelectric power, the mining industry expanded rapidly. Confirmed high rates of investment in the region after 1926 further stimulated manufacturing and construction industries, particularly in the major port of Vancouver.[17]

In the Atlantic provinces, the interwar period was also one of readjustment. Encouraged to expand during the First World War, many of its industries experienced subsequent excess capacity, even in the boom years of 1926-29. This was particularly so in the steel industry, centred on Sydney in Nova Scotia. This industry lacked markets and was inefficient:

1) the market demand for rails and railway material contracted;
2) Montreal and Ontario were located closer to large markets for the new steel products;
3) as scrap steel for resmelting became an important input, Ontario's

larger supply made scrap cheaper which put the Maritime producers at a disadvantage; and
4) with over-capacity in the world steel industry, export markets were developed only slowly and never sufficiently.

In another major industry, the shipments of lumber from British Columbia which were now feasible opened the area to greater competition. Only in the pulp and paper and electric-power industries did the manufacturers of the maritime region of Canada gain a greater share of markets.[18]

Much of the expansion of the 1920s was based on the new efficiency and falling cost of energy inputs, particularly hydroelectric power. With low cost and easy transmission of power, wood and metal resources, investment linkages to other manufacturing sectors expanded enormously, as noted earlier. Much of the growth in manufacturing occurred from 1925 to 1929: gross domestic-capital formation neared $6 billion, only slightly less than the record high levels, and current GNP rose about 28 per cent—the wholesale price index actually declined. During the mid-1920s, the pulp and paper industry became by value of production the largest manufacturing industry in Canada. Its major sector, newsprint, expanded phenomenally. In each period 1913-20 and 1920-29, newsprint production tripled and by 1929 Canadian newsprint exports constituted about 65 per cent of the world total. Almost all Canadian exports were destined for the United States. The newsprint industry had actually expanded so rapidly that it created substantial excess capacity which was evident by 1929. Had there been no Depression after 1929 the industry would still have had to make major adjustments.[19]

Another important industry which dates its prosperity to the 1920s is the automobile sector. In terms of gross value of production, the automobile industry rose from eighth place in 1921 to fourth place in 1929 among Canada's manufacturing industries. Better roads, lower automobile and fuel prices, and rising incomes contributed to the increased demand, and, as well, Canada exported about one-third of domestic production. Throughout the 1920s, Canada was second only to the United States in the per-capita consumption of automobiles. Finally, the automobile linked up directly with the tourist trade, growing urban and suburban living—with its demands on construction and retail trades—and supplies such as refineries and parts manufacturers.

Despite the growth of manufacturing in the 1920s the prosperity was not universal; there were some signs of weakness. The agricultural sector had remained depressed throughout the early twenties and had only recovered in the later years of the decade. As seen earlier, the capital account had taken on a completely different profile in the aftermath of the First World War. Residential construction although rapid in the twenties had not yet adjusted to accommodate the population increase brought about by the waves of immigration in the prewar years. On the other hand, the construction of plant in many industries had gone well beyond the level sustainable in the short run. In addition, Great Britain, although no longer Canada's principal market but still a substantial one, was not expanding throughout most of the twenties. Then beginning in 1928 the international economy, as a whole, began to contract. By 1929, Canada along with most of the economies with whom trade took place, was entering a depression of totally unprecedented severity.

The Depression of the 1930s was so widespread that the economy in general, and manufacturing in particular, had barely recovered by 1939 its late 1920s momentum. During its contractionary phase, from 1929 to 1933, real GNP declined about 28.4 per cent while employment in manufacturing fell by one-fifth in the sixteen months prior to January 1931. Total exports declined almost immediately after the onset of the Depression and, indeed, constituted one of the major conditions responsible for its transmission as will be seen later in this chapter. The manner in which recovery began after 1934 was also principally through exports. However, exports recovered in such a way as to affect first the newer exporting regions of northern Ontario, Quebec, and British Columbia; exports of gold, other non-ferrous metals, pulp and paper, and lumber were considerably higher in 1937 than in 1929. But this type of recovery was not universal throughout the industry. Several major exports, by value, recovered more slowly: Animals and animal products, wood products, agricultural and vegetable products remained, even in 1939, well below pre-Depression levels. The general excess capacity in many sectors of manufacturing was evident, particularly in automobiles, steel, newsprint, and utilities. As a consequence, the recovery in real investment was slow relative to the recovery of output. By the beginning of the Second World War the structure of manufacturing in Canada had evolved little from its late 1920s pattern.[20]

During the period 1879-1939 the economy underwent a transformation. In terms of the manufacturing sector the transformation was that of absolute and relative growth as well as change *within* the various manufacturing sectors. Yet, there was surprisingly little structural alteration in the composition of manufacturing. Throughout, the effects of export-led growth transmitted themselves in a smooth fashion and there was no discontinuity associated with the emergence of the new staples. Nor does the National Policy tariff seem to have been instrumental in promoting manufacturing change. While the tariff protected many of the existing industries it appears to have had little effect in creating new ones and while output in Canada was higher than it would otherwise have been, the costs, in terms of efficiency, were undoubtedly borne by domestic consumers.

The New Commercial Order of the Post-1945 Economy

Attempts to protect manufacturing industries while negotiating bilateral tariff reductions, in order to provide markets for resource-intensive exports, were characteristic of Canadian commercial policy until after the Depression of the 1930s. In the vastly changed post-1945 economic conditions it took on new guises.[21] Of the changing framework within which commercial policy was set two circumstances predominated. First, Canada along with many other nations was a signatory to the General Agreement on Tariffs and Trade—GATT—by which Canada agreed to negotiate tariff reductions on a multinational basis. Second, the international environment in which Canada trades has been radically affected by the creation of economic unions or free-trade areas by other countries and the limited bilateral free-trade arrangements with the United States.

During the Second World War organizations and regular conferences were established to facilitate international trade. They were primarily precipitated by the glaring need to reduce the relatively high tariffs and non-tariff restrictions on trade introduced as a response to the Depression of the 1930s. All countries of Western Europe and North America erected substantial barriers to external trade during these years and exacerbated the widespread Depression rather than remedying it. Pledged never to react again with such beggar-my-neighbour policies, representatives from these countries met in 1946 and 1947 to formulate new rules for the international order. With respect to international trade, the creation of the GATT was the most important single result. It was intended that each member's trade policy be given a multinational basis instead of a bilateral one. Bilateral arrangements, such as those Canada initiated with the United Kingdom and the United States in the second half of the 1930s, were held to be too narrow in scope to spread equitably the strength of any recovery of trade and likely to lead to Depression. Multinational reductions in tariffs and other trade barriers could be accomplished in an orderly and just fashion through such an agency as GATT. Several principles were agreed upon but two were regarded as essential. First, in tariff negotiations, concessions granted to any individual country extended also to all other signatory countries; that is, most countries accepted the principle of the most-favoured-nation clause. Second, tariffs were only tolerated as a means of trade control and other trade barriers were to be gradually eliminated. The ambiguity of this last principle will not be lost on the reader. During subsequent years, but especially in 1947 and 1967, major tariff reductions, at least in nominal rates, were negotiated under these GATT principles. Because of its participation, Canada now has lower tariff rates than in 1939 which, in turn, were lower than those that prevailed just before the First World War.

Does the reduction in tariff rates mean that the degree of protection afforded Canadian manufacturing industry fell as a consequence of GATT? The answer is positive if the falling nominal rates also reflected falling effective rates. Information presented later in this section indicates that during the 1960s the effective rate of protection on many of Canada's manufactured products declined. But, on the other hand, tariff rates may have been higher than required; this depended on Canadian production costs relative to production costs elsewhere and, therefore, there may have been little or no effect because of an excess built into Canada's relatively high tariff rates of earlier decades. Successive cuts in nominal tariff rates ensures that the excess disappears, although the process can be protracted over many rounds of negotiations.

The period since the Second World War also witnessed the formation of a number of economic unions or free-trade areas of which the most important are the European Econonic Communities (EEC), the European Free Trade Association (EFTA), the Communist bloc countries, the Latin American Free Trade Association, and the Central American Common Market. Since all of these areas or unions discriminate in their tariff structure against non-member countries, is their formation not in contravention of GATT? An exception was made to the principle of non-discrimination. The framers of GATT argued that regional groupings could be compatible with multilateral trade negotiations when member countries recognize the desirability of increasing freedom of trade by the development of integrated economies and areas or unions which entail commitments, extending further than multilateral tariff reductions.

Since the creation of the EEC, Canadian exporters may have had more difficulty selling certain goods in the markets of Western Europe than formerly. As we have seen on several occasions before, both trade creation and trade diversion result from this kind of economic integration so that, for example, Canadian exporters to West Germany may find themselves at disadvantage in Europe, not because the treatment they receive is less favourable than before, but because the position of their competitors has improved. On balance, however, Canada's exports have not been very greatly affected by the formation of the EEC. Insofar as Canada's comparative advantage lies in agricultural and resource-based products and EEC tariffs against such products are relatively low, and even zero, they have been able to enter fairly freely. It has been estimated that if the EEC and EFTA had ended all discrimination against Canada in the early 1960s, Canada's exports would have risen by only about $223 million which would represent about 3 per cent of its total 1964 world trade flow. In comparison, the United States has been Canada's most important trading partner throughout the post-Second World War period, taking 56 per cent of its total exports in 1960.

Regional trade groupings raise a very interesting problem to commercial policy-makers. Canada has a comparative advantage in raw and processed consumer and industrial materials which generally receive favourable tariff treatment in foreign markets. In turn, Canada imports mainly manufactured goods and many sectors of its own manufacturing industry have received relatively high nominal and, probably, effective tariff protection since at least 1879. This being so, post-1946 tariff reductions gained Canada little in export markets yet promised to bring a large growth in imports, leading to a deterioration in the trade balance—the difference between commodity exports and imports. This is more clearly seen when effective rates on manufactured goods are examined. References have been made to effective tariff rates or changes in the effective rates in 1858-59 and 1879, but direct evidence is only available—or can be made available—for recent years, the 1960s. With these effective tariff rates it is now possible to analyse more fully their impact on the primary, tertiary, and manufacturing sectors.

Effective rates of protection in the primary and tertiary sectors, in the mid-1960s, as might be expected, were close to zero or even negative.[22] The sectors in which Canada has a comparative if not absolute advantage over its trading partners has seldom needed much protection in modern times. Services of the tertiary sector are, in addition, non-tradeable by their nature. In the manufacturing sector, however, while nominal rates of protection averaged about 12 per cent in the mid-1960s, effective rates were approximately 20 per cent. They ranged widely from about 2 per cent in transport equipment to over 48 per cent for petroleum and coal products. The manufacturing industries with the highest effective tariff rates were food and beverages, clothing and textiles, and petroleum and coal products but many others, such as furniture and fixtures, electrical and some chemical products also registered rates in excess of 20 per cent. Food and beverages and petroleum and coal products need special attention because they bear moderate tariffs on the finished product but relatively low tariffs on inputs. Clothing and textiles were protected differently with relatively high import duties on the finished product. Perhaps in contrast to the apogee of the National Policy, the primary metal industries had effective rates of only about 10

Table 12:4 Distribution of Manufactured Value Added, by Province, 1958-1974

(per cent)

Province	1958	1963	1974
(1)	(2)	(3)	(4)
Newfoundland	0.7	0.6	0.8
Prince Edward Island	0.07	0.09	0.08
Nova Scotia	1.6	1.5	1.7
New Brunswick	1.5	1.4	1.7
Quebec	30.3	29.1	27.2
Ontario	51.7	51.9	51.7
Manitoba	2.9	2.6	2.6
Saskatchewan	1.0	1.0	1.1
Alberta	2.5	3.2	3.8
British Columbia	7.7	8.6	9.4
Yukon and Northwest Territories	0.01	0.01	0.009
Total Value Added (thousands of dollars)	7,993,069	12,272,734	35,084,752

Source: *Manufacturing Industries of Canada,* various issues.

per cent. Therefore, in the drive for freer trade in manufacturing, the sectors most affected are those which currently enjoy the highest degree of effective protection. When the manufacturing sector itself is viewed by its primary — 50 per cent of the inputs come from the primary sector of the Canadian economy — and secondary components the nominal tariff rates in the latter are about twice those in the former but the degree of effective protection is similar. In primary manufacturing effective protection is high because import duties on inputs were low.

With regard to the geographic distribution of manufacturing, the post-1945 era was one of relative stability. The earlier trend toward central Canada was halted. As seen in Table 12:4 from the provincial distribution of value added in manufacturing, Ontario remained dominant with slightly greater than one-half of all of the economy's manufacturing capability. In relative terms both Alberta and British Columbia expanded on the basis of intensive natural-resource exploitation but even here the changes were trifling. Similarly, the apparent decline in the relative contribution of Quebec's manufacturing industries was of insufficient magnitude to constitute a trend. Nor does it appear that, in relative terms, development programs of the federal government have increased manufacturing output in maritime Canada. This geographic stability among provinces of manufacturing masks some important geographic shifts within provinces as will be seen in Chapter 13. Nevertheless, at the regional level the structure of manufacturing changed little in the post-war era.

During the middle and late 1960s significant tariff revisions occurred during the so-called Kennedy Round of GATT negotiations. In addition Canada and the United States signed the Automotive Agreement in 1965 which took both countries far down the path to a free trade in automobiles and their parts among producers. As a consequence of these developments the manufacturing sector had lower nominal and effective rates at the end of the 1960s than at the start. After the Automotive Agreement, effective rates on motor vehicles and motor vehicle parts became almost zero. In only a few manufacturing industries did policymakers reverse the trend: dairy factories, fish products, shoe factories, printing and publishing, copper fabrication, petroleum, and coal products. Effective rates in all clothing and textile industries and in most food and beverage industries fell, but many still had rates in excess of 20 per cent.

This dramatic reduction in the degree of effective protection to the Canadian automobile industry had its foundation in what was a rare act, an agreement between Canada and another country, in this case the United States, for the reduction of tariff barriers. The only precedent was the earlier free trade agreement between the two countries with respect to agricultural machinery. This agreement was the product of several forces and the long frustration at the inactivity of the GATT negotiations of the time. In the first place, it was argued that for some products the North American market was separate from markets in the rest of the world so that the granting most-favoured nation status to non-participating countries would only slightly affect markets in Canada and the United States. Also, many Canadian manufacturers realized that multilateral tariff reductions were occurring too slowly and were too uncertain to provide them with the incentive needed to change production patterns from multi-product ones for the Canadian market to more specialized production for a larger world market. The net result was the Canada-United States Automotive Agreement of 1965. Its significance lies in the adjustments caused by the substantial reduction in the rate of effective protection.

By the 1920s the main structure of the current Canadian automobile industry was firmly in place with domination by the "Big Three", substantial foreign investment, and a great variety of models and styles of automobiles. The Ford Motor Company entered Canada in 1904, General Motors took over a Canadian-owned firm in 1918, and the Chrysler Corporation of Canada was incorporated in 1925. Production of about 100,000 automobiles and trucks in 1918 expanded to over 260,000 units by 1929. Canada's production was second only to the United States and was greater than that of the United Kingdom, France, and Germany and the growth took place behind high nominal tariffs against imports from the United States—35 per cent—and British Commonwealth preferences. Both tariff devices encouraged foreign firms to establish production facilities in Canada rather than export their products to Canada. While the tariff was lowered to 27.5 per cent in 1926, production continued to expand behind this barrier plus the special duty drawbacks. In 1936 the duty rate was reduced further to 17.5 per cent for most-favoured nations and to zero under the British Preferential Tariff and automotive parts were admitted free as long as certain "content" requirements were met. Because of the depressed economic conditions of the 1930s and the onset of war in 1939, it is difficult to measure the effect of this reduced protection on the industry, but by 1939 Canada faced competition from the automobile exporting nations of Western Europe as well as from the United States.

After reaching a peak in production during the Korean War the Canadian automobile industry entered what can only be called a period of stagnation between 1955 and 1961 as yearly production fell by 15 per cent, while imports rose by a staggering 31 per cent. By 1960 almost 40 per cent of all automobiles sold in Canada were manufactured abroad. The magnitude of this change prompted the federal government to appoint a Royal Commissioner, Vincent Bladen, to study the plight of the industry.[23] He recommended various tariff and content requirements which would have more closely integrated Canadian and U.S. production. The choices available at the time (the early 1960s) appeared to be twofold: integrate more closely with the United States or rationalize production for the Canadian market. Bladen's recommendations were not implemented, but in 1962 and 1963 the federal government instituted two duty-remission plans—like export bounties—which caused difficulties because under the GATT rules the United States was required to impose countervailing duties. This more or less forced the United States to enter into bilateral discussions with Canada out of which emerged the Automotive Agreement.

The agreement sought to rationalize the production of automobiles in North America by greatly reducing barriers to trade in vehicles and their parts.[24] But while the United States agreed to permit unconditional duty-free Canadian automobile imports, Canada insisted on certain guarantees for the Canadian domestic industry, in particular that Canadian production remain above the dollar value of automobiles and parts produced in Canada and above the ratio of production in the auto industry to sale of North American cars sold in Canada in 1964.

These safeguards were expected to assure stability in Canada's assembly and parts industries, but they provided for no absolute growth. For this, the federal government obtained assurances from the Canadian automobile subsidiaries that they would expand domestic production over the next three years in return for partial relief from the import duties. Over the first half dozen or so years of the agreement it had dramatic effects on Canadian vehicle assembly parts and accessories production. In the absence of the agreement, the value added in parts and assembly would have risen less dramatically than it did; the same is true for employment in the parts industry, although employment at the assembly stage appears to have been unaffected. Average hourly earnings also rose about 6 per cent as a consequence of the agreement. But the most striking effect occurred in trade flows. In 1961, the assembly operation exported 2.3 per cent of total Canadian production, while the parts sector exported about 6 per cent; by 1970, the respective figures were 77.8 and 69.6 per cent. Although imports into Canada from the United States also increased, the trade deficit against Canada in the entire automobile industry was reduced. The overall impact of the agreement on the Canadian economy cannot be accurately gauged, but it served to raise the gross national product. This integration of North American automobile production forced the Canadian industry to be more efficient; this followed from the reductions in number of vehicle models produced and the higher volumes for specific lines. On the negative side, while the difference in the factory list price of automobiles narrowed between 1965 and 1969—with price always higher in Canada—the differential then widened to at least 1972. This may have been caused by the safeguards in the agreement which in a sense give non-tariff protection to the domestic industry. Only licensed dealers may import automobiles free of duty.

Any major change in the agreement would have a relatively larger effect on the Canadian industry, which was reorganized and expanded after 1965 to attain scale economies, than the U.S. industry. It was relatively efficient at the time of the agreement and so changed little. In a real sense Canadian dependence on decisions made in the United States rose. In the labour market, the United Automobile Workers now negotiate a single contract which covers both countries, and they may have a stake in seeing that not many jobs in the industry migrate to Canada. In general, the agreement fits well with some traditional commercial-policy characteristics and in particular attaches Canada to a large market.

A certain pattern of commercial policy emerged in the period 1946 to the 1970s, premised on the fact that Canada is the only major industrial country without ready access to a large market for all its manufactured products—the Western European countries founded the EEC and Japan and the United States have large domestic markets. Partly to overcome this problem, Canada negotiated special trade arrangements with the United States—for example, the auto pact and defence-production-sharing arrangements—and defended the continuation of the Commonwealth preferential system. Finally, Canada's import duties, being higher than those in most of the so-called industrialized countries, may be classified as protective duties. The appropriateness is far from evident although some have advocated the establishment of a free trade and/or customs union between Canada and the United States. Equally vocal have been others who argue that such a policy would totally undermine Canadian-based manufacturing and bring Canada entirely within the economic and political jurisdiction of the United States.[25]

In the early nineteenth century the Canadian economy was profoundly altered as the export of staples stimulated the creation of a commercial economy. Later, staples provided the impetus for rapid structural change based on the growth of manufacturing. This was most evident in the mid-nineteenth century and the period from approximately 1896 to 1929. The twenty-five years after 1946, however, rivalled any early economic transformation. Real domestic product increased at an annual average rate of 4.8 per cent compounded. The more than threefold increase of real output which such a growth rate represents was accompanied by increases in industrial production averaging no less than 5.8 per cent. Like earlier periods of rapid economic change that of the post-1945 era was one of marked alterations in the structure of the economy, the manner in which it responded to external pressures, and in its absorption of international flows of savings and labour.

Representative of the pace and economic change in the post-1945 period was the rapid expansion of manufacturing activity in Ontario and Quebec, the development of new non-ferrous metal resources, the first major exploitation of iron-ore reserves, the appearance and extensive growth of new industries, such as petroleum and natural gas, and the construction of major new transport systems like the St. Lawrence Seaway which opened the Great Lakes to ocean-going vessels. Some of these developments had antecedents in the previous periods of growth and some were entirely new. Many of the new manufacturing industries grew so rapidly in the immediate postwar years that by the early 1950s they were firmly established as manufacturing industries of major importance. The petroleum and petro-chemicals industries are typical; their growth was fuelled by the new oil discoveries in Alberta, the vigorously expanding demand brought about by the return of peace without recession and the onset of the Korean War.

Table 12:5 Ten Leading Manufacturing Industries, Ranked by Value of Factory Shipments, 1954-1974

1954	1964	1974
(1)	(2)	(3)
1. Pulp & paper	Pulp & paper	Pulp & paper
2. Non-ferrous metal smelting & refining	Motor Vehicles	Motor Vehicles
3. Petroleum products	Petroleum products	Petroleum products
4. Slaughtering & Meatpacking	Slaughtering & Meatpacking	Slaughtering & Meatpacking
5. Motor Vehicles	Iron & Steel Mills	Iron & Steel Mills
6. Sawmills	Dairy products	Sawmills
7. Butter & Cheese	Sawmills	Motor Vehicle parts
8. Primary iron & steel	Smelting & refining	Dairy products
9. Aircraft & parts	Misc. Machinery & Equipment	Misc. Machinery & Equipment
10. Misc. food preparations	Motor Vehicle parts	Smelting & refining

Source: *Manufacturing Industries of Canada*, various issues.

Yet, despite the rapidity of growth in these new industries from 1946 to 1954 the structure of manufacturing took on very stable features thereafter. This is clearly evident for manufacturing in Table 12:5 which shows the dominant role still occupied by natural-resource-based industries accounting for about half of the top ten manufacturing industries. To be sure there was not complete stability; the automobile industry under the aegis of the United States-Canada Automotive Agreement expanded rapidly in the 1960s and in recent years smelting and refining have become less important. While export-led growth might still stimulate economic growth, as it did secularly during the 1950s and 1960s, it no longer induced much change in the overall structure of manufacturing (see Table 12:6). This, of course, is not to assert that new products and new types of manufacturing activity did not emerge, they did. Rather, the changes took place for the most part within the existing structure. Indeed, in the very broad perspective, the power of staple booms to alter the structure of manufacturing became successively weaker as the economy became more complex. The power of the staple was to increase the strength of inter-industry linkages as much as it was to change them.[26]

Instability, Growth, and Dependence
The persistence of trends in economic behaviour over long periods of time is only as remarkable as the many variations from these trends. At

Table 12:6 Distribution of Manufactured Value Added, by Industry Group, 1958-1974

(per cent)

Industry Group	1958	1963	1974
(1)	(2)	(3)	(4)
Food and Beverages	16.0	15.5	12.7
Tobacco Products	1.0	1.1	0.9
Rubber Products	1.9	1.6	2.7
Leather Products	1.3	1.3	0.8
Textile Products	3.4	4.0	3.2
Knitting Mills	0.9	0.9	0.8
Clothing Products	3.7	3.5	2.8
Wood Products	4.4	4.7	4.9
Furniture and Fixtures	1.7	1.7	2.0
Paper and Allied Products	9.7	9.6	11.1
Printing-Publishing	5.3	5.1	4.8
Primary Metals	10.8	8.1	8.1
Metal Fabricating	7.1	7.5	8.6
Machinery Products	2.9	3.7	4.5
Transport Equipment	9.2	9.1	10.0
Electrical Products	5.8	6.4	6.3
Non-Metallic Minerals Products	3.7	3.7	3.7
Petroleum and Coal Products	1.9	2.3	2.8
Chemical and Chemical Products	6.8	7.1	6.7
Miscellaneous	2.6	3.2	2.8

Source: *Manufacturing Industries of Canada*, various issues.

no time were they more evident than the interwar years of 1918-39. Even in the long run, as seen earlier in this chapter, economic development was never achieved at a steady pace. Accelerated economic progress was often followed by a relative decline in, say, rates of growth of real income per capita. Of course, some trends behave differently. Crude birth rates fell to their present stable, low level. The decline in the aggregate capital-output ratio in recent years has been very slight and very smooth. Yet, there are many measures of economic performance which display instability both for long- and short-run periods. Much of this instability appears linked to what are asserted to be regular fluctuations or cycles in economic behaviour.

Economic cycles are often held to be endemic in economies which developed under conditions of market capitalism. It is the nature of how markets clear that cycles are generated. Whether such exclusivity can be substantiated or not, it is certain that economies such as Canada's were subjected to economic forces which behaved in cyclical fashions. For instance, in Chapter 9 it was observed that the international capital flows of the late nineteenth and early twentieth centuries followed a cyclical pattern. The identification of aggregate cycles is however a complex matter. First, since there is no single economic indicator which satisfactorily describes the economy or its performance, a composite description must be attempted. Second, not all of the suggested types of cycles can be confirmed by the historical evidence with equal ease. Before going on to examine the various types of cycles, however the basic components of cycles must be recalled.[27]

Each individual cycle is composed of several components. The one commonly used to define the cycle is its length or *period*. Its duration is taken from peak to subsequent peak. The greater the period of the cycle, the less its *frequency*, which records the number of completed cycles over a fixed interval of time. Long-swings have a lower frequency but longer period than business cycles. Apart from information on the duration of cycles, a measure of how much a cyclical peak or trough departs from economic normality is also required in order to judge the buoyancy of the upturn or the severity of the downturn in economic performance being monitored. The *amplitude* of the cycle provides this measure (see Figure 12:1) at either the peak or the trough. Between amplitudes, the cycle moves through four distinct *phases*: I—the decelerating upswing; II—the accelerating downswing; III—the decelerating downswing; and IV—the accelerating upswing. Although no cycles in economic behaviour were the exact replica of predecessors, all had similar components.

In Canadian history there is strong evidence of three types of cyclical economic fluctuations:

1) the long-swing, or Kuznets cycle, usually of thirteen- to twenty-five-years' duration. Long-swings are most clearly evident in the economy of the nineteenth century and up until the outbreak of the First World War. Long-swing activity in the economy of more recent times seems, however, doubtful;
2) the business cycle, usually with a period of thirteen months to about seven years. These cycles have prevailed throughout most of modern industrial history, and perhaps earlier, and although government intervention with the appropriate fiscal and monetary policies may have dampened their effect there has been no lessening of the presence of business cycle activity; and
3) the seasonal fluctuations related to the annual weather cycle which influences both supply and demand for natural resources, construction, and other economic activities altered by climatic change. Typically, seasonal fluctuations have been greater in Canada than in its trading partners.

Figure 12:1 Cycles in Economic Behaviour

Amplitude

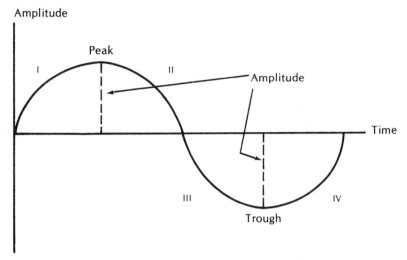

Note: The roman numerals represent the various parts of the cycle (see text).
The axis measuring the period of the cycle should be adjusted to incorporate
any underlying trend in the economy.

These three do not exhaust the period fluctuations in the economy. Some
observers have claimed evidence of cycles of approximately twenty-five
to fifty years' duration; others see shorter wave-like variations. Such
claims highlight two distinct problems. First, there is no economic theory
of cycles. Lacking any theoretical guidance, the existence of periodic
fluctuations can only be verified after repeated observation. Second,
satisfactory proof of very long cycles requires long reporting of
economic data uninterrupted by shocks to the economic system, such as
war or prolonged drought. Thus, searching history for periodic fluctuations is much like searching Loch Ness for monsters; the observers of a
single hump should not be surprised if scepticism still remains.

Long-swings in economic performance were an important pre-1914
phenomenon. The basis for such periodic fluctuations lay in the
geographic expansion of the world's economic frontiers, the movement
of goods and factors associated with the expansion, and the central role
played by Great Britain in the international capital market. Not surprisingly, when few geographic frontiers remained and when Great Britain's
ability to export capital contra-cyclically with domestic investment was
restricted, in the aftermath of the First World War, the moment for long-
swings was gone. Some features of frontier development, particularly

railway construction and the provision of other social-overhead capital, proved to be lumpy and discontinuous. Having suddenly increased the number of potentially profitable investment opportunities, the frontier expansion inevitably slowed down only to be quickened once again when, from a world point of view, the frontier was again shifted. Once the geographic frontiers were no longer pushed back discontinuously one of the principal sources of instability giving rise to the long-swings of the nineteenth- and early twentieth-century economies was gone.[28]

In the case of the long-swings, there is no convincing evidence to demonstrate that they survived the passing of the particular economic circumstances of the pre-1914 international economy. On the other hand, business cycles have proven resistant to a whole variety of structural changes in the domestic and international economies and are as prevalent today as they were over one hundred years ago. For instance, in the first half of the nineteenth century, the timber and wheat economies of British North America were intimately linked with the performance of the British economy. Building activity there, usually itself cyclical in nature, exercised the single strongest influence over timber prices and through the international transmission of price changes the domestic economy reacted. As the domestic economy began to diversify and as additional markets were found for Canadian produce in the United States, the responsiveness of staple outputs to cyclical economic activity in Great Britain began to weaken. However, the movements in the economy described by the business cycle were more than simply variations in staple outputs.

The best definition of the business cycle is achieved by the use of the so-called "reference cycle" which attempts to capture as many indicators of business and general economic activity as feasible. Peaks in the cycle, as well as troughs, are a consensus of the peaks or troughs displayed by the individual economic indicators. The reference cycle monitoring the performance of the Canadian economy confirms that business cycles have existed from at least Confederation. Also, the frequency of this cycle has changed little over the past century. As may be judged from Table 12:7, the average duration of Canadian business cycles during the period 1873-1961 was about 49 months. However, the expansionary phases of the business cycle—I and IV in Figure 12:1— tended to be much more prolonged than the contractionary phases, by about 3 to 2 on average. Business cycles were not a perfectly symmetrical periodic fluctuation of the economy.[29]

No single business cycle in modern history had a more profound effect on the pace of economic growth than that which spanned the greater part of the 1930s. The Depression which was traced out by this cycle (see

Table 12:7) was almost catastrophic in proportions. In the few years from the height of prosperity in 1929 to the depth of the Depression four years later GNP fell by almost 30 per cent. Although the economy began to recover in early 1934, the subsequent growth of output was slow. Impeded by a short recession in 1937-38 GNP had just reached the level of pre-Depression prosperity in 1939. By then the demand effects of a country preparing for war were beginning to be felt. The intervening years were ones of retrenchment for the economy.

The origins of the Depression of the 1930s lay not so much within Canada as in the whole fabric of the international economy.[30] After the Treaty of Versailles very few of the stabilizing features of the pre-1914 international order reasserted themselves. Great Britain defended an overvalued currency in an attempt to re-establish the gold standard and was no longer in a position to export capital as it had previously done. Similarly, the United States, whose balance of payments had not reached the mature stage of a capital exporter, was unable to substitute for Great Britain as a world lender. Furthermore, the war had left a vast and complex structure of war debts, including reparation payments by Germany, which left the international capital flows precariously balanced. It was also apparent, even by the 1920s, that the expansion of the international economy into new frontier areas in the pre-1914 epoch of development in Canada and elsewhere had given rise to a general excess supply of primary products. The prices of these commodities began to fall. Thus, when the stock markets in the United States crashed as stock prices fell dramatically in 1920s this was followed almost immediately by the same reaction in Toronto. It was a symptom rather than a cause of the instability in the world economy.

The initial effects of the Depression were transmitted to Canada in a variety of ways. As expectations about economic performance in the United States fell, so they fell in Canada. The realignment of world currencies, which was unsuccessfully carried out in the immediate post-1929 years, further exacerbated the pessimism about the economic climate. Monetary forces, as seen in Chapter 8, also played a role transmitting the depressing effects. However, probably no single element of the transmission mechanism was as critical to the spread of the depression as the foreign trade sector.

The fall in Canadian exports was as dramatic as it was unprecedented. In the first three years of the contraction exports declined by 57.6 per cent in value and 32.1 per cent in real terms. Canada was not alone in experiencing such a decline. Global trade fell every quarter from 1929 to mid-1934. The openness of the Canadian economy meant that it was especially vulnerable to the decline in income elsewhere being trans-

Table 12:7 Canadian Reference Cycle, 1870-1961

Peak (P) Trough (T)	Dates	Lead (-) or lag (+) in months of Canadian reference dates to comparable data of U.S.A.
(1)	(2)	(3)
P	11/73	+ 1
T	5/79	+ 2
P	7/82	+ 4
T	3/85	- 2
P	2/87	- 1
T	2/88	- 2
P	7/90	0
T	3/91	- 2
P	2/93	+ 1
T	3/94	- 3
P	8/95	- 4
T	8/96	-10
P	4/00	+10
T	2/01	+ 2
P	12/02	+ 3
T	6/04	- 2
P	12/06	- 5
T	7/08	- 1
P	3/10	+ 2
T	7/11	- 6
P	11/12	- 2
T	1/15	+ 1
P	1/18	- 7
T	4/19	+ 1
P	6/20	+ 5

mitted through the foreign-trade sector. But it was not falling incomes alone which led to the fall in Canada's exports. Many of the country's trading partners embarked on a beggar-my-neighbour tariff policy. The United States in particular led the rush to erect obstacles to trade which resulted in the highest tariffs in that country's history. The Smoot-Hawley tariff of 1930 was designed to protect both the U.S. manufacturing and primary producing sectors; all classes of Canadian exports were thus affected. Canada, for its part, enacted the Bennett tariffs.[31]

How much of the decline in exports was due to the increased tariffs against Canadian goods and how much was due to falling income in the United States is impossible to gauge. Nevertheless, exports to the United States fell and they fell by a greater amount than those to Great Britain. Of Canada's two major trading partners Great Britain suffered least from the Depression; real income actually rose by a modest amount (see Table

Table 12:7 Continued

Peak (P) Trough (T)	Dates	Lead (-) or lag (+) in months of Canadian reference dates to comparable data of U.S.A.
T	9/21	+ 2
P	6/23	+ 1
T	8/24	+ 1
P	a	—
T	a	—
P	4/29	- 4
T	3/33	0
P	7/37	+ 2
T	10/38	+ 4
P	a	—
T	2/46	+ 4
P	10/48	- 1
T	9/49	- 1
P	5/53	- 2
T	6/54	- 2
P	4/57	- 3
T	4/58	0
P	1/60	- 4
T	3/61	+ 1

Note: "a" indicates no Canadian equivalent of U.S. cycle. Data from Chambers and Hay—see bibliography.

Source: K. A. Hay, "Early Twentieth Century Business Cycles in Canada", *Canadian Journal of Economics and Political Science*, Vol. 32, no. 3 (1966), p. 362.

12:8). Overall there was a close correspondence with the United States from where the Depression spread to Canada. How much worse the decline in exports would have been without the British market is conjecture. Nevertheless, the Empire Conferences of the 1930s, which were convened to promote mutual assistance among members by the lowering of tariffs, gave Canadian goods access to the only relatively buoyant market of the times.

On the other hand, exports during the upturn of the cycle after 1933 did not have as immediate an impact on the recovery as they had had on the downturn. Internationally there was no significant abandonment of the high tariff policies pursued by most nations apart from those negotiated within the British Empire. World trade recovered very slowly. But domestically even the slow increase in exports did not give rise to any significant derived demand for investment. The excess capacity, evi-

Table 12:8 Indicators of Business Activity in Canada and Its Major Trading Partners, 1929-1933

Indicator	Percentage Changes		
	Canada	U.K.	U.S.A.
(1)	(2)	(3)	(4)
National Income[a]	−48.8	−10.0	−51.6
Real National Income[a]	−34.0	+ 6.4	−34.9
Industrial Production	−39.6	−18.3	−36.1
Mineral Production	−10.2	−13.2	−28.7
Electric Power Generation	− 3.4	+ 45.5	−12.3
Freight Carloadings	−42.5	—	−45.8
Farm Production	− 2.8	—	− 4.0
Residential Construction	−81.5	+ 40.8	−87.4
Non-residential Construction	−83.6	−25.9	−73.9
Manufacturing: Consumers' Goods	−15.7	−10.0	−24.5
Manufacturing: Producers' Goods	−52.5	−29.9	−43.8
Employment	−29.9	−10.6	−30.8
Wholesale Prices	−29.8	−26.1	−30.7

[a] refers to net national income since comparable measures of GNP are not available for all three countries. As noted in the text the decline of nominal GNP in Canada was −42.8 per cent and that of real GNP −29.8 per cent.

Source: V. W. Malach, *International Cycles and Canada's Balance of Payments, 1921-33* (Toronto, 1954), p. 91.

dent in most industries even in the 1920s, was simply reduced. Consequently, the building of plant in response to increased exports failed to materialize. The transmission mechanism of cyclical behaviour between countries had changed.

The transmission of business-cycle activity in general was part of a wider world pattern and Canada's economy tended to vascillate in sympathy with that of its trading partners. In the early nineteenth century, the source was Great Britain; later, the source was the U.S. economy. Over the past one hundred years, most business cycles in the United States have had a Canadian equivalent—more so than Great Britain with Canada. Furthermore, U.S. business cycles predate or antedate Canadian ones much more closely than the British and Canadian reference cycles. That is, the two cycles were closely *in phase* or matched with respect to the peaks and troughs. Nevertheless, the relationship between the business cycles of Canada and the United States was not always a completely synchronized one. For instance, there are a few cycles in Canada which have no counterpart in the U.S. economy (see Table 12:7). Also, it is evident from the individual indicators of economic performance that some cycles were more, and some less, severe in Canada than the United States.

The reference cycle measuring the period cannot be employed to measure the amplitude of the business cycle because it is simply a method of calculating the duration of an amalgam of indicators. However, individual measures, such as imports, do provide the comparison. They record that the downswing in the mid-1880s was, for instance, much less severe in Canada than in the United States due of course to the income-creating effects of the railway-construction expenditures. Also, it is apparent that the behaviour of exports, particularly agricultural ones, has been such that they have often offset or dampened other effects, that is, agricultural exports were often contra-cyclical. This was especially true in the early 1890s. In addition, the instability of the monetary base was less important in influencing Canadian flucuations than elsewhere. From a variety of economic indicators, and the amplitudes they recorded, it is apparent that the relationship between the Canadian and U.S. business cycle has often itself varied in a systematic manner. While Canadian cycles display dependence on the U.S. economy, in the proximity of peaks and troughs in the relevant reference cycles, that relationship varied with intensity; high amplitudes in one country are not necessarily associated with high ones in the other. A comparison of amplitudes of cycles in specific economic monitors of behaviour — building contracts started, imports, railway car loadings, and others — indicate that the relationship between the United States and Canada increased in intensity between 1900 and 1920, and has declined in intensity since the 1930s. This decreasing cyclical sensitivity recorded later in the twentieth century was a product of the changing method of transmission of cycles from the United States to Canada and the changing nature of the relationship between Canadian regions.[32]

It is necessary before proceeding to recall to mind that Canada is more a collection of regional economies than a single, homogeneous one. The reference cycle or the measure presented by any individual indicator is also an aggregate across regions. It may be inappropriate to gauge from their variations movements in the economy at large because they disguise information. For example, if there were only two regions and if, say, the exports of one were cyclically out of phase with those of the other, the resulting aggregate measure would demonstrate less cyclical variation than either of its components. Further, if the regional cycles were of equal amplitude and completely out of phase — the peak of one corresponding with the trough of the other — the national economy would display, through the indicator, no cyclical fluctuations whatsoever. Yet, it would be inaccurate to describe the economy as being without business-cycle movements.

The fact that the various regions in Canada historically behaved as different economies, stimulated and retarded, in part, by different external forces, suggests that the transmission mechanism of cycles in economic behaviour was complex. First, the impetus for a cycle may be endogenous and transferred from one region to another. Second, and more likely, the impetus for a cycle originated outside of Canada and was transferred to all regions of Canada simultaneously, or transferred to one region of Canada and subsequently spread to the others. Clearly, the overall Canadian response to any cyclical fluctuation in the United States may owe as much to the relationship between the regions of Canada as anything. Moments of cyclical instability were transmitted, between the regions or between the countries by very similar mechanisms. Real trade flows, not surprisingly, were important but not the only methods of transfer. Investment, capital flows, the effects of prices, and interest-rate behaviour have also proven to be important linkages transmitting the periodic fluctuations.[33]

The simpler the regional economy the more closely all indicators of economic performance move together. On the other hand, the more complex the regional economy, the greater the dispersion of, say, peaks of indicators. Round-aboutness dissipated some of the inital force of the cyclical movement throughout the greater length of lags in the complex system. For instance, for Canada as a whole in the interwar years of 1920-39, fluctuations in employment lagged behind fluctuations in imports. While this may be so for the regions of Ontario and Quebec, for individual regions the degree of correspondence between the deflationary effect of imports and employment was high. In British Columbia, for example as seen in Figure 12:2, imports, employment, new building starts, among other indicators, all peaked and troughed together. They were perfectly in phase. The prairie economy, too, usually displayed business-cycle activity less synchronized with the rest of the country than any other single region.[34]

Concentration of Industry

As manufacturing industries grew and evolved so some firms established market positions which were superior to others. In the first instance, market power is the firm's ability to control price which is itself related to the number of substitutes there are for the firm's output. If a few large firms account for a large proportion of an entire industry's output the industry is said to be "concentrated". If there are relatively few firms there is scope for explicit and implicit collusion between the firms to attempt control of prices. Concentration is only an indicator of the potential use of market power. There are many factors which might produce concentration in an industry; some of these were discussed in Chapter 9. To reiterate, they include government regulations, the firm's goals, barriers

**Figure 12:2 Regional and National Cycles, 1920-1939
(without regard to individual amplitudes)**

Amplitude

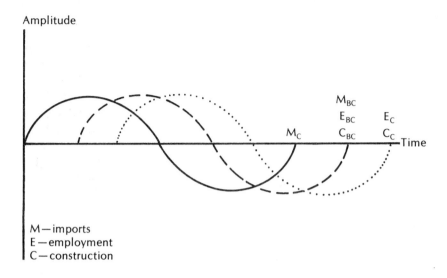

M_{BC}
E_{BC} E_C
M_C C_{BC} C_C
Time

M — imports
E — employment
C — construction

The subscripts C and BC indicate Canada, excluding British Columbia, and British Columbia, respectively. These cyclical fluctuations are based on business cycles of approximately 4.5 years' duration. See L. Blain, D. G. Paterson, and J. D. Rae, "The Regional Impact of Economic Fluctuations During the Inter-War Period: The Case of British Columbia", *Canadian Journal of Economics*, Vol. VII, no. 3 (1974):387.

to entry, the type of product being produced and, in the case of an open economy, the desire of a foreign company to establish a superior market position abroad by monopolizing a source of natural-resource inputs in Canada.

The evidence suggests that the manufacturing sector as a whole did become more concentrated in the late nineteenth and early twentieth centuries.[35] In 1890, about 63 per cent of manufacturing value added was produced by 2,879 plants. By 1922, about 66 per cent of manufacturing value added was produced by only 936 plants. Although there was no necessarily direct correspondence between the number of plants and the number of firms it is likely that overall concentration increased. During the interwar period there was no marked change in the degree of concentration but during the Second World War it increased yet again. This was followed by a rapid decline so that by 1948 the degree of plant concentration was actually below the level of the interwar years. From this variable long-run trend, it is evident that apart from "true" concentration changes within industries there are other factors which influence the size distribution of firms. Shifts in the relative size of industries with high and low concentration might account for part of the aggregate as does the distribution of average plant sizes in different industries.

The complexity of the shifts in concentration is well illustrated by an examination of some of the sub-periods within the years 1922 to 1948. Since concentration declined slightly from 1922 to 1929 and the relative importance to total output of some high concentration industries rose — automobiles, railway rolling stock — it can be concluded that there was a fall in plant concentration within industries. On the other hand, the substantial rise in plant concentration from 1939 to 1943 was due in large measure to shifts in the relative importance of war-related and highly concentrated industries — aircraft and shipbuilding, for instance. From 1943 to 1948, the decline in overall plant concentration reflected both a shift from wartime to peacetime with its trend towards less concentrated consumer-goods industries and a fall in concentration within industries with a general expansion of demand. As already noted, plant concentration was lower in 1948 than in 1922. Since the relative importance of highly concentrated industries to total output rose, plant concentration within industries fell over the period.

In recent times the trend in concentration once again reversed itself. For the forty manufacturing industries which are directly comparable in 1948 and 1964-65, the percentage of total value added by industries with twelve or fewer of the largest enterprises accounting for 80 per cent of factory shipments increased from 32.4 to 41.2 per cent. The number of industries with twenty-four or more of the largest enterprises accounting for 80 per cent of factory shipments declined slightly. There was clearly an increase in manufacturing-enterprise concentration. So too, in the mining industry, over the same period, the level of concentration was high. It was, in fact, more highly concentrated than manufacturing. Nevertheless, between 1950 and 1964, some mineral sectors maintained high concentration levels — potash, nickel, molybdenum, lead, iron ore; some experienced increased concentration — uranium, gypsum, coal; and some experienced reduced concentration — copper, asbestos, cement, crude petroleum.

Even in the service industries there were significant changes in concentrations. For instance, in the mass-communications industry, the concentration of ownership has become a problem. The number of urban areas served by more than two daily newspapers declined; in 1900, eighteen such areas had more than two papers, but by 1970 this had fallen to only five. In 1900, sixty-six daily newspapers were published in eighteen towns and cities with more than two newspapers; by 1958, fourteen out of ninety-nine daily newspapers were published in four cities with more than two newspapers. In comparison, in 1970, of 116 daily newspapers, about two-thirds were group-owned. That is, they were bought by a firm or individual who already controlled another newspaper, radio, or television station. In the television and radio broadcasting industry, ownership concentration was lower than for newspapers. Of 97 television stations, about 49 per cent were group-owned in 1970; the corresponding percentage for radio stations was 48. Of 485 units of mass communication in Canada for that year—newspapers, radio, and television stations—about half were part of an ownership groups across media types with highest concentrations in Quebec and British Columbia, and lowest concentrations in the Atlantic provinces and Manitoba.

The concentration of ownership within the daily newspapers raises the question of whether or not market power was reflected in price effects. In theory, the price per capita of newspaper space might be expected to vary inversely with the media competition if market power is being exercised providing there were no overriding factors. At least in the early 1970s television competition—a television station in the same city as the newspaper—and newspaper competition—at least one other daily paper published in the same language in the city—both significantly lowered the per-capita price of newspaper space. This supports the hypothesis that newspapers exercise some market power. But of course concentration in a highly sensitive industry which controls flows of information may well have a social cost beyond the realm of the private costs.

A variety of factors may contribute to changes in the general level of industrial concentration.[36] In addition, the merging or consolidation of firms often gave impetus to heightened industrial concentrations. As indicated in Table 12:9, there were three major periods between 1900 to 1961 during which mergers of firms took place rapidly. The merger movement of the later 1920s was one of the most intense. Almost two-thirds of all mergers between 1900 and 1948 occurred in the four years after 1924. Earlier, 1909-13, a similar movement exercised an important influence on Canadian industry with many consolidations taking place in the coal, iron and steel, pulp and paper, packing, and canning sectors. Third, the years 1959 to 1968 also witnessed a substantial increase in the number of mergers. By this later period, however, the relative importance of mergers had declined because of the growth of Canadian industry as a whole. In general, the effect of mergers on industrial concentration declined substantially over the long run.[37]

Despite the diminished impact of mergers, industrial concentration remains high in Canada. For instance, in most industries the degree of

Table 12:9 Mergers, Variously Defined, 1900-1961

Year	Consolida- tions	Enterprises Absorbed	Year	Consolida- tion	Enterprises Absorbed
(1)	(2)	(3)	(4)	(5)	(6)
1900	3	5	1925	31	79
1901	3	10	1926	33	69
1902	2	45	1927	46	86
1903	1	4	1928	87	179
1904	3	3	1929	74	148
1905	7	27	1930	44	74
1906	10	21	1931	26	37
1907	5	10	1932	16	16
1908	3	7	1933	18	21
1909	10	40	1934	14	19
1910	25	73	1935	16	22
1911	28	46	1936	12	16
1912	22	37	1937	9	11
1913	12	25	1938	13	16
1914	2	7	1939	10	13
1915	7	8	1940	7	8
1916	9	9	1941	6	6
1917	9	11	1942	12	12
1918	4	5	1943	18	21
1919	13	21	1944	25	29
1920	15	16	1945	30	56
1921	5	7	1946	32	49
1922	9	9	1947	16	20
1923	18	52	1948	18	20
1924	9	9			

Year	Acquisitions	Year	Acquisitions
(7)	(8)	(9)	(10)
1949	38	1956	135
1950	45	1957	103
1951	80	1958	140
1952	76	1959	188
1953	93	1960	203
1954	104	1961	234
1955	134		

Note: The upper and lower parts of the table are based on different definitions: see G. L. Reuber and F. Roseman, *The Take-Over of Canadian Firms, 1945-61* (Ottawa, 1969), p. 32 and J. C. Weldon, "Consolidations in Canadian Industry, 1900-1948", in L. A. Skeoch, ed., *Restrictive Trade Practices in Canada* (Toronto, 1966), p. 233.

Source: L. A. Skeoch, *Dynamic Change and Accountability in a Canadian Market Economy* (Ottawa, 1976), pp. 115-16.

potential market power represented by concentration is greater in Canada than in the United States. As early as 1889, this was of concern to legislators and the federal government instituted a policy to encourage competition among firms. Initially, it prohibited conspiracies and combinations in restraint of trade by making unlawful any agreement "to limit unduly the facilities for transporting, producing, storing, or selling any article, or to restrain commerce in it, or to unreasonably enhance its price". Agreements "to unduly prevent or lessen competition in relation to an article or to the insurance price upon persons or property" were also prohibited. These provisions became indictable offenses under the Criminal Code in 1892. Since then only minor alterations have been introduced into the provisions, although some new illegalities, such as minimum resale price maintenance and price discrimination, have been defined. In 1910 the first Combines Investigation Act established machinery for the investigation of alleged combines offences. As well, the words "merger, trust, or monopoly" were written into the Criminal Code for the first time.

Although industrial concentration has remained high the implementation and enhancement of regulations and laws to prevent concentration has been sporadic. In part this is due to the weaker constitutional power of the federal government in Canada to enact laws affecting commerce than in the United States. But two other factors are of greater importance. First, anti-combines prosecution has never been given a high priority by the federal government. As a result, few resources were devoted to investigation and prosecution. Second, as we have seen, Canada has always been a small, open economy with the result that it has been unwilling to sacrifice the apparent economic gains brought about by large-scale production units for other ends such as greater competition.[38]

CHAPTER THIRTEEN

Regional Growth and Retardation

Introduction

In both the short run and the long run there were often marked differences in the pace of economic growth and development among the various regions of the country. Differences in the cyclical pattern of economic activity, in the structure of regional exports, and in the pattern of internal migration, among others, all constitute evidence of regional distinctiveness. This can be found in many modern economies; however, in Canada, persistent differences in the pattern of regional incomes and unemployment were more marked than in most countries. For instance, in the United States there was a long-run convergence of real income per capita in the regions towards the national average.[1] This was also so in the history of other developed countries.[2] But in Canada the regional disparities in real income per capita showed only a slight tendency to diminish even though there were many forces of long duration acting so as to integrate the regional economies.

This chapter presents the evidence of regional economic disparities along with a framework for their examination. The economic performance of three distinct regions which exemplify the nature of the persistent economic problem will be be cast in this framework. These regions are the two largest provinces of Atlantic Canada, Nova Scotia and New Brunswick, Quebec which, although often classified as part of the central Canadian region, occupies a unique status as a region because of the many social and cultural differences which define it, and last, the province of British Columbia.

Regional Economic Disparities: The Framework

It is expected, in a historical context, that economic disparities in per-capita income and unemployment occurred. The different periods to which initial economic development dated and the variety of natural resource endowments alone would explain this discrepancy. What is surprising is the persistence of economic disparities among the regions in the face of the many forces which tend to integrate the regions with each other. The task, then, is to find a framework which explains this failure of regional economic differences to diminish on a significant scale.

Of all the forces which might be expected to reduce regional differences in per-capita income and unemployment, none are more important than the migration of labour and saving for investment. There are good grounds for arguing that if factors respond to differential economic opportunity there will be a reduction of regional income disparities.[3] For example, we can imagine a country with two regions, say A and B, each producing one product and both having identical economic structures and technologies; however, region A has a larger supply of labour and a smaller supply of saving, and therefore capital, than region B. As a result, region B pays higher wages to its workers and the price of capital is lower than in region A; therefore, region B is the higher-income region. If there are no barriers to the inter-regional movement of labour and capital and both factors respond to differential economic opportunities, some labour will migrate from region A to region B and some capital will move in the opposite direction. These factor flows would eliminate the original regional income inequality so long as there were no other significant changes.

An obvious expansion of the above one-sector model is to assume that there are two products produced in each region, a two-sector model. If the two products have different productivities associated with them, then one region may experience a lower per capita income because it has more resources committed to the lower-productivity product. A reduction of regional income inequality requires a shift of resources between sectors as well as from the low-wage to the high-wage region. Any persistence in regional inequality must be accounted for by other causes and/or factors which did not fully respond to the observed economic opportunity.

When a country such as Canada is in the early phases of economic development that development is usually characterized by a fragmentation of economic activity. Strong inter-regional linkages are as yet absent. In general, the larger the geographic spread of the country the more regional independence is displayed. In addition, more substantial economic growth and development of a particular region may set up forces which offset the wage-and-income-equalizing effect of labour and capital migration.[4] The demand and supply for labour and capital in the regions may shift so as to exacerbate the inter-regional wage differential;

for convenience, these offsetting forces can be categorized as the effects of labour growth and mobility, capital mobility, government policy, and inter-regional linkages.

As seen before, the flow of labour from low- to high-wage regions may close the real wage gap. However, the characteristics of labour growth and migration may also have other effects. On the supply side, for instance, a high rate of population growth in the low-wage region acts against the effects of the outward migration on real wages by increasing the supply of labour. The costs of moving may also be prohibitive and the probability of receiving the higher wage in the high-wage region is lower than that of receiving the low wage at home. Along with locational preferences, this may lead potential migrants to resist the temptation to move. All of these factors inhibit the supply-curve shifts described in the differential-opportunities model and could cause the wage differential to persist.

In addition, the migration of labour is likely to be selective. Because there are not simply high- and low-wage alternatives but a spectrum of high and low wages some workers can gain more than others by migrating. They generally are the highly educated, the skilled, and the employed of their own region. When the marginal physical product of labour rises in the high-wage region and falls in the low-wage one, a disparity is created; in terms of Figure 13:1, the labour-demand curve A shifts right while B shifts left. The wage differential may tend to increase. Since the educated, skilled, and employed workers have higher labour-force participation rates, not only wages but also per-capita income differentials increase. This was likely the case in Canada as valuable human capital flowed out of the relatively depressed regions.

As labour flows from one region to another it brings about a change in the structure of demand. The additional aggregate income, although not necessarily per-capita income, creates additional demand for particular types of goods and services—which cannot be traded: housing, educational, and government services, to name but a few. Since these could not be exported to those who have left the low-income region there is a shift in the derived demand for labour in each region (see Figure 13:1). If the demand for labour services in the non-traded goods and services sector is highly elastic either because labour has many substitutes or because labour costs are a high proportion of total costs, then aggregate income in the poorer region will fall and the wage disparity between the regions will increase.

With economic development may emerge more specialized production processes in the high-wage region relative to the low-wage one. This causes the division of labour to be carried further permitting more efficient use of the labour force with its higher marginal productivities

Figure 13:1 Labour Migration and Demand

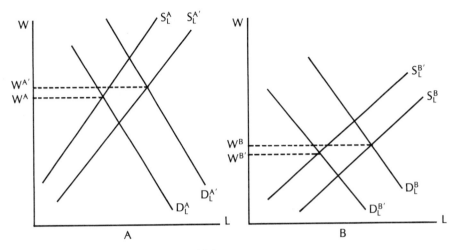

W—real wages   L—quantity of labour

Note: The migration causes shifts in the supply of labour which leads to a wage equality between regions. However, the increased demand in A and the decreased demand in B for non-traded goods and services causes shifts in the demand for labour which offset the convergent effects of the supply shifts. The resulting wage gap may be greater than that which prevailed before the migration but the exact extent of the gap depends on the elasticity of demand for labour services in the non-traded goods sector.

which, in turn, tend to widen the wage gap.

Even if the extent of the demand shifts for labour is less than the impact of the supply shifts through migration the reduction of the wage gap between regions may take place slowly. There may be obstacles to migration; these obstacles may take many forms, some of them non-pecuniary, such as the wish to remain in familiar surroundings. Or, these obstacles may take pecuniary forms, such as those created by the early development of unions and professional organizations with their mechanisms to control labour supply. So too, the skills required of the labour force in the fast-developing region may change and unless matched by those of the potential migrants further obstacles emerge to impede the closing of the inter-regional wage gap.

The inter-regional flow of capital may also be a force which tends to widen the wage differential between regions. External economies of scale and the benefits from agglomeration of capital projects in the expanding region may cause saving to leave the depressed region. This tends to raise the capital-labour ratio in the expanding region and lower it in the depressed region, causing similar changes in the regional marginal productivity of labour. The wage gap, therefore, increases. The lack of relative growth in the depressed region may increase the apparent riskiness of investing there and, if educated and skilled labour is emigrating, the region may face a scarcity of entrepreneurial talent. Even in the unlikely event that the marginal productivity of capital is higher in the depressed region, the capital market may be too immature to permit a flow of savings in that direction. However, capital scarcity in a depressed region is usually a sign of a relatively low marginal productivity of capital since production possibilities yield lower capital-labour ratios, lower output per worker, and lower wages.

Government policy, explicitly or inadvertantly, may cause regional disparities in economic performance. This, it might be argued, was especially so in Canadian history because the mechanisms for intervention in the economy were limited. In the drive to emulate other developing countries government attention, not unnaturally, was usually concentrated on the fastest-growing regions. Primarily through the investment in transport systems and communications and through the use of tariff policy some regions received a stimulus to economic growth denied to others. Whether or not the regional bias was justified on economic-efficiency grounds, it did serve to increase labour productivity at the margin in the fast-developing regions. In recent times, as seen later, this has not always been the case.

The fourth palpable cause of persistent regional differences in economic peformance is weak inter-regional linkages. Demand as well as technical and social change fail to spread from the fast- to the slow-developing regions if there are only few or weak links which bind the regional economies. For instance, Ontario was increasingly becoming the manufacturing centre of Canada in the nineteenth century but concomitantly developed a strong agricultural sector. Such specialization *within* regions necessarily limited the strength of inter-regional linkages. So too, inter-regional linkages may be weak if, in the prosperous economy, external economies of scale reduce average costs in exactly those industries which directly compete with the likely specialization of the low-income region.

So, inter-regional income levels may diverge during the country's formative period of growth and development. But in time, some obstacles to inter-regional wage and per-capita income convergence may of course be overcome. Indeed, the slight convergence of regional economic disparities of recent history may be a measure of the strengthening of inter-regional linkages, and the more efficient decision-making governing the flow of labour and capital. Yet even with the slight decline in inter-regional economic disparities, the gaps remain large. To solve this problem emphasis is increasingly being placed on government policy. For instance, a federal government may substitute equity for national-growth criteria and establish a policy of inter-regional income transfers. States often behaved in this way, instituting regional policies only after reaching a relatively high stage of economic development. Generally, a policy of income transfer can take two forms:

1) welfare transfers where income in the high per-capita income region is taxed and distributed, in some fashion, in the low per-capita income region; and
2) growth transfers where the government attempts to identify the sources of potential growth in the low-income region and subsidize them directly by investment grants and indirectly through tariffs and other measures.

Both such policies have been a feature of very recent Canadian history.

Regional Economic Disparities: The Evidence
Historical evidence from the late nineteenth century to the present traces out a clear contrast in the regional patterns of economic activity:

1) since at least 1890, regional differences in real per-capita income have existed. Overall, there has been no significant tendency of the regional income differences to disappear, and
2) the pattern of unemployment in Canada has differed by regions and these disparities have also persisted.

Regions with relatively high incomes, however, were not always the ones with the lowest levels of unemployment. Nor was the pattern static. For instance, inequality in regional income increased between 1890 and 1910 and although it diminished thereafter, the decline was slight. As a result, the degree of income disparity between the regions of Canada was approximately the same, in aggregate, in 1956 as it was in the last decade of the nineteenth century (see Table 13:1). This lends tentative support to the divergence-convergence model.

From Table 13:1 can be seen the tendency of income in the various provinces to converge toward or depart from the national average. The measure presented here, d, is the difference between the share of national income — gross value added — and the share of the employed labour force in the ith province or:

$$d_i = S_i^{GVA} - S_i^L$$

Table 13:1 Differences Between Income and Labour Force Share, by Region, in Constant 1935-39 Terms, 1890-1956

Area		Deviation of Gross Value Added from Labour Force Shares—d			
		1890	1910	1929	1956
(1)		(2)	(3)	(4)	(5)
P.E.I.		−0.4	−0.4	−0.4	−0.2
Nova Scotia		−1.7	−0.8	−1.3	−0.9
New Brunswick		−0.5	−0.7	−1.2	−0.7
Quebec		−1.9	−0.8	−0.3	−2.0
Ontario		+3.9	+5.0	+4.7	+1.7
Manitoba		+0.4	0.0	−0.5	−0.9
Saskatchewan		−0.1	−1.8	−1.5	−0.2
Alberta		a	−1.1	−0.3	+1.2
British Columbia		+0.3	+0.5	+0.7	+2.2
Total of above, disregarding sign		9.2	11.1	10.9	10.0
Total of Deviations of Gross Value Added from Population Shares disregarding sign		14.9	18.0	16.6	13.8

a The 1890 figure for Saskatchewan includes the entire, old Northwest Territories.

Source: A. G. Green, *Regional Aspects of Canada's Economic Growth* (Toronto, 1971), p. 43.

By subtracting the regional share of labour force from the relevant regional share of output, a weighted measure of the regional deviation of per-worker output from the national average results. A negative sign in Table 13:1 indicates that a particular region's average is less than the national average; a plus sign indicates a level greater than the national average; and zero means a level equal to the national average. Looking at these deviations over successive periods, an increase in regional deviation indicates a divergence away from the national average and a decreased deviation shows the opposite. Summing these deviations, disregarding sign, for any year, provides a measure of total regional inequality; an increase in this total—see the row of Table 13:1 called "Total of above, disregarding sign"—between periods indicates a move towards greater regional inequality and a reduction means the converse.

If d_i increased over time, a particular region's income grew at a faster rate than its labour force.[5] Conversely, when a province such as Quebec experiences a decline in its income per worker, as occurred between 1929 and 1956, the d measure in Table 13:1 declines. If instead of income per worker, the evidence of income per capita is examined then the regional inequality was apparently even greater than that suggested in

Table 13:1. As might be expected, from previous chapters, regional differences in the participation rate of the population in the labour force as well as differential fertility may well account for this difference between income per worker and income per capita.

In general, the pattern of regional income disparities changed little.[6] It can be seen that the measures of Table 13:2 confirm in more detail the evidence presented above. Ontario and British Columbia have always experienced per-capita incomes well above the national average. With equal persistence the Atlantic provinces and Quebec were below. The prairie region was for the most part an area where per capita incomes were close to the national average. Yet, within the prairie region, the province with the greatest proportion of its income derived from agriculture, Saskatchewan, was always less prosperous than its neighbours in terms of income per capita.

Historical disparities in regional income per capita must be considered, not alone, but in conjunction with unemployment disparities. In Chapter 6, for example, it was argued that the decision of a potential migrant to an area would likely be motivated by the level of income perceived and the probability of achieving it. Although all the estimated unemployment rates presented in Table 13:3 are not directly comparable, they do confirm the long history of relatively high unemployment in the Maritime provinces and Quebec, and the low unemployment in Ontario and to some extent in the prairie region. However, British Columbia, one of the richest regions in relative-income terms, was also an area with persistently high unemployment.

The evidence suggests that the underlying causes of the persistent income and unemployment disparities among regions can be best seen in the context of three historical case studies:

1) The Maritime provinces, with low income per capita and high unemployment;
2) Quebec which, although it followed a pattern similar to that of the easternmost provinces, was also influenced by special social and cultural factors; and
3) British Columbia, with its high income per capita and unemployment history.

Nova Scotia and New Brunswick: Relative Decline

The early prosperity of the two largest provinces of maritime Canada was based on what many have called "the economic triumvirate of wood, wind, and water". It was, however, insufficient to stimulate continued

Table 13:2 Personal Income Per Capita, by Region, as a Percentage of the Canadian Average, 1910-1973

Area	1910-11	1920-21	1926	1939	1955	1965	1973
(1)	(2)	(3)	(4)	(5)	(6)	(7)	(8)
Newfoundland	—	—	—	—	54	59	65
P.E.I.			57	53	55	69	69
Nova Scotia	64	69	67	76	73	75	78
New Bunswick			64	65	65	69	73
Quebec	77	84	85	88	85	88	90
Ontario	105	108	114	124	120	115	114
Manitoba			109	90	95	97	96
Saskatchewan	127	117	102	77	93	99	89
Alberta			113	87	103	99	102
British Columbia	186	121	121	125	122	115	108

Note: Columns (2) and (3) record participation income and are, therefore, not directly comparable to the rest of the table. Nevertheless, trends in participation income per worker were generally the same as trends in personal income per capita.

Sources: T. N. Brewis, *Regional Economic Policies in Canada* (Toronto, 1968), p. 92; R. M. McInnis, "The Trend of Regional Income Differentials in Canada", *Canadian Journal of Economics*, Vol. 1, no. 2 (1968), p. 447; and Statistics Canada, *Canadian Statistical Review*, Cat. no. 11-003.

economic development. As seen elsewhere, the area failed to capture or permanently hold enough of the West Indies trade for widespread linkages to influence the structure of domestic industry. With the coming of iron ships and marine engines, the traditional comparative advantage in the building of wooden sailing ships, too, was undermined and led to a decline in the industry. Although the decline was slow it was inevitable, as resources could not be transferred into the new techniques because of competitive disadvantage in the world shipbuilding markets. Apart from the fisheries only wood remained. But even the forest industries were forced to adjust to the changing structure of demand, as tariffs in foreign markets changed, as prime timber became more scarce, and as the demand for pulp and newsprint increased.[7] These changes were often protracted. In the immediate post-Confederation years, Nova Scotia and New Brunswick were areas where economic development was relatively slow. They persistently had per-capita incomes well below the national average and unemployment rates well above it.

More people migrated from Nova Scotia and New Brunswick than moved there during almost every decade since Confederation (see Chapter 6). There was only one exception. The Depression of the 1930s influenced the pattern of migration so that few left Nova Scotia and many from other parts of the Maritimes flocked there in the hope of finding a

Table 13:3 Estimated Unemployment Rates, by Region, 1921-1970
(per cent)

Region	1921	1931	1941	1947	1950	1954	1961	1966	1970
(1)	(2)	(3)	(4)	(5)	(6)	(7)	(8)	(9)	(10)
Maritime Provinces	13.2	13.3	4.7	4.7	7.8	6.6	11.1	6.4	7.6
Quebec	8.3	14.5	4.5	2.5	4.4	5.9	9.3	4.7	7.9
Ontario	10.0	13.4	2.5	1.8	2.4	3.8	5.5	2.5	4.3
Prairie Provinces	7.5	18.1	4.6	1.4	2.3	2.5	4.6	2.1	4.4
British Columbia	14.7	21.9	6.2	2.8	4.4	5.2	8.5	4.5	7.7
Canada	9.8	15.3	3.9	2.2	3.6	4.6	7.2	3.6	5.9

Note: The data for 1921, 1931, and 1941 use gainfully employed wage earners rather than the labour force which is used for all other years. The 1921 data are the percentage of the gainfully employed who stated that they were not at work on June 1, 1921. The 1931 and 1941 data are the percentage of the gainfully employed who stated that they had no job on the census date. The difference between the total not at work and the total with no job is usually small.

Sources: 1921—*Seventh Census of Canada, 1931*, Vol. 6, Appendix II, Table 1; 1931—ibid., Table 2; 1941—*Eighth Census of Canada, 1941*, Vol. 6, Table 14; Brewis (1968), p. 93 and Statistics Canada, Cat. no. 11-003.

job. This decade apart, the continental exodus from these two provinces was large. In the recent decade of 1951-61, for example, net emigration from New Brunswick to other parts of Canada was about 4.6 per cent of the average population of 690,000. Population growth in these two provinces, as well as other parts of Atlantic Canada, was clearly influenced by such a drain of people. In the twentieth century, the single most-favoured destination of the migrants was Ontario — 47 and 42 per cent of the internal migrants of Nova Scotia and New Brunswick respectively moved there in the period 1956-61. Labour supplies alone were shifting in such a manner as to induce a reduction of the wage disparity with Ontario. Of course, as seen in Chapter 6, Ontario itself was an area of net emigration until about 1901 which suggests that the forces, in general, were not necessarily strong enough to influence the inter-regional wage disparity between the two Maritime provinces and Ontario. Indeed, there may have been some increase in the wage or income gap in the late nineteenth century. Certainly, the pressure for convergence was stronger after the first decade of the twentieth century (Table 13:1).

Large though the migratory effect was, there were offsetting economic forces. Of these the effects of natural increase by region can be seen in Table 13:4. Higher birth rates giving rise to higher rates of natural increase in the low-income-per-capita regions dampened the shift in the supply of labour. Conversely, the lower rates of natural increase in Ontario, the major area of settlement of the migrants from the maritime

Table 13:4 Rates of Natural Increase of Population in Selected Provinces, 1901-1970
(per thousand of population)

Province	1901	1921-25[a]	1931	1951	1970
(1)	(2)	(3)	(4)	(5)	(6)
Nova Scotia	11.7	10.8	11.0	17.6	11.7
New Brunswick	14.4	15.3	15.1	21.8	10.5
Quebec	17.7	17.0	17.1	21.2	8.5
Ontario	8.7	12.4	9.8	15.4	10.3

[a] average. For a discussion of the birth rate of French Canadians in Quebec, see Chapter 6.

Sources: Census of Canada, 1901, Vol. 4, Table 9; D.B.S., Vital Statistics, 1931, (Ottawa, 1932), Tables 2 and 3; D.B.S., Vital Statistics, 1967 (Ottawa, 1967), Tables S5 and B1; and Statistics Canada, Canadian Statistical Review: Historical Summary, 1970, Cat. no. 11-505.

region, also acted against the equilibrating force. Yet, the migratory effect was much greater than the effects of fertility in all regions, with the possible exception of Quebec, and differential fertility cannot itself be held responsible for the persistent wage and income-per-capita differences. It was simply one of a variety of off-setting economic forces. There has been, in recent years, a diminution of inter-regional differences in the pattern of natural increase as there also has been a slight decrease in regional economic disparity. A causal relationship exists although its exact extent is unknown.

Fertility in relative terms, as was seen in Chapter 6, tends to diminish as the degree of urbanization increases. Nova Scotia and New Brunswick were both provinces where a greater proportion of the population lived outside the urban areas than in Ontario. Indeed, even the differences in the rate of natural increase *within* maritime Canada were directly proportional to the differences in the degree of urbanization (compare Nova Scotia and New Brunswick in Table 13:4 and Table 13:5). The extent of urbanization is, of course, a summary of the plethora of economic forces which give rise to the locational concentration of industry and population.[8] These forces, in turn, explain why workers in urban areas generally received higher wages than those in rural areas.

In 1851, New Brunswick, Quebec, and Ontario had similar proportions of their populations resident in urban places. In the following two decades the pattern changed little. However, the subsequent growth of the urban populations was rapid in central Canada but less so in New Brunswick. Nova Scotia, on the other hand, with a wider range of manufacturing industries than its immediate neighbours, also experienced a rising proportion of its population in towns and cities. Never-

Table 13:5 Population of Selected Provinces in Urban Areas, 1851-1971
(per cent)

Year	Nova Scotia	New Brunswick	Quebec	Ontario
(1)	(2)	(3)	(4)	(5)
1851	7.5	14.0	14.9	14.0
1871	8.3	17.6	19.9	20.6
1891	19.4	19.9	28.6	35.0
1911	36.7	26.7	44.5	49.5
1931	46.6	35.4	59.5	63.1
1951	54.5	42.8	66.8	72.5
1971	56.7	56.9	80.6	82.4

Sources: Census of 1971, *Population by Federal Electoral Districts* (Ottawa, 1972); Canada Year Book, 1969, Table 5; and M. C. Urquhart and K. A. H. Buckley, eds., *Historical Statistics of Canada* (Toronto, 1965), p. 14.

theless, the Maritime provinces never achieved the degree of urbanization found in central Canada. Today, almost one of every two persons in Nova Scotia and New Brunswick still lives in a rural area. In Ontario and Quebec, four persons of every five live in an urban area. In turn, the nature of industry in the region directly determined the degree of urbanization.[9]

The structure of industry in Nova Scotia and New Brunswick was always different from that of central Canada and has been reflected in the labour and capital differences between the regions. In general, the principal differences were that:

1) Nova Scotia employed much more of its work force in primary fishing than any other province;
2) the proportion of New Brunswick workers employed in primary forestry was large, even compared to British Columbia; and
3) central Canada had a proportionately larger manufacturing sector than either Nova Scotia or New Brunswick.

As seen in Table 13:6, the industrial structure of the various provinces changed little between 1911 and 1961. Indeed, there was a slight fall in the relative employment in manufacturing in both Nova Scotia and New Brunswick. Prior to 1911, neither of these two provinces had shifted resources from agriculture to the other industrial sectors as rapidly as Ontario; neither, of course, were as well endowed for cereal growing as central Canada and both had a smaller absolute and relative resource commitment in agriculture in the years immediately after Confederation.

Not only was the manufacturing industry of Nova Scotia and New

Table 13:6 Employment, by Industry, for Selected Provinces, 1911 and 1961

(per cent)

Industry	Nova Scotia		New Brunswick		Quebec		Ontario	
	1911	1961	1911	1961	1911	1961	1911	1961
(1)	(2)	(3)	(4)	(5)	(6)	(7)	(8)	(9)
Agriculture	28.1	5.2	38.1	7.2	31.4	7.6	31.0	7.2
Forestry	1.8	1.7	3.7	5.0	1.7	2.0	1.1	0.7
Fishing & Trapping	8.5	3.2	2.3	2.1	0.6	0.2	0.4	0.1
Mining	9.9	4.3	0.7	0.8	0.9	1.5	1.7	1.8
Manufacturing	15.1	14.2	16.9	16.0	21.7	26.5	23.3	26.9
Construction	7.3	6.2	9.8	5.8	10.4	6.7	8.4	6.1
Transport	6.6	10.4	6.7	11.8	6.6	9.1	7.7	8.2
Trade	7.9	15.6	8.1	16.7	10.9	14.1	11.3	15.5
Personal & Domestic Services	8.2	21.6	7.6	22.3	8.3	23.8	8.0	23.9
Government	2.7	15.9	1.8	10.1	2.8	5.6	2.8	7.7

Note: Minor differences in the classifications between 1911 and 1961 may introduce *slight* errors.

Sources: R. E. Caves and R. H. Holton, *The Canadian Economy: Prospect and Retrospect* (Cambridge, Mass., 1961), pp. 162 and 188, and E. C. C., *Second Annual Review*, p. 124.

Brunswick smaller than that of central Canada but it was more concentrated in the areas of the processing of primary products. Unlike Ontario, where diversification in manufacturing and a considerable degree of processing marked economic progress, the long-run development of manufacturing in the maritime region showed no such trend. The absence of processing industries generally meant that Nova Scotia and New Brunswick created employment in manufacturing more slowly than other areas. Even the iron and steel industry of Cape Breton, which became one of the major manufacturing industries of the region, did not stimulate ancillary production. Located in Cape Breton, because of its proximity to coal, the steel industry was inefficient by North American standards. The decreases in price of iron and steel inputs which might have been expected to promote other manufacturing were insufficient to compensate for the competitive disadvantage of location. Even primary iron and steel from Nova Scotia was uncompetitive without subsidies in the central Canadian market. The principal export market was, in fact, Great Britain. In general, the Maritime provinces had neither the natural resources nor any locational advantage in major markets to permit a diversification and growth of manufacturing in relative terms.

Table 13:7 Output per Worker in Manufacturing for Selected Provinces, 1871-1969

(percentage of output per worker in Ontario)

Province	1871	1891	1911	1931	1951	1969a
(1)	(2)	(3)	(4)	(5)	(6)	(7)
Nova Scotia	58.5	61.4	74.9	90.9	72.6	76.6
New Brunswick	73.2	61.1	58.4	87.3	91.1	83.8
Quebec	87.4	90.6	91.5	97.1	87.4	83.7
Ontario	100.0	100.0	100.0	100.0	100.0	100.0

a For 1969 the data are based on the value of shipments. All other calculations are based on the total value of output. The difference between the two measures is inventories of goods and was generally so small as not to influence the results presented here.

Sources: *Census of Canada, 1871*, Vol. 3, pp. 462-63; *Census of Canada, 1891*, Vol. 4, Table 6; *Census of Canada, 1911*, Vol. 3, Table 10; D.B.S., *The Manufacturing Industries of Canada, 1931*, tables 7 and 23; D.B.S., *The Manufacturing Industries of Canada, 1951*, Table 2; Statistics Canada, *The Manufacturing Industries of Canada, Atlantic Provinces, 1969*, Tables 20 and 26; as above, *Quebec, 1969*, Table 1; and as above, *Ontario, 1969*, Table 1.

The nature of the industrial composition of the regional economy, in general, and the manufacturing sector, in particular, created a capital-labour ratio which was low by comparison. In the private business sector as a whole, per-capita annual average investment, in the post-1945 years, was generally about one-half the Canadian average.[10] This led, for instance, to a very low stock of machinery and equipment per worker in manufacturing; in 1964, the index of this ratio recorded 43 and 60 for Nova Scotia and New Brunswick, respectively. The national average was 100 and that of Ontario 145.[11] As Table 13:7 indicates, output per worker — a crude measure of the average physical productivity of labour — was lower in the Maritime provinces than elsewhere. Since wages, and hence individual incomes, were directly proportional to capital-labour ratios, the differences in industrial structure explain much of the regional economic disparity.

Unlike most areas of Canada, the maritime region had few new types of natural resources which could be brought into production. Those which could be exploited were relatively abundant elsewhere. As a consequence, over the past one hundred years technical change both isolated Nova Scotia and New Brunswick from the rest of Canada and destroyed their isolation. In the former case, Nova Scotia and New Brunswick became less important as suppliers of goods and services both within Canada and in terms of international trade. In the latter case, local monopolies were broken as central Canadian and world goods entered the Maritimes market. At the heart of this paradox was the development of transport using steam and steel, ships and railways, from about the time of Confederation (see Chapter 10).

The larger size and greater economic efficiency of steel ships caused them to displace the sailing vessels which had been the mainstay of the pre-Confederation carrying trade of the Atlantic regional economy. With greater speed and some independence of weather new shipping patterns emerged using the new vessels. Increasing use was made of the St. Lawrence ports while the ports of Atlantic Canada were by-passed. Halifax harbour lost much of its attractiveness as locks and canals on the St. Lawrence and Great Lakes enabled ocean-going vessels to penetrate deeper into central Canada. So too, west-coast timber began to compete with that of Nova Scotia and New Brunswick due to reduced transport costs. On land, the railways from the seaboard of New England to central Canada reduced the overland distance from the Atlantic seaboard to these markets. This increasing isolation was exacerbated by the continual westward movement of the centre of gravity of the Canadian population as western Canada developed.[12]

At the same time, isolation of the maritimes domestic market was being destroyed. Improved transport into the region and changes in manufacturing and marketing techniques undermined local manufacturing. In general, the appearance of large-scale manufacturing created economic circumstances in which the location of economic activity became critical. Whether based on proximity to markets or resources its growth took place mainly in Ontario and Quebec.

Apart from the effects of transport costs there were other technical changes of note. Refrigeration, for instance, changed the nature of the world market in foodstuffs to the detriment of Nova Scotian fish exports in some European and North American markets. The opening of the northern forests of Ontario to road and rail allowed the timber industry to develop there whereas the capacity for expansion in the Maritimes was limited. The new mineral discoveries in the Canadian Shield and British Columbia became the basis for industrial expansion for which there was no counterpart in the Atlantic region. The development of hydroelectricity as a cheap source of energy further ensured that manufacturing expansion would be primarily located in central Canada (see Table 13:8). This difference was especially crucial up to the 1920s during the formative years of Canada's manufacturing sector. Although by 1931 New Brunswick, but not Nova Scotia, had closed the gap in horsepower per establishment as Table 13:8 demonstrates the absolute employment of motor power was much less. Even in the more traditional sector of agriculture the mechanization of farms in Nova Scotia and New Brunswick was generally much less prevalent than elsewhere in Canada.

Table 13:8 Electric Motors Installed in Manufacturing for Selected Provinces, 1901-1953

(horsepower per establishment)

Province	1901	1911	1931	1953
(1)	(2)	(3)	(4)	(5)
Nova Scotia	0.9	3.3	70.3	142.9
New Brunswick	0.5	3.2	142.0	251.2
Quebec	4.5	22.2	147.4	252.3
Ontario	3.3	19.9	128.6	269.3

Note: The substitution of primary power—steam engines and turbines, and internal combustion engines primarily—did not compensate in relative terms for the deprivation of cheap hydroelectric power in the Maritimes.

Sources: *Census of Canada, 1901*, Vol. 3, Table 6; *Census of Canada, 1911*, Vol. 3, Table 6; D.B.S., *The Manufacturing Industries of Canada, 1931*, tables 30 and 31; and D.B.S., *General Review of the Manufacturing Industries of Canada, 1958*, tables 2 and 54.

In 1901, the value of implements and machinery per improved acre was the following: Nova Scotia—2.55; New Brunswick—2.60; Quebec—3.63; Ontario—3.97. These relative differences persisted until at least 1921. But after 1931 the gap closed, especially in Nova Scotia[13] and its narrowing in recent years played some part in the convergence of incomes noted in Table 13:1. In summary, technological change served to dampen the potential economic growth of Nova Scotia and New Brunswick both because of the region's location with respect to markets and with respect to the relatively narrow range of opportunities enforced by a traditional natural-resource base.[14]

The industrial structure not only determined the characteristics of the labour force in Nova Scotia and New Brunswick but also helped to determine the characteristics of the migrants who left. It was the young, the well-educated, and the employed who were most likely to leave for other regions of Canada because of the higher opportunity cost of remaining at home. Mobility was greatest among those in the age group of twenty to forty years and also tended to rise with years of formal schooling and technical training. The employed, too, were more mobile than the unemployed in part because of the costs of moving.[15] Since the young, educated, and employed left the Maritimes in disproportionately high numbers the marginal physical productivity of labour would tend to fall in the region.

The migration between regions altered the profile of the regional labour forces. For instance, within Nova Scotia and New Brunswick there was continually a much greater proportion of the population which was outside of the labour force. Notably, the dependency ratio, defined here as the proportion of the population under 15 and over 64 years of age, to the total increased from 1881 to 1951 in comparison with that of Ontario. Only in very recent years has there been a slight tendency for the inter-regional discrepancy in dependency to decline. This discrepancy, of course, is a force causing inter-regional per-capita income differences. Even in the unlikely event that workers all received the same income, the higher number of dependents in the Maritimes would ensure a lower per-capita income.

Not unexpectedly, central Canada, in particular Ontario, experienced a higher labour-force participation in the work force than Nova Scotia and New Brunswick. Since it was the young who tended to leave the maritime region, the relative dependency ratio of the domestic population changed as noted above. But also, Ontario was generally an area which received a great deal of international migrants. They too were young. Since the young, especially the international migrants, also had a higher participation of females in the work force the overall participation was higher (see Table 13:9). While the greater participation of females in the workforce reduced average, regional *income per worker* it also raised the *income per capita* when it was not coincident, causally or otherwise, with any serious decline in male participation in the workforce. This was the case in Ontario. On the other hand, in Nova Scotia, male participation in the workforce fell from 85.6 to 65.8 per cent between 1901 and 1961, a figure well below the Canadian average.

Although high- and low-wage industries existed in both regions there was a greater proportion of employment in the Maritimes in the low-paying occupations. The relative scarcity of capital in industry thus led to a relatively lower standard of skills in the workforces of Nova Scotia and New Brunswick. Since the returns to any individual's investment in education were, on average, lower in the maritime region, it can be presumed that the demand for education was different from that in the more prosperous economy. On the supply side, the low-per-capita-income region was less capable of offering educational services than that region with the larger tax base. Even at the most basic levels of skill there were differences in the educational background of the regional labour supply. For instance, in 1891, while 86 per cent of the population over the age of four could read and write in Ontario, only about 75 per cent of the same group in Nova Scotia and New Brunswick could do likewise. This gap has tended to close in recent years.[16] Another dimension of education is the percentage of each province's population age seven to fourteen years that is at school for any period during the year. In 1911, 1921, and 1931, Ontario appears to have had significantly higher percentages of children at school than Nova Scotia and New Brunswick,

Table 13:9 Labour-Force Participation Rates, by Sex, For Selected Provinces, 1901-1961

(per cent)

Province	Participation Rate	1901	1911	1931	1951	1961
(1)	(2)	(3)	(4)	(5)	(6)	(7)
Nova Scotia	Total	49.4	51.5	50.7	49.7	45.3
	Male	85.6	86.6	83.1	79.5	65.8
	Female	12.0	14.8	16.1	19.4	24.4
New Brunswick	Total	50.7	51.0	51.2	49.6	46.1
	Male	87.7	87.8	84.1	79.3	67.3
	Female	12.7	14.4	16.6	20.0	24.8
Quebec	Total	48.9	51.2	53.4	53.4	51.6
	Male	83.3	85.3	85.1	83.2	75.9
	Female	14.7	16.1	21.3	24.5	27.8
Ontario	Total	48.9	54.1	53.1	55.1	55.7
	Male	83.6	88.1	84.7	84.1	79.0
	Female	14.1	17.5	20.1	26.1	32.6

Note: Percentage of the population 14 years and over gainfully employed or in the labour force.

Sources: *Census of Canada, 1951*, Vol. 4, Table 1 and G. W. Wilson, S. Gordon, and S. Judek, *Canada: An Appraisal of its Needs and Resources* (Toronto, 1965), Table 3.30.

although this difference too has disappeared over time. Duration of schooling during a year may be important also; up to at least 1931, Ontario had proportionately more students attending school seven to nine months per year while the maritime provinces had proportionately more students than Ontario attending school on a one-to-three months' basis only.[17] Even basic literacy was not as widespread in the maritime region as in Ontario and as late as 1961, while Ontario had only about 4 per cent of its labour force with less than four years of formal schooling, the percentage in New Brunswick was 10 per cent.[18] So too, formal vocational and academic training is more common elsewhere than in Nova Scotia and New Brunswick. In general, this low level of investment in education is both a symptom and a cause of the relative low per-capita income and high unemployment rates.

Not only did workers in the Maritimes have lower wages than their Ontario counterparts but they were also less sure in their employment. The seasonality of employment, because of the regional specialization in primary production, was about twice as important in the Maritime provinces as a cause of unemployment as in Ontario. Manufacturing, especially of the processing type, created a more continuous pattern of employment. For instance, since at least 1901 the number of weeks worked, on average, in manufacturing has been about one-third greater in Ontario than in Nova Scotia and New Brunswick.[19]

Regional economic disparities were also directly affected by government policy. As noted earlier, government expenditures at the federal level were motivated by either economic welfare or growth criteria. Through a number of tax-financed federal social security schemes, such as family allowances, old age pensions, unemployment insurance, and aid to farmers, a direct transfer of income from the more affluent to the less affluent regions took place. Without such transfers the regional disparities in real per-capita income would have been even greater than those observed. Such transfers, however, gave little stimulus to economic growth; they were intended only to shore up sagging incomes. More important for the pace of regional economic growth were the regional expenditures on social capital. Expenditures on social capital in the form of health, education, municipal services, and transport were carried out by all levels of government. Often, in the instance of transport, there was an attempt to strengthen inter-regional linkages and to integrate the regions with each other.

With respect to the expenditures of provincial and municipal governments there were great differences between the regions in both absolute expenditures and expenditures per capita. For instance, both Nova Scotia and New Brunswick committed themselves to the construction of a large road network in the first twenty-five years of the twentieth century. Ontario, with more apparent ease, financed its road-building, constructed a major railway, the Témiskaming and Northern Ontario Railroad, and spent over $130 million on the Ontario Hydro-Electric Power Commission.[20] While all provinces rapidly increased their per-capita outlays on social capital, especially after the 1930s, any narrowing in provincial differences in such expenditures only happened after about 1960. Even then provincial and municipal government expenditures per capita on each of education, health, and transport were higher in Ontario than in Nova Scotia or New Brunswick.[21] This, of course, is not surprising since per-capita income and tax capacity govern per-capita public expenditures.

Many types of municipal and provincial government services such as health and education are direct services to individuals. Thus, as migrations took place there was a shift in demand for these services from the low- to the high-income region as these services were incapable of being traded (see Figure 13:1). The demand for labour, derived from the demand for these services, was geographically shifted in aggregate terms. Since this was a force which exacerbated the wage and income per capita differences the role of government expenditures often was to contribute to regional economic disparity. It was an inevitable consequence of the provision of the services and the migration of people.

National government-expenditure patterns also contributed, from time to time, to the forces which caused regional economic disparity. These, in turn, were often bolstered by other elements of government policy which reinforced the effects of the expenditures. Elsewhere in this chapter the concern of the federal government for national growth and development during the early phases of economic expansion was noted. Such a concentration was almost myopic from the time of Confederation until at least the 1920s. Increased tariffs on manufactured imports, railway construction, and policies for the settlement of the prairies account almost exclusively for government intervention to promote economic growth. Nova Scotia and New Brunswick seldom figured in these national plans especially since the major centre of Canadian manufacturing was already well-established by the 1870s. National Policy measures strengthened the Montreal–Toronto area as the metropolitan centre of Canada.

Even measures intended to strengthen inter-regional linkages often had little or no effect in stimulating economic development. The Intercolonial Railway joining the Maritimes and central Canada destroyed the natural geographic protection that certain industries enjoyed, particularly in Nova Scotia and New Brunswick. In the desire of the national government to emulate the United States and to compete with that country the railway was built along an all-Canadian route; this increased transport costs above the next best alternative and put maritime industry at a further competitive disadvantage. Even by the beginning of the twentieth century the inter-regional linkages between New Brunswick–Nova Scotia and central Canada were still weak and few spreading effects from the prairie settlement and subsequent wheat boom permeated to the east-coast economy.

In 1879, the tariff on many manufactured goods was raised and remained high until after the Second World War. This had two effects of some importance on the development of the maritime region. First, it redirected purchases to goods made in Canada when, in the absence of tariffs, those articles could be more cheaply imported from abroad. Second, while the tariff encouraged the growth of steel and coal industries in the Maritimes, the long-run consequence of the tariff was to promote a different and less efficient distribution of resources than would have otherwise existed. In particular, resources were transferred from export industries, thus raising their costs and reducing their output, to the import-competing sector which was protected; the rate of growth of ex-

port trade was retarded and that of the protected industries was enhanced. Nova Scotia and New Brunswick specialized in the unprotected
export industries more than Ontario.

While the chief policies of the federal government prior to the 1920s
were national in scope, the Maritimes were not entirely neglected. The
chief forms of aid came either as money grants to the provinces from the
central government or as shared-cost schemes. The former were not
necessarily designed to promote economic development but when they
resulted in investment in infrastructure, such as for municipal services,
they had some beneficial effect. On the whole, however, the central
government was not favourably disposed towards greater aid for the
provinces in general or the Maritimes in particular. As suggested earlier,
the federal government's attitude only slowly changed but with it came
some convergence in provincial per-capita incomes. Before the 1960s,
the policy change tended to take the form of ad hoc aids: increased provincial transfers, increased emphasis on the management of the fisheries,
new grain elevators at Halifax, subventions for the coal industry, a subsidy to coke by-product plants using Canadian coal, and the reduction of
freight rates. During the 1960s, policies became more comprehensive.
Through agencies of the federal government such as the Department of
Regional Economic Expansion, the Area Development Agency, the Agriculture and Rural Development Act, and the Atlantic Development
Board, attempts have been made to identify and stimulate regional
specialization where it will produce the greatest benefit.[22] Whether there
have been effective consequences of the desire to remove the regional
economic disparity between the Maritimes and other regions of Canada
cannot yet be judged.

In conclusion, the relative backwardness of Nova Scotia and New
Brunswick can be seen to be the result of a large number of causes. Some
reach deep into the Canadian past while others are of more recent vin-
tage.

Quebec: The Special Economy

Because of the long association of the present provinces of Quebec and
Ontario, Quebec is often thought of as part of the region of central
Canada. But in terms of economic history Quebec has always been unique. Although its economic development was similar to Ontario's in
some respects, it, in others, more closely paralleled that of the maritime
region. For instance, the Montreal area appears to have grown with Ontario and to have had similar structures of labour force and factory enterprise. Yet on the whole, Quebec, since at least 1911 and probably earlier,
had a per-capita income lower than Ontario's (see tables 13:1 and 13:2).

At present the difference is approximately 30 per cent. Unemployment in Quebec was always higher than in Ontario and for the most part its pattern resembles that of Nova Scotia and New Brunswick (see Table 13:3). Alone these disparities in economic performance would mark Quebec as a region different from others. But Quebec also developed with a distinctive social and cultural base; the heritage of the French Canadians dictated that the pattern of economic activity would also be singular.[23]

Labour migration to and from Quebec is the first indication of uniqueness in the Canadian context. For instance, although Quebec experienced a net loss of people to other parts of the country during six of the nine decades between 1871 and 1961, there was no general exodus (see Table 6:11). Even in the period 1871-81 to 1921-31, when Quebec experienced negative net migration, its level was significantly below that of Ontario. On the other side of the internal migration ledger, from 1931-41 to 1951-61, the net migration into Quebec was actually positive despite relatively low per-capita income and high unemployment rates. Large inflows from New Brunswick took place and the French Canadians themselves were relatively immobile largely for non-pecuniary reasons. Quebec discharged only a relatively small number of its population through interprovincial migration and for the most part, this loss of population had little effect on the size of Quebec's population. The barrier of language and culture has acted so as to reduce labour mobility between Quebec and the other regions of Canada. While New Brunswick also had a relatively large French-speaking population, few left Quebec for New Brunswick which was, after all, a region with a generally low per-capita income. Too, it must be noted that there are cultural differences between the regions sharing the French language. In general then, there was little movement from the low-income region of Quebec so as to act as a force reducing inter-regional economic disparities. Therefore responses to differential economic opportunity likely failed to materialize in sufficient quantities to reduce income and employment differences in the manner set out earlier in this chapter.[24]

The birth-rate effect compounded the relative immobility of the Quebec labour force. Rates of natural increase in Quebec were, until about 1951, generally higher than elsewhere in Canada (see Table 13:4). This was reflected in the growth of the labour supply. For instance, from 1911 to 1951 Quebec's labour force grew at a faster rate than that of Ontario. Yet, the pattern of economic development was such that this labour could be absorbed only by depressing wage and income levels in relative terms.

The relative paucity of job opportunities in Quebec was not, as mentioned, mirrored in the low rates of out-migration from that province. Yet, language created an obstacle even within Quebec which influenced mobility. Those who spoke only French had lower rates of labour-force mobility than those who spoke both English and French or those who spoke only English. In this sense, literacy in the respective languages was less important that the ability to communicate orally. Since English was the usual language of commerce and industry an obstacle was created which prevented access to the relatively better-paying jobs by the solely French-speaking members of the Quebec workforce. While such a situation resembles a dual labour market in many respects its most lasting effect has been the long-term sense of frustration felt by a large portion of Quebec's labour force. Yet the lack of mobility within Quebec was undoubtedly caused by the lower levels of job creation in urban areas within the region. As seen in Table 13:5, with about the same proportion of the respective populations in urban places in 1871, a difference emerged over the following twenty years between Quebec and Ontario. If economies of agglomeration contribute to and are represented by increasing urbanization then the gap in relative per-capita incomes may well have increased from 1871 to 1891 and narrowed slightly thereafter, as the urbanization growth rate somewhat belatedly accelerated in Quebec. Despite the very different patterns of labour mobility and urbanization the broad features of industry in Quebec were remarkably similar to those of Ontario (see Table 13:6) in terms of employment. They were, however, only superficially so. In agriculture, for instance, the amount of machinery on farms both in terms of workers and acreage was significantly below that of Ontario. In 1911, the values per improved acre of implements and machinery in Quebec and Ontario were $3.63 and $3.97 respectively; by 1951, these had risen to $24.00 and $35.10 respectively. The productivity differences between the two regions in this sector never closed despite the transformation of Quebec agriculture in the mid-nineteenth century. Also, within manufacturing there were significant differences in the regional capital-labour ratios. From at least the time of the Census of 1871 Quebec lagged behind Ontario in the employment of capital goods. In 1964, the index of capital stock of machinery and equipment per capita in manufacturing was 90 for Quebec—the Canadian average was 100—and 145 for Ontario; the respective indexes for all industries were 77 and 112. As Table 13:7 indicates, Quebec's lower output per worker in manufacturing reflects this capital difference.

Both Quebec and Ontario remained throughout the post-Confederation period important areas for the production of natural-resource-based products. Flour and grist mills' production, dairy products, log and lumber products, and pulp and paper continued to rank within the ten most significant manufacturing industries of the two provinces in terms of value of product.[25] On the other hand, the importance of iron and steel products in Quebec fell while that of Ontario grew. By 1911, the foundry and machine industry, agricultural-implements manufacturing, and iron and steel production were among the major constituents of manufacturing in Ontario which had no Quebec counterpart. For its part, Quebec industry specialized in lighter manufacturing: cotton textiles, clothing, tobacco and cigar products, and a particularly efficient boot- and shoe-manufacturing sector. Two circumstances primarily determined the growth of regional specialization such as that noted above. First, the relative abundance of labour in Quebec kept wage rates lower than in Ontario thus encouraging the more labour-intensive industries to locate there. Second, the relative availability, and cost, of fuels imparted a regional bias. Both Ontario and Quebec have no domestic sources of coal; both import coal from the United States, as noted earlier. Because of transport costs, Ontario was the most efficient location for those industries which used a great deal of heat energy. Quebec, although a less efficient location for heat-using industries, was a more favoured location for those industries which required electric power. Hydroelectric power could of course be transported at a very low cost but the fact that many power-using industries, such as textiles, were also labour-intensive ones gave Quebec the competitive advantage of location. This trend in regional specialization in manufacturing is still evident: Quebec has more light industry and Ontario more heavy industry proportionally and this, in part, determined the relatively low output per worker in Quebec.

There were other contributing causes to the particular type of light manufacturing which became predominant in Quebec. It will be recalled, for instance, that many French-speaking Canadians emigrated to the New England region of the United States. There they were employed primarily in the textiles and boot- and shoe-making industries. Returning to Canada, as a sizeable number did, they gravitated towards and established firms in the trades they had acquired. The shoe-making industry of Quebec was one of the few which, for most of its modern history, was completely controlled by French Canadians.

During Quebec's so-called "era of industrialization" (1900 to the 1950s), natural resources played a key role. In these years economic and geographic factors were in Quebec's favour. Ample natural resources of the Canadian Shield, relatively inexpensive hydroelectricity, and expanding external markets, primarily in the United States, enhanced Quebec's economic position. The forest industry was at the forefront of this resource-based growth and development. In terms of gross value of production, it ranked first among the forty leading industries of Quebec from 1911 to 1951. It and its linkage industries employed a significant number of workers in a majority of Quebec's economic regions. Hydro-electrical developments, the transport networks, and a number of linkage industries experienced the effects of the growth of the forestry industry. The emergence of these industries gave more balance to the structure of industry relative to Ontario. Although the structure of industry, as argued above, was brought about, in part, by the different nature of the labour supplies, the output per worker difference between Quebec and Ontario was not as large as the difference in per-capita income. That is, the income per worker was distributed among more people in Quebec. There were three dimensions of participation in the work force which contributed to the lower per-capita income of Quebec.

First, when the birth rate in Quebec exceeded that of Ontario the number of dependent children was necessarily greater. Most exaggerated in the late nineteenth and early twentieth centuries, as seen in Chapter 6, was the difference between the birth rates evident in the higher dependency ratios of Quebec at this time (see Table 13:10). In addition, such emigration as occurred also raised the average number of dependents per worker. On such evidence alone, but supported by the actual performance of per-capita income disparities, we would expect that the relative discrepancy between Quebec and Ontario probably worsened in the late nineteenth century and improved slightly in the post-1945 years.

Second, there was a different pattern of labour-force participation in Quebec than in Ontario. Part of this is, of course, explained by the greater proportion of population either too young or too old to be members of the workforce. Part, however, is explained by the lower overall participation of the working-aged population. The different participation rates shown in Table 13:9 somewhat understate the nature of the discrepancy for the following reason. The non-Canadian born members of the workforce almost exclusively accounted for the major difference in the regional participation rates. Since most immigrants from outside Canada went to Montreal, Montreal's participation rates are similar to Ontario and buoy up the provincial average. Thus, within Quebec there were more varied patterns of labour participation than within Ontario where the immigrant population spread itself more evenly. The proportion of foreign-born individuals to the total population has varied from time to time in the regions. Nevertheless, it was quite stable in the long-run: 27 compared to 6.6 per cent for the respective provinces of Ontario and Quebec in 1871 and about 20 to 6 per cent thereafter.[26] As a consequence, the fall in the dependency rate in Quebec has not removed a large difference—about 4 per cent currently—in

Table 13:10 Dependency in Quebec and Ontario, 1881-1961
(percentage of the population under 15 or over 64 years of age)

Year	Quebec	Ontario
(1)	(2)	(3)
1881	44	42
1901	43	37
1921	43	36
1951	39	36
1961	41	40

Note: For an elaboration of the structure of births which determined in part the structure of dependency, see Chapter 6.

Sources: *Census of Canada, 1931*, Vol. 1, Table 9; *Census of Canada, 1951*, Vol. 1, Table 19; and E.C.C., *Second Annual Review*, Table 5-7.

labour participation between Quebec and Ontario. Per-capita incomes in Quebec were necessarily lower.

As in both Nova Scotia and New Brunswick one of the dimensions of low per-capita income in Quebec was the pattern of unemployment. In the recent years of 1954-59, for instance, unemployment in Quebec in the summer was 4.0 per cent and in the winter, on average, 10.6 per cent — in both instances double that of Ontario. Seasonality in Quebec exaggerated the annual cycle of employment and while less severe than those fluctuations experienced in the Maritimes they were characteristic of a less urbanized society with lower capital ratios in manufacturing and a somewhat greater dependence on natural-resource processing. As a consequence employment was, on average, less continuous in nature than in Ontario. Even in 1911, workers in manufacturing in Quebec tended to spend about two weeks fewer per year in employment than their equivalents in the neighbouring province to the west.

It has often been argued that the peculiarities of the Quebec educational system somehow retarded the development of a skilled labour force which, in turn, could earn high wages. Certainly there were historic differences in the level of educational attainment and the type of skills required. As late as 1891, for example, only 62 per cent of the population over five years of age could read and write any language.[27] On the other hand, about 86 per cent of Ontario's population over five years of age was literate. There is also evidence to suggest that in the first half of the twentieth century, a smaller percentage of Quebec's population ages seven to fourteen attended school for any part of the year and of those who did attend, they went for a shorter period of the year than the corresponding cohort in Ontario. For another parallel with at least New Brunswick, as late as 1961, about 10 per cent of Quebec's labour force had less than five years of formal education; this compares with about 4 per cent in the case of Ontario. Since there was a close correspondance between the ability to communicate in a second language, in this case English, and basic literacy in a first language, French, then the lack of basic education, evident in the later part of the nineteenth century, was in part responsible for the lack of occupational mobility in Quebec.

Despite this lack of occupational mobility, there is no strong evidence to suggest that this was an impediment to the process of economic development. Although Quebec received fewer international or internal migrants than other parts of Canada, it did receive sufficient migrants to fill any educational gap or particular labour-market excess demand without altering the structure of wages. It was the generally low wages as well as the cost of other factors which determined the growth of industry. The principal result of differences in educational attainment in basic literacy or mechanical skills was not to impede the rate of economic development but to increase the amount of social resentment and con-flict between the non-English-speaking population and other elements of Quebec society.

The Church, for the most part, directed the educational system of Quebec. It has often been asserted without much foundation that the Church in Quebec was a force impeding industrial progress — presumably to keep the population rural and content in the highly structured parishes. However, as seen earlier, the Church certainly did respond to the agricultural crisis of the mid-nineteenth century Quebec by improv-ing technical training and disseminating knowledge about agricultural methods. While it is possible to indicate particular churchmen who wished little change, industrial or otherwise, it was also true that many bishops took a keen interest in industrial development, such as Bishop Taschereau who devoted a great deal of energy to industrial relations and the plight of workers in Montreal. Indeed, by the 1920s the Roman Catholic Church was actively engaged in attracting industry to Quebec. Last, while education in Quebec stressed liberal arts to a greater extent than, say, Ontario, it was not evident that this was the basis of a profound labour-market problem. Rather, where the educational system of Quebec seems to have been deficient was in the provision of basic literacy brought about by too few schools and educational opportunities in some rural areas. However, this was a deficiency which had been largely resolved by the first decade of the twentieth century. In summary, the Church in Quebec cannot be singled out as a retarding force of the pace of industrial development of long-run consequence.[28]

The various governments of Quebec were historically less committed to government expenditures than most provincial governments in Canada. Particularly in the sphere of public works and utilities the governments were slow to invest at the same rates as elsewhere. For instance, in the period 1920-25 Quebec contributed only 12 per cent to the aggregate investment of all provincial governments.[29] Of course Quebec accounted for much more than 12 per cent of the Canadian population. Particularly in the early twentieth century, the investment in educational facilities was often insufficient, even when that investment by the Church is accounted for to provide the comprehensive coverage necessary to raise wages by promoting labour mobility—which, in turn, would probably have dampened birth rates because increased mobility generally meant increased urbanization. As a consequence of the apparent reluctance of successive provincial governments of Quebec to commit themselves, the pattern of public expenditures in per-capita terms was well below the average for Canada and undoubtedly contributed to the low per-capita income of the region. Not until the early 1960s was this situation remedied.

British Columbia: The Pacific Province
Far removed in terms of geography from Quebec and the maritime provinces, British Columbia is dissimilar in terms of economic development. Unlike Quebec and the Maritimes, British Columbia's pace of economic expansion and structural change has been rapid since Confederation. As persistently as Quebec and the Maritimes have experienced a real per-capita income below the Canadian average that of British Columbians has been above average. The Atlantic region has been one which continuously experienced out-migration. British Columbia has usually experienced positive net immigration (see Table 6:11). The relative economic backwardness of the Maritimes can in general be attributed to the lack of staples available to replace the timber trade given that that region had no comparative advantage in other manufacturing. On the other side of the continent, British Columbia's economic development has been based on the successive emergence of new staples with the continued importance of the old.[30]

British Columbia also stands in marked contrast to the economy of central Canada. The Ontario–Quebec economy became diverse, evolving around its staple base, while the far western economy of Canada did not. Two important economic characteristics appear to explain the markedly different development of these two regions. First, the agricultural potential of British Columbia, even with modern technology, is extremely limited. No more than 2 per cent of the land surface supports any agrarian activity. In central Canada the agricultural economy has assumed an historically important role. The different capacities were, of course, significant in their respective contributions to aggregate income, small in the case of British Columbia and large in the case of central Canada. However, in central Canada the agricultural sector proved a complement to early natural-resource-based growth and later became the source of cheap inputs, such as in the timber trade (see Chapter 3). Agriculture, particularly in Ontario, also was a continuing force for specialization and in the process created cheap inputs which the natural-resource-intensive sector could use. Secondary manufacturing was, as a consequence, stimulated. Not unconnected with this is the second reason for the differences. Central Canada had always been the main consumer market in the country and, with the aid of tariff protection, secondary manufacturing of consumer goods quickly evolved. In modern times, as Canadian industry became more efficient or where bilateral trade agreements with the United States directed trade, central Canada's locational advantage in the entire North American market reinforced this national locational advantage. Compared with central Canada, British Columbia derived only a very small proportion of its regional income from value added in secondary manufacturing and only a small proportion of its labour force has ever been employed in that sector.

Of all the Canadian regional economies which have evolved from non-agricultural staple-export origins only British Columbia has continued to be an economy directed by the export performance of the natural-resource sector. As such it is a unique region in Canada whose industrial structure is like no other (see Table 13:11). Not only has British Columbia's real income per capita been persistently greater than the Canadian average, as noted earlier, but in the short run fluctuations in that income have been greater than elsewhere. Why British Columbia's economy is both more prosperous and more vulnerable than most other regions of the country can be answered in the context of its economic development.

British Columbia joined the Confederation of Canada in 1871. At the time there was no overwhelming sentiment in favour of Confederation and in some quarters there was a considerable desire to join the United States. Pro-Confederation forces, led by a man who had given himself the delightful name of Amor de Cosmos, carried the issue after the Macdonald government agreed to link the Pacific region with central Canada by rail. As is well known, it was only in 1886 that the promise made to British Columbia was fulfilled. Until that time there were extremely few real links between British Columbia and the rest of Canada. At this time, the economy was still a small coastal trading centre exploiting resources

Table 13:11 Distribution of the British Columbian and Canadian Workforces, by Industrial Activity, 1911 and 1961
(per cent)

| | 1911 | | 1961 | |
| | B.C. | Canada (incl. B.C.) | B.C. | Canada (incl. B.C.) |
Industry				
(1)	(2)	(3)	(4)	(5)
Agriculture	11.5	34.2	4.0	9.9
Fishing and Trapping	5.7	1.3	3.7	0.5
Forestry	2.2	1.6	0.8	1.7
Mining	7.1	2.1	1.4	1.9
Primary Manufacturing[a]	10.8	5.3	13.4	7.7
Secondary Manufacturing	5.9	12.1	6.2	14.1
Electricity and Gas	0.5	0.4	0.9	1.0
Construction	15.0	7.3	6.9	7.2
Transportation	8.9	6.7	8.5	7.0
Trade	9.3	9.5	17.2	15.3
Finance, Insurance, etc.	2.5	1.4	3.9	3.5
Services	12.2	12.1	21.4	19.5
Public Administration	5.4	2.9	8.8	8.2
Others	3.0	3.2	2.9	2.5
Total	100.0	100.0	100.0	100.0

[a] Defined as the following industries: food, wood products, pulp and paper, primary steel, non-ferrous metal smelting, and non-metallic minerals.

Sources: R. M. McInnis supplied the data; see also R. M. McInnis, "Long-Run Changes in the Industrial Structure of the Canadian Work Force", *Canadian Journal of Economics*, Vol. 4, no. 3 (1971), pp. 353-61.

of the sea, the coastal forests, and the coal deposits of Vancouver Island. For the most part, markets for these products were found in Great Britain and on the west coast of the United States. A prosperous coal trade, for instance, developed between Vancouver Island and San Francisco. More and more, however, the railway shifted the focus of economic activity.

Prior to the coming of the railway the capital city of Victoria was the principal trading centre. Afterward the town of Vancouver assumed more and more of the shipping traffic. On the natural harbour of Burrard Inlet the harbour-rail terminus took an increasing amount of the trade with the interior replacing New Westminster, the port on the Fraser River, as the principal commercial centre. Apart from the coastal areas and the Fraser Valley, few parts of the province were extensively settled. The gold rushes into the Upper Fraser River and the Cariboo District had proven spasmodic. It was not until the 1890s with the development of the mining industry of the interior that the regional economy significantly spread. Later, as a lumber industry developed in response to the construction boom on the prairies, it reinforced the basis of economic development in the interior. Cattle ranching and fruit farming also began at this time.

As in the case of Nova Scotia and New Brunswick a bulk trade with the rest of Canada did not develop. Exports from the region generally were destined for foreign countries.[31] However, quite unlike the situation in the Maritimes the natural-resource base was much broader and industries, in the long run, could exploit these resources relatively efficiently. For instance, the mineral deposits in British Columbia proved to include many separate ores and fuels. Coal exports from the interior now constitute an important item in the regional-export bundle. So too, deposits of natural gas have become the basis of an important primary industry. The region is also well endowed with sources of hydroelectric power. In summary, the British Columbia economy has had a well-diversified primary-resource-using industry in contrast to that of the Maritimes. While this has generated per-capita income well above the Canadian average it has not, however, generated a stable pattern of employment.

More than most regions of Canada the economy is subject to seasonal fluctuations which directly influence employment. In addition, the primary sector is open to perturbations in demand for its products. The performance of the U.S. construction industry, for example, has a direct effect on lumber shipments. To the extent that the economy diversified among various natural-resource-using industries the effects of changes in demand did not always have a simultaneous impact which accounted for the lower average unemployment in British Columbia with respect to the Maritimes (see Table 13:3). Because primary production in the region has tended to develop with a high capital-labour ratio the unemployment impact was proportionately more severe in the tertiary sector much of which directly services the primary sector. Periods of employment, thus, were more discontinuous in British Columbia despite the high income per capita.

> There ain't no luck in town today,
> There ain't no work down Moodyville way.
> *Traditional Song.*

In summary, this chapter has focused attention on the regional economic disparities which have persisted throughout Canadian history. Of particular importance in this regard are those regions which have continually experienced economic performance which was markedly different from the national pattern: hence, our emphasis on Atlantic Canada and Quebec. Yet, it is also necessary to note, in a somewhat more cursory manner, that a region such as British Columbia which has persistently experienced a high per-capita income relative to the national average, shares some of the same problems. Unemployment in the western-most province has been traditionally high and variable.

Although in recent years there has been some reduction in the amount of regional inequality it has been small relative to the experience of other nations. The inter-regional movement of factors and government policy to promote more equality has not brought about the substantial changes in regional economic development necessary to close the gap.

CHAPTER FOURTEEN

Epilogue

The foundations of the Canadian economy rest in the colonial periods of the seventeenth and eighteenth centuries. However, it was not until the nineteenth century that the process of modern economic development began. At first it was evident in the growing commercial economy and by the 1850s and 1860s economic change took on some of its irreversible characteristics, the characteristics of structural change examined in this study. By then the economy was no longer a simple agricultural and natural-resource-exploiting enclave of settlement. Within a short period of time, by historical comparison, a geographically large nation was established whose economy afforded its citizens one of the highest standards of living ever achieved. Yet Canada was, and still remains, an open economy of modest size. Development of the open economy, as seen throughout this study, was complex and subject to the patterns of economic change in the international order. However, the Canadian economy was more than simply the product of international economic forces and a unique endowment of natural resource.

Today, countries which wish to initiate and stimulate economic development often adopt strategies to guide and hasten the process. These plans can be supported by international agencies, such as the World Bank, and by the more developed countries which extend aid in a variety of forms. Systematic planning of economic development is, however, a modern concept and few strategies of this type predated 1945. Planning, it is argued, is necessary to hasten the process of economic development principally because it is a mechanism which shifts emphasis from short-term to long-term goals, goals which may be in conflict.

Historically, most governments have had a powerful influence on the shaping of the economies of which they were part. Yet, most often governments' intervention and regulation was unconcerned with economic development, as such, but animated by the prospects of achieving higher aggregate income in the short run. Often, of course, such policies had an inadvertent effect on economic development. For instance, the mercantilist policies of France under Colbert and the later free-trade policy of Great Britain had long-run consequences even though they were initiated to increase immediate prosperity. Occasionally, some governments did undertake specific action to promote economic development in some limited sphere. The judicious use of tariffs in the early nineteenth century was found by many countries to be a particularly useful instrument for promoting domestic industry of one type or another. Canada itself was protected by the Baltic timber duties and given favoured treatment under the Corn Laws in order to stimulate economic expansion. This was felt to be in the imperial power's best interest. Yet few countries until the twentieth century ever produced policies in such a manner that in retrospect could be called a development strategy. Canada was an exception.

The early evolution of a development strategy in Canada stemmed from one unalterable fact—the proximity of Canada to the United States. Because of the similar natures of natural-resource endowments, relative factor scarcities, the openness of the early economies, and various other reasons, the more advanced economy of the United States was both an exemplar and a competitor. With the model of the U.S. economy, Canadian policy-makers invariably were drawn to make comparisons. Through such comparisons insights into the nature of economic development were garnered by political and industrial leaders and action upon them gave Canada a strategy of economic development, albeit an unplanned one. As we have seen throughout this study, such a strategy was not always coherent nor internally consistent. After all it was well appreciated that the simple imitation of the United States would not take into account the vastly different scales of the two economies. Furthermore, not only were the two competitors in many final-goods markets but they were also competitors for immigrants and savings from abroad.

The origin of the Canadian development strategy can be traced to the canal-building era. In emulating the example of the highly successful Erie Canal, in particular, Canadians of the time were also attempting to capture trade from the mid-western part of the continent. Naturally, those who most strongly supported the canal-building projects, both inside and outside of government, had the most to gain and, as noted, conflict did arise between the different economic interests. However, the pragmatism of self-interest was so strongly shaped by the performance of the southern neighbour that the unstated goal of rapid economic development was readily adopted. Expansion was also felt to be the only method of frustrating the northward shift of economic and political power. The United States was in some sense also a threat to sovereignty. The strategy which was to emerge from this beginning has been called by the historian Hugh Aitken one of "defensive-expansion".[1] It was adopted to protect and enhance market positions while expanding on the U.S. pattern of proven success.

Those who shaped the development strategy often had ill-defined immediate goals. For instance, governments were only reluctantly drawn into the railway business by often well-conceived but poorly executed projects. So too, there were only very crude mechanisms of control, mechanisms which were not effective enough to prevent the over-capitalization of railways several times in Canadian history, for instance. Even when long run goals were well understood and control could be exhibited, the various policies which comprised the strategy were sometimes inconsistent with the achievement of the highest possible income per capita. Thus, it may be argued that the themes of commercial policy caused duplication in Canada of similar secondary-manufacturing plant facilities to those found in the United States. But the scale of the Canadian economy could not justify such a structure of multi-product plants and Canadian consumers necessarily paid for the cost of such inefficiencies.

The highest expression of a strategy for economic development came in the form of the national policy. As noted earlier, this was not a single well-articulated policy but rather a set of policies brought down in the last quarter of the nineteenth century with some later additions. It had three main elements: the protection of Canadian manufacturing, the creation of a transcontinental railway, and the peopling of the Canadian west. This triad did not lack a certain amount of internal contradiction as we have seen. Other problems were also unforeseen. While the attempt to create employment in manufacturing in both the short- and long-run periods was recognized as a positive incentive to foreign direct investments, it was not appreciated that that type of investment might itself alter economic development. Natural-resource-exploiting foreign investments, with little or no manufacturing capacity in Canada, might thwart the efforts to develop manufacturing capacity very effectively. Not until later, as noted, was this particular problem perceived.

A cornerstone of the development strategy was the various attempts to integrate Canada's interests with some large trading area. During the colonial phase of development the link was, naturally, with Great Britain.

However, the experience of reciprocal free trade with the United States, although limited, left an indelible impression on the minds of Canadian policy-makers because of its apparent success. Reciprocity with the United States was long regarded as a panacea for all economic ailments. In a more limited sense, there can be little doubt that certain bilateral free-trade arrangements with the United States produced more and more efficient manufacturing in certain commodities — agricultural implements and automobiles, for example — than would otherwise have existed. However, whether a broadly defined free-trade arrangement with the United States would prejudice the long-run development of manufacturing or not is a matter of considerable controversy. Because of the proximity of the U.S. market and the historically free movement of factors between Canada and the economy to the south, attachment to the U.S. economy was sought by successive Canadian governments. U.S. policy-makers, on the other hand, were generally cautious about the possibility of admitting foreign goods and often raised tariffs to protect their domestic market. Thus, much of Canada's policy was a reaction to U.S. policy. There was no inconsistency in the minds of those who advocated free trade with the United States and subsequently pressed for an increase in tariffs. From time to time, government sought to extend its attachment from one larger trading unit to other areas. In the 1930s, for instance, there was a partly successful attempt to rejuvenate British empire trade on a preferential basis. More recently, Canadian governments have made overtures to the European Economic Community in an attempt to widen the Canadian export base as well as to increase the potential for manufacturing industry.

In contrast to the planned strategies for economic development of today, the Canadian unplanned strategy necessarily was limited both by internal and external economic conditions. Failure to appreciate the full implications of these constraints often led to a failure of policy. For instance, both industrialists and governments seem to have overestimated the extent of maturity of the domestic capital market at various times. Frequently projects, especially in the transport sector, could not be financed from domestic savings despite the expectation that they might be. Also, the state of the international economy severely limited the types of policy which succeeded. Particularly noticeable is the success and failure of the various immigration policies which depended so much on the relative prosperity and availability of land in the United States and other areas of new settlement. Although the international forces of economic change permitted the economy to grow rapidly when favourable, if they were not there were limits to the power of policy to shape the economy. Much of Canada's apparent development strategy then was to insulate the economy to some degree from the ill-effects of perverse economic forces stemming from the international economy: the creation of a market for domestically produced manufactured goods.

Motivating much of the attitude towards the desired nature of economic development was the fear of what is now known as "the staple trap". A staple trap is said to exist when an economy specializes in the production and export of staples with a low degree of processing. In turn, this leads to a commercial rather than an industrial economy. The economy then has only one potential dynamic sector which, of course, is vulnerable to the impact of long-run income-elasticity conditions. A trap, it is argued, exists because in such situations entrepreneurship and technical skills atrophy and this creates conditions which retard the development of a capital market in particular and all other markets in general. Also because of the relatively advanced state of industrial development elsewhere an economy can only exploit any latent comparative advantage in secondary manufacturing by absorbing high start-up costs; costs which a so-called trapped economy cannot bear.

During certain periods of Canadian history the economy did at least superficially resemble one caught in a staple trap. The troubled decade of the 1830s best displays such characteristics. Yet, such examples are rare and confined to early Canadian history. As seen throughout this study, conditions of the staple trap were avoided for two principal reasons. First, many new natural resources were brought into production and technical change often transformed the use of the more traditional ones. Second, the process of exploiting staples itself created a stimulus for the growth of capital-intensive transport in the tertiary sector and all sectors of manufacturing. After all, the economy changed most rapidly in structure when staple exploitation was most rapid. The broad strategy of economic development which was conceived in the second half of the nineteenth century laid down the framework which guided and accelerated this process of economic growth and structural change.

The interpretation of Canada's past which is presented here is directed towards a better understanding of the forces of economic growth and structural change. To serve such an end it has been necessary to concentrate attention on the broad themes of economic development and thereby to confine examination to the principal long-run causes and effects of economic change. It is the nature of inquiries into history that they can never be complete and never definitive; it is the quality which gives the study of economic history its fascination.

Notes

Chapter 1 (pages 1-9)

1. B. E. Supple, "Economic History, Economic Theory and Economic Growth", in B. E. Supple, ed., *The Experience of Economic Growth* (New York: Random House, 1963), pp. 1-46 and W. Parker, "Economic Development in Historical Perspective", *E.D.C.C.*, Vol. 10, no. 4 (1961), pp. 1-7.

2. J. R. T. Hughes, "Fact and Theory in Economic History", *E.E.H.*, Vol. 3, no. 2 (1966), pp. 75-100; H. A. Innis, "The Teaching of Economic History in Canada", in M. Q. Innis, ed., *Essays in Canadian Economic History* (Toronto: University of Toronto Press, 1956), pp. 3-16 and T. W. Schultz, "On Economic History in Extending Economics", in M. Nash, ed., *Essays on Economic Development and Cultural Change in Honor of Bert F. Hoselitz* (Chicago: University of Chicago Press, 1977), pp. 245-53.

3. In Canada the contribution by geographers has been particularly strong. Those not familiar with the historical geography of Canada may wish to consult D. G. Kerr, *Historical Atlas of Canada*, 3rd rev. ed. (Toronto: Nelson [Canada] Ltd., 1975).

4. For instance, see W. T. Easterbrook, "Long Period Comparative Study: Some Historical Cases", *J.E.H.*, Vol. 17, no. 4 (1957), pp. 571-95 and J. H. Young, "Comparative Economic Development: Canada and the United States", *A.E.R.*, Vol. 45, no. 1 (1955), pp. 80-93.

5. O. J. Firestone, *Canada's Economic Development, 1867-1953* (London: Bowes and Bowes, 1958) and S. Kuznets, *Modern Economic Growth* (New Haven: Yale University Press, 1966). The principal source of economic statistics of Canada's past is M. C. Urquhart and K. A. H. Buckley, eds., *Historical Statistics of Canada* (Toronto: Macmillan of Canada, 1965).

Chapter 2 (pages 10-41)

1. For bibliographic detail, see also chapters 3 and 11.

2. This is the definition most commonly used: see R. Caves and R. Holton, *The Canadian Economy: Prospect and Retrospect* (Cambridge, Mass.: Harvard University Press, 1959), p. 31.

3. See for example: W. A. C. Mackintosh, *The Economic Background of Dominion-Provincial Relations*, Royal Commission on Dominion-Provincial Relations (Ottawa: King's Printer, 1939; reprinted Toronto: McClelland and Stewart, 1964), Appendix 3 and "Economic Factors in Canadian History", *C.H.R.*, Vol. 4, no. 1 (1923), pp. 12-25; D. North, "Location Theory and Regional Economic Growth", *J.P.E.*, Vol. 62, no. 3 (1955), pp. 243-58; and M. H. Watkins, "A Staple Theory of Economic Growth", *C.J.E.P.S.*, Vol. 29, no. 2 (1963), pp. 141-58. In a wider context, see, for example: A. E. Hirschman, *Strategy of Economic Development* (New Haven: Yale University Press, 1958) and "A Generalized Linkage Approach to Development, with Special Reference to Staples", *E.D.C.C.*, Vol. 25, Supplement (1977), pp. 67-98.

4. See Chapter 3.

5. The open economy multiplier is the factor by which a net change in exports gives rise to a change of national income.

6. See Watkins, "A Staple Theory of Economic Growth" (1963).

7. H. A. Innis, "Transportation as a Factor in Canadian Economic History" and "Unused Capacity as a Factor in Canadian Economic History", in M. Q. Innis, ed., *Essays in Canadian Economic History* (Toronto: University of Toronto Press, 1956), pp. 62-77 and 141-55.

8. Production functions of this type measure the gross value of production. Later in this chapter, we shall have occasion to employ a value-added production function. The latter is based on the assumption that resource inputs are given and is, thus, compatible with the above when relatively short periods of history are being analysed.

9. Among the histories which emphasize this theme are: D. G. Creighton, *Dominion of the North: A History of Canada*, rev. ed. (Toronto: Macmillan of Canada, 1962) and *The Commercial Empire of the St. Lawrence, 1760-1850* (Toronto: Ryerson Press, 1937); A. R. M. Lower, *Colony to Nation: A History of Canada*, 4th ed. (Toronto: Longmans, 1964); and M. Zaslow, *The Opening of the Canadian North, 1870-1914* (Toronto: McClelland and Stewart, 1971).

10. A. D. Scott, "The Development of the Extractive Industries", *C.J.E.P.S.*, Vol. 28, no. 1 (1962), pp. 70-87.

11. K. Buckley, "The Role of Staple Industries in Canada's Economic Development", *J.E.H.*, Vol. 18, no. 4 (1958), pp. 429-50 and discussion by H. G. J. Aitken, in the same issue, pp. 451-52.

12. R. E. Caves, " 'Vent for Surplus' Models of Trade and Growth", in R. E. Caves, et al., eds., *Trade, Growth and the Balance of Payments: Essays in Honor of Gottfried Haberler* (Chicago: University of Chicago Press, 1965), pp. 95-115 and "Export-Led Growth and the New Economic History", in J. Bhagwati, et al., eds., *Trade, Balance of Payments, and Growth* (Amsterdam: North-Holland Press, 1971), pp. 403-42.

13. National income accounts for the years prior to 1926 were constructed by Firestone for the period 1851-1926 and Buckley for the period 1896-1930. See the citations throughout.

14. O. J. Firestone, *Canada's Economic Development, 1867-1953* (London: Bowes and Bowes, 1958), and "Development of Canada's Economy, 1850-1900", *Trends in the American Economy in the Nineteenth Century* (Princeton: N.B.E.R., 1960), pp. 217-52.

15. S. Kuznets, *Modern Economic Growth* (New Haven: Yale University Press, 1966), pp. 86-159.

16. The income elasticity measures the percentage change in consumption of a good relative to the percentage change in income at given prices. An income elasticity of unity means that a, say, ten per cent rise of income gives rise to a ten per cent increase in consumption of the good in question. A low income elasticity generally means one between zero and unity.

17. In the post-1945 decade the increased consumption of durable goods, housing, clothing, and foodstuffs was 135, 70, 53, and 43 per cent, respectively. M. C. Urquhart and K. A. H. Buckley, eds., *Historical Statistics of Canada* (Toronto: Macmillan of Canada, 1965), p. 134.

18. Kuznets, *Modern Economic Growth* (1966), pp. 19-113. Kuznets has shown that $r_i = a_i (1 + r_t) - 1$ where r is the rate of growth of output per decade of sector i and the whole economy t, and a_i is the ratio of the share of the ith sector in total product to its share a decade earlier. The a_i is the measure of industrial structure. Since the income elasticity of demand in a closed economy is $\xi_i = r_i/r_t$, it can be shown that $a_i = (1 + \xi_i r_t)/(1 + r_t)$. That is, the industrial structure is, in part, determined by the income elasticity. Of course, in an open economy there will be other influences which might temporarily reduce the impact of ξ_i domestically.

19. M. Abramovitz and P. David, "Economic Growth in America: History, Parables and Realities", *De Economiste*, Vol. 121, no. 3 (1973), pp. 251-72.

20. The Canadian results presented here are those of H. Lithwick, *Economic Growth in Canada* (Toronto: University of Toronto Press, 1967) and "Labour, Capital and Growth: The Canadian Experience", in T. N. Brewis, ed., *Growth and the Canadian Economy* (Toronto: McClelland and Stewart, 1968), pp. 65-75. For comparative U.S. studies see: E. F. Denison, *The Sources of Economic Growth in the United States* (New York: Committee for

Economic Development, 1962) and J. W. Kendrick, *Productivity Trends in the United States* (Princeton: N.B.E.R., 1961).

21. G. Bertram, *The Contribution of Education to Economic Growth*, Economic Council of Canada, Staff Study No. 12 (Ottawa: Queen's Printer, 1966) and discussion in Chapter 6.

22. For an examination of residual contributions by sector in a comparative context see E. Domar, *et al.*, "Economic Growth and Productivity in the United States, Canada, United Kingdom, Germany and Japan in the Post-War Period", *R.E. Stat.*, Vol. 46, no. 1 (1964), pp. 33-40.

23. J. Schmookler, *Invention and Economic Growth* (Cambridge, Mass.: Harvard University Press, 1966) and E. Mansfield, *The Economics of Technical Change* (New York: Norton, 1968).

24. O. J. Firestone, "Innovations and Economic Development—The Canadian Case", *The Review of Income and Wealth*, Series 18, Vol. 8 (1972). Also see H. G. Johnson, *Technology and Economic Interdependence* (London: Trade Policy Research Centre, 1975).

25. "Report of the Experimental Farms, Appendix to the Report of the Minister of Agriculture", *Sessional Papers of Canada* (Ottawa: King's Printer, various issues).

26. A. Faucher, "The Decline of Shipbuilding at Quebec in the Nineteenth Century", *C.J.E.P.S.*, Vol. 33, no. 2 (1957), pp. 195-215 and C. K. Harley, "On the Persistence of Old Techniques: The Case of North American Wooden Shipbuilding", *J.E.H.*, Vol. 33, no. 2 (1973), pp. 372-98.

27. Y. Kotowitz, "Capital-Labour Substitution in Canadian Manufacturing 1926-39 and 1946-61", *C.J.E.*, Vol. 1, no. 3 (1968), pp. 619-32 and "Technical Progress, Factor Substitution and Income Distribution in Canadian Manufacturing, 1926-39 and 1946-61", *C.J.E.*, Vol. 2, no. 1 (1969), pp. 106-14.

28. J. E. LaTourette, "Trends in the Capital-Output Ratio: United States and Canada, 1926-65", *C.J.E.*, Vol. 2, no. 1 (1969), pp. 35-51 and "Aggregate Factors in the Trends in Capital-Output Ratios", *C.J.E.*, Vol. 3, no. 2 (1970), pp. 255-75.

29. W. C. Hood and A. D. Scott, *Output, Labour, and Capital in the Canadian Economy*, Royal Commission on Canada's Economic Prospects (Ottawa: Queen's Printer, 1957).

Chapter 3 (pages 42-73)
1. M. Clawson, ed., *Natural Resources and International Development* (Baltimore: The Johns Hopkins Press, 1964); C. W. Clark, *Mathematical Bioeconomics: The Optimal Management of Renewable Resources* (New York: Wiley, 1976); D. W. Pearce, ed., *The Economics of Natural Resource Depletion* (London: Macmillan, 1975); and A. D. Scott, *Natural Resources: The Economics of Conservation* (Toronto: McClelland and Stewart, 1973).

2. D. G. Paterson, "Rights and Regulations: The North Pacific Seal Hunt, 1886-1910", *E.E.H.*, Vol. 14, no. 2 (1977), pp. 97-119 and D. G. Paterson and J. Wilen, "Depletion and Diplomacy: The North Pacific Seal Hunt, 1886-1910", in P. Uselding, ed., *Research in Economic History* (Greenwich, Conn.: JAI Press, 1977), Vol. 2, pp. 81-140.

3. Economic rent is a pure surplus after all costs, both explicit and implicit, have been subtracted from total revenue.

4. The major source of information in this section is H. A. Innis, *The Cod Fisheries: The History of an International Economy*, rev. ed. (Toronto: University of Toronto Press, 1954).

5. Ibid. Also see Innis's essays "An Introduction to the Economic History of the Maritimes, Including Newfoundland and New England" and "The Rise and Fall of the Spanish Fishery in Newfoundland", in M. Q. Innis, ed., *Essays in Canadian Economic History* (Toronto: University of Toronto Press, 1956), pp. 27-42 and 43-61, respectively.

6. The southern coast of Newfoundland was ceded to the British as exclusive territory in 1713. The French retained landing rights on the northeast coast until 1763 and on the west coast until 1904. See G. Graham, *The Empire of the North Atlantic: The Maritime Struggle for North America* (Toronto: University of Toronto Press, 1950).

7. See G. T. Cell, *English Enterprise in Newfoundland, 1577-1660* (Toronto: University of Toronto Press, 1969) and J. Gilchrist, "Exploration in Enterprise: The Newfoundland Fishery, c. 1497-1677", in D. S. Macmillan, ed., *Canadian Business History* (Toronto: McClelland and Stewart, 1972), pp. 27-43.

8. T. E. Norton, *The Fur Trade in Colonial New York, 1686-1776* (Madison, Wisc.: University of Wisconsin Press, 1974).

9. J. F. Crean, "Hats and the Fur Trade", *C.J.E.P.S.*, Vol. 28, no. 3 (1962), pp. 373-86 and M. Lawson, "The Beaver Hat and the Fur Trade", in M. Bolus, ed., *People and Pelts* (Winnipeg: Pequis Publishers, 1972), pp. 27-38.

10. J. McManus, "An Economic Analysis of Indian Behaviour in the North American Fur Trade", *J.E.H.*, Vol. 32, no. 1 (1972), pp. 36-53 and A. J. Ray, *Indians in the Fur Trade* (Toronto: University of Toronto Press, 1974).

11. H. A. Innis, *The Fur Trade in Canada*, rev. ed. (Toronto: University of Toronto Press, 1956), pp. 2-83.

12. W. J. Eccles, *The Canadian Frontier: 1534-1760* (New York: Holt, Rinehart and Winston, 1968).

13. H. P. Biggar, *The Early Trading Companies of New France* (New York: Argonaut Press, 1965).

14. Ray, *Indians in the Fur Trade* (1974), pp. 3-26.

15. Innis, *The Fur Trade in Canada* (1956), pp. 149-280.

16. H. A. Innis, "Interrelations between the Fur Trade of Canada and the United States", in Innis, ed., *Essays in Canadian Economic History* (1956), pp. 97-107; D. McKay, *The Honourable Company: A History of the Hudson's Bay Company*, rev. ed. (Toronto: McClelland and Stewart, 1949), pp. 121-48; F. Merk, *Fur Trade and Empire: George Simpson's Journal*, rev. ed. (Cambridge, Mass.: Belknap Press, 1968), p. 189.

17. K. G. Davies, "The Years of No Dividend: Finances of the Hudson's Bay Company, 1690-1718", in Bolus, ed., *People and Pelts* (1972), pp. 65-82 and E. E. Rich, *The Hudson's Bay Company*, 2 vols. (London: Hudson's Bay Society, 1958-59).

18. A. R. M. Lower, *Great Britain's Woodyard: British America and the Timber Trade, 1763-1867* (Montreal: McGill-Queen's University Press, 1973), pp. 3-26.

19. The discriminatory tariff against Baltic timber was raised from 11 shillings per load (50 cubic feet) to 22 shillings in the years 1802-05. It was then raised to 65 shillings in the late stages of the war and in the early 1820s this was partly offset by a small tariff of 2 shillings on colonial timber although the Baltic timber duty itself was reduced to 55 shillings in 1821. The high tariff on Baltic timber remained until 1842. It was then reduced systematically in the 1840s and by 1851 was only 1 shilling. The colonial tariff itself was revoked in 1842. A. R. M. Lower, "The Trade in Square Timber", in W. T. Easterbrook and M. Watkins, eds., *Approaches to Canadian Economic History* (Toronto: Macmillan of Canada, 1978), pp. 28-48. Also see R. G. Albion, *Forests and Sea Power: The Timber Problem of the Royal Navy, 1652-1862* (Cambridge, Mass.: Harvard University Press, 1926).

20. A. R. M. Lower, *The North American Assault on the Canadian Forest: A History of the Lumber Trade Between Canada and the United States* (Toronto: Ryerson Press, 1938), p. 3.

21. This theme is dealt with in most works on the timber industry as well as those on colonial agriculture; see Chapter 4.

22. It is assumed that output in agriculture is a simple function of land. As noted later, when capital in agriculture is also considered an input, savings generated from the timber trade can be used for investment purposes.

23. E. C. Guillet, *Early Life in Upper Canada* (Toronto: University of Toronto Press, 1933), pp. 232-51 and 277-78 and H. A. Innis and A. R. M. Lower, *Select Documents in Canadian Economic History, 1783-1885* (Toronto: University of Toronto Press, 1933), pp. 280-87.

24. J. W. Hughson and C. C. J. Bond, *Hurling Down the Pine* (Quebec: Historical Society of the Gatineau, 1964).

25. Lower, *Great Britain's Woodyard* (1973), pp. 261-62. Ocean freight rates between Quebec and Liverpool for a standard load of timber fell from 150 shillings in 1810 to 41 shillings in 1835 and by 1849-50 ranged between 26 and 31 shillings. P. D. McClelland, *The New Brunswick Economy in the Nineteenth Century*, Ph.D. thesis, Harvard University (1966), pp. 14-15.

26. H. A. Innis, "Unused Capacity as a Factor in Canadian Economic History", in Innis, ed., *Essays in Canadian Economic History* (1956), pp. 141-55.

Chapter 4 (pages 74-116)

1. For further reference see: C. Eicher and L. Witt, eds., *Agriculture in Economic Development* (New York: McGraw-Hill, 1964); J. W. Mellor, *The Economics of Agricultural Development* (Ithaca, N.Y.: Cornell University Press, 1966); and T. Schultz, *Transforming Traditional Agriculture* (New Haven: Yale University Press, 1964).

2. R. C. Harris and J. Warkentin, *Canada Before Confederation* (New York: Oxford University Press, 1974), pp. 65-109.

3. The best single source on the seigneurial system is R. C. Harris, *The Seigneurial System in Early Canada* (Madison, Wisc.: University of Wisconsin Press, 1968). Also see W. B. Munro, *The Seigneurial System in Canada: A Study in French Colonial Policy* (New York: Longmans, Green, 1907) and other works cited here.

4. For a review of the issues in a European context see: S. Fenoaltea, "Risk, Transaction Costs, and the Organization of Medieval Agriculture", *E.E.H.*, Vol. 13, no. 2 (1976), pp. 129-51; D. McCloskey, "English Open Fields as Behaviour Towards Risk", in P. Uselding, ed., *Research in Economic History* (Greenwich, Conn.: JAI Press, 1976), Vol. 1, pp. 124-70; as well as the debate between these two authors in *E.E.H.*, Vol. 14, no. 4 (1977), pp. 402-10.

5. Harris, *The Seigneurial System in Early Canada* (1968), pp. 20-40. Also see G. Frégault, *Canadian Society in the French Regime*, Canadian Historical Association, Booklet 3 (Ottawa, 1962) and M. Trudel, *The Seigneurial Regime*, Canadian Historical Association, Booklet 6 (Ottawa, 1971).

6. Even if the shadow price of land was zero a positive level of feudal dues would be appropriate because of the public-good characteristics of the system. For a discussion of the public-good aspect of feudal systems see: E. Domar, "The Cases of Slavery or Serfdom: A Hypothesis", *J.E.H.*, Vol. 30, no. 1 (1970), pp. 18-32 and L. E. David and D. C. North, *Institutional Change and American Economic Growth* (Cambridge, Mass.: Cambridge University Press, 1971).

7. The principal expression of this view is Munro, *The Seigneurial System in Canada* (1907). In part Munro's thesis rests on evidence such as that of a visit by the famous Swedish naturalist to New France. P. Kalm, *Travels into North America*, trans. J. R. Forster (London, 1771; reprinted Barre, Mass.:

Imprint Society, 1972). For a general introduction see M. Trudel, *Introduction to New France* (Toronto: Holt, Rinehart and Winston of Canada, 1968).

8. F. W. Burton, "The Wheat Supply of New France", in *Proceedings and Transactions of the Royal Society of Canada*, Vol. 30, 3rd series, Section 2 (1936), pp. 137-50 and "Wheat in Canadian History", *C.J.E.P.S.*, Vol. 3, no. 2 (1937), pp. 210-17; D. Delage, "Les Structures Economique de la Nouvelle-France et de la Nouvelle-York", *A.E.*, Vol. 46, no. 1 (1970), pp. 67-118; G. Frégault, *Le XVIIIᵉ Siècle Canadien* (Montreal: Editions H.M.H., 1970); and J. Hamelin, *Economie et Société en Nouvelle-France* (Québec: Les Presses de l'Université Laval, 1961).

9. A. J. E. Lunn, *Economic Development in French Canada, 1740-1760*, M.A. thesis, McGill University (1934), p. 72.

10. Among the principal church-owners were the Sulpicians, who held the seigneurie of *Ile de Montréal*, and the Bishop and Seminary of Quebec, with holdings which included the *St. Gabriel* seigneurie near Quebec. By far the single most important ecclesiastical holder of land was the Society of Jesus, the Jesuits. R. C. Dalton, *The Jesuits' Estates Question, 1760-1888* (Toronto: University of Toronto Press, 1968), pp. 60-77.

11. Harris, *The Seigneurial System in Early Canada* (1968), pp. 131-36, 145-46. By 1745, so many *rotures* had been further subdivided through inheritance that an edict was apparently needed setting the minimum width of a *roture* at one linear *arpent*, that is, about 192 feet. Only in the most densely populated seigneuries, however, was this a problem. Lunn, *Economic Development in French Canada, 1740-1760* (1934), p. 71.

12. For general works on the period see: F. Ouellet, *Histoire Economique et Sociale du Québec, 1760-1850: Structures et Conjuncture* (Montréal: Editions Fides, 1966) and M. Seguin, *La 'Nation Canadienne' et l'Agriculture, 1760-1850: Essai d'Histoire Economique* (Trois-Rivières: Editions Boréal Express, 1970).

13. R. L. Jones, "Agriculture in Lower Canada, 1792-1815", *C.H.R.*, Vol. 27, no. 1 (1946), pp. 35-61 and "French-Canadian Agriculture in the St. Lawrence Valley, 1815-1850", *A.H.*, Vol. 16, no. 2 (1942), pp. 141-48; G. McGuigan, "Economic Organization in Lower Canada, 1791-1809", in W. T. Easterbrook and M. Watkins, eds., *Approaches to Canadian Economic History* (Toronto: Macmillan of Canada, 1978), pp. 99-109; and P. Phillips, "Land Tenure and Economic Development: A Comparison of Upper and Lower Canada", *J.C.S.*, Vol. 9, no. 2 (1974), pp. 35-45.

14. R. C. Harris, "Of Poverty and Helplessness in Petite Nation", *C.H.R.*, Vol. 51, no. 1 (1971), pp. 25-50.

15. J. Hamelin et F. Ouellet, "Le Mouvement des Prix Agricoles dans la Province de Québec: 1760-1851", in C. Galarmeau et E. Lavoie, éds., *La*

France et le Canada Français du XVIᵉ au XXᵉ Siècle (Québec: Les Presses de l'Université Laval, 1966), pp. 35-48.

16. The debate about whether agriculture in Quebec was stagnating or simply slow to change is discussed in the writings of F. Ouellet and J. Hamelin, and G. Paquet and J.-P. Wallot, respectively. For an interpretation of the debate see T. J. A. Le Goff, "The Agricultural Crisis in Lower Canada, 1802-12: A Review of a Controversy", *C.H.R.*, Vol. 55, no. 1 (1974), pp. 1-31. Also see G. Paquet and J.-P. Wallot, "The Agricultural Crisis in Lower Canada, 1802-12: *Mise au Point*. A Response to T. J. A. Le Goff", *C.H.R.*, Vol. 56, no. 2 (1975), pp. 133-61 and T. J. A. Le Goff, "A Reply" in the same issue, pp. 162-68.

17. F. Ouellet, "L'Agriculture Bas-Canadienne Vue à Travers les Dimes et la Rente en Nature", *H.S./S.H.*, Vol. 8, no. 3 (1971), pp. 5-44.

18. See Ouellet, *Histoire Economique et Sociale du Québec, 1760-1850* (1966), and the works by R. L. Jones, F. Ouellet, and J. Hamelin, "La Crise Agricole dans le Bas-Canada, 1802-1837", *Canadian Historical Association Report* (1962), pp. 317-33.

19. G. Paquet and J.-P. Wallot, "Aperçu sur le Commerce International et les Prix Domestiques dans le Bas-Canada, 1793-1812", *R.H.A.F.*, Vol. 21, no. 3 (1967), pp. 447-73 and "Crise Agricole et Tensions Socio-Ethniques dans le Bas-Canada, 1802-1812: Eléments pour un Ré-interprétation", *R.H.A.F.*, Vol. 26, no. 2 (1972), pp. 185-237.

20. J. I. Little, "The Social and Economic Development of Settlers in Two Quebec Townships, 1851-1870", in D. H. Akenson, ed., *Canadian Papers in Rural History* (Gananoque, Ont.: Longdale Press, 1978), pp. 89-113.

21. R. L. Jones, *History of Agriculture in Ontario, 1613-1880* (Toronto: University of Toronto Press, 1946).

22. R. L. Gentilcore, "The Beginnings of Settlement in the Niagara Peninsula, 1782-1792", *C.G.*, Vol. 7, no. 3 (1963), pp. 72-82.

23. W. T. Easterbrook and H. G. J. Aitken, *Canadian Economic History* (Toronto: Macmillan of Canada, 1958), pp. 281-92 and R. L. Jones, "The Canadian Agricultural Tariff of 1843", *C.J.E.P.S.*, Vol. 7, no. 4 (1941), pp. 528-37.

24. O. J. McDiarmid, *Commercial Policy in the Canadian Economy* (Cambridge, Mass.: Harvard University Press, 1946), pp. 27-68.

25. D. G. Creighton, "The Economic Background of the Rebellions of 1837", *C.J.E.P.S.*, Vol. 3, no. 3 (1937), pp. 322-34 and W. H. Parker, "A New Look at Unrest in Lower Canada in the 1830's", *C.H.R.*, Vol. 4, no. 2 (1959), pp. 209-18.

26. L. F. Gates, *Land Policies of Upper Canada* (Toronto: University of Toronto Press, 1968) and A. Wilson, *The Clergy Reserves of Upper Canada: A Canadian Mortmain* (Toronto: University of Toronto Press, 1968), pp. 72-136.

27. Munro, *The Seigneurial System in Canada* (1907), pp. 224-51 and J.-P. Wallot, "Le Régime Seigneurial et Son Abolition au Canada", *C.H.R.*, Vol. 50, no. 4 (1969), pp. 367-93.

28. G. N. Tucker, *The Canadian Commercial Revolution, 1845-1851* (Toronto: McClelland and Stewart, 1964). Also see the notes to Chapter 5.

29. B. Johnston and P. Kilby, *Agriculture and Structural Transformation* (New York: Oxford University Press, 1975), pp. 182-239.

30. R. Pomfret, "The Mechanization of Reaping in Nineteenth-Century Ontario: A Case Study in the Pace and Causes of the Diffusion of Embodied Technical Change", *J.E.H.*, Vol. 36, no. 2 (1976), pp. 399-415.

31. M. C. Urquhart and K. A. H. Buckley, eds., *Historical Statistics of Canada* (Toronto: Macmillan of Canada, 1965), p. 373.

32. G. E. Reaman, *A History of Agriculture in Ontario* (Toronto: Saunders, 1970), pp. 67-172 and especially 122-23 and 142-44.

33. J. Hamelin et Y. Roby, *Histoire Economique du Québec, 1851-1896* (Montréal: Editions Fides, 1971), pp. 190-91 and Jones, "Agriculture in Lower Canada, 1792-1815" (1946), pp. 33-51.

34. Reaman, *A History of Agriculture in Ontario* (1970), pp. 86-87 and R. L. Jones, "The Agricultural Development of Lower Canada, 1850-1867", *A.H.*, Vol. 19, no. 2 (1945), pp. 212-24.

35. Explanation for the different levels of food productivity is threefold: the differences in farm size, the differences in productivity per acre, and the differences in the output levels of non-food items. J. Isbister, "Agriculture, Balanced Growth and Social Change in Central Canada Since 1850: An Interpretation", *E.D.C.C.*, Vol. 25, no. 4 (1977), pp. 673-97.

36. J. A. Ruddick, "The Development of the Dairy Industry in Canada", in H. A. Innis, ed., *The Dairy Industry in Canada* (Toronto: Ryerson Press, 1937), pp. 15-126.

37. H. A. Innis, "An Introduction to the Economic History of Ontario from Outpost to Empire", in M. Q. Innis, ed., *Essays in Canadian Economic History* (Toronto: University of Toronto Press, 1956), pp. 116-27.

38. O. E. Anderson, *Refrigeration in America: A History of a New Technology and Its Impact* (Princeton: Princeton University Press, 1953).

39. Ruddick, "The Development of the Dairy Industry in Canada" (1937), pp. 29-30.

40. The protection was removed in 1892 by new British quarantine regulations which required the slaughter of all Canadian cattle at the port of entry into Great Britain. The removal of protection notwithstanding, Canadian shipments of live cattle to Great Britain did not decline significantly until

about 1912. R. Perren, "The North American Beef and Cattle Trade with Great Britain, 1870-1914", *E.H.R.*, 2nd Ser., Vol. 24, no. 3 (1971), pp. 34-45.

41. D. A. Lawr, "The Development of Ontario Farming, 1870-1919: Patterns of Growth and Change", *O.H.*, Vol. 44, no. 4 (1972), pp. 239-51.

Chapter 5 (pages 117-48)

1. R. E. Caves and R. W. Jones, *World Trade and Payments* (Boston: Little, Brown and Co., 1973), pp. 227-314; H. G. Johnson, *Money, Trade and Economic Growth* (London: Allen and Unwin, 1962), Chapter 3; and S. Kuznets, *Modern Economic Growth* (New Haven: Yale University Press, 1966), pp. 285-358. On the subject of effective protection see J. Melvin and B. Wilkinson, *Effective Protection in the Canadian Economy*, Economic Council of Canada, Special Study No. 9 (Ottawa: Queen's Printer, 1968).

2. S. R. Weaver, "Taxation in New France: A Study in Pioneer Economics", *J.P.E.*, Vol. 22, no. 3 (1914), pp. 736-55.

3. H. G. J. Aitken, "The Changing Structure of the Canadian Economy", in H. G. J. Aitken, ed., *The American Economic Impact on Canada* (Durham, N.C.: Duke University Press, 1959), pp. 13-15.

4. O. J. McDiarmid, *Commercial Policy in the Canadian Economy* (Cambridge, Mass.: Harvard University Press, 1946), pp. 20-21.

5. M. C. Urquhart and K. A. H. Buckley, eds., *Historical Statistics of Canada* (Toronto: Macmillan, 1965), pp. 197-98.

6. B. W. Wilkinson and K. Norrie, *Effective Protection and the Return to Capital* (Ottawa: Information Canada, 1975).

7. C. D. W. Goodwin, *Canadian Economic Thought* (Durham, N.C.: Duke University Press, 1961), pp. 42-68.

8. For a discussion of anti-dumping and other trade policies see R. J. Wonnacott, *Canada's Trade Options*, Economic Council of Canada (Ottawa: Queen's Printer, 1975).

9. L. A. Harper, *The English Navigation Laws* (New York: Columbia University Press, 1939), and McDiarmid, *Commercial Policy in the Canadian Economy* (1946), pp. 11-33.

10. G. S. Graham, *British Policy and Canada, 1774-1791: A Study in 18th Century Trade Policy* (Westport, Conn.: Greenwich Press, 1974).

11. With respect to American shipments of produce to Great Britain before 1776, a lively literature includes: P. McClelland, "The Cost to America of British Imperial Policy", *A.E.R.*, *Papers and Proceedings*, Vol. 59, no. 2 (1969), pp. 370-85; J. Reid, "On Navigating the Navigation Acts with Peter McClelland: Comment", *A.E.R.*, Vol. 60, no. 5 (1970), pp. 949-55; R. P. Thomas, "A Quantative Approach to the Study of the Effects of British

Imperial Policy on Colonial Welfare: Some Preliminary Findings", *J.E.H.*, Vol. 25, no. 4 (1964), pp. 615-38; and G. Walton, "The New Economic History and the Burden of the Navigation Acts", *E.H.R.*, Vol. 24, no. 4 (1971), pp. 532-42.

12. J. F. Shepherd and G. Walton, *Shipping, Maritime Trade, and Economic Development of Colonial North America* (Cambridge: Cambridge University Press, 1972).

13. A. L. Burt, *Guy Carleton, Lord Dorchester, 1724-1808*, Canadian Historical Association, Booklet 5 (Ottawa, 1964).

14. J. B. Brebner, *North Atlantic Triangle* (Toronto: McClelland and Stewart, 1966), pp. 50-111.

15. W. T. Easterbrook and H. G. J. Aitken, *Canadian Economic History* (Toronto: Macmillan of Canada, 1958), pp. 153-59.

16. S. McKee, "Canada's Bid for the Traffic of the Middle-West", *Canadian Historical Association Report* (1940), pp. 26-35.

17. K. E. Knorr, *British Colonial Theories, 1570-1850* (Toronto: University of Toronto Press, 1944).

18. McDiarmid, *Commercial Policy in the Canadian Economy* (1946), pp. 34-60.

19. For the development of the customs in Upper Canada see F. H. Armstrong, "Ports of Entry and Collectors of Customs in Upper Canada", *Inland Seas*, Vol. 26 (Summer 1970), pp. 137-244.

20. D. G. Creighton, *The Commercial Empire of the St. Lawrence, 1760-1850* (Toronto: Ryerson Press, 1937), pp. 255-320.

21. R. L. Jones, "The Canadian Agricultural Tariff of 1843", *C.J.E.P.S.*, Vol. 7, no. 4 (1941), pp. 528-37.

22. C. D. Allin and G. M. Jones, *Annexation, Preferential Trade and Reciprocity* (Toronto: Musson, 1912) and G. N. Tucker, *The Canadian Commercial Revolution, 1845-1851* (Toronto: McClelland and Stewart, 1964).

23. D. C. Masters, *The Reciprocity Treaty of 1854* (Toronto: Longmans, Green, 1936).

24. L. H. Officer and L. B. Smith, "The Canadian-American Reciprocity Treaty of 1855 to 1866", *J.E.H.*, Vol. 28, no. 4 (1968), pp. 598-623.

25. R. Ankli, "The Reciprocity Treaty of 1854", *C.J.E.*, Vol. 4, no. 1 (1971), pp. 1-20.

26. S. A. Saunders, "The Maritime Provinces and the Reciprocity Treaty", *Dalhousie Review*, Vol. 14, no. 2 (1934), pp. 155-71 and "The Reciprocity Treaty of 1854: A Regional Study", *C.J.E.P.S.*, Vol. 2, no. 1 (1936), pp. 41-53.

27. The western British colonies of British Columbia and Vancouver Island were not parties to the treaty.

28. G. W. Brown, "The Opening of the St. Lawrence to American Shipping", *C.H.R.*, Vol. 7, no. 1 (1926), pp. 4-12.

29. Officer and Smith, "The Canadian-American Reciprocity Treaty of 1855 to 1866" (1968), pp. 619-22.

30. J. H. Young, *Canadian Commercial Policy*, Royal Commission on Canada's Economic Prospects (Ottawa: Queen's Printer, 1957), pp. 21-31.

31. D. F. Barnett, "The Galt Tariff: Incidental or Effective Protection?", *C.J.E.*, Vol. 9, no. 3 (1976), pp. 389-407.

Chapter 6 (pages 149 to 87)

1. W. E. Kalbach and W. W. McVey, *The Demographic Bases of Canadian Society* (Toronto: McGraw-Hill, 1971).

2. These are all summarized in the 1931 census.

3. Statistics Canada, *Vital Statistics*, Cat. no. 84-202.

4. For a discussion of the general issues see D. Heer, "Economic Development and the Fertility Transition", in D. V. Glass and R. Revelle, eds., *Population and Social Change* (New York: Edward Arnold, 1972), pp. 99-113.

5. See M. C. Urquhart and K. A. H. Buckley, eds., *Historical Statistics of Canada* (Toronto: Macmillan of Canada, 1965), p. 41, for both life-expectancy figures and death rates cited above.

6. H. Charbonneau et Y. Lavoie, "Introduction à la Réconstitution de la Population du Canada au XVIIe Siècle: Etude Critique des Sources de la Période 1665-1668", *R.H.A.F.*, Vol. 24, no. 1 (1971), pp. 485-571; R. C. Harris, "The French Background of Immigration to Canada before 1700", *Cahiers de Géographie du Québec* (Autumn 1972), pp. 313-24; and G. Langlois, *Histoire de la Population Canadienne-Française* (Montréal: Editions Lévesque, 1934).

7. J. Henripin, "From Acceptance of Nature to Control: The Demography of the French Canadians", *C.J.E.P.S.*, Vol. 22, no. 1 (1957), pp. 9-19 and J. Henripin and Y. Peron, "The Demographic Transition of the Province of Quebec", in Glass and Revelle, eds., *Population and Social Change* (1972), pp. 213-31.

8. R. M. McInnis, "Childbearing and Land Availability: Some Evidence from Individual Household Data", in R. D. Lee, ed., *Population Patterns in the Past* (New York: Academic Press, 1977), pp. 201-28 and N. B. Rao, "An Overview of Fertility Trends in Ontario and Quebec", *Canadian Studies in Population*, Vol. 1 (1974), pp. 37-42.

9. J. Henripin, "Observations sur la Situation Démographique des Canadiens Français", *A.E.*, Vol. 32 (March 1957), pp. 559-80; J. Henripin et Y. Peron, "Evolution Démographique Recente du Québec", *Annaire du Québec*, Vol. 152 (1972), pp. 8-122; and R. La Chapelle, "La Fécondité au Québec et Ontario: Quelques Eléments de Comparison", *Canadian Studies in Population*, Vol. 1 (1974), pp. 13-28.

10. See Heer, "Economic Development and the Fertility Transition" (1972), pp. 103-11 and P. A. Neher, "Peasants, Procreation and Pensions", *A.E.R.*, Vol. 61, no. 3, Part 1 (1971), pp. 380-89.

11. W. B. Hurd, "The Decline in the Canadian Birth Rate", *C.J.E.P.S.*, Vol. 3, no. 1 (1937), pp. 40-57; W. B. Hurd and J. C. Cameron, "Population Movements in Canada: Some Further Considerations", *C.J.E.P.S.*, Vol. 1, no. 2 (1935), pp. 222-45; A. H. Neveau and Y. Kasahara, "Demographic Trends in Canada, 1941-56, and Some of Their Implications", *C.J.E.P.S.*, Vol. 24, no. 1 (1958), pp. 9-20.

12. Urquhart and Buckley, eds., *Historical Statistics of Canada* (1965), p. 39.

13. J. Henripin, *Trends and Factors of Fertility in Canada*, Census Monograph (Ottawa: Information Canada, 1972) and Statistics Canada, *Vital Statistics*, Cat. no. 84-202.

14. M. J. Brennan, "A More General Theory of Resource Migration", in M. J. Brennan, ed., *Patterns of Market Behaviour* (Providence, R.I.: Brown University Press, 1965), pp. 45-64 and L. Sjaastad, "The Costs and Returns to Human Migration", *J.P.E.*, Vol. 70, no. 5, Part 2 (1962), pp. 80-93.

15. Because of individual differences in evaluating non-pecuniary benefits and because of individual differences in access to information, the flow will gradually increase or decrease rather than simply occur or not occur.

16. The best estimate is that approximately 10,000 immigrants came from France during the French regime. Of these, about 1,100 were marriageable young girls, almost 900 of which arrived between 1665 and 1673 as *filles du roi*. M. Trudel, *Introduction to New France* (Toronto: Holt, Rinehart, and Winston, 1968), p. 67, 136. J. Hamelin, *Economie et Société en Nouvelle-France* (Québec: Les Presses de l'Université Laval, 1961), pp. 75-114 and E. Salone, *La Colonisation de la Nouvelle-France* (Paris: Editions G.-P. Maisonneuve et Larose, 1905).

17. E. J. Ashton, "Soldier Land Settlement in Canada", *Q.J.E.*, Vol. 39, no. 2 (1925), pp. 488-98; H. I. Cowan, *British Immigration to British North America: The First Hundred Years*, rev. ed. (Toronto: University of Toronto Press, 1961) and *British Immigration Before Confederation*, Canadian Historical Association, Booklet 22 (Ottawa, 1968); and A. R. M. Lower, "Immigration and Settlement in Canada, 1812-1820", *C.H.R.*, Vol. 3, no. 1 (1922), pp. 37-47.

18. F. Landon, *Western Ontario and the American Frontier* (Toronto: McClelland and Stewart, 1967), pp. 12-61; N. MacDonald, *Canada, 1763-1841: Immigration and Settlement, The Administration of the Imperial Land Regulations* (London: Longmans, Green, 1939); and L. Upton, ed., *The United Empire Loyalists: Men and Myths* (Toronto: Copp Clark, 1967).

19. H. A. Innis, "Unused Capacity as a Factor in Canadian Economic History", in M. Q. Innis, ed., *Essays in Canadian Economic History* (Toronto: University of Toronto Press, 1956), pp. 141-55.

20. R. S. Langley, "Emigration and the Crisis of 1837 in Upper Canada", *C.H.R.*, Vol. 17, no. 1 (1936), pp. 29-40.

21. It is entirely likely that the general incidence of disease and death on the immigrant ships carrying the Irish was much higher than that on the typical slave ships of a century earlier.

22. G. N. Tucker, "The Famine Immigration to Canada, 1847", *A.H.R.*, Vol. 36, no. 3 (1931), pp. 533-49 and C. Woodham-Smith, *The Great Hunger* (New York: Harper and Row, 1962), especially chapters XI and XII.

23. General reviews of this period are found in D. C. Corbett, *Canada's Immigration Policy* (Toronto: University of Toronto Press, 1957) and N. MacDonald, *Canada: Immigration and Colonization, 1841-1903* (Toronto: Macmillan of Canada, 1966).

24. The principal statistical evidence is that of: N. Keyfitz, "The Growth of the Canadian Population", *Population Studies*, Vol. 4 (1950), pp. 47-63; D. M. McDougall, "Immigration into Canada, 1851-1920", *C.J.E.P.S.*, Vol. 27, no. 2 (1961), pp. 162-76; and J. Pickett, "An Evaluation of Estimates of Immigration into Canada in the Late Nineteenth Century", *C.J.E.P.S.*, Vol. 31, no. 4 (1965), pp. 499-508.

25. For a more complete discussion of these issues see Chapter 11 and K. H. Norrie, "The Rate of Settlement of the Canadian Prairies, 1870-1911", *J.E.H.*, Vol. 35, no. 2 (1975), pp. 410-27.

26. G. Paquet, "L'Emigration des Canadiens Français vers la Nouvelle-Angleterre, 1870-1910", *Récherches Sociographiques*, Vol. 5 (December 1964), pp. 319-70.

27. Corbett, *Canada's Immigration Policy* (1957), pp. 4-11 and M. Timlin, "Canada's Immigration Policy, 1896-1910", *C.J.E.P.S.*, Vol. 26, no. 4 (1960), pp. 517-32.

28. T.-F. Cheng, *Oriental Immigration into Canada* (Shanghai: The Commercial Press, 1931).

29. A. Green, *Immigration and the Post-War Economy* (Toronto: Macmillan of Canada, 1976) and W. L. Marr, "Canadian Immigration Policy Since 1962", *Canadian Public Policy*, Vol. 1, no. 2 (1975), pp. 196-203.

30. R. H. Coats, "Canada", in W. F. Wilcox, ed., *International Migration* (New York: N.B.E.R. 1931), Vol. 1, pp. 357-70; R. H. Coats and M. C. MacLean, *The American-Born in Canada* (Toronto: Ryerson Press, 1943); A. R. M. Lower, "The Case Against Immigration", *Queen's Quarterly*, Vol. 37 (Summer 1930), pp. 557-74 and *Census of Canada, 1931*, "Summary", Vol. 1.

31. M. Percy, "Immigration and Emigration During the Decade of the Canadian Wheat Boom, 1901-1911", *C.J.E.*, forthcoming.

32. R. Caves and R. Holton, *The Canadian Economy: Prospect and Retrospect* (Cambridge, Mass.: Harvard University Press, 1959), pp. 51-59; B. Thomas, *Migration and Economic Growth*, 2nd ed. (Cambridge: Cambridge University Press, 1973), pp. 244-89; and M. Timlin, *Does Canada Need More People?* (Toronto: Oxford University Press, 1951).

33. I. Anderson, *Internal Migration in Canada, 1931-1961*, Economic Council of Canada, Staff Study No. 13 (Ottawa: Queen's Printer, 1966) and L. O. Stone, *Migration in Canada*, Census Monograph (Ottawa: Queen's Printer, 1961).

34. R. Wilson, "Migration Movements in Canada, 1868-1925", *C.H.R.*, Vol. 13, no. 2 (1932), pp. 157-82.

35. K. Buckley, "Historical Estimates of Internal Migration in Canada", in E. Beach and J. Weldon, eds., *Conference on Statistics, 1960* (Toronto: University of Toronto Press, 1962), pp. 1-37.

36. L. O. Stone, *Urban Development in Canada*, Census Monograph (Ottawa: Queen's Printer, 1968).

37. L. Tuesdall, *The Canadian-Born in the United States* (New Haven: Yale University Press, 1943).

38. J. Spelt, *Urban Development in South Central Ontario* (Toronto: McClelland and Stewart, 1972). Also see Chapter 12.

Chapter 7 (pages 188-221)

1. For an introduction into the study of labour market operations see S. G. Peitchinis, *Canadian Labour Economics* (Toronto: McGraw-Hill Ryerson, 1970).

2. S. Ostry, "The Canadian Labour Market", in R. V. Miller and F. Isbister, eds., *Canadian Labour in Transition* (Scarborough: Prentice-Hall, 1971), pp. 15-23 and Peitchinis, *Canadian Labour Economics* (1970), pp. 23-24.

3. S. Ostry and M. A. Zaidi, *Labour Economics*, 2nd ed. (Toronto: Macmillan of Canada, 1972), pp. 60-61.

4. See R. C. Harris and J. Warkentin, *Canada Before Confederation* (New York: Oxford University Press, 1974), pp. 55-62.

5. Calculated from Canada, *Census of Canada, 1871*, Vol. 5, p. 90.

6. Ibid., pp. 90-92.

7. Wagner's Law is outlined and discussed in R. M. Bird, "Wagner's Law and Expanding State Activity", *Public Finance*, Vol. 26, no. 1 (1971), pp. 1-26.

8. S. T. J. Kulshreshtha, "Measuring the Relative Income of Farm Labour, 1941-1961", *C.J.A.E.*, Vol. 4, no. 1 (1967), pp. 28-43 and R. M. McInnis, "Long-Run Changes in the Industrial Structure of the Canadian Work Force", *C.J.E.*, Vol. 4, no. 3 (1971), pp. 353-61.

9. The regional structure of Canada's labour force is dealt with in A. G. Green, *Regional Aspects of Canada's Economic Growth* (Toronto: University of Toronto Press, 1971), pp. 45-60. Also see Chapter 13.

10. S. Kuznets, *Modern Economic Growth* (New Haven: Yale University Press, 1966), pp. 168-69.

11. T. Copp, *The Anatomy of Poverty: The Conditions of the Working Class in Montreal, 1897-1929* (Toronto: McClelland and Stewart, 1974), pp. 30-43.

12. The Department of Labour budget studies were based on the typical requirements of working families in a variety of Canadian cities. See also Canada, *Labour Gazette* (Ottawa, 1910-29) and Canada, *Report of the Board of Inquiry into the Cost-of-Living in Canada* (Ottawa: King's Printer, 1915), familiarly known as the Coats Report after its principal investigator, R. H. Coats.

13. G. Bertram and M. Percy, "Real Wage Trends in Canada, 1900-26: Some Provisional Estimates", *C.J.E.*, Vol. 12, no. 2 (1979), pp. 300-12.

14. S. M. Jamieson, *Industrial Relations in Canada*, 2nd ed. (Toronto: Macmillan of Canada, 1973); A. M. Kruger, "The Direction of Unionism in Canada", in Miller and Isbister, eds. *Canadian Labour in Transition* (1971), pp. 85-118; and H. A. Logan, *Trade Unions in Canada: Their Development and Functioning* (Toronto: Macmillan of Canada, 1948).

15. This classification is from J. T. Dunlop, "The Development of Labor Organization: A Theoretical Framework", in R. L. Rowan, ed., *Readings in Labor Economics and Labor Organization* (Homewood, Ill.: Irwin, 1972), pp. 66-81.

16. See the documentary collection M. S. Cross, ed., *The Workingman in the Nineteenth Century* (Toronto: Oxford University Press, 1974).

17. There is a large literature on the subject of Canadian-American unions. It includes: J. Crispo, *International Unionism: A Study in Canadian-American Relations* (Toronto: McGraw-Hill, 1967); J. T. Montague, "International Unions and the Canadian Labour Movement", *C.J.E.P.S.*, Vol. 23, no. 1 (1957), pp. 69-82; and J. N. Ware and H. A. Logan, *Labour in Canadian-American Relations: The History of Labour Interaction* (Toronto: Ryerson Press, 1937).

18. Thus reducing the number of commonly used acronyms. But see: E. Forsey, "The Movement Towards Labour Unity in Canada", *C.J.E.P.S.*, Vol. 24, no. 1 (1958), pp. 70-83; H. C. Pentland, "The Development of the Capitalistic Labour Market in Canada", *C.J.E.P.S.*, Vol. 28, no. 2 (1962), pp. 204-24; and other sources cited here.

19. M. Robin, *Radical Politics and Canadian Labour, 1880-1930* (Kingston: Industrial Relations Centre of Queen's University, 1968).

20. H. Espessat, J.-P. Hardy, et T. Ruddell, "Le Monde du Travail du Québec au XVIIIe et au XIXe Siècles: Historiographie et Etat de la Question", *R.H.A.F.*, Vol. 25, no. 1 (1972), pp. 499-539 and J. Hamelin et F. Harvey, *Les Travailleurs Québécois, 1941-1971*, Cahiers de l'Institut Supérieur des Sciences Humaines (Québec: Les Presses de l'Université Laval, 1976).

21. See Jamieson, *Industrial Relations* (1973), throughout.

22. N. H. Lithwick, *Economic Growth in Canada* (Toronto: University of Toronto Press, 1967), pp. 21-36.

23. For a description of nineteenth-century labour conditions see Canada, *Report of the Royal Commission on the Relations of Labor and Capital* (Ottawa: Queen's Printer, 1889).

24. J. D. Wilson, et al., eds., *Canadian Education: A History* (Scarborough: Prentice-Hall, 1970).

25. D. Stager, "The Economics of Education", in J. Chant, ed., *Canadian Perspectives in Economics* (Toronto: Collier Macmillan, 1972), B3.

26. M. Stamp, "Technical Education, the National Policy, and Federal-Provincial Relations in Canadian Education", *C.H.R.*, Vol. 52, no. 4 (1971), pp. 404-23.

27. O. J. Firestone, *Industry and Education* (Ottawa: University of Ottawa Press, 1969), pp. 177-96.

28. G. W. Bertram, *The Contribution of Education to Economic Growth*, Economic Council of Canada, Staff Study No. 12 (Ottawa: Queen's Printer, 1966), pp. 7-39.

29. The calculation of improvements in quality of the labour force as a result of formal education requires the empirical relationship between earnings and years of schooling. This relationship is taken from data in the 1961 Canadian Census and is combined with a distribution of males in the labour force by amount of education to arrive at quality improvements for 1941-51 and 1951-61. This is then extrapolated and interpolated to provide estimates for the period 1926-56. See Lithwick, *Economic Growth in Canada* (1967), pp. 11-13, 88-90.

30. S. Jamieson, *Times of Trouble: Labour Unrest and Industrial Conflict in Canada, 1900-66*, Task Force on Labour Relations, Study No. 22 (Ottawa: Queen's Printer, 1968).

31. J. D. Bercuson, "The Winnipeg General Strike, Collective Bargaining and the One Big Union", *C.H.R.*, Vol. 51, no. 2 (1970), pp. 164-76 and D. C. Masters, *The Winnipeg General Strike* (Toronto: University of Toronto Press, 1950).

32. S. Jamieson, "Militancy and Violence in Canadian Labour Relations: 1900-1975", forthcoming.

Chapter 8 (pages 222-64)

1. The two best sources are: K. A. H. Buckley, *Capital Formation in Canada, 1896-1930* (Toronto: University of Toronto Press, 1955) and O. J. Firestone, *Canada's Economic Development, 1867-1953* (London: Bowes and Bowes, 1958).

2. Buckley, *Capital Formation in Canada, 1896-1930* (1955), pp. 1-17 and S. Kuznets, *Modern Economic Growth* (New Haven: Yale University Press, 1966), pp. 1-33.

3. The lack of good evidence on the 1880s means that this is debatable. However, the increased railroad mileage as well as the gross immigration noted in Chapter 6 strongly suggest some basic strength in the economy, especially in the early years of the decade.

4. See later in this chapter as well as in Chapter 11.

5. Domestic service as an industry in the nineteenth century has dwindled in importance and now accounts for a trivial part of GNP. In 1870, the industry produced an estimated $6.2 million worth of services or about 1.53 per cent of GNP. Firestone, *Canada's Economic Development, 1867-1953* (1958), p. 263.

6. Interest-rate differentials between regions or industries are extremely difficult to measure. Nevertheless, there is ample circumstantial evidence that these differentials narrowed. See, for instance, Canada, *Report of the Board of Inquiry into the Cost-of-Living in Canada* (Ottawa: King's Printer, 1915).

7. Arbitrage may be defined as taking advantage of different prices in different markets or traffic in bills of exchange or stocks for profit.

8. E. P. Neufeld, *The Financial System of Canada: Its Growth and Development* (Toronto: Macmillan of Canada, 1972), pp. 176-219.

9. The most recent expression of this viewpoint is found in T. Naylor, *The History of Canadian Business* (Toronto: James Lorimer and Co., 1975).

10. See Chapter 3.

11. See G. N. Tucker, *The Canadian Commercial Revolution, 1845-1851* (Toronto: McClelland and Stewart, 1964).

12. C. Nish, *François-Étienne Cuget, 1719-1754: Entrepreneur et Entreprises en Nouvelle-France* (Montréal: Editions Fides, 1975).

13. H. G. J. Aitken, "A New Way to Pay Old Debts: A Canadian Experience", in W. Miller, ed., *Man in Business* (New York: Harper and Row, 1952), pp. 71-90.

14. See A. W. Currie, "The First Dominion Companies Act", *C.J.E.P.S.*, Vol. 28, no. 3 (1962), pp. 387-404 for a review of the legal basis of company organization.

15. See the various railway histories noted in Chapter 9.

16. The major financial journal of the period — *The Monetary Times,* Toronto — recorded the new exchanges.

17. This view has been promulgated by J. K. Galbraith, *The New Industrial State* (Boston: Houghton-Mifflin Co., 1967).

18. See Chapter 9.

19. T. W. Acheson, "The Social Origins of the Canadian Industrial Elite, 1880-1885", in D. S. Macmillan, ed., *Canadian Business History* (Toronto: McClelland and Stewart, 1972), pp. 144-74 and "Changing Social Origins of the Canadian Industrial Elite, 1880-1910", *B.H.R.*, Vol. 47, no. 2 (1973), pp. 189-217. Also see G. Tulchinsky, "The Montreal Business Community, 1837-1853", in Macmillan, ed., *Canadian Business History* (1972), pp. 125-43.

20. For a treatment of the social and economic background of the present-day so-called elites see J. A. Porter, *The Vertical Mosaic: An Analysis of Social Class and Power in Canada* (Toronto: University of Toronto Press, 1965) and W. Clement, *The Canadian Corporate Elite: An Analysis of Economic Power* (Toronto: McClelland and Stewart, 1975).

21. The literature on this subject is voluminous. Interesting comparisons with the Canadian literature, however, can be drawn from R. Andreano, "A Note on the Horatio Alger Legend: Statistical Studies of the Nineteenth Century Business Elite", in L. P. Cain and P. Uselding, eds., *Business Enterprise and Economic Change: Essays in Honor of Harold F. Williamson* (Kent, Ohio: Kent State University Press, 1973), pp. 227-46.

22. For example see: J. M. Careless, "The Business Community in the Early Development of Victoria, British Columbia", in J. Freisen and H. K. Ralston, eds., *Historical Essays on British Columbia* (Toronto: McClelland and Stewart, 1976), pp. 177-200; D. G. Paterson, "European Financial Capital and British Columbia: An Essay on the Role of the Regional Entrepreneur", *B.C. Studies*, Vol. 11 (Spring 1974), pp. 33-47; D. S. Macmillan, "The New Men in Action: Scottish Mercantile and Shipping Operations in the North American Colonies, 1760-1825", in Macmillan, ed., *Canadian Business History* (1972), pp. 44-103. Also see the fine bibliographic essay, F. H. Armstrong, "Canadian Business History: Approaches and Publications", in Macmillan, ed., *Canadian Business History* (1972), pp. 253-87.

23. The most vituperative account is also the most readable: G. Myers, *A History of Canadian Wealth* (Toronto: James Lewis and Samuel, 1972).

24. A quasi-rent is a rent (pure surplus) which is temporary in nature because it can be easily eroded by entry into the activity where it is generated.

25. J. Lorne MacDougall, "The Character of the Entrepreneur: The Case of George Stephen", in Macmillan, ed., *Canadian Business History* (1972), pp. 192-96.

26. R. M. Breckenridge, *The Canadian Banking System, 1817-1890* (New York: Macmillan, 1895).

27. By far the most comprehensive source of information is E. P. Neufeld, *The Financial System of Canada: Its Growth and Development* (Toronto: Macmillan of Canada, 1972).

28. Among the authored histories are: M. Denison, *Canada's First Bank: A History of the Bank of Montreal* (Toronto: McClelland and Stewart, 1966); J. Schull, *One Hundred Years of Banking: A History of the Toronto-Dominion Bank* (Toronto: Copp Clark, 1958); and R. Victor, *The History of the Canadian Bank of Commerce* (Toronto: Oxford University Press, 1920), 2 vols. with a third volume of this history by A. St. L. Trigge, 1934. None of the above, however, are critical evaluations. For a full description of Canadian banks and banking see *A Bibliography of Canadian Banking* (Toronto: The Canadian Bankers' Association, 1970).

29. See for example T. S. Ashton and R. S. Sayers, eds., *Papers in English Monetary History* (Toronto: Oxford University Press, 1953).

30. See E. Neufeld, ed., *Money and Banking in Canada* (Toronto: McClelland and Stewart, 1964), pp. 1-148; E. C. Guillet, "Pioneer Banking in Ontario: The Bank of Upper Canada", *C.B.*, Vol. 55, no. 1 (1948), pp. 114-32; as well as the many papers by A. Shortt published in *The Canadian Bankers' Association Journal*, between 1896 and 1906.

31. R. A. Lester, "Playing Card Currency of French Canada", in Neufeld, ed., *Money and Banking* (1964), pp. 9-23. Also see A. Shortt, *Documents Relating to Currency, Exchange and Finance in Nova Scotia with Prefactory Documents, 1675-1748*, Board of Historical Publications (Ottawa: King's Printer, 1933).

32. The Bank of Montreal's charter was directly fashioned after that of Alexander Hamilton's First Bank of the United States.

33. See for example P. Temin, *The Jacksonian Economy* (New York: Norton, 1969).

34. D. E. Bond and R. A. Shearer, *The Economics of the Canadian Financial System* (Scarborough: Prentice-Hall, 1972), chapters 9, 10, 12, and 16.

35. Neufeld, *The Financial System of Canada* (1972), pp. 71-139 and Appendix A.

36. Although the chartered banks have often been accused of directing funds from the slow-growing to fast-growing regions of Canada (or central Canada), the case has never been proven.

37. See T. J. Courchene, "An Analysis of the Canadian Money Supply, 1925-1934", *J.P.E.*, Vol. 77 (May 1969), pp. 363-91. High-powered money is defined as the monetary base which includes bank reserves (inside money) and currency outside the banks (outside money).

38. Bond and Shearer, *The Economics of the Canadian Financial System* (1972), pp. 257-74.

39. Courchene, "An Analysis of the Canadian Money Supply, 1925-1934" (1969) and G. Macesich, "Determinants of Monetary Velocity in Canada, 1926-1958", *C.J.E.P.S.*, Vol. 28, no. 2 (1962), pp. 245-54, as well as other works by the same author in the same source.

40. Neufeld, *The Financial System of Canada* (1972), pp. 176-219.

41. See Buckley, *Capital Formation in Canada, 1896-1930* (1955); O. J. Firestone, *Residential Real Estate in Canada* (Toronto: University of Toronto Press, 1951); and J. Pickett, "Residential Capital Formation in Canada, 1871-1921", *C.J.E.P.S.*, Vol. 29, no. 1 (1963), pp. 40-58.

42. Canada, "Reports of the Superintendent of Insurance", *Sessional Papers of Canada* (Ottawa: Queen's Printer, 1870-1929).

43. I. M. Drummond, "Life Insurance Companies and the Capital Market, 1890-1914", *C.J.E.P.S.*, Vol. 28, no. 2 (1962), pp. 204-24.

44. Neufeld, *The Financial System of Canada* (1972), pp. 490-541, and, for example, Y. Roby, *Alphonse Desjardins et les Caisses Populaires, 1854-1920* (Montréal: Editions Fides, 1964).

Chapter 9 (pages 265-301)
1. K. A. H. Buckley, *Capital Formation in Canada, 1896-1930* (Toronto: University of Toronto Press, 1955), p. 99.

2. H. C. Pentland, "The Role of Capital in Canadian Economic Development Before 1875", *C.J.E.P.S.*, Vol. 16, no. 4 (1950), p. 459.

3. See Chapter 10.

4. See for example C. P. Kindleberger, *The World in Depression, 1929-1939* (Los Angeles: University of California Press, 1973).

5. The relative importance of all North American capital inflows from Great Britain is well documented in J. G. Williamson, *American Growth and the Balance of Payments, 1820-1913* (Chapel Hill, N.C.: University of North Carolina Press, 1964).

6. M. C. Urquhart and K. A. H. Buckley, eds., *Historical Statistics of Canada* (Toronto: Macmillan of Canada, 1965), pp. 171-72.

7. The reader might wish to refer to D. E. Bond and R. A. Shearer, *The Economics of the Canadian Financial System* (Scarborough: Prentice-Hall, 1972), Chapter 7.

8. E. C. Wright, "Life and Hard Times", in L. Upton, ed., *The United Empire Loyalists: Men and Myths* (Toronto: Copp Clark, 1967), pp. 76-82.

9. Urquhart and Buckley, eds., *Historical Statistics of Canada* (1965), pp. 160-63.

10. Cited in J. Viner, *Canada's Balance of International Indebtedness, 1900-1913* (Cambridge, Mass.: Harvard University Press, 1924; reprinted Toronto: McClelland and Stewart, 1975), p. 41.

11. See Chapter 10.

12. G. N. Tucker, *The Canadian Commercial Revolution, 1845-1851* (Toronto: McClelland and Stewart, 1964), pp. 47-48.

13. W. T. Easterbrook and H. G. J. Aitken, *Canadian Economic History* (Toronto: Macmillan of Canada, 1958), p. 318, 372.

14. See A. W. Currie, *The Grand Trunk Railway of Canada* (Toronto: University of Toronto Press, 1957).

15. M. Simon, "New British Investments in Canada, 1865-1914", *C.J.E.*, Vol. 3, no. 2 (1970), pp. 238-54.

16. F. W. Field, *Capital Investments in Canada,* 3rd ed. (Montreal: Monetary Times of Canada, 1914).

17. See for example A. I. Bloomfield, *Patterns of Fluctuations in International Investments Before 1914*, Princeton Studies in International Finance No. 21 (Princeton, N.J., 1921) and B. Thomas, *Migration and Economic Growth: A Study of Great Britain and the Atlantic Community* (Cambridge: Cambridge University Press, 1973).

18. A. H. Imlah, *Economic Elements in the Pax Britannica* (New York: Russell and Russell, 1958), pp. 42-81.

19. C. K. Harley, "Transportation, the World Wheat Trade and the Kuznets Cycle, 1850-1913", in R. Caves, et al., eds., *Exports and Economic Growth* (Princeton, N.J.: Princeton University Press, forthcoming).

20. For a thorough review of this issue see J. P. Lewis, *Building Cycles and Britain's Growth* (London: Macmillan, 1965).

21. See Figure 7:1.

22. See Buckley, *Capital Formation in Canada, 1896-1930* (1958); Thomas, *Migration and Economic Growth* (1973); Lewis, *Building Cycles and Britain's*

Growth (1965); and J. Pickett, "Residential Capital Formation in Canada, 1871-1921", *C.J.E.P.S.*, Vol. 29, no. 1 (1963), pp. 40-58.

23. The classic treatment of this subject is Viner, *Canada's Balance of International Indebtedness, 1900-1913* (1924). Interpretations and critiques include A. Cairncross, *Home and Foreign Investment, 1870-1913* (Cambridge: Cambridge University Press, 1953); J. C. Ingram, "Growth and Capacity in Canada's Balance of Payments", *A.E.R.*, Vol. 117, no. 1 (1957), pp. 93-104; G. M. Meier, "Economic Development and the Transfer Mechanism", *C.J.E.P.S.*, Vol. 19, no. 1 (1953), pp. 1-19; and J. A. Stovel, *Canada in the World Economy* (Cambridge, Mass.: Harvard University Press, 1967).

24. Stovel, *Canada in the World Economy* (1967), pp. 156-62.

25. See Meier, "Economic Development and the Transfer Mechanism" (1953) and Stovel, *Canada in the World Economy* (1967), pp. 199-213.

26. Cairncross, *Home and Foreign Investment, 1870-1913* (1953), Chapter 7 and C. A. E. Goodhart, *The New York Money Market and the Financing of Trade, 1900-1913* (Cambridge, Mass.: Harvard University Press, 1969), pp. 139-56.

27. See for example D. G. Paterson, *British Direct Investment in Canada, 1890-1914: Estimates and Determinants* (Toronto: University of Toronto Press, 1976) and M. Wilkins, *The Emergence of Multinational Enterprise: American Business Abroad from the Colonial Era to 1914* (Cambridge, Mass.: Harvard University Press, 1970).

28. G. A. D. MacDougall, "The Benefits and Costs of Private Investment from Abroad: A Theoretical Approach", in J. Bhagwati, ed., *International Trade* (Middlesex: Penguin Books, 1969), pp. 341-69.

29. Canada, *Foreign Ownership and the Structure of Canadian Industry*, Report of the Task Force on the Structure of Canadian Industry, Privy Council Office (Ottawa: Queen's Printer, 1968) and K. Levitt, *Silent Surrender: The Multinational Corporation in Canada* (Toronto: Macmillan of Canada, 1970).

30. See Chapter 4.

31. H. Marshall, F. A. Southard, and K. W. Taylor, *Canadian-American Industry* (New Haven: Yale University Press, 1936), p. 6.

32. C. Lewis, *America's Stake in International Investments* (Washington: The Brookings Institution, 1938) and other works cited here.

33. Paterson, *British Direct Investment in Canada, 1890-1914* (1976), pp. 23-79.

34. O. W. Main, *The Canadian Nickel Industry* (Toronto: University of Toronto Press, 1955).

35. Ontario, *Report of the Royal Ontario Nickel Commission*, Royal Ontario Nickel Commission, Legislative Assembly of Ontario (Toronto, 1917).

36. Marshall, Southard, and Taylor, *Canadian-American Industry* (1936) and Wilkins, *The Emergence of Multinational Enterprise* (1970), pp. 70-79, 135-48.

37. M. Bliss, "Canadianizing American Business: The Roots of the Branch Plant", in I. Lumsden, ed., *Close the 49th Parallel: The Americanization of Canada* (Toronto: University of Toronto Press, 1970), pp. 27-42 and S. Scheinberg, "Invitation to Empire: Tariffs and American Economic Expansion in Canada", *B.H.R.*, Vol. 47, no. 2 (1973), pp. 218-38.

38. D.B.S., *Canada's International Investment Position, 1926-1954* (Ottawa, 1954).

39. Marshall, Southard, and Taylor, *Canadian-American Industry* (1936), pp. 24-27, 28-29, 80-86.

40. C. H. Aikman, *The Automobile Industry of Canada* (Toronto: Macmillan, 1926) and references cited in Chapter 12.

41. Canada, *Report of the Royal Commission on Pulpwood*, Chairman J. Picard (Ottawa: King's Printer, 1924).

42. E. S. Moore, *The American Influence in Canadian Mining* (Toronto: University of Toronto Press, 1941) and D. Slater, *Canada's Imports*, Royal Commission on Canada's Economic Prospects (Ottawa: Queen's Printer, 1957).

43. I. Brecher and S. S. Reisman, *Canada–United States Economic Relations* (Ottawa: Queen's Printer, 1957), Part II.

44. J. Fayerweather, *Foreign Investment in Canada: Prospects for National Policy* (Toronto: Oxford University Press, 1974).

45. Canada, *Foreign Direct Investment in Canada* (Ottawa: Queen's Printer, 1972), pp. 41-43, 229-36.

46. This view finds expression in Lumsden, ed., *Close the 49th Parallel* (1970).

47. See the various studies of the Royal Commission on Canada's Economic Prospects (1957).

Chapter 10 (pages 302-38)

1. For a general introduction to transport economics see: A. W. Currie, *Canadian Transportation Economics* (Toronto: University of Toronto Press, 1967) and H. Hunter, "Resources, Transportation and Economic Development", in J. J. Spengler, ed., *Natural Resources and Economic Growth* (Washington: Resources for the Future, 1961).

2. See A. A. Walters, *The Economics of Road User Charges* (Baltimore: The Johns Hopkins Press, 1968), Chapter 5, for more details of the model used here.

3. The social-savings concept was first employed in economic history in a discussion of U.S. railroad development. See A. Fishlow, *American Railroads and the Transformation of the Ante-Bellum Economy* (Cambridge, Mass.: Harvard University Press, 1965), pp. 23-32 and R. W. Fogel, *Railroads and American Economic Growth* (Baltimore: The Johns Hopkins Press, 1964), pp. 12-48.

4. E. C. Guillet, *The Story of Canadian Roads* (Toronto: University of Toronto Press, 1966).

5. A. F. Burghardt, "The Origin and Development of the Road Network of the Niagara Penninsula, 1770-1851", *Annals of the Association of American Geographers*, Vol. 59, no. 2 (1969), pp. 417-40.

6. G. P. de T. Glazebrook, *A History of Transportation in Canada*, 2 vols. (Toronto: McClelland and Stewart, 1964), Vol. I, pp. 101-46.

7. For a general history of the early postal service see W. Smith, *History of the Post Office in British North America* (Cambridge: Cambridge University Press, 1920).

8. T. F. McIlwraith, "The Adequacy of Rural Roads in the Era Before Railways: An Illustration from Upper Canada", *C.G.*, Vol. 14, no. 2 (1970), pp. 344-60 and W. H. Breidhaupt, "Dundas Street and Other Early Upper Canada Roads", Ontario Historical Society, *Papers and Records*, Vol. 21 (1924), pp. 5-10.

9. As cited in Glazebrook, *A History of Transportation in Canada* (1964), Vol. I, p. 136.

10. E. C. Guillet, *Pioneer Inns and Taverns*, 4 vols. (Toronto: Ontario Publishing Co., 1956).

11. For a particularly good view of early travel see J. J. Talman, "Travel in Ontario Before the Coming of the Railway", Ontario Historical Society, *Papers and Records*, Vol. 29 (1933), pp. 85-102.

12. C. Goodrich, *Canals and American Economic Development* (New York: Columbia University Press, 1961), pp. 7-66 and R. W. Filante, "A Note on the Economic Viability of the Erie Canal", *B.H.R.*, Vol. 48, no. 1 (1974), pp. 95-102.

13. T. F. McIlwraith, "Freight Capacity and Utilization of the Erie and Great Lakes Canals Before 1850", *J.E.H.*, Vol. 36, no. 4 (1976), pp. 852-75.

14. On finances, see H. G. J. Aitken, *The Welland Canal Company: A Study in Canadian Enterprise* (Cambridge, Mass.: Harvard University Press, 1954), pp. 77-109.

15. R. F. Legget, *Rideau Waterway*, rev. ed. (Toronto: University of Toronto Press, 1972).

16. T. C. Keefer, *The Canals of Canada: Their Prospects and Influence* (Toronto: Armor and Co., 1850).

17. G. N. Tucker, *The Canadian Commercial Revolution, 1845-1851* (Toronto: McClelland and Stewart, 1964), pp. 48-64.

18. As above and also see G. J. J. Tulchinsky, *The River Barons: Montreal Businessmen and the Growth of Industry and Transportation, 1837-53* (Toronto: University of Toronto Press, 1977), pp. 35-106.

19. Glazebrook, *A History of Transportation in Canada* (1964), Vol. I, pp. 86-96.

20. For the metropolitan thesis see: J. M. S. Careless, "Frontierism, Metropolitanism, and Canadian History", *C.H.R.*, Vol. 34, no. 1 (1954), pp. 1-21, "Metropolitanism and Nationalism", in P. Russell, ed., *Nationalism in Canada* (Toronto: McGraw-Hill, 1966), pp. 271-83, and "Aspects of Metropolitanism in Atlantic Canada", in M. Wade, ed., *Regionalism in the Canadian Community, 1867-1967* (Toronto: University of Toronto Press, 1969), pp. 117-29.

21. For details, see Glazebrook, *A History of Transportation in Canada* (1964), Vol. I, pp. 140-79. Also see O. D. Skelton, *The Railway Builders: A Chronicle of Overland Highways* (Toronto: Glasgow-Brook, 1916) and other works cited here.

22. For details on the commodities carried on the Great Lakes system from 1870 to 1911 see S. H. Williamson, "The Growth of the Great Lakes as a Major Transportation Resource, 1870-1911", in P. Uselding, ed., *Research in Economic History* (Greenwich, Conn.: JAI Press, 1977), Vol. II, pp. 173-248.

23. W. T. Easterbrook and H. G. J. Aitken, *Canadian Economic History* (Toronto: Macmillan of Canada, 1958), pp. 298-99 and 314-16.

24. There are many histories which document early railway development, among which are: Canada, *A Statutory History of the Steam and Electric Railways of Canada, 1836-1937* (Ottawa: Department of Transport, 1938); A. W. Currie, *The Grand Trunk Railway of Canada* (Toronto: University of Toronto Press, 1957); and G. R. Stevens, *The Canadian National Railways*, Vol. I (Toronto: Clark, Irwin, 1960).

25. J. S. Martell, "Intercolonial Communications, 1840-1867", *Canadian Historical Association Report* (1938), pp. 41-61.

26. See Stevens, *The Canadian National Railways* (1960), Vol. I.

27. P. Berton, *The National Dream: The Great Railway, 1871-1881* (Toronto: McClelland and Stewart, 1970) and *The Last Spike: The Great Railway, 1881-1885* (Toronto: McClelland and Stewart, 1971); and H. A. Innis, *A History of the Canadian Pacific Railway* (Toronto: University of Toronto Press, 1971).

28. P. D. McClelland, "Social Rates of Return on American Railroads in the Nineteenth Century", *E.H.R.*, Vol. 25, no. 3 (1972), pp. 471-88.

29. P. J. George, "Rates of Return in Railway Investment and Implication for Government Subsidization of the Canadian Pacific Railway: Some Preliminary Results", *C.J.E.*, Vol. 1, no. 4 (1968), pp. 740-62 and "Rates of Return and Government Subsidization of the Canadian Pacific Railway: Some Further Remarks", *C.J.E.*, Vol. 8, no. 4 (1975), pp. 591-600, and L. J. Mercer, "Rates of Return and Government Subsidization of the Canadian Pacific Railway: An Alternate View", *C.J.E.*, Vol. 6, no. 3 (1973), pp. 428-37.

30. H. A. Innis, "The Location of the Route of the C.P.R.", *C.H.R.*, Vol. 18, no. 1 (1937), pp. 87-89 and F. G. Roe, "An Unsolved Problem of Canadian History", *Canadian Historical Association Reports* (1936), pp. 65-77.

31. L. J. Mercer, "Building Ahead of Demand: Some Evidence for the Land-Grant Railroads", *J.E.H.*, Vol. 34, no. 2 (1974), pp. 492-500.

32. The Hon. W. Laurier, *House of Commons Debates*, July 30, 1903, p. 7659.

33. T. D. Regehr, "The Canadian Northern Railway: The West's Own Product", *C.H.R.*, Vol. 51, no. 2 (1970), pp. 177-87.

34. Canada, *Report of the Royal Commission to Inquire into Railways and Transportation in Canada* (Ottawa: King's Printer, 1917), known popularly as the Drayton-Acworth Report.

35. H. J. Darling, "Transport Policy in Canada: The Struggle of Ideologies *vs.* Realities", in K. W. Studnicki-Gizbert, ed., *Issues in Canadian Transport Policy* (Toronto: Macmillan of Canada, 1974), pp. 3-46.

36. For a discussion of contemporary attitudes see K. Norrie, "Western Economic Grievances: An Overview with Special Reference to Freight Rates", Economic Council of Canada Conference on the Political Economy of Confederation (Kingston, 1978).

37. H. L. Purdy, *Transportation Competition and Public Policy in Canada* (Vancouver: University of British Columbia Press, 1972), pp. 175-82.

38. A. W. Currie, "Freight Rates and Regionalism", *C.J.E.P.S.*, Vol. 14, no. 3 (1948), pp. 427-40; J. L. McDougall, "The Relative Levels of Crow's Nest Grain Rates in 1899 and in 1965", *C.J.E.P.S.*, Vol. 32, no. 1 (1966), pp. 46-54; and E. P. Reid, "Statutory Grain Rates", *Royal Commission on Transportation* (Ottawa: Queen's Printer, 1962), Vol. 3.

39. Canada, "Georgian Bay Ship Canal: Report Upon Survey with Plans and Estimates of Cost", *Sessional Papers of Canada, 1908* (Ottawa: King's Printer, 1909).

40. L. P. Sydor, "The St. Lawrence Seaway: National Shares in Seaway Wheat Benefits", *C.J.E.*, Vol. 4, no. 4 (1971), pp. 543-55.

41. Currie, *Canadian Transportation Economics* (1967), pp. 254-70.

42. C. A. Ashley, *The First Twenty-five Years: A Study of Trans Canada Air Lines* (Toronto: Macmillan of Canada, 1963).

Chapter 11 (pages 339-374)

1. The depression of 1873 is often referred to as "the Great Depression" both because of its long length in some countries and its widespread nature. There has long been considerable controversy over the depth of the depression in various countries, although the United States, where it first became evident in the financial crash of 1873, experienced a short but profound depression. Elsewhere it was not so profound but lasted, it is claimed, until about 1896 in some areas.

2. The prevailing view of the last quarter of the nineteenth century as one of relatively poor economic performance coupled with bouts of depression was that of O. D. Skelton, "General Economic History, 1867-1912", in A. Shortt and A. G. Doughty, eds., *Canada and Its Provinces: A History of the Canadian People and Their Institutions* (Toronto: Publishers' Association, 1914), Vol. IX, pp. 110-90.

3. W. E. Vickery, "Exports and North American Economic Growth: 'Structuralist' and 'Staple' Models in Historical Perspective", *C.J.E.*, Vol. 7, no. 1 (1974), pp. 32-58.

4. O. J. Firestone, "Development of Canada's Economy, 1850-1890", *Trends in the American Economy in the Nineteenth Century* (Princeton: N.B.E.R., 1960), Vol. 24, pp. 277-52, and in the same volume: O. J. Firestone, "Canada's External Trade and Net Foreign Balance, 1851-1900", pp. 757-71 and Hartland, "Canadian Balance of Payments since 1868", pp. 717-55.

5. The spread of the world wheat economy at this time is well described in C. K. Harley, "Transportation, the World Wheat Trade and the Kuznets Cycle, 1850-1913", in R. Caves, *et al.*, eds. *Exports and Economic Growth* (Princeton: Princeton University Press, forthcoming).

6. R. W. Murchie, *Agricultural Progress on the Prairie Frontier* (Toronto: Macmillan of Canada, 1936), pp. 22-50.

7. A. S. Morton and C. Martin, *History of Prairie Settlement and "Dominion Lands" Policy* (Toronto: Macmillan of Canada, 1938), pp. 394-434 and M. C. Urquhart and K. A. H. Buckley, eds., *Historical Statistics of Canada* (Toronto: Macmillan of Canada, 1965), p. 310.

8. This argument is set out in W. Marr and M. Percy, "The Government and the Rate of Canadian Prairie Settlement", *C.J.E.*, Vol. 11, no. 4 (1978), pp. 757-62; K. Norrie, "The Rate of Settlement of the Canadian Prairies, 1870-1911", *J.E.H.*, Vol. 35, no. 2 (1975), pp. 410-27; and K. Grant, "The Rate of Settlement of the Canadian Prairies, 1870-1911: A Comment", *J.E.H.*, Vol.

38, no. 2 (1978), pp. 471-72. For an earlier discussion see J. Stabler, "Factors Affecting the Development of a New Region: The Canadian Great Plains, 1870-1897", *Annals of Regional Science*, Vol. 7, no. 2 (1973), pp. 75-87.

9. C. Southey, "The Staple Thesis, Common Property, and Homesteading", *C.J.E.*, Vol. 11, no. 3 (1978), pp. 547-59.

10. K. Bicha, *The American Farmer and the Canadian West, 1876-1914* (Lawrence, Ka.: Coronado Press, 1968) and M. Percy and T. Woraby, "The Determinants of American Migration by State to the Canadian Prairies: 1899 and 1909", *E.E.H.*, forthcoming.

11. Canada Yearbook, 1914, p. 91.

12. J. W. Dafoe, *Clifford Sifton in Relation to His Times* (Toronto: Macmillan of Canada, 1931).

13. D. A. MacGibbon, *The Canadian Grain Trade* (Toronto: Macmillan of Canada, 1932) and W. Malenbaum, *The World Wheat Economy, 1885-1939* (Cambridge, Mass.: Harvard University Press, 1953).

14. K. A. H. Buckley, *Capital Formation in Canada, 1896-1930* (Toronto: University of Toronto Press, 1955), p. 16 and O. J. Firestone, *Canada's Economic Development, 1867-1953* (London: Bowes and Bowes, 1958), p. 156.

15. E. J. Chambers and D. F. Gordon, "Primary Products and Economic Growth: An Empirical Measurement", *J.P.E.*, Vol. 74, no. 4 (1966), pp. 315-22; J. H. Dales, J. C. McManus, and M. H. Watkins, "Primary Products and Economic Growth: A Comment", *J.P.E.*, Vol. 75, no. 6 (1967), pp. 876-79; F. Lewis, "The Canadian Wheat Boom and Per Capita Income: New Estimates", *J.P.E.*, Vol. 83, no. 6 (1974), pp. 1249-53; G. W. Bertram, "The Relevance of the Wheat Boom in Canadian Economic Growth", *C.J.E.*, Vol. 6, no. 4 (1973), pp. 545-66.

16. M. Zaslow, *Reading the Rocks: The Story of the Geological Survey of Canada, 1842-1972* (Toronto: Macmillan of Canada, 1975).

17. D. M. LeBourdais, *Sudbury Basin: The Story of Nickel* (Toronto: Ryerson Press, 1953) and *Metals and Men* (Toronto: McClelland and Stewart, 1957) and W. O. Main, *The Canadian Nickel Industry* (Toronto: University of Toronto Press, 1955).

18. J. Davis, *Mining and Mineral Processing in Canada*, Royal Commission on Canada's Economic Prospects (Ottawa: Queen's Printer, 1957), pp. 9-18, 28-42.

19. G. B. Langford, *Out of the Earth: The Mineral Industry of Canada* (Toronto: University of Toronto Press, 1954).

20. British Columbia, *The Mineral Province of Canada, 1905* (Victoria, B.C.: Provincial Bureau of Mines, 1905).

21. Davis, *Mining and Mineral Processing in Canada* (1957), p. 375.

22. See E. S. Moore, *American Influence in Canadian Mining* (Toronto: University of Toronto Press, 1941).

23. A. R. M. Lower, *The North American Assault on the Canadian Forest: A History of the Lumber Trade Between Canada and the United States* (Toronto: Ryerson Press, 1938), pp. 160-84.

24. Ibid., pp. 195-96.

25. W. A. Carrothers, "Forest Industries of British Columbia", in Lower, *The North American Assault on the Canadian Forest* (1938), pp. 227-344 and H. N. Whitford and R. D. Craig, *Forests of British Columbia* (Ottawa: Commission of Conservation, 1918).

26. K. H. Burley, *The Development of Canada's Staples, 1867-1939: A Documentary Collection* (Toronto: McClelland and Stewart, 1970), pp. 332-76 and A. R. M. Lower, *Settlement and the Forest Frontier in Eastern Canada* (Toronto: Macmillan of Canada, 1936).

27. E. Forsey, "The Pulp and Paper Industry", *C.J.E.P.S.*, Vol. 1, no. 3 (1935), pp. 501-09 and C. Southworth, "The American-Canadian Newsprint Paper Industry and the Tariff", *J.P.E.*, Vol. 30, no. 5 (1922), pp. 681-97.

28. See Chapter 3 and its references.

29. J. H. Dales, "Fuel, Power and Industrial Development in Central Canada", *A.E.R.*, Vol. 43, no. 2 (1953), pp. 181-98.

30. W. J. A. Donald, *The Canadian Iron and Steel Industry: A Study in the Economic History of a Protected Industry* (Boston: Houghton Mifflin, 1915); D.B.S., *Report on the Coal Trade, 1918* (Ottawa, 1919); and Canada, *Report of the Royal Commission on Coal, 1946*, Chairman W. F. Carroll (Ottawa: King's Printer, 1947).

31. A. E. D. Grauer, "The Export of Electricity from Canada", in R. M. Clark, ed., *Canadian Issues: Essays in Honour of Henry F. Angus* (Toronto: University of Toronto Press, 1961), pp. 248-85.

32. H. V. Nelles, *The Politics of Development: Forests, Mines, and Hydro-Electric Power in Ontario, 1849-1941* (Toronto: Macmillan of Canada, 1974), pp. 215-375.

33. Grauer, "The Export of Electricity from Canada" (1961), p. 259. Drayton qualified his conclusions somewhat because American producers were also important to the war effort. Also see Nelles, *The Politics of Development* (1974).

34. J. Davis, *The Canadian Chemical Industry*, Royal Commission on Canada's Economic Prospects (Ottawa: Queen's Printer, 1957), pp. 5-18; A. W. G. Wilson, *Development of Chemical, Metallurgical, and Allied Industries in*

Canada (Ottawa: Department of Mines, 1924), pp. 58-68 and for the political history of this conflict see Nelles, *The Politics of Development* (1974), pp. 307-81.

35. Davis, *Mining and Mineral Processing in Canada* (1957), pp. 144-45 and Wilson, *Development of Chemical, Metallurgical, and Allied Industries in Canada* (1924), pp. 180-82. For the history of the industry in Quebec, see J. H. Dales, *Hydroelectricity and Industrial Development in Quebec, 1898-1940* (Cambridge, Mass.: Harvard University Press, 1957).

36. Davis, *Mining and Mineral Processing in Canada* (1957), p. 343. The complex ores of British Columbia gave rise to a classic example of what economists know as "the joint-product problem", the essence of which is the apportioning of costs when two outputs are produced as a consequence of trying to produce one.

37. J. F. Due, *The Intercity Electric Railway Industry in Canada* (Toronto: University of Toronto Press, 1966).

38. In recent years electric buses and subways have come into use in some cities. Ibid., pp. 37-38.

39. The average cost of electricity for industrial purposes in 1964 in Norway, Canada, the United States, and Great Britain was 0.4, 0.6, 0.9, and 1.6 cents per kilowatt hour, respectively. N. B. Guyol, *The World Electric Power Industry* (Berkeley: University of California Press, 1969), pp. 31-76.

Chapter 12 (pages 375-417)
1. See Chapter 5.

2. "Mr. Speaker, I go heartily for the union, because it will throw down the barriers of trade and give us the control of a market of four million people." Hon. George Brown, cited in P. B. Waite, ed., *The Confederation Debates in the Province of Canada, 1865* (Toronto: McClelland and Stewart, 1963), p. 68.

3. Canada, *Report of the Select Committee on the Causes of the Present Depression, House of Commons Journal* (Ottawa: Queen's Printer, 1876).

4. The United States, in fact, made a more rapid recovery from the Depression of 1873 than did Canada despite the deeper nature of the depression in that country.

5. J. H. Perry, *Taxes, Tariffs and Subsidies: A History of Canadian Fiscal Development* (Toronto: University of Toronto Press, 1955), Vol. I, pp. 66-105.

6. Sir John A. Macdonald, *House of Commons Debates*, March 7, 1878, pp. 857, 859.

7. J. H. Dales, "Some Historical and Theoretical Comments on Canada's National Policies", *Queen's Quarterly*, Vol. 71, no. 3 (1964), pp. 297-316 and *The Protective Tariff in Canada's Development* (Toronto: Ryerson Press, 1966).

8. The original view of this period was incorporated into W. W. Rostow, *The Stages of Economic Growth: A Non-Communist Manifesto* (Cambridge: Cambridge University Press, 1965) and rebutted by G. Bertram, "Economic Growth and Canadian Industry, 1870-1915: The Staple Model and the Take-Off Hypothesis", *C.J.E.P.S.*, Vol. 29, no. 2 (1963), pp. 162-84.

9. D. M. McDougall, "Canadian Manufactured Commodity Output, 1870-1915", *C.J.E.*, Vol. 4, no. 1 (1971), pp. 21-36 and "The Domestic Availability of Manufactured Commodity Output, Canada, 1870-1915" *C.J.E.*, Vol. 6, no. 2 (1973), pp. 189-206.

10. G. Bertram, "Historical Statistics on Growth and Structure of Manufacturing in Canada, 1870-1915", and J. H. Dales, "Estimates of Canadian Manufacturing Output by Markets, 1870-1915", both in J. Henripin and A. Asimakopolus, eds., *Conference on Statistics, 1962-3*, Canadian Political Science Association (Toronto: University of Toronto Press, 1964), pp. 83-151 and 61-91, respectively, as well as E. J. Chambers and G. Bertram, "Urbanization and Manufacturing in Central Canada, 1870-1915", in S. Ostry and T. K. Rymes, eds., *Conference on Statistics, 1964*, Canadian Political Science Association (Toronto: University of Toronto Press, 1964), pp. 225-58.

11. V. C. Fowke, "The National Policy—Old and New", *C.J.E.P.S.*, Vol. 18, no. 3 (1952), pp. 271-86; "National Policy and Western Development in North America", *J.E.H.*, Vol. 14, no. 4 (1956), pp. 461-79; and *The National Policy and the Wheat Economy* (Toronto: University of Toronto Press, 1957).

12. K. H. Norrie, "Agricultural Implements Tariffs, the National Policy, and Income Distribution in the Wheat Economy", *C.J.E.*, Vol. 7, no. 3 (1974), pp. 449-62.

13. M. Bliss, "Canadianizing American Business: The Roots of the Branch Plant", in I. Lumsden, ed., *Close the 49th Parallel: The Americanization of Canada* (Toronto: University of Toronto Press, 1970), pp. 27-42.

14. D. C. Masters, *Reciprocity, 1846-1911*, Canadian Historical Association, Pamphlet 12 (Ottawa, 1961).

15. J. R. H. Wilbur, *The Bennett Administration, 1930-35*, Canadian Historical Association, Pamphlet 24 (Ottawa, 1969) and J. H. Young, *Canadian Commercial Policy* (Ottawa: Queen's Printer, 1957), pp. 35-47.

16. M. C. Kemp, *The Demand for Canadian Imports, 1926-55* (Toronto: University of Toronto Press, 1962); G. L. Reuber, "Anglo-Canadian Trade: Prices and the Terms of Trade, 1924-1954", *R. E. Stat.*, Vol. 41, no. 2, Part 1 (1959), pp. 196-99 and *Britain's Export Trade with Canada* (Toronto: University of Toronto Press, 1960).

17. R. Caves and R. Holton, *The Canadian Economy: Prospect and Retrospect* (Cambridge, Mass.: Harvard University Press, 1961), pp. 216-32.

18. R. E. George, *A Leader and a Laggard: Manufacturing Industry in Nova Scotia, Quebec and Ontario* (Toronto: University of Toronto Press, 1970).

19. J. H. Dales, "Fuel, Power and Industrial Development in Central Canada", *A.E.R.*, Vol. 43, no. 2 (1953), pp. 181-98 and J. A. Guthrie, *The Newsprint Paper Industry: An Economic Analysis* (Cambridge, Mass.: Harvard University Press, 1941).

20. A. E. Safarian, *The Canadian Economy in the Great Depression* (Toronto: University of Toronto Press, 1959), pp. 109-60.

21. For overviews of this period see: B. Balassa, *Trade Liberalization Among Industrial Countries* (Toronto: McGraw-Hill, 1967), chapters 4 and 5; H. C. Eastman, "Canada in an Interdependent North Atlantic Economy", in C. P. Kindleberger and A. Shonfield, eds., *North American and Western European Economic Policies* (London: Macmillan, 1971), pp. 31-56 and T. N. Brewis, "Canada's International Economic Relations", in T. N. Brewis, *et al.*, eds., *Canadian Economic Policy* (Toronto: Macmillan of Canada, 1961), pp. 259-82.

22. B. W. Wilkinson and K. Norrie, *Effective Protection and the Return to Capital* (Ottawa: Information Canada, 1975), pp. 26-53.

23. Canada, *Report of the Royal Commission on the Automotive Industry*, Chairman V. W. Bladen (Ottawa: Queen's Printer, 1960) and G. P. Wonnacott, "Canadian Automotive Protection: Content Provisions, the Bladen Plan and Recent Tariff Changes", *C.J.E.P.S.*, Vol. 31, no. 1 (1965), pp. 98-116.

24. C. E. Beigie, *The Canada–U.S. Automotive Agreement: An Evaluation* (Montreal: The Canadian-American Committee, 1970).

25. For contrasting arguments see: G. P. Wonnacott and R. J. Wonnacott, *Free Trade Between the United States and Canada: The Potential Economic Effects* (Cambridge, Mass.: Harvard University Press, 1967) and Lumsden, ed., *Close the 49th Parallel* (1970).

26. R. E. Caves, "The Inter-Industry Structure of the Canadian Economy", *C.J.E.P.S.*, Vol. 23, no. 3 (1957), pp. 313-30 and M. Percy and F. Vaillancourt, "The Vulnerability of the Canadian Economy, 1949-1966: Caves Revisited", *C.J.E.*, Vol. 9, no. 2 (1976), pp. 351-59.

27. M. W. Lee, *Economic Fluctuations* (Homewood, Ill.: Irwin, 1955), especially pp. 15-108.

28. J. P. Harkness, "A Spectral Analytic Test of the Long-Swing Hypothesis in Canada", *R.E. Stat.*, Vol. 50, no. 4 (1968), pp. 429-36.

29. C. L. Barber, *Inventories and the Business Cycle, with Special Reference to Canada* (Toronto: University of Toronto Press, 1958); E. J. Chambers, "Late Nineteenth Century Business Cycles in Canada", *C.J.E.P.S.*, Vol. 30, no. 3

(1964), pp. 391-412 and "Canadian Business Cycles Since 1919: A Progress Report", *C.J.E.P.S.*, Vol. 24, no. 2 (1958), pp. 166-89; K. Hay, "Early Twentieth Century Business Cycles in Canada", *C.J.E.P.S.*, Vol. 32, no. 3 (1966), pp. 354-55 and "Money and Cycles in Post-Confederation Canada", *J.P.E.*, Vol. 75, no. 3 (1967), pp. 263-71.

30. C. P. Kindleberger, *The World in Depression, 1929-1939* (Los Angeles: University of California Press, 1973).

31. V. W. Malach, *International Cycles and Canada's Balance of Payments, 1921-33* (Toronto: University of Toronto Press, 1954).

32. G. Rosenbluth, "Changing Structural Factors in Canada's Cyclical Sensitivity, 1903-54", *C.J.E.P.S.*, Vol. 24, no. 1 (1958), pp. 21-43.

33. L. Blain, "Regional Cyclical Behaviour and Sensitivity in Canada, 1919-1973", *J.E.H.*, Vol. 38, no. 1 (1978), pp. 271-73.

34. L. Blain, D. G. Paterson, and J. D. Rae, "The Regional Impact of Economic Fluctuations During the Inter-War Period: The Case of British Columbia", *C.J.E.*, Vol. 7, no. 3 (1974), pp. 381-401.

35. G. Rosenbluth, "Industrial Concentration in Canada and the United States", *C.J.E.P.S.*, Vol. 20, no. 3 (1954), pp. 332-46 and *Concentration in Canadian Manufacturing Industries* (Princeton, N.J.: N.B.E.R., 1957).

36. L. A. Skeoch, *Dynamic Change and Accountability in a Canadian Market Economy* (Ottawa: Supply and Services Canada, 1976); L. G. Reynolds, *The Control of Competition in Canada* (Cambridge, Mass.: Harvard University Press, 1940); and M. D. Stewart, *Concentration in Canadian Manufacturing and Mining Industries* (Ottawa: Economic Council of Canada, 1970).

37. G. L. Reuber and F. Roseman, *The Take-Over of Canadian Firms, 1945-61*, Economic Council of Canada, Special Study No. 10 (Ottawa, 1969) and J. C. Weldon, "Consolidations in Canadian Industry, 1900-1948", in L. Skeoch, ed., *Restrictive Trade Practices in Canada* (Toronto: McClelland and Stewart, 1966), pp. 228-79.

38. G. Rosenbluth, "The Relation Between Foreign Control and Concentration in Canadian Industry", *C.J.E.*, Vol. 3, no. 1 (1970), pp. 14-38.

Chapter 13 (pages 418-49)
1. A. G. Green, "Regional Economic Disparaties", in L. H. Officer and L. B. Smith, eds., *Issues in Canadian Economics* (Toronto: McGraw-Hill, 1974), pp. 357-60 and H. S. Perloff, E. S. Dunn, *et al.*, *Regions, Resources and Economic Growth* (Lincoln, Neb.: University of Nebraska Press, 1960).

2. J. G. Williamson, "Regional Inequality and the Process of National Development", *E.D.C.C.*, Vol. 13, no. 4 (1965), Part II.

3. See G. H. Borts and J. L. Stein, "Regional Growth and Maturity in the United States: A Study of Regional Structural Change", in L. Needleman,

ed., *Regional Analysis* (Harmondsworth, Mddsx.: Penguin Books, 1968), pp. 159-97 and T. N. Brewis, *Regional Economic Policies in Canada* (Toronto: Macmillan of Canada, 1968), pp. 1-94.

4. This relies on Myrdal's model of circular causation with cumulative effects, in G. Myrdal, *Economic Theory and Underdeveloped Regions* (London: Duckworth, 1957), chapters 2 and 3.

5. A. G. Green, *Regional Aspects of Canada's Economic Growth* (Toronto: University of Toronto Press, 1971), pp. 110-11.

6. E. Chernick, *Interregional Disparaties in Income,* Economic Council of Canada, Staff Study No. 14 (Ottawa, 1966).

7. For pre-Confederation history see: W. S. McNutt, *The Atlantic Provinces: The Emergence of Colonial Society, 1712-1857* (Toronto: McClelland and Stewart, 1965) and W. M. Whitelaw, *The Maritimes and Canada Before Confederation* (Toronto: Oxford University Press, 1966).

8. For a good brief history see R. Caves and R. Holton, *The Canadian Economy: Prospect and Retrospect* (Cambridge, Mass.: Harvard University Press, 1961), pp. 141-94.

9. L. O. Stone, *Urban Development in Canada* (Ottawa: Queen's Printer, 1968), pp. 36-41, 127-42.

10. R. D. Howland, *Some Regional Aspects of Canada's Economic Development* (Ottawa: Queen's Printer, 1958), pp. 95-97.

11. Economic Council of Canada, *Second Annual Review* (Ottawa: Economic Council of Canada, 1965), p. 121.

12. J. M. S. Careless, "Aspects of Metropolitanism in Atlantic Canada", in M. Wade, ed., *Regionalism and the Canadian Community, 1867-1967* (Toronto: University of Toronto Press, 1969), pp. 117-29.

13. Calculations of value per farm and per improved acre are made from data in *Census of Canada, 1931,* Vol. 8, Table 5 and *Census of Canada, 1951,* Vol. 6, Table 1.

14. B. S. Keirstead, "Temporal Shifts in Location: The Case of the Maritime Provinces", in B. S. Keirstead, ed., *The Theory of Economic Change* (Toronto: Macmillan of Canada, 1940), pp. 267-313.

15. This is, in part, conjecture, although based on recent evidence in W. L. Marr D. McCready, and F. Millerd, "Canadian Resource Reallocation: Interprovincial Labour Migration, 1966-1971", *Canadian Studies in Population,* Vol. 4 (1977), pp. 17-32.

16. Calculated from data in *Census of Canada, 1901,* Vol. 4, Table 13; *Census of Canada, 1911,* Vol. 2, Table 28; and *Census of Canada, 1931,* Vol. 1, Table 63.

17. See *Census of Canada, 1921*, Vol. 2, Table 102 and *Census of Canada, 1931*, Vol. 1, Table 69.

18. Economic Council of Canada, *Second Annual Review*, p. 178.

19. Data on weeks worked and average hours of working time are in *Census of Canada, 1901*, Vol. 3, Table 3; *Census of Canada, 1911*, Vol. 3, Table 4; *Census of Canada, 1931*, Vol. 6, Table 16; and *Census of Canada, 1951*, Vol. 5, Table 15.

20. K. A. H. Buckley, *Capital Formation in Canada, 1896-1930* (Toronto: University of Toronto Press, 1955), pp. 177-78, 187-88.

21. T. K. Shoyama, "Public Services and Regional Development in Canada", *J.E.H.*, Vol. 26, no. 4 (1966), pp. 498-513.

22. For the history of the federal government's regional growth policy see L. O. Gertler, *Regional Planning in Canada* (Montreal: Harvest House, 1972), pp. 72-82.

23. R. Durocher et P.-A. Linteau, éds., *Le "Retard" du Québec et l'Inferiorité Economique des Canadiens-Français* (Trois-Rivières: Editions Boréal Express, 1971); W. L. Marr, "Economic and Social Structure of Quebec, 1896-1960", *Quarterly of Canadian Studies*, Vol. 3, no. 1 (1973), pp. 34-47; and M. Saint-Germain, *Une Economie à Liverer, le Québec Analyse dans ses Structures Economiques* (Montréal: Les Presses de l'Université de Montréal, 1973).

24. Unless otherwise noted the material in the text is from the same sources as the comparable material of the previous section.

25. Caves and Holton, *The Canadian Economy* (1961), pp. 179 and 190-91.

26. Calculated from data in *Census of Canada, 1871*, Vol. 5, pp. 28-29; *Census of Canada, 1891*, Vol. 1, Table 5; *Census of Canada, 1911*, Vol. 2, Table 17; *Census of Canada, 1931*, Vol. 1, Table 24; and *Census of Canada, 1951*, Vol. 1, Table 45.

27. For the pre-twentieth century see A. Greer, "The Pattern of Literacy in Quebec, 1745-1899", *H.S./S.H.*, Vol. 11, no. 22 (1978), pp. 293-335.

28. W. F. Ryan, *The Clergy and Economic Growth in Quebec, 1896-1914* (Québec: Les Presses de l'Université Laval, 1966) and N. W. Taylor, "French-Canadians as Industrial Entrepreneurs", *J.P.E.*, Vol. 68, no. 1 (1960), pp. 37-52.

29. M. C. Urquhart and K. A. H. Buckley, eds., *Historical Statistics of Canada* (Toronto: Macmillan of Canada, 1965), pp. 581-603.

30. There is no good general economic history of this region, but for good studies of particulars see Caves and Holton, *The Canadian Economy* (1961), pp. 216-32; R. A. Shearer, "The Economy of British Columbia", in R. A. Shearer, *et al.*, eds., *Trade Liberalization and a Regional Economy: Studies of*

the Impact of Free Trade on British Columbia (Toronto: Private Planning Association, 1971), pp. 3-42. Also see the general history M. Ormsby, British Columbia: A History (Toronto: Macmillan of Canada, 1958).

31. J. E. Peters and R. A. Shearer, "The Structure of British Columbia's External Trade, 1939 and 1963", B.C. Studies, Vol. 8 (Winter 1970-71), pp. 34-46 and K. Ralston, "Patterns of Trade and Investment on the Pacific Coast, 1867-1892: The Case of British Columbia Salmon Canning Industry", B.C. Studies, Vol. 1 (Winter 1968-69), pp. 37-45.

Chapter 14 (page 450-54)

1. H. G. J. Aitken, "The Changing Structure of the Canadian Economy, with Particular Reference to the Influence of the United States", H. G. J. Aitken, ed., The American Economic Impact on Canada (Durham, N.C.: Duke University Press, 1959) and J. H. Young, "Comparative Economic Development: Canada and United States", A.E.R., Vol. 45, no. 1 (1955), pp. 80-93.

Selected Bibliography*

Abbreviations

A.E.	l'Actualité Economique
A.H.	Agricultural History
A.E.P.	Australian Economic Papers
A.E.R.	American Economic Review
A.H.R.	American Historical Review
B.H.R.	Business History Review
C.B.	The Canadian Banker
C.H.R.	Canadian Historical Review
C.G.	Canadian Geographer
C.J.A.E.	Canadian Journal of Agricultural Economics
C.J.E.	Canadian Journal of Economics
C.J.E.P.S.	Canadian Journal of Economics and Political Science to 1967, followed by C.J.E.
D.B.S.	Dominion Bureau of Statistics
E.D.C.C.	Economic Development and Cultural Change
E.E.H.	Explorations in Economic History
E.H.R.	Economic History Review
E.J.	Economic Journal
H.S./S.H.	Histoire Sociale/Social History
J.C.S.	Journal of Canadian Studies
J.E.H.	Journal of Economic History
J.P.E.	Journal of Political Economy
M.S.	Manchester School
N.B.E.R.	National Bureau of Economic Research
O.H.	Ontario History

* Items are listed by subject and not necessarily according to the chapter of their first citation.

Q.J.E.   Quarterly Journal of Economics
R.E. Stat.   Review of Economics and Statistics
R.H.A.F.   Revue d'Histoire de l'Amerique Française
S.E.J.   Southern Economic Journal
Y.E.E.   Yale Economic Essays

Chapter 1: Introduction

A. General

Aitken, H. G. J. "Defensive Expansion: The State and Economic Growth". In H. G. J. Aitken, ed. The State and Economic Growth. New York: Social Science Research Council, 1959, pp. 79-114.

Bladen, V. W. An Introduction to Political Economy. Toronto: University of Toronto Press, 1941.

Brebner, J. D. North Atlantic Triangle. Toronto: McClelland and Stewart, 1966.

Burley, K. H. The Development of Canada's Staples, 1867-1939: A Documentary Collection. Toronto: McClelland and Stewart, 1970.

Caves, R. E. and R. H. Holton. The Canadian Economy: Prospect and Retrospect. Cambridge, Mass.: Harvard University Press, 1961.

Clark, S. D. The Social Development of Canada: An Introductory Study with Select Documents. Toronto: University of Toronto Press, 1942.

Creighton, D. G. The Commercial Empire of the St. Lawrence, 1760-1850. Toronto: Ryerson Press, 1938.

_____. Dominion of the North: A History of Canada. rev. ed. Toronto: Macmillan of Canada, 1962.

Currie, A. W. Canadian Economic Development. Toronto: Nelson (Canada) Ltd., 1963.

Dick, T. J. O. Economic History of Canada: A Guide to Information Sources. Detroit: Gale Research, 1978.

Dickey, J. S. The United States and Canada. Englewood Cliffs: Prentice-Hall, 1964.

Easterbrook, W. T. and H. G. J. Aitken. Canadian Economic History. Toronto: Macmillan of Canada, 1958.

_____ and M. H. Watkins, eds. Approaches to Canadian Economic History. Toronto: Macmillan of Canada, 1978.

Harris, R. C. and J. Warkentin. Canada Before Confederation. New York: Oxford University Press, 1974.

Innis, H. A., ed. Select Documents in Canadian Economic History, 1497-1783. Toronto: University of Toronto Press, 1929.

_____ and A. R. M. Lower, eds. Select Documents in Canadian Economic History, 1783-1885. Toronto: University of Toronto Press, 1933.

_____ and A. F. W. Plumptre, eds. The Canadian Economy and Its Problems. Toronto: Ryerson Press, 1934.

Innis, M. Q. An Economic History of Canada. Toronto: Ryerson Press, 1935.

_____, ed. *Essays in Canadian Economic History*. Toronto: University of Toronto Press, 1956.

Kuznets, S. *Modern Economic Growth*. New Haven: Yale University Press, 1966.

Lower, A. R. M. "Two Ways of Life: The Primary Antithesis of Canadian History". *Canadian Historical Association Report* (1943), pp. 5-18.

_____. *Colony to Nation: A History of Canada*. 4th ed. Toronto: Longmans (Canada), 1964.

Saunders, S. A. *Studies in the Economy of the Maritime Provinces*. Toronto: Macmillan of Canada, 1939.

Shortt, A. and A. G. Doughty, *Canada and Its Provinces: A History of the Canadian People and Their Institutions*. 23 vols. Toronto: Publishers' Association of Canada, 1913-17.

Skelton, O. D. *General Economic History of the Dominion, 1867-1912*. Toronto: Ryerson Press, 1913.

Warkentin, J., ed. *Canada: A Geographical Interpretation*. Agincourt: Methuen Publications, 1968.

Wilson, G. W., S. Gordon, and S. Judek. *Canada: An Appraisal of Its Needs and Resources*. Toronto: University of Toronto Press, 1965.

Young, J. H. "Comparative Economic Development: Canada and United States". *A.E.R.*, Vol. 45, no. 1 (1955), pp. 80-93.

Zaslow, M. *The Opening of the Canadian North, 1870-1914*. Toronto: McClelland and Stewart, 1971.

B. Statistical Sources

Canada. *Census of Canada*. Ottawa: Queen's Printer, various years.

_____. *The Canada Yearbook*. Ottawa: Queen's Printer, annually since 1905.

_____. *Statistical Abstract and Record*. Ottawa: Department of Agriculture, 1885-1904.

D.B.S. *The Canadian Balance of International Payments: A Compendium of Statistics from 1946 to 1965*. Cat. no. 67-505. Ottawa: 1967.

Denton, F. and S. Ostry. *Historical Estimates of the Canadian Labour Force*. Ottawa: D.B.S., 1967.

Firestone, O. J. *Canada's Economic Development, 1867-1953*. London: Bowes and Bowes, 1958.

Kerr, D. G. *Historical Atlas of Canada*. 3rd rev. ed. Toronto: Nelson (Canada) Ltd., 1975.

Kubat, D. and D. Thornton. *Statistical Profile of Canadian Society*. Toronto: McGraw-Hill Ryerson, 1974.

Minville, E. *Etudes du Notre Milieu*. 4 vols. Montréal: Ecole des Haute Etudes Commerciales, 1942-44.

Statistics Canada. *Canadian Statistical Review*. Cat. no. 11-003. Ottawa: continuing series.

_____. *Canadian Statistical Review: Historical Summary, 1970*. Cat. no. 11-505. Ottawa: 1972.

_____. *Canada's Balance of International Indebtedness*. Cat. nos. 67-201 and 67-505. Ottawa, 1968 and 1974.

_____. *Quarterly Estimates of the Canadian Balance of International Payments.* Cat. no. 67-001. Ottawa: quarterly.

Taylor, K. W. and H. Michell. *Statistical Contributions to Canadian Economic History.* 2 vols. Toronto: Hunter-Rose, 1931.

Urquhart, M. C. and K. A. H. Buckley, eds. *Historical Statistics of Canada.* Toronto: Macmillan of Canada, 1965.

C. Methodology

Hughes, J. R. T. "Fact and Theory in Economic History". *E.E.H.*, Vol. 3, no. 2 (1966), pp. 75-110.

Innis, H. A. "The Teaching of Economic History in Canada". In Innis, ed. *Essays in Canadian Economic History* (1956), pp. 3-16.

Parker, W. "Economic Development in Historical Perspective". *E.D.C.C.*, Vol. 10, no. 4 (1961), pp. 1-7.

Schultz, T. "On Economic History Extending Economics". In M. Nash, ed. *Essays on Economic Development and Cultural Change in Honor of Bert F. Hoselitz.* Chicago: University of Chicago Press, 1978, pp. 245-53.

Supple, B. E. "Economic History, Economic Theory and Economic Growth". In B. E. Supple, ed. *The Experience of Economic Growth.* New York: Random House, 1963, pp. 1-46.

Chapter 2: Patterns of Aggregate Economic Change

A. The Staple Thesis

Aitken, H. G. J. "Myth and Measurement: The Innis Tradition in Economic History". *J.C.S.*, Vol. 12, no. 5 (1977), pp. 96-105.

Baldwin, R. E. "Patterns of Developments in Newly Settled Regions". *M.S.*, Vol. 24, no. 2 (1954), pp. 161-79.

_____. "Export Technology and Development from a Subsistence Level". *E.J.*, Vol. 63, no. 1 (1963), pp. 80-93.

Britnell, G. "Underdeveloped Countries in the World Economy". *C.J.E.P.S.*, Vol. 23, no. 4 (1957), pp. 453-66.

Buckley, K. A. H., "The Role of the Staple Industries in Canada's Development". *J.E.H.*, Vol. 18, no. 4 (1958), pp. 439-50.

Caves, R. " 'Vent for Surplus' Models of Trade and Growth". In R. Caves, et al., eds. *Trade, Growth and the Balance of Payments: Essays in Honor of Gottfried Haberler.* Chicago: Rand-McNally, 1965, pp. 95-115.

_____. "Export-Led Growth and the New Economic History". In J. Bhagwati, ed. *Trade, Balance of Payments, and Growth.* Amsterdam: North-Holland Publishing, 1971, pp. 95-115.

Hirschman, A. O. *Strategy of Economic Development.* New Haven: Yale University Press, 1958.

_____. "A Generalized Linkage Approach to Development with Special Reference to Staples". *E.D.C.C.*, Vol. 25, Supplement (1977), pp. 67-98.

Innis, H. A. *The Problems of Staple Production in Canada.* Toronto: Ryerson Press, 1933.

_____. "Significant Factors in Canadian Economic Development". In Innis, ed. *Essays in Canadian Economic History* (1956), pp. 200-10.

Kuznets, S. "Quantative Aspects of the Economic Growth of Nations: IX. Level and Structure of Foreign Trade: Comparisons for Recent Years". *E.D.C.C.*, Vol. 13 (1964), Part II.

_____. "Quantative Aspect of the Growth of Nations: X. Level and Structure of Foreign Trade: Long-Term Trends". *E.D.C.C.*, Vol. 15 (1967), Part II.

Levin, J. V. *The Export Economies: Their Pattern of Development in Historical Perspective*. Cambridge, Mass.: Harvard University Press, 1960.

Mackintosh, W. A. "Economic Factors in Canadian History". *C.H.R.*, Vol. 4, no. 1 (1923), pp. 12-25.

_____. *The Economic Background of Dominion-Provincial Relations*. Appendix no. 3. Report of the Royal Commission on Dominion-Provincial Relations. Ottawa: King's Printer, 1939; reprinted Toronto: McClelland and Stewart, 1964.

North, D. C. "Location Theory and Regional Economic Growth". *J.P.E.*, Vol. 63, no. 3 (1955), pp. 243-58.

Spengler, J., ed. *Natural Resources and Economic Growth*. Washington: Resources for the Future, 1961.

Trebout, C. M. "Exports and Regional Economic Growth". *J.P.E.*, Vol. 64, no. 2 (1956), pp. 160-69.

Watkins, M. H. "A Staple Theory of Economic Growth". *C.J.E.P.S.*, Vol. 29, no. 2 (1963), pp. 141-58.

_____. "The Staple Theory Revisited". *J.C.S.*, Vol. 12, no. 5 (1977), pp. 83-95.

See also Caves and Holton. *The Canadian Economy* (1961) and various works cited elsewhere.

B. *Economic Change*

Barber, C. L. "The Quantity Theory and the Income Expenditure Theory in an Open Economy, 1926-1958: A Comment". *C.J.E.P.S.*, Vol. 32, no. 3 (1966), pp. 375-77.

Bertram, G. *The Contribution of Education to Economic Growth*. Economic Council of Canada. Staff Study No. 12. Ottawa: 1966. See also Chapter 7.

Brecher, I. and S. S. Reisman. *Canada–United States Economic Relations*. Royal Commission on Canada's Economic Prospects. Ottawa: Queen's Printer, 1957.

Brewis, T. N., ed. *Growth and the Canadian Economy*. Toronto: McClelland and Stewart, 1965.

Brown, J. J. *Ideas in Exile: A History of Canadian Invention*. Toronto: McClelland and Stewart, 1967.

Careless, J. M. S. "Frontierism, Metropolitanism and Canadian History". *C.H.R.*, Vol. 35, no. 1 (1954), pp. 1-21.

Domar, E. D., *et al.* "Economic Growth and Productivity in the United States, Canada, United Kingdom, Germany and Japan in the Post-War Period". *R.E. Stat.*, Vol. 46, no. 1 (1964), pp. 33-40.

Due, J. M. "Consumption Levels in Canada and the United States". *C.J.E.P.S.*, Vol. 21, no. 2 (1955), pp. 174-82.

Easterbrook, W. T. "Long-Period Comparative Study: Some Historical Cases". *J.E.H.*, Vol. 17, no. 4 (1957), pp. 571-95.

Faucher, A. "The Decline of Shipbuilding at Quebec in the Nineteenth Century". *C.J.E.P.S.*, Vol. 21, no. 2 (1957), pp. 195-215.

Firestone, O. J. "Development of Canada's Economy, 1850-1890". In *Trends in the American Economy in the Nineteenth Century*. Princeton: N.B.E.R., 1960, pp. 217-46.

———. "Innovations and Economic Development—The Canadian Case". *The Review of Income and Wealth*, Series 18, Vol. 8 (1972), pp. 399-419.

Furniss, I. E. "Productivity of Canadian Agriculture, 1935-1960: A Quarter Century of Change". *C.J.A.E.*, Vol. 12, no. 2 (1964), pp. 41-53.

Goldberg, S. A. "Long-Run Changes in the Distribution of Income by Factor Shares in Canada". In *The Behavior of Income Shares*. Princeton: N.B.E.R., 1964, pp. 189-237.

Grant, G. P. *Technology and Empire*. Toronto: Anansi, 1969.

Harley, C. K. "On the Persistence of Old Techniques: The Case of North American Wooden Shipbuilding". *J.E.H.*, Vol. 33, no. 2 (1973), pp. 372-98.

Hartland, P. E. "Factors in Economic Growth in Canada". *J.E.H.*, Vol. 15, no. 1 (1955), pp. 13-22.

Hood, W. C. and A. D. Scott. *Output, Capital and Labour*. Royal Commission on Canada's Economic Prospects. Ottawa: Queen's Printer, 1957.

Hope, E. C. "Agriculture's Share of the National Income". *C.J.E.P.S.*, Vol. 9, no. 3 (1943), pp. 384-93.

Hotson, J. H. "The Constancy of the Wage Share: The Canadian Experience". *R. E. Stat.*, Vol. 45, no. 1 (1963), pp. 84-91.

Johnson, H. G. *Technology and Economic Interdependence*. London: Trade Policy Research Centre, 1975.

Kemp, M. C. *The Demand for Canadian Imports, 1926-55*. Toronto: University of Toronto Press, 1962.

Kotowitz, Y. "Capital-Labour Substitution in Canadian Manufacturing 1926-39 and 1946-61". *C.J.E.*, Vol. 1, no. 3 (1968), pp. 619-32.

———. "Technical Progress, Factor Substitution and Income Distribution in Canadian Manufacturing 1926-39 and 1946-61", *C.J.E.*, Vol. 2, no. 1 (1969), pp. 106-14.

LaTourette, J. E. "Trends in the Capital-Output Ratio: United States and Canada, 1926-65", *C.J.E.*, Vol. 2, no. 1 (1969), pp. 35-51.

———. "Aggregate Factors in the Trends in Capital-Output Ratios". *C.J.E.*, Vol. 3, no. 2 (1970), pp. 255-75.

Lerohl, M. L. and G. A. MacEachern. "Factor Shares in Agriculture: The Canada-U.S. Experience". *C.J.A.E.*, Vol. 15, No. 1 (1967), pp. 1-20.

Lithwick, H. "Labour, Capital, and Growth: The Canadian Business Experience". In Brewis, ed. *Growth and the Canadian Economy* (1965), pp. 65-75.

———. *Economic Growth in Canada: A Quantitative Analysis*. Toronto: University of Toronto Press, 1967.

Mackenzie, W. "The Terms of Trade, Productivity and Income of Canadian Agriculture". *C.J.A.E.*, Vol. 9, no. 2 (1961), pp. 1-13.

Maddison, A. "Productivity in an Expanding Economy". *E.J.*, Vol. 62, no. 3 (1952), pp. 584-94.

Maizels, A. *Industrial Growth and World Trade: Empirical Studies of the Trends in Production, Consumption, and Trade in Manufactures from 1899-1959*. London: N.I.E.S.R., 1963.

Maywald, K. "National Saving and Changing Employment in Canada, 1926-54". *C.J.E.P.S.*, Vol. 22, no. 2 (1956), pp. 174-82.

Safarian, A. E. *The Canadian Economy in the Great Depression*. Toronto: University of Toronto Press, 1958.

Scott, A. D. "Economic Effects of Changing Technology and Population in a Hostile Climate". *Proceedings and Transactions of the Royal Society of Canada*. Ser. IV, Vol. 8 (1970), pp. 61-74.

Sinclair, B., N. R. Ball, and O. J. Peterson. *Let Us Be Honest and Modest: Technology and Society in Canadian History*. Toronto: Oxford University Press, 1974.

Slater, D. W. "Changes in the Structure of Canada's International Trade". *C.J.E.P.S.*, Vol. 21, no. 1 (1955), pp. 1-20.

———. *Canada's Imports*. Royal Commission on Canada's Economic Prospects. Ottawa: Queen's Printer, 1957.

———. *World Trade and Economic Growth: Trends and Prospects with Applications to Canada*. Toronto: Private Planning Association, 1968.

Smith, J. M. *Canadian Economic Growth and Development from 1939 to 1955*. Royal Commission on Canada's Economic Prospects. Ottawa: Queen's Printer, 1957.

Sutton, G. D. "Productivity in Canada". *C.J.E.P.S.*, Vol. 19, no. 2 (1953), pp. 185-201.

Walters, D. *Canadian Income Levels and Growth: An International Perspective*. Economic Council of Canada. Staff Study No. 23. Ottawa: 1968.

———. *Canadian Growth Revisited, 1950-1967*. Economic Council of Canada. Staff Study No. 28. Ottawa: 1970.

Wampack, J. "Les Tendences dans la Productivité Totale dans l'Agriculture: Canada, Ontario, Québec, 1926-1964". *C.J.A.E.*, Vol. 15, no. 1 (1967), pp. 119-30.

Zaslow, M. "The Frontier Hypothesis in Canadian Historiography". *C.H.R.*, Vol. 29, no. 2 (1948), pp. 153-66.

Chapter 3: The Early Staples

Albion, R. G. *Forests and Sea Power: The Timber Problem of the Royal Navy, 1652-1862*. Cambridge, Mass.: Harvard University Press, 1926.

Biggar, H. P. *The Early Trading Companies of New France*. New York: Argonaut Press, 1965.

Cell, G. T. *English Enterprise in Newfoundland, 1577-1660*. Toronto: University of Toronto Press, 1969.

Christy, F. and A. D. Scott, *The Common Wealth in Ocean Fisheries*. Baltimore: The Johns Hopkins Press, 1965.

Crean, J. F. "Hats and the Fur Trade". *C.J.E.P.S.*, Vol. 28, no. 3 (1962), pp. 373-86.

Davies, K. G. "The Years of No Dividend: Finances of the Hudson's Bay Company, 1690-1718". In M. Bolus, ed. *People and Pelts*. Winnipeg: Pequis Publishers, 1972, pp. 65-82.

Eccles, W. J. *The Canadian Frontier, 1534-1760*. New York: Holt, Rinehart and Winston, 1968.

_____. "The Social, Economic, and Political Significance of the Military Establishment in New France". *C.H.R.*, Vol. 52, no. 1 (1972), pp. 1-22.

Galbraith, J. S. *The Hudson's Bay Company as an Imperial Factor, 1821-1869*. Toronto: University of Toronto Press, 1957.

Gilchrist, J. "Exploration in Enterprise: The Newfoundland Fishery, c. 1497-1677". In D. S. Macmillan, ed. *Canadian Business History*. Toronto: McClelland and Stewart, 1972, pp. 27-43.

Graham, G. *The Empire of the North Atlantic: The Maritime Struggle for North America*. Toronto: University of Toronto Press, 1950.

Grant, R. F. *The Canadian Atlantic Fishery*. Toronto: Ryerson Press, 1934.

Guillet, E. C. *Early Life in Upper Canada*. Toronto: University of Toronto Press, 1933.

Hughson, J. W. and C. C. J. Bond. *Hurling Down the Pine*. Old Chelsea, P.Q.: Historical Society of the Gatineau, 1964.

Innis, H. A. *Peter Pond, Fur Trader and Adventurer*. Toronto: Ryerson Press, 1930.

_____. *The Cod Fisheries: The History of an International Economy*. rev. ed. Toronto: University of Toronto Press, 1954.

_____. *The Fur Trade in Canada*. rev. ed. Toronto: University of Toronto Press, 1956.

_____. "An Introduction to the Economic History of the Maritimes, Including Newfoundland and New England". In Innis, ed. *Essays in Canadian Economic History* (1956), pp. 27-42.

_____. "The Rise and Fall of the Spanish Fishery in Newfoundland. In Innis, ed. *Essays in Canadian Economic History* (1956), pp. 43-61.

_____. "Interrelations between the Fur Trade of Canada and the United States". In Innis, ed. *Essays in Canadian Economic History* (1956), pp. 97-107.

_____. "Unused Capacity as a Factor in Canadian Economic History". In Innis, ed. *Essays in Canadian Economic History* (1956), pp. 141-55.

_____. "The Lumber Trade in Canada". In Innis, ed. *Essays in Canadian Economic History* (1956), pp. 242-51.

Lawson, M. G. *Fur: A Study in English Mercantilism, 1700-1755*. Toronto: University of Toronto Press, 1943.

_____. "The Beaver Hat and the Fur Trade". In Bolus, ed. *People and Pelts* (1972), pp. 27-38.

Lower, A. R. M. *Settlement and the Forest Frontier in Eastern Canada*. Toronto: Ryerson Press, 1936.

_____. *The North American Assault on the Canadian Forest: A History of the Lumber Trade Between Canada and the United States*. Toronto: Ryerson Press, 1938.

_____. "The Trade in Square Timber". In W. T. Easterbrook and M. H. Watkins, eds. *Approaches to Canadian Economic History*. Toronto: Macmillan of Canada, 1978, pp. 28-48.

_____. *Great Britain's Woodyard: British America and the Timber Trade, 1763-1867*. Montreal: McGill-Queen's University Press, 1974.

Lunn, J. "The Illegal Fur Trade out of New France, 1713-60". *Canadian Historical Association Report* (1939), pp. 61-76.

MacKay, D. *The Honourable Company: A History of the Hudson's Bay Company*. rev. ed. Toronto: McClelland and Stewart, 1949.

Macmillan, D. S. "The 'New Men' in Action: Scottish Mercantile and Shipping Operations in the North American Colonies, 1760-1825". In D. S. Macmillan, ed. *Canadian Business History*. Toronto: McClelland and Stewart, 1972, pp. 44-103.

McClelland, P. D. *The New Brunswick Economy in the Nineteenth Century*. Ph.D. thesis. Cambridge, Mass.: Harvard University, 1966.

McManus, J. "An Economic Analysis of Indian Behaviour in the North American Fur Trade". *J.E.H.*, Vol. 32, no. 1 (1972), pp. 36-53.

Merk, F. *Fur Trade and Empire: George Simpson's Journal*. rev. ed. Cambridge, Mass.: Belknap Press, 1968.

Norton, T. E. *The Fur Trade in Colonial New York, 1686-1776*. Madison, Wisc.: University of Wisconsin Press, 1974.

Paterson, D. G. "The North Pacific Seal Hunt, 1886-1910: Rights and Regulations". *E.E.H.*, Vol. 14, no. 2 (1977), pp. 97-119.

_____ and J. Wilen. "Depletion and Diplomacy: The North Pacific Seal Hunt, 1886-1910". In P. Uselding, ed. *Research in Economic History*. Greenwich, Conn.: JAI Press, 1977, Vol. 2, pp. 81-140.

Phillips, P. C. *The Fur Trade*. 2 vols. Norman, Oklahoma: University of Oklahoma Press, 1961.

Pritchard, J. "Commerce in New France". In Macmillan, ed. *Canadian Business History* (1972), pp. 27-43.

Ray, A. J. *Indians in the Fur Trade*. Toronto: University of Toronto Press, 1974.

Rich, E. E. *The Hudson's Bay Company*. 2 vols. London: Hudson's Bay Society, 1958-59.

_____. "Trade Habits and Economic Motivation Among the Indians of North America". *C.J.E.P.S.*, Vol. 26, no. 1 (1960), pp. 35-63.

Scott, A. D. *Natural Resources: The Economics of Conservation*. Toronto: McClelland and Stewart, 1973.

Searle, R. and K. Dobbs. *The Great Fur Opera*. Toronto: McClelland and Stewart, 1970.

Shepherd, J. "Commodity Exports from British North American Colonies to Overseas Areas, 1768-1772". *E.E.H.*, Vol. 8, no. 1 (1970), pp. 5-76.

_____. *Staples and Eighteenth-Century Canadian Development: A Comparative Study*. Unpublished paper. Whitman College (1973).

_____ and G. Walton. *Shipping, Maritime Trade, and the Economic Development of Colonial North America*. London: Cambridge University Press, 1972.

_____ and S. H. Williamson. "The Coastal Trade of the British North American Colonies, 1768-1772". *J.E.H.*, Vol. 32, no. 4 (1972), pp. 783-810.

Chapter 4: Agricultural Development in Central Canada to 1914

Burton, F. W. "The Wheat Supply of New France". In *Proceedings and Transactions of the Royal Society of Canada*, Vol. 30, 3rd Ser., Section 2 (1936), pp. 137-50.

_____. "Wheat in Canadian History". *C.J.E.P.S.*, Vol. 3, no. 2 (1937), pp. 210-17.

Clark, A. H. *Three Centuries and the Island: A Historical Geography of Settlement and Agriculture in Prince Edward Island*. Toronto: University of Toronto Press, 1959.

Creighton, D. G. "The Economic Background of the Rebellions of 1837". *C.J.E.P.S.*, Vol. 3, no. 3 (1967), pp. 322-34.

Dalton, R. C. *The Jesuits' Estates Question, 1760-1888*. Toronto: University of Toronto Press, 1968.

Delage, D. "Les Structures Economique de la Nouvelle-France et de la Nouvelle-York". *A.E.*, Vol. 46, no. 1 (1970), pp. 67-118.

Fowke, V. C. "An Introduction to Canadian Agricultural History". *C.J.E.P.S.*, Vol. 8, no. 1 (1942), pp. 56-68.

Frégault, G. *Canadian Society in the French Regime*. Canadian Historical Association. Booklet No. 3. Ottawa: 1962.

_____. *Le XVIIIe Siècle Canadien*. Montréal: Editions H.M.H., 1970.

Gates, L. F. *Land Policies of Upper Canada*. Toronto: University of Toronto Press, 1968.

Gentilcore, R. L. "The Agricultural Background of Settlement in Eastern Nova Scotia". *Annuals of the Association of American Geographers*, Vol. 44 (1954), pp. 292-314.

_____. "Lines on the Land". *O.H.*, Vol. 61, no. 2 (1969), pp. 57-63.

_____. "The Beginnings of Settlement in the Niagara Peninsula, 1782-1792". *C. G.*, Vol. 7, no. 3 (1963), pp. 72-82.

Hamelin, J. *Economie et Société en Nouvelle-France*. Québec: Les Presses de l'Université Laval, 1961.

_____. "Le Crise Agricole dans le Bas-Canada, 1802-1837". *Canadian Historical Association Report* (1962), pp. 317-33.

_____ et F. Ouellet. "Le Mouvement des Prix Agricoles dans la Province du Québec: 1760-1851". En C. Garlarmeau et E. Lavoie, éds. *La France et le Canada Francais du XVIe au XXe Siècle*. Québec: Presses de l'Université Laval, 1966, pp. 35-48.

_____ et Y. Roby. *Histoire Economique du Québec, 1851-1896*. Montréal: Editions Fides, 1971.

Harris, R. C. *The Seigneurial System in Early Canada: A Geographical Study*. Madison: University of Wisconsin Press, 1968.

_____. "Of Poverty and Helplessness in Petite-Nation". *C.H.R.*, Vol. 51, no. 1 (1971), pp. 23-50.

Innis, H. A. "An Introduction to the Economic History of Ontario from Outpost to Empire". In Innis, ed. *Essays in Canadian Economic History* (1956), pp. 116-27.

_____. "The Historical Development of the Dairy Industry in Canada". In Innis, *Essays in Canadian Economic History* (1956), pp. 211-19.

Isbister, J. "Agriculture, Balanced Growth and Social Change in Central Canada Since 1850: An Interpretation". *E.D.C.C.*, Vol. 25, no. 4 (1977), pp. 673-97.

Jones, R. L. "French-Canadian Agriculture in the St. Lawrence Valley, 1815-1850". *A. H.*, Vol. 16, no. 1 (1942), pp. 141-48.

_____. "The Agricultural Development of Lower Canada, 1850-1867". *A.H.*, Vol. 19, no. 2 (1945), pp. 212-24.

_____. "Agriculture in Lower Canada, 1792-1815". *C.H.R.*, Vol. 27, no. 1 (1946), pp. 33-51.

_____. *History of Agriculture in Ontario, 1613-1880.* Toronto: University of Toronto Press, 1946.

_____. "French-Canadian Agriculture in the St. Lawrence Valley, 1815-1850". In Easterbrook and Watkins, eds. *Approaches to Canadian Economic History* (1978), pp. 110-26.

Kalm, P. *Travels into North America.* trans. J. R. Forster. London: 1771; reprinted, Barre, Mass.: Imprint Society, 1972.

Kelly, K. "Wheat Farming in Simcoe County in the Mid-Nineteenth Century". *C.G.*, Vol. 15, no. 2 (1971), pp. 95-112.

Lawr, D. A. "The Development of Ontario Farming, 1870-1919: Patterns of Growth and Change". *O.H.*, Vol. 44, no. 4 (1972), pp. 239-51.

Le Goff, T. J. A. "The Agricultural Crisis in Lower Canada, 1802-12: A Review of a Controversy". *C.H.R.*, Vol. 55, no. 1 (1974), pp. 1-31.

Lemelin, C. "The State of Agriculture". In J. C. Falardeau, ed. *Essays on Contemporary Quebec.* Québec: Les Presses de l'Université Laval, 1953, Chapter III.

Letourneau, F. *Histoire de l'Agriculture, Canada Français.* Montréal: L'Imprimerie Populaire, 1950.

Little, J. I. "The Social and Economic Development of Settlers in Two Quebec Townships, 1851-1870". In D. H. Akenson, ed. *Canadian Papers in Rural History.* Gananoque, Ont.: Langdale press, 1978, pp. 89-113.

Lizars, R. and K. MacFarlane. *In the Days of the Canada Company.* Belleville, Ontario: Mika Publishing, 1973.

Long, M. H. *A History of the Canadian People.* Vol. 1, New France. Toronto: Ryerson Press, 1942.

Lunn, A. J. E. *Economic Development in French Canada, 1740-1760.* M.A. thesis. McGill University (1934).

Macdonald, N. *Canada, 1763-1841: Immigration and Settlement; The Administration of the Imperial Land Regulations.* London: Longmans, 1939.

McGuigan, G. "Economic Organization in Lower Canada, 1791-1809". In W. T. Easterbrook and M. H. Watkins, eds. *Approaches to Canadian Economic History.* Toronto: Macmillan of Canada, 1978, pp. 99-109.

Munro, W. B. *The Seigneurial System in Canada: A Study in French Colonial Policy.* New York: Longmans-Green, 1907.

Ouellet, F. et J. Hamelin. "La Crise Agricole dans le Bas-Canada". *Canadian Historical Association Report* (1962), pp. 317-33.

_____. *Histoire Economique et Sociale du Québec, 1760-1850: Structures et Conjuncture.* Montréal: Editions Fides, 1966.

_____. "L'Agriculture Bas-Canadienne Vue à Travers Les Dimes et la Rente en Nature". *H.S./S.H.*, Vol. 8, no. 3 (1971), pp. 5-44.

Paquet, G. et J.-P. Wallot. "Aperçu Sur le Commerce Intérnational et les Prix Domestiques Dans la Bas-Canada, 1793-1812". *R.H.A.F.*, Vol. 31, no. 2 (1967), pp. 447-73.

_____ and _____. "International Circumstances of Lower Canada, 1786-1810". *C.H.R.*, Vol. 52, no. 4 (1972), pp. 371-401.

_____ et _____. "Crise Agricole et Tensions Socio-Ethniques dans le Bas-Canada, 1802-1812: Eléments pour un Ré-intérprétation". *R.H.A.F.*, Vol. 26, no. 2 (1972), pp. 185-237.

_____ and _____. "The Agricultural Crisis in Lower Canada, 1802-12: *Mise au Point.* A Response to T. J. A. Le Goff". *C.H.R.*, Vol. 56, no. 2 (1975), pp. 133-61 and "A Reply", pp. 162-68.

Parker, W. H. "A New Look at Unrest in Lower Canada in the 1830's". *C.H.R.*, Vol. 40, no. 2 (1959), pp. 209-18.

Perrin, R. "The North American Beef and Cattle Trade with Great Britain, 1870-1914", *E.H.R.*, 2nd Ser., Vol. 24, no. 3 (1971), pp. 430-44.

Phillips, P. "Land Tenure and Economic Development: A Comparison of Upper and Lower Canada". *J.C.S.*, Vol. 9, no. 2 (1974), pp. 35-45.

Pomfret, R. "The Mechanization of Reaping in Nineteenth Century Ontario: A Case Study of the Pace and Causes of the Diffusion of Embodied Technical Change". *J.E.H.*, Vol. 36, no. 2 (1976), pp. 399-415.

Reaman, G. E. *A History of Agriculture in Ontario.* Toronto: Saunders, 1970.

Ruddick, J. A., *et al. The Dairy Industry in Canada.* Toronto: Ryerson Press, 1937.

Seguin, M. *La 'Nation Canadienne' et l'Agriculture, 1760-1850: Essai d'Histoire Economique.* Trois-Rivières: Editions Boréal Express, 1970.

Trudel, M. *Introduction to New France.* Toronto: Holt, Rinehart and Winston of Canada, 1968.

_____. *The Seigneurial Regime.* Canadian Historical Association. Booklet 6. Ottawa: 1971.

Wallot, J.-P. "Le Régime Seigneurial et Son Abolition au Canada". *C.H.R.*, Vol. 50, no. 4 (1969), pp. 367-93.

Wilson, A. *The Clergy Reserves of Upper Canada: A Canadian Mortmain.* Toronto: University of Toronto Press, 1968.

Chapter 5: Commercial Policy Before Confederation

Aitken, H. G. J. "The Changing Structure of the Canadian Economy, with Particular Reference to the Influence of the United States". In H. G. J. Aitken, ed. *The American Economic Impact on Canada.* Durham, N.C.: Duke University Press, 1959, pp. 3-35.

Allin, C. D. and G. M. Jones. *Annexation, Preferential Trade and Reciprocity.* Toronto: Musson, 1912.

Ankli, R. E. "The Reciprocity Treaty of 1854". *C.J.E.*, Vol. 4, no. 1 (1971), pp. 1-20.

Annett, D. R. *British Preference in Canadian Commercial Policy.* Toronto: Ryerson Press, 1948.

Armstrong, F. H. "Ports of Entry and Collectors of Customs in Upper Canada". *Inland Seas,* Vol. 26, no. 2 (1970), pp. 137-44.

Balls, H. R. "Quebec 1763-1774: The Financial Administration". *C.H.R.,* Vol. 41, no. 3 (1960), pp. 203-14.

Barnett, D. F. "The Galt Tariff: Incidental of Effective Protection". *C.J.E.,* Vol. 9, no. 3 (1976), pp. 389-407.

Blake, G. "The Customs Administration in Canadian Historical Development". *C.J.E.P.S.,* Vol. 22, no. 4 (1956), pp. 497-508.

———. *Customs Administration in Canada: An Essay in Tariff Technology.* Toronto: University of Toronto Press, 1957.

Brown, G. W. "The Opening of the St. Lawrence to American Shipping". *C.H.R.,* Vol. 7, no. 1 (1926), pp. 4-12.

Burt, A. L. *Guy Carleton, Lord Dorchester, 1724-1808.* Canadian Historical Association. Booklet 5. Ottawa: 1964.

Careless, J. M. S. *The Union of the Canadas.* Toronto: Macmillan of Canada, 1967.

Creighton, D. G. "The Economic Nationalism and Confederation". *Canadian Historical Association Report* (1942), pp. 44-51.

———. "The Commercial Class in Canadian Politics, 1792-1840". Canadian Political Science Association. *Papers and Proceedings* (1933), pp. 43-61.

Earl, D. W. L., ed. *The Family Compact: Aristocracy or Oligarchy?* Toronto: Copp Clark, 1967.

Faucher, A. "Some Aspects of Financial Difficulties of the Province of Canada". *C.J.E.P.S.,* Vol. 26, no. 4 (1960), pp. 617-24.

Goodwin, C. D. W. *Canadian Economic Thought.* Durham, N.C.: Duke University Press, 1961.

Graham, G. S. *British Policy and Canada, 1774-1791: A Study in 18th Century Trade Policy.* Westport, Conn.: Greenwood Press, 1974.

Harper, L. A., *The English Navigation Laws.* New York: Columbia University Press, 1939.

Heaton, H. *The History of Trade and Commerce with Special Reference to Canada.* Toronto: Nelson (Canada) Ltd., 1939.

Hermmeon, J. C. "Trade and Tariffs in the British North American Provinces Before Confederation". Canadian Political Science Association. *Papers and Proceedings* (1934), pp. 51-59.

Jones, R. L. "The Canadian Agricultural Tariff of 1843". *C.J.E.P.S.,* Vol. 7, no. 4 (1941), pp. 528-37.

Knorr, K. E. *British Colonial Theories, 1570-1850.* Toronto: University of Toronto Press, 1944.

Masters, D. C. *The Reciprocity Treaty of 1854.* Toronto: Longmans, Green, 1936.

———. *Reciprocity, 1846-1911.* Montreal: Quality Press, 1961.

McDiarmid, O. J. *Commercial Policy in the Canadian Economy.* Cambridge, Mass.: Harvard University Press, 1946.

McKee, S. "Canada's Bid for the Traffic of the Middle West", *Canadian Historical Association Report* (1940), pp. 26-35.

McLean, S. J. "The Tariff History of Canada". In *Toronto University Studies in Political Economy*. Toronto: University of Toronto, 1895.

Officer, L. H. and L. B. Smith. "The Canadian-American Reciprocity Treaty of 1855 to 1866". *J.E.H.*, Vol. 28, no. 4 (1968), pp. 598-623.

Perry, J. H. *Taxation in Canada*. Toronto: University of Toronto Press, 1953.

_____. *Taxes, Tariffs and Subsidies: A History of Canadian Fiscal Development*. Toronto: University of Toronto Press, 1955.

Poritt, E. *Sixty Years of Protection in Canada, 1846-1907*. London: Macmillan, 1908.

Saunders, S. A. "The Maritime Provinces and the Reciprocity Treaty". *Dalhousie Review*, Vol. 14 (1934), pp. 155-71.

_____. "The Reciprocity Treaty of 1854: A Regional Study". *C.J.E.P.S.*, Vol. 2, no. 1 (1936), pp. 41-53.

Tucker, G. N. *The Canadian Commercial Revolution, 1845-1851*. Toronto: McClelland and Stewart, 1964.

Weaver, S. R. "Taxation in New France: A Study in Pioneer Economics". *J.P.E.*, Vol. 22, no. 8 (1914), pp. 736-55.

Whitelaw, W. M. *The Maritimes and Canada Before Confederation*. Toronto: Oxford University Press, 1934.

Young, J. H. *Canadian Commercial Policy*. Royal Commission on Canada's Economic Prospects. Ottawa: Queen's Printer, 1957.

See also chapters 3 and 12.

Chapter 6: Population Growth in Canada

Anderson, I. B. *Internal Migration in Canada, 1931-1961*. Economic Council of Canada. Staff Study No. 13. Ottawa: 1966.

Ashton, E. J. "Soldier Land Settlement in Canada". *Q.J.E.*, Vol. 39, no. 2 (1925), pp. 488-98.

Brebner, J. B. *The Neutral Yankees of Nova Scotia*. Toronto: McClelland and Stewart, 1969.

Buckley, K. "Historical Estimates of Internal Migration in Canada". In E. Beach and J. Weldon, eds. *Conference on Statistics, 1960*. Toronto: University of Toronto Press, 1962, pp. 1-37.

Charbonneau, H. et Y. Lavoie. "Introduction à la Reconstitution de la Population du Canada au XVIIe Siècle: Etude Critique des Sources de la Période, 1665-1668". *R.H.A.F.*, Vol. 24, no. 1 (1971), pp. 485-571.

Cheng, Tien-Fang. *Oriental Immigration into Canada*. Shanghai: The Commercial Press, 1931.

Coats, R. H. "Canada". In W. F. Wilcox, ed. *International Migration*. New York: N.B.E.R., 1931, Vol. 1, pp. 357-70.

_____ and M. C. MacLean. *The American-Born in Canada*. Toronto: Ryerson Press, 1943.

Corbett, D. C. "Immigration and Economic Development". *C.J.E.P.S.*, Vol. 17, no. 3 (1951), pp. 360-68.

_____. *Canada's Immigration Policy*. Toronto: University of Toronto Press, 1957.

Cowan, H. I. *British Immigration to British North America: The First Hundred Years*. rev. ed. Toronto: University of Toronto Press, 1961.

_____. *British Immigration Before Confederation*. Canadian Historical Association. Booklet 22. Ottawa: 1968.

Dales, J. "Protection, Immigration and Canadian Nationalism". In P. Russell, ed. *Nationalism in Canada*. Toronto: McGraw-Hill, 1966.

Denton, F. T. and B. G. Spencer. "Population and its Economic Aspects". In J. Chant, ed. *Canadian Perspectives in Economics*. Toronto: Collier Macmillan, 1972.

George, M. V. *Internal Migration in Canada: Demographic Analysis*. Ottawa: Queen's Printer, 1970.

Green, A. *Immigration and the Post-War Canadian Economy*. Toronto: Macmillan of Canada, 1976.

_____ and M. C. Urquhart. "Factor and Commodity Flows in the International Economy of 1870-1914: A Multi-Country View". *J.E.H.*, Vol. 36, no. 1 (1976), pp. 217-52.

Hansen, M. L. and J. B. Brebner. *The Mingling of the Canadian and American Peoples*. New Haven: Yale University Press, 1940.

Harris, R. C. "The French Background of Immigration to Canada before 1700". *Cahiers de Géographie du Québec* (Autumn 1972), pp. 313-24.

Heer, D. M. "Economic Development and the Fertility Transition". In D. V. Glass and R. Revelle, eds. *Population and Social Change*. New York: Edward Arnold Ltd., 1972, pp. 99-113.

Henripin, J. "From Acceptance of Nature to Control: The Demography of the French Canadians". *C.J.E.P.S.*, Vol. 23, no. 1 (1957), pp. 9-19.

_____. "Observations sur la Situation Démographique des Canadiens Français". *A.E.*, Vol. 32 (March 1957), pp. 559-80.

_____. *Trends and Factors of Fertility in Canada*. Census Monograph. Ottawa: 1972.

_____ and Y. Peron. "The Demographic Transition of the Province of Quebec". In Glass and Revelle, eds. *Population and Social Change* (1972), pp. 213-31.

_____ et _____. "Evolution Démographique Recente du Québec". En *Annuaire du Québec*, Vol. 152 (Québec: 1972), pp. 80-122.

Hurd, W. B. *"The Decline in the Canadian Birth Rate"*. *C.J.E.P.S.*, Vol. 3, no. 1 (1937), pp. 40-57.

_____ and J. C. Cameron. "Population Movements in Canada: Some Further Considerations". *C.J.E.P.S.*, Vol. 1, no. 2 (1935), pp. 222-45.

Kalbach, W. E. and W. W. McVey. *The Demographic Bases of Canadian Society*. Toronto: McGraw-Hill, 1971.

Keyfitz, N. "The Growth of the Canadian Population". *Population Studies*, Vol. 4 (1950), pp. 47-63.

_____. "Population Problems". In J.-C. Falardeau, ed. *Essays on Contemporary Quebec*. Québec: Les Presses de l'Université Laval, 1953, Chapter 4.

La Chapelle, R. "La Fecondité au Québec et Ontario: Quelques Eléments de Comparaison". *Canadian Studies in Population*, Vol. 1 (1974), pp. 13-28.

Lamontagne, M. and J. C. Falardeau. "The Life-Cycle of French Canadian Urban Families". *C.J.E.P.S.*, Vol. 13, no. 2 (1947), pp. 233-47.

Landon, F. *Western Ontario and the American Frontier*. Toronto: McClelland and Stewart, 1967.

Langlois, G. *Histoire de la Population Canadienne-Française*. Montréal: Editions Lévesque, 1934.

Longley, R. S. "Emigration and the Crisis of 1837 in Upper Canada". *C.H.R.*, Vol. 17, no. 1 (1936), pp. 29-40.

Lower, A. R. M. "Immigration and Settlement in Canada, 1812-1820". *C.H.R.*, Vol. 3, no. 1 (1922), pp. 37-47.

_____. "The Case Against Immigration". *Queen's Quarterly*, Vol. 37 (Summer 1930), pp. 557-74.

Macdonald, N. *Canada: Immigration and Colonization 1841-1903*. Toronto: Macmillan, 1966.

Marr, W. L. "Canadian Immigration Policy Since 1962". *Canadian Public Policy*, Vol. 1, no. 2 (1975), pp. 201-203.

Martell, J. S. *Immigration to and Emigration from Nova Scotia, 1815-1838*. Halifax: Public Archives of Nova Scotia, 1942.

McDougall, D. M. "Immigration into Canada, 1851-1920". *C.J.E.P.S.*, Vol. 27, no. 2 (1961), pp. 162-76.

McInnis, R. M. "Census Survival Ratio Estimates of Net Migration for Canadian Regions". *Canadian Studies in Population*, Vol. 1 (1974), pp. 93-116.

_____. "Childbearing and Land Availability: Some Evidence from Individual Household Data". In R. D. Lee, ed. *Population Patterns in the Past*. New York: Academic Press, 1977, pp. 201-28.

Neveau, A. H. and Y. Kasahara. "Demographic Trends in Canada, 1941-56, and Some of Their Implications". *C.J.E.P.S.*, Vol. 24, no. 1 (1958), pp. 9-20.

Paquet, G. "L'Emigration des Canadiens Français vers la Nouvelle Angleterre, 1870-1910". *Récherches Sociographiques*, Vol. 5 (December 1964), pp. 319-70.

_____ and J.-P. Wallot. "International Circumstances of Lower Canada, 1786-1810: Prolegomenon". *C.H.R.*, Vol. 53, no. 4 (1972), pp. 317-401.

Parai, L. *Immigration and Emigration of Professional and Skilled Manpower During the Post-War Period*. Ottawa: Queen's Printer, 1965.

Percy, M. "Immigration and Emigration During the Decade of the Wheat Boom". *C.J.E.*, forthcoming.

Pickett, J. "An Evaluation of Estimates of Immigration into Canada in the Late Nineteenth Century". *C.J.E.P.S.*, Vol. 31, no. 4 (1965), pp. 499-508.

Pope, D. "Empire Migration to Canada, Australia and New Zealand, 1910-1929". *A.E.P.*, Vol. 7, no. 1 (1968), pp. 167-88.

Rao, N. B. "An Overview of the Fertility Trends in Ontario and Quebec". *Canadian Studies in Population*, Vol. 1 (1974), pp. 37-42.

Richardson, H. W. "British Emigration and Overseas Investment, 1870-1914". *E.H.R.*, Vol. 25, no. 1 (1972), pp. 99-113.

Salone, E. *La Colonisation de la Nouvelle-France*. Paris: Editions G.-P. Maissonneuve et Larose, 1905.

Scott, A. D. "The Brain Drain — Is a Human-Capital Approach Justified?" In W. L. Hansen, ed. *Education, Income, and Human Capital*. New York: Columbia University Press, 1970.

Statistics Canada. *Vital Statistics*. Cat. no. 84-202. Ottawa: annual.

Stone, L. O. *Urban Development in Canada*. Census Monograph. Ottawa: 1968.

_____. *Migration in Canada*. Census Monograph. Ottawa: 1969.

Studness, C. M. "Economic Opportunity and the Westward Migration of Canadians during the Late Nineteenth Century". *C.J.E.P.S.*, Vol. 30, no. 4 (1964), pp. 570-84.

Thomas, B. *Migration and Economic Growth*. Cambridge: Cambridge University Press, 1954.

Timlin, M. *Does Canada Need More People?* Toronto: Oxford University Press, 1951.

_____. "Canada's Immigration Policy, 1896-1910". *C.J.E.P.S.*, Vol. 26, no. 4 (1960), pp. 517-32.

Tucker, G. N. "The Famine Immigration to Canada, 1847". *A.H.R.*, Vol. 36, no. 3 (1931), pp. 533-49.

Tuesdell, L. *The Canadian-Born in the United States*. New Haven: Yale University Press, 1943.

Upton, L., ed. *The United Empire Loyalists: Men and Myths*. Toronto: Copp Clark, 1967.

Vedder, R. K. and L. E. Gallaway. "Settlement Patterns of Canadian Emigrants to the United States, 1850-1960". *C.J.E.*, Vol. 3, no. 3 (1970), pp. 476-86.

Wallot, J.-P. et G. Paquet. "La Liste Civile du Bas-Canada, 1794-1812: Un Essai d'Economie Historique". *R.H.A.F.*, Vol. 23 (September 1969), pp. 209-30; (December 1969), pp. 361-92; Vol. 24 (June 1970), pp. 3-43; (September 1970), pp. 251-86.

Wilson, R. "Migration Movements in Canada, 1868-1925". *C.H.R.*, Vol. 13, no. 2 (1932), pp. 157-82.

Woodham-Smith, C. *The Great Hunger*. New York: Harper and Row, 1962.

Chapter 7: Labour

Abella, I. M. "American Unionism, Communism and the Canadian Labor Movement: Some Myths and Realities". In R. A. Preston, ed. *The Influence of the United States on Canadian Development*. Durham: Duke University Press, 1972.

Bercuson, D. J. "The Winnipeg General Strike: Collective Bargaining and the One Big Union". *C.H.R.*, Vol. 51, no. 2 (1970), pp. 164-76.

_____. *Confrontation at Winnipeg: Labour Industrial Relations and the General Strike*. Montreal: McGill-Queen's University Press, 1974.

Bertram, G. W. *The Contribution of Education to Economic Growth*. Economic Council of Canada. Staff Study No. 12. Ottawa: 1966.

_____ and M. Percy. "Real Wage Trends in Canada, 1900-26: Some Provisional Estimates". *C.J.E.*, Vol. 12, no. 2 (1979), pp. 300-12.

Canada. *Report of the Board of Inquiry into the Cost-of-Living in Canada*. Ottawa: King's Printer, 1915.

_____. *Report of the Royal Commission on the Relations of Labour and Capital*. Ottawa: Queen's Printer, 1889.

Copp, T. *The Anatomy of Poverty: The Conditions of the Working Class in Montreal, 1897-1929*. Toronto: McClelland and Stewart, 1974.

Crispo, J. *International Unionism: A Study in Canadian-American Relations*. Toronto: McGraw-Hill, 1967.

Cross, M. S., ed. *The Workingman in the Nineteenth Century*. Toronto: Oxford University Press, 1974.

Denton, F. T. and P. J. George. "An Exploratory Statistical Analysis of Some Socio-economic Characteristics of Families in Hamilton, Ontario, 1871". *H.S./S.H.*, Vol. 5 (April 1970), pp. 16-44.

Espessat, H., J.-P. Hardy, et T. Ruddell. "Le Monde du Travail du Québec au XVIIIe et au XIXe Siècles: Historiographie et Etat de la Question". *R.H.A.F.*, Vol. 25, no. 1 (1972), pp. 499-539.

Firestone, O. J. *Industry and Education*. Ottawa: University of Ottawa Press, 1969.

Forsey, E. "The Movement Toward Labour Unity in Canada". *C.J.E.P.S.*, Vol. 24, no. 1 (1958), pp. 70-83.

Hamelin, J. et F. Harvey. *Les Travailleurs Québécois, 1941-1971*. Cahiers de l'Institut Superieur des Sciences Humaines. Québec: Université Laval, 1976.

Hammed, S. "Canadian Collective Bargaining: Analysis and Prospect". In R. U. Miller and F. Isbister, eds. *Canadian Labour in Transition*. Scarborough: Prentice-Hall, 1971, pp. 174-77.

Innis, H. A. "Labour in Canadian Economic Development". In Innis, ed. *Essays in Canadian Economic History* (1956), pp. 176-99.

Jamieson, S. *Industrial Relations in Canada*, 2nd ed. Toronto: Macmillan of Canada, 1973.

_____. *Times of Trouble: Labour Unrest and Industrial Conflict in Canada, 1900-66*. Task Force on Labour Relations. Study No. 22. Ottawa: 1968.

_____. "Militancy and Violence in Canadian Labour Relations: 1900-1975", forthcoming.

Katz, M. B. *The People of Hamilton, Canada West: Family and Class in a Mid-Nineteenth Century City*. Cambridge, Mass.: Harvard University Press, 1975.

Kruger, A. M. "The Direction of Unionism in Canada". In Miller and Isbister, eds. *Canadian Labour in Transition* (1971), pp. 85-118.

Kulshreshtha, S. T. J. "Measuring the Relative Income of Farm Labour, 1941-1961". *C.J.A.E.*, Vol. 15, no. 1 (1967), pp. 28-43.

Logan, H. A. *Trade Unions in Canada: Their Development and Functioning*. Toronto: Macmillan, 1948.

_____. *State Intervention and Assistance in Collective Bargaining: The Canadian Experience 1943-1954*. Toronto: University of Toronto Press, 1956.

Lower, A. R. M. *Canada and the Far East*. New York: Institute of Pacific Relations, 1940.

Marsh, L. C. *Canadians In and Out of Work: A Survey of Economic Classes and Their Relation to the Labour Market*. Toronto: Oxford University Press, 1940.

Masters, D. C. *The Winnipeg General Strike*. Toronto: University of Toronto Press, 1950.

McInnis, R. M. "Long-Run Changes in the Industrial Structure of the Canadian Work Force". *C.J.E.*, Vol. 4, no. 3 (1971), pp. 353-61.

Montague, J. T. "International Unions and the Canadian Labour Movement". *C.J.E.P.S.*, Vol. 23, no. 1 (1957), pp. 69-82.

Ostry, S. "The Canadian Labour Market". In Miller and Isbister, eds. *Canadian Labour in Transition* (1971), pp. 15-23.

_____ and M. A. Zaidi. *Labour Economics in Canada*. 2nd ed. Toronto: Macmillan of Canada, 1972.

Peitchinis, S. G. *Canadian Labour Economics*. Toronto: McGraw-Hill, 1970.

Pentland, H. C. "The Development of the Capitalistic Labour Market in Canada". *C.J.E.P.S.*, Vol. 25, no. 4 (1959), pp. 450-61.

Robin, M. *Radical Politics and Canadian Labour, 1880-1930*. Kingston: Industrial Relations Centre of Queen's University, 1968.

Stager, D. "Economics of Education". In J. Chant, ed. *Canadian Perspectives in Economics*. Toronto: Collier Macmillan, 1972.

Stowp, M. "Technical Education, the National Policy, and Federal Provincial Relations in Canadian Education". *C.H.R.*, Vol. 52, no. 4 (1971), pp. 404-23.

Ward, P. "British Columbia and the Japanese Evacuation". *C.H.R.*, Vol. 57, no. 2 (1976), pp. 289-308.

Ware, J. N. and H. A. Logan. *Labour in Canadian-American Relations: the History of Labour Interaction*. Toronto: Ryerson Press, 1937.

Wilson, J. D., ed. *Canadian Education: A History*. Scarborough: Prentice-Hall, 1970.

See also Chapter 6.

Chapter 8: Capital Formation and Mobilization

Acheson, T. W. "The Social Origins of the Canadian Industrial Elite, 1880-1885". In D. S. Macmillan, ed. *Canadian Business History*. Toronto: McClelland and Stewart, 1972, pp. 144-74.

_____. "Changing Social Origins of the Canadian Industrial Elite, 1880-1910". *B.H.R.*, Vol. 47, no. 2 (1973), pp. 189-217.

Aitken, H. G. J. "A New Way To Pay Old Debts: A Canadian Experience". In W. Miller, ed. *Men in Business*. New York: Harper and Row, 1952, pp. 71-90.

_____. "A Note on the Capital Resources of Upper Canada". *C.J.E.P.S.*, Vol. 18, no. 4 (1952), pp. 525-32.

Armstrong, F. H. "Canadian Business History: Approaches and Publications". In Macmillan, ed. *Canadian Business History* (1972), pp. 263-74.

Bliss, M. " 'Dyspepsia of the Mind': The Canadian Businessman and His Enemies". In Macmillan, ed. *Canadian Business History* (1972), pp. 175-91".

Bond, D. E. and R. A. Shearer. *The Economics of the Canadian Financial System: Theory, Policy and Institutions*. Scarborough: Prentice-Hall, 1972.

Brecher, I. *Monetary and Fiscal Thought and Policy in Canada, 1919-1939*. Toronto: University of Toronto Press, 1957.

_____. *Capital Flows Between Canada and the United States*. Montreal: Canadian-American Committee, 1965.

Breckenridge, R. M. *The Canadian Banking System 1817-1890*. New York: Macmillan, 1895.

Buckley, K. A. H. "Urban Building and Real Estate Fluctuations in Canada". *C.J.E.P.S.*, Vol. 18, no. 1 (1952), pp. 41-62.

_____. *Capital Formation in Canada, 1896-1930*. Toronto: University of Toronto Press, 1955.

_____. "Capital Formation in Canada". In *Problems in Capital Formation*. Princeton: N.B.E.R., 1957, pp. 91-145.

Canada. "Reports of the Superintendant of Insurance". *Sessional Papers of Canada*. Ottawa: Queen's Printer, 1870-1929.

Careless, J. M. "The Business Community in the Early Development of Victoria, British Columbia". In J. Freisen and K. Ralston, eds. *Historical Essays on British Columbia*. Toronto: McClelland and Stewart, 1976, pp. 177-200.

Clement, W. *The Canadian Corporate Elite: An Analysis of Economic Power*. Toronto: McClelland and Stewart, 1975.

Courchene, T. J. "An Analysis of the Canadian Money Supply, 1925-1934". *J.P.E.*, Vol. 77 (May 1969), pp. 363-91.

Currie, A. W. "The First Dominion Companies Act". *C.J.E.P.S.*, Vol. 28, no. 3 (1962), pp. 387-404.

Curtis, C. A. "Evolution of Canadian Banking". *Annals of the American Academy of Political and Social Science*, Vol. 253, pp. 115-24.

Denison, M. *Canada's First Bank: A History of the Bank of Montreal*. Toronto: McClelland and Stewart, 1966.

Drummond, I. M. "Government Securities on Colonial New Issue Markets: Australia and Canada, 1895-1914". *Y.E.E.*, Vol. 1, no. 1 (1961), pp. 137-75.

_____. "Canadian Life Insurance Companies and the Capital Market, 1890-1914". *C.J.E.P.S.*, Vol. 28, no. 2 (1962), pp. 204-24.

Easterbrook, W. T. *Farm Credit in Canada*. Toronto: University of Toronto Press, 1938.

Faucher, A. and C. Vaillancourt. *Alphonse Desjardins: Pionnier de la Coopera-tion d'Eparque et de Credit en Amerique*. Lévis: Edition le Quotidien, Ltée., 1950.

Firestone, O. J. See works cited elsewhere.

Guillet, E. C. "Pioneer Banking in Ontario: The Bank of Upper Canada". *C.B.*, Vol. 55, no. 1 (1948), pp. 114-32.

Hammond, B. "Banking in Canada Before Confederation, 1792-1867". In his *Banks and Politics in America from the Revolution to the Civil War*. Princeton, N.J.: Princeton University Press, 1957, Chapter 20.

Hood, W. C. *Financing of Economic Activity in Canada*. Royal Commission on Canada's Economic Prospects. Ottawa: Queen's Printer, 1959.

Jamieson, A. B. *Chartered Banking in Canada*. Toronto: Ryerson, 1955.

Kuznets, S. "Long-Term Trends in Capital Formation Proportions". *E.D.C.C.*, Vol. 9, no. 4, Part 2 (1961), pp. 1-124.

Lester, R. A. "Playing Card Currency of French Canada". In Neufeld, ed. *Money and Banking in Canada* (1964), pp. 9-23.

MacDougall, J. L. "The Character of the Entrepreneur: The Case of George Stephen". In Macmillan, ed. *Canadian Business History* (1972), pp. 192-96.

Macesich, G. "Determinants of Monetary Velocity in Canada, 1926-1958". *C.J.E.P.S.*, Vol. 28, no. 2 (1962), pp. 245-54.

———. "The Quantity Theory and the Income Expenditure Theory in an Open Economy: Canada, 1926-1958". *C.J.E.P.S.*, Vol. 30, no. 3 (1964), pp. 368-90.

Macmillan, D. S. "The New Men in Action: Scottish Mercantile and Shipping Operations in the North American Colonies, 1760-1825". In Macmillan, ed. *Canadian Business History* (1972), pp. 44-103.

McCalla, D. "Peter Buchanan, London Agent for the Great Western Railway of Canada". In Macmillan, ed. *Canadian Business History* (1972), pp. 197-216.

McIvor, R. C. *Canadian Monetary, Banking and Fiscal Development.* Toronto: Macmillan of Canada, 1958.

Moogk, P. "A Pocketful of Change at Louisbourg". *Canadian Numismatic Journal.* Vol. 21, no. 3 (1976), pp. 97-103.

Naylor, T. *The History of Canadian Business*, 2 vols. Toronto: Lorimer, 1975.

Neufeld, E. P. *Bank of Canada Operations, 1935-1954.* Toronto: University of Toronto Press, 1955.

———, ed. *Money and Banking in Canada.* Toronto: McClelland and Stewart, 1964.

———. *The Financial System of Canada.* Toronto: Macmillan of Canada, 1972.

Nish, C. *François-Etienne Cuget, 1719-1754: Entrepreneur et Entreprises en Nouvelle-France.* Montréal: Fides, 1975.

———. *Les Bourgeois — Gentils hommes de la Nouvelle-France, 1729-1748,* Montréal: Fides, 1968.

Paterson, D. G. "European Financial Capital and British Columbia: An Essay on the Role of the Regional Entrepreneur". *B.C. Studies*, Vol. 11 (Spring 1974), pp. 33-47.

Pentland, H. C. "The Role of Capital in Canadian Economic Development Before 1875". *C.J.E.P.S.*, Vol. 16, no. 4 (1950), pp. 457-74.

———. "Further Observations on Canadian Development". *C.J.E.P.S.*, Vol. 19, no. 3 (1953), pp. 403-10.

Pickett, J. "Residential Capital Formation in Canada, 1865-1914". *C.J.E.P.S.*, Vol. 29, no. 1 (1963), pp. 40-58.

Porter, J. *The Vertical Mosaic.* Toronto: University of Toronto Press, 1966.

Quinn, M. "Les Capitaux Français et le Québec, 1855-1900". *R.H.A.F.*, Vol. 24, no. 1 (1971), pp. 527-66.

Rice, R. "The Wrights of Saint John: A Study of Shipbuilding and Shipowning in the Maritimes, 1839-1855". In Macmillan, ed. *Canadian Business History* (1972), pp. 317-37.

Roby, Y. *Alphonse Desjardins et les Caisses Populaires, 1854-1920.* Montréal: Fides, 1964.

Roy, P. E. "The Fine Arts of Lobbying and Persuading: The Case of the B.C. Electric Railway". In Macmillan, ed. *Canadian Business History* (1972), pp. 239-54.

Schull, J. *One Hundred Years of Banking: A History of the Toronto-Dominion Bank.* Toronto: Copp Clark, 1958.

Shortt, A. *Documents Relating to Canadian Currency, Exchange and Finance During the French Period.* 2 vols. Board of Historical Publications. Ottawa: King's Printer, 1925.

_____. *Documents Relating to Currency, Exchange and Finance in Nova Scotia, 1675-1758.* Board of Historical Publications. Ottawa: King's Printer, 1933.

Skelton, O. D. *Fifty Years of Banking Service.* Toronto: Toronto-Dominion Bank, 1922.

Tulchinsky, G. "The Montreal Business Community, 1837-1853". In Macmillan, ed. *Canadian Business History* (1972), pp. 125-43.

Victor, R. *The History of the Canadian Bank of Commerce.* Toronto: Oxford University Press, 1920.

See also chapters 2 and 9.

Chapter 9: Foreign Investment in Canada

Aikman, C. H. *The Automobile Industry of Canada.* Toronto: Macmillan, 1926.

Aitken, H. G. J. *American Capital and Canadian Resources.* Cambridge, Mass.: Harvard University Press, 1961.

_____, et al. *The American Economic Impact on Canada.* Durham: Duke University Press, 1961.

Bliss, M. "Canadianizing American Business: The Roots of the Branch Plant". In I. Lumsden, ed. *Close the 49th Parallel.* Toronto: University of Toronto Press, 1970, pp. 27-42.

Bloomfield, A. I. *Short-Term Capital Movements Under the Pre-1914 Gold Standard.* Princeton Studies in International Finance. No. 11. Princeton: 1963.

_____. *Patterns of Infrastructure in International Investment Before 1914.* Princeton Studies in International Finance. No. 21. Princeton: 1968.

Blyth, C. D. and E. B. Carby. "Non-Resident Ownership of Canadian Industry". *C.J.E.P.S.*, Vol. 22, no. 4 (1956), pp. 449-60.

Brayer, H. O. "The Influence of British Capital on the Western Range-Cattle Industry". *J.E.H.*, Vol. 9, Supplement (1949), pp. 85-98.

Brecher, I. *Capital Flows Between Canada and the United States.* Montreal: Canadian-American Committee, 1965.

_____ and S. S. Reisman. *Canada–United States Economic Relations.* Royal Commission on Canada's Economic Prospects. Ottawa: Queen's Printer, 1957.

Cairncross, A. K. *Home and Foreign Investment, 1870-1913.* Cambridge: Cambridge University Press, 1953.

_____. "Investment in Canada, 1900-1913". In A. R. Hall, ed. *The Export of Capital from Britain, 1870-1914.* London: Methuen, 1968, pp. 153-68.

Canada. *Foreign Direct Investment in Canada.* Ottawa: Queen's Printer, 1972.

_____. *Foreign Ownership and the Structure of Canadian Industry.* Report of the Task Force on the Structure of Canadian Industry. Privy Council Office. Ottawa: Queen's Printer, 1968.

D.B.S. *Canada's International Investment Position, 1926-1954.* Ottawa: 1954.

Fayerweather, J. *Foreign Investment in Canada: Prospects for National Policy.* Toronto: Oxford University Press, 1974.

Field, F. W. *Capital Investment in Canada.* Toronto: Monetary Times, 1914.

Firestone, O. J. "Canada's External Trade and Net Foreign Balance 1851-1900". In *Trends in the American Economy in the Nineteenth Century*. Princeton: N.B.E.R., 1960, pp. 757-71.

Goodhart, C. A. E. *The New York Money Market and the Financing of Trade, 1900-1913*. Cambridge, Mass.: Harvard University Press, 1969.

Harley, C. K. "Transportation, the World Wheat Trade and the Kuznets Cycle, 1850-1913". In R. Caves and D. North, eds. *Exports and Economic Growth*. Princeton: Princeton University Press, forthcoming.

Hartland, P. "Private Enterprise and International Capital". *C.J.E.P.S.*, Vol. 19, no. 1 (1953), pp. 70-80.

———. "Factors in Economic Growth in Canada". *J.E.H.*, Vol. 15, no. 1 (1955), pp. 13-22.

———. "Canadian Balance of Payments since 1868". In *Trends in American Economy in the Nineteenth Century*. Princeton: N.B.E.R., 1960, pp. 717-55.

Helleiner, G. K. "Connection Between United States and Canadian Capital Markets, 1952-60". *Y.E.E.*, Vol. 2 (Autumn 1962), pp. 351-400.

Ingram, J. C. "Growth and Capacity in Canada's Balance of Payments". *A.E.R.*, Vol. 27, no. 1 (1957), pp. 93-104.

Knox, F. A. "*Excursus*: Canadian Capital Movements and the Canadian Balance of Payments, 1900-1934". In Marshall, *et al. Canadian-American Industry* (1976), pp. 296-324.

Levitt, K. *Silent Surrender*. Toronto: Macmillan of Canada, 1970.

Lewis, C. *America's Stake in International Investments*. Washington: The Brookings Institution, 1938.

Lumsden, I., ed. *Close the 49th Parallel: The Americanization of Canada*. Toronto: University of Toronto Press, 1970.

MacDonald, N. *Canada: Immigration and Colonization 1841-1903*. Aberdeen: Aberdeen University Press, 1966.

Main, O. W. "International Nickel: The First Fifty Years". In Macmillan, ed. *Canadian Business History* (1972), pp. 255-61.

Marshall, H., F. A. Southard, and K. W. Taylor. *Canadian-American Industry*. New Haven: Yale University Press, 1936; reprinted Toronto: McClelland and Stewart, 1976.

Meier, G. M. "Economic Development and the Transfer Mechanism: Canada 1895-1918". *C.J.E.P.S.*, Vol. 19, no. 1 (1953), pp. 1-19.

Moore, E. S. *The American Influence in Canadian Mining*. Toronto: University of Toronto Press, 1941.

Paterson, D. G. *British Direct Investment in Canada, 1890-1914: Estimates and Determinants*. Toronto: University of Toronto Press, 1976.

Reuber, G. L. and F. Roseman. *The Take-Over of Canadian Firms, 1945-61: An Empirical Analysis*. Economic Council of Canada. Special Study No. 10. Ottawa: 1969.

Roy, P. "Direct Management from Abroad: The Formative Years of the British Columbia Electric Railway". *B.H.R.*, Vol. 47, no. 2 (1973), pp. 239-59.

Safarian, A. E. "The Exports of American-Owned Enterprises in Canada". *A.E.R., Papers and Proceedings*, Vol. 54, no. 3 (1964), pp. 449-58.

_____. *Foreign Ownership of Canadian Industry.* Toronto: McGraw-Hill, 1966.

Scheinberg, S. "Invitation to Empire: Tariffs and American Economic Expansion into Canada". *B.H.R.*, Vol. 47, no. 2 (1973), pp. 218-38.

Simon, M. "New British Investment in Canada, 1865-1914". *C.J.E.*, Vol. 3, no. 2 (1970), pp. 238-54.

_____. "The Pattern of New British Portfolio Investment, 1865-1914". In J. H. Adler, ed. *Capital Movements and Economic Development.* London: Macmillan, 1967, pp. 33-60.

Slater, D. *Canada's Imports.* Royal Commission on Canada's Economic Prospects. Ottawa: Queen's Printer, 1957.

Stopford, J. M. "The Origins of British Multinational Manufacturing Enterprises". *B.H.R.*, Vol. 47, no. 3 (1974), pp. 303-35.

Stovel, J. A. *Canada in the World Economy.* Cambridge, Mass.: Harvard University Press, 1959.

Thomas, B. *Migration and Economic Growth: A Study of Great Britain and the Atlantic Community.* Cambridge: Cambridge University Press, 1973.

Viner, J. *Canada's Balance of International Indebtedness, 1900-1913.* Cambridge, Mass.: Harvard University Press, 1924.

Wilkins, M. *The Emergence of Multinational Enterprise: American Business Abroad from the Colonial Era to 1914.* Cambridge, Mass.: Harvard University Press, 1970.

_____. *The Maturing of Multinational Enterprise: American Business Abroad from 1914 to 1970.* Cambridge, Mass.: Harvard University Press, 1974.

Wonnacott, P. *The Canadian Dollar, 1948-1958.* Toronto: University of Toronto Press, 1960.

Chapter 10: Transport: Investment in Infrastructure

Aitken, H. G. J. *The Welland Canal Company: A Study in Canadian Enterprise.* Cambridge, Mass.: Harvard University Press, 1954.

_____. "Government and Business in Canada: An Interpretation". *B.H.R.*, Vol. 38, no. 1 (1964), pp. 4-21.

Ashley, C. A. *The First Twenty-Five Years: A Study of Trans Canada Air Lines.* Toronto: Macmillan of Canada, 1963.

Berton, P. *The National Dream: The Great Railway, 1871-1881* and *The Last Spike: The Great Railway, 1881-1885.* Toronto: McClelland and Stewart, 1971.

Breithaupt, W. H. "Dundas Street and Other Early Upper Canada Roads". Ontario Historical Society, *Papers and Records*, Vol. 21 (1924), pp. 5-10.

Burghardt, A. F. "The Origin and Development of the Road Network of the Niagara Peninsula, Ontario, 1770-1851". *Annals of the Association of American Geographers*, Vol. 59, no. 3 (1969), pp. 417-40.

Canada. *Report of the Royal Commission to Inquire into Railways and Transportation in Canada.* Chairman, J. de L. Tache. Ottawa: King's Printer, 1917.

_____. *Report of the Royal Commission to Inquire into Railways and Transportation in Canada, 1931-2.* Chairman, F. A. Acworth. Ottawa: King's Printer, 1932.

_____. *A Statutory History of the Steam and Electric Railways of Canada, 1836-1937*. Ottawa: Department of Transport, 1938.

Careless, J. M. S. "Aspects of Metropolitanism in Atlantic Canada". In M. Wade, ed. *Regionalism in the Canadian Community 1867-1967*. Toronto: University of Toronto Press, 1969, pp. 117-29.

Carr, D. W. "Truck-Rail Competition in Canada". In *Royal Commission on Transportation*. Vol. 3. Ottawa: Queen's Printer, 1962.

Cousins, G. V. "Early Transportation in Canada". *University Magazine*, Vol. 8, no. 4 (1909), pp. 607-28.

Currie, A. W. "Freight Rates and Regionalism". *C.J.E.P.S.*, Vol. 14, no. 3 (1948), pp. 427-40.

_____. *The Grand Trunk Railway of Canada*. Toronto: University of Toronto Press, 1957.

_____. *Canadian Transportation Economics*. Toronto: University of Toronto Press, 1967.

_____. "The Post Office Since 1867". *C.J.E.P.S.*, Vol. 24, no. 2 (1958), pp. 241-50.

Darling, H. J. "Transport Policy in Canada: The Struggle of Ideologies vs. Realities". In K. W. Studnicki-Gizbert, ed. *Issues in Canadian Transport Policy*. Toronto: Macmillan of Canada, 1974.

Filante, R. W. "A Note on the Economic Viability of the Erie Canal". *B.H.R.*, Vol. 48, no. 1 (1974), pp. 95-102.

Gentilcore, R. L. "The Beginnings of Settlement in the Niagara Peninsula (1782-1792)". *C. G.*, Vol. 7, no. 2 (1963), pp. 72-82.

George, P. J. "Rates of Return in Railway Investment and Implications for Government Subsidization of the Canadian Pacific Railway: Some Preliminary Results". *C.J.E.*, Vol. 1, no. 4 (1968), pp. 740-62.

_____. "Rates of Return and Government Subsidization of the Canadian Pacific Railway: Some Further Remarks". *C.J.E.*, Vol. 8, no. 4 (1975), pp. 591-600.

Glazebrook, G. P. de T. *A History of Transportation in Canada*. Toronto: Ryerson, 1938.

Guillet, E. *Pioneer Inns and Taverns*. 4 vols. Toronto: Ontario Publishing Co., 1956.

_____. *The Story of Canadian Roads*. Toronto: University of Toronto Press, 1966.

Harvey, D. C. "Hopes Raised by Steam in 1840". *Canadian Historical Association Report* (1940), pp. 16-25.

Hilton, G. W. and J. F. Due. *The Electric Interurban Railways in America*. Stanford: Stanford University Press, 1964.

Innis, H. A. "The Location of the Route of the C.P.R.". *C.H.R.*, Vol. 18, no. 1 (1937), pp. 87-89.

_____. *A History of the Canadian Pacific Railway*. Toronto: University of Toronto Press, 1971.

_____. "Transportation as a Factor in Canadian Economic History". In Innis, ed. *Essays in Canadian Economic History* (1956), pp. 52-77.

_____. "Transportation in the Canadian Economy". In Innis, ed. *Essays in Canadian Economic History* (1956), pp. 220-32.

Keefer, T. C. *The Canals of Canada, Their Prospects and Influence.* Toronto: Armor and Co., 1850.

Kraft, G., J. R. Meyer, and J.-P. Valetti, *The Role of Transportation in Regional Economic Development.* Toronto: D. C. Heath, 1971.

Legget, R. F. *Rideau Waterway.* rev. ed. Toronto: University of Toronto Press, 1972.

_____. *Canals of Canada.* Vancouver: Douglas, David and Charles, 1976.

Lukasiewiez, J. *The Railway Game.* Toronto: McClelland and Stewart, 1976.

Martell, J. S. "International Communications, 1840-1867". *Canadian Historical Association Report* (1938), pp. 41-61.

Masters, D. C. "T. C. Keefer and the Development of Canadian Transportation". *Canadian Historical Association Report* (1940), pp. 36-43.

McClelland, P. D. "Social Rates of Return on American Railroads in the Nineteenth Century". *E.H.R.*, Vol. 25, no. 3 (1972), pp. 471-88.

McDougall, J. L. "The Relative Levels of Crow's Nest Grain Rates in 1899 and in 1965". *C.J.E.P.S.*, Vol. 32, no. 1 (1966), pp. 46-54.

McIlwraith, T. F. "The Adequacy of Rural Roads in the Era before Railways: An Illustration from Upper Canada". *C.G.*, Vol. 14, no. 1 (1970), pp. 344-60.

_____. "Freight Capacity and Utilization of the Erie and Great Lakes Canals before 1850". *J.E.H.*, Vol. 36, no. 4 (1976), pp. 852-75.

Mercer, L. J. "Rates of Return and Government Subsidization of the Canadian Pacific Railway: An Alternate View". *C.J.E.*, Vol. 6, no. 3 (1973), pp. 428-37.

_____. "Building Ahead of Demand: Some Evidence for the Land Grant Railroads". *J.E.H.*, Vol. 34, no. 2 (1974), pp. 492-500.

Norrie, K. "Western Economic Grievances: An Overview with Special Reference to Freight Rates". Conference on the Political Economy of Confederation. Kingston: Economic Council of Canada, 1978.

Purdy, H. L. *Transport Competition and Public Policy in Canada.* Vancouver: University of British Columbia Press, 1972.

Regehr, T. D. "The Canadian Northern Railway: The West's Own Product". *C.H.R.*, Vol. 51, no. 2 (1970), pp. 177-87.

Reid, E. P. "Statutory Grain Rates". In *Royal Commission on Transportation*, Vol. 3. Ottawa: Queen's Printer, 1962.

Roe, F. G. "An Unsolved Problem of Canadian History". *Canadian Historical Association Report* (1936), pp. 65-77.

Skelton, O. D. *The Railway Builders: A Chronicle of Overland Highways.* Toronto: Glasgow-Brook, 1916.

Smith, W. *History of the Post Office in British North America.* Cambridge: Cambridge University Press, 1920.

Stevens, G. R. *The Canadian National Railways.* 2 vols. Toronto: Clarke-Irwin, 1962.

Studnicki-Gizbert, K. W. "The Structure and Growth of the Canadian Air Transport Industry". In E. F. Beach and J. C. Weldon, eds. *Conference on Statistics 1960.* Toronto: University of Toronto Press, 1962.

Sydor, L. P. "The St. Lawrence Seaway: National Shares in Seaway Wheat Benefits". *C.J.E.*, Vol. 4, no. 4 (1971), pp. 543-55.

Talman, J. J. "Travel in Ontario Before the Coming of the Railway". Ontario Historical Society, *Papers and Records*, Vol. 29 (1933), pp. 85-102.

Tulchinsky, G. J. J. *The River Barons: Montreal Businessmen and the Growth of Industry and Transportation, 1837-53.* Toronto: University of Toronto Press, 1977.

Chapter 11: Natural Resource Development to 1929: The New Generation of Staples

Armstrong, C. and H. V. Nelles. "Private Property in Peril: Ontario Businessmen and the Federal System, 1898-1911". *B.H.R.*, Vol. 47, no. 2 (1973), pp. 158-76.

Bertram, G. W. "The Relevance of the Wheat Boom in Canadian Economic Growth". *C.J.E.*, Vol. 6, no. 4 (1973), pp. 545-66.

Bicha, K. *The American Farmer and the Canadian West, 1896-1914.* Lawrence, Ka.: Coronado Press, 1968.

Britnell, G. E. *The Wheat Economy.* Toronto: University of Toronto Press, 1939.

_____ and V. Fowke. *Canadian Agriculture in War and Peace, 1935-50.* Stanford: Stanford University Press, 1962.

Burton, T. L. *Natural Resource Policy in Canada.* Toronto: McClelland and Stewart, 1972.

Canada. *Report of the Royal Commission on Coal, 1946.* Chairman, W. F. Carroll. Ottawa: King's Printer, 1947.

Carrothers, W. S. "Forest Industries of British Columbia", in Lower. *The North American Assault on the Canadian Forest* (1938), pp. 227-344.

Chambers, E. J. and D. F. Gordon. "Primary Products and Economic Growth: An Empirical Measurement". *J.P.E.*, Vol. 74, no. 4 (1966), pp. 315-32.

Dafoe, J. E. *Clifford Sifton in Relation to His Times.* Toronto: Macmillan of Canada, 1931.

Dagenais, M. G. "The Short-Run Determination of Output and Shipments in the North American Newsprint Paper Industry". *Y.E.E.*, Vol. 4, no. 2 (1964), pp. 281-328.

Dales, J. H. "Fuel, Power and Industrial Development in Central Canada". *A.E.R.*, Vol. 43, no. 2 (1953), pp. 181-98.

_____. *Hydroelectricity and Industrial Development in Quebec, 1898-1940.* Cambridge, Mass.: Harvard University Press, 1957.

_____, J. C. McManus, and M. H. Watkins. "Primary Products and Economic Growth: A Comment". *J.P.E.*, Vol. 75, No. 6 (1967), pp. 876-79.

Davis, J. *The Canadian Chemical Industry.* Royal Commission on Canada's Economic Prospects. Ottawa: Queen's Printer, 1957.

_____. *Mining and Mineral Processing in Canada.* Royal Commission on Canada's Economic Prospects. Ottawa: Queen's Printer, 1957.

D.B.S. *Report on the Coal Trade, 1918.* Ottawa: 1919.

Denison, M. *Harvest Triumphant: The Story of Massey-Harris.* Toronto: McClelland and Stewart, 1948.

_____. *The Barley and Stream: The Molson Story.* Toronto: McClelland and Stewart, 1955.

Donald, W. J. A. *The Canadian Iron and Steel Industry: A Study in the Economic History of a Protected Industry.* Boston: Houghton Mifflin Co., 1915.

Due, J. F. *The Intercity Electric Railway Industry in Canada.* Toronto: University of Toronto Press, 1966.

Firestone, O. J. "Canada's External Trade and Net Foreign Balance, 1851-1900". In *Trends in the American Economy in the Nineteenth Century.* Princeton: N.B.E.R., 1960, Vol. 24, pp. 757-71.

Forsey, E. "The Pulp and Paper Industry. *C.J.E.P.S.*, Vol. 1, no. 3 (1935), pp. 501-09.

Fowke, V. "The National Policy—Old and New". *C.J.E.P.S.*, Vol. 17, no. 3 (1952), pp. 271-86.

_____. "National Policy and Western Development in North America". *J.E.H.*, Vol. 14, no. 4 (1956), pp. 461-79.

_____. *The National Policy and the Wheat Economy.* Toronto: University of Toronto Press, 1957.

Galbraith, J. S. "Land Policy of the Hudson's Bay Company, 1870-1913". *C.J.E.P.S.*, Vol. 22, no. 1 (1951), pp. 1-21.

Grant, K. "The Staple Theory and Its Empirical Measurement". *J.P.E.*, Vol. 82, no. 6 (1974), pp. 1249-53.

_____. "The Rate of Settlement of the Canadian Prairies, 1870-1911: A Comment". *J.E.H.*, Vol. 38, no. 2 (1978), pp. 471-72.

Grauer, A. E. D. "The Export of Electricity from Canada". In R. Clark, ed. *Canadian Issues: Essays in Honour of Henry F. Angus.* Toronto: University of Toronto Press, 1961, pp. 248-85.

Hoffman, A. *Free Gold: The Story of Canadian Mining.* New York: Holt, Rinehart and Co., 1946.

Hunter, W. D. G. "The Development of the Canadian Uranium Industry: An Experiment in Public Enterprise". *C.J.E.P.S.*, Vol. 28, no. 3 (1962), pp. 329-52.

Innis, H. A. and A. F. W. Plumptre, eds. *The Canadian Economy and Its Problems.* Toronto: Canadian Institute of International Affairs, 1934.

_____. "The Canadian Economy and the Depression". In Innis, ed. *Essays in Canadian Economic History* (1956), pp. 123-40.

_____. "The Canadian Mining Industry". In Innis, ed. *Essays in Canadian Economic History* (1956), pp. 309-20.

_____. "The Wheat Economy". In Innis, ed. *Essays in Canadian Economic History* (1956), pp. 273-79.

Kerton, R. R. "Price Effects of Market Power in the Canadian Newspaper Industry". *C.J.E.*, Vol. 6, no. 4 (1973), pp. 602-06.

Langford, G. B. *Out of the Earth: The Mineral Industry of Canada.* Toronto: University of Toronto Press, 1954.

LeBourdais, D. M. *Sudbury Basin: The Story of Nickel.* Toronto: Ryerson Press, 1953.

_____. *Metals and Men.* Toronto: McClelland and Stewart, 1957.

Lewis, F. "The Canadian Wheat Boom and Per Capita Income: New Estimates". *J.P.E.*, Vol. 83, no. 6 (1975), pp. 1249-57.

Lower, A. R. M. and H. A. Innis, *Settlement and the Forest and Mining Frontiers*. Toronto: Macmillan of Canada, 1936.

MacGibbon, D. A. *The Canadian Grain Trade*. Toronto: Macmillan of Canada, 1932.

Mackintosh, W. A. *Prairie Settlement: The Geographical Setting*. Toronto: Macmillan of Canada, 1934.

Main, O. W. *The Canadian Nickel Industry*. Toronto: University of Toronto Press, 1955.

Malenbaum, W. *The World Wheat Economy, 1885-1939*. Cambridge, Mass.: Harvard University Press, 1953.

Marr, W. L. and M. Percy. "The Government and the Rate of Canadian Prairie Settlement". *C.J.E.*, Vol. 11, no. 4 (1978), pp. 757-62.

Mathewson, G. F. "A Note on the Price Effects of Market Power in the Canadian Newspaper Industry". *C.J.E.*, Vol. 5, no. 2 (1972), pp. 298-301.

Morrell, W. P. *The Gold Rushes*. London: A. and O. Black, 1940.

Morton, A. S. and C. Martin. *History of Prairie Settlement and 'Dominion Land' Policy*. Toronto: Macmillan of Canada, 1938.

Murchie, R. W. *Agricultural Progress on the Prairie Frontier*. Toronto: Macmillan of Canada, 1936.

Nelles, H. V. *The Politics of Development: Forest, Mines and Hydro-Electric Power in Ontario, 1849-1941*. Toronto: Macmillan of Canada, 1974.

Norrie, K. H. "Agricultural Implement Tariffs, the National Policy, and Income Distribution in the Wheat Economy". *C.J.E.*, Vol. 7, no. 3 (1974), pp. 449-62.

_____. "The Rate of Settlement of the Canadian Prairies, 1870-1911". *J.E.H.*, Vol. 35, no. 2 (1975), pp. 410-27.

Phillips, W. G. *The Agricultural Implements Industry in Canada: A Study in Competition*. Toronto: University of Toronto Press, 1956.

Plewman, W. R. *Adam Beck and Ontario Hydro*. Toronto: Ryerson Press, 1947.

Safarian, A. E. *The Canadian Economy in the Great Depression*. Toronto: University of Toronto Press, 1959.

Scott, A. D. "The Development of the Extractive Industries". *C.J.E.P.S.*, Vol. 27, no. 1 (1962), pp. 70-87.

Southey, C. "The Staple Thesis, Common Property and Homesteading". *C.J.E.*, Vol. 11, no. 3 (1978), pp. 547-59.

Southworth, C. "The American-Canadian Newsprint Paper Industry and The Tariff". *J.P.E.*, Vol. 30, no. 5 (1922), pp. 681-97.

Stabler, J. C. "Factors Affecting the Development of a New Region: The Canadian Great Plains, 1870-1897". *Annals of Regional Science*, Vol. 7, no. 2 (1973), pp. 75-87.

Studness, C. M. "Economic Opportunity and the Westward Migration of Canadians During the Late Nineteenth Century". *C.J.E.P.S.*, Vol. 30, no. 4 (1964), pp. 570-84.

Vickery, E. "Exports and North American Economic Growth: 'Structural' and 'Staple' Models in Historical Perspective". *C.J.E.*, Vol. 7, no. 1 (1974), pp. 32-58.

Whitford, H. N. and R. D. Craig. *Forests of British Columbia*. Ottawa: Commission of Conservation, 1918.

Wilson, A. W. G. *Development of Chemical, Metallurgical and Allied Industries in Canada*. Ottawa: Department of Mines, 1924.

Zaslow, M. *Reading the Rocks: The Story of the Geological Survey of Canada, 1842-1872*. Toronto: Macmillan of Canada, 1975.

See also chapters 2, 3, and 12.

Chapter 12: Manufacturing and Commercial Policy

A. Commercial Policy

Beigie, C. E. *The Canada–U.S. Automotive Agreement: An Evaluation*. Montreal: The Canadian-American Committee, 1970.

Brewis, T. N. "Canada's International Economic Relations". In T. N. Brewis, et al., eds. *Canadian Economic Policy*. Toronto: Macmillan of Canada, 1961, pp. 259-82.

Brown, R. C. *Canada's National Policy, 1883-1900*. Princeton: Princeton University Press, 1964.

Canada. *Report of the Royal Commission on the Automotive Industry*. Chairman, V. W. Bladen. Ottawa: Queen's Printer, 1960.

Dales, J. H. "Some Historical and Theoretical Comments on Canada's National Policies". *Queen's Quarterly*, Vol. 71, no. 3 (1964), pp. 297-316.

_____. "The Cost of Protectionism with High International Mobility of Factors". *C.J.E.P.S.*, Vol. 30, no. 4 (1964), pp. 512-25.

_____. "Protection, Immigration and Canadian Nationalism". In P. Russell, ed. *Nationalism in Canada*. Toronto: McGraw-Hill, 1966, pp. 164-77.

_____. *The Protective Tariff in Canada's Development*. Toronto: University of Toronto Press, 1966.

Drummond, I. M. *Imperial Economic Policy 1917-1939*. London: Allen & Unwin, 1974.

Eastman, H. C. "Canada in an Interdependent North Atlantic Economy". In C. P. Kindleberger and A. Shonfield, eds. *North American and Western European Economic Policies*. London: Macmillan, 1971, pp. 31-56.

Elliot, G. A. *Tariff Procedures and Trade Barriers: A Study of Indirect Protection in Canada and the United States*. Toronto: University of Toronto Press, 1955.

Ellis, L. E. *Reciprocity, 1911: A Study in Canadian-American Relations*. New Haven: Yale University Press, 1939.

Emerson, D. L. *Production, Location and the Automotive Agreement*. Ottawa: Information Canada, 1975.

Kemp, M. C. *The Demand for Canadian Imports, 1926-1955*. Toronto: University of Toronto Press, 1962.

Kildruff, V. R. "Economic Factors in the Development of Canadian-American Trade". *S.E.J.*, Vol. 8, no. 2 (1941), pp. 201-17.

Reuber, G. "Anglo-Canadian Trade: Prices and the Terms of Trade, 1924-1954". *R.E. Stat.*, Vol. 41, no. 2, Part 1 (1959), pp. 196-99.

_____. *Britain's Export Trade with Canada*. Toronto: University of Toronto Press, 1960.

Wilbur, J. R. H. *The Bennett Administration, 1930-35*. Canadian Historical Association. Pamphlet 24. Ottawa: 1969.

Wilkinson, B. W. and K. Norrie. *Effective Protection and the Return to Capital*. Ottawa: Information Canada, 1975.

Wilton, D. A. *An Econometric Analysis of the Canada-United States Automotive Agreement*. Ottawa: Information Canada, 1976.

Wonnacott, G. P. "Canadian Automotive Protection: Content Provisions, the Bladen Plan, and Recent Tariff Changes". *C.J.E.P.S.*, Vol. 31, no. 1 (1965), pp. 98-116.

Wonnacott, R. J. *Free Trade Between the United States and Canada: The Potential Economic Effects*. Cambridge, Mass.: Harvard University Press, 1967. *See also* chapters 5 and 11.

B. Manufacturing

Bertram, G. W. "Economic Growth in Canadian Industry, 1870-1915: The Staple Model and the Take-Off Hypothesis". *C.J.E.P.S.*, Vol. 29, no. 2 (1963), pp. 162-84.

_____. "Historical Statistics on Growth and Structure of Manufacturing in Canada, 1870-1957". In J. Henripin and A. Asimakopulas, eds. *Conference on Statistics 1962 and 1963*. Canadian Political Science Association. Toronto: University of Toronto Press, 1964, pp. 83-146.

Bliss, M. "Another Anti-Trust Tradition: Canadian Anti-Combines Policy, 1889-1910". *B.H.R.*, Vol. 47, no. 2 (1973), pp. 158-76.

Canada. *Report of the Select Committee on the Causes of the Present Depression, House of Commons Journal*. Ottawa: Queen's Printer, 1876.

_____. *Words, Music and Dollars*. Report of the Special Senate Committee on the Mass Media. 3 vols. Ottawa: Queen's Printer, 1970.

_____. *Concentration in the Manufacturing Industries of Canada*. Ottawa: Department of Consumer and Corporate Affairs, 1971.

Caves, R. E. "The Inter-Industry Structure of the Canadian Economy". *C.J.E.P.S.*, Vol. 23, no. 2 (1957), pp. 313-30.

Chambers, E. J. and G. Bertram. "Urbanization and Manufacturing in Central Canada, 1870-1915". In S. Ostry and T. K. Rymes, eds. *Conference on Statistics, 1964*. Canadian Political Science Association. Toronto: University of Toronto Press, 1964, pp. 225-58.

Dales, J. H. "A Comparison of Manufacturing Industry in Quebec and Ontario". In W. Wade, ed. *Canadian Dualism*. Toronto: University of Toronto Press, 1960, pp. 203-22.

_____. "Estimates of Canadian Manufacturing Output by Markets, 1870-1915". In Henripin and Asimakopulos, eds. *Conference on Statistics, 1962 and 1963* (1964), pp. 61-91.

Easterbrook, W. T. "Industrial Development in Canada". In *Encyclopedia Americana*, Vol. 5, pp. 347-53.

Economic Council of Canada. *Interim Report on Competition Policy.* Ottawa: 1969.

Fullerton, D. H. and H. A. Hampson. *Canadian Secondary Manufacturing Industry.* Royal Commission on Canada's Economic Prospects. Ottawa: Queen's Printer, 1957.

Gilmour, J. M. *Spatial Evolution of Manufacturing: Southern Ontario, 1851-1891.* Toronto: University of Toronto Press, 1972.

Guthrie, J. A. *The Newsprint Paper Industry: An Economic Analysis.* Cambridge, Mass.: Harvard University Press, 1941.

Hay, K. "Trends in the Location of Industry in Ontario, 1945-59". *C.J.E.P.S.*, Vol. 31, no. 3 (1965), pp. 368-81.

McDougall, D. M. "Canadian Manufactured Commodity Output, 1870-1915". *C.J.E.*, Vol. 4, no. 1 (1971), pp. 21-36.

_____. "The Domestic Availability of Manufactured Commodity Output, Canada 1870-1915". *C.J.E.*, Vol. 6, no. 2 (1973), pp. 189-206.

Percy, M. and F. Vaillancourt. "The Vulnerability of the Canadian Economy, 1949-1966: Caves Revisited". *C.J.E.*, Vol. 9, no. 2 (1976), pp. 351-59.

Reuber, G. L. and F. Roseman. *The Take-Over of Canadian Firms, 1945-61.* Economic Council of Canada. Special Study No. 10. Ottawa: 1969.

Reynolds, L. G. *The Control of Competition in Canada.* Cambridge, Mass.: Harvard University Press, 1940.

Rosenbluth, G. "Industrial Concentration in Canada and the United States". *C.J.E.P.S.*, Vol. 20, no. 3 (1954), pp. 332-46.

_____. *Concentration in Canadian Manufacturing Industries.* Princeton: N.B.E.R., 1957.

_____. "The Relation Between Foreign Control and Concentration in Canadian Industry". *C.J.E.*, Vol. 3, no. 1 (1970), pp. 14-38.

Safarian, A. E. *The Canadian Economy in the Great Depression.* Toronto: University of Toronto Press, 1959.

Skeoch, L. A. *Dynamic Change and Accountability in a Canadian Market Economy.* Ottawa: Department of Supply and Services, 1976.

Stewart, M. C. *Concentration in Canadian Manufacturing and Mining Industries.* Economic Council of Canada Background Paper. Ottawa: 1970.

Vout, T. R. "The Canadian Manufacturing Industry, 1900-1957". In E. F. Beach and J. C. Weldon, eds. *Conference on Statistics, 1960.* Canadian Political Science Association. Toronto: University of Toronto Press, 1962, pp. 295-314.

Weldon, J. C. "Consolidations in Canadian Industry, 1900-1948". In L. A. Skeoch, ed. *Restrictive Trade Practices in Canada.* Toronto: McClelland and Stewart, 1966, pp. 228-79.

See also chapters 2, 8, 9, and 11.

C. *Economic Cycles*

Barber, C. L. *Inventories and the Business Cycle with Special Reference to Canada.* Toronto: University of Toronto Press, 1958.

Blain, L. "Regional Cyclical Behavior and Sensitivity in Canada, 1919-1973". *J.E.H.*, Vol. 38, no. 1 (1978), pp. 271-73.

_____, D. G. Paterson, and J. D. Rae. "The Regional Impact of Economic Fluctuations during the Inter-War Period: The Case of British Columbia". *C.J.E..* Vol. 7, no. 3 (1974), pp. 381-401.

Chambers, E. J. "Canadian Business Cycles Since 1919: A Progress Report". *C.J.E.P.S.,* Vol. 24, no. 2 (1958), pp. 166-89.

_____. "Late Nineteenth Century Business Cycles in Canada". *C.J.E.P.S.,* Vol. 30, no. 3 (1964), pp. 391-412.

Harkeness, J. P. "A Spectral Analytic Test of the Long-Swing Hypothesis in Canada". *R.E. Stat.,* Vol. 50, no. 4 (1968), pp. 428-36.

Hay, K. A. "Early Twentieth Century Business Cycles in Canada". *C.J.E.P.S.,* Vol. 32, no. 3 (1966), pp. 354-65.

_____. "Money in Post-Confederation Canada". *J.P.E.,* , Vol. 75, no. 3 (1967), pp. 263-71.

Lee, M. W. *Economic Fluctuations.* Homewood, Ill.: Richard D. Irwin Inc., 1955.

Malach, V. W. *International Cycles and Canada's Balance of Payments, 1921-1933.* Toronto: University of Toronto Press, 1955.

Marcus, E. *Canada and the International Business Cycle, 1927-1939.* New York: Bookman Associates, 1954.

Rosenbluth, G. "Changes in Canadian Sensitivity to United States Business Cycles". *C.J.E.P.S.,* Vol. 23, no. 3 (1957), pp. 480-503.

_____. "Changing Structural Factors in Canada's Cyclical Sensitivity, 1903-54". *C.J.E.P.S.,* Vol. 24, no. 1 (1958), pp. 21-43.

White, D. A. *Business Cycles in Canada.* Economic Council of Canada. Staff Study No. 17. Ottawa: 1957.

Chapter 13: Regional Growth and Retardation

A. *General*

Brewis, T. N. *Regional Economic Policies in Canada.* Toronto: Macmillan of Canada, 1968.

Chernick, E. *Interregional Disparities in Income.* Economic Council of Canada. Staff Study No. 14. Ottawa: 1966.

Currie, A. W. "Freight Rates and Regionalism". *C.J.E.P.S.,* Vol. 14, no. 4 (1948), pp. 427-40.

George, R. E. *A Leader and a Laggard.* Toronto: University of Toronto Press, 1970.

Gertler, L. O. *Regional Planning in Canada.* Montreal: Harvest House, 1972.

Green, A. "Regional Aspects of Canada's Economic Growth, 1890-1929". *C.J.E.P.S.,* Vol. 33, no. 2 (1967), pp. 232-45.

_____. *Regional Aspects of Canada's Economic Growth.* Toronto: University of Toronto Press, 1971.

_____. "Regional Economic Disparaties". In L. H. Officer and L. B. Smith, eds. *Issues in Canadian Economics.* Toronto: McGraw-Hill Ryerson, 1974, pp. 354-70.

Howland, R. D. *Some Regional Aspects of Canada's Economic Development.* Ottawa: Queen's Printer, 1958.

Marr, W. L., D. McCready, and F. Millerd. "Canadian Resource Reallocation: Interprovincial Labour Migration, 1966-1971". *Canadian Studies in Population*, Vol. 4 (1979), pp. 17-32.

McInnis, M. "The Trend of Regional Income Differentials in Canada". *C.J.E.*, Vol. 1, no. 2 (1968), pp. 440-70.

Schultz, T. W. "Reflections on Poverty Within Agriculture". *J.P.E.*, Vol. 58, no. 1 (1950), pp. 1-15.

Shoyoma, T. K. "Public Services and Regional Development in Canada". *J.E.H.*, Vol. 26, no. 4 (1966), pp. 498-513.

B. The Maritimes

Archibald, B. "Atlantic Regional Underdevelopment and Socialism". In L. LaPierre, ed. *Essays on the Left*. Toronto: McClelland and Stewart, 1971, pp. 103-20.

Careless, J. M. S. "Aspects of Metropolitanism in Atlantic Canada". In M. Wade, ed. *Regionalism in the Canadian Community, 1867-1967*. Toronto: University of Toronto Press, 1969, pp. 117-29.

Keirstead, B. S. "Temporal Shifts in Location: The Case of the Maritime Provinces". In B. S. Keirstead, ed. *The Theory of Economic Change*. Toronto: Macmillan of Canada, 1940, pp. 267-313.

Whitelaw, W. M., *The Maritimes and Canada Before Confederation*. Toronto: Oxford University Press, 1966.

For a more complete listing see the following:

Taylor, H. A., ed. *New Brunswick History: A Checklist of Secondary Sources*. Fredericton: Provincial Archives of New Brunswick, 1971.

Vaison, R., ed. *Nova Scotia Past and Present, A Bibliography and Guide*. Halifax: Department of Education, 1976.

C. Quebec

Blanchard, R. *Le Centre du Canada Français: 'Province du Québec'*. Montréal: Librairie Beauchemin, 1947.

Breton, A. "The Economics of Nationalism". *J.P.E.*, Vol. 72, no. 4 (1964), pp. 376-86.

Dorocher, R. et J.-P. Linteau. *Le "Retard" du Québec et l'Inferiorité Economique des Canadiens-Français*. Trois-Rivières: Editions Boréal Express, 1971.

Falardeau, J. C., ed. *Essays on Contemporary Quebec*. Québec: Les Presses de l'Université Laval, 1953.

Faucher, A. "The Decline of Shipbuilding at Quebec in the Nineteenth Century". *C.J.E.P.S.*, Vol. 33, no. 2 (1957), pp. 195-215.

———— and M. Lamontagne. "History of Industrial Development". In Falardeau, ed. *Essays on Contemporary Quebec* (1953), Chapter III.

Greer, A. "The Pattern of Literacy in Quebec, 1745-1899". *H.S./S.H.*, Vol. 11, no. 22 (1978), pp. 293-335.

Hamelin, J. *Economie et Societé en Nouvelle-France*. Québec: Les Presses de l'Université Laval, 1960.

Hughes, E. C. "Industry and the Rural System in Quebec". *C.J.E.P.S.*, Vol. 4, no. 3 (1938), pp. 341-49.

Marr, W. L. "Economic and Social Structure of Quebec, 1896-1960". *The Quarterly of Canadian Studies*, Vol. 3, no. 1 (1973), pp. 34-47.

Melancon, J. "Retard de Croissance de l'Enterprise Canadienne-Française". *A.E.*, Vol. 31, no. 3 (1956), pp. 503-22.

Ouellet, F. *Histoire Economique et Sociale du Québec, 1760-1850*. Montréal: Fides, 1966.

Raynauld, A. *Croissance et Structure Economique de la Province de Québec*. Quebec: Province of Quebec, 1961.

Ryan, W. F. *The Clergy and Economic Growth in Quebec (1896-1914)*. Québec: Les Presses de L'Université Laval, 1966.

St.-Germain, M. *Une Economie à Liberer: Le Québec Analyse Dans Ses Structures Economiques*. Montréal: Les Presses de l'Université de Montréal, 1973.

Taylor, N. W. "French Canadians as Industrial Entrepreneurs". *J.P.E.*, Vol. 68, no. 1 (1960), pp. 37-52.

For a more complete listing see the following bibliographies:

Durocher, R. et P.-A. Linteau. *Histoire du Québec: Bibliographie Selective, 1867-1970*. Trois-Rivières: Editions Boréal Express, 1970.

Nish, C. "Bibliographie des Bibliographies Relatives a l'Histoire Economique du Canada Français". *A.E.*, Vol. 40, no. 4 (1964), pp. 456-66.

————. "Bibliographie sur l'Histoire Economique du Canada Français". *A.E.*, Vol. 40, no. 2 (1964), pp. 200-09.

D. Prairie Provinces

Archer, J. H. *A Bibliography of the Prairie Provinces to 1953 (with Supplements)*. 2nd ed. Toronto: University of Toronto Press, 1973.

Swanson, D., ed. *Historical Essays on the Prairie Provinces*. Toronto: McClelland and Stewart, 1970.

See also chapters 6, 10, and 11.

E. Ontario

Goheen, P. *Victorian Toronto*. Chicago: University of Chicago Press, 1971.

Innis, H. A. "An Introduction to the Economic History of Ontario from Outpost to Empire". In Innis, ed. *Essays in Canadian Economic History* (1956), pp. 108-22.

Kerr, D. and J. Spelt. *The Changing Face of Toronto*. Ottawa: Queen's Printer, 1965.

Masters, D. C. *The Rise of Toronto, 1850-1890*. Toronto: University of Toronto Press, 1947.

Spelt, J. *Urban Development in South Central Ontario*. Toronto: McClelland and Stewart, 1972.

For a more complete listing see the following bibliographies:
French, G. S. and P. Oliver. *Ontario Since 1867: A Bibliography*. Ontario
Historical Studies Series. Toronto: Ontario Ministry of Colleges and
Universities, 1973.
Granatstein, J. L. and P. Stevens. *Canada Since 1897: A Bibliographical Guide*.
Toronto: Hakkert, 1974.

F. British Columbia
Carrothers, W. A. "The Barter Terms of Trade between British Columbia and
Eastern Canada". *C.J.E.P.S.*, Vol. 1, no. 4 (1935), pp. 568-77.
Elliot, G. R. "Frontier and Forms of Enterprise: The Case of the North Pacific,
1785-1825". *C.J.E.P.S.*, Vol. 24, no. 2 (1958), pp. 251-61.
MacDonald, N. "Seattle, Vancouver, and the Klondyke". *C.H.R.*, Vol. 49, no. 3
(1969), pp. 234-46.
Norris, J. *Strangers Entertained: A History of the Ethnic Groups of British
Columbia*. Vancouver: U.B.C. Press, 1971.
Ormsby, M. *British Columbia: A History*. Toronto: Macmillan of Canada, 1958.
Paterson, D. G. "European Capital and British Columbia: An Essay on the Role
of the Regional Entrepreneur". *B.C. Studies*, Vol. 21 (1974), pp. 33-47.
Peters, J. E. and R. A. Shearer. "The Structure of British Columbia's External
Trade, 1939 and 1963". *B.C. Studies*, Vol. 17 (Winter 1970-71), pp. 34-46.
Pfister, R. L. "External Trade and Regional Growth: A Case Study of the Pacific
Northwest". *E.D.C.C.*, Vol. 11, no. 1 (1963), pp. 134-51.
Ralston, K. "Patterns of Trade and Investment on the Pacific Coast, 1867-1892:
The Case of British Columbia Salmon Canning Industry". *B.C. Studies*, Vol.
15, no. 1 (Winter 1968-69), pp. 37-45.
_____. "The Lowe Brothers, 1852-70: A Study in Business Relations on the North
Pacific Coast". *B.C. Studies*, Vol. 15, no. 2 (Summer 1969), pp. 1-18.
Shearer, R. A. "The Economy of British Columbia". In R. A. Shearer, *et al.*, eds.
*Trade Liberalization and a Regional Economy: Studies of the Impact of Free
Trade on British Columbia*. Toronto: Private Planning Association, 1971, pp.
3-42.
For a more complete listing see the following:
B.C. Studies, continuing bibliography.
Cuddy, M. L. and J. J. Scott. *British Columbia in Books*. Vancouver: J. J.
Douglas Ltd., 1974.

INDEX